The Rise of
Neo-Confucianism
in Korea

Neo-Confucian Studies
SPONSORED BY THE REGIONAL SEMINAR
IN NEO-CONFUCIAN STUDIES
COLUMBIA UNIVERSITY

The Rise of Neo-Confucianism in Korea

Wm. Theodore de Bary and JaHyun Kim Haboush, Editors

Columbia University Press   New York   1985

This volume results from a conference partially supported by the Committee on Studies of Chinese Civilization, of the American Council of Learned Societies, with funds provided by the Ford Foundation and the National Endowment for the Humanities.

Library of Congress Cataloging in Publication Data
Main entry under title:

The Rise of Neo-Confucianism in Korea.

(Neo-Confucian studies)
Includes bibliographies and index.
1. Neo-Confucianism—Korea—Addresses, essays, lectures.   I. de Bary, William Theodore, 1918–
II. Haboush, JaHyun Kim.   III. Series.
B5253.N45R57   1985   181'.09512   85-364
ISBN 0-231-06052-1

Columbia University Press
New York   Guildford, Surrey
Copyright © 1985 Columbia University Press
All rights reserved

Printed in the United States of America

Clothbound editions of Columbia University Press books are Smyth-sewn and printed on permanent and durable acid-free paper.

Neo-Confucian Studies

Preface

THE STUDIES CONTAINED in this volume were first presented to the Conference on Neo-Confucianism in Korea, held in August 1981 at the Rockefeller Foundation Conference Center in Bellagio, Italy, under the joint auspices of the American Council of Learned Societies' Committee on the Study of Chinese Civilization, and the Korean Studies Program and Committee on Oriental Studies of Columbia University.

In recent years there has been increasing recognition of the importance of Korea in East Asian civilizations, first as playing a major role in the great age of Buddhism from the fourth to the twelfth centuries, and then in the premodern period (twelfth to nineteenth centuries) as an active contributor to the new Neo-Confucian culture. Several conferences have already been held, and publication programs undertaken, focusing on the eminent Korean philosopher Yi T'oegye (1501–70). In the present conference an attempt has been made to broaden the discussion of Neo-Confucianism so as to deal with the larger process of its introduction and establishment as a new way of life in Yi dynasty Korea (1392–1910). In this we have had the advantage of drawing upon new studies of Neo-Confucianism in China made available through several ACLS-sponsored conferences in recent years. The fresh historical and comparative approaches suggested by the latter enable us also to view Korean developments in a new light and thus provide a more adequate baseline for the further study of premodern developments.

Whether we have succeeded in this aim or not, the conference itself was a success in bringing together scholars of quite diverse backgrounds. It benefited from the participation, not only of leading Korean scholars, but of specialists from China, Japan, and Europe expert in various aspects of Neo-Confucian thought and culture. Even in a volume of this substantial size, however, we have been unable to include all of the matters discussed at our meeting. It is appropriate therefore to acknowledge the contributions to the conference of some scholars whose work is not included here: Professor Koh Byong-ik, then President of the Academy of

Korean Studies and formerly President of Seoul National University, whose scholarship and leadership were both much appreciated at our meeting; Professor Gari Ledyard of Columbia University; Professors Lee Nam-young, Shim Jaeryong, and Yi T'aejin of Seoul National University; and Professor Kim Youngkun of the City University of New York; Professor Dieter Eikemeier, whom illness prevented from attending but who shared with us a draft study of the community-compacts *(hyangyak)* in Korea; and Professor Irene Bloom, who produced a synopsis of our discussions remarkable for its lucidity and conciseness.

To Professor Edward Wagner of Harvard University and Dr. Martina Deuchler of the University of Zürich we owe a special debt. In the editing of several of the papers herein Professor Wagner was most generous with his time and expertise in Korean history. Dr. Deuchler, a leading scholar in Korean Neo-Confucianism, has shared the fruits of her pioneering researches not only in her paper for this volume and in her contribution to the conference discussion but also in reviewing substantial portions of this book in preparation for publication.

We should also like to acknowledge here our appreciation to the Ministry of Education, Republic of Korea, and the Korean Traders' Scholarship Foundation, for providing travel funds for our Korean participants. At the Bellagio Center itself the graciousness of our host Dr. Robert Celli and his staff added considerably to the success of the conference. In all phases of the project Emma Rockwell's assistance has been invaluable, and in preparing the conference papers for publication we enjoyed and appreciated the help of Marie Guarino.

Explanatory Note

CONSISTENCY IN THE translation of terms, always a desirable goal, is difficult when applied to Chinese philosophical concepts which are often so broad and flexible in meaning as to justify diverse renderings in different contexts. One cannot say that each concept should have but one English equivalent, nor can we impose uniformity of usage upon scholars whose translations may be quite consciously intended to bring out nuances neglected by others. This is all the more true in the study of Neo-Confucianism, a neoclassical movement which used old terms in new ways and appropriated for its own purposes concepts borrowed from other teachings. Still more is this the case with Neo-Confucianism in Korea, which underwent stages of assimilation, domestication, and independent growth that left it in an ambivalent relation to the original tradition.

Our practice in this volume has been to keep to standard renderings as much as possible, but to allow variations by individual authors where they are specifically marked at the point of first occurrence by romanization and identification in the glossary. For this purpose a general glossary is provided at the end of the book, with Chinese romanization according to the Wade-Giles system, Japanese according to the Hepburn, and Korean according to the McCune-Reischauer system.

Historical personages are referred to by their own names (*ming/myŏng*) rather than their style (*hao/ho*) or courtesy names (*tzu/cha*). Exceptions are made for Yi Hwang and Yi I who are respectively referred to as T'oegye and Yulgok, as is by now the accepted style.

Contemporary Korean scholars do not necessarily romanize their names according to the McCune-Reischauer system. As far as possible we have followed individual preferences. In the glossary, however, Chinese characters for Korean names will be found under their McCune-Reischauer romanizations.

The romanized form may be given in either Korean or Chinese, depending on the nationality of the author cited. When both Chinese and Korean forms are given, the Chinese form precedes the Korean with a

slash between. Departures from this practice in the case of Japanese renderings are identified by the prefix J.

In romanizing Korean names, we have omitted hyphens between
characters (syllables) since other Korean words are not romanized with
hyphens. Thus Kim Yongguk rather than Kim Yong-guk.

Contributors

DANIEL BOUCHEZ is a research scholar at the Centre National de la Recherche Scientifique and teaches at the École Pratique des Hautes Études in Paris. His special interest is Neo-Confucian thought as it is expressed in Korean literature. He has studied seventeenth-century fiction, particularly that of Kim Manjung.

WING-TSIT CHAN is Anna R. D. Gillespie Professor of Philosophy Emeritus at Chatham College and Professor Emeritus of Chinese Philosophy and Culture at Dartmouth College. His numerous works on Chinese philosophy include A Source Book in Chinese Philosophy (1963), a translation of Wang Yang-ming's Instructions for Practical Living and Other Neo-Confucian Writings (1963), and a translation of Chu Hsi's Reflections on Things at Hand (1967).

JULIA CHING is a Professor of Religious Studies at the University of Toronto. She received her Ph.D. at Australian National University and has taught there as well as at Columbia and Yale. Her principal publications include To Acquire Wisdom: The Way of Wang Yang-ming (1976), Confucianism and Christianity (1977), and The Philosophical Letters of Wang Yang-ming (1972).

CHUNG CHAI-SIK is now Professor of Sociology and the Director of the Institute of Humanities at Yonsei University in Seoul, Korea. Formerly he was Professor of Philosophy at Heidelberg College in Ohio. His main field of interest has been the role of religion in the modernization of Korea. He is the author of Religion and Social Change (1982) and is completing a monograph on intellectual history and problems of modernizing change in Korea.

WM. THEODORE DE BARY is John Mitchell Mason Professor of the University at Columbia University, where he has also served as Vice-President and Provost. His most recent works are Neo-Confucian Orthodoxy and the Learning of the Mind-and-Heart (1981) and the Liberal Tradition in China (1983). He is also the co-author and editor of Sources of Japanese

Tradition (1958), *Sources of Chinese Tradition* (1960), *Sources of Indian Tradition* (1960), *The Buddhist Tradition* (1969), *Self and Society in Ming Thought* (1970), *The Unfolding of Neo-Confucianism* (1975), *Principle and Practicality* (1979) and *Yüan Thought* (1982).

MARTINA DEUCHLER is a research fellow of the Swiss National Science Foundation and is also teaching Korean history and language at the University of Zürich. She received her Ph.D. from Harvard University. Her research interests concentrate on the social and intellectual history of late Koryŏ and early Yi Korea. Among her publications are *Confucian Gentlemen and Barbarian Envoys* (1977), "The Tradition: Women during the Yi Dynasty" in *Virtues in Conflict* (1977), and several articles on Korean Neo-Confucianism.

JAHYUN KIM HABOUSH is a visiting Assistant Professor at the University of Illinois at Urbana-Champaign. She has taught at the State University of New York at Albany and at Columbia University, where she received her doctorate. Her special interests include the intellectual and institutional history of Yi Korea and comparative political thought and institutions. She is preparing a monograph on Confucian kingship in Korea.

HAN YOUNG-WOO is Professor of Korean History at Seoul National University in Korea. His fields of interest include the social and political thought and historiography of the early Yi dynasty. He has completed several books including *Chŏng Tojŏn sasang ŭi yŏn'gu* (A Study of Chŏng Tojŏn's Thought, 1973), *Chosŏn chŏn'gi sahaksa yŏn'gu* (A Study of the Historiography of Early Yi Korea, 1981), *Chosŏn chŏn'gi sahoe sasang yŏn'gu* (Studies on the Social Thought of the Early Yi Dynasty, 1983), and *Chosŏn chŏn'gi sahoe kyŏngje yŏn'gu* (Studies on Early Yi Society and Economy, 1983).

MICHAEL KALTON is Assistant Professor of Comparative Religion and Chairperson of the Department of Religion at Wichita State University, Wichita, Kansas. His doctoral degree in Comparative Religion and East Asian Languages and Civilization is from Harvard University. His publications include: "An Introduction to Sirhak" (1975), "Korean Ideas and Values" (1979), and "Chŏng Tasan's Philosophy of Man" (1981). He is currently working on a translation and commentary on the *Ten Diagrams on Sage Learning by Yi Hwang* (T'oegye).

PETER H. LEE, who is Professor of Korean and Comparative Literature at the University of Hawaii at Manoa, has also taught at Columbia and the

University of California, Berkeley. A Guggenheim Fellow, his publications include *Songs of Flying Dragons* (1975), *Celebration of Continuity: Themes in Classic East Asian Poetry* (1979), and *Anthology of Korean Literature* (1981). In 1982 Lee was decorated with the Order of Merit by the Republic of Korea for his contributions to Korean studies.

MIURA KUNIO is Professor of Chinese Thought at Osaka City University, having previously served at Tohoku University, Sendai, Japan. His special interest is in Neo-Confucianism in China and Korea, on which he has published many articles. With Yoshikawa Kōjirō he edited an anthology of the works of Chu Hsi.

SAKAI TADAO is Professor Emeritus at Tsukuba University and former Professor of Chinese History at Tokyo Kyōiku University. He is an expert in Chinese popular religion, with special emphasis on Taoism, and has been president of several major scholarly associations in the field of East Asian history, thought, and religion. His *Chūgoku zensho no kenkyū* (Research in Chinese Morality Books) is a classic in its field. He has also edited several volumes of the proceedings from the *International Conference on Taoist Studies* held in 1972.

TOMOEDA RYŪTARŌ, Professor Emeritus of Chinese Philosophy at Hiroshima University, currently teaches at Seinan Gakuin University in Fukuoka. He is the author of a major study of the development of Chu Hsi's philosophy (*Shushi no shisō keisei*, 1969), and editor of source readings on Chu Hsi (in *Shushigaku taikei*, vols. 4 and 5, 1983), Lu Hsiang-shan (in *Yōmeigaku taikei*, vol. 4, 1973), and Kumazawa Banzan (in *Nihon shisō taikei*, vol. 30, 1971). He has been active in the promotion of Yi T'oegye studies in Japan.

WEI-MING TU is Professor of Chinese History at Harvard University, where he received his doctorate. He has also taught at Princeton and the University of California, Berkeley. His fields of interest are Confucianism, Chinese intellectual history, and the religious philosophies of Asia. He has written *Neo-Confucian Thought in Action: Wang Yang-ming's Youth (1472–1509)* (1976), and *Humanity and Self-Cultivation* (1979).

YI SŎNGMU is Professor of Korean History at the Academy of Korean Studies in Korea. He received his doctorate from Seoul National University. He has specialized in the social history of the early Yi dynasty, particularly the *yangban* and the civil service examination. He has written *Han'guk ŭi kwagŏ chedo* (The Civil Service Examination Service in Korea, 1976),

Chosŏn chŏn'gi yangban yŏn'gu (A Study of the Yangban in Early Yi Korea, 1980), and *Kwagŏ* (The Civil Service Examination, 1981).

YOUN SA-SOON is Professor of Korean Philosophy at Koryŏ University in Seoul, where he received his doctorate. He is a specialist in Neo-Confucianism in Korea, especially in T'oegye's philosophy. His publications include *T'oegye ch'ŏrhak ŭi yŏn'gu* (A Study in T'oegye's Philosophy, 1980), *Han'guk yuhak yŏn'gu* (Studies on Korean Confucianism, 1980), and *Tongyang sasang ŭi hyŏndaejŏk ihae* (A Modern Understanding of Oriental Thought, 1983).

Contents

Contents

Wm. Theodore de Bary

Introduction

DESPITE ITS MODEST size and marginal situation on the edge of Asia, Korea has played a key role in the development of East Asian civilization. Without challenging China's claim to be the Central Kingdom, or dreaming, as Japan at times has done, that it could become the dominant power in Asia, Korea has afforded again and again throughout its history, not only a meeting ground and sometime battlefield for its larger neighbors, but also cultural achievements to rival those of China and Japan. It is only recently, however, that its stellar contributions to the rise of Neo-Confucian culture have gained the recognition they deserve.

Three personal experiences, on visits to disparate points in East Asia, have brought in upon me the unpredictable ways in which this Korean contribution has been made. The first occurred in 1960 when I visited the Confucian Society in what was then known as Saigon. Officers of the Society showed me, with a sense of real achievement in difficult circumstances, a new publication of theirs. It was a bilingual edition, in romanized Vietnamese and Chinese characters, of a traditional Confucian primer that had been highly regarded in their country, the *Minh-tam bao-giam*. On examination it proved to be, not a Chinese work, but the *Myŏngsim pogam*, a "classic" compiled by the Korean scholar Ch'u Chŏk (Nodang) at the end of the thirteenth century. Much admired as a primer in Korea down into modern times,[1] its diffusion throughout East Asia and the high regard in which it was held for summing up the wisdom of the East even led to its translation into Spanish and introduction to Europe in the seventeenth century. Clearly the ascending star of Neo-Confucianism in the late Koryŏ and early Yi dynasties had shed its light far beyond what Westerners have called the Hermit Kingdom.

My second visit was to the library of Yi T'oegye, the Tosan Sŏwŏn in the mountains near Andong, Korea, where I found the writings of the scholar Chen Te-hsiu (1178–1235), a Neo-Confucian scholar-statesman in the next generation after Chu Hsi (1130–1200), the great synthesizer of Neo-Confucianism. Though widely influential in the early centuries of the Neo-Confucian movement, these writings had been largely ignored by modern scholarship. Once recognized, however, for their importance to Korean philosophers and kings in the thirteenth to eighteenth centuries, these works and their historical significance for China itself could be recovered and appreciated.

My third visit was to the Cabinet Library (Naikaku Bunko) in Tokyo. There one could examine the charred and smoke-soiled remains from Edo fires of works studied by the Hayashi family mentors to seventeenth century Tokugawa shoguns. Among them were Neo-Confucian texts, written or commented on by Korean scholars like Yi T'oegye (1501–70), and reprinted or recopied with handwritten comments in the margin by their Japanese understudies. Here one could see in textual transmission the process by which the seed of Neo-Confucian discourse was propagated from one fertile soil to another across East Asia.

Neo-Confucianism has usually been thought of as a scholastic teaching and philosophy, but as it spread in the thirteenth to seventeenth centuries it carried a new form of cultural and religious contagion—a dynamic way of life which only later settled down into more fixed patterns. To the restless, impatient eyes of the nineteenth and twentieth centuries, Neo-Confucianism has appeared all stuck in a rut—an immovable mass of tradition and rigid dogma. Yet viewed from the other end, as it arose in the thirteenth century, the new movement is most striking for its burgeoning vitality and reformist zeal.

True, Neo-Confucianism was far from a *mass* movement. Its first signs of life appear in the relative seclusion of schools and academies in South China, where Chu Hsi's disciples quietly propagated his teachings. In those early days of the thirteenth century the odds were against their achieving any wide success. Chu Hsi's doctrines had been proscribed by the state as heterodox, and when this inquisition abated, China found itself locked with the Mongols in what seemed to be a life-and-death struggle for the survival of Chinese civilization.

Of this the surprising outcome was that the Mongols themselves, though hardly dedicated to the propagation of Chinese culture, became the unpremeditated sponsors and purveyors of Neo-Confucianism. To them it was a secular teaching, not necessarily in conflict with their adherence to Buddhism or with Khubilai's patronage of Taoist masters. Once the Grand Khan had reconciled himself to governing China through a dyarchy of Mongol tribal and Chinese bureaucratic institutions, he became persuaded by the scholar-statesman Hsü Heng (1209–81) that Neo-Confucianism could serve as the ideological basis for the new hybrid state. Thus Hsü became entrusted with organizing a new educational system based on Chu Hsi's texts and teachings. Thereafter its successful propagation led in 1313–15 to the adoption of a Neo-Confucian curriculum for the civil service examinations—a system which would largely channel the energies and intelligence of educated Chinese down into the twentieth century.

If this were all that Khubilai and his Mongols had done, it might explain how Chinese ideas and institutions endured in their homeland, but would not account for the almost revolutionary impact of Neo-Confucianism on the rest of East Asia. What differentiated his situation from the typical dynastic order was that Khubilai's ambitions and power reached well beyond the traditional limits of China proper. His was a conquest regime, and Peking served as the capital not only of China but of a larger empire with other Mongol dependencies. A cosmopolitan city, it housed residents from Central Asia, Korea, Vietnam, and elsewhere who participated in the cultural life at the hub of a universal empire. Among them were kings and heirs-apparent to the Korean throne, obliged to reside in Peking as virtual hostages of the Mongols. They and a retinue of scholarly compatriots had access to the new learning from the South, first brought to the Yüan capital in 1235 by another captive of war, Chao Fu (c.1206–c.1299), who lectured on Chu Hsi's teachings and his commentaries on the Four Books at the recently opened Academy of the Supreme Ultimate. Until then, for years before the Mongols extended their conquest to the South, North China and Korea had been largely (though not totally) cut off from the Southern Sung. There was a pent-up interest in the latest of Sung scholarship and philosophy, especially among Confucian activists like the charismatic Hsü Heng (himself a student of Chao Fu). As an advisor to Khubilai and rector of the Imperial Academy, Hsü was in a position to direct the cultural policies of the Yüan state and to manifest his missionary zeal in teaching not only Chinese, but Mongols, Central Asians, and Koreans as well.

When eventually Neo-Confucian texts were incorporated in the new civil service examination system, Koreans were among those eligible to take part in the ethnically diverse and highly cosmopolitan field of candidates. Among the non-Chinese the Koreans were no doubt the best prepared and the most adept of students, as well as the most avid collectors of books for transmission back home. It was from these expatriate subjects of the Koryŏ dynasty that a new generation of scholars was to come, who would, with the introduction to their homeland of the new "Learning of the Way," first stir up an intellectual and educational revolution, and then help to bring down the Koryŏ dynasty itself.

The Neo-Confucianism thus introduced to Korea was highly specific in form and in its historical development. It drew of course on a large body of tradition, and in much of its content could simply be described as Confucian. Nevertheless, its history begins with Chu Hsi, and can be traced in precise detail (as Yi T'oegye and more recently Professor Wing-tsit Chan have done) from Chu's disciples down into the Yüan period[2] and then to Koryŏ. It spread through identifiable academies, pursuing a well-defined curriculum. Its texts, largely from the hand of Chu, contained new doctrines concerning human nature and the social order, which at a certain point in time began to displace the traditional subjects in schools and examinations, first in China, then in Korea. Indeed one can trace its rise in the course of ideological and political struggles at the Yüan court, from which the new teaching emerged triumphant over older forms of Chinese learning.[3]

This, then, is not just a case of the old Confucianism reaching maturity, developing a comfortable middle-aged spread and then slumbering off into dreams of China's ancient glories. It is rather a new offspring, full of energy and ambition to take on the world. Not content simply to reclaim the Central Kingdom for Chinese culture, it reached out to embrace a multicultural world extending beyond even the Mongol empire.

SPEAKING OF NEO-CONFUCIANISM

In the historical instance just described the new movement had a quite specific content and character as the Ch'eng-Chu Learning or School of the Way (*tao-hsüeh*). This was itself, however, just part of a larger process, and even its centrality in the mainstream of the new social and cultural trend can be appreciated only in relation to the whole enterprise known as "Neo-Confucianism." Though of Western coinage, this term has gained some acceptance even in East Asia to designate the groundswell of new thought which arose with the Confucian revival in the Sung period (960–1279) and flowed down into modern times.

Much of this term's currency in the West may be attributed to its use by scholars like Fung Yu-lan, Carsun Chang, and Alfred Forke, whose historical surveys were among the first to draw attention to the later development of Confucian thought.[4] Fung's translator, Derk Bodde, adopted "Neo-Confucianism" as a rendering for *tao-hsüeh*, the Chinese term used by Fung in his *History of Chinese Philosophy (Chung-kuo che-hsüeh shih)* vol. 2.[5] In the latter work, as also in his later *Short History*, Fung took a comparatively broad view of *tao-hsüeh*. He did not restrict it to the so-called Ch'eng-Chu School, as the *Sung History (Sung-shih)* had done, but included within its scope such independent thinkers as Lu Hsiang-shan (1139–93) and Wang Yang-ming (1472–1529). Further, Fung extended the discussion of Neo-Confucian developments down into the Ch'ing period (1644–1911), viewing even critics of the Ch'eng-Chu school as variant expressions of a philosophical dialogue initiated in the Sung. In his treatment of *tao-hsüeh* in the Sung, on the other hand, Fung was less inclusive. No doubt constrained by the selectivity demanded in writing a general history of Chinese philosophy, he focused on the metaphysicians who contributed to the synthesis of Chu Hsi, and neglected large areas of Sung thought which earlier had been represented in *Case Studies of Sung and Yüan Confucians (Sung Yüan hsüeh-an)*, the classic account of Sung thought by Huang Tsung-hsi (1610–95) and Ch'üan Tsu-wang (1705–55).

Beside the fact of its having come into general use in the West, the name "Neo-Confucianism" has the advantage of being broadly inclusive of different schools and successive phases in the later development of Confucian thought, rather than being narrowly identified with one particular view of it. At the same time, as one aspect of the larger Confucian tradition Neo-Confucianism includes much that is basic to Confucian thought as a whole. Thus some scholars may well question why elements identifiable with the ethical and political core of a perennial Confucianism, should not simply be called "Confucian" rather than "Neo-Confucian." Why not indeed! The coexistence of old and new, of perennial "fundamentalism" as well as of distinctive new elements in later thought, must be allowed for.

Among the latter, Neo-Confucians often invoke ancient phrases or traditional concepts while putting them to new uses. Thus, for instance, the ancient virtue of "reverence" or "respect" _(ching),_ became super-charged in the Sung with a new moral and intellectual "seriousness" as well as with a sense of religious awe and mindfulness or "concentration," each reflecting a different side of Neo-Confucianism's flanking attacks on Buddhism. This is also the case with the central Confucian concept of humanity or humaneness _(jen),_ the interpretation of which was greatly amplified by Chu Hsi and others. There are, too, such formulations as the "five moral relations" _(wu-lun),_ and "three mainstays" _(san-kang-ling)_ among other expressions from the classics especially dear to Neo-Confucians and invested by them with a new importance. One can, of course, identify any of these as Confucian in the larger sense, but often their significance in the context of later thought lies in how and why they were singled out for special emphasis by Neo-Confucian thinkers. In such cases—and others will be cited below—one is warranted in underscoring the "Neo-Confucian" character of even traditional values.

The appropriateness of such distinctions varies from period to period. In the late Sung and Yüan there was open conflict between old style, conservative Confucians and liberal Neo-Confucians who were quite free in their interpretation of the classics. Later in the Ming and Ch'ing, after specifically Neo-Confucian formulations had become institutionalized and sometimes officially sanctioned, these recently established interpretations themselves became subject to a still newer brand of criticism which exposed the license taken by Sung thinkers in their reading of the classics. As to whether such purist or fundamentalist criticism in the late Ming and Ch'ing should be called Neo-Confucian or Confucian, it is perhaps a case of six of one or half a dozen of another, depending on whether one views this scholarship as a further extension of the Neo-Confucian's critical reinterpretation of received tradition or whether one sees it as a fundamentalist return to an original, and supposedly "pure," form of Confucianism that should remain a fixed standard of literal interpretation for all times.

One would underestimate the actual complexity of the problem, however, if one did not take into account the ways in which the great neoclassicists of the seventeenth century, among them Huang Tsung-hsi and Ku Yen-wu (1613–82), were heirs to, as well as critics of, Sung-Ming Neo-Confucianism. It was no doubt in recognition of this that Fung Yu-lan spoke of Ch'ing learning as a continuation of Sung and Ming Neo-Confucianism, the major contribution of which lay in new answers and interpretations to the latter's traditional problems and texts. . . . Hence those adherents of the Han Learning [in the Ch'ing] who concentrated on philosophy should, despite outward opposition to Neo-Confucianism, properly be regarded as its perpetuators and developers.[6]

To point out these nuances in the use of terms is also to acknowledge that Neo-Confucianism underwent successive modifications from its very beginning. Neo-Confucians differed among themselves as to whether the Way or Tao should be conceived of as a mainstream of fluid thought, with many tributaries and side-currents, or whether it should be seen as a fixed legacy to be handed down intact to later generations. Demonstrably Neo-Confucianism first struggled, and then flourished, as a dynamic intellectual movement before it settled down to become an established tradition. When finally it did assume scholastic form, the tradition survived primarily as a dialogue or body of discourse, built up by citing earlier texts and historical cases as a way of defining issues for discussion. An example of this, and also of the Confucian/Neo-Confucian dichotomy referred to above, is the new attention given to the so-called Four Books. These texts were "Confucian" in the sense of being drawn from the earlier Confucian classics, but interpreted and repackaged as they were by Chu Hsi, they came to have a new meaning and significance in Neo-Confucian discourse. Unless one is quite familiar with Chu Hsi's commentaries on the *Great Learning (Ta-hsüeh)*, for instance, as well as with the intense discussion which his interpretations aroused in ensuing generations, one might miss the specific point of later references to Chu Hsi's views (as in Wang Yang-ming's *Inquiry into the Great Learning*) and fail to recognize in what way the Neo-Confucian dialogue was being advanced.

A scholar's identification with tradition depends not only on his avowed loyalties or antipathies, but also on which earlier writers he chooses to converse with over time, and which texts we must be conversant with if we are to comprehend him. He may be more or less of a "traditionalist" and more or less "orthodox" according to current definitions of that term, but he would be working within, or out of, Neo-Confucian tradition as long as it provides him with his basic frame of discursive reference and he does not call into question its underlying assumptions.

A case in point is the Japanese philosopher of the Tokugawa Period, Miura Baien (1723–89), who has been cited in recent years as a highly original thinker, one who departed from orthodox Neo-Confucianism and anticipated modern scientific thought. Yet on more careful reflection in the perspective of East Asian thought as a whole, Professor Shimada Kenji finds little in Miura's thought that is not already anticipated by Sung and Ming Neo-Confucians. Miura's philosophy, he concludes, "was hardly anything more than a variation on the philosophy of *ch'i* formulated by Sung philosophers."[7] It is ignorance of the latter, more than a failure to recognize Miura's distinctive achievements, which distorts the picture.

Philosophically speaking, what may be considered irreducibly "Neo-Confucian" in these cases will vary according to one's reading of Chu Hsi's, or the other Sung masters', thought as a whole. Yet as a system of thought undergoing historical development, Neo-Confucianism was a tangible body of discourse with definable characteristics; we are not without signposts by which to gauge directions or to measure continuity and change in the system. Among these reference points internal to the tradition itself are the new names scholars themselves coined to designate the Confucian Way, and the new concepts with which they explained it—names and concepts not previously identified with Confucian tradition, which I shall discuss below. Another set of indicators is the texts accepted by them as authoritative, the shared basis of their common discourse. A third consists in institutions closely identified with the life of Neo-Confucianism, either those which promoted the discourse or those promoted by it—i.e., which were produced by Neo-Confucians themselves as a means of giving practical shape to their ideas. Finally there are the specific interests served by Neo-Confucianism, or those it was made to serve through its official adoption by the state, etc.

A. Neo-Confucian Designations for the Way *(tao)* or Learning *(hsüeh)*

1. *Tao-hsüeh/tohak*

Although the term "Neo-Confucianism" embraces many trends of thought, it was used in the Fung-Bodde translation to render *tao-hsüeh,* which in Chinese (indeed, in East Asian) usage has generally been identified with the Ch'eng-Chu school and often with a narrow definition even of that. Literally translatable as "the Learning of the Way" or "School of the Way," depending upon whether one emphasizes its thought content or its scholarly transmission, this term has had a special importance in the history of Neo-Confucianism. As used by the Ch'eng brothers and

Chu Hsi it conveyed the sense of ultimate value and the commitment to it which we usually associate with religion. Not surprisingly this claim to ultimate truth and its followers' intense dedication to it evoked a comparably strong reaction from those who rejected the claim. Hence the ironic use of the term among the critics of the Ch'eng-Chu school or the characterization of it as false or spurious learning *(wei-hsüeh)* in the Sung period, when the *tao-hsüeh*, far from constituting the officially approved learning, was on the contrary ridiculed and officially condemned.[8] It was only later, at the end of the Sung and in the Yüan period, as a reflection of Chu Hsi's increasing influence in the scholarly community, that official acceptance of Chu's teaching gave *tao-hsüeh* the connotation of an established orthodoxy.[9] This is the sense in which the term appears in the *Sung History (Sung-shih)*, wherein a special section is devoted to Neo-Confucian thinkers who qualify as bearers of the True Way, with the implication of their being a breed apart from other Confucian scholars treated in the *Ju-chia* section of biographical accounts.

Given this usage of *tao-hsüeh*, I suggest that it be translated as Learning or School of the Way and that it be understood to represent orthodox Neo-Confucianism insofar as this would differentiate a subset of those thinkers officially considered "orthodox" from the larger numbers of those who accept the basic terms of, and participate in, the wider Neo-Confucian discourse. One must bear in mind, however, that many thinkers claimed to represent the authentic Ch'eng-Chu teaching, though not all had official support for their claim.

In the *Unfolding of Neo-Confucianism* and in *Principle and Practicality* I have pointed out that even those who resist official orthodoxy, or a narrow definition of it, rarely go so far as to reject any standard for "true teaching" at all.[10] A radical skepticism of this latter sort may sometimes be found in Taoist or Buddhist thought, but Neo-Confucians, for their part, hold to a belief in the existence of "real" values *(shih)*, the possibility of knowing and communicating them, and the correlative obligation to follow a definable Way. One can understand this as "orthodoxy" in the broadest and most liberal understanding of the term, or one can think of it as "Neo-Confucian tradition" in contradistinction to "Orthodox Neo-Confucianism" in the more limited *tao-hsüeh* sense. Huang Tsung-hsi's conception of the unity and variety of the Way, set forth in his discussion of *i-pen wan-shu* in *Case Studies of Ming Confucians (Ming-ju hsüeh-an)*,[11] conveys his idea of Neo-Confucian thought as carrying on a Way

(distinguishable from Buddhism and Taoism) with its own basic integrity
and coherence, while at the same time it generates innumerable differentiations in individual schools and thinkers. It is this broad conception
of the Confucian tradition, as well as its inherent power of creative di-
versification, which Huang celebrates in the sweeping panorama of Sung,
Yüan, and Ming thought presented in *Case Studies of Sung and Yüan
Confucians* and *Case Studies of Ming Confucians*. Objective though Huang
tried to be in his exposition of Neo-Confucian thinkers, it would have
been inconceivable to him that such objectivity could be altogether "value-
free" or noncommittal. The Way still provided a definite guide or standard for human life, and Huang decidedly rejected the notion that one
could be all things to all men.

2. *Shih-hsüeh/sirhak*

A less frequent characterization of Neo-Confucianism than *tao-hsüeh*
is *shih-hsüeh*, meaning "solid," "real," "substantial," or "practical" learning. This differentiated Neo-Confucianism from the "emptiness" of
Buddhism and Taoism. It asserted the substantiality and knowability of
Confucian values, in contrast to the mutability and uncertainty which
governed all ordinary existence and cognition in the Buddhist view. For
Neo-Confucians *shih-hsüeh* was the study of enduring moral, social, and
cultural values, together with the practical benefits that could accrue from
acting upon them or from studying their role in the historical process. It
is noteworthy that Chu Hsi especially employs this term in his advocacy
of an education that would be truly rooted in humane values and be of
practical benefit to human society, and in Korea Chŏng Tojŏn (1342–
98) echoes this when he refers to Neo-Confucianism as "the real learning
of the ancients which manifests the moral nature and renews the people." [12]

As the social and cultural context changed, so too did the view of
"reality" in this tradition. This was particularly true in the field of learning, a matter which involved virtually all Neo-Confucians, and in the
political and social affairs which concerned many of them. Here the processes of steady differentiation in human affairs produced a "reality" of
increasing complexity. From a view of "real learning" which had focused
on the human mind as embodying value principles and performing an
integrative function in the conduct of life, there was a gradual shift to-

ward the other pole of Neo-Confucian scholarship, the study of principles in things and affairs, with emphasis on their concrete particularity. The later stages of this process then converged on forms of Western learning which produced a utilitarian view of reality or a pragmatism much in contrast to the earlier holistic conception of Chu Hsi.

3. Hsin-hsüeh/simhak or hsin-fa/simpŏp

The Learning of the Mind-and-Heart (hsin-hsüeh) and the System of the Mind-and-Heart (hsin-fa) are terms developed in the eleventh and twelfth centuries to characterize the Neo-Confucian doctrine of the mind and its proper discipline. They appear in the writings of Shao Yung (1011–77), the Ch'eng brothers, and Chu Hsi, and refer to a Neo-Confucian view of the mind, distinct from the Buddhist, which was in turn key to the Neo-Confucian political doctrine that the way to govern men was through individual self-discipline and the key to self-cultivation was mind-rectification. I have discussed this development in Neo-Confucian Orthodoxy and the Learning of the Mind-and-Heart.[13] Here I wish only to stress that these terms were applied to the Neo-Confucian philosophy of mind as a whole and especially to the Ch'eng-Chu school's central teaching concerning the "Mind of the Way" (tao-hsin) and the "Mind of Man" (jen-hsin). In the thirteenth and fourteenth centuries this Learning of the Mind-and-Heart spread through China and into Korea as an integral part of the Learning of the Way, i.e., orthodox Neo-Confucianism. Students of Neo-Confucianism in Korea will be familiar with this aspect of the tradition, so clearly echoed in writings of Yi T'oegye (Yi Hwang) like the Ten Diagrams of the Sage Learning (Sŏnghak sipto), of which the seventh is entitled "Diagram of the Learning of the Mind-and-Heart"[14] (Simhak to). Coming from a sharp critic of Wang Yang-ming, this Learning is unquestionably of the Ch'eng-Chu School and not the so-called Lu-Wang School.

In the latter case there has been some confusion because of the recent tendency to speak of the "School of the Mind" as something passed down from Lu Hsiang-shan to Wang Yang-ming, and opposed to the Ch'eng-Chu school as the School of Reason or Principle (li-hsüeh). To some extent this is reflected in the treatment of the subject in Fung Yu-lan's History of Chinese Philosophy, where the Learning of the Mind-and-Heart is most prominently identified with Lu Hsiang-shan and Wang Yang-ming in chapter 14.[15] Actually Fung himself cautions against drawing too sharp a dichotomy between Chu and Lu in this respect. In his comparison of the two Fung says, as Bodde has translated it:

A popular way of contrasting Chu Hsi with Lu Chiu-yüan is to say that the former emphasizes the importance of study, whereas the latter emphasizes the "prizing of one's virtuous nature". . . . What it overlooks, however, is that the final goal of Chu Hsi, no less than of all other Neo-Confucianists, is to explain the nature and functioning of the inner self.[16]

This last expression, "the nature and functioning of the self," is actually a quotation drawn from a key section of Chu Hsi's discussion of the method of the *Great Learning*. It appears in the *Words and Phrases from the Great Learning (Ta-hsüeh chang-chü)* and *Questions on the Great Learning (Ta-hsüeh huo-wen)*, in a context which refers to the System of the Mind-and-Heart *(hsin-fa)*.[17] What Bodde has rendered as "the nature and functioning of the inner self" might be translated more literally as "the whole substance and great functioning of our mind-and-heart *(wu hsin chih ch'üan-t'i ta-yung)*.[18] This is a central concept in Chu's thought and assumes the importance of a "technical term" much discussed in the later Chu Hsi school. Here it underscores the significance of Fung's observation in the Chinese text that "the final goal of Chu Hsi was to explain the nature and function of the mind-and-heart." In early Neo-Confucianism and even in much of the later school, there would have been no disposition to concede this crucial area to Lu and Wang as their special property. To avoid further confusion it may be wise to translate *hsin-hsüeh* as "Learning of the Mind-and-Heart" when it is used in this most general Neo-Confucian sense, and to recognize "School of the Mind" as an attempt retroactively to link Wang Yang-ming's teaching to the thought of Lu Hsiang-shan. In this latter case it would be seen as one significant outgrowth of the earlier Learning of the Mind-and-Heart, along with others like Ch'en Hsien-chang's, which reflect a changed perception of the mind in the Ming Period.

Another consideration here is that our term "school" may only be equated with the Chinese term *hsüeh*, "learning," in a very loose sense. In fact, "Lu-Wang School" can only mean a loose affinity of ideas, not an intellectual lineage from teacher to disciple or scholar to scholar. Wang Yang-ming's "learning" or "thought" is akin to Lu Hsiang-shan's, but Wang did not receive it from a line of teachers coming down from Lu. In the case of the Ch'eng-Chu "Learning of the Mind-and-Heart," however, there is usually some scholastic filiation, some personal link involved. By this criterion Wang would have to be identified more with Ch'eng-Chu.

4. Sheng-hsüeh/sŏnghak

"Sage Learning" (sheng-hsüeh) has several different connotations. It is of course the learning which comes from the sages of the past, i.e., "the Learning of the Sages," but Chu Hsi particularly emphasized it as the Way of learning to be a sage, or learning for sagehood. For him the important thing was that sagehood could be a practicable ideal in the Sung, that one could transform one's wayward mind-and-heart into a Way-ward one, through a definite process of self-cultivation. Chu Hsi's lifework and much of Neo-Confucian literature is premised on this idea. Unless one renders it as something like "Learning for Sagehood," rather than simply "Learning of the Sages," one misses perhaps the most dynamic element in the Neo-Confucian version of this traditional conception.

The alternative rendering, "Way of the Sages and Worthies" (sheng-hsien chih tao) conveyed the idea that worthies of recent times, like the Sung masters, came close enough to achieving sagehood as to be spoken of in the same breath with the ancients. It suggested the possibility that such attainment remained within anyone's reach. Inscriptions still hanging in the Royal Confucian College (Sŏnggyun'gwan) in Seoul today bear witness to the power of this ideal among the early Neo-Confucians in Korea.

Sagehood was understood in two principal forms. Classically it had strong associations with the sage-rulers of the remote past and with the Way of the Sage-kings. This perennial political concern of Confucians is still prominent in the minds of Neo-Confucians, whether as proponents of programmatic, institutional reform or as advocates of the intellectual and moral self-reformation of the ruler. Many Neo-Confucian leaders also served as ministers to the ruler, counseling him on how he might revive and follow the Way of the Sage Emperors and Early Kings. From this a new kind of "traditional" learning arose in the eleventh century, along with the Learning of the Way (tao-hsüeh), which was known as the "Learning of the Emperors and Kings" (ti-wang chih hsüeh) or, for short, "Learning of the Emperors" (ti-hsüeh). Scholars who propounded it, often in the lectures on the classics at court, were active in the same scholarly and official circles as the adherents of the Learning of the Way. Important among them were Fan Tsu-yü (1041–98), a colleague of Ch'eng I

(1033–1107) and Ssu-ma Kuang (1019–86), and Chen Te-hsiu, a leader of the School of the Way in the generation after Chu Hsi.[19]

Sagehood was also conceived as the ideal form of, or model for, the self. Not everyone could expect to be a sage-ruler but anyone could aspire to sageliness in virtue and wisdom. When Chou Tun-i, the Ch'eng brothers, Chu Hsi, and other Neo-Confucians talked about learning to become a sage or transforming oneself into a sage, they were said to be pursuing "learning for the sake of one's self" (wei-chi chih hsüeh), as Chu Hsi had put it using the language of the *Analects* (14:25): "The ancients pursued learning for one's own sake; nowadays they learn for the sake of [pleasing] others."

Whether as sage-ruler or as ideal self, the Neo-Confucian concept of sagehood exhibited certain perennial Confucian features as well as others particular to the Sung. As Neo-Confucian ideas made their way into the Ming and other periods, problems of continuity and discontinuity arose with both conceptions. Some of these will be discussed later but for illustration's sake one can imagine the difficulties that would arise with a "learning for the emperor," intended to activate the consciences of Sung rulers, if one tried to apply it to Japanese emperors who reigned but did not rule. Differences between Chinese and Korean monarchies would no doubt present their own problems.

5. Li-hsüeh/ihak and hsing-li-hsüeh/sŏngnihak

In the later development of Neo-Confucianism and in modern works, the Learning or School of Principle (li-hsüeh) has been one of the most common terms for Neo-Confucianism. Li, as principle, order, inner structure, was unquestionably a central concept in Neo-Confucian metaphysics. Yet its full significance only emerged with the passage of time. The Ch'eng brothers and Chu Hsi do not refer to their doctrine in this way, probably because they saw such a concept as only explanatory of, or instrumental to, the study of the Way and pursuit of sagehood. Chen Te-hsiu, fully appreciative of the historic contributions of the Ch'engs and Chu to the philosophy of principle, also recognized that the concept of li itself had little standing in classical Confucian literature and was not even mentioned in the original text of the Ch'eng-Chu school classic, the *Great Learning*.[20]

When it came into wider use in the Ming and in Korea, li-hsüeh was closely associated with the Learning of Human Nature (hsing-li-hsüeh) and the Learning of the Mind-and-Heart. It stressed principle as human nature, and principles as inherent in the mind. The imperial Ming *Compendium on Human Nature and Principle (Hsing-li ta-ch'üan)*, widely circulated in Korea, reinforced the idea that Ch'eng-Chu teaching was to be understood as a philosophy of "human nature and principle." In the first general accounts of Ming Neo-Confucian thought, the *Authoritative Transmission of the Learning of Principle (Li-hsüeh tsung-ch'uan)* by Sun Ch'i-feng (1585–1675) and *Case Studies of Ming Confucians* by Huang Tsung-hsi, references to *li-hsüeh* were understood to include *hsin-hsüeh* within its scope. Yi T'oegye, as mentioned before, also speaks of *li-hsüeh* and *hsin-hsüeh* as complementary terms, although by his time he felt the need to exclude Wang Yang-ming from the company of orthodox Neo-Confucians, which neither Sun nor Huang were prepared to do.[21]

There may be no harm in identifying *li-hsüeh* with reason or rationalism so long as this does not imply a merely logical ratiocination or conjure up a Western-style antithesis of reason versus intuition or emotion. According to Ch'eng-Chu teaching, the moral principles which constituted the nature of Heaven in the mind of man were humane feelings and impulses. It was the ordered structure and inherent rationality of these natural feelings that gave the Learning of the Mind-and-Heart its confidence in men's spontaneous intuitions, and it was the reliability of basic human instincts—their universality and predictability among all peoples—that underlay the rationalism of the Learning of Principle.

A somewhat similar problem is met in describing the relation between principle *(li)* and ether (or material force, *ch'i)* in Neo-Confucianism. The language used for this by Professor Takahashi Tōru in his early accounts of Korean Neo-Confucianism has an aptness which is difficult to reproduce in English usage. The Japanese *shuri-ha* and *shuki-ha* can be understood as tending to put a relative emphasis on principle or ether (material force) respectively, without implying a necessary antithesis between monism and dualism.[22]

It is significant that no such term as *ch'i-hsüeh* came into use among either Neo-Confucians or the critics of Ch'eng-Chu *li-hsüeh* despite the rising importance of *ch'i* (material force) in later Neo-Confucianism. In this century great attention has been paid to what in seventeenth- and eighteenth-century Chinese thought has been called by "Marxist" writers "materialism" or by Japanese scholars like Yamanoi Yū the "ch'i philosophy" or "ch'i thought" *(ki no tetsugaku* or *ki no shisō).*[23] Traditionally,

however, it would not have been considered appropriate to view learning
as primarily aimed at study of matter or ether apart from the reason or
principle inherent in it.

6. *Tao-t'ung/tot'ong*—THE "ORTHODOX WAY"

Tao-t'ung was a term widely used among Neo-Confucians after Chu
Hsi applied it to the orthodox Way which he believed had been revived
by the Ch'eng brothers. In *Neo-Confucian Orthodoxy* I have already pointed
out significantly different uses of this term in the Ch'eng-Chu school,
depending on whether one stresses, as Chu Hsi did, the inspirational and
prophetic elements in the revival and reinterpretation of the Way, or authoritative transmission and scholastic filiation. Both of these have an important role in later Neo-Confucianism, but it is significant that when
Neo-Confucians wish specifically to express the idea of transmission, *tao-
t'ung* alone is not seen as sufficient and therefore *tao-t'ung chih ch'uan*
has been used to specify the "transmission of the orthodox Way."

T'ung itself does not necessarily imply direct succession. In the related use of *cheng-t'ung* as "legitimate succession," there is no necessary
implication that legitimate dynastic rule is something handed on or directly conferred by one dynasty on its successor. Similarly, when Chu
Hsi spoke of *tao-t'ung* he emphasized the lack of continuous succession
and stressed rather the repossession of the Way after a long lapse in transmission. In both of these cases *t'ung* has the primary meaning of "control," "bring together," "coordinate." With Chu Hsi it is effective repossession or reconstitution of the Way which is conveyed by *tao-t'ung*, just
as *cheng-t'ung* meant effective repossession or reconstitution of the empire, often after a period of disunity. For Chu Hsi *cheng-t'ung* constituted
a recognition of a dynasty's political legitimacy without necessarily conferring on it the moral legitimacy of *tao-t'ung*. In this respect Chu Hsi
remained true to the earlier Sung view that the Han and T'ang, though
great dynasties in asserting their effective political control of the empire,
had failed to fulfill the Way of the Early Kings. Thus the purity of the
Sages' Way was upheld while political common sense was not flouted.

In *Neo-Confucian Orthodoxy* I have stressed *tao-t'ung* as the active
repossession of the Way partly in order to bring out the significance of
Neo-Confucian orthodoxy's being promoted under Mongol rule in ways
that had no precedent in the Sung or Chin dynasties. The Yüan dynasty's
achieving of legitimate rule by actively reintegrating the whole Empire

after long years of division had a seeming analogue in the "repossessing of the Way" *(tao-t'ung)*, achieved when the Learning of the Way *(tao-hsüeh)* became the established teaching in the Yüan schools and examination system.

Some acceptance of this idea would seem to have been implied when Korean converts to Neo-Confucianism sought to establish it as the orthodox teaching of Korea in the fourteenth and fifteenth centuries. Yet this same conception of the Way as "broken off" for centuries and only regained late in time by the Ch'eng brothers and Chu Hsi, meant that Koreans too could think of it as something they were capable of repossessing directly without the need for any intermediation by the Chinese. Indeed some Korean writers would think of their own active reconstituting of the Way as retrieving a long lost Tao originally implanted in Korea by the sage-statesman Kija (Chi Tzu), variously identified in classical sources as a survivor of the Shang dynasty who either came to northern Korea as a vassal of the Chou or chose exile there rather than serve under a new dynasty.[24] In this view the Koreans could be seen as resuming an indigenous "broken" transmission of the Tao, sharing in a larger world order based on Confucian values, while developing their own authentic version of the Way. Here there was room for a Korean identity to assert itself, eventually claiming for the Yi dynasty that it was more orthodox than the Ming itself in fidelity to that shared Way.

B. Concepts Conveying the Essence of the Way

Along with the foregoing names for the Way or for Neo-Confucian learning, there were other terms taken to express central truths or values in the Neo-Confucian teaching. Many ideas could be included here which individual thinkers and schools advocated as, in their eyes, keys to all others in the system. Humaneness, reverence, filiality *(hsiao)*, innate knowing *(liang-chih)* are typical examples. Other concepts or doctrines may be identified with individual thinkers as their own distinctive contribution to the development of Neo-Confucian thought: e.g., Chou Tun-i's "Non-finite and yet the Supreme Ultimate" *(wu-chi erh t'ai-chi)* or his "stressing quiescence" *(chu-ching)*, teachings which might be taken by some as central to Neo-Confucian metaphysics or spiritual praxis, but accepted by others only with reservations.

Korean thinkers, no less than Chinese and Japanese, held diverse views on these matters. Certain ideas and practices were seen to have a special meaning for individual scholars and teachers depending on their own life-experience; indeed their learning would be thought superficial if it conformed simply to one model and did not reflect some personal struggle to "get" or find the Way for one's self *(tzu-te)*. This idea is not uncommon among Korean Neo-Confucians, but it is most evident in Yi Yulgok's (Yi I, 1536–84) frequent reference to "getting it oneself" *(chadŭk,* for the Chinese *tzu-te).* As Han Young-woo's study of the Kija myth (herein) shows, Yulgok particularly emphasized the Korean role of Kija as a sage comparable to Confucius and Mencius and, by equating Korea with the native states of the latter sages, Lu and Ch'i, he naturalized the Way of the Sage Kings with Kija as its spiritual patriarch. Paradigmatically Kija thus served to demonstrate that "getting the Way oneself" was not finding it outside and internalizing it, but finding the Way within and affirming it as universal.

Beyond these core ideas and individual concepts, however, there are formulations which attempt to characterize the tradition in a broader and more balanced way. Such formulations represent the Way as a comprehensive process or pattern in which it is vital to maintain a balance between polar values. "To abide in reverence and fathom principle" *(chü-ching ch'iung-li)* expresses the idea that learning should link scholarly study and moral/spiritual cultivation. "To spend half the day in quiet-sitting and half in the study of books" *(pan-jih ching-tso, pan-jih tu-shu)* conveys the same idea in more concrete terms. In a similar vein there is the classic formulation taken from the *Mean (Chung-yung)* which speaks of "honoring the moral nature and pursuing intellectual inquiry" *(tsun te-hsing, tao wen-hsüeh).* There has been some tendency recently to dichotomize these values in such terms as intellectualism vs. anti-intellectualism, or to identify one with Chu Hsi and the other with his "antagonist" Lu Hsiang-shan, but traditionally both elements were seen as equally necessary, and indeed complementary, aspects of the Way.

Each of these formulations conveys a sense of the Way as embracing certain universal values or developing basic human faculties, while at the same time each can be associated with the particular moral and intellectual concerns of the Sung scholar-official *(shih-ta-fu).* Thus "abiding in reverence" may take the form for the Sung scholar of quiet-sitting, since he is heir to Buddhist and Taoist meditation techniques (whether professedly so or not) as well as to Confucian ritual. For him too "fathoming principle" is more often pursued in bookish learning than in systematic observation of nature. As it happens the Korean *yangban* aristocracy, also scholar-officials with Buddhist influences deeply embedded in their native tradition, inclined toward many of the same pursuits as Sung scholars, e.g., office holding, "quiet-sitting" and classical studies. In principle, however, the expression of religious/moral concern or intellectual inquiry need not, and did not, adhere strictly to Sung models, for Chu Hsi himself had acknowledged that such practices would vary with individual circumstances.[25]

On a more theoretical level there is the expression of Chu Hsi referred to above (p. 12) which is found in his *Words and Phrases from the Great Learning* and his *Questions on the Great Learning*: namely, "the whole substance and great functioning" [of the nature as expressed in the mind-and-heart *(ch'üan-t'i ta-yung)*]. This formulation appears frequently in the writings of the early Ch'eng-Chu School in the late Sung, Yüan, and early Ming, and conveys the sense of Neo-Confucian Learning as completely integrating the ideal of man's moral nature with its practical realization in fulfilling the needs of mankind.

As Chen Te-hsiu explained it, there could be no separation of principle and practice, no discussion of "substance" that did not take human needs into account, and no resort to practices (functions) that did not conform to the moral nature of man and the Way.[26] Here the concept is broad enough to implicate the entire Ch'eng-Chu system of metaphysics as the basis for one's understanding of the moral nature, as well as to connote a large body of historical and social experience considered relevant to the "functioning" of that nature in particular human situations.

Professor Kusumoto Masatsugu has written a long essay on this recurrent theme in Chinese Neo-Confucian thought, which also had its Japanese proponents.[27] Korean Neo-Confucians, too, were familiar with this doctrine, and for them also it tended to define the essential tradition. Clearly "substance" and "function" would have to be understood in terms of the Neo-Confucian discourse and are not comprehensible in classical terms alone.

On the same level of theoretical abstraction is the formula of Ch'eng I: "principle is one, its particularizations diverse" or "the unity of principle and diversity of its particularized functions" *(li-i fen-shu)*.[28] This served especially to distinguish Neo-Confucian teaching from Buddhism and Taoism, affirming the reality both of the immutable principle or substance of the nature—in man, his "humanity"—and the innumerable forms of action in which this virtue was given concrete expression. One could also view it as a way of emphasizing the unity of substance and function.

Some persons held that there was no essential difference in principle between Confucianism and Buddhism, since Confucian "humaneness" could be equated with Buddhist "compassion" (tz'u). According to this view the only significant difference between the two teachings lay in the functional aspect; i.e., Buddhism's lack of a practical program such as Confucianism offered for dealing with the needs of human society. Li T'ung (1093–1163), Chu Hsi's teacher, contended that the difference in practice also pointed to a difference in principle. One could not expect Confucian practice to follow from Buddhist principle nor could one accept as true principle what did not lead.to Confucian ethical practice. Hence, there could be no dichotomizing, as in Buddhism, of principle and practice to represent two different orders of reality, principle real and undifferentiated, practice less real because it pertained to the world of differentiation and discrimination. To substantiate principle, one must realize one's humanity in the midst of practice, i.e., by fulfilling one's individual lot (fen) or station in life with its differentiated duties. This is what was meant by realizing "the unity of principle and the diversity of its particularizations."

For Neo-Confucians this doctrine served to distinguish their "real or practical learning" from the "empty learning" of Buddhism, which viewed the world of moral action as a secondary or qualified order of reality in contradistinction to the essential Truth of Buddhist Emptiness.[29] Li T'ung was unwilling to concede either the Buddhist bifurcation of reality on two levels of truth or the need for transcendental Enlightenment as the precondition for coping with the world. For him, on the contrary, true spiritual freedom was to be attained in the performance of the moral task. In Yi T'oegye such ideas resurfaced with special intensity as he held Li T'ung in even higher respect than Chu Hsi had done (see pp. 279–88).

"Principle is one, its particularizations diverse" was much discussed by Hsü Heng, the leading Neo-Confucian teacher of the Yüan period in China, who was such a seminal force in the spread of the Learning of the Way.[30] Since his influence was strong in Korea, as well as in seventeenth-century Japanese Neo-Confucianism,[31] one may take frequent reference to Li T'ung, Hsü Heng, and this concept as confirming the underlying continuity from Chinese Neo-Confucianism to Korean and

Japanese. It is understandable that a doctrine linking universal values to particular applications, and recognizing the differentiated expression in social and cultural life of one underlying Way, would have special significance for Koreans and Japanese, whose adherence to Neo-Confucian teaching was not taken to entail a loss of their own cultural identity.

Still another expression for the same basic idea is Ch'eng Hao's (1032–85) "Humaneness which forms one body with Heaven-and-Earth and all things" *(t'ien-ti wan-wu i-t'i chih jen)*.[32] According to this holistic view one's self-fulfillment was achieved by engendering a state of mind and following a way of conduct in which there was no longer any consciousness of a distinction between self and others. Such a view was quite prominent in Ming thought and in Tokugawa Neo-Confucianism. Professor Shimada Kenji in his early studies of modern thought in China saw an essential link between this ideal of Sung-Ming Neo-Confucianism and late nineteenth-century reformers like T'an Ssu-t'ung (1865–98)—a continuity running down through almost a millennium of Neo-Confucian thought in China. More recently, in comparing the differing outlooks of the seventeenth-century Japanese thinkers Kaibara Ekken (1630–1714) and Yamazaki Ansai (1611–82) in relation to Ch'eng-Chu thought, Professor Okada Takehiko cited this doctrine of the "Humaneness which forms one body with Heaven-and-Earth and all things," and its importance in Ekken's thought, as the crucial element of continuity in Neo-Confucianism and the key criterion by which to distinguish Ekken's essential orthodoxy from the skepticism of Kogaku thinkers, which in some other respects Ekken shared.[33]

As a last example of this type of formulation I offer the doctrine of "self-cultivation for the governance of men" *(hsiu-chi chih-jen)* or "ordering the state through self-discipline" *(hsiu-shen chih-kuo)*. This was an outgrowth of the ethicopolitical thought developed during the Sung in connection with the *Great Learning*, and particularly in the lectures on the classics at the Sung court. The appeal of this idea lay in its utter simplicity and rich ambiguity. Its primary meaning was that the responsibility for self-discipline fell first of all on the ruler (or his surrogates) who had to set the model for others' self-cultivation, but its plausibility rested on the idea that truly to govern men was not possible except through their voluntary cooperation and self-discipline.[34] *Hsiu-shen chih-kuo* was shorthand for the eight steps *(pa-t'iao-mu)* of the *Great Learning*, and one might refer back to the latter for a fuller idea of what "self-cultivation" consisted in. But shorthand lent itself to oversimplification, and problems could arise from simplistic thinking about governmental administration. Perhaps in periods of decline or transition, when institutions failed, there was some advantage in putting everyone on their own and something hopeful about making a virtue of necessity in the midst of rapid political and social change. At any rate, this may have been the case in the late Sung, Yüan, and early Ming, when the idea of "ordering the state through self-discipline," especially as advocated by Chen Te-hsiu and Hsü Heng, seems to have played a large role in gaining acceptance for Neo-Confucianism as the dominant public philosophy.

A similar phenomemon is observable in the writing of Fujiwara Seika as a proponent of this philosophy in Japan during the transition from the Warring States Period to the founding of the Tokugawa shogunate.[35] From my own reading in the thought of early Neo-Confucians in Korea, and from the work of Martina Deuchler,[36] I conclude that this aspect of Neo-Confucianism had much the same appeal: it was par excellence an answer to the need for an explicit political philosophy, flexible enough to be adapted to varied circumstances. Yet by the mid-Ming period in China, and Yi Yulgok's time in Korea, the idea was wearing a little thin; one sees a groping for something less moralistic and more substantial, more concrete, to work with. In response to this there developed the institutional studies and "solid learning" *(shih-hsüeh)* that became identified with "practical statecraft" *(ching-shih chih yung)*. In Korea too this seems to have prepared the way for the practical learning known as *sirhak*.

To conclude this discussion of key concepts I offer as a contrasting example of ostensible continuity in Neo-Confucianism what may, in the end, prove to be a case of discontinuity, the Japanese expression *taigi meibun*, or *meibun taigi*, which asserted that the "highest duty is to perform one's allotted function (i.e., to fulfill the obligations of loyalty to one's lord or ruler)." This doctrine was developed among the followers of the school of Yamazaki Ansai, especially Asami Keisai (1652–1711), citing Chu Hsi's writings on the threat of foreign conquest in the Sung. By the nineteenth century in Japan *taigi meibun* had come to be regarded as a cardinal teaching of Chu Hsi and indeed the very essence of Neo-Confucian teaching on duty and loyalty. Today one can read through any number of Chinese works on Neo-Confucian thought and philosophy without finding any mention of it. From this one might adjudge *taigi meibun* to have been a peculiarly Japanese appropriation of Neo-Confucianism. Elsewhere I have suggested that it may be more reasonable to "take it as a distinctive Japanese formulation of an ethicoreligious attitude which finds diverse expression within and among the cultural traditions sharing the Neo-Confucian legacy."[37]

This would seem to be confirmed in the Korean case. Korea was threatened, and to an even greater degree than were China or Japan, with the danger of foreign conquest and the loss of its national identity. There, however, a heightened sense of loyalty and resistance to foreigners elicited from Neo-Confucians an intense feeling of fidelity to principle and a self-sacrificing devotion, often spoken of in terms of *chŏrŭi*, "integrity and righteousness," which inspired many acts of self-martyrdom. This was not clearly identified with supreme loyalty either to one's own ruler or one's own nation, but would present itself, for instance, as resistance to the Manchus out of loyalty to the Ming,[38] or resistance to the ruler in the name of fidelity to principle. For all the acts of heroism which one might cite in the name of *chŏrŭi*, however, it remains only an intense Korean expression of a concept, and an ethicoreligious attitude, shared among Neo-Confucians in China and Japan as well. *Taigi meibun* on the other hand seems not to have been known or at least much talked about in Korea until modern times when the Japanese repaid, in their own coin, some of Yamazaki Ansai's debt to Yi T'oegye.

C. Authoritative Texts

Another measure of continuity in a tradition is the transmission of texts that establish the terms of the ongoing discourse, and are generally accepted as standard or canonical works. Views on which texts can claim primacy vary with individual participants in the Neo-Confucian dialogue, even when they accept in general the authority of the tradition. An illustration of this is given in the paper by Yamazaki Michio for the Conference on Chu Hsi's Philosophy and Korean Confucianism in Seoul, September 1980, wherein he presents the differing views of Yi T'oegye, Yamazaki Ansai, and Miyake Shōsai on the priority to be assigned to the *Elementary Learning (Hsiao-hsüeh)* and *Reflections on Things at Hand (Chin-ssu lu)* as basic texts.[39] Neither of these works compiled under Chu Hsi's direction would have been thought canonical by Chu himself, but among his followers they became virtual "classics," with a social and educational importance far beyond their derivative status as "scriptures." The

Elementary Learning served, for instance, as the proximate scriptural authority for the adoption of the community compact and village wine-drinking ceremony, widely practiced in rural Korea. Indeed there were times in the political history of the Yi dynasty when the standing of the Neo-Confucians at court was closely correlated to the status of the *Elementary Learning* and its acceptance as a basis for economic and social reform.[40]

Competing in these same circles for priority as an introductory text or primer was a third neoclassical work, Chen Te-hsiu's *Classic of the Mind-and-Heart (Hsin-ching)*, which I have discussed in *Neo-Confucian Orthodoxy and the Learning of the Mind-and-Heart*, and which Professor Yamazaki also cites in this connection. This *Heart Classic*, as I learned after a chance encounter with the text in Yi T'oegye's library at the Tosan Sŏwŏn had set me off on the path to rediscovery of its roots in earlier tradition, had once carried great weight in the Learning of the Mind-and-Heart transmitted from China to Korea and Japan.

Another new classic of the greatest practical importance was the *Family Ritual of Master Chu (Chu-tzu chia-li, or Wen-kung chia-li)*. Compiled under Chu Hsi's direction but left unfinished at his death (i.e., he had hoped to do more refining and polishing of it), the *Family Ritual* reflected Chu's sense that the ancient ritual texts, prescribing elaborate ceremonial observances for the Chou aristocracy, were unsuited to the life-situations of scholars in the Sung. The rites needed to be simplified and their costs brought within the considerably reduced means of the Sung literatus. For this purpose Chu sought to synthesize writings of Sung masters like the Ch'eng brothers, Chang Tsai (1020–77), and Ssu-ma Kuang, believing that their recommendations on ritual would serve as a more practical guide in the contemporary circumstances than would ritual classics literally adhered to. Of all the East Asian peoples, during the Neo-Confucian age, the Koreans seem to have embraced this approach most enthusiastically. They made the *Family Ritual* virtually the law of the land and Ritual Studies *(yehak)* a major field of Confucian studies.

Apart from helping us to fill in the early history of Neo-Confucianism, the *Family Ritual, Heart Classic*, and similar works illustrate how this school of thought was constantly creating and recreating its own past in the attempt to remake the present. In a basic sense it made up "classics" as it went along—partly with pieces of old fabric from the ancient canon and partly out of the whole cloth of new commentaries which laced these fragments together. This was of course true of the Four Books, which owed their existence as such to Chu Hsi, and especially true of the *Great Learning* and the *Mean*, to which he gave a new interpretation and a central position. Another example of a popular classic, but of less consequence to the canonical tradition, is the aforementioned syncretic work of the Korean Ch'u Chŏk, the *Precious Mirror for Clarifying the Mind-and-Heart (Myŏngsim pogam, or Vietnamese Minh-tam bao-giam)*, which appeared to sum up the wisdom of the ages in regard to mind cultivation and the conduct of life.

It would be misleading, however, to suggest that this improvisation knew no limits and that there are no objective tests by which to ascertain the consensus of tradition in respect to its core curriculum. Though this was still a tradition in the making, already by Hsü Heng's time the *Elementary Learning* had won a place as a text virtually on a par with the Four Books and Five Classics in the basic curriculum of the Imperial College and other state schools during the Yüan dynasty. Indeed Hsü spoke of it as sacred scripture.[41] This only reflected a consensus already established in the local academies where instruction in the new teaching was flourishing well before its acceptance by the state.[42] When the Yüan dynasty, after much debate, finally resurrected the examination system and installed the Four Books with Chu Hsi's commentaries as required texts for the first time, the *Elementary Learning* did not make it into this official company, perhaps because it was regarded as something to be studied on the elementary level. But in the eyes of Wu Ch'eng (1249–1333), the leading classicist of his day, it was eminently worthy of inclusion in the curriculum which he unsuccessfully proposed for adoption at that time.[43]

Against this background it becomes relevant to ask whether there was much debate over the content of the examinations later adopted in Korea, and what selectivity, if any, was shown in the fixing of curricula for state and local schools. Did these tend to follow lines already laid down in China? The Ming Dynasty, certainly, followed the Yüan system almost to the letter, without any questions being asked worthy of mention in the record. Having once become fixed in the Ming "constitution," i.e., in the official enactments of the dynasty's founder, the content of the examinations was of course not readily subject to change by his heirs, but even the succeeding Ch'ing dynasty did not exercise a new regime's normal option to install different texts.

In Korea the examination system underwent many changes, as the paper of Professor Yi Sŏngmu herein (pp. 125–60) indicates, but if the *Great Statutes for the Governance of the State (Kyŏngguk taejŏn)* may be taken as a standard for Yi dynasty Korea, the five Classics and Four Books became required texts for one part of the examinations (the other part being the various literary styles) for both the lower and higher civil service degrees. No candidate could successfully complete either stage of the exams without showing his mastery, at the lower level, of the *Family Ritual* and the *Elementary Learning*, and at the higher level, of the *Family Ritual*.[44]

Another kind of official certification is found in the *Great Compendia on the Five Classics, Four Books, and [the Philosophy of] Human Nature and Principle (Wu-ching, ssu-shu, hsing-li ta-ch'üan)*, compiled in 1415 on the order of Ming Ch'eng-tsu (r. 1403–25). This went beyond simply confirming the position of the Five Classics and Four Books. It strongly endorsed many writings of the Sung philosophers, and gave the imperial imprimatur to such texts as Chou Tun-i's *Diagram of the Supreme Ultimate Explained (T'ai-chi-t'u shuo)* and his *Penetrating the Book of Changes (T'ung-shu)*, Chang Tsai's *Western Inscription (Hsi-ming)*, *Correcting Youthful Ignorance (Cheng-meng)*, and many writings of the Ch'eng brothers and Chu Hsi. In 1426 a set of these *Compendia* was given by the Emperor Hsüan-tsung (r. 1426–36) to the Korean king,[45] and to judge from the frequency with which they were reprinted and appear in the classical collections of Korean libraries, they would seem to have had wide influence.[46]

As is well-known the Ch'ing dynasty not only reprinted these compendia but sponsored an official abridgement of the *Great Compendium on Human Nature and Principle* under the title of *Essential Ideas of Nature and Principle (Hsing-li ching-i)*, published in 1715.[47] Comparing the comprehensive scope of the original version (70 *chüan*) with the later one (12 *chüan*), one can see two rather different approaches to the perpetuation of the tradition: the earlier one expansive and comprehensive, the later one much more selective and trim. Contrary to the conventional view, traditions do not simply accumulate heirlooms from the past. From time to time they feel the need to sort out their possessions and clean house to get some room to live and work in. In the process they reveal what adjustments are being made in their own priorities. Sometimes too there is a need to adapt to the level of practical comprehension on the part of a new master in the house, like the non-Chinese rulers of the Ch'ing (Manchus), just as had been done by Hsü Heng in educating the Mongols to Neo-Confucianism.[48] Thus there was ample precedent within the tradition for such adjustments on the part of the Koreans. Even before the *Great Compendium on Human Nature and Principle* was abridged under the Manchus, it had been reduced to more manageable proportions by the Koreans. As Martina Deuchler reports, "The famous symposium of Sung philosophy, the *Great Compendium on Human Nature and Principle* was printed several times during Sejong's reign (r. 1418–50) but seems to have reached its full significance for the development of Neo-Confucian thought in Korea only after it was excerpted by Kim Chŏng-guk (1485–1541) at the beginning of the sixteenth century."[49]

If historical circumstances warrant such adjustments, however, we must remember that Chu Hsi himself set a prime example of how one consolidates and encapsulates a tradition for educational purposes, as he did in his commentaries on the Four Books, his simplification of the ritual in the *Elementary Learning* and *Family Ritual*, his concise anthology of the Sung masters in *Reflections on Things at Hand*, his condensation of Ssu-ma Kuang's history, etc.

In Japan the nature of the "official orthodoxy" (what I call Bakufu orthodoxy" in contrast to the Mandarin orthodoxy of China)[50] was much looser, with the state less directly involved in education, with no civil examination system comparable to the Chinese, and with individual scholars taking more independent initiatives. Accordingly, the ruling regime rarely got into the business of defining and publishing an approved canon of Neo-Confucian literature. Indeed the contrast is so sharp between the Japanese and Chinese cases as to raise similar questions about the Koreans. In the matter of approved texts is there anything to establish the "official" content of the canon? And among independent scholars, or in the libraries of their academies, is there any consensus concerning the standard works that are seen to represent the core of tradition?

Such questions are not easily answered on the basis of existing scholarly studies, but judging from the holdings of academy libraries (mainly post-1590s and the Hideyoshi invasions) the indispensable texts would appear to have been the Four Books, Five Classics, Chinese dynastic histories, Chu Hsi's works including the *Basic Structure and Selected Details of the General Mirror (T'ung-chien kang-mu)*, Chen Te-hsiu's *Heart Classic* and *Extended Meaning of the Great Learning (Ta-hsüeh yen-i)*, and the aforementioned *Great Compendium of Human Nature and Principle.*[51]

In the early days of the Neo-Confucian movement in Korea scholars and officials drew freely on a considerable body of classical and historical literature for whatever sanction it might offer their plans for reform. They invoked especially the three ritual classics of the Confucian tradition: the *Book of Rites (Li-chi)*, *Rites of Chou (Chou-li)*, and *Ceremonial Rites (I-li)*. But they did not stop there. Chu Hsi's *Family Ritual* had almost greater authority for them, not despite but indeed because of its being a recent adaptation, better suited to their own times than the classic rites prescribed for Chou aristocracy which had long since disappeared. As precedents for governmental institutions, classically subsumed under the concept of religiosocial liturgies (i.e., "rites"), Korean Neo-Confucians did not hesitate to cite later historical encyclopedias such as the *Comprehensive Institutes (T'ung-tien)* of Tu Yu (735–812) and the *Comprehensive Inquiry into Recorded Institutions (Wen-hsien t'ung-k'ao)* by Ma Tuan-lin (1254–1325) in the scholarly lineage of Chu Hsi and Chen Te-hsiu. Also, more for historical precedents than institutions, they consulted Chu Hsi's *Basic Structure and Selected Details of the General Mirror.*[52] In this process, by consensus among scholars rather than by official prescription, the Koreans participated in the identification of Neo-Confucian classics that would have as much effective authority as the original classics in the actual conduct of affairs and of life.

D. Neo-Confucian Institutions

In the corporate life of Neo-Confucianism, political institutions loomed large. This was not because scholar-officials had effective control over them or much opportunity to impress on them a specifically Neo-Confucian character, but simply because, with the Confucian commitment to public service, they had to live with them and make the best of it. Institutions of state tended to follow the persistent patterns of dynastic rule; for the most part they remained typical of the centralized bureaucracies of the past, much at variance with Neo-Confucian ideals of a Chou restoration and return to decentralized feudalism.

To this generalization the new civil service examinations of the Yüan dynasty stand as only a partial exception. Neo-Confucian reformers at Khubilai's court resisted plans to reestablish the examinations, preferring to recruit, train, and bring up leaders through a system of public schools. When, in a later reign, they finally compromised, accepting a system in which the examinations' content, and to some extent the form, were of Neo-Confucian authorship, the concession was rather typical of the Neo-Confucian's adjustment to the hard facts of political life and the stubborn persistence of dynastic institutions.

Another partial exception, yet only a qualified success by the Neo-Confucian's own standards, is the institution at court of lectures from the "classics mat." These constituted a serious effort to promote Neo-Confucian ideas of rulership, giving leading scholars an opportunity in the presence of the Emperor to discuss classical principles in relation to contemporary affairs. We know that Chu Hsi seized this opportunity to stress the importance of the *Great Learning* as a manual of imperial self-cultivation, often in direct reference to urgent political problems of the day. We also know that Fan Tsu-yü's *Learning of the Emperor (Ti-hsüeh)* and Chen Te-hsiu's *Extended Meaning of the Great Learning* are byproducts of this kind of imperial instruction, and that recourse was had in these "imperial seminars" (as Robert Hartwell has called them) to manuals of statecraft and political histories which became classics in their own right, offering a practical wisdom for the guidance of rulers rather in contrast to the Four Books. These included the *Essence of Government in the Chen-kuan Era (Chen-kuan cheng-yao)*, the *Imperial Pattern (Ti-fan)* of T'ang T'ai-tsung (r. 627–50), the *General Mirror for Aid in Government (Tzu-chih t'ung-chien)* of Ssu-ma Kuang, and the *Mirror of T'ang (T'ang-chien)* of Fan Tsu-yü.[53]

The importance of these works in the political literature of early Neo-Confucianism has not been well recognized in recent times. Perhaps a realization that the classics mat as an institution and these texts as political classics, along with Chen's *Heart Classic* and *Classic of Government (Cheng-ching)*, played a prominent role at the Korean court, will direct new attention to the Chinese prototypes. As it is, there has been some disposition to believe that Neo-Confucian political thinking was largely limited to well-worn clichés of self-cultivation drawn from the Four Books.[54] One cannot dispute this view altogether, inasmuch as the latter texts were basic to the intellectual formation of scholar-officials in later centuries, and the idea of "self-cultivation for the governance of men" or "self-discipline for the ordering of the state" certainly led in this direction. Nevertheless Chen Te-hsiu's *Extended Meaning* covered extensive historical

ground and went into many political problems never dealt with in the
Great Learning itself. Chen did this by embracing a great deal of practical political lore under the rubric of "the investigation of things and affairs" and the "learning to be pursued by the ruler." Thus it is significant
that Chŏng Tojŏn (1342–98), in proposing a new constitutional order at
the inception of the Yi dynasty, should identify the lectures from the classics
mat as one of the most essential institutions of the royal court, and should
specify Chen Te-hsiu and his *Extended Meaning of the Great Learning*
as the model for these discussions.[55]

Chen's scholarly enterprise in this connection reminds us that "broad
learning" was one of the twin aims of Neo-Confucian cultivation, along
with moral and spiritual discipline. For Chu Hsi to stress "self-cultivation" did not necessarily imply a moralistic reductionism on his part, for
he was equally emphatic on the need for intellectual inquiry. And even
though Chu, like Mencius, spoke disparagingly of the pursuit of "systems" or institutions in a utilitarian sense, he did not neglect institutions
intended to serve "humane" or "righteous" causes. Chu himself devoted
much attention to the workings of institutions which could benefit people
on the local level. The community compact (*hsiang-yüeh*) and local
granaries (*she-tsang-fa*) became classic Neo-Confucian examples of this.[56]

It may be that such institutions do not loom large in the thinking of
scholars for whom practical statecraft is almost entirely an affair of the
court and central government, and who look somewhat indifferently on
problems of lower-level administration. But Chu Hsi's brand of realism
and practicality accepted the need for grass-roots organization and for
dealing with people in their actual condition. Thus he pursued this interest in the only way feasible to him (given his non-participation for most
of his career in service at court), that is, through statecraft practiced on
the local level. In this way Chu remained true to his own belief in the
importance of "great functioning" or "great usefulness" (*ta-yung*) as a
necessary complement to the cultivation of the "whole substance" of the
mind. This "great usefulness" may be seen as all the more complementary to self-cultivation, if we consider that one of the implications of "ordering the state through self-discipline" was a recognition that the only
practical way to administer a vast and teeming empire was to allow for a
large measure of local autonomy or self-governance.

It should be no surprise to us that this kind of practicality took diverse
forms among Chu's followers. For some, like the historians Wang Ying-

lin (1223–1296) and Ma Tuan-lin, it meant directing their "broad learning" to the study of social and political institutions in their historical development. For others, like the Neo-Confucian reformers at the court of Khubilai, it meant strengthening Han Chinese institutions under Mongol rule, even those of a traditional dynastic sort, for which they became known as exponents of "practical statesmanship" (ching-shih chih yung).[57]

Among such institutions in the Yi dynasty the censorate may be cited as one which Neo-Confucians powerfully reinforced as a means of restraining royal power. Recognition of the Confucian censors' right and duty to censure the king became such a feature of Yi politics as to effect a real sharing of power. According to Edward Wagner, this equilibrium of power "at its finest point of balance represented a constitutional monarchy."[58] For others still, in the Ming dynasty, practical statecraft meant grafting the Neo-Confucian "community compact" onto the local system of collective security (pao-chia). And in Korea too the practice of Neo-Confucian statecraft on this level apparently proved adaptable to local conditions and of "great usefulness" in meeting practical needs. As the papers in this volume testify, the community compact was for many Neo-Confucians in Korea a key institution, widely practiced on the local level. Curiously enough the authority often invoked on its behalf was Chu Hsi's Elementary Learning, which cited the community compact as an "exemplary practice" (shan-hsing).[59]

Another set of distinctively Neo-Confucian institutions were the four major rituals prescribed in Chu Hsi's Family Ritual: "capping" (coming of age), wedding, funeral, and sacrifices for the ancestors. For the perpetuation of these rituals it was essential in the eyes of Ch'eng I and Chu Hsi that each family set some land aside to support an ancestral shrine, where filial respect would be shown to the dead and gratitude expressed for the blessings of life received through them. This was to be a modest approximation of the shrines and rites prescribed in the ancient ritual texts for the Chou aristocracy; by T'ang times these could be maintained by only a few great clans and by the Sung period they were only a vestigial memory of scholars concerned over the fragmentation of property by equal inheritance and the consequent atomization of the social and political structure before the growing power of the state. In China it remained difficult for any but a few clans to keep up the appearances of the aristocratic lineages (tsung) of the past, or even to preserve the simplified version Chu had adapted to the situation of the Sung family or household *(chia).* But in Korea the hereditary prerogatives and propertied status of the *yangban* scholar-aristocracy put them in a better position to practice this system and fulfill Chu Hsi's intentions.

For all this, Korean use of the *Family Ritual,* according to Martina Deuchler, remained quite selective. The parts most faithfully followed were the ones on ancestor worship (although there were long, and in the end, inconclusive debates about the number of ancestral generations which should be venerated) and on funerals. Capping was most often performed, if at all, as a preliminary to the wedding ceremony, and the latter remained Korean into modern times (just as weddings in Japan have kept to Shinto rites).[60]

One of the most talked-of institutions in Neo-Confucian literature is the well-field system. It appears also to have been one of the least practicable as a system of agricultural organization, though its "utility" may from the beginning have been more symbolic and pedagogical than practical, i.e., it was a vivid illustration of the principles of economic equality and communal cooperation rather than a workable system of land management. Already by Chu Hsi's time he had tended to belittle Chang Tsai's attempt to recreate a well-field system as rather idiosyncratic and ineffectual.[61] One does not hear much of it thereafter as an actual institutional form in China. In Korea too it was often held up as a model for reform but never, it seems, actually instituted in its classic form. Curiously, in Japan there were symbolic reenactments of the system in feudal domains of Neo-Confucian-minded *daimyo,* and one can still see vestiges of nine-squared plots in public parks which had once been gardens of the daimyo[62]—nostalgic evocations of an arcadian ideal somewhat reminiscent of the rustic cottages of the Bourbons at Versailles. Perhaps the ultimate adaptation of this idea to the aesthetic tastes of the Japanese is the miniature well-field incorporated into a few square feet of the garden at the Zen temple of Tōfukuji in Kyoto.

Of more practical significance in the corporate life of Neo-Confucians was the academy *(shu-yüan),* in which Chinese Neo-Confucian thought first germinated, was then earnestly cultivated, and eventually came to full flower. Several features of Neo-Confucianism reflect this "academic" provenance. Academies (as the name *shu-yüan* indicates) were for the keeping and study of books. Thus book-learning and the preservation of the cultural heritage were central to the Neo-Confucian enterprise even before it became known for its speculative philosophy. Second, academies were for teaching, and played a large part in the spread of education in the Sung, taking up some of the slack from the failure of state schools to fulfill the need for public education. Third, academies were local institutions. Though sometimes winning a wide reputation and attracting students from a considerable distance, they depended essentially on local initiative and support. "Private" in the sense that they were not part of the official state system, and had the voluntary support of the community, academies still needed the cooperation of local officials and occasionally received grants from the state. Thus they had somewhat less independence from officialdom than the word "private" would suggest in the West. So far as I know, no Neo-Confucian championed academies as "private," in contrast to "public," schools. Universal education through state-supported schools remained the ideal, as Chu Hsi's writings clearly implied. In both China and Korea, however, academies provided the institutional base for Neo-Confucian scholarship and teaching; they afforded a measure of intellectual autonomy, if not financial independence, and kept alive a spirit of both voluntarism and community involvement in the life of learning.

As a typical social and cultural institution of the Chinese scholar-official class *(shih-ta-fu)* in their home setting, the local academy could well serve a similar function for even the more aristocratic *yangban* class in Korea, who identified themselves in the same terms as Confucian *sa-daebu*. In Japan, however, the ruling elite or *samurai* class had military functions, feudal allegiances, and often religious loyalties, much in contrast to the Chinese and Korean cases. Hence the academy could not function in the same way as a meeting place of an upper-class conscious of upholding its traditions and position vis-à-vis the ruler. In such circumstances it is not surprising that the *shoin* (equivalent term for the Chinese *shu-yüan* and Korean *sŏwŏn*) should be transmuted into a cultural adornment of the Japanese aristocracy, known best as an architectural feature in a new style of residential villa *(shoin tsukuri)* and thus assimilated, like the "well-field," as an aesthetic element in the new culture of the Edo period. Meanwhile the educational functions of the local academy were served by private schools *(shijuku)* including schools for townspeople *(chōnin)*, as well as by schools (often known as *gakkō*) maintained by Japanese daimyo as domainal *(han)* institutions. This difference did not, in the end, prevent such schools from serving many of the same cultural services as the academies, and yet they could not quite stand as the embodiment of a class-conscious culture in the way the latter had done in the Ming and Yi dynasties.

As regards the Korean case, several papers in this volume testify to the major role of local academies in the development of Yi dynasty education and culture, a role perhaps even greater than that of their Chinese counterparts. Moreover, Korea is probably unique in having preserved the academies so well with their collections of books largely intact.

For all that, the full significance of the academies can only be measured against the failure of the Neo-Confucians to achieve their stated objective of establishing a universal public school system. Neo-Confucians in the Sung, Yüan, and early Ming stressed education as a prerequisite to good government, and called repeatedly for rulers to establish official schools on all levels from the court down to the village. Yet actual measures to accomplish this under all three dynasties eventually lapsed into ineffectuality. Thus, by default, the local academy was left to perform a function it had limited capacity to fulfill. This too was a pattern to be repeated in Korea.

E. The Uses of Neo-Confucianism

In its long Chinese life Neo-Confucianism has served many purposes—educational, political, social, philosophical, and ideological. At its inception in the Northern Sung, it was a movement among scholars and would-be officials of a regime strongly oriented toward civil bureaucratic rule. Hu Yüan (993–1059), an early leader of the movement, was particularly known for his commitment to the education of scholar-officials in both classical learning and practical governmental skills.[63]

This was well after the Sung dynasty had established itself, so the new thought and scholarship, instead of ideologically spearheading the drive to power of a new dynasty, responded rather to the needs of a centralized civil administration following a period of contentious warlordism.

In this situation Neo-Confucians tended to take power for granted and were more concerned about its legitimate uses. Their scholarship celebrated the civil virtues, their culture the arts of peace. Already by the time of Li K'ou (1009–59), a scholar patronized, like Hu Yüan, by the statesman Fan Chung-yen (989–1052), Li could complain about the failure of contemporary scholars to give due attention to power factors, and especially to military affairs.[64] This state of affairs was not untypical of

Neo-Confucians in later times. Rarely did they give much thought to the seizing and organizing of power or the founding of new dynasties, yet often they found themselves serving as custodians of a power and managers of a state they had not themselves created.

Historically speaking Neo-Confucianism was a class phenomenon in several important respects. Its rise in the Sung was concomitant with the rise to new heights of power of a professional scholar-official class, whose scholarship and cultural activities were the beneficiaries of the new affluence, material means and leisure enjoyed by that class. Its concerns reflected their heightened sense of responsibility for political leadership and for preserving the essential values—"this culture"—on which they believed the polity should rest.. With one foot in the land as a kind of landed gentry, and the other in the halls of power as bureaucrats, they had a measure of independence from the ruler and fought hard to maintain their own status and integrity, with the alternative of repairing to their home base if need be. Yet often it was not much of a propertied base they returned to. Many Neo-Confucians were not well off, and to maintain their independence required heroic struggle of the kind Confucius spoke of when he said, "Poverty and low estate are what every man detests, but if they can only be escaped at the expense of the Way, [the Noble Man] will not try to escape them" (*Analects* 4:5).

To a degree Neo-Confucians functioned as buffers or mediators between dynastic power and the common people. But the insecurities of both property and power were such that scholar-officials could only act as a countervailing force, a kind of political "middle class," because of the solidarity maintained among the *shih-ta-fu* as sharers in a common mission and culture. Education was a crucial factor in developing that sense of common identity. In the case of the leading Neo-Confucian thinkers, who sometimes experienced great hardships, they could sustain themselves in poverty or dismissal from office only because of the moral and physical support of their own class.

On this basis they tried to express in their philosophy the highest ideals of that class and their common aspiration for self-fulfillment. As a program of self-cultivation Neo-Confucianism gave meaning and direction to their individual lives; as institutionalized instruction, first in schools and then in government, it became the public philosophy of the educated elite. As philosophy it was subscribed to by generations of later scholars; as ideology it was resorted to by dynasty after dynasty, irrespective of ethnic and even cultural differences among them—by Mongols in the Yüan, Chinese in the Ming, and Manchus in the Ch'ing.

Perhaps the most remarkable thing in the extension of this system to other lands and peoples is its ability to transcend the limitations of the class that produced it. Its first purveyors to Japan were Zen monks, whose social and political role contrasted sharply with that of the scholar-officials of China and whose interest in Neo-Confucianism was cultural in the narrow sense (if not actually commercial, as a commodity in the China trade engaged in by Zen monasteries). Truly transmitters of the teaching, rather than its proponents or creative interpreters, the Zen monks were superseded as sponsors of Neo-Confucianism by professional Confucian advisers to the Tokugawa aristocracy, a military elite whose social circumstances differed markedly from the Chinese mandarin. So little did the Tokugawa military government have in common with Chinese civil bureaucracy that it strains credulity to think of Neo-Confucianism as offering explicit ideological support to established institutions in cases as dissimilar as the Ming and Tokugawa. In fact, Neo-Confucianism lent little to the ideological justification or legitimization of Tokugawa rule itself,[65] though ethically and philosophically it contributed much to filling a vacuum left by the silence of Zen and Pure Land Buddhism in the social arena. Yet, adapted as it was to the way of the warrior, to the new cultural needs of a reunified Japan, and to the native religious traditions of Shinto, Neo-Confucianism was able to play a substantial role in the social and cultural life of premodern Japan.

More significant in this process than political or economic structures was the spirit of voluntarism and self-determination implicit in much of Neo-Confucian teaching. Here the emphasis lay on individual initiative and local autonomy. It did not renounce formal structures, but saw them as growing from within rather than being superimposed from without. This allowed the Koreans and Japanese (and I would suppose Vietnamese too) to adjust Neo-Confucian views on the primacy of moral relationships to their own social and political structures, and adapt Neo-Confucian concepts of self-cultivation to indigenous traditions of moral and spiritual discipline.

NEO-CONFUCIANISM IN KOREA

In its own historical development Korean Neo-Confucianism appears to be unique. The case of the Yi dynasty would seem to be a singular instance in which Neo-Confucians played a large role in the creation of a new regime and in the formulating of its institutions. For any comparative study of continuity and change in Neo-Confucianism, the founding of the Yi dynasty and remolding of Korean society at this time offer a fascinating test case for some of the generalizations offered above.

Though unique in the depth of its political involvement, the role of Neo-Confucianism in fourteenth-century Korea is not without significant parallels in other dynastic situations close at hand: e.g., in its relation to the Yüan state and then to Koryŏ. Here Neo-Confucian social values, as appropriated by both dynasties, may have afforded them some degree of legitimacy, but in the not too long run rationalistic and idealistic tendencies in Neo-Confucianism probably worked as a leaven to undermine these regimes and hasten their replacement.[66] This reflects an ambivalence in Neo-Confucianism toward any ruling power; i.e., whether one's primary loyalty should be to one's royal masters or to higher ideals often at odds with the status quo. Indeed Khubilai himself seems to have sensed this ambivalence. He had his own suspicions and premonitions concerning the dependability of Confucian support. When urged to adopt Confucianism, he pointedly asked if the weakness of the preceding Chin dynasty, and its defeat by his Mongols, were not attributable in part to the softening effects of Confucian humanistic teachings.[67] In the end there were committed Neo-Confucians who gave their service to the Yüan, and others to the Ming, some to Koryŏ and others to the Yi. In both cases, too, Neo-Confucianism survived the demise of its official sponsors.

The issue of course is not solely one of Neo-Confucian influence. Both Yüan and Koryŏ remained deeply involved with Buddhism, and were also heavily dependent on structures of authority, imposed by conquest, which would be jeopardized by reformism of any kind. In this respect these dynasties faced the classic dilemma of authoritarian regimes which are never so endangered as when compelled to accept a measure of liberalization. There are parallels here to the late Tokugawa shogunate, undone in the midst of its own efforts to reform and modernize in the 1850s and 60s, and to the reforms of the declining Manchu dynasty in the early twentieth century. How to manage change, without letting it get out of hand, is a problem for military regimes whose rule has not actually been predicated, as Confucian theory requires, on the consent of the governed.

As regards coexistence or conflict with Buddhism, there is more than one parallel: to the Confucian revival in the Northern Sung period, to the intellectual and political ascendance of Neo-Confucianism in Yüan

China, the early Ming, and early Tokugawa Japan; and to a concurrent pattern of ideological syncretism drawing on Buddhism as well as Neo-Confucianism for purposes of dynastic legitimation in these same settings. We are not yet in a position to handle, in more than a suggestive manner, the complex questions that arise in the comparative analysis of such cases, but it is perhaps significant that both of the papers herein dealing with Neo-Confucians in the early years of the Yi dynasty revert to the persisting influence of Buddhism as an important challenge to Neo-Confucian reform efforts.

Chung Chai-sik's contribution to this volume deals with a reform-minded statesman, Chŏng Tojŏn, whose name, meaning "Way-transmitter," is suggestive of the Neo-Confucian sense of mission so prominent in its early apostles. Chŏng, credited with substantially engineering the Yi dynasty's rise to power, embodied many of the themes we have identified with Neo-Confucianism. He espoused the orthodox tradition *(tao-t'ung)* as the active repossession of the Way in the broadest sense, i.e., under its several aspects as the Way to sagehood, the Learning of the Mind-and-Heart, the Way of the Sage Ruler, the Learning of the Emperor (as exemplified in the lectures from the classics mat), and above all as the practical or substantial learning which emphasized, contra Buddhism, dealing with moral and social realities.

Chŏng understood the meaning of Chu Hsi's (and Confucius') "learning for the sake of one's self: and Mencius' "getting it [the Way] oneself."[68] Hence he did not adhere slavishly to any one Neo-Confucian model. Though conversant with the Neo-Confucian institutions identified with Chu Hsi, he went beyond them to draw on the whole spectrum of Sung institutional reforms and statecraft thought—including Wang An-shih's (1021–86) New Laws and military and legal affairs well beyond the typical interests of Neo-Confucians. Further, Chŏng reached back to the highest antiquity in order to gain greater leverage on the present for radical change. Thus he put before Yi Sŏnggye (1335–1408, r. 1392–98), founder of the Yi dynasty, the model of Kija, the sage-statesman who had reputedly established the Way in early Korea just as the Duke of Chou had promulgated it in China. In other words Chŏng was asserting his right to "find the Way for himself" on native soil and in Korean terms. For instance, while deferential to the Ming and acknowledging its suzerainty, he avoided wholesale imitation of the Ming and devised a constitutional order far bolder in conception than anything the Ming could offer. An indication of this is Chŏng's emphasis on institutions which would strengthen the hand of scholar-officials at court and limit the power of the king. Key to this was enhancing the executive authority of the prime minister vis-à-vis the ruler, contrary to the Ming founder's abolition of the premiership and concentration of all authority in his own person. Chŏng advocated no wholesale decentralization of power, no dismemberment of the central state, but only arrangements which would strengthen it by curbing the arbitrary rule of dynastic despots.[69] On this and other points Chŏng established himself as one of the most incisive Neo-Confucian critics of autocratic rule. He was an eloquent proponent of a welfare state, land and tax reforms, and such typical Neo-Confucian institutions as those found in the *Family Ritual of Master Chu*, which would provide the social base for an independent scholar aristocracy[70] balancing the power of the king without impairing the essential authority of the state.

If Professor Chung is right, however, in the end Chŏng Tojŏn became convinced that none of this could be successful without a frontal attack being made on Buddhism. According to this view, Buddhism remained a serious obstacle, not so much because of its entrenched social and economic position (which already by the late fourteenth century had been considerably reduced) as because its basic values—or lack of such—undercut the social conscience, moral consensus, and political commitment needed to mobilize men for the attainment of reformist goals. Hence Chŏng devoted his last years increasingly to ideological struggle against Buddhism, which, in the account of Professor Chung, stressed the economic exploitation, social evils, and political corruption of the Buddhist establishment as stemming from inherently false views of the world.

Though Chŏng Tojŏn has not been ranked among the great philosophers of Korea, Professor Chung argues that he should be acknowledged as a major thinker who articulated a thoroughgoing, well-rounded political philosophy based on Neo-Confucian principles. The full results of Chŏng's ideological compaign were not immediately felt in his own time, but in Professor Chung's view, Chŏng Tojŏn prepared the soil for the later flowering of Neo-Confucianism in the fifteenth and sixteenth centuries.

Another contributor to this result was Kwŏn Kŭn (1352–1409), the subject of Michael Kalton's study. Kwŏn, a contemporary of Chŏng Tojŏn, was a leading statesman of the early Yi dynasty, a vigorous exponent of Neo-Confucian philosophy, and a scholar in the field of rites, both classical and Neo-Confucian (especially *The Family Ritual of Master Chu*). Kalton's focus is not, however, on the political program of Kwŏn Kŭn but on his Neo-Confucian "Learning of the Mind-and-Heart" as a positive alternative to Buddhism. He points to the problems of implementing Neo-Confucian reforms in an uncongenial atmosphere still permeated by Buddhist thought. Kwŏn saw this as a struggle for the hearts and minds of men, and dealt with it on several levels. One was the level of accommodation with Buddhist contemporaries and with the Buddhist proclivities of the royal house. In this area, as a state ideologist and drafter of royal pronouncements, he could make conciliatory gestures toward Buddhism and indeed write of it with apparent sympathy, while on another level, as a convinced Neo-Confucian, like Chŏng Tojŏn, he could compose virulent refutations of Buddhism expressing full confidence in the eventual triumph of Neo-Confucian principles. Kalton's view is that Kwŏn, though primarily dedicated to transforming the social order through ritual, recognized the difficulty of gaining acceptance for the latter without first converting Koreans from a Buddhist to Neo-Confucian world view. For this he resorted to Neo-Confucian doctrines which themselves had emerged in the philosophical dialogue with Buddhism, e.g., the unity of principle and diversity of its particular applications, which was predicated on the unity of all existence (as in Mahayana Buddhism) but offered a realistic view of ethical practice to complement it. As this process of education and conversion unfolded, Neo-Confucians like Kwŏn moved from a policy of reluctant co-existence with Buddhism to one of increasing insistence on Neo-Confucian orthodoxy, looking to the gradual implementation of Neo-Confucian institutions and practices once a change in ideological climate had rendered them more acceptable.

Regardless of such tactical adjustments or the allowances made for prevailing religious attitudes, Korean Neo-Confucians did not conceive of the problem as a matter solely of translating Chu Hsi's ideas into Korean terms. From the start they took most seriously the transplantation of Neo-Confucian institutions as well. This is shown, as in the cases of Chŏng Tojŏn and Kwŏn Kŭn, by the readiness to espouse radical reforms, to adapt selectively major Yüan or Ming institutions, and beyond that to put into effect many of Chu Hsi's practical proposals not even widely adopted in China itself.

Here we must take into account a special feature of Neo-Confucianism that has not always been well understood. Ch'eng-Chu teaching put primary emphasis on the individual rather than on institutions, on self-renewal from within rather than on organizational constraints externally imposed. On the other hand, Chu Hsi recognized the importance of the people's education and moral uplift of certain types of institutions on the local level, e.g., family and community organizations. His concern with these reflected Chu's own longer service and greater involvement in local administration than in central government, his brief time at court having been devoted more to preceptorial than to administrative duties. Generally speaking, Korean Neo-Confucians seem to have easily identified with those institutions and practices specifically associated with Chu Hsi.

In the area of education, however, the first steps had been taken in direct response to Yüan initiatives, when the Korean scholars An Hyang (1243–1306) and Paek Ijŏng (fl. 1310–20) reported back to Koryŏ the momentous changes that were taking place in Chinese education and in the new examination system adopted by the Yüan in 1313–15. Later the Korean scholar Yi Saek (1328–96), who had studied in Peking, was appointed educational intendant for the Yüan in Korea. His mission was to promulgate Neo-Confucian education on the curricular pattern set for the Mongols by Hsü Heng. This called for "renewal" of the general populace through a universal school system and the recruiting of talented scholars into the Yüan service on a multiracial basis.

Yi Sŏngmu's study of "Education and Examination in the Early Yi Dynasty" recounts the stages by which education in the capital and the provinces was reformed, first according to the Yüan system and then in ways thought to be more in accordance with Chu Hsi's own ideas. The twists and turns of successive reforms and counterreforms suggest that even a fundamentalist and literalist approach to the reading of Chu's intention was not proof against different interpretations being drawn to serve divergent power interests. Schools and examinations, playing a key role as avenues to power and influence, quickly became subject to partisan controversy and strife.

A special feature of the Korean situation was the *yangban* aristocracy's almost exclusive prerogative of admission to the examinations, in contrast to the more open, egalitarian, and meritocratic system in China. Chu Hsi himself, like other Neo-Confucians before him, had not set much store by the civil service examinations as such. He preferred to train up talented persons through the schools, observe their conduct and moral character at firsthand, and then have meritorious candidates personally recommended for government service. A similar rationale seems to have lain behind the substitution of oral, for written, examinations in Korea—a practice never sanctioned in China. Written examinations were favored by scholars at the capital, oral by candidates from the countryside. The latter might lack literary skills and intellectual sophistication, but their moral character could be discerned in personal interviews. Understandably sharp cleavages developed along these lines, as oral examinations were alleged to be too subjective and liable to favoritism, while written exams were said to favor those highly literate in the Chinese tradition.

In education, on the other hand, there were marked similarities between China and Korea in the gradual decline of the public schools and the rise of private study halls (sahak)[71] and later local academies as centers of learning and social influence among the yangban,[72] a role academies had also served among the local gentry in China. Here too the contest for power between the king and the yangban aristocratic bureaucracy was reflected in the king's support for public schools as a counterweight to yangban influence, while the latter supported academies as bastions of local power and culture.[73] Ironically enough one would be hard put to find any endorsement in Chu Hsi's writings for academies versus state schools. The rise in importance of the former simply reflected the failure to carry out what Chu had urged be done for the latter.

One of the most distinctive Neo-Confucian institutions at the Chinese court during the Sung, Yüan, and Ming dynasties was the lectures from the Classics Mat, in which distinguished scholar-ministers lectured to and carried on discussions with the ruler concerning lessons to be drawn from the Confucian classics for contemporary affairs. This role had been performed by several of the great Neo-Confucian teachers who had the greatest influence on the Koreans: Ch'eng I, Chu Hsi, Chen Te-hsiu, and Hsü Heng.[74] For their part, Korean Neo-Confucians went even further in the systematic conduct of these lectures, which emphasized the importance of the scholar-minister as mentor to the throne and sought to enhance the latter's influence vis-à-vis the increasing concentration of power in the hands of the ruler.

A natural corollary to this kind of royal education in Korea was the provision for the education of the heir apparent. Dr. JaHyun Kim Haboush, who has already reported on the conduct of the royal lectures under the Yi dynasty,[75] has undertaken in her article for this symposium to study the education of the crown princes of the Yi dynasty during the fourteenth to eighteenth centuries. The significance of the subject lies in the key Neo-Confucian doctrines on which the instruction was premised: the goodness of man's nature and his potentiality for sagehood; the special responsibility of those who exercise great power to learn how to use it well and commit themselves to becoming sage-rulers; and the importance of the ruler's self-cultivation as setting an example for others to follow (i.e., fulfilling the basic aim of Neo-Confucian political doctrine: to govern men by "renewing" them through exemplary self-cultivation).

Since adequate studies have not yet been made of the Chinese counterpart to this system of education at court, we are in no position to make comparative assessments. Judging from Dr. Haboush's evidence alone, which includes many striking individual cases, the results in Korea were at best mixed. Dr. Haboush suggests that three special factors may have affected the outcome. One was the lack of significant motivation on the part of princes whose future seemed assured simply by hereditary right. A second was the lack of real leverage on the part of the tutor in dealing with such a privileged student. The third consisted of the attractive diversions from study which were readily available to the crown prince. No doubt other considerations pertaining to the content of instruction played a part. The more his preceptors stressed the heavy responsibility of the ruler, the greater could become the prince's resistance to this kind of moral overload. In any case Dr. Haboush's detailed case studies provide us with fascinating illustrations of the problems encountered at this crucial juncture in the relations of the king and his Neo-Confucian mentors.

The next group of papers represents the golden age of Korean Neo-Confucian philosophy in the sixteenth century, following upon a period of substantial progress in the development of Neo-Confucian institutions and culture in the fifteenth century, especially during the reign of the renowned King Sejong. Sejong was responsible for marked advances in several areas of cultural life. One of these was the devising of the Korean phonetic alphabet, a unique creative achievement which contributed to the growth of vernacular literature. This development shows how Neo-Confucian influence, though always implying some measure of siniciza-tion, did not necessarily inhibit the growth of native traditions. In fact it sanctioned and stimulated cultural activity in general, and encouraged a people's natural self-expression.[76] In keeping with its central conception of "the unity of principle and diversity of its functional applications," Neo-Confucianism accepted cultural diversity and, rather than insisting simply on conformity to things Chinese, helped to strengthen the Korean people's sense of themselves and encourage their distinctive expression of the Way *(tzu-te)*.

The philosopher Yi T'oegye has attracted much attention in East Asia and, since there is already a considerable literature devoted to him, it was unnecessary for our conference to dwell particularly on his achievements. Nevertheless the papers here reflect the true dimensions of Yi's scholarly and philosophical stature. Professor Wing-tsit Chan, a leading authority on Chinese thought and Chu Hsi in particular, examines the scholarly work of Yi T'oegye in regard to Chu Hsi's life and writings. He finds that Yi, while holding Chu in highest respect, was most thorough and critical in his scholarly annotations of Huang Kan's (1152–1221) account of Chu's "conduct of life" *(hsing-chuang)*, being particularly attentive to details of Chu's movements and whereabouts, his relationship to his teacher Li T'ung (1093–1163), his deep interest in religious and ritual matters, and his serious concerns over national defense—matters relatively neglected by other writers. In the last three respects Professor Chan's observations have heightened significance in that these particular emphases in Yi's scholarship may well have had a part in shaping Japanese perceptions of Chu Hsi.

Three other papers on T'oegye deal with his philosophical contributions. Tomoeda Ryūtarō shows how Yi T'oegye sought to bring greater clarity and precision to Chu Hsi's discussion of the Supreme Ultimate in relation to the creative processes of yin and yang. There were ambiguities enough in Chu's handling of the matter so as to evoke further questioning among Chu's followers. Professor Tomoeda believes that Chu Hsi's view of principle and the Supreme Ultimate was basically a structural theory of existence, not an emanational or creation theory; it remained, however, for T'oegye to make this distinction clear without detracting from principle's priority over material force in respect of value, by virtue of which principle still plays a dominant role in the creative process.

This same question underlies Youn Sa-Soon's discussion of the relation of *li* as natural law, or principle of being, and *li* as normative law or principle of "oughtness," i.e., what should be. Since the purpose of one's ethical cultivation is to realize one's nature, and thereby to unite man and Heaven, it is important that the capability to realize human nature be seen as inborn, a fact and not just a possibility, something active and not merely a passive, quiescent potential. In this light it may be understood why T'oegye emphasized the "issuance of principle" in the mind as something active. At the same time he recognized that the failure to realize one's nature, which was understood as due to the intervention of external forces or circumstantial factors *(shih/se)*, could only be explained adequately on the basis of a holistic cosmology in which all things are seen as occurring both naturally and purposefully. "The cultivation of self-governing human beings," through the recognition of reason and order in the universe, "is the basic intention of T'oegye's theory," according to Professor Youn.

In a similar vein Tu Wei-ming discusses the centrality in T'oegye's thought of the famous "Four-Seven Debate." This concerned the relation of principle and material force (or ether) in the issuance of the Four Beginnings (feelings or impulses which constitute the inherent tendency to goodness in human nature) on the one hand, and the Seven Emotions which may work for either good or evil, on the other. Professor Tu analyzes in detail the views expressed by T'oegye and a junior colleague in a continuing exchange on this question. Out of this developed T'oegye's more mature and refined views on the active or dominating character of principle and the crucial agency of the mind in coordinating reason and emotion. This dialogue in Korea, according to Professor Tu, represented an authentic, independent development of the Neo-Confucian discourse, notable for its thoroughness, frankness, and civility, "a model of scholarly communication for [later] generations."[77] From it Professor Tu suggests there emerged a clarified perception of the human feelings, marked by a precision and finesse not often matched in China.

Not long after T'oegye's time the dialogue was resumed by Yi Yulgok, a powerful thinker and worthy rival of T'oegye in the interpretation and propagation of Chu Hsi's philosophy. Yulgok stressed the primacy of material force in the dialogue he carried on with a friend about the "Four-Seven" issue. This segment of the continuing controversy is presented in Julia Ching's paper, "Yi Yulgok on the Four Beginnings and Seven Emotions," emphasizing the complementary relationship or dialectical unity of the "beginnings" and emotions, rather than their opposition. Without attempting here to recapitulate the argument in detail, we can report Professor Ching's conclusion that Yulgok, like T'oegye, has detected and clarified certain ambiguities in Chu Hsi's thought and "has made a real contribution on an issue that Chinese thinkers had not clearly settled."[78] Further, we note that this clarification, though it sometimes has the appearance of hair-splitting, actually deals with a central issue for Neo-Confucians engaged in self-cultivation, whose conscientiousness in regard to moral imperatives and the disciplining of selfish desires was still meant to express the spontaneous goodness of man's moral nature. It demonstrates too the intellectual, as well as moral, seriousness which Koreans brought to their practical realization of Neo-Confucian principles.

Another indication of the Koreans' active pursuit of Neo-Confucian goals is found in the attention both T'oegye and Yulgok gave to Chu Hsi's recommendations for the setting up of community compacts—voluntary local charters in the nature of social contracts, by which people subscribed to a code of conduct and various forms of cooperation and mutual aid. Chu Hsi had recommended a model compact worked out in 1076 by Lü Ta-chün, whose family in Shensi had been associated with Ch'eng I. It was one of several schemes for self-governing communities experimented with by such early Neo-Confucians as Chang Tsai. Chu Hsi had written a modified version of the Lü family compact, adapted to his own time and situation, the text of which was included in his collected works. The Lü version was also reproduced in the official early Ming compilation, *Great Compendium of Human Nature and Principle* (1415).

This is an aspect of Chu Hsi's thought which seems not to have attracted much notice in the early days of the Neo-Confucian movement in Korea, when reform centered on the organization of central government, schools and examinations, the land system, and the conduct of family affairs according to the prescriptions of Chu Hsi's *Family Ritual*. According to Sakai Tadao, in his paper "Yi Yulgok and the Community Compact," interest in this compact arose after the texts had become available in Korea during the early fifteenth century,[79] and actual institution of the system was not officially sanctioned until the early sixteenth century. In China itself adoption of the compact had spread from the mid-fifteenth into the sixteenth century. Thus the Korean development could possibly be seen as an extension of the compact's propagation in China. If this is so, however, it is more a matter of stimulus than of substantive replication, since the early form of the compacts in Korea follows, if anything, Sung models and only later incorporates certain Ming adaptations. In other words, the Korean phenomenon followed its own internal lines of development from shared premises.

In the compacts devised successively by Yi T'oegye and Yi Yulgok, the detailed specifications are based on community consultation and adapted to local conditions, especially to the existing social structure and the tradition of covenant associations which had deep roots in Korea. Professor Sakai speculates that the community compact idea in China had sprung from similar roots in local covenants, and that in Korea too an attempt was made to ground the compact organization in such indigenous structures and practices. Organizationally the Korean compacts were fitted into the pattern of *yangban* leadership in the local community, though Sakai sees Yulgok as more egalitarian than T'oegye and more progressive in emphasizing education in the vernacular for commoners and in linking the administrative direction of the compacts to that for the communal granary and local school, as Chu Hsi himself had done. However, for Chu Hsi the local school had been the official or public school in the districts, whereas by Yulgok's time in Korea the public schools had seriously declined and been largely superseded by local academies, quasiprivate schools maintained by the *yangban*. Nevertheless, according to Sakai, where T'oegye had tended to buttress *yangban* authority and uphold class privilege, Yulgok promoted the upward mobility of commoners and cooperation between upper and lower classes. This he sees as reflecting Yulgok's more pragmatic and realistic approach, which in turn is linked to his empirical philosophy of material force or ether.

However this may be, we should not fail to note the normative, didactic content of the compact texts and the natural association of the compacts with schools. This shows the strong continuing interest of these major Korean thinkers in education, and in the plurality of means by which this was to be accomplished on different levels of society. In this T'oegye and Yulgok were carrying on a major and indeed central commitment of the Neo-Confucian tradition as it came down from Chu Hsi. There may be differences from one Neo-Confucian to another as to their elitism or egalitarianism, but none in respect to the fundamental need for the "renewal of the people" (as Chu Hsi had put it) through education.

Sakai concludes with a brief comparative discussion of similar institutions in Japan as well as China, and suggests that a more thoroughgoing historical and comparative study would confirm the impression that this trio of Neo-Confucian institutions—the community compact, communal granary, and local academy—had a much fuller development and more lasting significance in Korea than in either China or Japan.

This then provided the background for the flowering of Neo-Confucian culture, as expressed especially in the teachings of T'oegye and Yulgok, and in their personal involvement with the community compact. Finally, this development is linked to the flourishing of the local academies as centers of *yangban* culture, which Professor Sakai has already pointed to in connection with Yulgok's plan for the administration of the community compact, with its significant outreach to the lower classes.

If in these respects Professor Sakai draws attention to progressive features of the Neo-Confucian movement, he concedes that more than one class, party, or faction sought to exploit Neo-Confucian ideas and institutions for their own purposes, some of them certainly protective of their own interests and often conservative of the status quo in the midst of economic and social change. In such circumstances it was only natural that controversy would arise as to who could legitimately claim to speak for Neo-Confucianism as either authoritative teaching or official ideology.

Thus political struggle, factional rivalry, and disputes concerning orthodoxy and heterodoxy may be seen as inseparable concomitants of Neo-Confucianism's rise to dominance in Korea. Along with this there was a change in the way "orthodoxy" was conceived or asserted in the course of Neo-Confucianism's becoming the established teaching.

For Chŏng Tojŏn and Kwŏn Kŭn in the late fourteenth century the problem had been how, in order to achieve their social goals, the positive values or "correct learning" of Neo-Confucianism could be propagated in the face of entrenched Buddhist influence. The Neo-Confucian scholar Kim Koengp'il (1454–1504), following after Chŏng Tojŏn and Kwŏn Kŭn, felt a need to press the case for a public philosophy centered on a view of the self defined in rational, moral, and social terms, as opposed to the nonrational and essentially private experience of "nothingness" or "emptiness" in Buddhism.[80] By the sixteenth and seventeenth centuries, however, with the new teaching firmly established, the question had become, rather, which brand of Neo-Confucianism could claim to represent itself as the authentic heir of Confucius and Chu Hsi. It is this problem in variant forms that Martina Deuchler, Miura Kunio, and Daniel Bouchez address in the studies which follow.

Further, there was the vexed issue of the Korean relationship to China and the extent to which political loyalty required Korean acceptance of the latter's ideological authority. Koryŏ had identified closely with the Yüan at a time time when the Yüan court stood as the principal sponsor of Neo-Confucianism, to such an extent indeed that the Mongol collapse in 1368 undermined Koryŏ's own authority. The Yi dynasty, though initially identified with the Ming, experienced repeated difficulties in its relations with the latter, and while professing loyalty to its suzerain, strongly implied that the exemplary virtue of the Koreans in this respect showed them to be the truer of the two as custodians of the Confucian heritage. Thus total devotion to Chu Hsi became a badge not only of Korean fidelity to the Way but of its independence from the decadent Ming—a form of subtle nationalistic self-assertion worthy of the Neo-Confucian claim to have "gotten" the Way for oneself.

Further advances in Korean thought during the fifteenth and sixteenth centuries, discussed by Dr. Deuchler, confirmed this autonomous capability. Yi T'oegye developed his own orthodox "learning of the mind-and-heart" which preempted much of the ground taken up in China by Wang Yang-ming, while Yulgok's dual emphasis on the creative mind and concrete reality kept within the orbit of the Chu Hsi school tendencies that in late Ming China veered off from the Neo-Confucian center of gravity. T'oegye thus became the great symbol of a conservative orthodoxy and Yulgok of a more liberal one—both claiming fidelity to Chu Hsi and both exemplifying the autonomy and authenticity so central to Neo-Confucianism. Official confirmation of these claims came in 1610 with the enshrinement in the Confucian temple of leading Korean Neo-Confucians, who symbolized Korean independence of China and rejection of the allegedly corrupt, heterodox thought that permeated the late Ming.

It has become commonplace to speak of Korean Neo-Confucianism as burning with a spirit of fanatic orthodoxy, embittered by partisanship and wracked by intolerant factionalism. Such is the view confirmed by Professor Miura Kunio, and expressed in his discussion of the fatal clash between Song Siyŏl (1607–89) and Yun Hyu (1617–80). Professor Miura is inclined to view Song's total, and extremely literalist, devotion to Chu Hsi as characteristic of those who stand as defenders of a faith on its frontiers, the more dogmatic and conservative as they are removed in time and space from the original fountainhead of religious inspiration. The paradox one encounters here is that both Song and Yun, mortal enemies ideologically and politically, professed loyalty to the same masters: Chu Hsi and Yi Yulgok. What we have then is not a blind loyalty to rival sources of authority, but an insistence on differing personal interpretations of the same authority.

The nature of this conflict is highlighted by the attention which Dr.

Deuchler draws to the idea of individual inspiration in both T'oegye and Yulgok.[81] T'oegye acknowledged no single teacher as the direct source of his views, but rather thought of himself as the true successor to Chu Hsi. In this respect he was casting himself in the same role as Chu Hsi had cast the Ch'eng brothers (and by implication himself), who had discerned the true meaning of the Way after the tradition had lapsed for more than a thousand years after Mencius.

Elsewhere I have identified this view of tradition as a "prophetic" one, stressing the unique insight of one who rediscovers and repossesses the long-lost Way, as contrasted to the "scholastic" or apostolic emphasis on lineal transmission from teacher to disciple.[82] Typical of the prophetic role is its powerful self-assurance, its sense of direct access to truth, as well as dogmatic conviction of its own hold on the Way and rejection of others'. This was as true of their Sung predecessors as of their Korean emulators, and since there could be no inherent limit on such claims, rivalry and partisanship were the almost certain consequences.

Ironically, Yulgok availed himself of the same privilege by declaring his independence of T'oegye, whom he accused of being too slavish in his devotion to Chu Hsi. For Yulgok the key to authentic possession of the Way was "getting it oneself."[83] It would appear too from Professor Miura's account of Yun Hyu that he exercised a similar freedom of interpretation, with no less a sense of deep personal conviction.[84]

In this light many of the leading Korean Neo-Confucians would appear to be acting out roles already modeled for them by their Sung predecessors, though no doubt doing it their own way and reacting to situations in Korea for which there could be no exact parallel in China. The outcome, while an autonomous development within Korea and not merely a response to external stimuli, was in significant part, as Dr. Deuchler has put it, a "result of the intellectual challenge inherent in Neo-Confucian philosophy."[85] Hence, while further research may well differentiate the historical conditions or social forces impinging on this process, there would seem to be nothing in the Neo-Confucian discourse itself to mark the Korean sense of orthodoxy as unique, except in the Neo-Confucian sense that all human activity partakes of both commonness and distinctiveness, i.e., the underlying unity of principle and diversity of its manifestations.

The three remaining essays in this collection illustrate how that same principle manifested itself in different aspects of the evolving Korean tradition. The first, by Daniel Bouchez, deals with a most striking case of Neo-Confucian orthodoxy coming to terms with some of its most fundamental values in the encounter with Buddhism. Kim Manjung (1637–92), a disciple of Song Siyŏl, was in public life an upholder of Neo-Confucian orthodoxy and critic of Yun Hyu, who served as custodian of the tradition by virtue of his office at court as lecturer from the Classics Mat. It was not untypical of the careers of such scholar-officials as Kim that they should encounter disappointments, dismissals, exile, and even untimely death. What is unusual about Kim Manjung is that in his own disillusionment his private thoughts should turn increasingly toward Buddhism, the religion his mother had inculcated in him as a youth. Kim's authorship of the *Nine-Cloud Dream (Kuunmong)*, an allegorical novel based on the *Diamond Sutra*, has recently been established. Bouchez goes on to show how Kim's more personal reflections about the nature of Buddhism were expressed in the informal style of the random essays or desultory jottings *(manp'il)*. In these writings Kim's aim is not to preach Buddhism but to do simple justice to it. He is critical of many Neo-Confucian objections to Buddhism, showing how they are based on a double standard of judgment; Neo-Confucianism itself would fail to pass the same tests. Kim also brings out the ways in which Neo-Confucianism was influenced by Buddhism, putting itself in actual (though unacknowledged) debt to the latter.

In the end Kim appears as something of a syncretist, asserting the distinctive and complementary character of the two teachings. More than this, he reveals in his thought processes how Neo-Confucian historical analysis and critical method can, in his hands, be redirected toward a more self-conscious, as well as more broadly sympathetic, study of human religious experience without regard to rigid sectarian allegiances. Openness, fairness, skeptical inquiry allied to rational analysis, a disposition to study human experience in historical context and to consider the effect of historical processes on the manner of human expression—all these are traits of the Sung learning which, at this later stage and in a broader perspective, have been brought to a finer point so as to produce a new humanism embracing both Neo-Confucianism and Buddhism.

Kim does not articulate this attitude into a systematic methodology or scientific approach, but a kind of critical thinking emerges here which would become even more characteristic of the practical or solid learning in seventeenth-century Korea. Something of the same cast of mind is also found in Peter Lee's essay on the more literary work of Ŏ Sukkwŏn (fl. 1525–54), whose *Story-teller's Miscellany (P'aegwan chapki)* is in form and spirit similar to Kim's *Random Essays*. Indeed the rise of this genre, with its informal, anecdotal character, was contemporaneous with the rise of Neo-Confucianism, and, in avoiding a moralistic and didactic tone, was meant to be expressive of a self-cultivation and character-formation that prized naturalness and spontaneity. Ŏ, though an illegitimate son and thus barred from holding office in Korea's peculiarly birth-conscious bureaucracy, nevertheless shared most of the values of the *yangban* class. He upholds Neo-Confucian orthodoxy, the conventional virtues of loyalty and filiality, and a constitutional order that aims at a balance of power between the king and the bureaucracy.[86]

Ŏ's purpose in the *Miscellany*, however, is not to promote such values overtly, but to show how he has assimilated them in a thoroughly individual and creative way—to share what he has "gotten for himself" of the Way. His culture encouraged this kind of self-revelation, just as it gave the highest priority (even in politics) to individual self-cultivation. Further, it set great store by naturalness and unfeigned sincerity, and had a special appreciation for literature which let the self be exposed in a seemingly unguarded way, leaving the reader to form his own estimate of the author's character and sensibility. The test of this kind of literature then is whether the author's voice rings true, not whether he persuades us by marshaled arguments, mounds of historical evidence, or quotations from the classics. As a leading scholar not only in Korean but in East Asian literature, Peter Lee demonstrates his remarkable erudition and gifts for comparative study, in bringing out the distinctive qualities of a genre so revealing of the Neo-Confucian personality.

From the papers in our volume one will not get the full story of Neo-Confucianism in the early Yi dynasty, nor even of the particular topics touched upon. If the conference and this symposium have been true to their purpose, they will show that the depth and complexity of the Korean experience with Neo-Confucianism goes far beyond what can be reported here.

For all that, at least some tentative conclusions may be arrived at. One is that the Koreans showed a remarkable capacity for assimilating both Neo-Confucian thought and institutions, as well as their social and cultural adjuncts. Another is that the process of assimilation was not merely one of skilled copying, but from the beginning involved creative adaptation to Korean needs and conditions. Individual thinkers and statesmen achieved a thorough grasp of different aspects of Neo-Confucian thought as well as their historical antecedents in China and the relevant background in Korea. Early on a statesman like Chŏng Tojŏn, and later on a scholar like Yi Yulgok, could make highly original contributions to Neo-Confucian statecraft thought (unfortunately not fully represented here) which bear favorable comparison to, and often anticipate the handling of similar problems by, leading Chinese thinkers. Because of their native versatility and the range of fields they were prepared to deal with, Koreans at the end of Koryŏ and the inception of the Yi dynasty were able to undertake ambitious reforms in their national life beyond anything attempted in China. Though many of these were subject to later modification, the experience gained in a massive program of political and social engineering, as found in the record kept of it, must be considered one of the richest chapters in East Asian, if not world, history. This is especially true of the efforts to implement Chu Hsi's political and social thought, which often go beyond anything attempted in China and Japan, e.g., the implementation of his *Elementary Learning* and *Family Ritual*, his recommendations for the community compact, communal granary, village ceremonies, schools, etc. Truth to tell, in many instances little attention has been given to their counterpart ideas or institutions in China, and it is only their inescapable importance in Korea, once one gets around to looking at them, that compels us to reexamine these neglected areas of Chinese—and perhaps Japanese—intellectual and social history. If the papers here stimulate others to press forward with such further search and reflection, they will have served their purpose.

NOTES

1. See Taga Akigoro, ed., *Kinsei Ajia kyōiku shi kenkyū* (Tokyo: Bunrui shoin, 1966), Appendix 2, article in Japanese by Lothar Knauth, "Meishin hōgan no ryūtsū to Hispania Yaku no mondai" (The *Myŏngsim pogam*: its diffusion and translation into Spanish), pp. 851–79. See also Sakai Tadao, *Chūgoku zensho no kenkyū* (Tokyo: Kōbundō, 1960), pp. 451, 483; Kim Chung-Kuk, *Myung-Sim-Bo-Kam: Mirror of Clear Mind* (Seoul: Sŏnggyun'gwan University, 1959), pp. 1–11; *Kosŏ mongnok* (Seoul: Sŏnggyn'gwan University, 1979), p. 50; Richard Rutt, "Chinese Learning and Pleasures" in *Transactions of the Korea Branch of the Royal Asiatic Society* (April 1960), 36:37. Despite its syncretic character as a popular morality book, quotations from Ch'eng-Chu school masters down to Chen Te-hsiu suggest that it was an outgrowth of the spread of Neo-Confucianism from Yüan China to Korea, in which Chen's writings figured prominently.
2. See Wing-tsit Chan, "Chu Hsi and Yüan Confucianism" in H.L. Chan and W.T. de Bary, eds., *Yüan Thought* (New York: Columbia University Press, 1983).
3. See Wm. Theodore de Bary, *Neo-Confucian Orthodoxy and the Learning of the Mind-and-Heart* (New York: Columbia University Press, 1981), pp. 1–66. Hereafter abbreviated as *Neo-Confucian Orthodoxy*.
4. Fung Yu-lan, *History of Chinese Philosophy*, vol. 2, tr. by Derk Bodde (Princeton: Princeton University Press, 1953); Carsun Chang, *The Development of Neo-Confucian Thought* (New York: Bookman Associates, vol. 1, 1957; vol. 2, 1962); Alfred Forke, *Geschichte der neueren Chinesischen Philosophie* (Hamburg: Cram, De Gruyter, 1964), Book One, chapter 1.
5. Fung Yu-lan, *Chung-kuo che-hsüeh shih* (Shanghai: Commercial Press, 1934), vol. 2 chaps. 10–15.
6. Fung and Bodde, vol. 2, p. 631.
7. Shimada Kenji, "The Thought of Miura Baien," in *Tōyōshi kenkyū* (December 1979), 38(3):1, 23–24.
8. See Conrad Schirokauer "Neo-Confucianism Under Attack: The Condemnation of Wei-hsüeh" in John W. Haeger, ed., *Crisis and Prosperity in Sung China* (Tucson: University of Arizona Press, 1975), pp. 163–98.
9. See pp. 28–38.
10. Cf. Wm. Theodore de Bary and Irene Bloom, eds., *Principle and Practicality* (New York: Columbian University Press, 1979), pp. 5–15, and Wm. Theodore de Bary et al., eds., *The Unfolding of Neo-Confucianism* (New York: Columbia University Press, 1975), pp. 15–22.
11. In the explanatory note *(fan-li)* of the *Ming-ju hsüeh-an.*
12. See his "Personal Proposals for Schools and Examinations" in *Hui-an hsien-sheng Chu Wen-kung wen-chi* (SPPY ed.), 69:24ab. For Chŏng To-chŏn, see herein, Chung Chai-sik, pp. 81.
13. See note 8.

14. *Yi T'oegye chŏnjip* (Tokyo: Ri Taikei kenkyūkai, 1975), vol. 2, pp. 260-61.
15. Fung, *History*, vol. 2, chap. 14.
16. *Ibid.*, p. 585.
17. Chu Hsi, *Ssu-shu chi-chü, Chung-kuo tzu-hsüeh ming-chu chi-ch'eng chen-pen ch'u-pien* (Taipei: 1978), p. 18. *Ta-hsüeh huo-wen, Kinsei kanseki sōkan*, 3d series (Kyoto: Chūbun shuppansha, 1976), pp. 20b-21a (pp. 40–41).
18. Fung, *Chung-kuo che-hsüeh shih*, vol. 2, p. 938.
19. *Neo-Confucian Orthodoxy*, pp. 28–35, 91–98.
20. Chen Te-hsiu, *Hsi-shan wen-chi* (KHCPTS ed.), 24: 409–10.
21. Yi T'oegye, *Songgye Wŏn Myŏng ihak t'ongnok* in *T'oegye chŏnjip* (Seoul: Sŏnggyun'gwan University, 1959), vol. 3, pp. 249–551, esp. pp. 254, 513.
22. Takahashi Tōru, "Richō-jugakushi ni okeru shuriha shukiha no hattatsu," in *Chōsen Shina bunka no kenkyū* (Keijō [Seoul]: Keijō teikoku daigaku, 1934), pp. 141–281.
23. Yamanoi Yū, in Onozawa Seiichi et al., *Ki no shisō* (Tokyo: Tokyo University Press, 1978), pp. 355–513; and his *Min-shin shisōshi no kenkyū* (Tokyo: Tokyo University Press, 1980), esp. pp. 149–99.
24. See Martina Deuchler, "Neo-Confucianism: The Impulse for Social Action in Early Yi Korea" *Journal of Korean Studies* (1980), 2:80, 94 and Han Young-woo, *Chosŏn chŏn'gi ŭi sahoe sasang* (Seoul, 1976), pp. 53–61.
25. See my introduction and article in de Bary and Bloom, *Principle and Practicality*, pp. 12–13, 132–35, 141, 178–79.
26. Chen, *Hsi-shan wen-chi*, 25:425.
27. Kusumoto Masatsugu, *Chūgoku tetsugaku kenkyū* (Tokyo: Kokushikan daigaku, 1975), pp. 353–90.
28. *I-ch'uan wen-chi* (SPPYed.), 5:12b.
29. Chu Hsi, *Yen-p'ing ta-wen*, in *Kinsei kanseki sōkan, shisōhen* (Kyoto: Chūbun shuppansha, 1972), pp. 70, 89–92, 99–103, 111.
30. Hsü Heng, *Hsü Lu-chai hsin-fa* (Ming ed. of 1522), p. 1b.
31. See de Bary and Bloom, *Principle and Practicality*, pp. 93–6, 129, 131, 165, 273–75, 286–87, 421, 433.
32. Ch'eng Hao, *Erh-Ch'eng i-shu* (SPPYed.), 24:2a.
33. Okada Takehiko, "Practical Learning in the Chu Hsi School," in *Principle and Practicality*, p. 283.
34. Cf. *Neo-Confucian Orthodoxy*, pp. 44–47, 54–55, 125.
35. *Principle and Practicality*, p. 26; R. Tsunoda, W.T. de Bary, and D. Keene, *Sources of Japanese Tradition* (New York: Columbia University Press, 1958), pp. 348–50.
36. Martina Deuchler, "Self-cultivation for the Governance of Men: The Beginnings of Neo-Confucian Orthodoxy in Yi Korea," *Asiatische Studien* (1980), 34(2):9–39.
37. *Principle and Practicality*, p. 32.
38. See JaHyun Kim Haboush, *A Heritage of Kings: One Man's Monarchy in the Confucian World* (Ph. D. Diss. Columbia University; Ann Arbor, Mich.: University Microfilms, 1978), pp. 36–40.

39. Proceedings of the 2nd Academic Conference for Asiatic Studies (Seoul: Sŏng-gyun'gwan University, 1980), pp. 82–99, 273–88.

40. Yi T'aejin, "The Socioeconomic Background of Neo-Confucianism in Fif-teenth- and Sixteenth-Century Korea," draft prepared for the Conference on Korean Neo-Confucianism, August 1981, pp. 27–28.

41. Neo-Confucian Orthodoxy, p. 136–41.

42. Makino Shūji, "Gendai no jugaku kyōiku," in Tōyōshi kenkyū (March 1979), 37(4):64–76.

43. [Tsao-lu], Wu Wen-ch'eng kung ch'üan-chi (1756 ed.), chüan shou 34b; suppl. ch. 1:1a–8b.

44. Kyŏngguk taejŏn (reprint 1934), pp. 212, 214.

45. Ming Hsüan-tsung shih-lu, Chung-yang yen-chiu yüan ed. 22:4b Hsüan-te, 10th mo., hsin-wei.

46. Kosŏ mongnok, Catalogue of the Central Library, Sŏnggyun'gwan, (Seoul, 1979), p. 205. Lee Choon-hee, Yijo sŏwŏn mun'go ko (Seoul: Sŏnggyun' gwan, 1969), pp. 8, 60, 80, 110.

47. See Wing-tsit Chan, "The Hsing-Li Ching-i and the Ch'eng-Chu School of the Seventeenth Century," in de Bary, ed., Unfolding, pp. 543–79.

48. Neo-Confucian Orthodoxy, pp. 61, 134–35.

49. Deuchler, "Neo-Confucianism," p. 86.

50. Neo-Confucian Orthodoxy, pp.188–91.

51. See Lee Choon-hee, Yijo sŏwŏn, passim.

52. Deuchler, "Neo-Confucianism," pp. 87–88, 90–91.

53. The foregoing are discussed in Neo-Confucian Orthodoxy, pp. 28–35, 93–94.

54. This is a main theme in Ray Huang's 1587, a Year of No Significance (New Haven: Yale University Press, 1980).

55. Chŏng Tojŏn, Chosŏn kyŏnggukchŏn, in Sambongjip (Seoul: Kuksa p'yŏn-ch'an wiwŏnhoe, 1961), p. 227.

56. These are discussed extensively in Kusumoto Masatsugu, Chūgoku tetsugaku kenkyū, pp. 327–52, 359–60.

57. Neo-Confucian Orthodoxy, pp. 24, 133.

58. Edward W. Wagner, The Literati Purges: Political Conflict in the Early Yi Dynasty (Cambridge: Harvard University Press, 1974), p. 2.

59. Uno Seiichi, ed., Shōgaku (Hsiao-hsüeh), sec. 6, Shinshaku kambun taikei, 3 (Tokyo: Meiji shoin, 1965), p. 377.

60. See Martina Deuchler, "The Tradition: Women During the Yi Dynasty" in Sandra Mattielli, ed., Virtues in Conflict (Seoul: Royal Asiatic Society, Ko-rea Branch, 1977), pp. 1–47.

61. Chin-ssu lu chi-chu (Taipei: I-wen reprint, Ssu-k'u shan-pen tsung-shu, 9:72a–73b; Wing tsit Chan, tr., Reflections on Things at Hand (New York: Colum-bia University Press, 1967), p. 237.

62. E.g., the Kōrakuen Park in Okayama.

63. Huang Tsung-hsi and Ch'üan Tsu-wang, Sung Yüan hsüeh-an (Taipei, Ho-lo t'u-shu ed., n.d.), 1:26.

64. Cf. Etienne Balazs, *Chinese Civilization and Bureaucracy* (New Haven: Yale University Press, 1964), pp. 278–86.
65. Cf. Hermans Ooms, "Neo-Confucianism and the Formation of Early Tokugawa Ideology: Contours of a Problem," in Peter Nosco, ed., *Responses to Neo-Confucianism in Tokugawa Japan* (Princeton: Princeton University Press, 1984).
66. In the Korean case it is obviously not a question of original legitimization but of the Confucian sense that a dynasty's mandate must be constantly renewed by moral effort and political reform if it is to survive. On the Chinese case see the important studies of John Dardess on the Yüan and Ming respectively: *Confucians and Conquerors* (New York: Columbia University Press, 1973); and *Confucianism and Autocracy* (Berkeley: University of California Press, 1983).
67. See my *Neo-Confucian Orthodoxy*, p. 41.
68. For the significance of these concepts, see my *Liberal Tradition in China* (New York: Columbia University Press, 1983), pp. 21–24, 45–48.
69. A fuller discussion in English of the significance of Chŏng's reforms in historical context may be found in the review article by James Palais, "Early Chosŏn Intellectual History," *Journal of Korean Studies* (1980), 2:199–22.
70. See Martina Deuchler, "Neo-Confucianism," pp. 91–98.
71. *Ibid.*, p. 74
72. See Sakai, "Yi Yulgok and the Community Compact," pp. 332–34.
73. To the extent that Neo-Confucians promoted local interests in the academies, it would presumably derive from their preference for political decentralization, emphasizing the dispersion and sharing of power, not from any common rural background or personal identification with the local landed aristocracy. Edward Wagner in "The Social background of Early Yi Dynasty Neo-Confucianists" calls into question their having a common social background and emphasizes instead, as the defining characteristic of the *sarim* group, their common outlook as Neo-Confucians. See the proceedings of the Ninth International Seminar, October 1981, entitled *Neo-Confucianism* (Taegu: Kyungpook National University, 1982), pp. 155–75.
74. See my *Neo-Confucian Orthodoxy*, pp. 31–37.
75. See JaHyun Kim Haboush, "A Heritage of Kings," p. 92.
76. See Lee Ki-moon, "Foundation of Hunmin chŏngŭm," in *Korea Journal* (June 1983), 23 (6):4, 8.
77. See Tu, "Yi T'oegye's Perception of Human Nature," pp. 244, 260.
78. See Julia Ching, "Yi Yulgok on the 'Four Beginnings and the Seven Emotions,'" pp. 318–19.
79. The earliest text reported by Professor Eikemeir is dated 1475. (D. Eikemeir, "Some Thoughts Surrounding the Community Pacts in Korea," draft prepared for the Conference on Korean Neo-Confucianism, August 1981.)
80. Deuchler, "Reject the False and Uphold the Straight," here in p. 376.
81. Deuchler, "Reject the False and Uphold the Straight," pp. 388, 392.
82. See *Neo-Confucian Orthodoxy*, pp. 9–13.

83. Deuchler, "Reject the False and Uphold the Straight," pp. 392–93.
84. See Miura Kunio, "Orthodoxy and Heterodoxy in seventeenth-Century Korea," pp. 427–33.
85. Deuchler, "Reject the False and Uphold the Straight," p. 381.
86. Peter Lee, "Versions of the Self," pp. 484–86, 491.

Chai-sik Chung

Chŏng Tojŏn: "Architect" of Yi Dynasty Government and Ideology

HAVING WITNESSED THE collapse of the Yüan empire and the rise of the Ming dynasty, General Yi Sŏnggye (r. 1392–98), who had been sent to attack the Ming in 1388, instead withdrew his army from the Yalu River, marched against the Koryŏ capital, and seized power. Subsequently with support from members of the rising scholar-official class, he ascended the throne himself, bringing the Koryŏ dynasty (918–1392) to an end after 474 years of rule. Among his supporters was Chŏng Tojŏn (1342–98), to whom major credit must be given for assisting Yi Sŏnggye's ascent to power. Chŏng was not only a supreme "meritorious subject" *(kaeguk kongsin)* of Yi Sŏnggye, but also a close friend of this founder of the Yi dynasty.[1] Chŏng is said to have remarked once, in a drunken frolic, that "it was not Kao-tzu of the Han who used Chang Liang, but Chang who used Kao-tzu,"[2] implying that he himself was the power behind Yi Sŏnggye. As a matter of fact, it was through the instrumentality of Yi Sŏnggye that Chŏng and his Confucian colleagues succeeded in establishing Neo-Confucianism as the leading ideology of Yi Korea.

Yi, being a military man rather than a scholar, does not seem to have been much interested in Confucianism and was, at best, ambivalent about it. Indeed he was more inclined to remain faithful to Buddhism, and he spoke out publicly, not against Buddhist doctrine, but only to condemn its involvement in land holdings, its ownership of slaves, and the profligacy of its monks.[3] Nevertheless the Confucian literati, by taking advantage of Yi Sŏnggye's rise to power, were able to establish Neo-Confucianism as the state ideology, the dominant system of beliefs and values about man, society, political legitimacy, and authority. In this process Chŏng was the leading figure among the Confucian literati.

Many of the historic buildings which survive in Seoul today as remnants of ancient glory bear the names originally given them by Chŏng Tojŏn when they were first built at the beginning of the new dynasty.[4] Chŏng not only participated prominently in the erection of the physical edifices of the new dynasty but also, more importantly, as the architect of the new government, he provided a blueprint for the polity and social order of Yi Dynasty Korea. Included in his political writings were *Statutes for the Governance of Chosŏn (Chosŏn kyŏnggukchŏn)* 1394; *Historical Mirror for Statecraft (Kyŏngje mun'gam)* 1395, describing Chinese Government functions from the prime minister to local magistrates; a supplement to the preceding *(Kyŏngje mun'gam pyŏlchip)* n.d.; and *A Compendium for Inspectors (Kamsa yoyak)* 1397. These writings later formed the basis for the final codification of *Great Statutes for the Governance of the State (Kyŏngguk taejŏn)* 1471—the basic constitution of Yi Korea.

It was Chŏng who thus laid the foundations of the key institutional structures of the new dynasty and it was he too who gave Neo-Confucianism a firm foothold as the ideology of Yi Korea. The two groups of people whose interests came into conflict with those of the artistocratic class of large landholders allied with Buddhism were the oppressed peasantry and the new class of Confucian-educated middle-level and petty landowners. As the disorder and confusion resulting from the break-up of Koryŏ society became more evident in the fourteenth century, educated scholar-officials increasingly viewed a corrupt Koryŏ Buddhism, serving the interests of a decadent aristocracy, as the spiritual source of Korea's ills. To these men, who were keenly conscious of the social and economic contradictions of the time, Confucianism offered the hope of creating order out of the wreckage of the old society. It was in the changeover from Koryŏ to a new type of society that the Confucian literati played their crucial part. Invoking the authority of a transcendent morality expressed in Neo-Confucian doctrines, the literati questioned Koryŏ's legitimacy and provided a new set of goals to legitimize the political authority of the new government. At the center of this transition was Chŏng Tojŏn, and by grasping the main features of his thought we may come to understand the ideological character of Neo-Confucianism in early Yi Korea.

1. A BIOGRAPHICAL SKETCH

Chŏng Tojŏn was born in the village of Sambong[5] in Tanyang in Southern Ch'ungch'ŏng Province. His childhood name was Chongji, and he acquired the pen name of Sambong after his birthplace in the village of the same name.[6] Chŏng's father, Un'gyŏng, a native of Ponghwa *hyŏn* in northern Kyŏngsang Province, came from a long line of obscure local officials *(hyangni)*. Un'gyŏng was the first in his line to receive a fairly respectable appointment as honorary director of the security council *(kŏmgyo milchik chehak)*, but despite this he remained an impoverished scholar with apparently little ambition for success in political life.[7] About Chŏng Tojŏn's childhood his biography tells us only that from his early years he was very bright and had a real love of learning, but no teacher made a strong impression on him until he met Yi Saek (1328–96), a celebrated Confucian scholar.

While a student of Yi Saek, Chŏng met with a number of young men who were to be major influences on the intellectual life of his time, among whom Chŏng Mongju (1337–92) was the best known. At Yi's school Chŏng Tojŏn acquired some close friends with whom he studied the Chinese classics and could exchange ideas. In 1362 Chŏng passed the *chinsa* (Doctor of Letters) examination and in 1367 the Royal College, Sŏnggyun'gwan, was reestablished as the highest national academy for Confucian learning, with Yi Saek as its head, and, from 1370, with Chŏng Tojŏn as a member of the faculty. Among the faculty were such men as Chŏng Mongju, Kim Kuyong (1338–84), Pak Sangch'ung (1332–75), and Yi Sungin (1349–92). The Royal College had become a center for the study of Chu Hsi's philosophy, then rising to prominence,[8] and during his five years there Chŏng Tojŏn devoted himself to achieving a mastery of Neo-Confucian teachings.

In 1368 the Ming rose to power, supplanting the alien Mongols who had ruled China as the Yüan dynasty from 1279. With the establishment of Ming rule over China, Neo-Confucianism had been confirmed as the dominant philosophy. Chŏng and the Confucian literati in Korea embraced the new teaching, partly no doubt as an opportunity to enhance their own power, and they supported the Korean King Kongmin's (r. 1351–74) pro-Ming, anti-Mongol policy. In 1374, however, as King U (r. 1374–88) ascended the throne, the Koryŏ government controlled by Yi Inim shifted its position, adopting an anti-Ming, pro-Mongol stance. At this point Chŏng and his associates who had supported the pro-Ming policy were driven into exile.[9]

Chŏng spent the first three of his nine years of exile, from 1375 to 1383, at Kŏp'yŏng, a village designated by the government as a dwelling place for the low-born (pugongmin), in Naju, Chŏlla Province. Vilified and bereft of his friends, Chŏng lived at Kŏp'yŏng in abject poverty and loneliness. Some of the essays he wrote at Kŏp'yŏng—for example, Kanan (Family Woes)[10] and Sojaedonggi (Reminiscences of Sojae Village);[11]— reveal the agony of despair and loneliness he suffered. Living in almost complete isolation from the surrounding world, Chŏng came to learn firsthand the plight of the peasantry in the rural areas. Mistrust and hatred of the ruling establishment ran deep in the veins of these people who groaned under heavy burdens of taxation while trying to provide sustenance for their families. To these poor people, the Confucian literati, with high-bred manners and superior airs, seemed a breed apart and not to be trusted. In such circumstances Chŏng experienced the misery of those left forgotten in the bottom ranks of society, and came to feel a deep sympathy for the poor. These sentiments later found expression in his writings.[12]

After three years at Kŏp'yŏng, Chŏng moved during the next six years from Ponghwa hyŏn to Samgaksan, Pup'yŏng, and Kimp'o, one after the other. During these years of exile, he devoted himself entirely to studying, teaching, and writing, with much time for soul-searching and self-reflection. Refusing to despair, he lived in the hope that some day his integrity would be vindicated and he could return to active political life.

In the fall of 1383, Chŏng went to see Yi Sŏnggye, then military commander of the Northeastern Area (Tongbungmyŏn tojihwisa), at his military camp in Hamju, a remote town in Hamgyŏng Province. By this time the Koryŏ regime had lost its authority, and Buddhism, which till then had been patronized by the government, was becoming discredited. Chŏng appears to have sensed that the time was ripe for the emergence of a new political force to take over from the tottering Koryŏ dynasty,[13] and he hoped to make a political comeback in the course of staging a coup d'état by General Yi. Chŏng's personal history at this point became inseparable from the dynastic upheaval which brought the fall of Koryŏ and the rise of Yi.

In 1388 Yi Sŏnggye abruptly seized control of the government and Chŏng found himself in a position to play a leading role in reforming the system of land tenure and military organization. By preparing the way for the appointment of Yi Sŏnggye as the commander-in-chief *(toch'ongjesa)* of the Central High Command of Armed Forces *(Samgun toch'ongjebu)*, Chŏng masterminded Yi's ascent to the throne as the first king of the Yi dynasty in 1392. Later Chŏng himself was appointed to the position of commander-in-chief of the Joint Command of the Armed Forces *(Ŭi-hŭngsamgunbu)*. During his tenure in office, by abolishing the private military guards illegally acquired by princes or powerful families, Chŏng built up a national army under the control of a civilian prime minister. Chŏng also wrote many treatises on military command and tactical formations. He is credited with a plan to build up an effective defense against foreign encroachment and to regain Liao-tung, a former territory of both ancient Chosŏn and Koguryŏ, though his untimely death in 1398 prevented him from living to see this accomplished.[14] For the first seven years of the new dynasty until his tragic death, Chŏng not only designed the fundamental institutional structure of the government but also played a decisive part in establishing Neo-Confucianism as the philosophy of Yi Korea. Chŏng wrote the first draft of a history of Koryŏ which was to become the basis for the official history of that dynasty, known as the *Koryŏsa*.[15]

Chŏng's rise to power and fame came to an abrupt halt in 1398 as a result of another coup d'état. T'aejo, the dynastic founder, had eight sons. Yi Pangwŏn (1367–1422, r. 1400–18), the fifth, was the most ambitious and able of all. But T'aejo named as crown prince *(seja)* Yi Pangsŏk (1382–98) the youngest son by T'aejo's second wife, and Chŏng, who had played an important part in this designation of the crown prince was appointed to the position of teacher for the prince. In retaliation, Yi Pangwŏn staged a coup in 1398, during which he killed Chŏng, the crown prince, and many of their supporters. Two years later Yi Pangwŏn assumed the throne as King T'aejong. Meanwhile Chŏng had died in ignominy, having been accused of plotting against Yi Pangwŏn by supporting T'aejo's youngest son. Thus Chŏng became the victim of his own involvement in the politics of succession to the throne.[16]

2. TOWARD A NEW GOVERNMENT MODEL

One of the greatest accomplishments of Chŏng was the compilation of the aforementioned *Statutes for the Governance of Chosŏn*, which outlined a new constitutional order for the state of Chosŏn. Chŏng based his ideal government on several Chinese models: the *Rites of Chou (Chou-li)*, the idealized governmental structure attributed to the Chou dynasty in China; the *Ming Code (Ta Ming lü)*; the governmental structures of various dynasties in China; and the *Six Administrative Statutes (Liu-tien)*.[17] At the outset of his *Statutes* Chŏng defined the source of sovereignty, the name of the dynasty, succession to the throne, enfeoffment of members of the royal family, and the form of royal pronouncements—in short, the constitutional basis of the dynasty.[18]

The name of Chosŏn was adopted at the suggestion of the Ming emperor and reflects Chŏng's view of diplomacy and foreign relations. Chosŏn had been first used for the ancient state of Chosŏn founded by Tan-gun, the legendary progenitor of the Korean people. However, though Chŏng referred to Tan'gun Chosŏn, he did not really have much to say about it in any substantial way. Instead, Chŏng explained that the adoption of Chosŏn as the dynastic name derived from the ancient state of Chosŏn founded by Kija, who had received Korea as his fief from King Wu of Chou. Kija was a sage who had helped King Wu to develop the Chou dynasty's great culture by drawing up the Great Plan *(Hung-fan)*, described in the *Book of History* or *Documents (Shu-ching)*. According to Chŏng, it was also Kija who promulgated the eight main tenets underlying the Great Plan, which became the basis for the spread of Chinese civilization. Drawing a parallel between Kija's enfeoffment by King Wu and the legitimation of Yi Sŏnggye by the Ming emperor, Chŏng promoted the idea that Yi Korea was a legitimate restoration of Kija Chosŏn, which had been modeled on the glorious age of Chou. With particular pride Chŏng emphasized that Yi Korea was founded upon a standard of Confucian culture such as no later dynasty, Chinese or Korean, had ever actually attained.

This way of regarding Confucian culture reflected Chŏng's conception of tributary relations in diplomacy and foreign relations. He maintained that, as a nation dedicated to Confucian values, Korea's relationship with Ming China should be to "serve the great" *(sadae)*, in order properly to maintain the hierarchy of the universal Confucian world order. Thus Korea's tributary relationship with Ming China was to be different from its earlier relationships with the Jurchen and Mongols. Relations with the Ming were to be grounded on the acceptance of common Confucian cultural values, whereas those with the non-Chinese had been based on sheer military subjugation. In fact, Chŏng's posture of defining the cultural identity of Korea in the context of *sadae*, or tributary relations with the Ming, was at the time the most realistic one for Korea to take if it were to maintain a measure of autonomy within the bounds of dependency on a powerful Ming China. Indeed the long-term realism of this view was borne out as it came to characterize the fundamental cultural orientation and diplomatic posture of Yi Korea for the ensuing centuries.[19]

Chŏng elaborated more specific items in further subsections of his work. In the Code of Rulership *(Ch'ijŏn)*, he defined the duties of the sovereign and the ministerial subjects and stipulated that government officials be recruited on the basis of talent rather than by birth.[20] The aristocratic structure of the late Koryŏ dynasty was, in Chŏng's view, lamentable. A social hierarchy based on heredity and privilege lent itself to such corrupt practices in state service as marriages of convenience, nepotism, and the securing of government positions through bribery. Chŏng called for elimination of these evils by establishing a more equitable and efficient bureaucracy that would extend even to commoners (though not slaves) an equal opportunity to serve as officials in the state bureaucracy. To this end he proposed establishing qualifications for office solely on the basis of merit attested by official examinations *(kwagŏ)*. With the exception of the *munŭm*, i.e., the privilege of exemption from examination granted to a descendant of a *yangban* who had rendered meritorious services to the state, access to officialdom was to be conditioned only on the passing of the civil and military examinations. While the limited opportunity through the *munŭm* provided some continuity of family in a status-oriented society, the examination system was an apparatus for the "circulation of elites," which served the interests of a newly rising class of scholar-officials and commoners.

Greater emphasis was put on the study of the Classics (the Four Books and the Five Classics) as the way for the "true Confucian" to cure the ills of man and society. Also, much stress was laid on literary learning and practical policy study, replacing the traditional emphasis on fossilized literary skills and belles-lettres which had formerly been a requisite for the civil service examination.[21] Chŏng believed that, in order to establish a more efficient bureaucracy, the meritocratic examination system exemplified in the *Rites of Chou* and other historical experiences related to bureaucracy should be imitated. For the enhancement of both the examination system and Confucian learning for moral education, Chŏng supported the promotion of the school system, which ranged from the local district schools *(hyanghak)* to the Royal College (Sŏnggyun'gwan) in Seoul.[22]

His Tax Code *(pujŏn)* dealt with the means of increasing the national income, reducing the expense of government, and securing the livelihood of the people.[23] Defining ritual and ceremonial *(ye)* as the key to a harmonious social order, Chŏng presented in the Ceremonial Codes *(Yejŏn)* the principles of court ceremonies and rituals, royal sacrifices, the calendar, education, a recruitment system based on merit attested by civil service examination, open channels of information, foreign relations "serving the great [China]," and rites of passage and ancestral shrines.[24] The Code of Governance *(Chŏngjŏn),* which was really a code of military affairs *(Pyŏngjŏn),* provided the practical means to implement the military organization, weaponry, training, examination, rewards and punishments, palace guard, territorial defense, corvée, administration of land to be reserved for military garrisons, and so forth. The reason Chŏng referred to military affairs under the heading of the Code of Governance is because he was convinced that war should be resorted to only to rectify evil and injustice. Confucian principles of humanity and righteousness should be the moral basis of the military leadership and the governance of men.[25]

The Code of Justice *(Hŏnjŏn)* was necessary to complement the governance of men through moral means. It is better to govern men by moral persuasion, but sometimes it becomes necessary to resort to laws and punishments in order to keep people in line. In Chŏng's view, such administrative functions as personnel management, revenue, ceremonies, governance, and public works could not be properly carried out without the backing of some legal sanction. Laws and punishments were to be used for their deterrent effect, i.e., to obviate their own use. Laws have a deterrent as well as didactic function, and punishments are to be carefully administered in the spirit of humane love. In compiling the Code of Justice Chŏng drew upon the Ming Code, which was the most complete legal formulation based on Confucian moral norms.[26] It seems that Chŏng's legal philosophy reflected Chu Hsi's idea that law and punishment served to reinforce moral cultivation for the governance of men.[27]

The Code of Works *(Kongjŏn)* stipulated that in public works people should be mobilized in a loving spirit, and in producing goods resources should be used sparingly. Under the five categories outlined above Chŏng further elaborated his plans for governing the country and set forth a fundamental policy for the Yi government.[28]

The Code of Rulership in the *Statutes for the Governance of Chosŏn* gives only general directions for ruling the country, but in the *Historical Mirror for Statecraft* Chŏng presented more detailed models for government officials.[29] Outlining how the functions and duties of ministers came to be defined over the course of China's long history, Chŏng described desirable role models for local magistrates. Chŏng presented vignettes of exemplary and evil ministers in China so that one might derive from them ideas of what good deeds one should perform and what evil acts one should avoid. Chŏng wrote this book as a guide of conduct for ministers and government officials. He attributed the successful governance that existed, for example, in the classical "Three Dynasties" to the ideal ministers who helped the kingly rule of the monarch. In the establishment and maintenance of the harmony of yin and yang, and in keeping peace in the state and all-under-heaven, the prime minister's role is pivotal. The state's punishments and rewards and administrative orders all should come from the prime minister.[30] Chŏng maintained that administrative authority must be given to the prime minister, not to the king:

Not even for one day can there be any lapse in the administrative authority held by the court [i.e., the state government or civil administration]. If not held by the court, it will be in the hands of the Censorate *(Taegak)*; and if not in the Censorate, it will be found in the inner palace. If administrative authority resides in the court, the nation will enjoy order. If it lies in the censorate, the nation will be in disorder. If it falls to the inner palace, the nation will be in ruins.[31]

Chŏng found in the *Rites of Chou* an ideal model for political reform. In the classical ages of Hsia, Shang, and Chou the rulers and their prime ministers were both saintly and wise men, able to rule their countries in prosperity and peace through mutual cooperation. But during the Ch'in-Han dynasties, or the age of conquerers,[32] the model system of antiquity had been abandoned in favor of an imperial system based on the anti-Confucian Legalist principle, which elevated the emperor to an unchallenged position. Thereafter the throne had used the machinery of the state to dominate society, with an inevitable tendency toward tyranny. In the age of conquerors it was a stark reality that the ideal philosopher-king with high intellectual and moral qualifications was hard to come by. Longing for the ideal pattern of the past, Chŏng, like the Neo-Confucians, bewailed the abandonment of the ancient system by the Ch'in-Han dynasties and the late Koryŏ dynasty. Under the circumstances Chŏng thought the best way out was to find a man of wisdom from among the people and give him actual authority to conduct the government through the six ministers who were to run the state apparatus.[33]

Chŏng's ideal of giving the prime minister actual authority over the government would have made the king a mere symbol or figurehead. Yi Pangwŏn, however, who later became King T'aejong, was committed to the idea of centralized monarchical authority. He had tried to weaken the power of the state council (controlled by the prime minister) in an effort to extend and buttress royal power. This conflict of interests and differences in political philosophy may have been behind the assassination of Chŏng by King T'aejong. Chŏng's ideal was rejected by T'aejong who wished to regain monarchical control, but the next king, Sejong, restored the active role of the state council. Then his son, King Sejo, again reversed his father's stance by restoring monarchical centralism. Thus during the ensuing period in Yi Korea the political scene was characterized by the recurring conflict between Chŏng's Neo-Confucian ideal and the monarchical centralism meant to shore up royal power.[34]

In the second half of the *Historical Mirror* Chŏng traces how the functions of the censorate, the central military command, the inspector, and the local magistrate had developed in China and Korea. Chŏng wanted to see their powers expanded. Functioning as the eyes and ears of the king, the censorate was to have the authority to examine the wrongdoing of officials and ministers, and even the misrule of the monarch. The authority of the censorate was to be strengthened, but it was not to exceed that of the prime minister. The central military command was to defend the palace and the capital. the inspector would keep close watch on the misconduct of powerful families and abuses of corrupt officials in order to protect helpless people against them. It was also to be the responsibility of the inspector to recommend able scholars for government service. The local magistrates were to be responsible for the livelihood of the people, for "they are the parents of the people."[35] The magistrates constitute "the foundation of the people,"[36] for upon them depends the achieving of an increase of cultivable land, growth in population, the rise of schools, morality, law and order, a just system of corvée, and economizing of expenditures.[37]

Chŏng was in the mainstream of Neo-Confucianism, which emphasized both the inward concern of the sage for the moral transformation of the human mind and the outward role of the king in establishing order in the world. However, Chŏng seems to have put greater emphasis on the latter problem of achieving order in the outer realm of state and society. While Chŏng's admiration of the *Rites of Chou* as a model for political reform and his suspicion of the Han-T'ang trend toward heavy monarchical centralism reflect his commitment to Neo-Confucian political philosophy, one may suspect that his deep concern for the outer world of political economy and his stress on enriching and strengthening the state reveal an interest in practical statecraft that may owe something to Chinese legalist thought or the statecraft thinkers of the Eastern Chekiang school in the southern Sung.

Chŏng frequently referred to the *Rites of Chou* as a model for institutional reforms. In the Sung it was Wang An-shih who had stressed the *Rites of Chou* to justify his reforms. Later, Chu Hsi still believed in the political ideals and institutions prescribed in the *Rites of Chou*, but along with the Ch'eng brothers, he disapproved of Wang's use of authoritarian methods of statecraft to achieve his political goals and fiscal reforms. For Chu Hsi the reforming of society ultimately hinged upon the moral education of the people. With his active interest in political reform, Chŏng Tojŏn, too, accepted the ideals of the *Rites of Chou*, but considered Wang An-shih to have departed from Confucian orthodoxy with its reliance on self-cultivation and moral education as a means of ordering society. Interestingly, however, Chŏng did not just keep to Ch'eng-Chu moral cultivation but also drew upon institutional models and precedents from Chinese and Korean history at large.[38]

In the *Historical Mirror* Chŏng largely defined the duties of officials, but in the *Supplement to the Historical Mirror* he discussed the duties of the sovereign.[39] The following statement by Chŏng, which Kwŏn Kŭn (1352–1409) quoted in his preface to the *Supplement*, shows clearly the purpose for which Chŏng wrote the Supplement:

The mind of the king is the foundation of government. In discussing the ways of governance, if the mind of the king is not treated as the most fundamental consideration, is it not tantamount to leaving the source of a stream unclean and still expecting the water downstream to be pure? How could this be?[40]

To Chŏng, the legendary rulers of the classical Three Dynasties had set a standard in the model of the sage kings.[41] But in his attitude toward later rulers in China, Chŏng was not uncritical.[42] He understood Chinese history largely through the historical writings of Chu Hsi and other Sung historians. Morever, following his evaluations of the merits and demerits of successive rulers in China from the perspective of the Ch'eng-Chu philosophy, Chŏng reviewed the lives and deeds of all the Koryŏ kings in a similar moralistic vein.[43]

Chŏng conceptualized an ideal society in which the king would retain the right to rule but would accept severe restraints on any tendency toward royal despotism. The king would be advised on all questions of state by the prime minister, who would have the actual authority to decide most matters. The king would be open to the avenues of public opinion, so as to understand what the majority of the people think. He would seek men of wisdom to serve the government. With their help the king would rule the country through a moral leadership that comes from self-cultivation, for the monarch's moral example was the key to good government. In order to explain the moral responsibility of the king, Chŏng attached a discourse of Ch'eng I on the fifth hexagram in his *Commentary on the Book of Changes*, which is a key to understanding the king's role.[44]

By surveying the main outlines of Chŏng's politicoeconomic writing we can glimpse his vision of a new sociopolitical order for Chosŏn. Through these writings Chŏng addressed an enormous task: to define the *raison d'état* so as to establish the legitimacy of the new dynasty; to rebuild the central bureaucracy and local administrative apparatus; to push through land reforms; and to give a new sense of direction and order to society.

The new leadership that came from the coalition of military men (represented by Yi Sŏnggye) and the emergent Confucian scholar-officials (represented by Chŏng Tojŏn) faced the formidable task of winning the support of the peasantry and legitimizing the Yi's overthrow of the Koryŏ dynasty. The new leaders had to demonstrate that they could win popular support by their adherence to the ideal, the Kingly Way of caring for the well-being of the people. As a theoretician of the new leadership, Chŏng rationalized that Yi Sŏnggye had overthrown the Koryŏ dynasty in accordance with the Mandate of Heaven and the wishes of the people, just as the Chou had done when they overthrew the Shang in China. Without popular support the legitimacy of the new dynasty would remain in question and Chŏng was convinced that the way to win that support was neither through brute power nor deception but only through the humane rule of which Mencius spoke.[45]

To Chŏng the peasantry was indeed the foundation of the state,[46] for whom nothing was more urgent and necessary than to secure the means of sustenance. Moral man and the good society, for which government exists (a Neo-Confucian ideal), were possible only when people were fed and the means of their livelihood was secured (the ideals of Kuan Chung and Mencius).[47] In order to ensure the livelihood of the people a political and economic structure had to be formed that would promote the general welfare of the people against the hereditary and privileged claims of the dominant aristocratic families. Under the economic domination of the aristocratic families the peasantry had been reduced to utter penury, usually having to divide the harvest with the landlord half and half. The state itself was bankrupt, lacking adequate control over land and manpower. It also lacked the necessary grain reserves for the army, since these were under the control of the aristocratic families.

Chŏng proposed radical reform measures to attack the entrenched position of a hereditary landed aristocracy which enjoyed privileged access to both land and bureaucratic office and even had private military guards. Chŏng advocated the abolition of the arbitrary private ownership of land and unjust land-tenure relations in favor of a system of public land *(kongjŏn)*, and a militia system of peasant-soldiers *à la* the ideal set forth in the *Rites of Chou*. He asserted that the state alone should be allowed to levy taxes on land. This would replace the 50 percent rate and other arbitrary levies with a simple tithe. With state control of the land, the revenue of holdings that had previously been exploited by aristocratic families would now be available to the state for meeting its essential needs.

The aim of Chŏng's reform measures was to equalize the incomes of the people by the state's redistribution of all land in relatively equal proportions, on a per capita basis. Chŏng believed that a wealthy and strong nation could be built only on the foundation of a well-fed peasantry. His reform measures, however, were so radical that they encountered opposition not only from the landed aristocracy but also from such Neo-Confucian scholars as Yi Saek, Kwŏn Kŭn, and others of the middle-level landlord class. Thus, Chŏng's aspirations for a society that would serve the welfare of the people as a whole were frustrated, and the land policy of early Yi Korea took a different direction from the one he had envisioned.[48]

It may be difficult to argue that Chŏng's impulse for land reforms came from the *Rites of Chou* and Neo-Confucian ideals alone, since a majority of Neo-Confucian scholar-officials in his own time and after did not share his egalitarian ideas. We may also speculate that Chŏng was better able to sympathize with the plight of the peasantry than most of his Neo-Confucian cohorts because of his own experience in exile, living as a marginal person in society. Through his daily contact with the low-born, Chŏng learned firsthand the wretched conditions and poverty of the downtrodden people. But Chŏng's populist stance was more than a re-flection of his own life experience and his exposure to Neo-Confucian ideals. He was first and foremost an ideologue, who sought primarily to legitimize the authority of the new state and consolidate its power.[49] To him, the welfare of the people was a prerequisite for the consolidation of state power. A wealthy and strong state required a strong bureaucratic government and military defense. Thus the immediate purpose of his land reform proposal was probably to increase the revenues of the state to meet the expense of bureaucratic administration and military defense.[50]

From this one could argue the case for Chŏng as a "tough-minded" political realist. But along with this Chŏng Tojŏn can still be seen as a "tender-hearted" Neo-Confucian moralist. For him government was still not an end in itself but a means to provide for good people and a moral society. The good society was one in which both the ruler and his sub-jects lived in accordance with the Confucian Way.[51] Ideally, good gov-ernment would rule the people neither by the external controls of the Legalists nor by the utilitarian manipulation of reward and punishment (though at times these might be necessary), but primarily through moral suasion. To govern was to educate. Moral education and government were one and the same. A sense of moral responsibility, which comes from the consciousness of the ontological unity of man, society, and the universe, was the foundation of social order. The monarch and the scholar-officials *(yu)* were to implant a sense of moral responsibility in the people's minds through their own internalizing of moral norms in their respective per-sons.[52]

Chŏng characterized the ideal Confucian scholar-official as a man who cultivates in himself Confucian morality and expresses it in his po-litical leadership. He is a morally conscious scholar, as well as a man of politics, who participates in the governance of the country.[53] He is, as Chŏng himself was, a versatile man with many intellectual interests in literature, history, philosophy, and morality. But he is also quite knowl-edgeable about such technical areas as astronomy, medicine, divination, geography, and military strategy.[54] To Chŏng, the ideal Confucian scholar-official was not simply a Confucian moralist but a man of social action with a broad background of technical knowledge to be used for the enrichment and strengthening of the country.[55]

Governing was essentially a process of moral education of the self and moral rectification of society. But in the actual public realm the regulative process of laws and institutions was necessary in order to realize ideal Confucian values.[56] Chŏng was the key person at the beginning of the new dynasty, who provided a workable legal framework for the concrete manifestation of ideal Confucian values as the normative system of the Chosŏn dynasty.

3. TOWARD A CONFUCIAN NORMATIVE SOCIETY

During the Koryŏ dynasty (918–1392) Buddhism was patronized by the government as the mainstay of the country's religion, along with Taoist geomancy, yin-yang theory, and the ancient native cults of the heavenly gods, mountain spirits, and the dragon god.[57] Although Confucianism was introduced to Korea as early as the Three Kingdoms period (c. 57 B.C. to A.D. 668), it had long been overshadowed by the above-mentioned religions.[58] It served mainly to provide the state with educated civil servants. Through private schools that flourished from the second half of the eleventh century, Confucianism was able to sustain its life and produce outstanding scholar-officials for the state.[59]

Neo-Confucianism had been introduced to Korea by An Hyang (1243–1306) and Paek Ijŏng around the beginning of the fourteenth century,[60] yet it was not until the end of the fourteenth century that Neo-Confucianism had grown strong enough to become a real counterbalance to Buddhism. In 1367, the Royal College, Sŏnggyun'gwan, had been established under the leadership of Yi Saek and Chŏng Mongju, and there, for the first time, Chu Hsi's commentaries on the Four Books were taught.[61] Although the Royal College was the highest national academy for Confucian learning, the private schools continued to train civil service candidates. Now, however, in contrast to earlier Confucian learning, which had become fossilized by its emphasis on formal literary skills and belles-lettres, Neo-Confucianism taught the Chinese classics as the scriptural basis for the ontologically grounded moral principles underlying society. This new normative system which linked man and society to the cosmic order was able to evoke the interest of intellectuals who had been longing for a functional religion or philosophy that would bring order and direction to a society floundering in moral decline and social disorder.[62] Neo-Confucianism offered its followers a set of goals and values in terms of which some critique could be made of Koryŏ's failings and the prevalent moral decay. In effect the Neo-Confucians attributed Koryŏ's collapse to Buddhism.

During the Koryŏ dynasty Buddhism had reached the apex of its influence. Buddhist monasteries, richly endowed with lands and exempted from taxation, held religious ceremonies on national festivals in their capacity as guardians of the state religion.[63] The dominant doctrines of Koryŏ Buddhism were inherently congenial to the maintenance of the status quo and established institutions. T'ien-t'ai and Chogye Sŏn (Zen) had been the leading Buddhist sects since the earlier phase of the dynasty. T'ien-t'ai emphasized the mutual interdependence of universal emptiness and phenomenal existence. Stressing the idea of totality and mutual harmony, T'ien-t'ai saw no essential dichotomy between, for example, the king and his people. Each phenomenon was viewed as a complementary part of the harmonious whole. This teaching in effect rationalized the status quo and masked social conflicts and tensions.[64]

The central element in the Chogye school, which drew on the idealistic metaphysics of the *Avatamsaka* (or *Hua-yen*) *sutra*, was a noumenal, immutable mind or emptiness, considered to be the basis of all phenomenal manifestations. In the Hua-yen school's doctrine of the unity of the self and the world in noumenal emptiness, the givenness of this world was affirmed as the ultimate reality or manifestation of an all-inclusive, universal emptiness. Hence the Chogye school lacked transcendent universals that could stand in critical tension with the institutions of this world. Easily accommodating to the world, Koryŏ Buddhism became an important prop to the status quo.[65]

Koryŏ Buddhism also contained much ritualism and magic that could be exploited for ulterior ends. Because of its exceedingly fluid accommodation to such beliefs and practices as geomancy, the yin-yang theory, and shamanism, Buddhism became too diluted and adulterated to stand on its own and give deep spiritual or universal meaning to things.

To the Neo-Confucians, moreover, the Buddhists seemed to be too preoccupied with the problems of life after death and individual salvation to be very mindful of their social responsibilities to family and state here on earth. This then became the standard formula for Neo-Confucian criticism of Buddhism. But what bothered the Neo-Confucians most was that, as Buddhism lost its spiritual vigor under the patronage of the state, monks were increasingly tempted to invade the political and economic realms that traditionally were considered the Confucian sphere of action. The monk Sin Ton's involvement in Koryŏ politics, the moral depravity of the monks, the expense of Buddhist state festivals, the tax exemptions that drained off the national wealth, and the evils associated with "monastic landlordism," became targets of bitter criticism.[66]

As early as the tenth century Ch'oe Sŭngno (927–89) and others had criticized Buddhism for the evils associated with expensive festivals, the frequent mobilization of laborers to build monasteries, attempts at profiteering, and other corrupt practices.[67] Toward the Buddhist belief system, however, Ch'oe's criticism was rather restrained. To him Buddhism was mainly interested in the otherworldly salvation of the individual, wl.ereas Confucianism served as "the basis for regulating the state" here and now. He simply wondered whether it was not a mistake for the Buddhists to give up what is of immediate significance today for whatever may be promised in the remote future.[68]

In 1352 Yi Saek, the Confucian scholar and statesman, also asserted that there were too many Buddhist temples and monks. Yet, critical though he was of the evils of monastic landlordism from the standpoint of state policy, he remained vague about Buddhism itself and even found it a religion congenial and compatible with Confucianism.[69] Even his famous disciple, Chŏng Mongju, and others, held somewhat ambiguous attitudes toward Buddhism.[70] As they saw it toward the end of Koryŏ, Buddhism and Confucianism, though differing greatly in their beliefs and interests, had coexisted in relative harmony for many years.[71]

After 1391, however, the Confucian scholar-officials launched an all-out attack on Buddhism. Now they blamed Buddhism for society's decadence. It was Chŏng Tojŏn who broke with the pattern of coexistence between the two religions and worked with sophisticated and systematic doctrinal arguments against Buddhism for the rejection of the latter and the encouragement of Confucianism. What was his reason for doing this? In the Statutes for the Governance of Chosŏn, Chŏng declared categorically that the sacrifice in Confucius' Temple (Munmyo) should be the cult of the state and that Confucianism should provide the basic normative orientation of Yi society. Accordingly, all superstitious and lewd practices associated with the cults of the Bodhisattvas and the native cults of the various gods and spirits, were to be forbidden. Only the cults of the morally exemplary sages and of the spirits of the mountains, the dragon god, and the spirits of the soil that bring forth crops, were to be excepted.[72]

As a prerequisite to the promotion of Confucianism as an ideology that explains social change and provides an alternative blueprint for the reorganization of society, a complete repudiation of Buddhism was deemed necessary. Reform of the existing society could only be pressed through criticism of the prevailing belief system that had supported it. With this clear end in view Chŏng elaborated a comprehensive philosophical attack on Buddhism and Taoism in the following works: *Questions and Answers between the Mind and Heaven (Simmun ch'ŏndap)* 2 *p'yŏn*, 1375; *On the Mind, Material Force, and Principle (Simgi ip'yŏn)* 3 *p'yŏn*, 1394; and the celebrated *Arguments Against Mr. Buddha (Pulssi chappyŏn)* 20 *p'yŏn*, 1398, which was the principal anti-Buddhist writing produced during the Yi dynasty.

In *Questions and Answers* Chŏng presented a critique of the Buddhist doctrine of karma with a view to explaining the principle of ethical compensation from the perspective of Neo-Confucianism. In Chŏng's view, principle *(i)* is identified with the enduring Way, while material force *(ki)* is associated with finite physical beings subject to change. When material force comes into contact with external things in the phenomenal world, it is manifested in many different ways. Differences among individuals are ascribed to an inequality in their material endowment. The fact that human beings deviate from goodness, and that good deeds do not always bring happiness nor evil deeds suffering, is attributable to disparities in material force. Behind the individual manifestation of material force (which is subject to change, according to Chŏng) Confucianism can find an ethically and ontologically constant principle that gives structure and meaning to the seemingly contradictory and meaningless phenomena of this world. Principle is a concrete standard of value that eventually distinguishes what is right from what is wrong. And with this belief in the eventual ethical compensation of the good by the eternal principle, man can overcome both the lack of immediate retributive justice in this world and the pragmatic response to this in the Buddhist doctrine of karma.[73]

Chŏng wrote this essay during the first year of his exile. Separated from kin and friends, stripped of his former high position and worldly glory, Chŏng, the lonely exile, may have written this essay in order to ground his personal conviction on the ontological conception of the ultimate victory of goodness over evil.

On the Mind, Material Force, and Principle is a comparative study of Buddhism, Taoism, and Confucianism from the perspective of Neo-Confucianism. Chŏng wrote this tract to affirm his belief that Neo-Confucianism is superior to both Buddhism and Taoism. The gist of his argument is that the mind with which the Buddhists are so concerned is actually composed of both principle and material force, but, in Chŏng's view, it is material force that is primary. By this Chŏng aims to correct the Buddhist tendency to put excessive emphasis on the subjectivity of the mind at the expense of objective reality.

At the same time, however, Chŏng maintains that there must be principle before there can be material force to constitute the mind. Principle is the reason for the existence *(so-i-yŏn)* of material force. The mind and material force cannot exist apart from principle. The Taoists, excessively concerned with the attainment of longevity through the nourishment of material force, and the Buddhists, preoccupied with the subjective calmness of the mind, are both concerned with material force and the mind in a realm "within form" *(hyŏng-i-ha)*, and are not mindful of the principles of personal moral relations in the realm "above form" *(hyŏng-i-sang)*. What distinguishes man from the beasts, however, is his capacity to live a moral life. If man is solely motivated by human feelings and selfish desires, he is not much different from the beasts. The Taoist doctrine of the nourishment of the self and the Buddhist view of the enlightenment of the mind, therefore, are heterodox doctrines that delude people with false teachings.[74]

In *On the Mind, Material Force, and Principle* Chŏng denounced Buddhism and Taoism in general terms. In his *Arguments Against Mr. Buddha* he singled out doctrines of Buddhism for more detailed criticism so as to justify installing Chu Hsi orthodoxy as the ideology of the state. *Arguments Against Mr. Buddha* was written in the summer of 1398 shortly before Chŏng's murder. This was the last of Chŏng's writings for which he "exerted all the strength in his life." According to Chŏng, this book was written with the clear objective of refuting Buddhism once and for all lest it destroy morality and eventually humanity itself.[75]

Kwŏn Kŭn, who wrote a preface to this work, spoke of Chŏng Tojŏn as indeed the successor of Mencius, who had repudiated Yang Chu and

Mo Tzu.[76] Among the fifteen items he covered, Chŏng attacked with a special emphasis the Buddhist theory of knowledge that regarded the phenomenal world as an illusion. Strong ethical concern for the organization and maintenance of the status-oriented society governed by Confucian values permeate the entire work, but this is especially the case in the section that deals with the differences between Confucianism and Buddhism.[77]

Chŏng's motive was no doubt more political than philosophical—the total discrediting of organized Buddhism, along with the conservative aristocratic elements associated with it. Thus, it may be questioned whether in *Arguments Against Mr. Buddha* he really sought to elaborate as comprehensive a Neo-Confucian theory of cosmology and human nature as Chu Hsi had provided. For his refutation of Buddhism, however, Chŏng seems to have drawn mainly on what was found in Chu Hsi's arguments against it, since he himself apparently had a greater familiarity with Chu Hsi than with the doctrines of Hua-yen and Zen Buddhism.[78]

First, Chŏng criticized the Buddhist doctrine of the transmigration of the soul. In order to refute the notion of the soul's survival after death, Chŏng resorted to the Neo-Confucian ontological conception of the continuing creative production of material force. He also rejected the doctrine of the transmigration of the soul by asserting that once the human spirit and body are respectively dispersed in heaven and earth they cannot be reintegrated into a living soul.[79] As an alternative to the Buddhist concept of karma, Chŏng explained the inequalities among men and things in nature as attributable to differences in the purity and opacity of the material force with which nature was endowed. The alternation of yin and yang and the concentration and dispersion of the Five Elements, rather than differences in karma, were responsible for inequalities among men in intelligence, wealth, and position.[80]

Drawing upon Chu Hsi's philosophy of principle and material force Chŏng directed his attack mainly at the Buddhist theory of knowledge and at a conception of the mind as one with nature or ultimate reality. Buddhism, according to Chŏng, distinguishes the phenomenal world from nature or ultimate reality, which is the mind in its absolutely pure state of consciousness. The phenomenal world of facts and human affairs is only the imagination of the mind, and so it is an empty illusion. All things—both beings and values—are fabricated by the mind. In Chu Hsi's thought, however, principle is the ultimate "being" or "nature" of things as well as of man.[81] If man and the world function according to this organizing principle inherent in them, they do so in conformity with the permanent and orderly laws that govern man and the objective world. In this sense, they are moral beings.[82] Man should seek the highest good in external things and human affairs that possess in themselves a fixed or concrete standard of value. For example, man should seek the virtue of filial piety in serving his parents, and similarly observe the various moral obligations attaching to the relations between parent and child, ruler and minister, older and younger, husband and wife, and friends. All things have their ultimate nature, and the question is not whether this nature exists, but whether or not the fixed standard of this nature is preserved. Man's greatest obligation is to strive to safeguard his inborn good nature, or principle, and to extend this act of moral cultivation to the governance of the outer world in accordance with the moral dictates of principle.[83]

In brief, Chŏng concludes that whereas Buddhism maintains that all things, being fabrications of the mind, are empty and devoid of self-nature, Confucianism affirms that all things have a concrete nature. Whereas Buddhism insists on the duality of absolute emptiness and the world of illusion, Confucianism maintains the unity of one ultimate principle that links the individual, society, and the world. Whereas Buddhism views the mind and principle as two, Confucianism considers the mind and principle as one.[84] Chŏng accuses Buddhism of seeking a noumenal self that transcends all relative concepts, standards, and discriminations, and thus of not abiding by any fixed principle of value. Since there is no central organizing principle, there are no true moral distinctions. Buddhism knows only emptiness or subjective imagination and does not know the objective, universal principle. Buddhism completely disregards the morality of social relations between father and son, ruler and minister, older and younger, husband and wife, and friends.[85]

More specifically, Chŏng charges that the Buddhist notion of compassion, despite its resemblance to Confucian humanity (in) and its expression in the feeling of commiseration (ch'ŭgŭn), is actually applied quite differently. Buddhist compassion takes the form of an abstract, universal love among men, disregarding the natural inclination of man to love his own immediate family and relatives.[86] Furthermore, Chŏng repeated the standard Confucian criticism of the Buddhist conception of rewards and punishments, calling its doctrine of heaven and hell deceptive, egoistic, and amoral.[87] He also averred that Buddhist mendicancy is self-contradictory, unethical, and parasitical.[88] It is interesting to note that

Sŏn (Ch'an or Zen) Buddhism, the dominant form of Buddhism in eleventh- and the twelfth-century China, was especially singled out for attack as a most dangerous teaching, which led people astray by emphasizing the subjective mind and meditative practice instead of upholding explicit philosophical doctrine.[89]

To Chŏng, Buddhism is even more dangerous than the philosophies of Mo Tzu and Yang Chu, which Mencius had condemned as heterodox. Mo Tzu's universal love, which gives no priority to the family as does Confucianism, becomes a vague abstraction which allows for no intimate warmth of love between parents and children. Hence Chŏng condemns Mo Tzu's love as having no place for parents—as being "without father"—and thus as destroying the family. Chŏng also charges Yang Chu's unrestrained egoism as seeking only one's own salvation. It is an anarchistic rejection of rulership, a denial of the importance of state and society. Buddhism, however, is even more harmful than the heterodox teachings of Mo Tzu and Yang Chu because it deludes people with its lofty and mystical notions about nature, destiny, and morality. The Mohist conception of universal love, the Taoists' anarchic and hedonistic egoism, and the Buddhists' escapism from the painful cycle of existence, all are antithetical to the Confucians' moral imperative. Therefore, he lumps them together as "deviant" (idan, Ch. i-tuan, literally the "other strand") and "unorthodox" (sa, Ch. hsieh, morally off the correct path)—condemning them all as heterodox.[90]

It was Han Yü who used the terms "deviant" and "unorthodox" in contrast to cheng (K. chŏng, meaning "right," "straight") or cheng-tao (K. chŏngdo, meaning the right path). Han Yü used these terms in the ninth century A.D. to stigmatize Buddhism, and later they were used to attack the doctrines of Lao Tzu, Chuang Tzu, Yang Chu, and Mo Tzu. Thus they came to be juxtaposed as "heterodoxy" and "orthodoxy." After Chŏng Tojŏn used the terms, and especially after Chu Hsi's philosophy became the state ideology of the Yi dynasty, the Koreans used them to brand as heterodox not only Buddhism, Taoism, and even unorthodox Confucian schools within their own camp, but also any ideas that challenged the established ideology and legitimacy of the state.[91]

The keynote of Chŏng's thought is the affirmation of orthodox Confucian ethics and society, that is, the moral imperative to order human society according to the model of nature or principle. With this Chŏng set the fundamental direction of Yi dynasty ideology.

4. CONCLUSION

A common theme in the philosophical writings of Chŏng Tojŏn is his affirmation of the reality of this world as against Buddhism's tendency to turn away from the "real" world of community and ethical responsibilities in the contemplative pursuit of individual salvation through mystical enlightenment. He characterized Neo-Confucianism as the "real learning of the ancients which manifests the moral nature and renews the people" *(koin myŏngdŏk sinmin chi sirhak) (The Great Learning).*[92] In Buddhism's search for quiescence and emptiness, according to Chŏng, it neglected the real responsibilities of moral man to his society. Chŏng's aim was to appropriate the "real" *(sil)* or "practical" spirit of Confucian teaching in order to set a new direction for Yi Korean society. In contrast to Buddhism's preoccupation with the self and its engagement in contemplation, Chŏng's thought concentrated on such concrete matters as social morality, the polity, the economy, and the legal system.

To Chŏng, Buddhism was the ideology of the Koryŏ dynasty which had served the interests of the privileged classes; its individualistic and egotistic *Weltanschauung* was worlds apart from the Confucian value system promoted by the rising scholar-official class. The disintegration of Koryŏ society and its loss of intellectual unity called for a new system of thought to replace the old. It was no longer possible for these incompatible doctrines to live in the same symbolic universe or function in the same socioeconomic world. A conflict between these divergent world views and social orders was inevitable. What had been a simple distrust in the initial stage of conflict now became, more explicitly, an antagonistic confrontation. Accordingly, Confucian criticisms of Buddhism now assumed a deeply urgent and emotive tone. The scholar-officials, with a new set of Neo-Confucian values, were no longer content to take an assigned place and subordinate role within the old order. In order to achieve a new social order in which they could play a leading politicoeconomic role, it was necessary to engage in a systematic discrediting of the adversary, to rebut in detail the specific beliefs and practices of Buddhism.

As Mannheim remarked,

Only in a world in upheaval, in which fundamental new values are being created and old ones destroyed, can intellectual conflict go so far that antagonists will seek to annihilate not merely the specific beliefs and attitudes of one another, but also the intellectual foundations upon which these beliefs and attitudes rest.[93]

From the beginning Chŏng's approach to Buddhism was not meant to come to terms with the philosophy itself. To him, Buddhism was the ideology of the Koryŏ dynasty and of the privileged classes, and their whole world view was to be replaced. Chŏng's approach stands in contrast to that of Hamhŏ (Kihwa, 1376–1433), who wrote *On the Manifestation of the Truth (Hyŏnjŏngnon)* in defense of Buddhism. Hamhŏ discussed the differences between Buddhism and Confucianism, exhibiting an attitude of mutual understanding and respect.[94]

In the past, students of Chu Hsi philosophy in Korea often neglected Chŏng Tojŏn and Kwŏn Kŭn when they were tracing the lineage of Korean Neo-Confucianism. It was Chŏng Mongju and Kil Chae (1353–1419), not Chŏng Tojŏn, who have long been considered as the founding fathers of Neo-Confucian philosophy in Yi Korea.[95] The orthodox teaching in Korea consisted of the Learning of Human Nature and Principle *(sŏngnihak)* and the Ritual Studies *(yehak)*, which were primarily concerned with studying the rites of passage (capping, wedding, mourning, and ancestor worship).[96] With the heavy emphasis on morality in the Learning of Human Nature and Principle, Korean scholars from generation to generation have admired as founding fathers of Chu Hsi orthodoxy Chŏng Mongju and Kil Chae, who, out of loyalty to Koryŏ, refused to be reconciled to the coup d'état by Yi Sŏnggye.

Chŏng Tojŏn did not, however, give exclusive attention to the Learning of Human Nature and Principle. His primary concern was statecraft, the practical side of the Neo-Confucian tradition. For this reason, but more importantly for the reason that he took part in the overthrow of Koryŏ, Chŏng has been thought to have no place in the lineage of Neo-Confucian orthodoxy. Nevertheless, Chŏng was an important Neo-Confucian thinker in his own right.[97] Though not a philosopher in the usual sense, his thought was intimately connected with the vicissitudes of his own time, the political affairs of his day, and his commitment to a definite set of political and moral values. In this sense he was truly a prominent Neo-Confucian representative of real or practical learning *(sirhak)*.

Ideology can be variously used to characterize a constellation of concepts, ideas, beliefs, values, *Weltanschauung*, and so forth. As compared with the prevailing cognitive or moral ideas, ideologies take a different attitude toward the same phenomena. They are not purely intellectually oriented. They serve a variety of interests. Ideologies come into existence either to promote or reject a particular set of goals and values, either to legitimize or undermine the existing pattern of society and its culture. Ideologies are unavoidably political or *engagé*. "An ideology arises because there are strongly felt needs, which are not satisfied by the prevailing outlook, for an explanation of important experiences, for the guidance of conduct, and for a fundamental indication or legitimation of the value and dignity of the persons who feel these needs."[98] This was the case with Neo-Confucianism in a crisis situation at the end of the Koryŏ dynasty.

For an ideology to exist, there must be not only a rejection of the existing society and the dominant symbol systems that support it but also an accompanying vision of an alternative society and culture that can be legitimized by some transcendent principle or sacred authority. It was not enough simply to reject Buddhism and give a meaningful account of the confusing social situation. It was also necessary to provide a philosophical direction for society and matrices for the formation of a new political and social order.[99] Chŏng Tojŏn was an ideologist who met these requirements with distinction. If we fail to notice the central importance of ideology in Chŏng's thought we cannot fully understand either the thought itself or the ideological character fundamental to Yi Neo-Confucianism from its beginning.

NOTES

1. Chŏng Tojŏn, *Sambongjip* (Writings of Chŏng Tojŏn) (Han'guk saryo ch'ongsŏ, no. 13) (Seoul: Kuksa p'yŏnch'an wiwŏnhoe, 1961), p. 386.
2. *T'aejo sillok* (The Veritable Records of the Reign of T'aejo) (Seoul: Kuksa p'yŏnch'an wiwŏnhoe, 1968), 14:27a.
3. Yi Sangbaek, "Yubul yanggyo kyodae ŭi kiyŏn e kwanhan il yŏn'gu" (A Study of the Occasion for the Supplanting of Buddhism by Confucianism) in *Han-guk munhwasa yŏn'gu non'go* (Studies in the Cultural History of Korea), vol. 1 of *Yi Sangbaek chŏjakchip* (1947; reprint ed., Seoul: Ŭryu munhwasa, 1978), pp. 63–80, 80–88; Han Woo-keun (Ugŭn), "Yŏmal Sŏnch'o ŭi pulgyo chŏngch'aek" (The Policy toward Buddhism During the Interregnum of Koryŏ and Yi Dynasties), *Seoul taehakkyo nonmunjip* (December 1957), 6:3–80.
4. Chŏng, *Sambongjip*, pp. 100–3.
5. Han Young-woo (Yŏngu), *Chŏng Tojŏn sasang ŭi yŏn'gu* (A Study of the Thought of Chŏng Tojŏn) (Han'guk munhwa yŏn'gu ch'ongsŏ, no. 15) (Seoul: Han'guk munhwa yŏn'guso, 1973), pp. 13–21.
6. Except as otherwise noted, the biographical sources for Chŏng Tojŏn are from "Sasil" (Biographical Facts) in *Sambongjip*, kwŏn 14.
7. Chŏng, *Sambongjip*, pp. 116–21.
8. *Ibid.*, p. 370; Yi Pyŏngdo, "Charyo Han'guk yuhaksa ch'ogo" (A Draft History of Confucianism in Korea), mimeographed in 3 parts (Seoul: Seoul taehakkyo, 1959), 1:89–102.
9. Chŏng, *Sambongjip*, pp. 370–71.
10. *Ibid.*, pp. 109–10.
11. *Ibid.*, pp. 96–97.
12. *Ibid.*, pp. 108–9.
13. *Ibid.*, p. 372; *T'aejo sillok*, 14:26b-27a.
14. For Chŏng's military reform ideals, see Chŏng, *Sambongjip*, pp. 178–89, 211, 233–39, Chŏng Tuhŭi, "Sambongjip e nat'anan Chŏng Tojŏn ŭi pyŏngje kaehyŏgan ŭi sŏngkkyŏk," (The Characteristics of Chŏng Tojŏn's Military Reform Ideals in *Sambongjip*) (Papers delivered at the Eighth Korean Classics Symposium, Seoul, Korea, November 1, 1980); Han, *Chŏng Tojŏn sasang ŭi yŏn'gu*, pp. 133–42.
15. Chŏng, *Sambongjip*, p. 389.
16. Yi Sangbaek, *Han'guk munhwasa yŏn'gu non'go*, pp. 277–368.
17. Chŏng, *Sambongjip*, pp. 70–71, 239, 247, 252.
18. *Ibid.*, pp. 204–7.
19. *Ibid.*, p. 205. It may be maintained that Chŏng Tojŏn was at heart nationalistically minded in spite of the fact that he has often been identified with the policy of *sadae*. One may make the point, as Han Young-woo persuasively did, that Chŏng supported the adoption of the name Chosŏn because of its association not only with Kija Chosŏn but with the Ancient Chosŏn

founded by Tan'gun. But one can make such a case only by reading into the historical context more nationalistic sentiments than Chŏng himself expressed. In terms of the given text alone, such an interpretation seems to be less than warranted. See Han, *Chŏng Tojŏn sasang ŭi yŏn'gu*, pp. 142–48, 148–53.

20. Chŏng, *Sambongjip*, pp. 207–12.
21. *Ibid.*, pp. 209–10, 227–28.
22. *Ibid.*, p. 227.
23. *Ibid.*, pp. 212–22.
24. *Ibid.*, pp. 222–32.
25. *Ibid.*, pp. 233–39.
26. *Ibid.*, pp. 239–47.
27. Chu Hsi and Lü Tsu-ch'ien, *Reflections on Things at Hand*, tr. by Wing-tsit Chan (New York: Columbia University Press, 1967), pp. 202–17; William R. Shaw, "The Neo-Confucian Revolution of Values in Early Yi Korea: Its Implications for Korean Legal Thought" (unpublished paper).
28. Chŏng, *Sambongjip*, pp. 247–53.
29. *Ibid.*, pp. 128–203.
30. *Ibid.*, pp. 150–51, 161.
31. *Ibid.*, pp. 161–62.
32. *Ibid.*, p. 85.
33. *Ibid.*, p. 209.
34. See Edward W. Wagner, *The Literati Purges: Political Conflict in Yi Korea* (Cambridge: Harvard University Press, 1974), p. 2; Asanuma Takekami, "Richō no kenkoku to seiken no suii," (The Founding of the Yi Dynasty and Transfer of Power), *Chōsen gakuhō* (1956), 9:1–35.
35. Chŏng, *Sambongjip*, p. 200.
36. *Ibid.*, p. 196.
37. *Ibid.*, pp. 195–203; Han, *Chŏng Tojŏn sasang ŭi yŏn'gu*, p. 127.
38. For Wang's reforms and the reactions of orthodox Neo-Confucians to Wang's attempts see Wm. Theodore de Bary, "A Reappraisal of Neo-Confucianism," in Arthur F. Wright, ed., *Studies in Chinese Thought* (Chicago & London: University of Chicago Press, 1953), pp. 100–6. For Chŏng's view of Wang's reforms see *Sambongjip*, pp. 334–35. For Chŏng's appropriation of past institutional models and precedents, see *Samgongjip*, p. 201.
39. Chŏng, *Sambongjip*, pp. 295–358.
40. *Ibid.*, p. 295.
41. *Ibid.*, pp. 296–98.
42. *Ibid.*, pp. 298–329, 330–41.
43. *Ibid.*, pp. 431–52.
44. *Ibid.*, pp. 353–58.
45. *Ibid.*, pp. 204–5, 296, 298, 302–3.
46. *Ibid.*, p. 214.
47. *Ibid.*, pp. 215–16, 222, 244.

48. *Ibid.*, pp. 214–15; Yi Sangbaek, *Yijo Kŏn'guk ŭi yŏn'gu* (A Study in the Founding of Yi Korea), vol. 2 of *Yi Sangbaek chŏjakchip* (1947; reprint ed., Seoul: Ŭryu munhwasa, 1978), pp. 137–265.

49. In his review of Han Young-woo's *Chŏng Tojŏn sasang ŭi yŏn'gu*, James Palais found fault with Han's "unwitting" philosophical eclecticism, the simultaneous commitment to a materialist view of history and belief in the independent role of ideas as primary and causal forces. Palais especially charged that Han "put an unquestioning faith in class analysis as a legitimate tool of historical interpretation." While I share Palais's feeling that it is difficult to look at the late-fourteenth-century situation in terms of class struggle, I think Chŏng's ideas do relate to his life experience and political motivations. James B. Palais, "Han Yŏng-u's Studies of Early Chosŏn Intellectual History," in *The Journal of Korean Studies* (1980), 2:199–224.

50. According to Yi Sangbaek, the immediate and primary reason for Yi Sŏnggye's land reforms was to increase the military grain reserves supplying his army. Chŏng was one of Yi Sŏnggye's henchmen in carrying out the reforms. See Yi Sangbaek, *Yijo kŏn'guk ŭi yŏn'gu*, pp. 188–200, 200–11.

51. Chŏng, *Sambongjip*, pp. 64, 296.

52. *Ibid.*, pp. 87, 239–40, 247, 296, 355.

53. *Ibid.*, p. 87.

54. *Ibid.*, pp. 1–2.

55. *Ibid.*, pp. 87, 108–9.

56. *Ibid.*, pp. 239–40.

57. *Koryŏsa* (History of Koryŏ) (reprint ed., Seoul: Yŏnse taehakkyo tongbang yŏn'guso, 1955), 2:15a–17a. For the religious situation antedating the coming of Neo-Confucianism to Koryŏ, see Yun Yonggyun, *I bungakushi ikō* (The Posthumous Writings of Yun Yonggyun, B.A.) (Seoul, 1933), pp. 3–19.

58. Yi Pyŏngdo, "Han'guk yuhaksa," 1:1–62.

59. Lee Woo-song, (Yi Usŏng), "Koryŏjo ŭi i e taehayŏ" (On the Official of the Koryŏ Dynasty) in *Yŏksa hakpo* (April 1964), 23:1–26; Yi Pyŏnghyu, "Yŏmal Sŏnch'o ŭi kwaŏp kyoyuk" (Education for the Civil Service Examination in the Late Koryŏ and the Early Chosŏn Dynasty) in *Yŏksa hakpo* (September 1975), 67:45–70.

60. According to Yun Yonggyun, it was Paek Ijŏng and not An Hyang who first brought Neo-Confucianism to Korea around 1314. Yun, *I bungakushi ikō*, pp. 20–31.

61. *Koryŏsa*, 115:10b–11a; Chŏng, *Sambongjip*, p. 370; Yi Pyŏngdo, "Han'guk yuhak sa," 1:89–102.

62. Yi, "Han'guk yuhak sa," 1:102–7; Yun, *I bungakushi ikō*, pp. 35–37; Chŏng, *Sambongjip*, p. 87.

63. Hatada Takashi, "Kōrai chō ni okeru jiin keizai," (The Monastic Economy in the Koryŏ Dynasty), *Shigaku zasshi* (1932), 43 (5):557–93, especially 562–63.

64. For Koryŏ Buddhism, see Takahashi Tōru, *Richō bukkyō* (Buddhism in the

Yi Dynasty) (Tokyo: Hobunkan, 1929), pp. 30–43. For T'ien-t'ai, Tamura Yoshirō and Umehara Takeshi, eds., *Zettai no shinri, Tendai* (Absolute Truth, T'ien-t'ai), vol. 5 of *Bukkyō no shisō* (Buddhist Thought), (Tsukamoto Zenryū et al., eds.) (Tokyo: Kodansha shoten, 1970), see esp. pp. 182–86.

65. For Hua-yen, *Mugen no sekaikan, Kegon* (View of the Infinite World, Huayen), ed. Kamata Shigeo and Ueyama Shunpei, vol. 6 of *Bukkyō no shisō*, ed. Tsukamoto et al., pp. 60–152, 157–64.

66. Yi Nŭnghwa, *Chosŏn pulgyo t'ongsa* (Outline History of Korean Buddhism) (reprint ed., Seoul: Kyŏngin sŏrim, 1968), 1:317–26, 328; Min Hyŏn'gu, "Sin Ton ŭi chipkwŏn kwa kŭ chŏngch'ijŏk sŏngkyŏk" (The Seizure of Power by Sin Ton and its Political Character), *Yŏksa hakpo* (August 1968), 38:46–88; (December 1968), 40:53–119; Hatada, "Kōrai chō ni okeru jiin keizai," pp. 557–93; for "monastic landlordism," Max Weber, *The Religion of India: The Sociology of Hinduism and Buddhism*, tr. by Hans H. Gerth and Don Martindale (Glencoe, Ill.: Free Press, 1959), pp. 222–23.

67. *Koryŏsa* 93:8ab.

68. *Ibid.*, 93:19a.

69. *Ibid.*, 115:7b–8b. For Yi Saek's ambiguous attitude toward Buddhism, see also Yi Hwang, *T'oegye chŏnsŏ* (Complete Works) (Seoul: Sŏnggyun'gwan taehakkyo, 1958), 1:75b.

70. Chŏng, *Sambongjip*, pp. 71–73; *Koryŏsa*, 117:10b–11b.

71. Yi Pyŏngdo, "Han'guk yuhak sa," 1:96–107; Yi Nŭnghwa, *Chosŏn pulgyo t'ongsa*, 1:329–38.

72. For the religious policy, Chŏng, *Sambongjip*, pp. 224, 225, and also 67. For the attack against Buddhism, see Chŏng Tojŏn's letter to Chŏng Mongju in *Sambongjip*, pp. 71–73; Kwŏn Kŭn's preface to *Pulssi chappyŏn* in *Sambongjip*, pp. 277–78. See also *Koryŏsa*, 119:13b–15a; Yi Nŭnghwa, *Chosŏn pulgyo t'ongsa*, pp. 333–34. For the methods by which the founders of the Yi dynasty sought to implement Confucianism in Korean society, see Martina Deuchler, "Neo-Confucianism: The Impulse for Social Action in Early in Korea," *The Journal of Korean Studies* (1980), 2:71–111.

73. Chŏng, *Sambongjip*, pp. 288–94.

74. *Ibid.*, pp. 280–88.

75. *Ibid.*, p. 274.

76. *Ibid.*, p. 278.

77. *Ibid.*, pp. 258–59, 267–69.

78. Ch'ien Mu, *Chu Tzu hsin-hsüeh-an* (A New Comprehensive Study of Chu Hsi) (Taipei: San-min shu-chü, 1971), 3:489–579.

79. Chŏng, *Sambongjip*, pp. 254–56.

80. *Ibid.*, pp. 256–58.

81. *Ibid.*, pp. 258–59, 262–64.

82. *Ibid.*, pp. 259–60; Chung-hua Shu-chü edition of *Chu Tzu ta-ch'üan* (Complete Literary Works of Master Chu), 58:13–15.

83. Chŏng, *Sambongjip*, pp. 260–61.

84. *Ibid.*, pp. 258–59, 268.

85. Ibid., pp. 261, 261–62, 267–69; Chu Tzu ta-ch'üan, 56:17, 36–38, 67:19–20.
86. Chŏng, Sambongjip, pp. 261–62.
87. Ibid., pp. 264–65.
88. Ibid., pp. 265–66.
89. Ibid., p. 266–67.
90. Ibid., pp. 273–77, 277–78.
91. See Chai-sik Chung, "Christianity as Heterodoxy: An Aspect of General Cultural Orientation in Traditional Korea," in Korea's Response to the West, ed. Yung-Hwan Jo (Kalamazoo, Michigan: Korea Research and Publications, 1971), pp. 57–86; Paul A. Cohen, China and Christianity: The Missionary Movement and the Growth of Chinese Antiforeignism, 1860–1870 (Cambridge: Harvard University Press, 1963), pp. 4–5.
92. Chŏng, Sambongjip, p. 269.
93. Karl Mannheim, Ideology and Utopia: An Introduction to the Sociology of Knowledge, tr. by Louis Wirth and Edward Shils (New York: Harcourt, Brace, 1936), p. 64.
94. Hamhŏ Hwasang Hyŏnjŏngnon, vol. 5 of Han'guk ŭi sasang taejŏnjip (The Great Series of Korean Thought) (Seoul: Tonghwa ch'ulp'ankongsa, 1972), pp. 485–90.
95. Actually Yi Chehyŏn (1287–1367) and his disciple, Yi Saek—and for that matter, An Hyang and Paek Ijŏng—were earlier Neo-Confucians.
96. Yi Ik, Sŏngho saesŏl (Minute Explanations on Various Topics by Yi Ik) (Seoul: Kyŏnghŭi ch'ulp'ansa, 1967), 2:56.
97. Youn Sa-Soon, (Yun Sasun), "Chŏng Tojŏn sŏngnihak ŭi t'ŭksŏng kwa kŭ p'yŏngka munje," (The Characteristics of Chŏng Tojŏn's Philosophy of Nature and Principle and Problems of their Evaluation) (Paper delivered at the Eighth Korean Classics Symposium, Seoul, Korea, November 1, 1980).
98. Edward Shils, "The Concept and Function of Ideology," in David L. Shils, ed., International Encyclopedia of the Social Sciences (New York: MacMillan and Free Press, 1968), 7:69.
99. Ibid., pp. 67–69.

Michael C. Kalton

The Writings of
Kwŏn Kŭn:
The Context and Shape
of Early Yi Dynasty
Neo-Confucianism

INTRODUCTION

WHEN YI SŎNGGYE ascended the throne in 1392 and thus finally brought the decrepit Koryŏ dynasty to its close, at his side were a group of young Neo-Confucians who had been the support and architects of his rise to power. Under their guidance the new Yi dynasty underwent an ideological shift which was to have a profound and lasting effect on Korean life for the next five hundred years. Hitherto, from the formative period of a high culture on the Korean peninsula in the fourth century A.D. onwards, Buddhism had been the principal spiritual and intellectual force in this society; Confucianism likewise had been present from the earliest years as a form of professional training in the Chinese classics and in literary form which was part of the equipment of the civil servant. But while the Confucian civil service examinations established minimal qualifications, they were not the major route to positions of wealth and power in pre-Yi dynasty Korea, nor did Confucian learning function as a decisive arbiter in political and social life. That was to come only with the Yi dynasty.

It is to the Neo-Confucianism of this period of dynastic and ideological transition that this paper is addressed. One hears much of Korea's strict and rigid adherence to the "orthodox" Ch'eng-Chu school of Neo-Confucian thought, but orthodoxy is a term which could have had but little meaning in this period, for the serious intellectual appropriation of Chu Hsi's complex Neo-Confucian synthesis had been underway hardly more than a generation before Yi Sŏnggye came to power.[1] What were the features of Chu Hsi's thought which Koreans in their Buddhist environment found most compelling and most serviceable in this initial stage? What were the problems they faced and what were the assumptions about those problems which affected their appropriation of Neo-Confucian doctrine?

The reformers could easily legislate a new ideological framework for the Yi dynasty, but for this to become a reality they had to deal with the fundamental problem posed by the massive social-cognitive presence of Buddhism. The schools of Mahayana Buddhism had for at least eight centuries been this society's window on the world, the framework for understanding life, and the provider of the means of salvation both temporal and transcendental. Towards the end of the Koryŏ dynasty there had been an overreaching of its power, particularly in the debacle of a Buddhist monk, Sin Ton, assuming virtually royal authority.[2] There were, too, economic dysfunctions connected with the draining of land and manpower resources by heavily patronized monasteries, and there was the corruption of monastic life which came with overweening political and economic power. Still, one could not say that Buddhism was thereby fundamentally discredited or that the basic plausibility of a Buddhist world had been seriously undermined.

At the beginning of the Yi dynasty the members of the young Korean Neo-Confucian movement were a small minority operating in an environment in which Buddhist institutions and ideas were deeply entrenched. One part of the problem with which this situation presented them was objective, that is, how to bring about a change in other people's traditional practices and customary ways of thinking. The other part of the problem, however, was subjective, the transformation of their own practices and ways of thought. The orthodox Neo-Confucian rejection of all things Buddhist is not a difficult matter in an environment which is already largely Confucian; but a much different form of cognitive engineering, so to speak, is called for when the views and practices with which one is breaking have a high degree of acceptance in the surrounding society. Beliefs and values have a strong claim to be taken seriously when those who hold and practice them are not faceless "heretics," but one's own parents, brothers, and kinsmen, and when one is in personal contact with outstanding representatives of those beliefs whose attainments cannot lightly be dismissed. In such circumstances, an outright rejection of Buddhism as utter nonsense would lack plausibility; on the other hand, an overaccommodating attitude would sap the vigor of a movement toward Confucian orthopraxis, and this did in fact occur.

This paper will attempt to convey a sense of the social-cognitive environment of the early Yi dynasty, elucidate the problem areas or tensions attending the rise of Neo-Confucianism, and finally examine how this affected the shape of Neo-Confucianism as it was appropriated and lived in this period.

Our vehicle for investigating this period will be the writings of Kwŏn Kŭn (1352–1409), the foremost Neo-Confucian scholar and literary figure of the early decades of the Yi dynasty. Kwŏn's *Diagrammatic Treatise for Entering Upon Learning (Iphak tosŏl)* is one of the earliest Korean expositions of Neo-Confucian thought. His work on rearranging and commenting on the *Book of Rites*[3] and his annotated edition of Chu Hsi's *Family Ritual (Chia-li)*[4] are the first Yi dynasty endeavors in the field of ritual scholarship, which was to predominate over all other Neo-Confucian intellectual concerns during the first century of the dynasty. Kwŏn also wrote commentaries on the other classics which are now lost,[5] but which in his day contributed greatly to his reputation for scholarship. His collected literary works *(munjip)* in forty fascicles *(chüan/kwŏn)* contain a wealth of historical information and are invaluable as many-faceted reflections of his times. Finally, Kwŏn's name is closely linked with the most important anti-Buddhist literature of the times, three tractates[6] composed by Chŏng Tojŏn (1342–98).

Chŏng Tojŏn, the chief strategist in Yi Sŏnggye's rise to power, became the new dynasty's highest merit subject and was the real power behind the throne until his losing out in the young dynasty's first succession struggle brought his career to a close in 1398. He had a capacity for harboring long-lasting resentments, a rigid and unforgiving temperament which nonetheless did not hinder his abilities as a brilliant political tactician. Buddhism was a particular object of his animosity, and he was one of the most extreme anti-Buddhists of the time. Although Kwŏn's relationship with Chŏng was less than cordial, Kwŏn wrote prefaces and long annotations for Chŏng's anti-Buddhist tracts, and after the *Diagrammatic Treatise* these are perhaps the best source for Kwŏn's Neo-Confucian thought.

Kwŏn Kŭn was a member of the Andong Kwŏn clan, one of the

most illustrious families of the Koryŏ dynasty. Four of Kwŏn's five immediate ancestors had held posts of either the first or second rank in the Koryŏ government, and his great grandfather, Kwŏn Po (1262–1346), was one of the earliest and most notable of Korean Neo-Confucians. Kwŏn himself passed the civil service examinations with second-place honors when he was only seventeen, and by the time he was thirty-five he had already served both as headmaster of the Confucian Academy and as minister of the Board of Rites. He had studied with Yi Saek (1328–96), the leading Neo-Confucian scholar of the day and the Grand Old Man of the conservative, loyalist faction which was trying to preserve the dynasty during its tumultuous final years. Kwŏn was closely associated with this faction, and in 1389 was exiled for his vigorous defense of a leading loyalist minister, Yi Sungin (1349–92). Further, though already in exile, he was implicated in a loyalist attempt in 1390 by the Yi Saek faction to block the rise of Yi Sŏnggye by alerting the Chinese emperor and bringing in the Ming army. His life was spared, however, when a sudden flood disrupted the trial proceedings against the conspirators and was taken as a sign the proceedings should be dropped.

Kwŏn's exile was ended in late 1390 and he retired to Yangch'on in the Ch'ungju district, whence came his pen name, Yangch'on. Yi Sŏnggye had virtually total control of the government after 1388, and in 1392 finally ascended the throne himself as founder of the Yi dynasty. Kwŏn remained in retirement until 1393, when a personal interview with Yi convinced him to devote his talents and lend his prestige to the new dynasty. His role in the new government was at first constricted and uncomfortable since his earlier associations with the loyalist faction had earned him the resentment of Chŏng Tojŏn and the other Neo-Confucians who had been active in supporting Yi Sŏnggye. All of this was changed, however, when Chŏng and his fellow revolutionaries were wiped out in the bloody succession struggle among the sons of Yi Sŏnggye in 1398. Thereafter until his death in 1409, Kwŏn occupied a succession of posts which made him the supreme arbiter in aspects of government dealing with scholarly and literary affairs.

In this position Kwŏn used his influence to redirect the educational system towards literary accomplishments. At the founding of the dynasty enthusiastic Neo-Confucians had systematically suppressed the traditional literary orientation; one of their most important measures had been to remove all composition from the first stage of the civil-service examination, making it instead an oral exam on the classics. Kwŏn sympathized with this concern to stress character formation in learning; in fact, he instigated the adoption of Chu Hsi's *Elementary Learning (Hsiao-hsüeh)*, the Neo-Confucian moral primer *par excellence*, as a mandatory school text. But a decade of close experience with the new system showed him that it was not producing the desired results: its product was not a profound understanding and personal appropriation of the classics, but merely the rote memorization of texts and commentaries. Further, skills in poetic and literary composition were in serious decline. In his view these were not a matter of empty artifice, but practical skills imperative for successful diplomatic relations with China. Thus in 1407 he presented a memorial to the king which in effect reintroduced the strong literary component.[7] Essay examinations on the classics replaced the oral exam, and a system in which the abilities of junior officials in literary and poetic composition were promoted by periodic reviews and mandatory competitions was put into effect.

What will concern us in this paper is not so much Kwŏn's activities in office—important though these were—as the social situation reflected in his writings and the form his Neo-Confucianism took in response to that situation. The first section will discuss the nature and extent of the Buddhist presence in order to assess its cognitive impact upon the problems faced by the would-be makers of a Neo-Confucian society in Korea. The second section will deal with the form taken by early Yi dynasty Neo-Confucianism in this situation. The major source for the first part of this study will be the *Collected Writings of Kwŏn Kŭn*[8] *(Yangch'onjip)*; passages quoted from this source will be followed immediately by fascicle and page references in parentheses. The second part will use Kwŏn's more theoretical Neo-Confucian writings, the *Diagrammatic Treatise* and his annotations to Chŏng Tojŏn's anti-Buddhist tracts, as well as the *Collected Writings*.

I. THE BUDDHIST AMBIENCE

Kwŏn, in his preface to Chŏng Tojŏn's *Arguments Against Mr. Buddha (Pulssi chappyŏn)*, quotes a communication he received from Chŏng in 1398, the year of his death:

The Buddhists damage and ruin proper ethics; this will certainly eventuate in people's becoming like animals and proper human relationships will perish. Those with Confucian responsibilities must regard them as enemies and attack them forcefully. Formerly I told myself that if I ever got in a position to have my way, I would certainly be able to repulse them with ease. Now I have the king's confidence and he listens to what I say and follows my proposals; I now have my way—and still am not able to repulse them. This, then, means that to the very end I cannot expect to succeed in repulsing them. (17.13a)

When I first read this passage I was inclined to regard it as hyperbole; having read through the *Collected Writings*, however, I am now inclined to take it at face value. Chŏng, the vehement anti-Buddhist, had every reason to feel thoroughly frustrated: he wished to draw a clear line between the true and the false, the Confucian and the Buddhist, but trying to draw such a distinction in his society must have felt like writing with one's finger on the surface of water. From our historical vantage point the dynastic change seems to be a demarcation between Buddhist and Neo-Confucian societies, but from the circumstances around him it would have been very hard for Chŏng to be confident that any corner had been decisively turned. The situation was ambiguous and complex, and the ambiguity was present at the very heart of the new government.

A. The Legitimation of the Yi Dynasty

Governments commonly appeal to some sort of religious legitimation as a justification of their exercise of authority and as a support for the well-being of the nation and the continuation of that authority. Christian kings have claimed to rule by the will of God, Muslims by the will of Allah, and Confucians by the will of Heaven. Such legitimation is a public matter, expressed in ceremonies and rituals, documents, monuments, and dedications. It has little to do with personal faith. A ruler may burn incense before a statue of Buddha in the privacy of his inner quarters, but if he sticks to exclusively Confucian rituals in public the sacred canopy[9] sheltering his regime will be Confucian.

Knowing that the Yi dynasty adopted Neo-Confucianism as its official ideology, one would expect its early rulers to have restricted any personal Buddhist convictions to a more or less private sphere. In fact, however, quite the contrary was the case: they made every effort to legitimize their government in a Buddhist as well as a Confucian mode.

The paradigmatic legitimation of a new dynasty in Confucian terms attributed degenerate or incompetent rule to the preceding dynasty and claimed a Heavenly Mandate for a virtuous new ruler, who accepts it unwillingly at the insistence of the people and upright officials, voicing the will of Heaven in a way that cannot be denied. Needless to say, this legitimation was fully employed at the founding of the Yi dynasty; it appeared as a matter of course in documents touching on the founding of the dynasty and was engraved in the tomb inscriptions written for members of the royal family by Kwŏn Kŭn.

That Kwŏn should have been entrusted with the composing of these most public and enduring justifications of the new dynasty was but a reflection of his reputation as the foremost scholar and most talented literary pen (or brush) of the time. His was the hand that gave the royal will its elegant public expression in many prefaces, commemorations, memorial monuments, and in the public prayer life of the country. It is not without irony, however, that the majority of such compositions produced at the royal behest were prefaces for gold-ink copies of Buddhist sutras, commemorations of Buddhist temple constructions or reconstructions, and of major Buddhist rituals performed on the ruler's behalf, memorial inscriptions for notable monks, and prayers to the Buddhas and Bodhisattvas for the protection of the country and assistance in times of crisis.

Buddhism, ostensibly a nonworldly religious tradition, has no ready-made legitimations for dynastic revolutions. On occasion, however, the Buddha may simply replace Heaven in the stock narrative of dynastic change, as in the following passage of a prayer offered as the new dynasty embarked upon the construction of a new capital city: "Presumptuously this unworthy person, relying on Your [i.e., the Buddha's] trustworthy assistance and urged on by the support of ministers and subjects, has ascended the throne" (28.4a). But more typical of the way Buddhism assumes the role of sacred canopy over the government is the enshrinement of Buddhas and Bodhisattvas as the protectors of the nation and its rulers, with temples erected at government expense dedicated to this end, government-sponsored rituals and prayer services, and recourse to the Buddha in times of public need. Kwŏn Kŭn's *Collected Writings* contain many examples of Buddhism in precisely this role in the early Yi dynasty;[10] the following is typical of the tone and sentiments which run throughout these compositions:

At the time of the former dynasty's decline and disorder I was fearful that I could not even fulfill my duties as prime minister, but meeting with the urging of the multitude of subjects I was unable to avoid the throne. Now as I presume with my unworthiness to govern the people, my anxiety is as one who attempts to control a horse with rotten ropes. And what is more, when the whole political order has undergone such change there cannot but be resentments in the hearts of the people, and this has brought ominous portents in Heaven and Earth. In such circumstances we rely on the Buddhist dharma and offer our prayer; thus we have come out to [Hoeam temple] for the special purpose of holding this assemblage in honor of [the Bodhisattva] Manjusri. Although what we have prepared [for this offering] is but little, may your response be swift. Prostrating myself I beg that Heaven on High may extend its protecting Mandate and that all blessings may follow, that the people may travel the path of humanity and long life, and may trust in you forever. (27.7b–8a)

If Korean governments had ever had a purely Confucian legitimation, one would say that this passage reflects a deep Buddhist encroachment on Confucian territory. As it is, the above conflation of Confucian and Buddhist ideas was probably typical of Korean civil religion for many centuries. The Heavenly Mandate of the Confucians becomes an aspect of the protective goodwill of the Buddha, and Confucian omenology occasions a resort to Buddhist remedies.

In a Confucian context one of the most important ongoing legitimations of government was the responsive involvement of Heaven in the person and deeds of the ruler as indicated by portents and omens. Auspicious portents accompanied the rise of a sage ruler[11] and confirmed the wisdom of important decisions, while inauspicious portents such as drought, famine, unseasonable weather, or other "unnatural" phenomena signified something amiss; in either case there was an important public affirmation of the connection between the ruler and the Ultimate. Buddhism was able to leave the cosmological framework of this Confucian doctrine intact and simply subsume it under the transcendence of the Buddha Nature or Dharma, thus placing a Buddhist soteriology at the center of civil religion. The need to repent and correct misgovernment in good Confucian fashion is not denied, but becomes associated with gaining the compassionate protection of the Buddha. This is then supplemented with more mundane Buddhist methods of getting good results such as performing meritorious deeds and reciting scriptures and mantric formulas which have a special potency:

Have I unknowingly committed a crime against Heaven and Earth? I am anxious as one walking [on the edge of] a gulf or on [thin] ice. To be rid of the shoots of disaster [i.e., evil portents] one must rely on Your supporting and protecting strength. Thus in the inner chambers I have especially prepared a place for prayer, reading the true and efficacious scriptures, and reciting the auspicious and mysterious mantras. (27.6b)

King T'aejo (the posthumous title of Yi Sŏnggye), disheartened by the bloody fratricidal struggle for the succession among his sons, resigned the throne and retired to a Buddhist monastery in 1398. His intentions as communicated to Kwŏn were as follows:

I have with the assistance of the accumulated virtue of my ancestors and the hidden aid of Buddha (pulch'ŏn) founded this dynasty and established its unending succession; but I am now too worn out for diligent effort and have put off the heavy burden, wishing only to devote myself entirely to the service of Buddha, prostrating myself before him morning and night, that above I might repay the heavy debt of gratitude to my ancestors and below I might assist the unending peace of the country, washing off the sins of my past and planting the roots of virtue for the future. (22.13b–14a)

The combination of old age and unhappy experience may have deepened the Buddhist sentiments here, but the framework of assumptions which connect Buddha with the founding of the dynasty and the welfare of the country has long been operative; it is, in fact, a direct continuation of conceptions which obtained throughout the Koryŏ dynasty and before. As Kwŏn comments in 1393 at the completion of an expensive temple-rebuilding project by T'aejo: "Thinking of Buddhism's compassion and love for all creatures as something beneficial to the nation, he therefore has preserved the praised and honored dharma and has not destroyed it" (12.5b).

This small sample of Kwŏn's public compositions in a Buddhist vein illustrates how the deeply ingrained Buddhist tradition contributed to one of the highest and most public Confucian functions, that of legitimating the king's rule in terms of the ultimate governing power of the universe. At the very least it reflects on this level a large degree of initial continuity between the early "Neo-Confucian" Yi dynasty and its Buddhist predecessor, and suggests the magnitude of the problem faced by Neo-Confucian ministers who desired to reshape their government and society in a Confucian mold.

Kwŏn Kŭn, the exemplary Neo-Confucian scholar of the time, the man regarded as the most knowledgeable authority on the practice of Confucian ritual and propriety, cooperated as a loyal minister in producing these official pronouncements and others in the same vein. Kwŏn was a man of principle who did not hesitate to risk his life in frank remonstrance when he felt it necessary, yet he appears to have had no compunction about this application of his talents. It seems clear that the mentality of Neo-Confucian officialdom during this period cannot be characterized as rigidly orthodox. On the other hand there must have been a sufficiently strong conviction regarding the rightness and superiority of the Neo-Confucian vision to fuel a gradual transition away from this kind of Buddho-Confucian synthesis.

Thus far we have seen Kwŏn speaking mainly in the persona of a Buddhist ruler. It is now time to let him speak for himself, and to trace further some of the ambiguities and tensions which mark this period of transition.

B. The Neo-Confucian and the Buddhists: How Many Ways?

In the interaction of religious traditions which compete in offering explanations for the ultimate nature of our existence and the final meaning of our lives, one may discern the mind working on the questions and issues in two relatively distinct modes: the first is the abstract mind, cogitating chiefly in terms of the concepts, ideas, presuppositions, etc., which constitute a system of thought; the second is the concrete, engaged mind alive to and responding to cognitive currents which are socially rather than conceptually grounded. This is not a literal and final distinction; these modes are simply an analytic construct with some grounding in experience. I propose them as a heuristic device which may enable us to make sense of various statements in Kwŏn's works regarding Buddhism which at first blush might otherwise seem irreconcilable.

1. The Abstract Mode

Religious traditions which share a single cultural milieu commonly develop internal means of accounting for one another. In East Asia it is common to speak of the Three Teachings, Confucianism, Taoism, and Buddhism; each teaching is a way with its own distinctive doctrines and life-style. However, another constant feature of East Asian thought is the proposition that there is only one Way. How then do the Way and the ways relate?

This question can be answered in a variety of ways and with many levels of subtlety and sophistication. At the risk of oversimplification, I would suggest three major types of response: (1) the three Ways are variant and valid expressions of a transcendent Way or Truth which is beyond words or conceptualization; (2) the three are complementary and partial expressions of the one Way; (3) the fundamentalist stance: there is one Way and we have it; the others are wrong, or better, right only insofar as they also conform to our way.

In the first case, one can rest content with differences, although a tendency to create a hierarchy of expressions often manifests itself. Buddhists have often used this approach in accounting for the wide variety of schools and practices within their own tradition and also easily extended it to other traditions.

The second position is reflected in the inclination to utilize the resources of the various traditions to meet the diverse needs of different periods or situations in life. When presented as an intellectual proposition, however, this position is inherently unstable, since it logically leads to the formation of a synthetic super-teaching which would then move in the direction of the third position.

To some extent one might see such dynamics at work in the Neo-Confucian synthesis, in which Confucians supplemented their own strong social orientation with inner resources analogous to Buddhist meditation and a metaphysical framework of Taoist proportions. Of course the synthesizing was not self-conscious and occurred rather under the rubric of the rediscovery of true Confucianism; but in the startling doctrine that the true Confucian Way had been lost for some thousand years, there is a tacit admission that in the absence of the supplements discovered or rediscovered by the early Neo-Confucians, Confucianism was indeed partial. Historically standing on the shoulders of earlier Confucians, Buddhists, and Taoists, Neo-Confucians might well regard themselves as endowed with the one full truth, in comparison to which other teachings were only one-sided and partial.

This analysis shows how it might have been possible for a Neo-Confucian to have a kind of fundamentalist faith in the complete adequacy of his way; it does not mean that such was indeed always the case. The presence of discordant Neo-Confucian schools of thought, the experience of personal frustration in trying to convert theory to practice, or the failure of Neo-Confucian recipes for government, etc., might well militate against such serene self-confidence.

But if ever there were conditions in which it is likely that this potential within Neo-Confucianism would be realized, these would seem to have obtained in the early Yi dynasty. The doctrines of the Ch'eng-Chu school come suddenly on the scene as a mature and integrated vision completely separated from the divisions, disagreements, and groping for more adequate expressions which characterized their historical development. There has not yet been time to experience failure and limitation, nor to grasp finer aspects of theory which might lead to diverse opinions and fragmentation. Further, while Koreans are self-consciously straining to attain an adequate understanding of the masters, any apparent inadequacies would naturally be attributed to their own lack of understanding, leaving faith in the perfection of the masters' work intact. The new doctrines open up vistas beyond anything offered by the limited Confucianism of Korea's earlier history, and simultaneously encompass ground formerly totally conceded to Buddhism; it is reasonable to suspect that the new Neo-Confucians would be deeply impressed with the fullness and completeness of this vision.

Chŏng Tojŏn in his *On the Mind, Material Force, and Principle (Simgi ip'yŏn)* argues the case for Neo-Confucianism over Buddhism and Taoism. Personifying the three teachings as Principle, Mind, and Material (Vital) Force, respectively, he lets each teaching argue its case in its own words. His presentation of Buddhist and Taoist views is very abbreviated and so less than totally fair, but Kwŏn's extensive annotations expand on Chŏng's presentation considerably and maintain the same objective tenor. If the result is less full and forceful a defense than the Buddhist or Taoist might mount, it is nonetheless a far fairer treatment than adversaries usually receive in apologetic literature. Kwŏn presents the rationale behind this methodology in his preface to the work; it expresses a faith in the fullness of Neo-Confucianism much in contrast to the partiality of the other teachings of which I have been speaking:

In speaking for the mind [i.e., Buddhists] and vital force [i.e., Taoists] it entirely uses the words of the two themselves to explain their meaning . . . one does not see a trace of criticism. Thus even if they were shown to followers [of those teachings] the latter likewise would regard them as perfectly accurate and happily accept them. Finally after principle's [i.e., Neo-Confucianism's] position is formulated, the partiality of the others and the correctness of our Way becomes clear of itself, with no need for argument. Even if they would wish to say something, what more could they do? (16.15a)

This is a method which bespeaks great self-confidence; undoubtedly a fundamental faith that Neo-Confucian doctrine is a fully rounded and adequate presentation of the truth is operative here.

There is, however, an ambiguity in the assumption that other teachings are partial as opposed to the fullness of one's own position. On the one hand the partiality of a teaching may mean that it is fundamentally flawed and therefore bound to lead to dire consequences. This is the tack most often taken in the heat of controversy, but it can also emerge when the mind is operating in a relatively abstract mode, enunciating the logical consequence of its own assumptions. This is the mode of Chŏng when he asserts that the Buddhists neglect the fundamental human relationships and thus bring humanity to ruins, or of Kwŏn when he summarizes the consequences of Buddhist and Taoist partiality in a statement such as, "This is why those who follow these teachings, if they are not beguiled into a trance-like Nirvana [lit.: becoming like dead wood in quiescent oblivion], tend [on the other side] to fall into dissoluteness and licentiousness."[12] Such statements may be mere rhetoric or expressions of sincere conviction; in either case they represent a rather abstract mode of analyzing the consequences of ideas. It is hard to believe that Kwŏn would seriously apply what he has just said to his Buddhist parents, to his elder brother who was a monk, or to the monk to whom he entrusted the instruction of his own children![13]

On the other hand being partial may also mean possessing a part of the truth; thus in other contexts Kwŏn is quite ready to recognize good qualities in the other traditions. For example, he has praise for Buddhist compassion as similar to Confucian humanity (12.16b), and can state that filial piety is considered of the greatest importance by all Three Teachings (22.16b). Although such statements are often motivated by recognizing the goodness of real people, they nonetheless are abstract insofar as they take the "full truth" as found in Neo-Confucianism as the norm for whatever good may be found in other teachings. Kwŏn's rationalization of the excellent qualities of the monk who tutored his children epitomizes this mode of thought: "The Heavenly Mandate being our nature, humanity and righteousness are rooted in our mind-and-heart; thus one can on occasion find those who without having had recourse to [Confucian] study yet develop and manifest these qualities in the course of their daily lives" (8.22a).

2. *The Social Mode*

The abstract mind sits like a judge sorting concepts and ideas, pursuing consequences, seeking the full satisfaction of truth. But in fact the mind forms its ideas and develops its feel for truth in a concrete social context.[14] In sifting ideas and beliefs the mind is inclined towards the more reasonable or plausible, but reasonableness and plausibility are heavily conditioned by culture. Voodoo may seem absurd while one is sitting in a Cambridge drawing room, but become compelling in its reality if one lives for long in Haiti. Mideastern Muslims in mid-America must form a subcommunity or soon feel the plausibility of the Quran's literal truth ebbing away. Anthropologists immersed in primitive cultures may "go native."

In a word, what is widely affirmed[15] in one's social context takes on an inherent plausibility, while what is not affirmed has a nisus towards implausibility and disbelief. Such socially grounded plausibility or implausibility is not absolutely determinative, but it is an unavoidable force at work in the cognitive situation and dealing with it one way or another leaves its mark on the shape of the mind. A man swimming towards a rock in a river can presumably reach the rock if he is strong enough and determined enough. But he will have to exercise different muscles depending upon whether the current is carrying him to the left or to the right, towards or away from his goal, and the stronger the current the more his course will deviate from a simple straight line. In the next section of this paper we shall consider which Neo-Confucian muscles are most developed in responding to the social-cognitive currents at work in Kwŏn's society; here we shall observe how it deflects him from a doctrinaire Neo-Confucian response in his interaction with Buddhists.

We have already seen something of this in his prefaces and notes for Chŏng's tracts, or in prefaces or commemorations of outstanding Neo-Confucian figures such as Yi Saek, wherein Kwŏn can speak of Buddhists anesthetizing themselves into oblivion or plunging into licentiousness, or he can repeat stereotyped Neo-Confucian accounts of civilizations becoming corrupted by Buddhism. In such passages conviction shades off into rhetoric and it is difficult to know exactly where to draw the line, but there is no reason to think that Kwŏn is fundamentally insincere in expressing such sentiments. In such contexts, however, he is moving easily with a Neo-Confucian current.

It is a quite different current which prevails in the wider context of Kwŏn's life. I have already mentioned that his own elder brother was a Buddhist monk, his parents were Buddhists, and the ruler he served was Buddhist. His writings reflect wide contact with Buddhist monks, and a number of them were men whose personal qualities and spiritual attainments commanded his respect. Further, broadly throughout all levels of his society Buddhist concepts such as rebirth, karma, accumulating merit, and nirvana were simply assumed to be real. Kwŏn could not but be affected by this environment. He does not, it is true, surrender his Neo-Confucian identity and simply accept all this, but neither can he shrug it off.

Among the many poems, commemorative pieces, and prefaces in his *Collected Writings* one finds a liberal sprinkling of pieces composed for monks. His attitude in these works ranges from reproof, to friendly criticism, to virtual acceptance. Kwŏn was not compulsively obliging—different relationships with different monks elicit from him greater or less sympathy—yet critical reproof is rare. One instance shows Kwŏn in his doctrinaire frame of mind, brought about by a monk's making the mistake of mentioning the proto-Neo-Confucian and anti-Buddhist scholar of the T'ang dynasty, Han Yü.[16] In this case the preface he requested for his collection of poems includes a disquisition on how China prospered under the true Confucian way and was ruined by Buddhism. It concludes as follows:

Your reverence does not seek the Way in the principle within your mind and the mandate of your nature, or in the proper human relationships of ordinary life, but sets off instead to wander every which way;[17] I fear you will be, as they say, "a traveller with no destination." I have emulated Han Yü's unwillingness to flatter, and so have ventured to speak thus. Whether this will please or distress your reverence lies with you; the blame is not mine. (16.5a)

This is Kwŏn in a totally unsympathetic mood. But for monks towards whom he feels greater friendship and respect Kwŏn can compose poems in which distinctively Buddhist values are affirmed: "Putting off the karma of the dusty world, his cultivation of the Way is profound" (7.20a); "The mind's ashes are now already cold; sitting facing the wall[18] how many springs has he spent?" (7.22b); "Suddenly the ten-thousand motives are put to rest, the traces of the mind cut off" (7.25a). The spiritual attainments Kwŏn here praises are those which elsewhere, in doctrinaire Neo-Confucian contexts, he stigmatizes as "becoming seduced into quiescent oblivion."

Such passages are not adequately explained as merely good manners on Kwŏn's part: as evidence in many of the other poems Kwŏn composed for monks, there are many ways of writing a gracious poem for a monk which avoid such affirmations of distinctive Buddhist values if one is so minded. What is at work here is something other than simple diplomacy. The qualities Kwŏn mentions are high attainments for a monk and in his society they are generally recognized as praiseworthy. Confronted with persons whose spirituality commands respect, Kwŏn sees their attainments and goals through the eyes of his society rather than through partisan spectacles; they are praiseworthy and he is willing to say as much. In this frame of mind theoretical differences may seem somewhat irrelevant, and in one passage Kwŏn even seems to say so: "Since the Way is the same *(hap)* what need is there to discuss the difference of paths? The mind is at rest and returns again to the great emptiness" (7.25a–25b).

Personal friendship and respect are strong restraining forces; in the abstract mode it is easy to say, "We are right and they are wrong," but such statements do not come easily in the context of a warm social relationship. There are several passages which present a fuller picture of Kwŏn in such circumstances. In 1392 a monk whom he had known for a long time and respected highly came to take his leave. He explains that there are two gates to the final Buddhist realization, meditation and travel. Not having met with final success in his meditative endeavors, he now feels a strong urge to try the alternative method of a life of wandering. Kwŏn responds:

Ah! the positions of your reverence and myself are as different as clouds and mud, and our intentions are set on different paths. There is no way I could change your mind, nor any way I could hold you back from going your way. And the sorrow that wells up within me at our parting likewise cannot be stopped; how can it not have a true basis? Looking into it from this perspective, your reverence and I have a single mind-and-heart, men and creatures have a single principle. Its origin is of itself; its manifestation has an order. Everything everywhere is endowed with it and each thing has that which it should be. How can you know that being active in the noise and dust of the world and yet always quiet, dwelling in the midst of dirt and impurity but not being soiled—that [the proper way] is not in just this? Then there would be no need to make one's mind like cold ashes, and to make its traces as trackless as a wandering cloud, in order to regard oneself as having attained a lofty purity.

After you have awakened and devoted yourself to the propagation of the Tao, if you happen in your pity for those in delusion and darkness to honor me with a visit, I will be rubbing my eyes waiting for you to have another discussion. (16.13a–b)

Kwŏn's self-confident Neo-Confucian identity is evident here, but so too is a restraint in his assertiveness which goes beyond mere politeness. His monk friend's way of life and its ultimate goals are commonly regarded as a high and difficult quest, and his own person adds to the weight of the plausibility of his way; one may have reservations and disagreements on one level, but it is impossible to dismiss it altogether out of hand. Kwŏn's final remarks may contain more reverent politeness than real substance, but in the context of his society one would not expect him to react with shock or disbelief if his friend were to return enlightened. Nor, we might add, would that shake his Neo-Confucian confidence.

A number of passages reflect the fact that Kwŏn assumes, along with the rest of his society, that there is something true and substantial going on in Buddhism. He has particular respect for Chogye, the Korean school of Ch'an (Zen) Buddhism, which he considers the height of the Buddhist way. Such respect was not a one-way street, however; many monks seem to be ready to accept words of wisdom from whatever source they come, and to seek them from well-known Confucians such as Kwŏn. Neo-Confucian homilies stretched slightly to fit a Buddhist context are common in the prefaces and commemorations Kwŏn writes for monks. The following three selections from one such preface exemplify Kwŏn's respect and show him sharing his Neo-Confucian wisdom in a sympathetic rather than a critical spirit:

Extreme indeed is the difficulty of transmitting the Way! Of the myriads who gathered on Vulture Peak, there were none who did not hear the Buddha's way, but only Kasyapa attained the full understanding and passed it on. At the Haeng-dan school [where Confucius first taught], of the 3,000 disciples there was no one who did not hear our Master's tao, but only Master Yen [i.e., Yen Hui] came close [to fully comprehending it]. (15.14a)

How Kasyapa understood the Buddha's wordless transmission is a well-known story concerning the founding of the Zen tradition. Certainly Kwŏn does not mean to identify Confucianism and Zen here, but in this context he assents to the common assumption that Kasyapa perceived the profound truth of the Buddha's message, becoming fully enlightened on the spot. Without such an assumption the passage is meaningless, since it is not just any way, but the true Way that is difficult to convey.

Further on, Kwŏn proceeds to give his Neo-Confucian homily:

Nevertheless, the Way is not separate from material forms [in which it is embodied]; it is not a matter of stillness and trance. But it is also not mixed up with material forms; it is not shallow and common or ignoble. Within, it is embodied in the mind; without, it is manifested in things and affairs. If one neglects the mind there is no foundation and the substance is not established; if one separates oneself from things and affairs it is incomplete and function cannot operate. The combined perfecting of both substance and function and the complementary cultivation of the inner and outer is what our Confucian learning is about. (15.14b)

The ideas here presented are an almost archetypical lineup of Neo-Confucian doctrines as they are formulated to preface a critique of Buddhist doctrine and practice. But instead of attacking Kwŏn goes on to give these ideas a Buddhist application:

The Buddhist way—although I really do not know anything about it—likewise does not depart from this mind, and the greatness of this mind is like empty space, without difference between the self and others, without the distinction of within and without. Your reverence's seeking [the Truth] in your mind and also seeking it in the name [given you by Yi Saek][19] means that you are able to recognize that the within and the without do not have two ultimate [separate principles]. As you in the future inquire about it of the already awakened [masters], there will certainly be one who fits [your need]. (15.14b)

Here Kwŏn selectively emphasizes the Neo-Confucian unity of principle to such an extent that it merges with the Buddhist's monistic transcendence of any final distinction between self and exterior universe. He is, as a matter of fact, giving good Buddhist advice.

Kwŏn is not a Buddhist but a Neo-Confucian. In more doctrinaire contexts we have seen him confidently use his Neo-Confucian doctrines to criticize Buddhism. But passages such as this illustrate another use of Neo-Confucian doctrine which is quite natural in a society in which the Buddhist tao has a high level of plausibility: convinced of the fullness of Neo-Confucian truth yet inclined to assume a substantial truth in Buddhism, he uses the former to *understand* the latter. How this affects his appropriation of Neo-Confucianism will be our next consideration.

II. THE SHAPE OF EARLY YI DYNASTY NEO-CONFUCIANISM

Neo-Confucianism is at once a philosophy and a way of life. Put simply, one is supposed to live according to the vision voiced philosophically. But historically the Ch'eng-Chu school of Neo-Confucian thought has in fact sponsored a variety of ways of life, ranging from an almost monklike preoccupation with self-cultivation to a social and political activism which entrusts personal development largely to the discipline of action. The ideal of course is the middle ground, but different historical contexts and/or doctrinal emphases may pull in one direction or the other, resulting in quite different styles of Neo-Confucianism. It will therefore be appropriate first to describe the doctrinal content and emphasis of Kwŏn's Neo-Confucianism and then consider how it was put into practice.

A. Metaphysics and Psychological Theory

Kwŏn's Diagrammatic Treatise is the only broad and systematic early Yi exposition of the Neo-Confucian vision of man and the universe. It circulated widely in two formats, one with twenty-six diagrams and one with forty diagrams.[20] In the rest of his works one finds very little in the way of technical elaboration that goes beyond what is presented in the Diagrammatic Treatise. It seems likely that for most of the following century Yi dynasty Neo-Confucians were more engaged in applying this vision to the transformation of their society than in the speculative probing of latent philosophical problems; certainly in Kwŏn's immediate milieu this seems to have been the case.

The essence of the *Diagrammatic Treatise*, what brought it attention in its own times and is of value to us now, is the first diagram and its accompanying text. Kwŏn created the diagram for some students who came to him while he was in exile in Ikchu in 1390. They were discussing Chou Tun-i's *Diagram of the Supreme Ultimate* and Chu Hsi's *Commentary on the Doctrine of the Mean*, the two texts which are the foundations of Neo-Confucian metaphysics and psychological theory respectively. The students were having difficulty, and Kwŏn conceived of a diagram which would enable them to grasp these complex ideas as a whole. The diagram proved a success; Kwŏn added an explanatory text and a section of questions and answers based on his experience with the students. Enthused by the success of the format he also reduced much of the other fundamental lore for Confucian students to a similar form; thus the *Diagrammatic Treatise* contains diagrams relating to the traditional Confucian classics, ritual matters, yin and yang, the fundamentals of the calendar, etc. Apart from the first diagram, the only two which have much bearing on things distinctively Neo-Confucian are diagrams of the *Great Learning* and the *Doctrine of the Mean*, and these add little to the overall doctrine presented in the first diagram.

The title of the diagram is, "Heaven and Man, Mind and Nature, Combine as One." The diagram itself is ingenious in the way it conflates the metaphysics of the *Diagram of the Supreme Ultimate* with the psychological theory of the *Doctrine of the Mean*.[21] Instead of the discrete circles of Chou's diagram, one finds the whole universe outlined in an apparently human shape, with Heaven as the head and earth as the square trunk, in the midst of which is a large outline of the Chinese character *sim (hsin)*, "mind-and-heart." Within the "nature" portion of this heart character are listed the four virtues which constitute human nature, corresponding to the four characteristics of Heaven listed in the cosmic head. In the more "physical" portion of the heart are the Seven Emotions which, unlike the Four Beginnings, may eventuate in either good or evil. The two legs of the diagram represent the two extremes of the human condition: the right leg, representing perfect accord with the virtues of human nature, culminates in sagehood; the left, the career of one ensnared in feelings corrupted by selfishness, culminates in a condition of near animality. A path linking the legs has at its center "mindfulness" *(ching/kyŏng)*, the essential method of Neo-Confucian self-cultivation which makes it possible to move from the imperfection of the left leg to the perfect condition of sagehood on the right.

Fundamentally this diagram, with its accompanying text, contain quite standard doctrines of the Ch'eng-Chu school. Its importance for its times does not lie in points of doctrinal uniqueness, though there happen to be several of these which merit brief attention. First, metaphysically Kwŏn appears to be an absolute monist in that he derives material force *(ch'i/ki)* from principle *(li/i)*; he mentions this in passing in the text,[22] and perhaps it is also implied in the diagram in that the Supreme Ultimate is not part of the figure itself but above it, virtually as the space in which the figure exists. Kwŏn, however, does not draw attention to this in his presentation, and seems to have taken the derivation of material force from principle more or less for granted. Second, he discriminates the Four Beginnings and the Seven Emotions in terms of principle and material force; far from being monistic, this is a rather extreme expression of the dualistic aspect of Neo-Confucian thought. This aspect of the diagram is eventually expressed in the thought of Yi T'oegye (1501–70) and be-

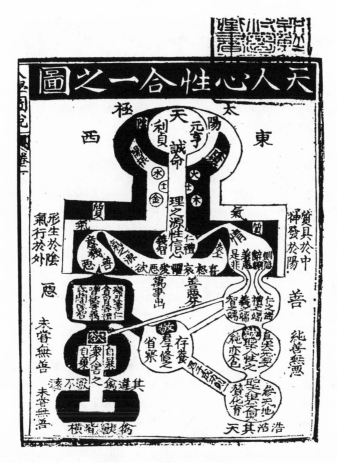

comes the center of the most famous and extended philosophical controversy in the history of Korean Neo-Confucian thought. Kwŏn, however,
is far from imagining any such controversy, and is also oblivious to the
philosophical tension between his monistic metaphysics of the universe
as a whole and the metaphysical dualism of his psychomoral analysis of
the mind and nature.

The absence of technical philosophical questioning of such points
either in Kwŏn's own work or in the immediately succeeding generations
during which his diagram circulated widely, reflects the level at which
the Neo-Confucianism of the Ch'eng-Chu school was appropriated at the
time. It *is* philosophical insofar as there is a deep interest in understanding and coordinating a set of concepts into a satisfactory vision of human

existence and the universe. But it is also religious, in the sense that it stops where religious interest stops: with a satisfactory picture of the whole which explains the whence and wherefore of life and its ultimate potential and meaning. The degree to which Kwŏn has done this in a single diagram is impressive; Koreans could see how the complex vision of the Ch'eng-Chu school worked, and grasp its essential implications; that was sufficient for the first century.

But what, we may ask, were the "essential implications" of this vision for early Yi dynasty Neo-Confucians? What is uppermost in Kwŏn's mind, and how does it meet the questions and needs of his social and cognitive environment?

We might begin to answer this by considering how he sums things up in the closing remarks of the initial portion of the accompanying text:

Thus the myriad creatures each is endowed with the one principle and the myriad principles proceed alike from the single origin. Each blade of grass and each tree [participates in] the one Supreme Ultimate and in the universe there is no creature outside [the scope of this] nature. Therefore the *Doctrine of the Mean* [ch. 21] says, if one is fully able to perfect his own nature, he will be able to perfect the natures of others persons, be able to perfect the natures of all creatures, and thereby assist in the transforming and nurturing activity of Heaven and Earth. Ah! this is indeed the ultimate![23]

The theme of the metaphysical unity of all things in terms of principle or the Supreme Ultimate drawn from the *Diagram of the Supreme Ultimate* is nicely combined with the vision of man's ultimate responsibility to take care of the world found in the *Doctrine of the Mean* (the relationship between these two being established by Chu Hsi's annotations which describe the mind and nature in terms of principle and material force). In the light of this, we might see a twofold point in Kwŏn's choice of a title for this diagram, "Man and Heaven, the Mind and Nature, Combine as One": first, he wishes to establish the unity of man and Heaven, a unity which runs through the whole universe; second, he wants to describe that unity in terms of a doctrine of mind and nature which imply the necessity of moral cultivation and social responsibility. Looked at from one point of view, these are simply conclusions which obviously emerge from the texts he is dealing with; from another point of view, one might say that it is a focus on these issues which leads him to combine these texts in the first place.

Some substantiation of this can be found in the section of questions and answers he appends to the text. Supposedly they are the questions his students asked him, but they are transparently a vehicle for Kwŏn to present what he has in mind regarding various aspects of his diagram. Two of the weightiest and most elaborately answered questions focus on our topic, asking, in essence, why he has muddled up a clear unity with all these other complications.

The first question has to do with Heaven:

Heaven on high is without sound and without smell; therefore in Chou's diagram he makes the form round and the middle empty and further adds the expression, "the Ultimateless." Now, if you had just written in the word "Heaven," it would have been enough; but you go on to write in the four characteristics and then fill out those with "integrity" and "the Mandate." Why are there so many terms? Why couldn't you stop with the mysteriousness of the single root [of all things]?[24]

Kwŏn responds with a long disquisition on how Heaven creates through principle and a detailed explanation of the correlation between the characteristics of Heaven, the four seasons, and the virtues which comprise human nature. He then concludes:

For beginners, if I did not explain it like that, but just directly called it "Heaven," some would think of it as a dark, vast emptiness without any order, and would not recognize it as the source of all principle. Others would be caught on the notion of Heaven as the blue vault covering everything, with its active ether transforming [things], and would not recognize its mysteriousness as the single root, or understand that what we call the nature has its origin entirely from Heaven but its principle present within oneself. Still others would drown in the emptiness of the Buddhists or the confusion of Yang [Chu].[25]

The second question has to do with the mind:

The mind's substance is originally empty, and consciousness is a unity and that is all. Thus before it is active it is perfectly still and may be said to be without either concept or image. Then after it is activated, its awareness follows the principle of things with a single unity running through all, and there is nothing it does not penetrate. But you divide the strokes [of the character, "mind"] into nature, mind, feelings, and will; further, beneath them you put the five constant [virtues of the nature], the four beginnings, the seven emotions, and two sorts of inner wellsprings. Consciousness is [here] not a unity; it is a complicated snarl, a mixed-up tangle, and its still and empty substance cannot be established; it is so categorized and bound up that its single, penetrating [active] function contains differentiation. Why is that?[26]

Kwŏn responds with an explanation of these various aspects of the mind as they are integrated into its substance and function, and then holds forth on the importance of knowing this kind of thing:

If one understands that [the mind] is still and empty but does not recognize the five constant virtues of the nature as its substance, then the mind becomes a great vastness with nothing in it and one falls into the Taoists' vacuous nonbeing or the Buddhists' emptiness and quiescence. If one considers its consciousness without realizing that in the wellsprings of its activation as the four beginnings and the seven emotions there is a distinction of good and evil, and so bringing discernment to bear, the mind will become the slave of things, moved by desire and overcome by feelings.[27]

The matters Kwŏn discusses in responding to these two questions are not mere secondary details; they pertain to the basic substance of the diagram, and one might well expect them to be explained in the initial explanatory text. But the question-and-answer format suits his purpose better: the questions establish the unitary aspects of Heaven and mind with a forcefulness that would be obtrusive in a purely expository text, and the answers allow Kwŏn to qualify that unity in just the way he wishes.

To say this is to say that at this early stage the Korean environment led to a "selective emphasis" on those doctrines which constitute the core of the Ch'eng-Chu thought. This might seem unremarkable and even disappointing to those searching for a distinctive essence in the Korean appropriation of Neo-Confucianism. Indeed the abstract intellectual profile appears here to be scarcely distinguishable from what one finds in Chinese masters of this school.

Such a line of thought misses the real issue, however, which is: why do these basic Neo-Confucian doctrines arouse such enthusiasm and inspire such conviction in the Korean context? If we can answer this, we will be in a position to understand better how, once introduced to Korea, Neo-Confucianism exercised such an immense attraction that it could supplant Buddhism as the ideological and spiritual center of the elite governing class of Yi dynasty society.

A large part of the answer, not surprisingly, has to do with Buddhism itself. Kwŏn's answers to the above questions concerning Heaven and mind both indicate that an important effect of understanding these correctly, that is, in a Neo-Confucian way, is that it will preclude falling victim to Buddhist errors. To conclude, however, that Neo-Confucianism was attractive as an instrument to refute the Buddhists and reduce their influence is probably to distort the situation by seeing it from a perspective which is already non-Buddhist. It presupposes a pre-existing *animus* against Buddhism which is hard to imagine. One could clearly understand and plan to remedy excessive Buddhist intrusions in the economic and political orders without having to become an ex-Buddhist to do so. As for refuting Buddhist errors, the notion of error arises only after one is either thoroughly alienated or has already become convinced of an alternative perspective.

Kwŏn certainly is acutely aware of how one must understand the unity of the universe in such a way as to avoid Buddhist "errors." But he is a Neo-Confucian, not because it enables him to avoid errors, but because he finds in Neo-Confucian doctrine a better, more accurate way of seeing things, and from this perspective he can identify Buddhist "error." In short, he now *knows better*.

The reason, I would suggest, that Kwŏn and many of his fellow officials find Neo-Confucian doctrine so persuasive is that Buddhism has prepared the way, not by its wrongness, but by its rightness. That is, the high plausibility of Buddhism in this cognitive milieu makes Neo-Confucian doctrines even more plausible. To understand this it will be useful to consider a Buddhist view of man and the universe as stated by Kwŏn when he writes for the king in his Buddhist *persona*:

The Buddhas and all living things are fundamentally one and the same mind, the only difference being between unenlightened and enlightened [conditions]. Therefore it is possible for the Buddhas to consider their mind as the mind of all living things and all living things can likewise consider their mind as the mind of the Buddhas. Since the million-bodied transformations [of the Buddhas] are all for the sake of approaching and saving living beings, does not the mind of all the Buddhas follow in accord with living beings? And since one good thought likewise can arouse [a response] in the Buddhas, are not the minds of living things united with the Buddhas? For although the delusion and depravity of the human mind be extreme, if the shoot of a single good thought arises within it, one depraved thought is removed. The removal of one depraved thought is the same as the appearance of the one Truth. It can be compared to boring through a wall and making a window; there is then illumination. Or as when one hollows out the earth and there is then an empty hole. The illumination and emptiness do not come from somewhere else; it is just a matter of removing what conceals them and then the integral substance of itself appears. It is just that the enlightened mind is always quiet, neither coming nor going; it is necessary that the human mind be aroused and then the spirit-response will come in a flash, For in the sincere desire of the human mind there is also the Buddha mind. . . . Sincerity arises in this [human mind] and the response appears from that [Buddha mind]; the mysterious arousing is not hasty, but [its effect comes] rapidly. The one mind can divide into the countless number of Buddhas and the countless number of Buddhas do not depart from the one mind; and even one's own mind may be regarded as the Buddha mind. (33.4a–b)

This is general Mahayana Buddhist doctrine cast into a form which relates it more to the layman than the monk; that is, although the theoretical basis for enlightenment and nirvana are not absent, the real focus is the way the One Mind theory serves as a framework for a retribution doctrine, which explains how faith and meritorious actions such as supporting temples can bring in response desired blessings. T'aejo's engaging in such activities for the welfare of his ancestors and the nation is in fact the occasion for this composition.

It does not require much imagination to see how Kwŏn in presenting such doctrines might have a self-satisfied sense of "knowing better" with every line he writes. The knowing better would result not so much in a total rejection of all this, as in covering the same general cognitive map with a more satisfactory explanation. Yes there is a unity, but it is the unity of principle not of the One Mind; the identity is not the mind of Buddha and my mind, but the mind of Heaven (principle) and the nature which is the substance of my mind. The differentiation is not the deluded craving which obscures the Buddha mind in me, but the selfish desire due to the opacity of an imperfect psychophysical endowment of material force which obscures the Heavenly principle of my nature. Ultimate perfection is already present within me, but it will shine forth only with serious and constant attention to principle in my conduct and the subduing of self-centered impulses. Blessings come as a natural response to moral conduct, not as the reward of actions manifesting faith in and reliance on the Buddha.

This is, of course, the same complex of ideas which we saw as the focus of Kwŏn's diagram. They stand out because they serve to explain features of man and the universe which are the assumed cognitive terrain of this society as it has been shaped by long centuries of Buddhist predominance. They are persuasive especially for those oriented outwards active life in government service because they not only illuminate the socially mediated cognitive map, but do so in a way that substantiates the Confucian values significant in the milieu of officialdom.

Thus Kwŏn, for example, can turn to these unitive ideas as the ultimate framework for understanding the proper functioning and ideal order in government and society. One part of the *Diagrammatic Treatise* is devoted to a diagram of the Grand Plan, a section of the classic *Book of Documents* which presents an ideal formula of government and society.[28] Perfection, for Kwŏn, immediately calls to mind the ultimate framework, and thus his diagram is entitled: "The Great Plan in Nine Divisions: Heaven and Man Combine as One." In the middle of the diagram, summing up its significance, we find the words: "The Ruler Establishes the Ideal Standard, Combining Heaven and Man and Making Them as One."[29] One can easily gather what he means by this from the following passage on kingship taken from a bell inscription:

The *Book of Changes* says: "The great virtue of Heaven and Earth is giving life; the great jewel of the Sage is the throne; how does one maintain the throne? By humanity."[30] This means that the sage [ruler] regards the disposition *(hsin/sim)* of Heaven and Earth to give life to creatures as his own mind-and-heart and dispenses it broadly, and therefore is able to protect his throne. This is because although Heaven and man are different, their mind-and-heart is one. (23.1b)

The primary significance of the unity between man and the Ultimate is thus the moral imperative of carrying forward the life-givingness of the universe in the conduct of one's own life among others.

B. Practice

The vision incorporated in these doctrines places a heavy stress on moral cultivation, as did traditional Confucianism. The unitary framework in terms of which the one principle, diversely manifested in all creatures, is fully and perfectly present as man's nature, the substance of his mind-and-heart, goes beyond traditional Confucianism, however, in that it establishes a foundation for a new kind of attention to human interiority. The traditional approach to self-cultivation was mainly a common-sense, active formation of good habits and fitting conduct through the inculcation of Confucian values and the development of the habits of discipline and self-control which enable one to live by those values. But in the Neo-Confucian framework discipline and control have not only an active application, but can be turned towards the inner life of the mind itself in order to attain a calm and undisturbed identity with principle as the substance of the mind. This complements the active side of cultivating oneself by discernment and restraint, and even perfects it insofar as when the mind-and-heart moves into an active condition ("function," in the Neo-Confucian terminology) from a basis of integration with its perfect substance, activity will naturally correspond to principle:

> Now what is called the mean has both substance and function: if before [one's mind] is aroused one makes its emptiness perfect in order to maintain the substance with its perfect equilibrium, then when the mind is aroused it will be perfectly moderated and will thereby become perfect in its function, with no excess or deficiency. (21.10b)

This theory invites a kind of meditative practice in order to "maintain the substance with its perfect equilibrium," and a practice called "quiet sitting" *(ching-tso/chŏngjwa)* consequently comes to have its place in the world of Neo-Confucian self-cultivation. It was difficult to strike a balance in which the reciprocal role of active and quiet cultivation was fully recognized, without undue attention being directed towards the quiet nurture of the substance of the mind. Finally in the Ch'eng-Chu school the term "mindfulness" emerged as a synthesis: when activity is in order, it is manifested as the exercise of discernment and attention to what is at hand; when nothing calls for activity, mindfulness takes the form of a calm, quiet mind, perhaps even the perfect equilibrium of objectless consciousness.

"Mindfulness," as a recollected, focused state of mind, thus comes to assume a central place in the Ch'eng-Chu lexicon of self-cultivation. This is evident in the position it occupies in Kwŏn's diagram, and as the foregoing passage indicates, he has a full grasp of this theory of self-cultivation, though his writings rarely expound it in any detail. In his critiques of Buddhism a "balanced" and "integral" attention to both cultivation of the mind and active engagement in affairs, substance and function, is a common theme; thus this aspect of Neo-Confucian doctrine strengthens his confidence in the greater fullness of the Neo-Confucian vision.

Mindfulness, whether applied to the active or quiet state, is a practice which involves a high degree of awareness and concern regarding one's mental condition. The following poem by Kwŏn Kŭn, composed for a palace official, Kang Inbu, reflects the values and lifestyle that come to the fore when this type of cultivation is pursued:

> Desire stilled, the Heavenly [endowed] light radiates;
> The mind being purified, the [nurturing] force of the night arises;[31]

In every circumstance being constant in maintaining this condition,
One's mind-and-heart of itself becomes empty and clear. (7.25a)

A commemorative piece on Kang tells us the following regarding his life-style:

In his residence he set aside a room which he cleaned spotlessly and made fra-
grant with incense; every time he returned from the palace, he would there settle
his mind and sitting still and erect would rid his mind of thoughts. (12.12a)

This is an excellent description of Neo-Confucian quiet sitting. In
the value orientation and lifestyle described here one sees how Neo-Confucianism can combine an active life-style with the kind of serious spiritual cultivation of the inner life of the mind ordinarily associated with
Buddhism. The same passage, as a matter of fact, indicates Kang's early
devotion to Buddhism: "Being deeply attached to Buddhism, he purified
his mind and for decades did not eat smelly vegetables or food with a
fishy odor" (12.11b). The implication seems to be that eventually he
changed his practice, since the imagery in the poem is Neo-Confucian
rather than Buddhist. Thus it seems likely that Kang discovered in Neo-
Confucianism an outlet for his originally Buddhist concern for spiritual
cultivation.

Considering the strength of Buddhism in this society, one might well
suppose that in the Neo-Confucianism of this period serious efforts would
be devoted to this mode of self-cultivation, which is an activist analogue
of the resources available for the serious-minded in Buddhism; Kang Inbu
would thus typify the concerns and lifestyle of the period. Every indication that one may gather from Kwŏn's works, however, points to the contrary: this aspect of Neo-Confucianism seems to have been important mainly
as a necessary element in the more fully rounded doctrinal edifice, and
had little real impact on the lifestyle of early Yi dynasty Neo-Confucians.

Kwŏn, as we have seen, is well aware of this theory of self-cultivation; indeed, it is so much an integral part of the core doctrines which
are foremost in his mind that he could hardly neglect it. But very little
attention is devoted to these matters in his works. In critiques of Buddhism he usually mentions the more balanced superiority of the Neo-
Confucian theory of self-cultivation, but he rarely discusses that theory in
other contexts. Further, I have not found a single passage in which he
discusses how one might actually put this theory into practice. Mindfulness is centrally located in his diagram, but one can read hundreds of

pages in the *Collected Writings* without encountering the term in its technical Neo-Confucian sense. And aside from the Kang Inbu passage quoted above, I find nothing that might be taken as a reference to quiet sitting.

Perhaps even more indicative than this doctrinal neglect is the fact that the characteristic values associated with this kind of cultivation do not appear in the many pieces which describe, discuss, or praise his contemporaries. If such practices were much pursued and their related fruits an object of high esteem, one would expect it to appear in this literature. As we have seen, poems for Buddhist monks frequently reflect the spiritual values and attainments characteristic of their way of life. But Kang Inbu is the only nonmonk about whom such things are mentioned, and the Buddhist roots of his orientation are evident. In any case, his attention to this type of self-cultivation was noteworthy and Kwŏn's two pieces on him clearly reflect the fact. The absence of any similar instances among a large number of examples[32] praising such traditional Confucian values as propriety, frugality, and filial piety, seems to indicate that this distinctive style of Neo-Confucian self-cultivation was not a significant part of the lives of most early Yi dynasty Neo-Confucians.

This suggests that the practical consequences in terms of a way of life that these men drew from Neo-Confucian doctrine was focused precisely on that area in which Neo-Confucianism distinguished itself from the Buddhist path, the area of active involvement in the government and affairs of their society. Here too, the Neo-Confucian philosophy of principle has its distinctive application. Faith in principle may lead to a cultivation of mind which is constantly responsive to principle as manifest in affairs, and which is a calm, transparent medium for the realization of the good impulses arising from the principle-informed substance of the mind. But when concern is not thus focused on the subjective and immediate apprehension of principle, the energy of faith may be directed to the objective aspect, principle as the objective and unchanging norm inherent in everything:

Whether it be in great matters such as ritual, music, laws, government, cappings, weddings, funerals and ancestor rites, or smaller one's such as the home life of husband and wife, plowing and farming, raising silk worms and weaving, the Way is never absent, nor can it be disregarded or abridged. Therefore our Confucian Way looks to the constant [principles] of everyday life and affairs, and each thing has its norm. (16.4b)

A norm for everything and everything with a norm! This was taken with great seriousness, but in lieu of cultivating a subjective, intuitive grasp of this norm, early Yi dynasty Neo-Confucians turn in the direction of seeking it out as authoritatively expressed in writings such as the *Rites of Chou*, the *Book of Rites*, and Chu Hsi's *Family Ritual*, intent on discovering the perfect norm for the "great matters" and applying it to their society.

CONCLUSION

In concluding this paper, I would like to suggest how the foregoing might help us to understand the dynamics of the transformation which took place in the century following Kwŏn's death, as Yi dynasty society gradually became less Buddhist and more Confucian.

In turning to the ancient norms of Confucian social institutions and practices with a mind to applying them to their society, the early Yi dynasty Neo-Confucians grasped the essential means for the Confucian transformation of their society. But if one looks only at the ritual norms it is difficult to understand the source of their power to bring about change. Clearly if such norms were taken seriously and put into practice the result would be a vast change from the largely Buddhist society which we have seen. But in a society in which Confucian practice is not deeply or widely rooted, those norms would have minimal plausibility. When very few people observe a given standard, it is simply unconvincing to claim that one is seriously deficient as a human being if one does not observe it. Legislation may be enacted, but if there is no deep conviction on the part of the legislators, a sustained effort at enforcement will be lacking. In this situation, how is the primary instrument of transformation energized to the point where it can transform?

The answer which emerges in this paper is that the orientation towards ritual is not primary but secondary and derivative. That is, ritual norms in themselves would lack plausibility in this society were it not for the fundamental core of of Neo-Confucian doctrine which explains the unity of man and the universe in terms of principle—a doctrine which has great plausibility as a "knowing better" in the cognitive context created by centuries of Buddhist predominance. Early Korean Neo-Confucians have few reasons to doubt the total adequacy and correctness of these doctrines, and much reason to be deeply impressed by them. Faith in a universe informed by principle points to an objective norm of the way things should be; the ideals expressed in the authoritative books on ritual, although socially implausible, are supported by the high plausibility of their foundation. The combination of deep conviction on the one hand and implausibility on the other is a fruitful one, providing not only the elasticity needed to deal with the "unorthodox" practices of one's family and sovereign, but also the sustained will to effect a transformation of them.

If this is accurate, one might look for a snowballing effect, but one with slow beginnings. In officialdom convictions concerning principle demand attempts to shape practice accordingly; the gap between ideal norm and actual practice is initially so great, however, that rigid orthopraxis is impracticable, and the response is slow. Nevertheless the new convictions are strong enough so that the attempt to change things persists, and gradually practice is modified. The more practice begins to reflect the norms, the more plausible the norms themselves become, until finally they can be taken seriously and observed strictly.

This model of cognitive dynamics is an abstract schematization of processes which in the flesh and blood of history would have neither the neatness nor the inevitability implicit in the abstraction. But if a high level of concern with questions of ritual and propriety and a strong orientation towards orthopraxis are indeed distinctive features of later Yi dynasty Neo-Confucianism, one might well see this as stemming from an initial appropriation of Neo-Confucianism which was unremarkable in its doctrinal features, but unusually strong in its convictions.

NOTES

1. According to Martina Deuchler, "Self-Cultivation for the Governance of Men: The Beginnings of Neo-Confucian Orthodoxy in Yi Korea," *Asiatische Studien* (1980), 34(2):9–39, Yi Saek (1328–96) presided over the first large-scale discussions of the basic Neo-Confucian literature. Kwŏn Kŭn was a disciple of Yi.
2. Sin Ton (?–1371) was an obscure Buddhist monk who gained the confidence of the mentally unstable King Kongmin; beginning about 1365 he rose rapidly to a position in which he was virtually the surrogate of the king, but aroused such opposition in pursuing the reform policies favored by the king that the king was compelled finally to assent to his exile, where he was quietly done away with.
3. He began the *Yegi ch'ŏn'gyŏnnok* (Commentary on the *Book of Rites*) in 1391, fulfilling a task entrusted to him by his teacher, Yi Saek, who felt the rectification of the order of the text was an urgent need. Kwŏn rearranged the text and supplemented his own work with the commentary of the Yüan dynasty Neo-Confucian scholar, Ch'en Hao. The work begun in 1391 was suspended when he took office in 1393 and was completed only in 1404.
4. The *Sangjŏl karye*. Chu Hsi's *Chia-li* was the most important ritual handbook for Yi dynasty Neo-Confucians. Martina Deuchler, in "Neo-Confucianism: The Impulse for Social Action in Early Yi Korea," *Journal of Korean Studies* (1980), 2:85, states that this annotated edition prepared by Kwŏn was the most widely used in the early period of the dynasty, citing a number of passages in the *Sillok* as her source. This would make it one of Kwŏn's most influential works, but it is nowhere mentioned in contemporary Korean sources on Kwŏn and his works, which appear to be unaware of its existence.
5. The *Ogyŏng ch'ŏn'gyŏnnok* (Commentaries on the Five Classics).
6. The *Pulssi chappyŏn*, the *Simgi ip'yŏn*, and *Simmun ch'ŏndap* (Questions and Answers between the Mind and Heaven). The *Pulssi chappyŏn* is a critique of various Buddhist doctrines and practices; the *Simgi ip'yŏn* is a Buddhist/Taoist/Neo-Confucian dialogue; *Simmun ch'ŏndap* is a dialogue between the mind and Heaven concerning the question of retribution.
7. A detailed analysis of this memorial may be found in Pak Ch'ŏn'gyu, "Yangch'on Kwŏn Kŭn yŏn'gu" (Research on Kwŏn Kŭn), *Sach'ong* (December 1964), 9: 1–50. This article is the best account of Kwŏn's political career and activities.
8. References will be to the text reprinted in the Korean translation of the *Yangch'onjip*, *Kugyŏk Yangch'onjip* (Kwŏn Kŭn's Works in Korean translation), *Kojŏn kugyŏk ch'ongsŏ*, vols. 173–76 (Seoul: Minjok munhwa ch'ujinhoe, 1979).
9. I borrow this term from a book which is one of the most penetrating works in a contemporary sociology of religion, *The Sacred Canopy: Elements of a*

Sociological Theory of Religion, by Peter L. Berger (New York: Anchor Books, 1969).

10. I find six commemorations *(chi/ki)* of royal temple building or temple reconstruction projects, three colophons for royal editions or copies of scriptures, and nineteen prayers *(shu/so)* for royal-sponsored Buddhist rituals and ceremonies among the Yi dynasty materials. Of course this reflects only a portion of the Buddhist activity of the early Yi rulers, since it is unlikely that Kwŏn was the only one called on for such compositions.

11. See, for example, Kwŏn's preface for T'aejo's grave inscription (36.5a and ff.), which he begins by recounting the omens or portents which from early on indicated Yi Sŏnggye's royal destiny.

12. *Sambongjip* (Chŏng Tojŏn's Collected Works), 6.10a.

13. Kwŏn notes that his father was a liberal supporter of such good works as rebuilding temples (14.3a). A number of passages mention his monk brother; Kwŏn wrote a colophon for a *Lotus Sutra* copied for the repose of his soul (22.12a). On the monk who tutored Kwŏn's children, see 8.21b.

14. An excellent analysis of the way society forms and informs our cognitive world is: Peter L. Berger and Thomas Luckmann, *The Social Construction of Reality* (New York: Anchor Books, 1967). This paper makes use particularly of their theory of plausibility and its social basis.

15. "Affirmation" here goes well beyond explicit verbal affirmation; all sorts of social interaction are based upon shared assumptions which are tacitly or indirectly affirmed in the very modes of the interaction.

16. Han Yü (768–824), one of the greatest literary figures of the T'ang dynasty, was also one of the few to take a stand against Buddhism when the "foreign" religion was at the height of its success; on the occasion of a great celebration in honor of the finger bone of the Buddha, he memorialized the emperor offering to throw the relic into the river. He was fortunate to be only exiled rather than executed.

17. This is both literal and figurative: the monk was about to set off on a life of wandering. Such travel was one of the Zen paths to enlightenment; it seems to have been quite popular at this period, for Kwŏn writes a number of prefaces for monks who, like this one, had collected a number of poems from Confucian literati on the eve of their departure.

18. A reference to Zen meditation. Bodhidharma, the sixth century Indian monk to whom the transmission of Zen (Ch'an) to China is attributed, is said to have sat unmoving and silent facing a wall for nine years, whence the use of the term.

19. In his petition to Kwŏn this monk indicates that he had sought and been given a style *(hao/ho)* in earlier years by Yi Saek, and sought enlightenment not only in meditation but in reflecting on the meaning of the style.

20. The shorter version was first published in 1397, and the longer version appeared in 1425. There have been at least two editions of the shorter version and three of the longer, including a Japanese edition published in 1648. In this paper references will be made to the shorter version as reproduced in a

modern paperback Korean translation, *Iphak tosŏl*, tr. by Kwŏn Tŏkchu (Seoul: Ŭryu munhwasa, 1974). References will include the page of this text as well as the *kwŏn (chüan)* and folio page numbers.

21. In the text which accompanies the diagram Kwŏn states that he has based it on these two works, but it is evident that he has freely used other sources to supplement or interpret them. One such source, as indicated by the position and description of "integrity" *(ch'eng/sŏng)* in the diagram, was Chou Tun-i's *T'ung shu.*

22. *Iphak tosŏl*, 1.5a, p. 145.

23. *Ibid.*, 1.2b–3a, pp. 138–39.

24. *Ibid.*, 1.5a, p. 145.

25. *Ibid.*, 1.5b, p. 146. Yang Chu (4th century B.C.) was known as the representative of an extreme form of egoism. Mencius says that he would not have parted with a single hair of his body to save the whole world.

26. *Iphak tosŏl*, p. 6b–7a, pp. 148–49.

27. *Ibid.*, 1.7a, p. 149.

28. The Great Plan *(Hung-fan)* is found in the *Book of Documents*, 5.4. As the earliest general schema of ideal government it was generally highly respected by Confucians, but even more revered in Korea because of its association with Kija (Chi Tzu), the Duke of Chi, who supposedly emigrated to Korea rather than serve the new rulers when the Chou dynasty was founded, and thus transmitted Chinese culture to the peninsula in the twelfth century B.C. This story, which gives Korea a very ancient Confucian heritage, understandably came into great currency in the early Yi dynasty.

29. *Iphak tosŏl*, 1.33b, p. 202.

30. *Book of Changes*, Great Appendix, B.1.

31. A reference to *Mencius*, 6A.8, where he describes the way the nurturing force of the calm night restores life to the good dispositions inherent in human nature.

32. The one part of the *Yangch'onjip* I have not had opportunity to read are the six *kwŏn* of poems which he composed before 1388. However, since the material I perused included four *kwŏn* of poetry and much other material from his earlier career, it is doubtful that the unexamined material would significantly alter the picture which emerges from the rest of his writings.

Yi Sŏngmu

The Influence
of Neo-Confucianism
on Education and the
Civil Service Examination
System in Fourteenth-
and Fifteenth-Century
Korea

I. INTRODUCTION

THE RULING IDEOLOGY of the Yi dynasty was Neo-Confucianism,
while that of the previous dynasty was Buddhism. Buddhism had been
the dominant ideology of the state since the era of the Three Kingdoms,
while Confucianism had been a system of practical ethics, concerning
itself with ongoing sociopolitical problems. Its role was to provide a way
of government based on the civil arts. During the Koryŏ dynasty (918–
1392), Buddhism and Confucianism maintained a mutually supportive
relationship, expressed in Ch'oe Sŭngno's (927–89) twenty-eight proposals for contemporary government *(simu isipp'al cho)* submitted to King
Sŏngjong (r. 981–97), which described Buddhism as the foundation for
personal cultivation, while Confucianism was called the foundation for
the governing of the state.[1] In other words, Buddhism was seen as a religion concerned with the spiritual and sacred, Confucianism as a way of
government concerned with the practical and profane. This partnership
was reenforced during the period of military control lasting from 1170 to
1270. Many civil officials schooled in Confucianism escaped to Buddhist

temples in remote mountain areas in order to avoid severe persecution from the military men at this time. Thus, Buddhist monks and Confucian scholars became exposed to one another's influence.

However, because Buddhism was the state religion of the Koryŏ dynasty, it enjoyed a privileged position. For instance, Buddhist ceremonies were frequently conducted by the state, and Buddhist temples were exempt from tax and public labor service. Consequently, Buddhist temples and monks increased in number. With the wealth which came from the donations of the royal family, nobility, and public, the monks succumbed to corruption. Eventually Buddhism was criticized for undermining the economic foundation of the state and causing a decline of public morality. This state of affairs was only exacerbated by the social upheaval caused by the calamitous invasions of Mongols and other ethnic groups, which aroused people's superstitious beliefs and led the Ch'oe military government to reenforce their policy of venerating Buddhism, a policy sustained even after the normalization of relations between the Koryŏ and Yüan dynasties.

During the Ch'oe regime, Confucian scholar-officials had risen to national prominence through the official examinations and when the old political order became weakened in consequence of the Mongol domination, they had an opportunity to seize power in the central government. But they found that they could not even be paid their government stipends because the nation's finances were completely exhausted. Much of the country's land and wealth had become concentrated in the hands of Buddhist temples and old aristocrats who were exempt from taxation. This, together with the extravagant Buddhist ceremonies conducted by the royal family, had contributed to the depletion of the national treasury. Consequently the newly risen scholar-officials formulated a policy to attack and remove the cause of these evils. For this, however, they needed a new and powerful philosophy to defeat the long-established Buddhism, and they found such a doctrine in Neo-Confucianism.

The extension of Yüan dynasty control over Koryŏ in the late thirteenth century had the consequence that many Koreans traveled to China and learned about the prevalence of Neo-Confucianism there. This new philosophy was then studied and gradually introduced to Koryŏ. In the beginning, the books of Neo-Confucianism were imported and carefully studied at the state schools *(kwanhak)*. Then, basing their arguments on the new philosophy, scholars at state schools began to attack Buddhism and the Buddhist establishment. In this they were joined by military men who had come to power in the course of battling against invading Red Turbans *(Honggŏnjŏk)* and marauding Japanese. They too turned against the old power structure, since the concentration of wealth in the hands of Buddhist temples and aristocrats deprived them of the economic resources needed for military expenditures. Thus the military generals and scholar-officials joined together to bring the Koryŏ dynasty to its end. This new power group inaugurated the Yi dynasty after General Yi Sŏnggye returned with his troops from Wihwa-do *(Wihwa-do hoegun)*[2] to the capital.

Since Neo-Confucianism now became the principal doctrine for governance of the state, the ideology and institutions of the dynasty were totally reviewed and reconstructed from this new perspective. Of course, the reconstruction could not be accomplished all at once and a complete reorganization was not possible. In fact, the rise of Neo-Confucianism involved some compromises with Buddhism, Taoism, and folk beliefs. This same accommodation was made in the introduction of new institutions. In other words, the policy of curbing Buddhism was not intended to expel Buddhism altogether but rather to rid it of its internal corruption and to return the economic wealth of Buddhism to the state. Following this principle, a policy of reducing the number of Buddhist temples was implemented during the reigns of King T'aejong (r. 1400–18) and King Sejong (r. 1418–50).

The land reform toward the end of the Koryŏ dynasty and the reduction in the number of Buddhist temples in the beginning of the Yi dynasty established a strong economic foundation for the new kingdom. This reformed economy enabled King Sejong to increase his military power, extend the territorial borders of the dynasty, and establish the bureau of rites *(Ŭirye sangjŏngso)*, where various institutions were studied and reformed.

Thus, an important cultural reformation took place in the reign of King Sejong. This reformation was a result of the struggle to make Neo-Confucianism an integral part of Korean thought after its introduction into the country almost a century earlier. This struggle in turn was in large part concerned with the relationship between the education and examination systems in the fourteenth and fifteenth centuries. Therefore I shall attempt here to discuss the acceptance of Neo-Confucianism and the influence of Neo-Confucianism on the systems of education and examination in the fourteenth and fifteenth centuries.

II. THE ACCEPTANCE OF NEO-CONFUCIANISM AND ITS ENTRENCHMENT AS THE DOMINANT IDEOLOGY

Neo-Confucianism was a new trend in Confucianism which had been brought to completion by Chu Hsi (1130–1200). From its infancy in the Sung dynasty, it had received support from the newly rising scholar-official class in the provinces south of the Yangtze River,[3] but it was not immediately adopted as the ideology of the Chinese state. In fact, five years before Chu Hsi's death, Neo-Confucianism was still officially anathematized as a pseudolearning. However, in 1230 the Southern Sung dynasty accepted Neo-Confucianism and appointed Chu Hsi posthumously as the head of the Confucian shrine. Thereafter Neo-Confucianism began to flourish. At first Mongol control in the North hindered it, but Khubilai of the Yüan dynasty soon recognized the limitations of Mongol methods of control and adopted the policy of encouraging Confucianism.

In 1235 Chao Fu, a prominent Neo-Confucian, had been brought as a prisoner of war to the capital of the Yüan dynasty where he was the first to introduce Neo-Confucianism. He then handed on his philosophy to Hsü Heng, and Hsü Heng in turn transmitted it to Wu Ch'eng (1249–1333), Wang Tsai, and Yao Sui (1238–1313).[4] This lineage helped to make Neo-Confucianism the dominant ideology of the Yüan dynasty.[5]

Following Koryŏ's surrender to the Mongols after thirty years of struggle, the relationship between the two nations rapidly improved. For instance, at Koryŏ's request, a daughter of Khubilai married the crown prince of Koryŏ (who later became King Ch'ungnyŏl) in 1270, and at Yüan request, a marriage bureau *(Kyŏrhon togam)* was established to arrange marriages between Korean girls and Yüan officials. Thus the relationships between the two dynasties became closer than ever. Koryŏ officials, willingly or otherwise, were required to travel to the Yüan, and before long began to bring back a knowledge of Neo-Confucianism.

There is some dispute over how Neo-Confucianism was introduced to Koryŏ: one school of thought maintains that it was introduced by An Hyang (1243–1306; later known as An Yu) during the reign of King

Ch'ungnyŏl (r. 1274–1308), another that it was first propagated by Paek Ijŏng (fl. 1310–20) during the reign of King Ch'ungsuk (r. 1313–30, 1332–39). The former claim is based on such writings as the biography of An Hyang in the *History of the Koryŏ Dynasty (Koryŏsa)*; the *Works of Hoehŏn (Hoehŏnjip)*; *The Odd Tales of Yŏgong (Yŏgong p'aesŏl)* (Yi Chehyŏn); *Inconsequential Tales and Trivial Records (Sumun soerok)* (Cho Sin); and the *Works of Kŭnjae (Kŭnjaejip)* (An Ch'uk). According to these writings, An Hyang's accomplishment consisted in (1) revitalizing the National Academy *(Kukhak)*; (2) creating the *Sŏmhakchŏn*, a scholarship fund donated by the king and higher officials; (3) purchasing books on Neo-Confucianism from China with this fund; (4) bringing these books back himself from the court of the Yüan after he accompanied King Ch'ungsuk on his royal trip to China; (5) taking his pen name, Hoehŏn, in homage to Chu Hsi, the character *hoe* being from Hoeam, Chu Hsi's pen name; and (6) in recognition of these accomplishments, being placed in charge of the Confucian shrine, *Munmyo*, in 1319. This is the basis for the view that An Hyang made the decisive contribution to the introduction of Neo-Confucianism to Korea.

An Hyang was one of the newly-risen scholar-official class and was a student of Yu Kyŏng (1211–98), a civil official who killed Ch'oe Ŭi (?–1258), the last power holder of the Ch'oe military regime, and restored royal rule. Apparently, An Hyang believed that the most effective strategy against the entrenched aristocrats and Buddhists was to adopt Neo-Confucianism and disseminate it widely. Consequently, he concentrated his efforts on bringing Neo-Confucian books to Korea and using them for the training of students. As a high government official he may have had little time to study Neo-Confucianism himself or to teach it directly to students, but it is certain that he believed strongly in the importance of creating a climate conducive to the adoption and dissemination of the philosophy. To do this, it was necessary to reenforce and expand the state schools, thus enabling them to compete with the private schools of the old nobility. To achieve these ends, An Hyang created a scholarship fund and expanded the state schools, an extraordinary feat accomplished while Buddhism was still dominant. It was also these factors which led directly to his appointment as head of the Confucian shrine.

The other theory, which maintains that Paek Ijŏng was the first to bring Neo-Confucianism to Koryŏ in 1314,[6] is based on his biography in the *History of the Koryŏ Dynasty*. According to this record, Paek Ijŏng was the first Korean to become learned in the Neo-Confucianism then flourishing under the Yüan dynasty. When he returned to Koryŏ, where it was not yet known, he taught it to Yi Chehyŏn (1287–1367), Pak Ch'ungjwa (1287–1349), and others. Paek Ijŏng had had an opportunity to stay with King Ch'ungsŏn (r. 1298, 1308–13) in the Yüan capital for a decade, and there he could engage in a thorough study of Neo-Confucianism.[7] There is no doubt, then that he mastered the new philosophy and, once back in Korea, communicated his knowledge to others.

So while An Hyang was a national political figure and scholar-official who created a situation favorable for the study of Neo-Confucianism, Paek Ijŏng was a scholar who himself studied and understood Neo-Confucianism. There are several reasons why history has given primary credit to An Hyang for the introduction of Neo-Confucianism to Korea. An Hyang was senior to Paek Ijŏng, and it was he who laid the groundwork for the propagation of Neo-Confucian doctrine while Buddhism was still strong. Moreover, An Hyang was able to rise to a position of power from which he could be placed in charge of the Confucian shrine. Nevertheless, it would not have been possible for foreign philosophy to penetrate a sociopolitical structure solely through the efforts of one or two individuals, had not the philosophy itself answered certain specific needs of that day.[8] It is reasonable to believe that one of these was for a weapon to employ in destroying the entrenched power of the high aristocrats and Buddhist temples.

Neo-Confucianism as introduced by An Hyang and Paek Ijŏng received strong support from the newly rising scholar-officials. Their activities in promoting the new doctrine may be described in terms of three stages: first, the period during the early fourteenth century when Neo-Confucianism was first introduced; second, the period of its increasing acceptance a half a century later; and third, the period of Neo-Confucian struggle against Buddhism near the end of the fourteenth century.

In the first period the National Academy was attended by such scholars as An Hyang, Paek Ijŏng, Yi Kok (1298–1351), Kwŏn Po (1262–1346), Yi Chin (1244–1321), An Ch'uk (1287–1348), Yi Chehyŏn (1287–1367), Kwŏn Han'gong (?–1349), Pak Ch'ungjwa, U T'ak (1263–1342), and Cho Kan (fl. 1301). During this period, ritual vessels for the Confucian shrine and Neo-Confucian texts were imported from China. For example, An Hyang sent Kim Munjŏng (fl. 1303) to China to bring back portraits of Confucius and his seventy-two disciples, ritual vessels, and scriptures.[9] In

1314 the Royal College (Sŏnggyun'gwan) sent Yu Yŏn and Yu Chŏk, two of its officers of instruction, to the Kiangnan area in China and had them bring back classics and other books numbering 10,800 volumes.[10] Furthermore, the late Yi *Reference Compilation of Documents on Korea (Munhŏn pigo)* mentions that in 1314 Emperor Jen-tsung (r. 1312–21) of the Yüan dynasty gave 4,071 copies of books from the Imperial Library (Pi-kao t'u-shu) of the Sung dynasty to Koryŏ.[11] Books thus imported were classified and studied in the Royal College by Kwŏn Po, Yi Chin, Kwŏn Han'gong, Cho Kan, and An Ugi (?–1329).[12] In particular, Kwŏn Po published the *Collected Commentaries on the Four Books (Ssu-shu chi-chu / Sasŏ chipchu)* with his own commentaries, and a biography of him states: "Korean commentaries on Neo-Confucianism began with Kwŏn Po."[13] A biography of U T'ak also comments that after he studied Chu Hsi's commentary on the *Changes (Chou-i)* seriously and taught it to students, Neo-Confucianism began to flourish.[14] Yi Chehyŏn—a son of Yi Chin, a son-in-law of Kwŏn Po, and a student of Paek Ijŏng—went to the Yüan capital and at the Man'gwŏndang, a library built there by King Ch'ungsŏn, he enjoyed the companionship of prominent scholars of the Yüan dynasty such as Yao Sui, Yen Fu, Yüan Ming-shan, and Chao Meng-fu. There he was also fully exposed to current Neo-Confucianism.[15] Nevertheless, Korean scholar-officials during this period were not completely converted to Neo-Confucianism.

The second period was when scholar-officials such as Yi Saek (1328–96), Chŏng Mongju (1337–92), Pak Sangch'ung (1332–75), Yi Sungin (1349–92), Pak Ŭijung (fl. 1388), and Kim Kuyong (1338–84) took their positions on center stage in the reigns of King Kongmin (r. 1351–74) and King U (r. 1374–88). They instituted state teaching of Neo-Confucianism, especially at the Royal College, and began to attack Buddhist education.

Yi Saek, a son of Yi Kok and a disciple of Yi Chehyŏn, had accompanied his father on a trip to the Yüan court. While there he took and passed an examination and was appointed as an official in the Yüan government. Thus, he was trained in Neo-Confucianism in the Yüan capital. This enabled him to revitalize Neo-Confucianism at the Royal College after his return to Koryŏ. When as education intendant *(Cheng-tung-hsing chung-shu-sheng ju-hsüeh t'i-chü)*, he was dispatched to Koryŏ from the Yüan in 1363, he insisted that a Neo-Confucian education at the Royal College be required of all who wished to sit for the official examination.

He also served on the staff of the magistrate of the capital, and in 1367, on the faculty of the Royal College. Also in 1367, by request of Im Pak, its rector, the Royal College was rebuilt on the ruins of the Sungmun' gwan and the number of its students was increased. The college's curriculum was changed and a course in the Four Books and Five Classics *(Sasŏogyŏngjae)* was instituted. Yi Saek, with his fellow scholars such as Chŏng Mongju, Kim Kuyong, Pak Sangch'ung, Pak Ŭijung, and Yi Sungin taught students energetically and regularly held discussions on Neo-Confucianism after school hours. Hence, more and more students enrolled at the Royal College and Neo-Confucianism continued to spread.[16]

Chŏng Mongju passed the civil service examination in 1360, and he, with Yi Saek, became an instructor at the Royal College in 1367. There he gave lectures on Neo-Confucianism. Yi Saek esteemed Chŏng Mongju's comprehension of Neo-Confucianism so highly that he once called Chŏng Mongju the father of Neo-Confucianism in the East.[17] For the purpose of propagating Neo-Confucian ethics, he advocated the practice of the *Family Ritual of Master Chu (Chu Tzu chia-li/Chuja karye)*. Chŏng Mongju himself observed three years of mourning at the death of his father instead of the traditional Buddhist one-hundred-day mourning period.[18] The Buddhist practice being well-accepted and less demanding, most people found the three-year mourning too difficult to practice. This is why Chŏng Mongju's observance of three years' mourning was especially noteworthy. Actually, the three years' mourning was observed by only a small group of scholar-officials.[19] So far as is known, according to surviving records, only Pak Sangch'ung, Chŏng Sŭbin, Yun Kwisaeng, and perhaps a few others observed the three-year mourning period.[20] Chŏng Mongju also strongly urged that every household establish a family shrine in accordance with the prescription of the *Family Ritual of Master Chu*.[21] This advocacy was supported by a number of radical scholar-officials led by Cho Chun (1346–1405).[22] Scholar-officials saw the observance of the three-year mourning period as crucial to changing from a social norm based on the Buddhist ethic to one based on Neo-Confucianism. However, the observance of the *Family Ritual of Master Chu* was not widely practiced until after the beginning of the Yi dynasty.[23]

As Neo-Confucianism began to gather momentum, especially in the Royal College, and many scholar-officials who believed in Neo-Confucianism took up positions in national politics, they gradually began to criticize Buddhism. However, these critics did not aim their protests at the basic tenets of Buddhism. Rather, they attacked the corrupt institutions and moral decay of Buddhism. This is illustrated by Yi Saek's statement that although the Buddha was a great saint, monks had corrupted the society and therefore a society dominated by Buddhist monks ought to be reformed.[24] This approach implicitly conceded that the Neo-Confucians lacked the political power to mount a frontal attack against Buddhism. In fact, a policy advocating the suppression of Buddhism did not become crystallized until after the military coup d'état in 1388 which cemented the ties between the military generals who had recently risen to prominence and the newly rising scholar-official class.

The third period came when Buddhism was openly denounced by the radical group of scholar-officials including Chŏng Tojŏn (1342–98), Cho Inok (?–1396), Kim Chasu (fl. 1374), Yun Sojong (1345–93), and Pak Ch'o (1367–1454). In the reign of King Ch'ang (r. 1388–89), Cho Inok asserted that the lands and slaves belonging to the Buddhist temples should be brought under state control; that an individual should be prohibited from becoming a monk without official approval; that a monk spending the night in a private home should be regarded as adulterous; and that a woman visiting a Buddhist temple should be regarded as having lost her chastity.[25] Chŏng Tojŏn also maintained that all the lands and slaves owned by the temples should be returned to the state and that all "licentious" (i.e., superstitious or shamanistic) religious practices should be proscribed.[26] Kim Ch'o (fl. 1391) asked that Buddhist monks be laicized and made liable for regular military service, that slaves of the temples should be repossessed by the state, and that those aspiring to become monks should be killed.[27] Kim Chasu also said that Buddhism and superstitious rituals should be severely restricted by the state.[28] Pak Ch'o, a student at the Royal College, charged that Buddhism was a religion which distorted human nature and produced no good and urged that, therefore, monks should be conscripted into the military, Buddhist texts burned, lands and slaves belonging to the temples returned to the state, and statues of Buddha melted down and made into weapons.[29]

Thus it is evident that the main thrust of these attacks on Buddhism was to claim the material wealth of the temples for the state. The reformation of the land system aimed at taking the land out of the hands of the old Buddhist aristocrats and returning it to the state. However, because of the entrenched power of Buddhism at that time, such a direct assault on the economic foundation of institutional Buddhism in Koryŏ had to await the opening of the Yi dynasty.

From the beginning of the Yi dynasty, Buddhism was subjected to both ideological attack and concrete restrictions. Chŏng Tojŏn wrote *Arguments Against Mr. Buddha (Pulssi chappyŏn)* and *On Mind, Material Force, and Principle (Simgi ip'yŏn)* in which he attacked both Buddhism and Taoism with systematic and devastating arguments.[30] Also, T'aejong initiated the first of a series of drastic reductions in the number of temples: in 1406, Buddhist institutions were reduced to 12 Buddhist sects and 242 temples;[31] in 1424, the number was further reduced to 2 Buddhist sects and 36 mother temples; all other temples not associated with these were disestablished.[32] The lands and slaves which belonged to the unauthorized temples were of course turned over to the state. Furthermore, a procedure for the licensing of monks *(toch'ŏpche)* was enforced. This policy sought to reduce the number of monks by requiring every monk-aspirant to pay a fee and get permission from the state in order to become a monk. Anyone failing to receive permission was prohibited from becoming a monk.[33]

Not only Buddhism, but Taoism also was repressed. By 1392, of the Taoist shrines dating from the Koryŏ period, only the Sogyŏkchŏn remained. All the rest, i.e., Pogwŏn'gung, Singyŏkchŏn, Kuyodang, Sojŏnsaek, Taech'ŏnggwan, and Ch'ŏnggye paesŏngso, were destroyed.[34] Thus, Sogyŏkchŏn was the only Taoist institution permitted to exist, so that the state could conduct rituals for drought, flood, and other national calamities.

Along with Buddhism and Taoism, superstitious religious practices *(ŭnsa)*—i.e., shamanistic rituals—were also controlled by the state. In 1392, Nam Chae, the inspector-general *(taesahŏn)*, asked that all shamanistic rituals except those approved by the state be prohibited.[35] However, folk beliefs deeply rooted in the public mind could not be so easily eradicated. This included the traditional folk belief that the destiny of an individual and a nation was determined by the power of gods who governed the cosmic order of sky and earth. For this reason, the scholar-officials of the Yi dynasty decided to establish an Altar of Grain and Millet *(Sajiktan)* in every county and a shrine *(isa)* in every village in order to allow these beliefs to be observed and controlled by the state.[36] This was an extension of the *sajikche*, the national worship of the founders of the dynasty. Thus, the scholar-officials intended to create a stable social order in the rural community by compromising with and exercising control over the traditional practices in agricultural society of worshiping deities found in the natural world, especially through rites at the village shrine. This, in turn, would give them a basis for the dissemination of Neo-Confucianism.[37] In 1393 the government conferred official titles on the Sŏnghwang deities (regional gods) of sacred mountains, rivers, and islands. Thus, the Sŏnghwang of Songak became Duke of Pacification of the Realm (Chin'gukkong), the Sŏnghwang of Hwaryŏng, Anbyŏn, and Wansan became Barons of Guidance of the Realm (Kyegukpaek), the Sŏnghwang of Chii, Mudung, Kŭmsŏng, Kyeryong, Kamak, Samgak, Paegak Mountains, and Chinju became Barons Protecting the Realm (Hogukpaek), while other Sŏnghwangs became Spirits Protecting the Realm (Hoguk chi sin). Thus, these deities were given a place within the new order in which they retained their functions of blessing and protecting the kingdom.[38] They were to replace Buddhism which, now discredited, had lost the ability to perform this role.

The rituals for Sŏnghwang gods were usually conducted by shamans; that is, shamans were the priests of the Sŏnghwang cults. However, from 1411, eunuch attendants at the palace (Naesi pyŏlgam) were dispatched to conduct the rituals for the Sŏnghwang deities.[39] This meant that the worship of these deities as guardian gods of the state was put under the control of the government. However, in 1437 the state withdrew the official titles granted the Sŏnghwang gods of sacred mountains, rivers, and islands.[40] This meant that the ideological foundation of the Yi dynasty, namely Neo-Confucianism, had been consolidated and that the government, no longer needing the support of other religions, could dispense with them.

Scholar-officials, as the power group of the dynasty, suppressed Buddhism, Taoism, and shamanism on the one hand and enforced the dissemination of the Confucian ethic throughout the kingdom on the other. The paradigm of the Confucian ethic was found in the Family Ritual of Master Chu. This prescribed specific social norms and ways of family life relating to initiation into adulthood, marriage, funerary observances, and ancestor rites. By these practices, scholar-officials sought to curb the individualistic tendencies in Buddhism and emphasize the social nature of the Confucian ethic.

To achieve this goal, two primary innovations were required: the establishment of the family shrine and the observance of the three-year mourning period. These two were meant to replace Buddhist funerary rituals and shamanistic rites. The institution of these practices, it was believed, would enable Confucianism to overcome its historical disadvantage as a mere "art of governing" *(yusul)* and eventually become firmly rooted as the ruling ideology of the Yi dynasty.

The establishment of family shrines had already been proposed in the late Koryŏ dynasty by Chŏng Mongju, Cho Chun, and Yi Tam,[41] and at the beginning of the Yi dynasty others added their support to this advocacy in growing numbers. For instance, Pae Kŭngnyŏm (1325–92) and Cho Chun, both Dynastic Foundation Merit Subjects, petitioned the king for the establishment of family shrines in 1392;[42] Min Yuŭi, the magistrate of Ikchu county, did the same in 1395;[43] and Yi Chi (?–1414), as inspector-general, repeated the request in 1401.[44] Moreover, in the *Kyŏngje yukchŏn*, the new dynasty's first attempt to codify its laws (completed in Taejo's reign), it was stipulated that all households, including those of the privileged class and of the common people alike, had a duty to establish family shrines. In 1403, examinations were begun on the *Family Ritual of Master Chu* as a basis for recruiting officials in the seventh and lower grades.[45] However, even after three years had passed, very few people had established a family shrine and inferably the situation improved little during the next two decades. Consequently, in the second month of 1427, the Board of Rites *(Yejo)* decreed that officials above the second degree in rank must establish a family shrine before year's end, those of sixth rank and above by 1430, and those below the sixth rank by 1433. Those who failed to do this were to be punished.[46] Nevertheless, the nationwide establishment of family shrines was not realized as quickly as might have been expected.

The three-year period of mourning was decreed in 1391,[47] even before the new dynasty was founded, but this also required a long time before it became widely observed. Once family shrines and observance of the three-year mourning period had become more or less established, scholar-officials endeavored to have such Confucian texts as the *Elementary Learning (Hsiao-hsüeh/Sohak)* and the *Practical Realization of the Three Bonds (San-kang hsing-shih/Samgang haengsil)* read widely among the common people, and also instituted a system of rewards to those who exemplified ideal Confucian conduct.[48] For example, in 1434 the government awarded honors to men of loyalty, men of filial piety, and virtuous women.[49]

We have seen the historical process by which Neo-Confucianism was introduced and adopted as the principal ideology of the Yi dynasty. In the process of establishing Neo-Confucianism as the dominant ideology, its proponents did not simply suppress Buddhism, Taoism, and shamanism. Instead, they achieved their goal in part through techniques of negotiation and compromise with the traditional religous practices.

III. THE NEO-CONFUCIAN INFLUENCE ON THE EDUCATIONAL SYSTEM

From the beginning of the Koryŏ dynasty there had been state educational institutions such as the National Academy (*Kukchagam or Kukhak*), and regional schools (*hyanggyo*). However there were deficiencies in the education available in the state schools in this period. One reason was that Confucianism was still overshadowed by Buddhism, another that the government was unable adequately to support a state system of education, which was entirely dependent on governmental aid. Instead of supporting state schools which were costly to maintain, the government simply relied on the examination system, which cost little to administer, as a means to recruit new officials. Thirdly, private schools were springing up in which the youth of the nobility were trained for the examinations.[50]

In the early Koryŏ dynasty, state education had been forced to expand, in spite of the enormous expense, in order to produce a new official class within the central government. As the kingdom achieved stability and the new power-holders themselves became an aristocratic class, government support of public education was reduced and the aristocratic class came to depend on the private schools for the education of their own children. Thus the state was no longer dependent on its own school system, since it could now recruit, through the examination system, as many officials as it needed from among those aristocrats trained in the private schools. In fact, private schools became exclusive academies for aristocratic youth and those trained in these academies were able to monopolize the examinations. By the middle of the Koryŏ dynasty twelve private schools, the *sahak sibido*, had developed and come to dominate national education.

The twelve private schools were founded by retired high officials and accepted only the youth of aristocratic families as students. The lecturers were those who had already passed the examinations. Every young aristocrat who intended to sit for the examination was expected to enroll in a private school.[51] The twelve private schools all adhered to a strictly exclusivistic policy, permitting no student to transfer from one academy to another. This policy was enforced by a government decreee that any student who transferred would forfeit his right to take the examination.[52]

As state schools declined and private schools thrived, the *kujae saksi,* an examination conducted at the twelve private schools, came to replace the examination at the Royal College, formerly the National Academy, by which candidates hitherto had qualified to take the final civil service examination (in 1317).[53] Furthermore, in 1352, Yi Saek proposed to make the twelve private schools the intermediate educational institutes between the local state schools and the Royal College.[54]

The exclusiveness of the private schools and the protégé relationship of disciple to master (*chwaju munsaengje,* the system of close ties between the examiner and the examinee) were two elements which prevented those outside the capital aristocracy from advancing into the higher governmental offices. Therefore, in the late Koryŏ dynasty, the class of newly rising scholar-officials felt a need to encourage state schools and oppose the private academies in order to extend the power of their own class. Consequently, in 1261, the Eastern and Western District Schools (*Tongbu, Sŏbu haktang*) were opened, and in 1304 a Confucian shrine (*Taesŏngjŏn*) was newly constructed within the Royal College and the *Sŏmhakchŏn,* a scholarship foundation, was created for the revitalization of the College.[55] The movement to reinvigorate the state schools was accelerated by King Kongmin's vigorous exercise of his sovereign power. In 1367, the Royal College was rebuilt, and classes in the Four Books and Five Classics were inaugurated. To further encourage the development of state schools such newly emerged scholar-officials as Yi Saek, Chŏng Mongju, and Pak Ŭijung were allowed to give lectures at the Royal College while simultaneously holding government offices. In addition, in order to encourage education at the local level, the construction of local schools was included as one of the seven duties of the local magistrates.[56] Finally, in 1391, the twelve private schools were closed.[57] The full revitalization of the state education system, however, could be fully realized only through the effort of the new Chosŏn dynasty.

At the beginning of the Yi dynasty, a strong program of state school construction and support were undertaken in order to disseminate Neo-

Confucian doctrine and produce a new generation of officials trained in Neo-Confucianism. Such a policy was exemplified by King T'aejo's (r. 1392–98) coronation edict, which decreed that the Royal College was to be constructed in the new capital at Seoul and the local schools on the county level.[58] In 1398, the Chosŏn's Royal College was built in ninety-eight *kan* in Hanyang (Seoul), the new capital,[59] and local state schools were established in each county.[60] In 1406 it was decreed that the construction of the local school was one of the seven duties which the magistrate of each county must fulfill, and that the degree of fulfillment of this duty would be a major criterion for evaluation of a magistrate's overall performance.[61] In 1412, in the capital, the Southern District School was constructed, in 1422, the Central District School, in 1435, the Western District School, and in 1438, the Eastern District School.[62] Thus the state education system, which consisted of the Royal College and the four district schools in the capital *(sabu haktang)*, and a local school in each county, was completed.

It is noteworthy that in the early Yi dynasty the four district schools in the capital and the local schools very largely made use of the physical facilities of the recently abolished twelve private schools and the Buddhist temples. In fact, when the private schools were abolished in 1391, they were absorbed into the state school system.[63] The sites of the Buddhist temples also were used in the new state school system. For instance, the Anhŭng temple was closed and rebuilt as the public school of Ich'ŏn county *(Ich'ŏn hyanggyo)* and Huam temple was rebuilt as the public school of Anŭm county *(Anŭm hyanggyo)*.[64] In the capital, at first, the premises of still existing temples were used for schools. For example, the Eastern District School was opened at Sunch'ŏn temple and used its facilities, and the Western District School those of the Mirŭk temple. However, because of the Confucian students' frequent violence towards the Buddhist monks, and their vandalism of the temple facilities, at one point the four capital district schools were closed and Yi Kyŏk, a teacher of Confucianism at the Eastern District School, was punished.[65] Furthermore, in the early period of the Yi dynasty there were many cases where the land and slaves once belonging to the abolished temples were turned over directly to the capital district schools and local schools. This happened in 1406, on the occasion of a massive reduction in the number of Buddhist temples,[66] and again in 1424 at the time of another large-scale disestablishment of Buddhist temples, when thirty of the confiscated slaves were

distributed to the Eastern and Western District Schools.[67] In addition, in
1411, all slaves that had belonged to the twelve private schools were bestowed on the state schools.[68] The property of the aristocratic private schools
of the late Koryŏ dynasty also was transferred to the state schools. By the
reign of King Sŏngjong (r. 1469–94), then, students in state schools had
increased to 15,550, while the land bestowed on the public schools
amounted to many thousand kyŏl and the number of their slaves also
reached many thousand.

In the course of establishing the state education system, a school for
the heir apparent (Wŏnja hakkung)[69] and a School for the Royal Clan
(Chonghak)[70] were created in the early Yi dynasty, in 1402 and 1428 respectively. The former was a special school for the education of the king's
eldest son during the years prior to his formal designation as crown prince,
while the latter was a school for the youth of the royal family. King T'aejong intended to educate his eldest son, Prince Yangnyŏng, under the
tutelage of a venerable monk at a remote mountain, in accordance with
the old Koryŏ tradition. However, the scholar-officials strongly asserted
that the prince should be educated in Neo-Confucianism together with
the children of scholar-officials at the Royal College.[71] The establishment
of the School for the Royal Clan was for the purpose of inculcating children of the royal family with a Neo-Confucian point of view and way of
thinking as taught by specially designated scholar-officials. Why then was
the School for the Royal Clan established independent of the state schools
in which the children of the yangban—the civil and military nobility—
were enrolled? It had a twofold purpose: it was to preserve the distinction
between the royal family and the yangban class, and it was to reinforce
the prohibition against members of the royal family occupying official posts
in the government. Young men of the yangban, after their education at
the Royal College, could take the state examinations and be appointed to
official posts, but those of the royal family, after their education at the
School for the Royal Clan, were not so privileged.[72] This restriction reflected the desire of the scholar-officials to keep in check the power of the
royal family.

The age of enrollment in the public schools was based on the prescription of Chu Hsi which appeared in the preface of the Words and
Phrases from the Great Learning (Ta-hsüeh chang-chü). Namely, at the
age of eight every male child except those of the base class (ch'ŏnmin)
would be enrolled in one of the state's elementary schools. At the age of

fifteen a student who had demonstrated exceptional promise and who passed a qualifying examination could enter the Royal College.[73] The *chaphak*, the schools for technical specialists in foreign languages, statute law, medicine, astronomy, geomancy, and accounting also were state institutions.[74] However, there was at this time no state facility for the training of military men. This was because the scholar-officials then in power more highly valued civil attainments.

The instructors at the state schools in the capital were appointed primarily from among those who had passed the civil examination (*munkwa*).[75] The instructors at the Royal Clan School and the four capital district schools held their primary teaching appointments at the Royal College, a system of dual appointment designed to maintain uniform quality of instruction.[76] In principle, instructors at the local schools also were to be appointed from among those who had passed the civil examination.[77] However, those who succeeded in passing this difficult examination did not wish to be instructors at the rural schools. Accordingly, those who passed the civil examination were sent down only to the more urbanized provincial centers (those designated administratively as *chu* and *pu*). For counties of more than five hundred households the government dispatched an instructor who had taken but not yet passed the examination.[78] To districts of smaller population the government appointed volunteer instructors, called *hakchang*, who received no salary but were allowed exemption from military duty.[79]

At the same time, every student in the state schools was exempt from military duty, since the students were regarded as a cadet corps from which future governmental officials would be selected. And despite the lower quality of education at the local schools, their enrollments increased markedly, primarily because of the military exemption student status carried.

The texts used in the state schools fell into four groups: (1) Confucian texts such as the *Elementary Learning*, the *Classic of Filial Piety*, the *Four Books: Great Learning (Ta-hsüeh/Taehak)*, the *Analects (Lun-yü/Nonŏ)*, *Mencius (Meng Tzu/Maengja)*, *Doctrine of the Mean (Chung-yung/Chungyong)*; the *Five Classics*: the *Book of Odes (Shih-ching/Sigyŏng)*, the *Book of Documents (Shu-ching/Sŏgyŏng)*, the *Book of Changes (Chou-i* or *I-ching / Chuyŏk* or *Yŏkkyŏng)*, the *Book of Rites (Li-chi/Yegi)*, the *Spring and Autumn Annals (Ch'un-ch'iu/Ch'unch'u)*; the *Family Ritual of Master Chu*, *Reflections on Things at Hand (Chin-ssu lu/Kŭnsarok)*, and the *Great Compendium on Human Nature and Principle (Hsing-li ta-ch'üan/Sŏngni taejŏn)*; (2) texts concerning history such as *The General Mirror for Aid in Government (Tzu-chih t'ung-chien/Chach'i t'onggam)*, the *Tso Commentary (Tso-chüan/Chwajŏn)*, *Essentials of Sung and Yüan History (Sung Yüan chieh-yao/Song Wŏn chŏryo)* and the *Summary History (Shih-lüeh/Saryak)*; (3) texts concerning literature such as the *Genuine Treasures of the Old Writing (Ku-wen chen-pao/Komun chinbo)*, the *Anthology (Wen-hsüan/Munsŏn)*, *Writing of the Eight Masters of the T'ang and Sung Dynasties (T'ang Sung pa-chia-wen/Tang Song p'algamun)* and the *Anthology of Korean Literature (Tongmunsŏn)*; and (4) other texts taught occasionally, such as the *Great Statutes for the Governance of the State*, the *Correct Rhymes for Korean Pronunciations (Tongguk chŏngun)*, the *Thousand Character Classic (Ch'ien-tzu-wen/Ch'ŏnjamun)* and the *Practical Realization of the Three Bonds*. However, the most important texts among the above were the *Elementary Learning*, *Four Books* and *Five Classics*, and *Great Compendium on Human Nature and Principle*.

The *Elementary Learning* was an introduction to basic education compiled under the direction of Chu Hsi, presenting Confucian ethical norms as they appeared in the classics and histories. It was of fundamental importance in the primary education of the capital district schools and local schools. One could not begin the study of the classics unless he had first mastered the *Elementary Learning* and one could apply to take the preliminary *(sokwa* or *samasi)* examinations only after successfully passing a qualifying examination on two primary texts, the *Elementary Learning* and *Family Ritual of Master Chu.*[80] The *Elementary Learning* had been emphasized by Hsü Heng, a prominent Neo-Confucian of the Yüan dynasty, and by Kwŏn Kŭn (1352–1409), a major Neo-Confucian scholar-official in the reign of King T'aejong.[81] And when regulations governing the state schools, including the Royal College, were drawn up and promulgated in 1439,[82] they were based on the principles expounded in the *Elementary Learning*. These were a synthesis of the five moral relations *(oryun)*, the five moral virtues, the regulations of the Academy of the White Deer Hollow (Po-lu-tung shu-yüan, the school created by Chu Hsi), and Hsü Heng's commentary on the *Elementary Learning*. The text next in importance was the *Classic of Filial Piety*,[83] a primer for the moral conduct of family relationships on the basis of Confucian principles. From the reign of King Sŏngjong, however, the *Practical Realization of the Three*

Bonds, a simplified text introducing Confucian ethics to women and people of the lower classes, was added to the list of basic readings.[84]

Since the *Elementary Learning, Classic of Filial Piety*, and *Practical Realization of the Three Bonds* were so widely read and used in the schools, the government had to make copies of these texts available in large quantities. To accomplish this, in 1425 one hundred copies of the *Elementary Learning, Collected and Completed (Chi-cheng Hsiao-hsüeh / Chipsŏng Sohak)* were brought from the Ming dynasty;[85] in 1429, the government printed and distributed 250 copies of the *Classic of Filial Piety*;[86] in 1441, it distributed 200 copies of the *Straightforward Explanation of the Elementary Learning (Chih-chieh Hsiao-hsüeh / Chikhae Sohak)* to local schools;[87] and in 1471, it bestowed a copy of the *Practical Realization of the Three Bonds* on each local school.[88]

A student who finished these texts was then supposed to read the Four Books and Five Classics, the *Great Compendium on Human Nature and Principle*, and Chu Hsi's *Reflections on Things at Hand*. The Four Books and Five Classics, however, constituted the basic subject matter for both the state education system and the official examinations, and since the Four Books included Chu Hsi's commentaries, they were regarded as particularly important. In this way, unlike the Koryŏ period when various forms of prose and poetic composition were highly valued, during the Yi dynasty the study of scriptural texts, especially the Four Books, was much esteemed. Most scholar-officials believed that one could not write good poetic prose without a knowledge of the classics. Furthermore, it was felt that the Four Books and Five Classics should only be read as interpreted by the Neo-Confucians of the Sung dynasty and that any interpretation of the texts or any position on Confucian philosophy which differed from those of the Sung dynasty should be discarded along with the writings of the philosophers of the hundred schools. Consequently, Neo-Confucian texts such as the *Great Compendium on Human Nature and Principle, Reflections on Things at Hand*, the *Heart Classic (Hsin-ching / Simgyŏng)* of Chen Te-hsiu, and *Great Compendium of Chu Hsi*, and others also had to be studied.

Because the Four Books, Five Classics, and the *Great Compendium on Human Nature and Principle* were so important in the state education system, copies were brought from China and then reprinted for distribution in Korea. For instance, in 1419 the government received 229 copies of the Four Books and Five Classics (1403 edition) from the Emperor

Yung-lo (r. 1403–24) of the Ming dynasty.[89] In 1426, it also received 120 copies of the *Great Compendia of the Four Books and Five Classics (Ssu-shu wu-ching ta-ch'üan)* from the Ming dynasty.[90] In 1427, the texts of the Yung-lo version of the Four Books, Five Classics, and the *Great Compendium on Human Nature and Principle* were then distributed to the governors of Kyŏngsang, Chŏlla, and Kangwŏn provinces to enable them to share the work of engraving the woodblocks necessary to reprint the texts. The woodblocks were then sent to a government facility for printing.[91] This agency printed the texts and distributed copies of the texts to the state schools, also printing copies for individuals who supplied their own paper.[92] Besides the Yung-lo version, there were older woodblock versions of the Four Books and Five Classics circulating widely, and copies of these older versions had been distributed to the Royal College, the four district schools, and the local schools before 1427.[93] Moreover, such works as the *Reflections on Things at Hand, Basic Structure and Selected Details of the General Mirror (T'ung-chien kang-mu / T'onggam kangmok), Records of the Grand Historian (Shih-chi/Sagi), History of the Former Han Dynasty (Han-shu/Hansŏ)* and *Correct Rhymes for Korean Pronunciations* were printed by metal movable type and copies widely distributed to the state schools and *yangban* officials on many occasions.[94]

In this period many other new works also were imported from China. The government sent envoys to China several times a year, and each time they asked the emperor for the gift of whatever new books had appeared at that time. Or they purchased newly published works themselves. For instance, in 1425 envoys bought one hundred copies of the *Elementary Learning, Collected and Completed*;[95] in 1435, they were given texts including the *General Mirror for Aid in Government with Commentaries of Hu San-hsing (Hu San-hsing chu Tzu-chih t'ung-chien)* by the Chinese emperor;[96] and in 1454 they were given the *History of the Sung Dynasty (Sung-shih/Songsa)*.[97]

The central government also ordered provincial governors to prepare woodblock editions of important texts. For instance, in 1425, the Kyŏngsang governor, Ha Yŏn (1376–1453), printed the Four Books and Five Classics[98] and in 1428 the governor of Kyŏngsang Province, Yi Sŭngjik, printed fifty copies of the *Great Compendium on Human Nature and Principle* for the government in Seoul.[99]

However, in the early Yi dynasty most books were printed with metal type at the government's printing bureau, which was founded in 1403.[100]

*

King T'aejong was so concerned with the difficulty of obtaining sufficient copies of textbooks that he used his private funds for this purpose.[101] A decade earlier, however, at the very end of the Koryŏ dynasty, a National Office for Book Publication (Sŏjŏgwŏn) had been established while metal movable type had been in some use since 1234.[102] However, movable metal type came into large-scale use from 1403, the cyclical year of kyemi, and the font cast at that time was called kyemija.[103] After the kyemija, the technique of casting type developed rapidly. Several castings were made in the ensuing decades: in 1420, the kyŏngja was made; in 1434, the kabinja; in 1452, the imsinja; in 1455, the ŭrhaeja; in 1484, the kapchinja; and in 1493, the kyech'ukcha.[104] Thus, with the development of this printing technology many books were published, including textbooks for the state schools.[105] The development of printing techniques constituted the driving force behind the blossoming of Korean culture during the fifteenth century, and it may also be viewed as a monument to the century-long cultivation of Neo-Confucianism by scholar-officials of the late Koryŏ dynasty.[106]

Thus, in the early Yi dynasty the government concentrated its efforts on developing the state schools, and this was an integral aspect of the scholar-officials' efforts to create a Confucian society. Their efforts succeeded to a considerable degree, but by the time the new dynasty's institutional structure achieved a semblance of completion in the late fifteenth century, the yangban elite already were in the process of making themselves into a new elite class, and as such they set about securing a number of special privileges for their sons in regard to matriculation at the state schools in the capital. For example, these youth were able to enter the Royal College without taking any kind of qualifying examination, or they registered as students at the Royal College while at the same time being on active military duty.[107]

The government also began utilizing the mechanisms of the examination system to select talent for state service in preference to relying on state education. As a result, state schools began to decline. This decline in turn discouraged able officials from taking positions as instructors in the state schools. Hence, an instructorship at one of the local schools came to be regarded as a position for a degraded official.[108] Thus, as the youth of the yangban class came to enroll in decreasing numbers, the students in the state schools were more and more non-yangban youth wishing to avoid military duty. The government too, in fact, from the beginning had encouraged not only state schools but also private schools. A clear example of this is the plan for revitalizing education devised by Kwŏn Kŭn and adopted in 1407, in which it was stipulated that private schools were to be protected and fostered.[109] From the sixteenth century, private schools such as academies (sŏwŏn) and study halls (sŏdang) began to thrive and to replace the state schools as the principal medium of education for the youth of the privileged class. These private schools became centers of Neo-Confucian instruction, where the philosophical doctrines of the Neo-Confucian school were taught. In other words, whereas the central concerns of Neo-Confucianism in the fourteenth and fifteenth centuries had been political and ethical, in the sixteenth century the emphasis shifted to academic and philosophical issues.

IV. THE INFLUENCE OF NEO-CONFUCIANISM ON THE EXAMINATION SYSTEM

In 958, a Chinese-style civil service recruitment examination was first administered in Korea.[110] During the Koryŏ dynasty the official examinations consisted of two courses: the civil examination (munkwa) and the specialist examination (chapkwa), there being no military examination (mukwa). Much more than the study of Chinese classical texts, the Koryŏ civil examinations emphasized mastery of literary skills—the ability to compose standard Chinese prose and poetical forms. Furthermore, the examination system during this period had a strongly aristocratic flavor, as has been observed above. Eventually, in fact, the protégé system that developed in the twelve private schools, which dominated education for the civil examinations, ensured that the examination would be monopolized by aristocratic youths in the capital. The Koryŏ examiner was called "examination master" (chwaju, or ŭnmun), and his student who passed the examination was called "disciple" (munsaeng), names expressive of the concept that the latter was a protégé of the former. The master and disciple were bound together in a relationship as close as that of father and son.[111] Consequently, the system became a key factor in the formation of academic cliques and political factions. This factious element of the system was criticized by Sin Ton (?–1371) who noted that Yi Che-hyŏn's disciples were placed everywhere from the capital to the remote provinces and their mutual ties of loyalty allowed them to determine their own policies.[112]

This exclusivistic nature of the Koryŏ examination system constituted an obstacle to the participation of a new class in national politics. Nevertheless, the infusion of new blood into national politics could not be completely blocked since the examination system itself was predicated on open access. Furthermore, during the period of military rule (1170–1258), large numbers of scholar-officials trained in practical politics, instead of factious aristocrats, were appointed to office. In the course of the ensuing century of Yüan domination, the old order of the Koryŏ regime in large part was destroyed and new power groups developed rapidly. Meanwhile, the adoption of new agricultural technology from Kiangnan Province in China increased agricultural production, and this strengthened the position of the rural landlords for entrance into national politics.[113] In the early fourteenth century, then, these groups slowly consolidated their political power vis-à-vis the aristocrats and the Buddhist temples.

A century earlier, in response to Yeh-lü Ch'u-ts'ai's proposal in 1237, the Yüan dynasty had conducted one round of examinations in China, but discontinued them thereafter until 1314, when they were permanently reestablished.[114] The major texts for the examination at this point were the *Collected Commentaries of Chu Hsi on the Four Books (Chu Tzu chi-chu)*.[115] As soon as the examinations were resumed in 1314, the Yüan dispatched an envoy to inform the Koryŏ government of the reinstitution of the examination system.[116] In the same year, the Central Secretariat of the Yüan sent Koryŏ a guidebook on the examinations, detailing its regulations and procedures.[117] Koryŏ then sent a high official, Kwŏn Han'gong, to congratulate the Yüan dynasty on its conduct of examinations in the sixth month of the same year.[118] In 1315, Koryŏ's civil examination was altered to allow it to serve as a kind of provincial examination (qualifying examination) of the Yüan empire, and three men among the thirty-three who passed the Koryŏ examination were allowed to take the metropolitan examination *(hui-shih)* in the Yüan capital.[119] From then on, the Koryŏ dynasty sent three men from among those who passed the official examination to the Yüan to take the special examination for non-Chinese *(chih-k'o)*. Those who passed this examination were An Chin (1318), Ch'oe Hae (1321), An Ch'uk (1324), Yi Kok (1333), Yi Inbok (1342), An Po (1344), An Chijung (1349), and Yi Saek (1354).[120] Also, in adopting the examination system of the Yüan, including its curriculum, the Koryŏ dynasty came to use Neo-Confucian books such as the *Elementary Learning* and the Four Books and Five Classics.[121]

When King Kongmin came to the throne in 1351 the Yüan empire was in a state of decline. He therefore instituted policies aimed at expelling the pro-Yüan forces in the government and recovering Koryŏ territories taken by the Yüan. In need of a new power group which would support his program, he appointed an unknown monk, Sin Ton, to a specially created and all-powerful post, curbed the old aristocratic factions, and reformed the examination system to enable him to recruit new scholar-officials on a large scale. From 1365, for instance, for the sake of fairness and impartiality examinees were not allowed to take books into the place of examination and scribes made a copy of each examination paper so that the examiners would be unable to recognize the handwriting of the examinee.[122] And in 1369, he adopted the Yüan triple-tier system consisting of a provincial examination *(hsiang-shih/hyangsi)*, a metropolitan examination *(hui-shih/hoesi)*, and a palace examination *(tien-shih / chŏnsi)* the significance of which would be reenforced by its being conducted by the king.[123] It was at this point, in 1370, that Ming held its first examination, informing Koryŏ of this fact and of the procedures that were followed, to which Koryŏ was expected to adhere.[124] It is not surprising that in the Ming examination Neo-Confucian texts were much used, the Four Books and Five Classics were emphasized, and the triple-tier examination system was maintained.

Due to these changes in the structure and procedures of the Koryŏ examination system, many new scholar-officials entered national politics. Obviously, then, King Kongmin's policies were threatening to the entrenched capital aristocracy, who eventually had him killed. As a result, the triple-tier examination system was abandoned in the reign of King U, to be restored only when Yi Sŏnggye and his fellow scholar-officials grasped political power in 1388.[125] This examination structure then became a permanent institution in the Yi dynasty.

Several features of the Koryŏ examination system thus had been changed in consequence of or subsequent to the introduction of Neo-Confucianism in the late Koryŏ dynasty. However, due to strong opposition from the entrenched aristocrats, the complete reformation of the examination system was delayed until the Yi dynasty. As soon as King T'aejo was crowned, he issued an edict declaring that (1) the government examinations would consist of both civil and military examinations; (2) the protégé system of master and disciple would be abolished; (3) the civil examination, which could test the candidates in the classics, would be conducted in three stages. The first would be administered by the Royal College and the second and the third by the Board of Rites. A list of thirty-three successful candidates would be sent to the Board of Personnel *(Ijo)* which would appoint them according to each candidate's talents. The military examination would test knowledge of the seven military texts and skills in archery and riding. It would be administered by the Military Training Administration *(Hullyŏnwŏn)* and a list of twenty-eight success-ful candidates would be sent to the Board of War *(Pyŏngjo)*; and (4) the qualifying examination that emphasized composition (called *Kukchagam si)* was to be discarded.[126] In the Koryŏ period, the military examination had been administered for twenty-four years from 1109 to 1133,[127] but it was soon abandoned because of strong opposition from the civil offi-cials.[128] In 1390, an effort to revive the military examination was at-tempted, but was not immediately carried out.[129] Thus it is reasonable to state that the inclusion of military examinations as part of the government service examination system effectively dates only from the Yi dynasty.

In regard to the abolition of the master-disciple system, once again a Koryŏ institution resisted immediate change. It was only in 1413 that a decisive step proposed by the Office of the Inspector-General *(Sahŏnbu)* ended this practice.[130]

Under the influence of Neo-Confucianism in the Yi dynasty, the preliminary examination for the literary licentiate degree *(chinsa si)* ini-tially was omitted from the examination structure. King T'aejo's corona-tion edict had so decreed, but in spite of objections from the Board of Rites, it was conducted once again in 1392.[131] In the twelfth month of 1393, then, the literary examination finally was discontinued, leaving the examination for the classics licentiate degree *(saengwŏn si)* as the only preliminary examination course.[132] Consequently, it was necessary to draw up regulations for the classics examination in great detail.[133] Because of its strong backing, however, the literary licentiate examination was re-vived in 1435,[134] to be again abolished in 1437[135] and once more revived in 1452.[136] Thereafter it remained a permanent institution.

The difficulties encountered by the literary licentiate examination during the early Yi dynasty stemmed from the attitude of the Neo-Con-fucians, who emphasized the study of canonical texts. This attitude led to frequent quarrels in the Royal College where older members who had passed the literary licentiate examination were given seats less prestigious than younger members who had passed the classics licentiate examination.[137] Another indication of the higher esteem in which learning in the classics was held is that applicants for the classics licentiate examination were required to take a screening test *(hangnyegang)* on the *Elementary Learning* and the *Family Ritual of Master Chu.*[138] Its purpose was to ensure the selection of students well-trained in Neo-Confucianism for places at the Royal College and future appointments to official positions.

The Neo-Confucian desire to emphasize the study of Chinese classical texts also was strongly imprinted on the content of the higher civil service examination. This examination normally was conducted in three stages: the first or provincial stage tested knowledge of the Four Books and Five Classics; the second or metropolitan stage tested skill in the composition of three literary genres—the prose-poem *(pu)*, memorials to Chinese emperors *(p'yomun)*, or communications expressing gratitude to Korean kings *(chŏn)*; and the third or palace stage tested the already successful candidate's ability to devise solutions to political problems *(ch'aengmun).*[139] Written tests were proper for the evaluation of literary skills (second stage) and of a candidate's ability to address himself to policy issues (third stage). However, written tests were not deemed adequate for the examination in the classics, because in a written examination a student with skill in composition but a limited knowledge of the classics might do well, while one having a profound knowledge of the classics but lacking skill in composition could not display his knowledge properly. Consequently, an oral test, in addition to a written test, was often required for the examination on the classics (first stage).[140] The written test was called "composition" *(chesul)* and the oral test "discussion of the classics" *(kanggyŏng).* In the Koryŏ dynasty the examination in literary composition *(chesul ŏp)* had required only a written test of knowledge of the classics, and the examination on the classics *(myŏnggyŏng ŏp)* consisted only of an oral test. However, in the Yi dynasty there were long discussions over which type of test should be given at the first stage in the civil examination. If the oral test came first, it would favor those who could recite the classics from memory and possessed a profound knowledge of them. If the written came first, it would favor those having skill in composition. The former criteria usually favored the newly emerging scholar-official class from the rural areas, the latter the sons of central government officials.

Furthermore, the oral and written tests each had its merits and drawbacks as a testing mechanism. Objections to the oral test included the following:

1. The oral test could not be conducted impartially, but rather was susceptible to personal influence.
2. Only vague grading criteria could be applied to an oral test.
3. The use of an oral test hampered the recruitment of men of letters.
4. The oral test took too long, removing applicants from their homes in the farming season.

Claims favoring the oral test included the following:

1. The use of written tests encouraged applicants to study only model answer sheets and so limited the scope of their study.
2. A thorough study of the classics was a prerequisite to good composition.
3. Study of the classics was the foundation of Confucianism, while the study of literature was merely a corollary.
4. Since the examination was an important national event, it should not be subject to restrictions as to time.

The lines of battle in the above controversy were drawn at the beginning of the Yi dynasty. King T'aejo's coronation edict, which reflected Chŏng Tojŏn's view, had placed the oral test at the first stage in the civil examination. However, in the first civil examination conducted by the Yi dynasty, in 1393, the written test was given the first position.[141] This was because the practice of using the written test had existed for five centuries, throughout the Koryŏ dynasty, and could not be abandoned all at once. But in the second examination, conducted in 1395, the oral test was given the first position.[142] At this time, the *munkwa ch'ojang kang-gyŏngpŏp*, a "law placing the oral test at the beginning of the civil examination," was promulgated in the *Six Canons of Law (Kyŏngje yuk-chŏn)*. Yet, in 1407, Kwŏn Kŭn again claimed the right to place the written test ahead of the oral test at the first stage of the examination. He insisted that the conduct of the oral test constituted a handicap for able men of letters.[143] From that time forward, the written test increased in popularity. Thus, the antagonism between the pro-oral test and pro-written test camps continued, and alterations of examination policy were made many times.[144] However, since Neo-Confucianism fundamentally valued knowledge of canonical texts over literary skills, those favoring oral tests gained ground as time went on. Accordingly, after 1453 the practice of placing the oral test at the first stage was legislated and this statute was included in the *Great Statutes for the Governance of the State*, the basic administrative code of the dynasty.[145]

The confrontation between the pro-oral test and pro-written test groups eventually produced a compromise called the System of Nine Courses *(kujaean)*. According to this plan, nine courses in the Four Books and Five Classics were instituted at the Royal College, and each student was to take all nine courses, but the written test was to be administered at the first stage of the civil examination. In 1465, the Board of Rites formulated the regulations governing the nine courses, and in 1467 King Sejo established the nine courses at the Royal College. However, in order to make this plan effective, it would have been necessary to integrate the system of state education and the examination system. Since, however, the two systems were not organized in such a way as to make this possible during the Yi dynasty, the administration of the nine courses was hardly effective.

After the reign of King Sejo, rural scholars who had training in the philosophical studies of Neo-Confucianism began to enter national politics and to step into governmental posts in large numbers. This was due to King Sŏngjong's extraordinary policy of appointing new groups of able men in order to reinforce his own authority. In this connection, the king established the examination in the classics, which opened the way for scholars to pass the civil examinations by taking only the oral test.[146] As a result, a new group of Confucians entered the government. They formed a power group which opposed the old power group of King Sejo's meritorious subjects, the *hun'gu p'a*. The new power group was called the *sarim p'a*.

Thus, the confrontation between the pro-oral test and the pro-written test groups developed into political antagonism between the group from the state schools, the *hun'gu p'a*, and the group from the private schools, the *sarim p'a*. It was this antagonism which resulted in the purges of scholars which occurred four times in the early sixteenth century. From that time on, the difference in opinion on this issue among Neo-Confucian scholar-officials intensified political factionalism.

V. CONCLUSION

In considering the influence of Neo-Confucianism on the state education and examination systems it has been observed that newly rising scholar-officials of the late Koryŏ and early Yi dynasties adopted Neo-Confucianism as an ideological weapon in their confrontation with the entrenched aristocracy and the Buddhist establishment. In Koryŏ, however, the opportunity to receive an education and to take the civil service examination was available predominantly to aristocratic youth through the twelve private schools and the master-disciple system. Therefore, the emerging class of scholar-officials tended to favor state schools over private ones and to seek to reform the examination system in order to insure continued access to office for their own youth.

The policy of fostering education at state schools in the early Yi dynasty was a definite factor in the successful establishment of Confucian culture. As the dynasty grew in strength and stability, however, the government began to neglect the system of state education. So long as the system was needed to educate new officials who would support the ideology of the new dynasty, the government supported it; but after the stability of the dynasty became assured in the late fifteenth century, state schools began to suffer from neglect. This led to the decline of the state schools and the rise of private schools. Local academies (sŏwŏn) and study halls (sŏdang) sprang up and spread rapidly from the mid-sixteenth century. The academies became not only educational institutions but also sanctuaries where the local patriarchs of the Confucian scholar community were sanctified and venerated. Furthermore, the government bestowed funds, including land and slaves, on each academy and waived the taxes due on the lands that supported their activities. Thus, the private academies came to receive the privileges and status formerly enjoyed by the Buddhist temples in the Koryŏ dynasty.

The examination system was also reorganized in the early Yi dynasty. At the outset, King T'aejo abolished the most baneful feature of the Koryŏ examination system, the all-important role of the master-disciple relationship, and also instituted a military examination. Moreover, under the influence of Neo-Confucianism, the government for a time discontinued the literary licentiate examination and administered instead only the saengwŏn examination, which tested knowledge of the classical texts, while the higher civil service examination was modified to give added emphasis to the classics.

The civil examination of the early Yi dynasty was conducted in three stages: the first tested knowledge of the classics, the second covered various forms of literary composition, and the third combined textual understanding with composition skill in an essay examination on a government policy topic. Putting the classics test first in the civil examination meant that primary weight was given to study of the Chinese classics, and this innovation was accomplished only after intense controversy. At the root of this dispute was the question of whether knowledge of the classics should be tested in an oral or a written examination. An oral test was widely believed to favor candidates from rural areas, and its adoption in the reign of King Sŏngjong was a major factor in the emergence of a new political force, the *sarim*—scholar-officials from the rural area. Before long, the *sarim* and the *hun'gu*, the old power elite, came into sharp confrontation. The four purges of scholar-officials which occurred between 1498 and 1545 were caused in large measure by this struggle.

The Neo-Confucian orthodoxy of the early Yi dynasty accomplished several positive ends. It reorganized the social order and governmental system, and stabilized the new dynasty's foundation. The cultural accomplishments of the fifteenth century stemmed directly from these sociopolitical reformations. From the sixteenth century onward, however, Neo-Confucianism became a dogmatic system of thought, and its rigidities contributed much to the endemic factional disputes that plagued the dynasty throughout its later centuries.

NOTES

1. *Koryŏsa* (Seoul: Asea munwhasa, 1972), 93:19a.
2. The term *Wihwa-do hoegun* refers to the return to the capital in 1388 of General Yi Sŏnggye and his forces from Wihwa-do, an island in the middle reaches of the Yalu, and his subsequent expulsion of Ch'oe Yŏng and seizure of political power.
3. Wm. Theodore de Bary, "The Rise of Neo-Confucian Orthodoxy in Yüan China," *Tōyōshi kenkyū* (1979), 37:4:1–2.
4. *Yüan-shih* (Peking: Chung-hua shu-chü, 1976), 8:4313.
5. de Bary, "Neo-Confucian Orthodoxy."
6. Yun Yonggyun, *Shushigaku no denrai to sono eikyō ni tsuite* (On the Transmission of the Chu Hsi Learning and its Influence) (Seoul, 1933), p. 21.
7. *Koryŏsa*, 106:2a–b.
8. Yun Yonggyun came to the conclusion that it was Paek Ijŏng, not An Hyang, who first transmitted Neo-Confucianism to Korea. However, this conclusion was based on inadequate evidence. See Yun Yonggyun, *Shushigaku.*
9. *Koryŏsa*, 105:30a.
10. They were shipwrecked, and Yu Yŏn alone survived. He made his way to Nanking where he met Hong Yak, a military official. Hong gave Yu Yŏn Yüan currency with which to purchase books. *Ibid.*, 34:20a–b. [Editors' note: Here and in what follows the Korean name *Sŏnggyun'gwan* is translated as Royal College, and the term *kukhak* as National Academy. Most often they refer to the same institution. "Royal" is used here to represent the ruling house (kingdom) of Korea in contrast to the Chinese Empire and its Imperial University (*t'ai-hsüeh*) at the Chinese capital. In the late Koryŏ and early Yi dynasties there were successive changes in nomenclature for the principal educational institution at the capital, the details of which are not gone into here.]
11. *Chŭngbo munhŏn pigo* (Seoul: Tongguk munwhasa, 1957), 202:12b.
12. *Ibid.*
13. *Koryŏsa*, 107:15a.
14. *Ibid.*, 109:21a.
15. *Ibid.*, 110:21b.
16. *Ibid.*, 115:10b–11a; 74:32b.
17. *Ibid.*, 117:16–2a.
18. *Ibid.*
19. *Ibid.*, 115:96.
20. *Ibid.*, 112:30b; 112:31b; 121:21a–b.
21. *Ibid.*, 117:19b.
22. *Ibid.*, 118:23b.
23. Martina Deuchler, "Neo-Confucianism: The Impulse for Social Action in Early Yi Korea," *Journal of Korean Studies* (1980), 2:73.
24. *Koryŏsa*, 115:7b–8a.

25. *Ibid.*, 113:34b–35a.
26. *Ibid.*, 119:15a–b.
27. Yun Yonggyun, *Shushigaku*, p. 56.
28. *Koryŏsa*, 120:32a–b.
29. *Ibid.*
30. Chŏng Tojŏn, *Sambongjip* (Seoul: Kuksa p'yŏnch'an wiwŏnhoe, 1951), *Pulssi chappyŏn*, 9:254–79; *Simgi ip'yŏn*, 10:280–94.
31. Han Ugŭn, "Yŏmal Sŏnch'o ŭi pulgyo chŏngch'aek" (Policy Toward Buddhism in Late Koryŏ and Early Chosŏn Korea), *Inmun, sahoe kwahak p'yŏn* (Seoul, 1957), 6:23.
32. Han Woo-keun, "Sejong-jo e issŏsŏ ŭi tae pulgyo sich'aek" (Policy toward Buddhism in the Reign of King Sejong), *Chindan hakpo* (1964) 25:98.
33. See notes 31 and 32.
34. *T'aejo sillok*, in *Chosŏn wangjo sillok* (Seoul: Kuksa p'yŏnch'an wiwŏnhoe, 1955–1958), 2:11a.
35. *Ibid.*, 2:4a–b.
36. *T'aejong sillok*, 11:27a–b.
37. Han Woo-keun, "Chosŏn wangjo ch'ogi e issŏsŏ ŭi yugyo yulli ŭi silch'ŏn kwa sinang chonggyo" (Relationship Between the Practice of Confucian Ethics and Traditional Religious Rituals in the Early Yi Dynasty) in *Han'guk saron* (1976), 2:166.
38. *T'aejo sillok*, 3:2a–b.
39. *T'aejong sillok*, 22:10b.
40. Han Woo-keun, "Yugyo yulli," p. 183.
41. When King Kongyang was crowned, Yi Tam, the rector of the Royal College, urged that Buddhism and shamanistic rituals be completely prohibited and that each household establish a family shrine. Anyone who violated this would be executed. Cf. *Koryŏsa*, 117:35a–b.
42. *T'aejo sillok*, 2:6a.
43. *Ibid.*, 8:17b.
44. *T'aejong sillok*, 2:22a–b.
45. *Ibid.*, 5:27b.
46. *Sejong sillok*, 35:14b.
47. *Koryŏsa*, 64:28b.
48. *Sŏngjong sillok*, 10:37b; 69:14b.
49. Yun Yonggyun, *Shushigaku*, p. 137.
50. Yi Sŏngmu, "Han'guk ŭi kwagŏje wa kŭ t'ŭksŏng" (The Characteristics of the Korean Government Service Examination System) in *Kwagŏ* (Seoul: Il-chogak, 1981), p. 120.
51. *Koryŏsa*, 74:34a–b.
52. *Ibid.*, 74:35a.
53. *Ibid.*, 74:21a.
54. *Ibid.*, 74:32a–b.
55. *Ibid.*, 74:31b.
56. *Ibid.*, 74:33a–b.

57. *Ibid.*, 74:35b.
58. *T'aejo sillok*, 1:45b.
59. Yang Taeyŏn, ed., *T'aehakchi* (Seoul, 1950), pp. 2–5.
60. Yi Sŏngmu, "Chosŏn ch'ogi ŭi hyanggo" (The County Schools in the Early Yi Dynasty) in *Yi Sangok paksa hoegap nonmunjip* (Seoul, 1969), p. 237.
61. *T'aejong sillok*, 1:37b.
62. Yi Kwangnin, "Sŏnch'o ŭi sabu haktang" (The Four District Schools in Early Yi Korea) in *Yoksa hakpo* (1961), 16:38. In 1390 it was announced that the Western and Eastern District Schools were to be augmented by three new schools, but one of them, the Northern District School, was never constructed. Thus four schools were established in the new capital in the early Yi dynasty.
63. *T'aejong sillok*, 22:12b.
64. Yi Sŏngmu, "Hanggyo," p. 238.
65. *Chŏngjong sillok*, 5:11a–b.
66. *T'aejong sillok*, 12:8b. Each *hyanggyo*, according to the size of the county in which it was situated, was given an allotment of land varying from 12 to 58 *kyŏl*. The total amount of land thus bestowed came to 5,000 *kyŏl*. Slaves were also given to the *hyanggyo*, the number again being determined by the size of the county. The numbers of slaves given ranged from 15 to 50 and the total number of slaves given numbered 6,700.
67. *Sejong sillok*, 24:13b.
68. *T'aejong sillok*, 22:12b.
69. *Ibid.*, 3:26a.
70. *Sejong sillok*, 4:3b.
71. *T'aejong sillok*, 2:8a–b.
72. Royal family members were treated simply as members of the *yangban* class from the fifth generation of descent from a monarch, but the ban against their sitting for the examinations and serving in the government remained in effect until that time. Because of this restriction, the School for the Royal Clan was beset by the problem of nonattendance. See JaHyun Kim Haboush, "The Education of the Yi Crown Prince," in this volume.
73. Yi Sŏngmu, "Sŏnch'o ŭi Sŏnggyun'gwan yŏn'gu (The Royal College in the Early Yi Dynasty) in *Yŏksa hakpo* (1967), 35/36:254–58.
74. Yi Sŏngmu, "Chosŏn ch'ogi ŭi jisulgwan kwa kŭ chiwi" (Technical Specialists and their Status in the Early Yi Dynasty) in *Yu Hongyŏl paksa hwagap kinyŏm nonch'ong* (Seoul, 1971), p. 197.
75. In a process called *pun'gwan*, those who passed the civil examination were assigned to the Sŏnggyun'gwan, Kyosŏgwan, or Sŭngmunwŏn (or Hongmun'gwan), in accordance with their performance on the examination and their attributes of character.
76. Yi Sŏngmu, "Sŏnggyun'gwan," pp. 249–54.
77. *T'aejong sillok*, 27:38a–b.
78. *Sejong sillok*, 6:3b.
79. *Ibid.*, 2:32a–b.

80. Yi Sŏngmu, "Sŏnggyun'gwan," pp. 258–59. Also see Song Chunho, *Yijo saengwŏn chinsasi ŭi yŏn'gu* (A Study of Saengwŏn and Chinsa Examinations in the Yi Dynasty) (Seoul: Kukhoe tosŏgwan, 1970), p. 31.

81. *T'aejong sillok,* 13:14b.

82. *Sejong sillok,* 86:42a.

83. *Ibid.,* 43:26b.

84. *Ibid.,* 69:18b–19a.

85. *Ibid.,* 30:27b.

86. *Ibid.,* 43:26b.

87. *Ibid.,* 94:6a.

88. *Sŏngjong sillok,* 9:37a.

89. *Sejong sillok,* 6:10a–b.

90. *Ibid.,* 34:10b.

91. Kim Tujong, *Han'guk koinswae kisulsa* (A History of Early Printing Technology in Korea) (Seoul, 1974), p. 142.

92. *Sejong sillok,* 43:22a.

93. Kim Tujong, *Han'guk,* p. 142.

94. *Ibid.,* p. 138.

95. *Sejong sillok,* 30:27b.

96. *Ibid.,* 69:18.

97. *Tanjong sillok,* 12:10b.

98. *Sejong sillok,* 30:8a.

99. *Ibid.,* 40:8b.

100. *T'aejong sillok,* 5:7a.

101. *Ibid.*

102. Kim Tujong, *Han'guk,* p. 134.

103. *T'aejong sillok,* 24:17b.

104. Kim Tujong, *Han'guk,* pp. 131-83.

105. *Ibid.*

106. The operations of the printing bureau were expanded and affiliated with the Kyosŏgwan, and its operations were begun in 1424. *Sejong sillok,* 24:14b.

107. Yi Sŏngmu, "Sŏnggyun'gwan," pp. 200–56.

108. Yi Sŏngmu, "Hyanggyo," p. 254.

109. *T'aejong sillok,* 13:14b.

110. *Koryŏsa,* 73:2a.

111. *Ibid.,* 73:2b–3a.

112. *Koryŏsa chŏryo* (Seoul: Asea munhwasa, 1972), 28:32a–b.

113. Yi T'aejin, "Sipsao segi nongŏp kisul ŭi paltal kwa sinhŭng sajok" (Emerging Scholar-Officials and the Development of Agricultural Technology in Fourteenth- and Fifteenth-Century Korea), *Tongyanghak* (1979), 9:344.

114. *Yüan-shih,* 4:2017.

115. *Ibid.,* 4:2019.

116. *Koryŏsa,* 34:17b.

117. *Ibid.,* 34:19b.

118. *Ibid.,* 34:20b.

119. *Koryŏsa choryo*, 24:5b.
120. *Koryŏsa*, 74:7b–8a.
121. *Ibid.*, 117:10b.
122. *Ibid.*, 73:11b.
123. *Ibid.*, 73:11b.
124. *Ibid.*, 42:10b–14a. Some of those who passed the Koryŏ examination were allowed to take the Ming examination, although a quota was not prescribed as it had been in the Yüan (*ibid.*, 74:9a). Accordingly, several men who had passed the Koryŏ examination in the same year of 1370 (Yi Sungin, Pak Sil, Kwŏn Kŭn, Kim To and Yu Paegyu), took the Ming examination, but Kim To alone passed it (*ibid.*, 74:8a–b). After that, there were few Koreans who passed the Ming dynasty's examination. This was because the Yüan dynasty had viewed Koryŏ as a subordinate entity within its vast empire, and for newly qualified Koryŏ officials to take the Yüan examination constituted a powerful symbol of Koryŏ's political integration with Yüan. On the other hand, although the Koryŏ and Ming dynasties enjoyed close ties, Ming did not directly exercise suzerain power over Koryŏ as Yüan had. This situation continued into the Yi dynasty. The Yi dynasty maintained its subordinate relationship to Ming as a matter of diplomatic form, while actually exercising internal autonomy. For Koreans to take Ming examinations, then, lacked any purpose or meaning.
125. The *kwagŏ samch'ŭngpŏp*—the triple-tier examination system—was abolished in 1376 and revived in 1379. It was again abolished in 1386 and revived again in 1388. See *ibid.*
126. *T'aejo sillok*, 1:43b.
127. Yi Sŏngmu, "Kwagŏje," pp. 117–18.
128. *Koryŏsa*, 74:9b.
129. *T'aejong sillok*, 25:1b–2a.
130. *Ibid.*, 25:25b.
131. *T'aejo sillok*, 3:7b.
132. *Ibid.*, 8:15b.
133. *Ibid.*, 9:6a.
134. *Sejong sillok*, 68:36a–b.
135. *Ibid.*, 77:32a.
136. *Munjong sillok*, 12:30b.
137. *Sejong sillok*, 83:13a–b.
138. *Ibid.*, 31:10b–11a.
139. *T'aejong sillok*, 1:43b.
140. Cho Chwaho, "Kwagŏ kanggyŏnggo" (A Study of the Oral Test on the Classics in the Civil Service Examination) in *Cho Myŏnggi paksa hwagap kinyŏm nonch'ong* (Seoul, 1965), p. 121. There were two kinds of oral tests on the classics (*kanggyŏng*), the *kuŭi* and the *chŏpkyŏng*. The *kuŭi* in turn was administered in two ways: one as an open book exam in which the examinee answered questions using the text, the other without a text and requiring that the examinee answer questions sitting with his back to the exam-

iner. The *chŏpkyŏng* tested knowledge of the context of isolated excerpts from canonical texts. The *chŏpkyŏng* was also often administered as a written test. In this case it consisted of two parts, the *mugŭi* and the *kyŏngŭi*. The *mugŭi* was similar to the *kuŭi*, in that it was an open book exam in which the answer was written using the text. The *kyŏngŭi* involved writing an exposition of the content of a given text.

141. *Sejong sillok*, 40:6a–b.
142. *T'aejo sillok*, 8:15b.
143. *T'aejong sillok*, 13:13b.
144. The testing method had been changed to the *kanggyŏng* in 1417, then to the *chesul* in 1425, and then back to the *kanggyŏng* in 1442. Finally the *chesul* was reinstituted in 1450.
145. Cho Chwaho, "Kwagŏ kanggyŏnggo," p. 360.
146. *Sŏngjong sillok*, 93:3b.

JaHyun Kim Haboush

The Education
of the Yi Crown Prince:
A Study in
Confucian Pedagogy

INTRODUCTION

EARLY IN OSCAR WILDE'S play, *The Importance of Being Earnest*, this exchange occurs:

> JACK: You're quite perfect, Miss Fairfax.
> GWENDOLEN: Oh! I hope I am not that. It would leave no room for development, and I intend to develop in many directions.

Oscar Wilde was not a student of the Confucian monarchy, but this exchange nonetheless illustrates one of the central problems of the educational apparatus in the Yi court. The perfection of the monarch was the central aim of the Yi educational establishment, but it was the imperfectness of the monarchical mind which justified its continuing existence.

The two principal institutions devoted to education in the Yi court were the Crown Prince Tutorial Office (*Sŏyŏn* or *Seja sigangwŏn*) and the Royal Lecture (*Kyŏngyŏn*). Both were motivated by a belief that man was perfectible and impelled by a sense that the ruler, who should be a paradigm to all men and from whose mind and heart flowed the welfare and well-being of the nation, was after all a man and hence could not approach perfection without continuous striving and development.

The ruler's imperfection at issue here was not just the common garden variety of imperfection, so often platitudinously summoned as an explanation for human fallibility. This was imperfection at the apex of the system—a cause for urgent concern and a source of profound anxiety. It was impurity at the center which, if it was not constantly dealt with, worked upon, and ameliorated, might spread out to the whole of the social order.

What gave rise to this concern and anxiety was the concept central to Neo-Confucian political thought that rectification of the monarchical mind was the basis of good government. This view, which seemed to have been widely shared by the eleventh-century Neo-Confucians, was aptly summarized by Fan Tsu-yü (1041–98): "Order and disorder in the world all depend on the heart-and-mind of the ruler. If his heart-and-mind are correct, then the myriad affairs of the court will not be incorrect."[1] While this view is treated as self-evident wisdom by Fan, for Chu Hsi (1130–1200), a century later, the immediate need for rectification of the imperial mind became a pressing and urgent matter. Consider, for example, this passage from his celebrated memorial of 1188 to Emperor Hsiao-tsung (r. 1163–90):

None of these six points can be neglected, but they all have their root in Your Majesty's mind-and-heart . . . Therefore this root of empire is also the most urgent of all urgent needs and cannot be put off even for a little while.[2]

This memorial comes as no surprise from a man who had made the *Great Learning (Ta-hsüeh)*, a prescription for achieving monarchical perfection in eight steps, the central element of his theory of Confucian pedagogy.[3]

Given the inherently imperfect nature of government, the state of the imperial mind of course could never really be seen as fully satisfactory. But then, Neo-Confucians believed in man's perfectibility. The sage kings of antiquity were the model for perfection in the ruler and the prescriptions of the *Great Learning* theoretically showed how to achieve this perfection. Since everything depended on the rectification of his mind, the ruler was burdened with the duty of emulating the sage kings and seeking perfection. This perfection, however, was not a state which could be attained definitively or permanently. It was an elusive goal to be pursued with ceaseless study and self-examination. The institution of the Royal Lecture or Classics Mat Lecture was designed to assist the ruler in this process. Neo-Confucian scholars, with their understanding of the classics and their duty to counsel the sovereign, emerged as his teachers.

In China, where it originated, the Classics Mat Lecture was, in some form, practiced sporadically from the Han to T'ang but it prospered and flourished under Neo-Confucianism.[4] From the eleventh century on, Neo-

Confucian scholars paid a great deal of attention to the learning of the emperors *(ti-hsüeh)* and this focus played an important role in the development of Neo-Confucian orthodoxy.[5] In Korea, the evolution of the Royal Lecture also paralleled a deepening commitment to Neo-Confucianism. Unfolding interpretations of Confucianism and the resulting changes in attitude were reflected in the form and content of the lecture sessions.

The Royal Lecture was first instituted in 1116 by King Yejong (1079–1122, r. 1105–22) of the Koryŏ dynasty (918–1392), and his son Injong (1109–46, r. 1123–46) continued the practice. The adoption of the Royal Lecture, however, was more a recognition of Confucian scholarship than an acceptance of Confucian ideology. Yejong and Injong, for instance, continued to patronize Buddhism and geomancy, and this did not change until the end of the Koryŏ.[6] Yejong's and Injong's curriculum consisted mainly of the Five Confucian Classics other than the *Spring and Autumn Annals (Ch'un-ch'iu)*. The *Great Learning* and the *Doctrine of the Mean (Chung-yung)* were presumably studied but as part of the *Book of Rites (Li-chi)*. Yejong also studied *Lao Tzu* and Injong some Sung historical works.[7] After Injong's death, the Royal Lecture was discontinued for two centuries until it was revived in the mid-fourteenth century with the ascendance of Neo-Confucianism. The Four Books were now included in the curriculum. Toward the end of the Koryŏ dynasty, officials of high rank were added to the instructional staff and censors and historians were permitted to attend the lecture sessions.[8]

When the Yi dynasty (1392–1910) was founded, the Royal Lecture retained essentially the same structure and Neo-Confucian orientation, but some time elapsed before the practice was reviewed and systematized. This lapse occurred mainly because of the political turmoil associated with the consolidation of dynastic power. With the adoption of Neo-Confucianism as state orthodoxy and the emergence of Neo-Confucian ideologues as the new ruling group, the early kings who were committed to the enhancement of the monarchical power seem to have viewed attending the Royal Lecture as a capitulation to the bureaucratic power. T'aejong (1367–1422, r. 1400–18), the third Yi king, who, among the Yi kings, was the first to rule long enough and with sufficient determination, seems to have held this view. It took his son Sejong (1397–1450, r. 1418–50), supremely confident of his administrative ability but equally devoted to Confucian scholarship, to patronize the Royal Lecture. During his reign, the Royal Lecture remained purely an academic pursuit. His son Munjong's (1414–52, r. 1450–52) brief reign saw the beginning of its politicization. Senior officials and censors attended the lecture sessions at regular intervals and policies were discussed. This practice was reversed by Sejo (1417–68, r. 1455–68), another champion of monarchical authority, who, soon after accession, ceased attending the Royal Lecture. During Sŏngjong's (1457–94, r. 1469–94) reign, the trend toward politicization accelerated. Every morning session was attended by several high officials and censors in addition to the lecturers. The Royal Lecture was no longer simply an institution which assisted royal scholarship; it now functioned as a forum for the reconciliation of principle and practice. Contemporary affairs were discussed and analyzed in light of the classics and policies were formulated.[9] During King Yŏnsan's (1476–1506, r. 1494–1506) reign, the Royal Lecture suffered another setback, but his successor Chungjong (1488–1544, r. 1506–44) restored it in full with all of its attendant political functions. The Royal Lecture continued, despite minor setbacks, essentially unchanged for the duration of the dynasty. In this sense, it was yet another forum in which the king and his officials, as representatives of opposing forces in the monarchical system, engaged in ritualized confrontation and debate. And the protocols were shaped by the ideological *raison d'être* of the institution—that it was a means through which the Confucian vision of society might be realized.

Just as the Royal Lecture was focused upon the state of the monarch's mind, efforts devoted to the mind of the future monarch were in no way spared. Confucians believed that rectification of the mind could be achieved only through a continuous and uninterrupted process of development. It is quite logical that they should have attempted to initiate this process through a carefully designed program of childhood education. The curriculum of the Royal Lecture as a rule began where the education of the Crown Prince ended.[10] In this sense, the education of the Crown Prince must be seen as the initiation of a life-long continuum of Confucian pedagogy whose ultimate purpose was the maintenance of as nearly perfect a state as possible in the mind of the monarch.

Like the bureaucratic structures related to the Royal Lecture the apparatus for the education of the Crown Prince was established in the first month of the Yi dynasty, and its evolution was subjected to many of the same forces that shaped the Royal Lecture. Still these forces were expressed in a different manner and in several crucial ways the education of the Crown Prince conformed to its own distinct pattern. First of all, while the Royal Lecture was based upon a bilateral relationship, the educational process for the Crown Prince was based on a trilateral relationship—in addition to the Crown Prince and his tutors, the king, often his father, played an important role in educating the heir. This added another layer of complexity. Obviously, the king's understanding of his own position, his relationship to his bureaucrats, his assessment of them, and his opinions and those of the tutors all contributed to the changing shape of the educational effort directed at the heir. The rivalry between monarchical and bureaucratic powers, however, had to be expressed differently in the education of the Crown Prince. One may assume that the monarch and the bureaucrats had different images of the ideal ruler. The king would have preferred an heir who would achieve his virtue mainly through competence and ability, while the bureaucrats, seeking a ruler ideal from the point of view of a bureaucratic operative, would seek an heir who sought virtue through consultation. Yet even those kings who were most concerned with monarchical power had to acknowledge the need to educate the heir. They could not abolish the educational apparatus for the Crown Prince as they cancelled the Royal Lecture. This meant that Crown Princes were all subjected to a Confucian education.

Furthermore, as is often the case with education of the young, the Crown Prince played a passive though essential role in formulating educational policies concerning him. Since the educational apparatus for the Crown Prince, like the Royal Lecture, was an institution whose entire function was addressed to one individual, it had to be reshaped, to a degree, in response to his character. He, however, had very little to say about the reshaping; this was done by others. The king appointed the tutors and between them they decided what and when to study. They also attempted to supervise other activities in his life. In fact he had no voice in determining the public aspect of his life, neither in the choice of his place of residence, the choice of his spouse and attendants, the choice of his clothing nor in the design of his schedule and curriculum of study.

The education of the Crown Prince began when he was a small child and it often continued into his maturity, depending on his age at accession. The examination of the Crown Prince's education offers opportunities to study Confucian pedagogy at work in the Yi court. I will first discuss the educational theory on which this education was based. Then

I will discuss its institutional evolution, curriculum, and pedagogy as well as the prince's daily life. Lastly, I will examine the performance of several Crown Princes who completed such an education.

EDUCATIONAL THEORY

Education, in its normative use, is a process for improving a man. An educational theory, especially a general theory which gives a comprehensive prescription for pedagogy, begins with an assumption about an educated man—that a certain kind of individual is what the education is to produce.[11] A properly educated man is usually conceived of as someone who has developed his intellectual abilities, attained a measure of emotional maturity, is aware of his actions and sensitive to the needs of others and his own responsibilities to society. He is someone possessed of an integrated knowledge, one in whom judgment and action cohere with this state of knowledge. This general picture of an educated man takes concrete shape within the specific social and political conditions of the time and society. Moreover, in ascribing certain characteristics to an educated man, a theorist unmistakably reveals his own values.

In the Neo-Confucian context, an ideal educated man was a moral man—a sage. He possessed moral knowledge and he practiced it in his actions. He cultivated humanity, righteousness, propriety, and wisdom, qualities similar to what Hume called "the sentiment of humanity," and he acted in accord with the rules of proper social behavior—expressing affection between parent and child, maintaining righteousness between ruler and minister, keeping the distinction between husband and wife, respecting the order of precedence between the elder and the younger and showing trust among friends.

In the Yi Crown Prince's education, this idea of an educated man was very much at work. Inasmuch as the object of the education was the future ruler, however, the ideally educated Crown Prince should also possess the attributes of a good king. Different political theorists of course had different ideas of what these attributes were. Chŏng Tojŏn (1342–98), for instance, who regarded the ministers as the mainstay of government, would delegate most of the responsibilities of rule to them while relegating to the ruler chiefly the duty of taking their counsel.[12] Yi Yulgok (1536–84) preferred a more activist king. Surely, the ruler needed virtuous ministers, without whose assistance good government was not possible.[13] But the ministers' role was to assist the king in governing and to guide him on the right path rather than to dominate him.[14] The king was to discern and select men of virtue as his ministers but ultimately it was his duty to maintain the welfare of his people by providing them with the means to earn an adequate livelihood and to protect them with reform.[15]

The qualities of an ideal ruler, however, were not seen as being distinct from those of a moral man. Rather they were a natural extension or a part of the condition of being a moral man. According to Yulgok: "The study of the Way is to make goodness clear through the investigation [of things] and the extension [of knowledge] and to cultivate one's self through sincerity [of thought] and rectification [of mind]. When [they are] contained in one's person, [they] become the virtue of Heaven and when [they are] carried out in government [they] become the Kingly Way."[16] The aim of the Yi Crown Prince's education was to cultivate just such a person, one who could contain virtue within himself and practice the Kingly Way.

In recommending certain pedagogical procedures, the theorist must proceed from his idea of how the recipient of this education will respond. This requires the theorist to make a second assumption to formulate an educational theory—his idea of human nature. Rousseau's idea of man as originally but not morally good or Locke's concept of man's mind as a *tabula rasa* were the points of departure for their respective educational theories. The Confucian concept of human nature is the subject of copious research and discussion and I will only mention the points pertinent to general educational theory. One of the first discussions of human nature is generally taken to be a statement from the *Doctrine of the Mean* traditionally attributed to Tzu-ssu (490–431 B.C.): "What Heaven (*T'ien*, Nature) imparts to man is called human nature. To follow our nature is called the Way (Tao). Cultivating the Way is called education."[17] This remark implies that man is originally good but the question of whether he is morally good is left unanswered. Mencius filled this gap with his famous idea of the Four Beginnings (*ssu-tuan/sadan*)—that the feeling of commiseration, the feeling of shame and dislike, the feeling of deference and compliance, and the feeling of right and wrong were inherent in man and that, in fact, these qualities were what made man man and were the beginnings respectively of humanity, righteousness, propriety, and wisdom, which were also contained in man.[18] Arguing from this essentially

optimistic postulate about human nature he inferred that a man would
be able to do good if he were left to his own natural inclinations,[19] thus
making man morally good as well.

The concept of man's nature was periodically revised by Sung Neo-
Confucians, particularly those of the Ch'eng-Chu school, ultimately integrating the concept of human nature into a universal cosmological
scheme. In this Confucian universe, principle was immanent in all things
but it could only be manifested through material force. Nature was seen
as principle and thus was devoid of any intrinsic dynamism. It required
material force for its expression.[20] What made a thing different from other
things was its material force. It followed that the moral quality of an entity was determined by the quality of its material force—whether it was
clear or turbid.[21]

This view posited by Ch'eng I (1033–1107) was further elaborated
by Chu Hsi. He introduced the concept of physical nature as opposed to
original nature to explain the moral phenomenon. For instance, man has
an original nature as well as a physical nature and only when he returns
to accord with his original nature does he act in accord with moral principle.[22] What determines the morality of human action is mind. Mind,
in Chu Hsi's view, is consciousness.[23] Through his mind man is cogni-
zant of his own self as well as of the external world. Moreover, this mind
contains an innate knowledge of moral law and has the cognitive capacity
to discern it. In its most developed state of full consciousness, mind can
comprehend everything in the universe with clarity.[24] The problem as he
defined it was that this capacity of mind can be prevented from functioning properly and consciousness might operate independent of moral law
when mind becomes clouded by selfish desire.[25] He used the concepts of
the human mind and the moral mind in explaining this phenomenon.
The human mind and the moral mind, however, were not ontologically
separate entities but rather descriptive terms referring to different states of
mind. The former referred to the state in which mind contained the seeds
of selfish desire and was prone to error while the latter referred to mind
rectified and consciously discerning moral law.[26] Chu Hsi never doubted
man's potential to achieve a moral mind. The question was not whether
man could do this but rather how he should do it. Chu Hsi rejected the
dualism of mind and body, seeing body as essentially ruled by mind.[27]
Hence, his affirmation of man's ability to achieve the moral mind was an

affirmation of his ability to act in accord with moral law. And education was seen as a process of initiating the development of the mind to its fullest consciousness.

While Chu Hsi saw education as a life-long process, the procedures he recommended seem to have been tailored to different stages of development. In childhood education, he stressed the role of adults and teachers in guiding and teaching the child. For him the issue was to nurture the goodness immanent in the child and to prevent it from being contaminated by impurity. At the earliest stages, he seems to have relied mainly on maintaining the right environment. It was of primary importance to provide the child with an environment in which he would be exposed only to good influences and shielded from evil influences and this should begin at the earliest possible moment. In fact, the regimen of prenatal care (t'ai-chiao/t'aegyo) made exacting demands on the expectant mother. She was expected to behave with the strictest decorum in the smallest minutiae of her conduct; she was not to think evil thoughts or to utter evil words; she was to recite poetry at night and to speak of proper things.[28] After the child was born, women who were generous, affectionate, kind, courteous, and careful in their speech were to be chosen to guide him.[29]

The right environment and a suitable paradigm were essential elements of Confucian education. Mencius' mother, who, according to the celebrated anecdote, moved three times before she settled near a school, was taken as the model for child rearing.[30] Even after one reached adulthood these factors, especially having a suitable paradigm, were regarded as important. Yet, exclusive reliance on these essentially passive aspects of education probably reflected an idea of the state of the child's mind. After all, in regard to its cognitive power to understand moral law the infant would be nearly totally undeveloped.

As the child grew, one stage at a time, he was taught to develop correct manners and basic intellectual abilities. Quoting from the Book of Rites, Chu Hsi illustrated the process. One was to instruct the child to use his right hand when he began to eat on his own and one was to teach the child the proper form of speech and dress according to sex. At the age of six,[31] he was to be taught numbers, directions, and the names of things. At seven, male and female children were no longer to be allowed to sit or eat together.[32] At eight, childhood education began formally through enrollment at an elementary school (hsiao-hsüeh).[33] The socialization of the child also accelerated. He was to be taught to concede to elders in passing through doors and at mealtimes. At nine, he was to be taught the numbers of the day, etc.[34]

What is noticeable in this progression in the instruction and socialization of the child endorsed by Chu Hsi is that behavioral training was emphasized. In fact, he opened a preface to the *Elementary Learning (Hsiao-hsüeh)* with this statement:

The elementary schools of ancient times taught manners of sprinkling and sweeping, and the ways of affection for parents, respect for elders, appreciation of teachers, and consideration for friends. It was because [they] regarded [these] as the foundation of self-cultivation, family regulation, the governance of the state and peace in the world. [They] made absolutely certain that instruction and practice [in these] would start in early years, so that while practicing, intelligence might develop, while changing, the mind might be formed and so there would be no problem of inability in overcoming obstacles.[35]

Chu Hsi seems to be suggesting that at this early age, the exercise of proper behavior would facilitate intellectual growth and that this was an effective means of developing the mind.

While behavioral development seems to have been stressed, the educational premise involved was not based on a mechanistic view of man.[36] That is, education was not regarded purely as a process of inculcating the values of the society by manipulating external behavior. Rather than viewing it as the imposition of social values on the child, Confucians viewed education as a development of what was already in the child. In fact heavy reliance on behavioral instruction in the early stages seems to have been devised in recognition of the internal state of the child rather than as a denial of it. After all, the intellectual abilities of the child at this stage were limited and the cognitive power of his mind to discern moral law was still undeveloped. At about ten years of age when the child had begun to learn reading and arithmetic, instruction in intellectual activities was accelerated, eventually becoming an equally important part of education.[37]

When the child reached about fifteen years of age, he was considered to have achieved adulthood. Now he entered college *(ta-hsüeh)* and Chu Hsi viewed the student as beginning his education as a scholar and ultimately a sage.[38] Chu Hsi believed that one could achieve this through continuous striving and moral cultivation. This was a subject that he was particularly concerned with. Unlike the *Elementary Learning*, which he compiled mainly of quotations from various books, he wrote copiously in his own words on the topic. His prescriptions were based on the premise that the student's mind was capable of reason and discernment and that he was equipped with basic intellectual abilities.

With this, Chu Hsi also shifted the emphasis in education from teaching to self-effort.[39] This transition was neither sudden nor final. In childhood education, the student was constantly exhorted to exert himself in order to understand and assimilate the teaching he received. Neither was it the case that Chu Hsi proposed that a fifteen-year-old youth should grope for truth completely on his own. In the Confucian tradition the teacher's role in transmitting the sage's teachings and in providing a paradigm for his students in his striving for moral perfection was particularly valued.[40] Surely, with his abilities reasonably developed, the student was now in a position to receive more meaningful instruction from his teacher. Thus, the assignment of a major role to the self in adult education was more a question of initiative and attitude. It was now he himself who should seek instruction from teachers and others as well and his progress depended on his effort. More importantly, this process was seen as unending. After all, the purpose of achieving full consciousness of mind was to be moral and this was a manner of living, not a project which could, after a certain span of time, be terminated. Moral cultivation that the student was to begin would continue long after any kind of formal education had ceased.

Chu Hsi's regimen for moral cultivation had as its point of departure Ch'eng I's dual dicta—seriousness in self-cultivation and the extension of knowledge as a basis for learning.[41] Seriousness and the extension of knowledge, which perhaps can be described as attitudinal and intellectual endeavors, were discussed separately but were seen as complementary processes in striving to be a moral man. That seriousness emerged as the central concept in Chu Hsi's moral cultivation, as Professor Wing-tsit Chan pointed out,[42] seems to have been an expression of concern for reflection as part of the process. The way to maintain seriousness was to be "correct in movement and appearance and to be orderly in thoughts and deliberations."[43] Seriousness was a state in which "the mind being its own master" was tranquil and the Principle of Nature would be perfectly clear.[44] If one were to succeed in preserving seriousness, then this would be born out in righteousness of action. But both seriousness and righteousness had to be reinforced through constant self-examination and reflection.[45]

If seriousness was seen as a way to achieve full consciousness of mind and morality of action through reflection, extension of knowledge was prescribed as a way to achieve the same goals through active enquiry. Unlike his discussion of seriousness, in which Chu Hsi seems to have regarded both mental and behavioral attitude as an inseparable unit, in this case he made a clear distinction between knowledge and action. In saying that "we must first know before we can act"[46] Chu Hsi was placing knowledge before action in sequential order.

As in the *Great Learning*, the investigation of things was seen as a necessary step in the extension of one's knowledge. And the first order of activity which Chu Hsi suggested in this process was the reading of books. He saw books as the repository of the sagacious wisdom of all ages, and so he placed a special emphasis on them.[47] As they contained moral principle, properly reading and understanding them would make principle clear to the student.[48] He states: "In learning, nothing takes precedence over the investigation of principle. The key to the investigation of principle certainly lies in reading books."[49] As might be expected, Chu Hsi's recommendation of how to read books was a mixture of method and attitude. He suggested reading a book with an empty mind free of preconceived notions, to be able to seek meaning therein. Encumbered by preconceived notions, no amount of reading would bear fruit—seeing everything through this barrier of prejudice, one would be unable to grasp the meaning contained in the book.[50] One should never hurry; one should be attentive to each word and phrase and return to it repeatedly until one penetrates and understands.[51] What was required to succeed in grasping each shade of meaning in the finest detail was seriousness and steadfast determination.[52] In addition to reading, he proposed that the student "discuss people and events of the past and present" and that he "handle affairs and settle them in the proper way."[53] They also offered opportunities for analysis and contemplation. The object of these activities was to develop one's understanding of "the reason for which things and affairs are as they are and the reason according to which they should be."[54]

Ultimately, the purpose of these activities was righteousness of action. On this Chu Hsi was very clear: "With respect to order, knowledge comes first, and with respect to importance, action is more important."[55] Chu Hsi's sequential priority of knowledge did not mean that he sanctioned delaying the student's exertions in daily behavior. This order was purely logical. He always maintained that knowledge and action reinforced each other and that they should develop, like two legs walking toward one destination, side by side.[56] If action required knowledge, knowledge which was not expressed in action was shallow and incomplete.[57]

It is clear that these endeavors, both attitudinal and intellectual, were intended to produce a man of integrated knowledge and moral action. Chu Hsi often warned the student lest he lose sight of the true aim of these activities. It was not enough to go through the motions of being serious even if he could always maintain this posture. This was a lifeless seriousness.[58] Nor was it satisfactory merely to read,, however widely, and to accumulate factual knowledge. This was pedantry.[59]

Chu Hsi does not seem to have made any meaningful distinction between moral cultivation and formal education, perhaps because he regarded the place of formal education as an appropriate setting for moral cultivation during a certain period of life. Considering how extensive the goal and procedures for moral cultivation were, this is not surprising. At any rate, his guidelines for the White Deer Hollow Academy (Po-lu-tung shu-yüan) were based on essentially the same concepts and procedures as his precepts for moral cultivation. At the beginning of the guidelines, the proper assimilation of the five relationships was set as a goal. Then he recommended five steps to achieve it—extensively study about them, rigorously scrutinize them, carefully reflect upon them, clearly discern them and faithfully carry them out. How they were to be faithfully carried out was by means of prescriptions for development in three areas:

Essentials for self-cultivation: Be loyal and trustworthy in one's word and faithful and serious in one's action. Restrain anger, check desire, do good and correct error.

Essentials for handling affairs: Affirm what is right, and do not seek mere profit. Clarify the [right] way and do not look for mere success.

Essentials for dealing with things: Do not do to others what one does not want done to oneself. When one's action does not attain [what it should], turn to oneself and seek [it] within oneself.[60]

Chu Hsi's theory of education seems to have been based on a belief in the rationality of the mind. Surely he acknowledged the existence of selfish desire which could obstruct perception of the moral law and lead to error in action. He saw continuous striving as necessary to guard against these threats. Despite his recognition of these corrupting forces, Chu Hsi seems to have implicitly assumed that since man had an innate knowledge of moral law, if his mind were properly developed, he would see the desirability of following moral law. In addition, the procedures prescribed for development were also based on an implicit assumption of the supremacy of rationality in the mind. Both preserving seriousness and the extension of knowledge required rationality of the mind. This was an optimistic view of man affirming his perfectibility. At the same time, this might lead to rather harsh judgments for those whose actions did not meet the expectations implied by this view.

By and large, Korean educational theories were variations of Chu Hsi's theory. Yi Koreans accepted both his idea of an educated man and the concept of human nature on which his theory was based, and they further accepted prescriptions for early and adult education. For instance, Chu Hsi's belief in the correlative link between behavioral and intellectual development in education was faithfully echoed in *Instructions to the Young (Kyemong)*, an educational manual written by the Korean scholar Pak Semu (1487–1564):

There is no evil in the nature with which a person is endowed in the beginning. The ways of affection for parents, respect for older brothers, loyalty to the ruler and deference to elders are all immanent in his mind. Therefore, one should not seek it from without, rather one should rely solely on industrious practice without interruption. If a person does not learn, it is difficult to know what constitutes filial piety, loyalty, respectfulness and truthfulness. For this reason, one must read books and investigate principles; one should seek guidance from the men of old and experience [it] in his own mind; one must acquire probity and energetically practice it. Then one's being filial, respectful, loyal and truthful would naturally correspond to the laws that Heaven sets forth.[61]

Nevertheless, within the framework of Chu Hsi's acknowledged supremacy, some modifications were inevitable. Yi T'oegye (1501–70), a seminal thinker of the Chu Hsi school, for instance, perhaps made seriousness a more central aspect of moral cultivation than even Chu Hsi had done.[62] While he did not deemphasize intellectual endeavors, the balance seems to have shifted more toward maintaining a serious attitude and correct behavior. His "Exhortations to Teachers and Students of the Four Academies" *(Yu sahak sasaengmun)* was entirely addressed to deviations from proper behavior and correct ritual that he had observed among the faculty and students at the four academies and the corrective measures he suggested were directed exclusively to these problems.[63]

This tendency to be particularly concerned with the student's attitude and behavior in daily life can also be found in the work of Yi Yulgok, a scholar whose stature among Korean Confucians was rivaled only by that of T'oegye. Deeply concerned with the need for systematization, he wrote a number of treatises on education, among them *Important Methods of Eliminating Ignorance (Kyŏngmong yogyŏl)* and *A Model for Schools (Hakkyo mobŏm)*. *Important Methods*, written in 1577, was meant for students of all ages. *A Model* was written in 1582 and it was commissioned by King Sŏnjo (1552–1608, r. 1567–1608). As the title suggests, *A Model for Schools* contains recommendations for the management of schools and academies but the greater part is devoted to instructions for students. Only in the later portion did he discuss practical measures such as the selection and financial remuneration of teachers, procedures for admission, expulsion and enrollment, student support, and procedures related to the civil service examinations.[64]

In both works, Yulgok began by prescribing resolution of will *(ipchi)* to study as the first step in the process of education. In this way he recognized the need for motivation in learning but the advice he offered was characteristic—man had original goodness in himself and so he needed only to seek it within himself. *Important Methods* then has nine more sections, each containing important prescriptions followed by methods and instructions for the student seeking to fulfill them. The contents of the nine sections are: (2) the elimination of bad habits such as vanity, frivolity, greed, etc.; (3) the proper attitude and manners; (4) methods of reading—what to read, in what order and how to read it; (5) how to serve one's parents; (6) behavior during funerals and the mourning period—the proper attitude, dress, manner, etc.; (7) rituals associated with the ancestral sacrifice—proper conduct on such occasions; (8) behavior within the family—proper conduct toward family members and servants, (9) proper behavior toward people generally; (10) proper conduct in society.[65] *A Model for Schools* was obviously addressed to students at the academies who were more educated and who would presumably become leaders of society. Consequently, in addition to most of the material in *Important Methods*, it discusses such topics as serving teachers, choosing friends, the kind of relationship one should maintain toward them, conduct at the dormitory, and more general ethical practices such as righteousness, loyalty, and seriousness.[66]

In general, both T'oegye's and Yulgok's writings suggest, at least in terms of the allocation of space, that they paid a great deal of attention to the behavioral and attitudinal aspects of education. In Yulgok's edu-

cational treatises, for instance, the only purely intellectual activity he
recommended was the reading of books. This apparent emphasis on behavior and attitude might be specific to Korean culture. Professors Tu
Wei-ming and Julia Ching point out, in their respective articles on T'oegye's and Yulgok's concepts on the Four Beginnings and Seven Emotions, that Koreans paid special attention to the role of emotion in the
learning process and in life. Interpreted in the context of education, this
may have found expression in concern with the experiential process of
learning.

Our concern here is to provide a certain theoretical framework with
which one can discuss the evolution and practices of the Yi Crown Prince's
education. Chu Hsi's theory of education was of course the basis, but it
was interpreted and applied by Koreans with the specific aim of producing a future king. In this sense, the censorial memorial concerning Prince
Yangnyŏng (1394–1462) presented to King T'aejong in 1405 is illumi-
nating. Since the memorial not only resulted in the adoption of important measures but also was an early statement of recurring themes in discussions of the prince's education throughout the dynasty, I shall present
it in full:

> The heir-apparent is the foundation of the nation and the state of order and
> disorder is linked to him. The goodness [of the heir-apparent] depends on early
> instruction and teaching as well as the [right] choice of those near [him]. This is
> why the Crown Princes of ancient times had Three Teachers and Three Guard-
> ians from the cradle. [They] resolutely made filial piety, benevolence, propriety,
> and righteousness clear [to him] and [they] made certain that he be practiced in
> the Way. Depraved men were expelled and eliminated from his presence and thus
> the Crown Prince did not see evil acts. This was accomplished by carefully choosing
> upright scholars who were filial and brotherly, broad in learning, and proficient
> in the classics and other arts, and having them live with and accompany the Crown
> Prince. Thereby the Crown Prince saw correct things, heard correct words, and
> behaved correctly. [While] practicing, his intelligence developed, and [while]
> changing, his mind was formed. This was the reason why the Three Dynasties
> lasted so long.
>
> As for our Crown Prince, his Heaven-endowed disposition is bright and pure
> and his learning improves daily. Yet, his teachers and mentors teach him only
> for a limited time and do not live with him or accompany him. Therefore, when
> the Crown Prince stays at his residence, he plays with eunuchs and attendants
> and does not exert himself in learning. In addition, because of their duties in
> office, the tutors cannot fully devote themselves to his instruction. Your servants
> secretly fear that there is nothing with which to cultivate and nourish [the prince]
> that he might attain brilliance.

We wish that Your Majesty would appoint more tutors and that the head tutor be relieved of the duties of office and made to attend [the prince] at his residence. Even during idle hours at his residence, let them always stay near [the prince]. Please also order that every day, two of them remain to exhort and advise [the prince] on everything in order to improve [his virtue]. As for attendants and eunuchs, please select ten honest and dutiful men and make them attend him by turns. As for the sycophantic and disreputable, please discern [their evil ways] and order their expulsion.[67]

The argument for more strict guidance in the memorial was based on familiar Neo-Confucian ideas and there are direct quotations from the *Elementary Learning*. The intense anxiety over the effects of evil and un-wholesome influences is striking. Chu Hsi was not unmindful of these issues and, considering Prince Yangnyŏng's age (twelve at the time), a request for careful guidance might not seem extraordinary. But anxiety over evil influences and this stress on incessant moral instruction were not limited to young princes, and both recurred as dominant themes in the Yi Crown Prince's education. To protect the prince from corrupting influences, the bureaucracy pressed further and further to isolate the heir in his educational environment at an ever earlier age. To insure that his moral development and behavioral training should progress appropriately, the court subjected the royal heir to ever more rigorous plans of study and programmed exercises of ceremonial activity.

INSTITUTIONAL EVOLUTION

In the beginning of the dynasty, there was a period of uncertainty concerning the young prince's education. This was a result of an unsettled atmosphere at court. The officials theoretically associated with the Crown Prince *(Seja kwansok)* in the bureaucracy of 1392 included two teachers *(chwau sa)*, two mentors *(chwau pin'gaek)*, six tutors *(chwau podŏk, chwau p'ilsŏn, chwau munhak)*, four perceptors *(chwau sagyŏng, chwau chŏngja)*, two attendants *(sijik)*, and four assistants *(sŏri)*.[68] In the same year, Yi T'aejo appointed his youngest son, Pangsŏk (1382–98), as heir-apparent but it was not until 1395 that two mentors were assigned to him.[69] Pangsŏk's tenure as Crown Prince was short lived. He was killed by his older half-brother Pangwŏn, T'aejo's fifth son, in 1398.

What was established from the beginning of the dynasty, however, was the practice of educating the Crown Prince in isolation apart from other royal children. This was not new to the Yi court. The Yi bureaucracy was, in large measure, based on that of the Koryŏ and the separate educational establishment of the Crown Prince had its precedent in the Koryŏ. This practice, which continued until the end of the Yi dynasty, was based on the assumption that since the Crown Prince was unique in his position, he had to be educated as such. This deeply influenced the nature of the education of the Crown Prince. It meant that he seldom enjoyed the companionship of other children of his age and was constantly the focus of the attention of the adults surrounding him. This must have played a significant role in his personality formation.

Yi Pangwŏn's coup, which led to Pangsŏk's death, also resulted in T''aejo's abdication to his second son, Panggwa, known as Chŏngjong (1357–1419, r. 1398–1400). In Chŏngjong's two-year reign, no activity was devoted to the education of the heir-apparent as Pangwŏn was appointed heir-apparent in 1400. He ascended the throne in the same year on Chŏngjong's abdication and retirement. Only after the dynastic line was established by Pangwŏn, known as T''aejong, did serious discussion concerning the education of his heir begin. Yangnyŏng, T''aejong's first Crown Prince, was the first instance of a lengthy educational effort devoted to the Crown Prince. As such, his education elaborates many of the themes that would emerge in the education of Crown Princes throughout the dynasty.

T''aejong was an eminently practical man and his idea of education was pragmatic rather than ideological. He wanted his heir well-spoken, well-read, and proficient in both literary and military arts. These were the attributes that he saw as useful in rulership. He was not overly concerned with who taught his son so long as they had the requisite skills. In 1401, when his oldest son Yangnyŏng was eight, he thought it appropriate that he begin his studies with Buddhist monks, following Koryŏ custom. When his close confidant and senior minister Pak Sŏngmyŏng (1370–1406) suggested the Royal College (Sŏnggyun'gwan) instead, he readily agreed. He must have seen the merit of Pak's implication that studying with monks had been practiced in the declining years of the Koryŏ because the academies had deteriorated. The monks could instruct only in petty versification, which had nothing to do with learning, and hence it would be better for the prince to enter the Royal College where he could participate in discussions with teachers and students. This would help to nurture his virtuous nature *(tŏksŏng)*. But rather than have his son stay at the dormitory like the other students, T'aejong ordered that a study hall *(hakkung)* be built for him to live in near the College, where the teachers could come to instruct him and students could attend his studies.

The bureaucracy viewed this arrangement with suspicion, believing it to be too informal and, in any case, unsuited to a future king. Censors in the Office of the Inspector-General *(Sahŏnbu)* soon submitted a memorial urging the swift appointment of Yangnyŏng as heir-apparent with separate teachers. Reminding the king that King Ch'eng of Chou had three teachers with separate roles, the memorial expounded upon the importance of guiding the prince to filial piety, humanity, ritual, decorum, and righteousness *(hyoin yeŭi)*, of expelling depraved persons from his sight, and preventing his exposure to evil acts. To this end, the prince should be educated within the palace precincts by teachers carefully chosen for their virtuous conduct *(tŏkhaeng)*.[70] This recommendation was, in time, put into practice, but T'aejong accepted it only slowly and incompletely.

The first concession T'aejong made was in 1402 when he formally appointed Yangnyŏng Primary Son *(wŏnja)* and selected six scholars to instruct him.[71] This precedent of formally designating the Primary Son was followed by later generations. Though T'aejong acquiesced to the argument that the future monarch required special education, he was not willing to isolate him completely from other students. Thus, when Pak Sŏngmyŏng, who had initially suggested the Royal College, now reversed his position arguing for study in the palace, T'aejong resisted it.[72] In the summer of 1402, the study hall was completed and in 1403 Yangnyŏng, now ten, entered the College. He performed a bowing ceremony at the Confucian Shrine *(Munmyo)* and presented cloth and dried meat *(soksu)* to two senior professors at the College signifying his student status.[73] But though Yangnyŏng's study was conducted at his study hall near the Royal College, the instructional staff seems to have included both professors from the College and other tutors, the latter holding other offices.

In addition, T'aejong selected a number of bodyguards from among the sons of the meritorious officials *(kongsin)* who had helped him to the throne. As a veteran of succession struggles, he apparently felt that it was important that the prince have a loyal coterie devoted to him personally and so he instructed his son to develop a close relationship to them. Bodyguards were to attend the prince at night while tutors were to limit their instruction to daylight hours. T'aejong seems to have made this arrangement out of concern that his son should, despite his position, have a balanced and normal life surrounded by boys of similar age. He also cautioned both tutors and bodyguards against excessive rigidity of schedule and overwork saying that, while adherence to regulations was a necessity in rearing children, it was harmful to bore them.[74] The bureaucracy, however, found this quite unsatisfactory. The Office of the Censor-General *(Saganwŏn)* submitted another memorial. Pointing out that the prince's becoming a sage *(chaksŏng)* depended upon correctness in daily guidance, it recommended the appointment of worthy teachers and elimination of corrupting influences such as eunuchs.[75]

Yangnyŏng's appointment as Crown Prince in 1404 brought some changes to his life. He now lived in the Crown Prince's residence, which was outside the palace. His instructional staff consisted of several layers of scholar-officials—teachers, mentors, and tutors.[76] The exact number cannot be ascertained but teachers and mentors were officials of high rank, and the tutors were all censors.

The turning point in arrangements for Yangnyŏng's life, however, came in 1405, when T'aejong accepted the suggestions made in the censorial memorial which I quoted in the previous section.[77] It is difficult to understand why T'aejong accepted this proposition. Confident of his hold on the bureaucracy and committed to the enhancement of monarchical power, T'aejong was not a king to be pressed into agreement by bureaucratic pressure. He must have thought that Yangnyŏng, now twelve, needed more supervision. At any rate, both the practice of attendance by full-time tutors and their night duty at the Crown Prince's residence began on this occasion at the Yi court, though they still did not enjoy as much access to the prince as they would have liked.

This change, however, had certain negative effects. Within months, Yangnyŏng's negligence in study emerged as a serious concern to the court. Kwŏn Kŭn (1352–1409), a respected scholar-official, serving as Yangnyŏng's mentor, went so far·as to discuss the dangers of illiteracy in the monarch which might lead to dynastic ruin.[78] T'aejong's various stratagems to correct the situation did not produce the desired effect. On the contrary, Yangnyŏng's dereliction in study was accompanied by other indiscretions which grew worse as the years went by. Finally, in 1418, in a dispute concerning his concubine, he openly defied his father.[79] This unfilial act, utterly unacceptable by the mores of the time and especially so for a future ruler, on top of other derelictions equally trying to the king and his officials, was the final blow. Yangnyŏng was judged to have lost his legitimacy[80] and so T'aejong deposed him and replaced him with his third son, Prince Ch'ungnyŏng. This unanimous choice was based on his perspicacity (hyŏn). Ch'ungnyŏng's intelligence and his delight in learning were qualities mentioned as indications of a capacity for rule.[81]

In the eighth month of 1418, two months after Ch'ungnyŏng's elevation, wishing to secure the new heir's position, T'aejong abdicated in his favor. The new king, known as Sejong, lived up to the expectations that had prompted his selection. Considered the most able king of the Yi dynasty, he was often referred to as the sage king of the Eastern Nation by scholars of later generations,[82] a truly rare distinction.

The next Crown Prince to experience a protracted tenure was Munjong, Sejong's first son and heir. Appointed Crown Prince in 1421 at the age of eight, he spent his next twenty-nine years in that position. Naturally, his life during this period was shaped largely by the atmosphere and the policies of the court over which his father presided. Unlike T'aejong, whose attitude toward education was rather straightforward and pragmatic, Sejong was deeply committed to learning. In addition to attending the royal lectures regularly himself,[83] he also expanded and strengthened the other educational apparatuses of the Yi court. He established the School for the Royal Clan (Chonghak). He further set a precedent in 1448 by appointing a Grand Heir (seson) along with the necessary educational establishment. Needless to say he actively oversaw his heir's education and devoted a huge effort to its improvement.

For his first ten years as Crown Prince, Munjong's instructional staff consisted of officials concurrently serving in office. Due to the only part-time attention which the staff was able to devote to his son's education, and the frequent changes in personnel, Sejong regarded this arrangement as inadequate. Thus, in 1431, he proposed that mentors and tutors devote their full time to the instruction of the Crown Prince and that their tenure be quite lengthy so that Munjong would feel comfortable with them. The proposals were accepted by the bureaucracy. Except for three teachers and two mentors, the remainder of the staff served exclusively in the Tutorial Office.[84] Four years later, the entire permanent staff of the Tutorial Office was granted membership in the Hall of Worthies (Chiphyŏnjŏn) and made a part of it.[85] This institution, which had been established in 1420 by Sejong, was an association of salaried scholars whose function had been to lecture to the king,[86] to engage in joint scholarly projects,[87] and to pursue independent study. At its inception in 1420, there were six honorary members and ten regular members.[88] In 1426, six more regular members were added. In 1435, the regular membership doubled in number. In addition to the Crown Prince's instructional staff, who totaled ten in number, six members were added to serve at the Royal Lecture, bringing the total to thirty-two.[89] In the following year, the number of scholars at the Hall was reduced to twenty and the Crown Prince's instructional staff now was drawn partly from the Hall and partly from other offices.[90] In 1438, all ten of them were again members of the Hall of Worthies,[91] and this arrangement lasted until Munjong's reign.

Under Sejong, many ceremonies and rituals were established, and those concerning the Crown Prince were no exception. The first such ceremony was devised when Munjong entered the Royal College in 1421. The Crown Prince's entrance to the College was a ceremonial act symbolizing his initiation into study. There were two ceremonies that he was required to perform—the Ceremony of Entrance _(iphak ŭi)_ and the Ceremony of Presenting Dried Meat _(soksu ŭi)_. The first was a ritual libation at the Confucian shrine, an affirmation of reverence to the sages and scholars of old. The latter was a ritual request for instruction from the professors of the College. The Crown Prince was not to be taught by them, but this was the ritual formalizing his student status. According to the plan formulated by the Board of Rites _(Yejo)_, the Crown Prince initiated the ceremony by sending a messenger requesting instruction from the professors. The professors were to refuse twice, pleading incompetence. Requested a third time, they were to reply that they could not disobey. They were to greet the Crown Prince, and the Crown Prince was to enter the gate of the College and bow twice, whereupon they too were to bow twice.[92] Very late in 1421, Munjong, clothed in a student robe, performed these ceremonies.[93]

After 1431, Munjong, now eighteen, was expected to participate in many court ceremonies. He was to assist in the ceremonial reception of the royal clan, his attendants, and the bureaucracy in separate groups on the New Year and at the winter solstice. Accordingly, elaborate rituals were worked out by the Board of Rites prescribing the position of each participant, the kind of bow, and the moment it was to be made.[94] On this occasion, the Board of Rites also devised details of the ceremony in which the Crown Prince and his teachers and mentors greeted each other _(sabu pin'gaek sanggyŏn ŭi)_.[95] Interestingly, in the former, the Crown

Prince was to nod his head twice in return for two deep bows from the officials. In the latter, however, the Crown Prince was required to bow deeply twice first. Then his teachers and mentors were to return the bows in the same number and degree. The Crown Prince was expected to continue in this deferential posture toward his teachers and mentors throughout.

In 1143, Sejong began to transfer some of the responsibilities of government to Munjong[96] and, consequently, the ritual with which Munjong greeted his teachers and mentors changed. The Crown Prince now returned their bows rather than bowing first.[97]

This transference of power was, however, just a step in a continuing process of apprenticeship which Munjong had begun in 1430. Sejong, who was deeply aware that he should train his son not only in the classics but also in practical affairs of government, required his presence at audiences and consultations with ministers from quite early on.[98] At any rate, by the time Munjong ascended the throne in 1450 at Sejong's death, he was quite proficient both in the theory and practice of the Confucian kingship. He did not have much chance to put his training into practice however. Munjong died after two years on the throne.

There was no institutional change in the arrangements for the Crown Prince's education during Munjong's short reign. His heir and successor Tanjong (1441–57, r. 1452–55) had already been appointed Grand Heir in 1448 at the age of eight (he was the first Grand Heir of the Yi dynasty) and was provided with four tutors.[99] When Munjong ascended the throne, Tanjong was made Crown Prince, inheriting the same educational institution that his father had passed through.

Changes came during the reign of Sejo, Sejong's second son, who usurped the throne from his young nephew Tanjong in 1455. The first was the abolition of the Hall of Worthies in 1456.[100] The scholars of the Hall, with the aim of restoring Tanjong, had unsuccessfully attempted a coup.[101] Now the Crown Prince's instructional staff consisted of ten tutors, six of whom were full-time staff in the Crown Prince Tutorial Office while the remaining four were drawn from scholars serving in office.[102]

While the staff did not change in number, the abolition of the Hall of Worthies probably resulted in shorter tenure for the tutorial staff. Sejong had been explicitly concerned with the lack of continuity which resulted from frequent changes in personnel in the prince's educational staff. The establishment of the Hall, in which prominent scholars enjoyed a long tenure as well as a close relationship to the king and the Crown Prince, alleviated this problem. With the abolition of the Hall, the lack of continuity in the prince's educational staff may very well have returned. After all, the Hall of Worthies had been the only conspicuous group of scholars continuously maintained primarily and almost exclusively for their commitment to scholarship and royal education.

Moreover, long tenure for the Crown Prince's instructional staff would be sought only if the king trusted his scholar-officials to instruct his heir correctly and also to serve his interests in doing so. In fact Sejong's court seems to have been characterized by a remarkable rapport between the king and his officials, especially the scholars of the Hall of Worthies. The attempt by the latter to restore Tanjong, Sejong's legitimate grandheir, beyond their Confucian sense of loyalty, was probably motivated by their personal allegiance to the deceased king who had invested so much trust in them.[103]

Sejo's court was altogether different. The usurpation, unforgivable by Confucian standards of morality, alienated many scholars.[104] This usurpation is usually attributed to Sejo's commitment to the restoration of a monarchy which he saw as having been eroded by the rise of a bureaucracy whose growing power he felt resulted from Sejong's and Munjong's patronage of scholars.[105] He had discontinued the Royal Lecture soon after his accession and his general mistrust of scholar-officials might explain the reduction of the Crown Prince's instructional staff by half in 1460. Of five tutors, three were full-time while two served concurrently in office.[106] By this time, Yejong (1441–69, r. 1468–69) was the Crown Prince, Tŏkchong (1438–57), Sejo's first son and heir-apparent, having died in 1457 at the age of twenty.

It was not that Sejo was against providing an adequate education for his son. He himself was well-versed and interested in the classics. Determined to bequeath his throne but not his stigma to his heir, he did not for a moment question that his son should be properly educated. He supervised his son's education quite carefully, participating, for example, in such decisions as the selection of books and the order in which they were to be read.[107] Rather, his sensitivity concerning royal authority and his suspicion of scholar-officials seem to have influenced his attitude toward the education of his Crown Prince. He tried to mitigate the sense that tutors, being the prince's teachers, were somehow superior to him in position or authority. Perhaps with this in mind, he limited the occasions on which his son's knowledge was tested. In 1464, for instance, he forbade tutors from requiring Yejong to read aloud, declaring that, since his son had made great progress in his studies, this was no longer necessary.[108] Sejo also reduced the number of plenary sessions (hoegang), which required the attendance of the prince's entire instructional staff, from three to one a month.[109]

Sejo's concern that tutors should not assume a superior attitude toward his son extended beyond the classroom. Once, at a reception following the plenary session, Yejong poured wine for his tutors and other officials. When Sejo noticed that a tutor remained seated while Yejong filled his cup, he burst out in a rage. He accused the tutor of ignorance of the most basic elements of propriety despite his status as a Confucian scholar.[110] All in all, Sejo appears to have been somewhat overprotective of his son, though it is difficult to tell how much of this impression is a result of the historiographical bias against Sejo. At any rate, Yejong reigned little more than a year and thus he never emerged as a distinct personality.

Matters took a somewhat different course at the court of Sŏngjong. Tŏkchong's second son. He was supposedly chosen to succeed his uncle on the basis of intelligence.[111] Sŏngjong ascended the throne at the age of thirteen but only in 1476, when he reached twenty, did his grandmother, Queen Dowager Chŏnghŭi (1418–83), Sejo's widowed queen and the acting regent, hand the government over to him. Having ascended the throne as a boy and being punctilious in matters of royal decorum, Sŏngjong chronically exhibited an exaggerated concern for propriety. Devoted to learning, he attended the Royal Lecture almost daily[112] and, in executing affairs of state, he consulted widely and at length with his officials before reaching a decision. And in this atmosphere, decisions were made concerning the education of his Crown Prince Yŏnsan.

At the outset, there were few substantial changes in the Crown Prince's education. Yŏnsan was appointed Crown Prince in 1483 at the age of eight. Rules for the Crown Prince Lecture were devised. Every morning one mentor, two officials of lower rank, and one member of the Censorate were to attend the session.s[113] Also, the number of the prince's instructional staff increased slightly. There were five full-time tutors in addition to three teachers and four mentors of very high rank including the Prime Minister.[114] In 1493, five part-time tutors were added.[115]

What is particularly noticeable about these changes is the manner in which they were brought about. Each decision was prefaced by official debates *ad infinitum*.[116] In addition, Yŏnsan's education was unusual for the concern over his state of development expressed by both the king and the bureaucrats. Sŏngjong seems to have been frequently apprehensive of his son's ability to deport himself properly.[117] Officials on their part repeatedly referred to Yŏnsan's need for extra guidance in his behavior.[118]

Yŏnsan responded to their concern, upon ascending the throne, by systematically destroying the system, practices, and scholar-officials who represented the system and carried on its practices. By his dethronement in 1506 in a coup by officials, only the barest skeleton of the structure of Yi government remained, if the *Yŏnsan'gun ilgi* is to be believed.

Intent though he appears to have been on rescinding Confucian precepts and dismantling the monarchical institutions that he inherited, Yŏnsan did not question the validity of the prescribed educational process for his heir. Crown Prince No (1497–1506) was subjected to the usual training for the future king. Appointed Crown Prince in 1502, No began to receive instructions from teachers and mentors in 1503 and performed the Entrance Ceremony at the Royal College in 1504.[119] Yŏnsan did abolish the Crown Prince Tutorial Office in 1505 but, obviously thinking that it was impossible for his son to be without tutors, he did not dismiss them. Perplexed, he was driven to ask: "The Crown Prince Tutorial Office has been abolished. What should these five tutors be called?"[120]

It was Chungjong's court that presaged the trends toward earlier instruction and increased instructional staff for the Crown Prince. Acceding after twelve destructive years of Yŏnsan's rule, Chungjong was burdened with two pressing tasks, the restoration of the institutions and practices his predecessor had discontinued and the rectification of any remaining corruption. Wishing to restore royal authority, which had been so deeply compromised by his half-brother's deposal, he sought to achieve this through moral rule. He turned to a younger generation of Confucian scholars committed to a vision of the Confucian state.[121] Beyond simple dedication to Confucian ideals, his bureaucracy had a vested interest in strengthening Confucian practices of government to insure, if possible, that the cataclysms which had been commonplace under Yŏnsan could not recur. Between them, new standards were set for the education of the Crown Prince. From Chungjong's point of view, early appointment of the Crown Prince would secure the dynastic line. Insofar as he believed that virtue was the basis of royal authority, the early initiation of his heir's education served his purpose. To the bureaucrats, the opportunity to mold the future ruler according to Confucian precepts from the earliest possible age also seemed in their best interests. Thus when Injong (1515–45, r. 1544–45) was born in 1515, the court hummed with frenzied concern for his proper development.

Debate over the education of the heir began almost immediately upon his birth. Chungjong, probably desiring clear guidelines, instructed the Office of Special Councillors to examine the classics and to prepare a report. Within three months, early in 1516, this effort materialized in a memorial containing seven items essential to education. These included early instruction, guidance in daily conduct, a strict regimen of study, etc.[122] Chungjong took this to heart and when his son reached three years of age he began to teach him to read. For this purpose, he appointed Four Guidance Officials (poyanggwan). Injong supposedly learned a number of characters and so the court, convinced of his intelligence, added more instructors.[123] By 1519, the five-year-old child had no less than seven teachers.[124]

In 1520, Injong was appointed Crown Prince. He was two years younger than the norm, and this caused some hesitation in Chungjong. Ultimately, the decision to appoint him was arrived at with no dissent.[125] The Crown Prince was immediately placed in the care of the tutorial staff which had already been appointed and was ready to "cultivate and cherish" (poyang) its charge. In 1522, Injong performed the capping and entrance ceremonies and, at eight, he was officially a student. As might be expected, Injong was the object of unremitting educational concern on the part of his father's court until his accession in 1544, but he died a year later.

The ideas concerning the education of the Crown Prince which were enunciated under Chungjong continued to dominate the thinking of the Yi court. No substantial changes in the institution of the Crown Prince, by now firmly set on course, were made except for occasional elaborations of ritual, increases in the number of instructional staff, earlier appointment of the Crown Prince and initiation of instruction, etc. These trends reached a culmination in the late seventeenth and early eighteenth centuries.

First, the heir was formally designated the Primary Son. This practice began with Prince Yangnyŏng in 1402.[126] In 1517, Chungjong conferred the title of Guidance Minister (Poyang chaesang),[127] which was later changed to Guidance Official,[128] upon the officials responsible for the education of the Primary Son. As their duties were mostly symbolic in nature, officials of the highest rank usually served in these posts. Their duties for the most part were certain ritual interactions with the Primary Son. These were recorded in the *Records of the Guidance Office (Po-yangch'ŏng ilgi)*. The first extant volume of this record chronicles ritual activities involving Kyŏngjong (1688–1724, r. 1720–24) after his designation by Sukchong (1661–1720, r. 1674–1720) as Primary Son at two months of age, and it continues until his elevation to Crown Prince.[129]

Sometime before he was eight years of age, the Primary Son was designated Crown Prince. At about eight he performed the Entrance Ceremony at the Royal College and his formal education by the Crown Prince Tutorial Office began. But both Sukchong and Yŏngjo (1694–1776, r. 1724–76) appointed their heirs Crown Prince much earlier than usual. Kyŏngjong was appointed Crown Prince in his third year, while Prince Sado (1735–62) was appointed at fourteen months of age. It appears that both Sukchong and Yŏngjo, for different reasons, wanted to secure the dynastic line by a timely designation of the Crown Prince.

The Crown Prince tutorial staff also increased in number but this too stabilized by the early eighteenth century. At this point the staff consisted of three teachers, four mentors, and thirteen full-time tutors.[130] This number as well as most of the other educational arrangements designed to serve the Crown Prince remained essentially unchanged until the end of the nineteenth century.[131]

CURRICULUM

Curriculum, as the content of education, is a direct expression of the concept of an educated man. It consists of the kind of knowledge and understanding that a society desires an educated man to possess.[132] After all, any society which considers itself civilized possesses a corpus of knowledge that it wishes to transmit to future generations to insure future progress and the continuity of its civilization.[133] The kind of knowledge that the Neo-Confucian Yi society regarded as essential for its future rulers was moral knowledge. The curriculum of the Yi Crown Prince's education thus consisted for the most part of studying those books the understanding of which was believed to lead to moral knowledge.

A discussion of Confucian epistemology is beyond the scope of this paper. Nonetheless it should be remarked that Chu Hsi believed that there was a unifying moral principle governing the phenomenal as well as the nonphenomenal world. In particular, it governed the human world as well and Chu Hsi believed that grasping how it operated in the human sphere and living on the basis of this understanding resulted in moral action. He believed that certain books illustrated this principle in all of its shades and manifestations, as well as how the sages perceived and penetrated it.[134] He recommended studying these books as a way of seeing into the minds of the sages and attaining sagehood.[135] Korean Neo-Confucian scholars accepted this view. Yulgok, for instance, professed an almost religious faith in the power of the texts to bring about changes in character and development. He states: "One should first read books. This is because examples of how the sages used their minds, and what should be emulated or avoided in goodness and evil are all contained in books."[136]

Certainly not all books belonged to this category. Moreover there should be an order in which important books were to be read, reflecting the state of development of the student's intellectual ability. Chu Hsi compiled the *Elementary Learning* for young students. When the student attained basic intellectual abilities, he recommended starting with the Four Books in a certain sequence—the *Great Learning* first, the *Analects (Lun-yü)*, the *Mencius (Meng Tzu)* and lastly the *Doctrine of the Mean*.[137] He held the Four Books in high esteem: "If one understands the Four Books, then there will be no book one cannot read, there will be no principle one cannot fathom and there will be no situation one cannot handle."[138] He apparently regarded them, with their different but complementary functions, as primary and essential texts. After the Four Books came the classics—the *Odes (Shih-ching)*, the *Documents (Shu-ching)*, the *Changes (I-ching)*, and then the *Spring and Autumn Annals*. The ritual texts, though certainly regarded as essential, were not given a specific place in this sequence.[139] Then Chu Hsi recommended other worthwhile books such as history and certain philosophical works.[140]

Given the Yi commitment to Neo-Confucianism in general and to the Ch'eng-Chu school in particular, it is not surprising that the curriculum of the Crown Prince's education consisted for the most part of studying the Four Books and the Confucian Classics. In their early years, the princes also studied such well-known Confucian primers as the *Elementary Learning*, the *Classic of Filial Piety (Hsiao-ching)*, etc. Neo-

Confucian philosophical and historical works were also included in the curriculum. While this much can be easily inferred from discussions concerning the princes' education,[141] it is not possible to ascertain the precise curriculum for each prince until the mid-seventeenth century. Before that, information about the Crown Prince's education is mainly drawn from the *Sillok* and, as the *Sillok* is essentially a chronicle of the activities of the king and his court, information in the *Sillok* concerning the Crown Prince is by no means exhaustive. For instance, we know for certain of only one book, the *Extended Meaning of the Great Learning (Ta-hsüeh yen-i)*, that Prince Yangnyŏng read and took six years to finish.[142] The only other title mentioned in connection with his education is the *Doctrine of the Mean*. In the *Sillok*, his tutors are recorded as having requested permission to lecture him on the book[143] but there is no indication of whether he read it or not. Other books studied by princes are mentioned in passing. For example, Tanjong began his study sessions as Grand Heir in 1448 with the *Elementary Learning*,[144] Yejong was reading the *Classic of Filial Piety* when he was appointed Crown Prince in 1457,[145] and Injong studied the *Excerpts from the Elementary Learning (Sohak ch'oryak)* when he was very young.[146]

The order in which books were to be studied in the Crown Prince Lecture was not discussed extensively for the first hundred years of the Yi dynasty. The only reference to the subject is a record of Sejo's order in 1460 that his heir, Yejong, should first read the *Great Learning* and then the *Analects*.[147] Reticence on this topic did not mean that the Yi court was unaware of it or that it was unconcerned. Sejong's and Sŏngjong's curricula for the Royal Lecture, for instance, show that the Four Books were read more or less, though not exactly, in the order that Chu Hsi recommended and that the Five Classics, historical works (both Korean and Chinese), and a number of Sung philosophical works were for the most part studied though not in any discernible order.[148] But in the sixteenth century, the order of books in the Crown Prince's curriculum began to receive more attention.

In 1528, apparently the fourteen-year-old Injong had great difficulty in understanding the *Great Learning* and the *Doctrine of the Mean*. When he expressed curiosity over people of the past, he was given the *General Mirror for Aid in Government (Tzu-chih t'ung-chien)*. This was severely criticized by Yi Ŏnjŏk (1491–1553), a renowned scholar. He maintained that in the education of the future king there should be a proper sequence from the basic to the peripheral. The classics should be basic while history should be peripheral. If one were to reverse the order, teaching the child history as basic, then his mind would be inclined toward shallowness. Yi further stressed that one should study historical works at one's leisure only after reaching a high level of understanding and after one's virtuous nature had become firmly established.[149]

The opinion that Yi professed here was not new to him nor to his period. If some scholars had been less vehement on the relative merits of history, Confucians generally maintained that history and the classics had separate roles in one's discovery of truth. Chu Hsi, for instance, viewed the *Spring and Autumn Annals*, the only work among the classics that can be regarded as history, as the sage's application of moral principles, while the *Odes* and the *Documents* were seen as "vehicles of moral principles."[150] He described its place in the Five Classics as "comparable to that of judgments in the sphere of law." He continues, "Laws merely prescribe rules of conduct. Not until judgments are made can the application of law be seen." In other words, other Classics were seen as discussing the "meaning of principle" while the *Spring and Autumn Annals* were viewed as applying principle to "practical affairs."[151] Thus, studying the *Annals* was seen as essential for the student's understanding of principle but, as befit its function as an explication, it was placed after other works.[152] Chu Hsi consistently viewed history in this way. He recommended the study of history after other essential texts as a way to understand the sages' intentions[153] and to perceive the principle behind historical and human events.[154] This way of using history was widely accepted among Confucians. Sometimes it was incorporated with works nominally philosophical in nature. The *Extended Meaning of the Great Learning*, which was much favored by Yi Koreans, especially during the earlier part of the dynasty, is a case in point. As might be expected of the author of the *Extended Meaning of the Great Learning*, Chen Te-hsiu (1178–1235) singled out the *Great Learning* as *the* text whose understanding held the key to the realization of the Confucian ideal.[155] But the *Extended Meaning* is full of references to historical and contemporaneous examples.[156]

Koreans accepted this view in principle. Their discourse was amply illustrated by history, both Korean and Chinese. While this continued to be true, sometime around the sixteenth century, they began to place a stronger emphasis on the Classics and the Four Books, relegating history to a secondary place. Sejong's and Sŏngjong's[157] curricula for the Royal

Lecture show that historical works of various kinds, mostly Chinese, were studied in formal sessions interspersed among the Classics, the Four Books, and other philosophical works.[158] Sejong seems to have been particularly fond of history. In 1425, for instance, he specifically sought and employed three scholars who could explicate historical texts to him at the Hall of Worthies.[159] But after the seventeenth century, historical works were studied in informal sessions *(sodae)*, reserving the formal Royal Lecture sessions mostly for the Classics, the Four Books, and a few Sung philosophical works such as the *Heart Classic (Hsin-ching)* and the *Reflections on Things at Hand (Chin-ssu lu)*.[160] Perhaps Koreans felt a greater affinity for the classics because they were universal while Chinese history may have seemed somewhat particular to that country. Even if this is true, they did not replace Chinese history with Korean history in formal sessions. Some additional works on Korean history were added in the eighteenth and nineteenth centuries but they were for the most part read only in informal sessions.[161] In any case in the sixteenth century history came to occupy a decidedly secondary role.

The relative value of the classics in relation to history was reconsidered in the sixteenth century out of an emerging concern for the exact place and role of each text. This apparently corresponded to a growing confidence among Koreans in their understanding of Confucianism. Yi Yulgok exemplified this phenomenon. Under the heading "Reading Books" *(Tokso)* in his *Important Methods of Eliminating Ignorance*, he specified the order in which books were to be read and he described what the student should seek to achieve through each:

First, read the *Elementary Learning*, noting therein the ways of serving one's parents, respecting one's brothers, being loyal to the ruler, being humble to one's elders, being reverent to one's teachers, and being affectionate to one's friends. Consider each of these scrupulously and diligently practice them.

Then read the *Great Learning* and [Chu Hsi's] *Questions on the Great Learning (Ta-hsüeh huo-wen)*, seeking therein the ways of investigating principle, rectifying the mind, cultivating the self, and governing others. Understand each of these things truly and seek to practice them.

After this, read the *Analects*, mindful of striving to seek benevolence as the basis for cultivating and nurturing the self. Calmly meditate upon these things and experience them deeply.

And then read *Mencius*, investigating therein the theory of discriminating between righteousness and profit, thereby restraining greed and maintaining the principle of Heaven. Discern these things clearly and understand them.

Then read the *Doctrine of the Mean*, considering therein the power of one's nature and emotions, of striving for the ultimate and the mysteries of the birth and growth [of myriad things]. Considering each of these things, seek to understand them.

Having done these things, read the *Odes*, learning therein what is perverse and what is right in nature and emotion and how to encourage what is good and thwart what is evil. Thoughtfully unravel these things, taking them passionately to heart, and stand firm in your vigilance.

Then read the Ritual Texts seeing in them the propriety of the principle of Heaven and the appropriateness of ceremonies and protocols. Investigate these things, establishing your opinion upon them.

Afterwards, read the *Documents*, discovering there the foundations of the great principles and methods with which the two emperors and the three sage kings governed the empire. Trace the origins of these things, grasping all the basic points.

Then, the *Changes*, considering there the auspicious and the inauspicious, life and death, advance and retreat, prosperity and decay. Observe these points and scrutinize them carefully.

And then, read the *Spring and Autumn Annals*, observing the sage's judgment as he praises and commends in his subtle phrases. Investigate these things conscientiously and understand him correctly.

Read these five books and these five classics scrupulously by turns, continuously striving for understanding, thus making their meanings and their principles clearer daily.

Then Yulgok recommends various Sung philosophical works, among them such books as the *Reflections on Things at Hand*, the *Family Ritual (Chia-li)* [of Chu Hsi], the *Heart Classic*, the *Great Compendium of the Two Ch'eng Brothers' Works (Erh Ch'eng ta-ch'üan)*, the *Great Compendium of Master Chu's Works (Chu Tzu ta-ch'üan)*, *Classified Conversations of Master Chu(Chu Tzu yü-lei)*, and other Neo-Confucian texts. Only after all of these texts have been studied does he recommend the reading of historical works. Even so, histories were to be studied with no more effort than was needed to "get acquainted with the ancient and the present and to become familiarized with events and changes so as to expand one's knowledge and opinions." Then he warns against reading, even for a moment, unsuitable books, either those that contain heterodox ideas or those of a vulgar sort.[162]

Yulgok's proposal did not contain anything new—his descriptions of books echo Chu Hsi, while his emphasis on the Classics and the Four Books echoes other Korean scholars. Nevertheless the careful ordering of the books chosen reflects a growing tendency in the mentality of his age, a belief that there was a right way to do everything and an obsession with finding and following it.

At any rate, from the mid-seventeenth century on, a survey of the Crown Prince's curriculum reveals that, with minor variations, this order was kept consistently. Some examples of the curricula follow:

HYOJONG (1619–59, r. 1649–59):	*Dates read and discussed*
Great Learning	10/3/1645–2/24/1646
Questions on the Great Learning	10/3/1645
Extended Meaning of the Great Learning	3/7/1646
Analects	3/10/1646–1/26/1648
Mencius	1/26/1648–4/12–1649
Doctrine of the Mean	4/28/1649

KYŎNGJONG:	
Classic of Filial Piety	3/9/1694–2/19/1694
[Pak Semu's]*Primer for the Young* (*Tongmong sŏnsŭp*)	1/21/1695–7/21/1695
Elementary Learning	8/6/1695–6/1/1696
General Mirror for Aid in Government	6/13/1696–6/24/1705
Great Learning	1/7/1702–1/26/1702 1/15/1704–2/3/1704 (repeat)
Analects	2/9/1702–2/18/1703 9/11/1710–5/22/1712 (repeat)
Mencius	11/12/1703–1/5/1704 3/14/1713–5/16/1713 (repeat)
Odes	2/18/1704–2/11/1705
Documents	2/20/1705–12/18/1705 5/27/1713

Heart Classic	1/8/1706–10/14/1706
Extended Meaning of the Great Learning	10/23/1706–12/13/1708
Reflections on Things at Hand	12/25/1708–8/20/1710

PRINCE SADO:

Primer for the Young	2/3/1741–5/19/1742
Elementary Learning	3/6/1742
Primer for the Young	4/2/1742–5/19/1742
Classic of Filial Piety	8/19/1742–9/16/1742
Elementary Learning	4/3/1743–7/6/1745
Great Learning	3/2/1746–11/3/1746
Analects	11/13/1746–9/14/1747
Mencius	9/15/1747–9/2/1748
Doctrine of the Mean	9/6/1748–12/27/1748
Odes	1/14/1749–6/3/1750
Documents	6/6/1750–12/26/1751
Elementary Learning	1/10/1752–11/24/1753
Great Learning	11/28/1753–12/18/1753
Analects	12/19/1753–11/2/1754
Mencius	11/10/1754–9/5/1758
Doctrine of the Mean	9/6/1758–12/8/1758
Changes	12/9/1760

CHŌNGJO (1752–1800, r. 1776–1800):

Elementary Learning	4/7/1758–6/23/1760
Great Learning	6/25/1760–8/29/1760 2/12/1769–3/6/1769 (repeat)

Analects	8/30/1760–11/4/1761
	3/12/1769–12/14/1769
	(repeat)
Mencius	11/8/1761–10/1/1763
	8/7/1768–2/3/1769
	(repeat)
Doctrine of the Mean	11/7/1763–3/14/1764
	1/6/1770–2/21/1770
	(repeat)
Documents	4/14/1764–8/10/1765
	2/26/1770-intercalary
	5/16/1770 (repeat)
[Yi Yulgok's] *Essential Guide to the*	1/17/1764
Learning of the Sage (Sŏnghak	
chibyo)	

The relatively stable character of the curriculum is readily noticeable. If one, in addition, follows the curriculum of the Royal Lecture, the pattern is even more obvious. Very few historical works are listed above but, true to the belief that they should be read in one's spare time, they were studied at informal sessions. And basically the same curriculum, with some deletions or additions of philosophical or Korean works for various princes, remained intact until the end of the Yi dynasty.[163]

Needless to say, an intellectual understanding of moral knowledge was to be accompanied by a corresponding development in behavior and conduct. Naturally, the prince's familiarization with and training in proper conduct was an important aspect of his education. What the prince did in his private life may have been beyond official control, but his public life was subjected to official regulation and much of it was governed by ritual. While most societies would have made certain demands of a ritual nature on the Crown Prince, in a Confucian society, ritual carried special significance. On a personal level, it was a formalization of the correct state of the mind. On a more general level, it was human conformance to universal order. At any rate, rituals governing the Crown Prince's life were quite extensive. They included his dealings with his parents and members of the royal clan, his contact with his tutors and other officials, and his attendance at ancestral sacrifices and other ceremonial functions. For rituals which he performed on special occasions, the Board of Rites drew up protocols often based on precedent. The Crown Prince was introduced to simple rituals when he was young and he was expected to attend to more of them as his sphere of activity enlarged. His mastery of the full range of rituals associated with his position signaled growth into his role and it was an essential part of his apprenticeship as a future ruler.

There were other rather utilitarian prerequisites for kingship, such as proficiency in martial arts. The founder of the dynasty, Yi Sŏnggye, was a general and the early Yi court devoted considerable attention to training the future ruler in the martial arts. Prince Yangnyŏng, for instance, initiated his training in archery and equestrianism in 1407,[164] at the age of sixteen, and, to the delight of his father, became quite skillful at both. In 1411, T'aejong invited him to view the biannual display of martial arts (kangmu) by military officers. Confucian scholars seldom took kindly to the enjoyment of martial arts and, even in this early period in the Yi, they conveyed to the king their disapproval of his having introduced the prince to this aspect of life unnecessarily early. But T'aejong, who had a rather different idea of what constituted an adequate education for the future ruler, ignored their objections. He maintained that the Crown Prince should be versed both in martial arts and in the rituals (ŭi) associated with them.[165] But clearly even he regarded expertise in martial arts as merely a supplementary rather than central aspect of education.

Still, during the early part of the dynasty, being a good horseman and archer was regarded as an asset. Sejo was supposed to have been a remarkable archer. His ability to hit every target in the hunt is cited as proof of his talent.[166] Sejo certainly did not neglect to train his heir in martial arts. One of his most enthusiastic boasts concerning his son was that Yejong did extremely well at an archery contest in 1463. Immensely pleased that his son had mastered the art, he exclaimed: "When I was his age [he was twenty-three], I was not as good as he. He is much more intelligent than his father."[167] Sejong, who was a much more devoted scholar than either his father T'aejong or his son Sejo, did not neglect to train his heir in this area either. In 1431, he made Munjong participate in the viewing of the display of martial arts.[168] Moreover, he occasionally practiced archery with his sons.[169]

But as Confucianism tightened its grip on the Yi court, attention to the martial arts dwindled. Viewing the martial arts, for all practical purposes, seems to have been discontinued by the sixteenth century. Kings and princes gradually settled into a more sedentary and bookish life. While basic skills in horseback riding and archery were still taught to the princes, these activities were kept to a minimum. Not only was excessive interest in the martial arts discouraged, any interest at all was held in suspicion as if it was detrimental to the development of virtue.[170] It was more or less assumed that if one were to follow scrupulously the appropriate regimen of study and to concentrate on learning moral principles and practicing them in daily behavior, there would be little time left for such activities as archery.

PEDAGOGY

Once the content of education is identified, the next question is how to transmit this body of knowledge to students. Transmission, by definition, is an act which requires participation of both the transmitter and the receiver. But questions remain concerning how and to what degree each party should participate in the process and this in part constitutes pedagogy. Pedagogy, in turn, is closely tied to the concept of man.[171] Neo-Confucians viewed man as possessing an innate moral knowledge and a potential to follow moral law. Education was meant to realize this potential inherent in man and consequently the role of the teacher was to provide the proper environment, stimulus, and guidance to the student to fulfill his potential.

Given this idea of education as a process of discovering truth by enhancing what was inherent, active participation by the student was viewed as essential. The role of the student thus was not the passive reception of knowledge and skills through a training process but a process of development through participation. The Confucian student was expected to explore and discover truth for himself,[172] though presumably with the assistance of his teacher. It must be remembered, however, that what he was to discover was a truth that was viewed as absolute and universal.[173] Confucians did not encourage experimentation or trial-and-error methods in the formulation of an individual value system.

In the Yi Crown Prince's education, where the educational effort was devoted to one individual, the prince's active participation was taken quite seriously. This required motivation. Confucian educators, like other educators, instinctively knew the importance of motivation. Chu Hsi, for instance, spoke of the necessity of arousing interest and expressed an intention to compose instructional poems to be sung by boys.[174] Those responsible for the prince's education at the Yi court frequently expressed concern with keeping the prince interested and avoiding boredom.[175] Yet, perhaps because they believed that man, properly guided, would naturally see the desirability of a moral course, they did not develop a coherent theory of motivation. Beyond passing references to keeping the prince interested, Yi Confucians did not probe deeply into this question. Nonetheless, stimulating and maintaining the prince's motivation seems to have been a major factor in devising and revising the format of his study sessions.

Contemporary scholarship on education usually divides motivational factors into two groups, intrinsic and extrinsic. Of extrinsic factors, the student's liking for his teachers—his desire to emulate and resemble them— is considered the strongest. Intrinsic factors are somewhat more complex. They are generally classified into two categories, general motivations and specific motivations. General motivations refer to the student's desires for discovery, exploration, a sense of control and, most importantly, his impulse toward achievement. Specific motivations are the pleasures and joys intrinsic to the task one is performing and these usually come into play after one has mastered the more routine aspects of the task. A writer's search for economy of expression or a mathematician's striving for an elegant proof, for example, belong in this category. These reinforce general motivation and act as incentives for excellence.[176]

Confucian educators did utilize all of these factors. The Yi court, for instance, seems to have chosen the prince's instructional staff not merely for scholarly qualifications but also for manners and speech, in the apparent hope that the prince would emulate them. The Yi court also seems to have stressed the achievement motive. According to the *Sillok*, at least, the king and his officials frequently praised the young prince when he learned a few characters[177] or displayed some inclination toward learning.[178] In fact, the teaching of basic skills such as writing and reading seems to have been motivated almost exclusively by this tactic. The use of the achievement motive continued as the prince grew older—in the form of constant references to the greatness of the sage kings, his ability to become one if he were to try, and the benefits for the nation if he were to achieve it. Yet, utilization of the achievement motive was vitiated by the fact that the reward for the achievement was nothing practical or tangible. Unlike most students who might wish to achieve a certain status in society, the Crown Prince was already the heir-apparent destined to become king.

Thus, the instruction of the Crown Prince had to rely more on specific motivation. Hence, the greater part of the instructional staff's efforts were devoted to transmitting the necessary knowledge, that is, to presenting and covering the required material in such a way as to kindle in the prince the joy of learning and the pleasures of discovery so that he would want to learn more and work harder. Achieving this was the object of the various efforts to devise methods of study and procedures for study sessions.

The first recorded debate on methods of study occurred in 1408 and it concerned Prince Yangnyŏng. The Censorate attacked the study method *(kanghakpŏp)* which had been in use—an acute concern with monitoring the number of pages read, recording scrupulously the amount covered each day even down to the number of phrases and characters. This method was termed suitable for ordinary persons preparing for an examination. What was most important in educating the Crown Prince, according to the memorandum, was that his original endowment be nurtured. Consequently there was no reason for him to read a new book every day. Studying the Four Books and the Classics, as was expected of the Crown Prince, should be based upon understanding principle and rectifying the mind. Then the memorandum prescribed a specific plan—the prince should read one or two passages and discuss the contents with his tutors, and the same methods should be applied through the session. This proposal—suggested more immediately to kindle Yangnyŏng's interest in book learning, for which the prince had been displaying an increasing distaste—was accepted. In addition to a reading session, there was a daily discussion session which allowed sufficient leeway for Yangnyŏng to discuss any matter that he might wish.[179]

When this method proved to be ineffectual because of Yangnyŏng's increasing dereliction in study, it was revised in 1413. Every morning, two or three pages were to be covered and this was to be done in ten rounds of discussion. The same procedure was to be repeated in the afternoon but there were to be only about five rounds of discussion.[180] This format recognized the necessity of having to cover a certain amount daily but it did not ignore the need for the prince's active participation and his understanding of the material presented.

Unfortunately the *Sillok* does not give much information on the evolution of the format that was used in the prince's study sessions. As a rule, it mentions those events and problems with which the court as a whole was particularly concerned at any given time and, unless a major change occurred, the study format is not mentioned. The next reference to it concerned Yŏnsan. A mentor was to lecture in the morning session and the tutors were to attend the prince in the afternoon to aid him in reviewing what he had studied that morning. In addition, they were to go over what the prince had studied in the last three days.[181] Except for the emphasis on reviewing the material already learned, it does not give a clear indication of exactly what went on in the study session.

The only descriptions of sessions available are private records kept by those who served Crown Princes. One such record from the mid-eighteenth century indicates a rather flexible format. A typical session was attended by several tutors. It began with the prince's reading of several paragraphs. Then the tutor responsible for his reading explained difficult words and characters. Other tutors by turn explicated the text and explained its meanings and morals. This was followed by discussion in which, as a rule, the prince asked questions and was answered by one or more tutors. Some questions were factual, some logical, and some concerned the meaning of certain passages. This process might be repeated many times but it could just as well end after only a few rounds or even only one if the prince had numerous questions and comments. There does not seem to have been a predetermined amount which should be covered in one session, though as a rule it averaged a few pages a day.[182]

What does emerge from these descriptions is that the prince's active participation was expected and encouraged and that there was a considerable amount of give and take between the student and his instructors. It appears that how the sessions proceeded depended greatly on the prince. He could passively listen to the tutors' explanations and avoid tutorial bait to engage him in discussion. Understandably, the tutors were not pleased by this. One of the more bitter charges against Yŏnsan was that he was too reserved and inattentive in his tutorial sessions.[183] The prince could also ask any question that came to mind and every question was answered with care.[184]

These methods seem to have been consistent with general Confucian pedagogy. Chu Hsi, for instance, regarded doubt as important, viewing it as the beginning of discovery.[185] Yet, while the Crown Prince was encouraged to doubt and question, he did not have the opportunity to resolve his doubts through discussions with his peers. In fact discussion with fellow students was seen as an important part of the student's learning process. Chu Hsi,[186] Yi T'oegye,[187] and Yi Yulgok[188] repeatedly stressed discussion. T'aejong tried, rather unsuccessfully, to mitigate this problem but afterwards no one broached the topic. That the prince had no opportunity to discuss or interact with peers and fellow students and that he was always the only student surrounded by adult tutors must have exerted considerable influence on his development. In China, the Ming court also educated the Crown Prince in isolation.[189] It would be interesting to see how this factor might have influenced the Ming Crown Prince by comparing him to Crown Princes of other Chinese dynasties who were educated in the company of other imperial children.

In the Yi court at least, this arrangement was not limited to the Crown Prince; it extended to other royal children as well. For a time, the royal princes attended the School for the Royal Clan which Sejong established in 1428.[190] But the School was beset by problems of attendance.[191] Since princes were forbidden to serve in office, unless they were interested in study for its own sake, they tended to lose motivation especially when they grew a little older. Every sort of device, ranging from ritual[192] and coercion[193] through beneficent persuasion,[194] was used in attempting to solve this problem but none was particularly successful. The School continued, on increasingly tenuous terms, until 1505 when Yŏnsan abolished it.[195] In 1511, Chungjong nominally reestablished it[196] but nothing seems to have come of it. The education of royal children reverted to individual instruction.[197] Though the restoration of the School for the Royal Clan was discussed intermittently, in 1655 and in 1676 for instance,[198] it was never realized.

Since the Crown Prince was to pursue learning solely in the company of his instructional staff, effort was devoted to promoting cordial relationships between them. For instance, Sejong ordered that a party should follow the plenary session.[199] The plenary session, which was initiated in 1427, was quite formal and ceremonial in nature and it was attended by the entire instructional staff, including teachers, mentors, and tutors. It began as a trimonthly session, and met on the first, the eleventh, and the twenty-first.[200] After 1431, it was always followed by a reception at which wine and food were served[201] and at which, presumably, participants interacted rather informally. Sejo reduced the number of sessions from three to one a month in 1455 but the basic features of the session and the gathering following it remained unchanged throughout the dynasty.

Undoubtedly, occasional close relationships developed between certain tutors and the prince. Yet, no matter how close the relationship may have been, the teacher, by definition, was an authority. He was an authority at least in the sphere of knowledge and that was the whole reason for his position. True, the prince was encouraged to explore and find truth for himself but within limits and under the guidance provided by the teacher. The teacher's role was to make certain that the prince would achieve proper understanding, develop a sense of judgment, and learn proper behavior and ritual within certain definite and established standards. Since the teacher was an authority on the knowledge that the prince was to acquire and as he was closer to the truth that the prince was to discover, the prince was invited to question but not to disagree with him, and discussion—not debate—was welcome.

While the teacher's status as an authority was accepted, it is dubious whether he actually had any authority over the prince. Given the difference in their respective social positions, there was bound to be some ambivalence in their relationship. Recognizing this problem, the ritual protocols for the study sessions emphasized the teacher's authoritative status. For example, these are the Ritual Protocols for the Crown Prince Lecture (*Sŏyŏn chin'gang ŭi*) that Sejong established: Each morning the Crown Prince was to go to his lecture hall, entering by the eastern steps and standing facing west. His teachers and mentors were to enter by the western steps and to stand facing east. The Crown Prince would then bow twice deeply. The teachers and mentors were to return his bows. Then they were to take their seats. The tutors now entered and took their seats. The Crown Prince would begin by summarizing what he had studied the previous day. The teachers and mentors would then lecture in the prescribed manner.[202]

Despite this ritual recognition of status, teachers had no means of forcing the prince to obey. First of all, the format of study sessions did not permit teachers to test the prince or to challenge him directly. If the prince was so inclined, he could just mumble yes and no throughout the session. Moreover, if the prince were to continue to be negligent of his studies, there was nothing the teacher could do. He had no way either to discipline or to punish the prince. No matter how inattentive and negligent the prince might be, the instructional staff had to be ready for the sessions. The Crown Prince, on the other hand, could cancel them. The worst punishment that was imposed on the Crown Prince was to remove him from his position, as sometimes happened, but this could be done only by the king. In the final analysis, the pedagogical practices addressed to the Yi Crown Prince, while they may have conformed to the tenets of Confucian pedagogy, were at least as strongly influenced by the unique status of the student.

DAILY LIFE

Important though formal education may have been in the development of the Crown Prince, perhaps it should be viewed in the total context of his life. Once appointed, the Crown Prince was moved to a completely separate establishment. His residence consisted of several buildings, one for living, one for holding study sessions, one for daytime use, etc. The Crown Prince Tutorial Office and the Crown Prince Protection Office (Şeja igwisa) were situated in proximity.[203] His establishment was managed by nine ladies-in-waiting and several tens of eunuchs, all holding special rank, and they jointly commanded an additional seventy to ninety slaves, most of them male.[204] The Crown Prince was taught by the tutors of the Tutorial Office and was escorted and guarded by fourteen military officers holding various ranks in the Protection Office.[205] Located within the palace precinct, his establishment was a scaled-down version of the king's establishment.

The Crown Prince usually married between age ten and twelve. The selection procedure for his wife was known as the threefold selection (samgant'aek). The king first promulgated an edict forbidding all marriages and requesting eligible families with daughters of marriageable age to send in their names. First the king chose about seven girls from the list. Then the royal family, after personal interviews, narrowed the list down to three finalists among whom one was chosen after further scrutiny. For some period before the wedding ceremony, the prospective bride was housed within the palace and was instructed in court manners and customs. After the ceremony, the prince and his wife had adjoining living quarters, but nuptial consummation did not take place until they reached about fifteen years of age. This was preceded by their capping ceremonies.[206] In addition to his primary wife, the Crown Prince could have secondary consorts who were given ranks ranging from junior second rank to junior fifth rank.[207]

There is little information on his living arrangements before appointment, but occasionally, in his early years, he was brought up outside the palace. Prince Yangnyŏng was made to stay at his study hall until his appointment as Crown Prince.[208] Yŏnsan and Injong spent their first several years outside the palace in the care of certain strangers, presumably with little occasion to see their parents.[209] Officials regarded this arrangement as quite dangerous and they urged the respective father-kings to keep their sons nearby and to guide them through love and example.[210] External domicile, however, was not usual and most Crown Princes grew up within the palace. But early appointment as Crown Prince again separated the heir-apparent from his parents. Ensconced in separate quarters, his contact with his parents, especially his father, tended to be quite formal and ceremonial. Some kings seem to have made a special effort to maintain a close relationship with their sons. Sejong, for instance, took three meals a day with Munjong.[211] But in most instances, the father-son relationship seems to have been rather distant.

As a rule the Crown Prince took his meals alone, though presumably he was attended by ladies-in-waiting. Women and persons of low position were not permitted to share his table. The meal was brought to him on a small low table and it usually consisted of rice, soup, pickles, meat and/or fish, and vegetables in rather small quantities.[212] On the days of commemoration for deceased royal ancestors or during the mourning period, meat or fish was omitted. The Crown Prince also slept alone while his ladies-in-waiting slept in adjoining rooms. When he wished, he visited his wife, whose quarters adjoined his, or he visited other secondary consorts in their respective apartments, which usually were not far from his own. Sexual abstinence was expected of him, as it was for others, during the period of mourning for parents or grandparents. Yŏngjo broke this taboo before he was appointed Crown Prince and supposedly earned the displeasure of his father Sukchong.[213]

The Yi Crown Prince dressed, assisted by his ladies-in-waiting, in the manner prescribed for the occasion. In the Yi dynasty strict sumptuary laws were the norm and deviation was frowned upon.[214] In fact, one

of the symptoms of insanity that Prince Sado developed was an inability
to dress. His wife attributed this to the fact that he had often been up-
braided for inappropriate attire by his father Yŏngjo.[215]

It is difficult to reconstruct the precise schedule which the Crown
Prince followed in his daily life, but a rough composite picture based on
various sources can be constructed. The Crown Prince rose at dawn, washed
and, in formal attire, paid regular visits to his elders—his father, his mother,
the queen if he was born of a secondary consort, and his grandmother.
He did not visit them every morning but by turns, and some more often
than others. He was frequently accompanied by his wife.[216] These visits
were short, consisting of bowing to them and inquiring after their health.
On those days when he did not pay a visit in person, he sent a note of
greeting.[217]

Upon returning, he changed into more informal dress. After break-
fast, he had a lecture session with his tutors. The session was repeated in
the early and late afternoon. Sometimes he had evening sessions. The
length of these sessions seems to have varied depending upon the individual prince, the weather, the time of day, etc.[218] The Crown Prince Lecture recessed during the hottest part of summer, though the prince was
encouraged to hold sessions on cooler days.[219] Aside from the summer
recess, there was no designated holiday but there seem to have been small
breaks between finishing one text and starting another.[220] When the Crown
Prince was ill he could cancel a session and, not surprisingly, some princes
often did so under this pretext.

On days of commemoration of royal ancestors, the lecture sessions
were usually canceled. Instead, the Crown Prince attended the sacrificial
ceremonies. He was also expected to perform other ceremonial functions
either familial or official in nature. If the Crown Prince was given some
governmental function, both his ritual and official duties increased.[221]

The Crown Prince was not permitted to go outside the palace at will
but only for specific reasons. When he did, he was escorted by his military guards. He sometimes accompanied his father when the king went
to view a display of martial arts. This was more common during the earlier part of the dynasty. Later, the Crown Prince's outings usually consisted of accompanying his father on visits to tombs of royal ancestors.

Most of the Crown Prince's leisure hours were spent in the company
of ladies-in-waiting and eunuchs. Having neither authority nor incentive
to discipline him, both groups seem to have indulged his whims.[222] Some

ladies-in-waiting of higher rank were somewhat educated and very well trained in court custom[223] and they might have tried to be rather strict with the prince. But since they had no authority over him, most likely he had his way.

In fact, the Crown Prince grew up unattended by any adult who might discipline him with both authority and affection for any extended period. Presumably his mother might fulfill this function to a limited degree but there is little information on her role in her son's education and upbringing. It appears, however, that there might have been a difference between having a mother who was the queen and a mother who was a secondary consort. The queen would have had more ceremonial duties of her own and her status would have placed her relationship to her son on a more formal basis. On the other hand, secondary consorts were usually drawn from lower social classes. In Yi society, where a mother's familial status was as important as a father's, Crown Princes born of secondary consorts seem to have suffered from a certain stigma. The prince's intellectual and behavioral guidance was left mostly to his tutors who, on the one hand, changed rather often, and on the other, enjoyed only limited access to him in the controlled atmosphere of the study sessions. They did little more than read books with him.

The Crown Prince's life, thus, seems to have had a rather schizoid character consisting of drastically differing situations, each with its own special expectations and demands. Toward his parents and in ceremonial functions the most exacting deference and propriety were expected of him; in his study sessions sincerity and studiousness were demanded, while at most other times his every whim was attended to by ladies-in-waiting and eunuchs. In these circumstances consistent reinforcement of values was not possible. After all, without appropriate reinforcement in private life, the educational effort directed toward the prince cannot be described as complete.

RESULTS

If the proof of the pudding is in the eating, perhaps the education of the Crown Prince as it was practiced at the Yi court should be evaluated in terms of the princes' ability to assimilate it, their responses and their respective performances. These may be said to fall into three categories, each conforming to a rather distinct pattern. The first consists of those princes who in fact acceded to the throne and reigned for some time with a measure of success. Hyŏnjong (1641–74, r. 1659–74), Sukchong, and Chŏngjo fall into this category. The second category consists of kings who died quite soon after their accession. Munjong reigned for two years, Injong for one, and Yejong a little more than a year. Finally there were Crown Princes who failed. Either their tenure as Crown Prince was terminated because of their unsuitability, as was the case with Princes Yangnyŏng and Sado or, if they did ascend the throne, their rule proved to be an unmitigated disaster, as with Yŏnsan and Kyŏngjong. These "failed" princes provide interesting case studies for identifying the possible causes of failure.

The Princes Yangnyŏng and Sado, whose tenures were terminated in disgrace, both spent many years as Crown Prince, Yangnyŏng from 1404 until his deposal in 1418 and Sado from 1736 until his execution in 1762. Sado is the more tragic character. Stark mad and a threat to the dynasty, he was killed by his father at the age of twenty-eight. Yangnyŏng, on the other hand, lived to the ripe age of sixty-nine, enjoying his life as an ordinary prince not in the line of succession. He was the first Crown Prince to have had a long tenure, and several features of his life were not typical of the lives of later Crown Princes. He was not appointed Crown Prince until he was eleven years of age and various aspects of his education were delayed. His father, T'aejong, was not ideological and, mindful of the several traps that might lie in wait for his son, he tried to prepare him for them. True, when Yangnyŏng blatantly neglected study, T'aejong resorted to such coercive measures as punishing his son's eunuch attendants and ordering the tutors to keep a close watch over him,[224] even threatening them with severe reprisals if he did not improve.[225] But on no occasion did he display personal hostility toward his son. On the contrary, he tried to encourage and to please him. He frequently took Yangnyŏng on outings, sometimes even against the prescribed rules.[226] In 1407, T'aejong went so far as to send the fourteen-year-old Yangnyŏng on an ambassadorial mission to China for seven months.[227]

Despite T'aejong's judiciousness and forbearance toward his son, he does not seem to have provided a great deal of personal parental care or supervision. Yangnyŏng lived away from his parents from a rather early age. T'aejong brushed aside the official suggestions that his son live closer to him, answering that such an arrangement would further mar the father-son relationship if his son were to continue to misbehave and he were to find it necessary to scold his son and interfere in his life constantly.[228] T'aejong was probably right because, by the time this emerged as a problem, Yangnyŏng was well on his way to adulthood, too old to be molded by parental supervision.

It would appear that Yangnyŏng, initiated into the structured life of a Crown Prince after his crucial formative years, was not deeply influenced by the formal education that he was subjected to. His tutors tried, but they were powerless to enforce strict measures. His father was conciliatory and he left daily guidance to others. Not interested in study, Yangnyŏng developed interests in other areas—areas seen as inconsistent with the qualities of a future ruler. In his mid-teens, he took up such things as falconry,[229] music,[230] calligraphy, [231] and, naturally, women, and he pursued these interests with gusto often against prescribed rules. Yangnyŏng's affair with a certain Yŏri, which cost him his position, was a case in point. According to the *Sillok*, Yangnyŏng forcibly took Yŏri into his residence. Since she had formerly been a minister's concubine, this was regarded as a serious offence. Despite a promise to his father that he would not see her again, he secretly took her back and had a child by her.[232] The discovery of this fact sent the court into an uproar. T'aejong carried out a ritual punishment of Yangnyŏng and sent Yŏri away.[233] At this point, Yangnyŏng openly protested his father's decision.[234] This sealed his fate. He was deposed as Crown Prince. Though T'aejong appears to have been rather hurt by his son's defiance, his decision to depose him does not seem to have been motivated by disenchantment; if anything he was of a mind to forgive him.[235] His decision was, rather, a political one born of a desire not to compromise the authority of the throne.[236]

The tragedy which afflicted Prince Sado was an instance of Yi educational practice gone awry. He was appointed Crown Prince at the age of two and instantly became the focus of the attentions of the entire court. His father, Yŏngjo, was quite unlike T'aejong. Though committed, like T'aejong, to the strengthening of the royal authority, unlike T'aejong, Yŏngjo faced the mid-eighteenth-century bureaucracy, thoroughly Confucianized and divided into factions with established power bases. An ideologue himself, Yŏngjo tried to achieve his aims through a quest for moral perfection.[237] Hoping to make his son into a latter-day sage, he subjected him to the most rigorous training at an early age. While he was very demanding toward his son, Yŏngjo was not inclined toward affectionate or conciliatory gestures. He frequently asked his son to explicate difficult passages in the presence of officials and he expressed open disapproval when he did not get the answer he wanted. He seldom took his son on outings and he was often critical of his manner and dress.[238] Nor did he provide adequate supervision for his son. From his appointment as Crown Prince at the age of two, Sado lived in his own residence in the care of ladies-in-waiting and eunuchs.[239] This life, in fact, left him unable to manage its disparate elements—an extremely demanding but equally distant father; a mother who provided neither the affection nor the discipline to overcome this; moralistic but quite powerless tutors; and indulgent attendants and servants who had neither the desire nor the authority to discipline him. By his mid-teens he began to display symptoms of insanity, and by the time of his death these had reached such extremes as the pointless killing of his servants and concubines and an utterly unrealistic and futile attempt on his father's life.[240] In the end, there appears to have been no alternative to his execution.

If Yangnyŏng and Sado played out their dissatisfactions at great personal cost, the same cannot be said for Kings Yŏnsan and Kyŏngjong. With the prerogatives of the monarchy at their disposal, they made others pay for their own discontents. Generally regarded as two of the lowest points of Yi Confucian rule, their reigns were punctuated by purges resulting in the deaths of numerous scholar-officials whom they seem generally to have hated.

Yŏnsan, who acceded at a younger age and reigned longer, mounted the greater spectacle and suffered the more precipitous fall. First there were the purges. Yŏnsan unleashed two, in 1498 and in 1504, killing many scholar-officials. He even meted out posthumous punishment to a number of officials, exhuming them and having their bodies sliced up.[241] And if one is to believe the *Yŏnsan'gun ilgi*, which was compiled in Chungjong's court in part to justify Yŏnsan's dethronement, Yŏnsan went on to dismantle the entire Confucian structure of the monarchy. First, there was his interruption of practices that Confucian officials held sacred—for example, keeping the "channel of expression (*ŏllo*)" open. He proscribed official admonitions to him for his misconduct and banned all criticisms of his rule. In 1505, he ordered that every official and attendant at court wear a plaque with this quatrain:

The mouth is a gate to disaster;
The tongue is a knife that stabs,
Your mouth tightly sealed, your tongue deeply concealed,
You'll preserve life and limb, stay safe and sound.[242]

To heap more humiliation on the officials, Yŏnsan then had the director of the Office of the Royal Decrees (Yemun'gwan) write a rhyme conceding all wisdom and power to the ruler and commanded that it be inscribed on the back of these plaques.[243] In 1506, he ordered that officials' caps be inscribed with the character "loyalty (ch'ung)" in front and "sincerity (sŏng)" in back.[244] Finally he abolished those offices representing the channel of expression, two of the three branches of the Censorate, and those offices conducting Confucian education such as the School for the Royal Clan, the Royal Lecture,[245] the Crown Prince Tutorial Office, the Royal College,[246] etc.·

Kyŏngjong, already feeble and in ill health when he began his four-year reign in 1720 at thirty-three, was no match for his predecessor of two hundred years, who had embarked on his twelve-year reign at the age of nineteen, full of vigor and determination. Born in an age of intense political strife, Kyŏngjong's conflicts were played out in the context of factional politics. His short reign is chiefly remembered for the purge of 1721–22 (Sinim sahwa), in which he killed over fifty officials of the Noron faction including four, known as the "four Noron ministers," who were the powerful nucleus of the faction.[247] The political impact of this purge would reverberate through the next half century of Yi court politics.

The two kings, however, share striking similarities of background. They were both born of women who had been secondary consorts before being elevated to the queenship by husbands supposedly in thrall to their charms, and both women were subsequently deposed and executed. Their sons, as the first issue of reigning monarchs, remained in their rightful positions, but not entirely free of the stigma resulting from their mothers' loss of legitimacy. Their fathers, presumably repentant of their youthful follies, are described as having viewed their sons, visible reminders of shameful lapses, with a certain suspicion and coldness. Yŏnsan'gun ilgi mentions that Sŏngjong often admonished Yŏnsan for stupidity and ignorance, while Yŏnsan came to fear and avoid his father.[248] Sukchong is said to have attributed Kyŏngjong's less desirable qualities to his mother's nature.[249] The bureaucracy also seems to have regarded these princes with disapproval. Disliking upstarts as they did, particularly beautiful ladies of dubious morality who led innocent men astray, the bureaucrats may well have let these princes know in what low esteem they held their parents.

Yet, it is not clear whether this suspicion and disapproval was the cause or the result of poor performance. Neither Yŏnsan nor Kyŏngjong excelled in study. Whatever the reasons for this might have been, Yi Confucians were not equipped to seek or find them beyond these princes' immediate educational environs. As far as they were concerned, they provided their princes as careful guidance and as thorough an education as any other Crown Prince had received. When the prince did not respond well, they just redoubled their efforts with existing procedures, providing more tutors or revising the format of the study sessions in the hope that the prince would improve. But if this concerted effort produced no result, Yi educators had no way to explain it other than to attribute it to the prince's nature. Thus, the *Yŏnsan'gun ilgi* cites, as reasons for Yŏnsan's downfall, perversity and vengefulness comparable to his mother's, an unintelligent nature and, finally, imperviousness to instruction and learning. It also mentions that, despite the effort his father and his tutors so lavished upon him, Yŏnsan could neither understand the principles contained in books nor discern proper behavior.[250] For all the *Yŏnsan-gun ilgi*'s apparent bias against Yŏnsan, this condemnation clearly reveals the mentality of the scholar-officials. As Kyŏngjong died in office, the *Kyŏngjong sillok* contains no explicit denunciation of the king. But by one official's account, Sukchong, displaying the same logic, attributed his son's deficiencies to his mother's nature.

Each of these four cases differs from the others and each has its own problems and complications. But in each instance, the schizoid character of the prince's life and the conflicting values represented by his public and private selves culminated in extreme crises. When these princes faltered in their performance, those responsible for their education responded in a predictable manner. At the extreme, the establishment found it necessary to remove individual princes from their positions, or even, as in the case of Yŏnsan, to dethrone him if they could. They did not, however, seek out alternative educational methods. Thus, the conduct of the Crown Prince's education evolved, with the best of intentions on the part of its sponsors, through increases in the number of instructional staff, more precise curricula, and ever earlier appointment of the Crown Prince. Yet this hardly brought the desired effect. In fact, the picture that emerges in the products of the system is quite grim. Even of the three kings who reigned for some time, only Chŏngjo can be viewed as an unreserved success. Hyŏnjong appears to have been a rather ineffectual ruler—his fifteen-year-reign is chiefly remembered for a rites controversy.[251] Sukchong ascended the throne at fourteen years of age, and was thus spared education as Crown Prince in his adult years. Viewed as an autocrat, he is remembered for the purges and bloodshed that marked his reign.[252]

The system of education for the Yi Crown Prince may have been rather inflexible, but this would seem to be a problem intrinsic to any traditional system of instruction proceeding from fixed premises. Held to certain assumptions concerning human nature and to consequent expectations of behavior, traditional practitioners seldom allowed for or experimented with alternative practices.

The education of the Crown Prince in the Yi dynasty represents a special case of Confucian pedagogy in that it had to accept on the one hand the unique position of the student and on the other a rigid conception of what he was to become. That Neo-Confucians viewed man as possessing an innate knowledge of moral principles and the potential to develop it did not mean that all men were seen as having equal capacity. According to Chu Hsi, each person had a different physical nature and some men's capacities were superior to others'. But those with a superior endowment did not necessarily fulfill their potential better than those less well endowed. It all depended on one's individual effort, and this in turn depended significantly on the society's ability to provide rewards which might stimulate the individual's motivation.[253] In China by the Ming dynasty the civil service examination had become the channel through which men gained access to the ranks of the official elite.[254] In Yi Korea, which had more rigid social classes, a somewhat more elaborate method had to be devised to reconcile birth and merit.[255] Nonetheless, entry into the ruling elite became the goal of education and qualifying in the civil service examinations the generally accepted criterion of success.

For the heirs-apparent discussed in this paper, however, birth was the primary criterion and merit could only have a questionable role to play. Because they were the first issue of reigning monarchs, heirs-apparent had nothing more to gain from education than their own moral improvement. This fact allowed neither the instructional staff nor the student much room for maneuver. True, not having to take the civil service examination freed the prince from studying in the formulaic manner associated with the examinations. Thus unencumbered, his education could well have aimed closer to the Confucian ideal of education—the single-minded pursuit of sagehood. Yet, this very fact also denied him some of the options open to others, such as the possibility of remaining a private scholar. In fact, almost everything was predetermined for him and the instructional staff too had little choice. No matter what their charge was like, his mentors could only teach him how to become a sage-ruler in the manner of the Confucian tradition, and this had to be done within the constraints imposed by the student's unique position.

The reality of history was such that, despite the Yi predilection for primogeniture, the majority of the Yi kings, especially the kings who reigned long and successfully, were not men who had been educated as heirs-apparent. T'aejong, Sejong, Sejo, Sŏngjong, Chungjoing, Sŏnjo, Hyojong, and Yŏngjo either were never Crown Princes at all or became so only briefly in their adult years. Unlike those Crown Princes who were designated early, strictly on the basis of birth, these kings were selected later because they had already shown some promise. Naturally, the odds of success were more in their favor since their capacities had already been recognized. Perhaps, too, this constituted a tacit recognition of an unpleasant reality. For those who underwent education as Crown Prince, it had proved impossible to fulfill the expectation, central to Confucian belief, that a proper education would produce a perfect ruler.

NOTES

1. *Fan t'ai-shih chi* (Ssu-ku chen-pen ed., 1st ser.; Shanghai: Commercial Press, 1935), 14:11a. Quoted from Wm. Theodore de Bary, *Neo-Confucian Orthodoxy and the Learning of the Mind-and-Heart* (New York: Columbia University Press, 1981), p. 30.
2. Chu Hsi, *Hui-an hsien-sheng Chu Wen-kung wen-chi* (SPTK ed.), 11:35b–36a. Quoted from de Bary, *Neo-Confucian Orthodoxy*, p. 34.
3. *Shushi gorui, Shushigaku taikei*, vol. 6 (Tokyo: Meitoku shuppansha, 1981), pp. 104–29.
4. For the Chinese Classics Mat Lecture, see Robert Hartwell, "Historical Analogism, Public Policy, and Social Science in Eleventh and Twelfth Century China," in *American Historical Review* (1971), 76(3):690–727.
5. de Bary, *Neo-Confucian Orthodoxy*, pp. 1–66.
6. Yon-Ung Kwon, "The Royal Lecture of Early Yi Korea (1), " in *Journal of Social Sciences and Humanities* (December 1979), 50:62–65.
7. *Ibid.*, p. 105.
8. *Ibid.*, pp. 67–69.
9. *Ibid.*, pp. 79–104.
10. See *Yŏlsŏngjo kye kang ch'aekcha ch'aje* (Sigangwŏn, Mss., Kyuganggak).
11. For a discussion of educational theory, see T. W. Moore, *Educational Theory: An Introduction* (London: Routledge & Kegan Paul, 1974).
12. Chŏng Tojŏn, *Chosŏn kyŏnggukchŏn* in *Sambongjip* (Seoul: T'amgudang, 1971), pp. 204–32.
13. Yi Yulgok, *Tongho mundap* in *Yulgok chŏnsŏ* (Seoul: Sŏnggyun'gwan taehakkyo Taedong munhwa yŏn'guwŏn, 1971), 15:2a–6a (1:314–16).
14. Yulgok saw ministerial power, which he felt sometimes exceeded that of the ruler, as one of the problems of Yi government. *Ibid.*, 15:13a–b (1:319).
15. *Ibid.*, 15:17b–27b (1:321–26).
16. *Ibid.*, 15:6b (1:316).
17. Wing-tsit Chan, *A Source Book in Chinese Philosophy* (Princeton: Princeton University Press, 1963), p. 98.
18. *Mencius*, 2A:6, 6A:6. Chan, *Source Book*, p. 65, p. 54.
19. *Mencius*, 6A:6. Chan, *Source Book*, p. 54.
20. Wm. Theodore de Bary et al., *Sources of Chinese Tradition* (New York: Columbia University Press, 1960), pp. 470–71.
21. *I-shu* in *Erh Ch'eng ch'üan-shu* (SPPY ed.), 19:4b; de Bary, *Chinese Tradition*, p. 473.
22. *Chu Tzu ch'üan-shu* (1714 ed.), 43:2b–3a, 43:4a; de Bary, *Chinese Tradition*, pp. 494–95.
23. *Chu Tzu ch'üan-shu*, 44:2a; de Bary, *Chinese Tradition*, p. 496.
24. *Chu Tzu ch'üan-shu*, 44:12b; de Bary, *Chinese Tradition*, pp. 497–98.
25. *Chu Tzu ch'üan-shu*, 44:13a–b; de Bary, *Chinese Tradition*, p. 498.
26. *Chu Tzu ch'üan-shu*, 44:28a–b; de Bary, *Chinese Tradition*, pp. 498–99.

27. *Chu Tzu ch'üan-shu*, 44:28a; de Bary, *Chinese Tradition*, p. 498.
28. Uno Seiichi ed., *Shōgaku* (Tokyo: Meiji shoin, 1965), pp. 16–17.
29. *Ibid.*, p. 18.
30. *Ibid.*, p. 177.
31. For age, I have adhered to the traditional Chinese and Korean method of counting *(sui/se)*. That is, the child is said to be one year old at birth and a year is added on each lunar new year. One should subtract at least one year to convert to the western equivalent.
32. *Shōgaku*, p. 18.
33. *Chu Tzu ta-ch'üan* (SPPY ed.), 74:11a.
34. *Shōgaku*, p. 18.
35. *Ibid.*, p. 5.
36. For a discussion of this view, see T. W. Moore, *Philosophy of Education: An Introduction* (London: Routledge & Kegan Paul, 1982), pp. 33–37.
37. *Shōgaku*, pp. 19–20.
38. *Chu Tzu ta-ch'üan*, 74:11a–b.
39. E.g., Chu Hsi and Lü Tsu-ch'ien compiled, Wing-tsit Chan translated, *Reflections on Things at Hand* (New York: Columbia University Press, 1967), p. 97.
40. Donald Munro, *The Concept of Man in Early China* (Stanford: Stanford University Press, 1969), pp. 98–99.
41. *I-shu*, 18:5b. Chan, *Source Book*, p. 605–6.
42. Chan, *Source Book*, *p.* 607.
43. *I-shu*, 15:5a, Chan, *Source Book*, p. 607.
44. *Chu Tzu ch'üan-shu*, 2:22a. Chan, *Source Book*, p. 606.
45. *Chu Tzu ch'üan-shu*, 3:1b–2a. Chan, *Source Book*, p. 608.
46. *Chu Tzu ch'üan-shu*, 3:8b. Chan, *Source Book*, p. 609.
47. Ch'ien Mu, *Chu Tzu hsin-hsüeh-an* (Taipei: San-min shu-chü, 1971), 3:613–87.
48. *Shushi gorui*, p. 85.
49. *Chu Tzu ta-ch'üan*, 14:11a.
50. *Shushi gorui*, p. 91. Also, *Chu Tzu hsin-huüen-an*, 3:643–44.
51. *Shushi gorui*, pp. 93–94. *Chu Tzu Hsin-hsüeh-an*, 3:649–54.
52. *Chu Tzu ta-ch'üan*, 14:11a.
53. *Reflections*, p. 92.
54. *Chu Tzu ch'üan-shu*, 3:34a. Chan, *Source Book*, p. 611.
55. *Chu Tzu ch'üan-shu*, 3:8a. Chan, *Source Book*, p. 609.
56. *Ibid.*
57. *Chu Tzu ch'üan-shu*, 3:12b. Chan, *Source Book*, p. 609.
58. *Chu Tzu ch'üan-shu*, 3:1b–2a. Chan, *Source Book*, p. 608.
59. *Reflections*, pp. 38–39.
60. *Chu Tzu ta-ch'üan*, 74:16b–17b.
61. Pak Semu, *Kyemong* in *Tongmong sŏnsŭp* (Seoul: Ŭryu munhwasa, 1971), pp. 124–26.
62. Chŏng Tonmok, "T'oegye kyohak sasang yŏn'gu (1)," in *T'oegye hakpo*, (1977), 16:12–74.

63. *T'oegye chŏnsŏ* (Seoul: Sŏnggyun'gwan taehakkyo Taedong munhwa yŏn-guwŏn, 1971), 2:338–40.
64. *Yulgok chŏnsŏ*, 15:33b–46a (1:329–36).
65. *Ibid.*, 27:3a–21b (2:82–91).
66. *Ibid.*, 15:34a–40b (1:330–33).
67. *T'aejong sillok* in *Chosŏn wangjo sillok* (Seoul: Kuksa p'yŏnch'an wiwŏnhoe, 1970–72, 48 vols. plus index vol.), 9:27a.
68. *T'aejo sillok* in *Chosŏn wangjo sillok*, 1:46a–b.
69. *Ibid.*, 7:12b.
70. *T'aejong sillok*, 2:8a–9a.
71. *Ibid.*, 3:22a.
72. *Ibid.*, 3:24a–b.
73. *Ibid.*, 5:16a–b.
74. *Ibid.*, 7:10a–b.
75. *Ibid.*, 7:17b–18a.
76. *Ibid.*, 8:3a–b.
77. See note 67.
78. *T'aejong sillok*, 10:22a.
79. *Ibid.*, 35:61a–63a.
80. *Ibid.*, 35:64a–65a.
81. *Ibid.*, 35:65a–67b.
82. E.g., *Tongho mundap*, 15:10a (1:318).
83. Yon-Ung Kwon, "The Royal Lecture (1)," pp. 82–87.
84. *Sejong sillok* in *Chosŏn wangjo sillok*, 54:24b.
85. *Ibid.*, 69:3a.
86. *Ibid.*, 7:29b–30a.
87. One of the more celebrated projects they completed was the invention of the Korean alphabet *(Hunmin chŏngŭm)*.
88. *Sejong sillok*, 7:30a.
89. *Ibid.*, 69:3a.
90. *Ibid.*, 73:2b.
91. *Ibid.*, 83:12b.
92. *Ibid.*, 14:17a–18b.
93. *Ibid.*, 14:18b–19a.
94. *Ibid.*, 52:34b–35a.
95. *Ibid.*, 52:35a–b.
96. *Ibid.*, 100:6b.
97. *Ibid.*, 100:16a–b.
98. *Ibid.*, 48:32a.
99. *Ibid.*, 119:19a.
100. *Sejo sillok* in *Chosŏn wangjo sillok*, 4:14b.
101. Those who attempted this coup came to be known as "the six who died" *(sayuksin)*. They were executed by Sejo.
102. *Sejo sillok*, 4:27b.
103. Sin Chihyŏn, "Sŏng Sammun—Taeŭi myŏngbun ŭi hwasin," in *Inmul Han'guksa*, (1965), 3:149–64.

104. E.g., six scholars known as "the six who lived" (saengyuksin). These six supposedly chose to live out their lives as hermits.
105. Yi Hyŏnhŭi, "Sejo (1427–68) P'aedo e ŏlkin ungji," in Inmul Han'guksa (1965), 3:116–34.
106. Sejo sillok, 20:27b.
107. Ibid., 19:44a–b.
108. Ibid., 33:2b.
109. Ibid., 2:8b.
110. Ibid., 31:4a.
111. Sŏngjong sillok in Chosŏn wangjo sillok, 1:2a–b.
112. Yon-Ung Kwon, "The Royal Lecture (1)," pp. 93–104.
113. Sŏngjong sillok, 151:6b.
114. This is based on the Kyŏngguk taejon which was published in 1485. Kyŏngguk taejŏn (Seoul: Pŏpchech'ŏ, 1962), vol. 1, p. 70.
115. Sŏngjong sillok, 284:15a–b.
116. E.g., ibid., 151:11a–b; 188:81b.
117. Sŏngjong wanted to postpone Yŏnsan's Entrance Ceremony at the Royal College because of this apprehension. Ibid., 187:1a; 189:6b.
118. E.g., ibid., 246:2b–3a; 246:4b.
119. Yŏnsan'gun ilgi in Chosŏn wangjo sillok, 52:10a.
120. Ibid., 58:15a.
121. Edward Wagner, The Literati Purges: Political Conflict in Early Yi Korea (Cambridge: Harvard University Press, 1974), pp. 80–104.
122. Chungjong sillok in Chosŏn wangjo sillok, 27:23b–29a.
123. Ibid., 28:49b–51a.
124. Ibid., 36:57b–58a.
125. Ibid., 38:22a–b.
126. T'aejong sillok, 3:22a.
127. Chungjong sillok, 8:49a–51b.
128. Ibid., 34:63b.
129. See Poyangch'ŏng ilgi (Sigangwŏn, 1689, Mss., Kyuganggak).
130. Soktaejŏn (Seoul: Pŏpchech'ŏ, 1965), pp. 37–39.
131. Taejŏn t'ongp'yŏn (Seoul: Pŏpchech'ŏ, 1963), pp. 52–53. See also Taejŏn hoet'ong (Seoul: Korea University Press, 1960), pp. 52–53.
132. See P. H. Hirst, Knowledge and the Curriculum (Routledge & Kegan Paul, 1974).
133. P. H. Hirst and R. S. Peters, The Logic of Education (Routledge & Kegan Paul, 1974), chap. 4.
134. Shushi gorui, pp. 84–85.
135. Chu Tzu hsin-Hsüeh-an, 3:615.
136. Yulgok chŏnsŏ, 27:8a (2:84).
137. Shushi gorui, pp. 104–5.
138. Ibid., p. 105.
139. Reflections, p. 88. Also Shushi gorui, pp. 148–88.
140. Shushi gorui, p. 91.

141. E.g., *T'aejong sillok*, 16:43a; *Sejong sillok*, 35:72a.
142. *T'aejong sillok*, 26:29b.
143. *Ibid.*, 32:16b.
144. *Sejong sillok*, 121:44b.
145. *Sejo sillok*, 10:20a–b.
146. *Chungjong sillok*, 31:58a.
147. *Sejo sillok*, 19:44a–b.
148. Yon-Ung Kwon, "The Royal Lecture (1)," pp. 106–7. But they both showed some interest in the Taoist works. Sejong had the *Chuang Tzu* printed and distributed copies to officials *(Sejong sillok*, 27:10a). Sŏnjong unsuccessfully tried to read *Lao Tzu*, *Chuang Tzu*, and *Lieh Tzu* at the Royal Lecture *(Sŏngjong sillok*, 150:11b).
149. *Chungjong sillok*, 64:13b–14b.
150. *Reflections*, p. 117.
151. *Ibid.*, pp. 117–18.
152. *Ibid.*, p. 118.
153. *Shushi gorui*, p. 91.
154. *Reflections*, p. 119.
155. de Bary, *Neo-Confucian Orthodoxy*, pp. 91–123.
156. *Ibid.*, p. 35.
157. Sŏngjong included several Korean historical works in his curriculum. Yon-Ung Kwon, "The Royal Lecture (1)," p. 97.
158. *Ibid.*, pp. 106–7.
159. *Sejong sillok*, 30:18b–19a.
160. *Yŏlsŏngjo kye kang ch'aekcha ch'aje.*
161. *Ibid.*
162. *Yulgok chŏnsŏ*, 27:8b–9b(2:84–5).
163. *Yŏlsŏngjo kye kang ch'aekcha ch'aje.*
164. *T'aejong sillok*, 18:14b.
165. *Ibid.*, 22:28a–29b.
166. *Sejo sillok*, 1:1a–3b.
167. *Ibid.*, 31:5a.
168. *Sejong sillok*, 51:17a.
169. *Ibid.*, 83:18b.
170. E.g., Kim Tonguk, ed., *Hanjungnok* (Seoul: Minjung sŏgwan, 1970), pp. 97–107.
171. T. W. Moore, *Philosophy of Education*, pp. 66–80.
172. *Reflections*, p. 97.
173. E.g., *ibid.*, pp. 5–34.
174. *Ibid.*, p. 263.
175. E.g., *T'aejong sillok*, 16:43a.
176. R. S. Peters, *Ethics and Education* (London: George Allen & Unwin, 1966), pp. 61–62.
177. E.g., *Chungjong sillok*, 28:49a–51b; 31:58a; *Yŏngjo sillok* in *Chosŏn wangjo sillok*, 43:15a.

178. E.g., *Sejong sillok*, 37:10b; *Yŏngjo sillok*, 90:22b–23a.
179. *T'aejong sillok*, 16:43a.
180. *Ibid.*, 26:25b.
181. *Sŏngjong sillok*, 151:6b.
182. Cho Ch'ŏngse, *Sŏyŏn kangŭi* (1762 ed., Kyujanggak).
183. *Sŏngjong sillok*, 246:2b–3a.
184. Cho Ch'ŏngse, *Sŏyŏn kangŭi*.
185. *Reflections*, p. 94.
186. *Ibid.*, pp. 92, 96.
187. *T'oegye sŏnsaeng ŏnhaengnok* in *T'oegye chŏnsŏ*, 1:1a–4b (4:169–70); 2:1a–9b (4:183–87).
188. See the section "Selecting Friends" *(T'aegu)* in *A Model for Schools in Yulgok chŏnsŏ*, 15:36b (1:332).
189. I learned of this fact from Professor Pei-yi Wu who is working on the childhood of the Chinese rulers.
190. *Sejong sillok*, 41:3b.
191. *Ibid.*, 61:47a; 72:9a–b; 97:20b–21a.
192. *Sejong sillok*, 47:26a; *Sŏngjong sillok*, 17:1b.
193. *Sejong sillok*, 97:20b–21a; 100:33b; *Munjong sillok* in *Chosŏn wangjo sillok*, 6:32a; *Sŏnjong sillok*, 90:12a.
194. *Sejong sillok*, 101:35a–b; *Sŏngjong sillok*, 173:1a–b; 248:1b.
195. *Yŏnsan'gun ilgi*, 60:11b–12a.
196. *Chungjong sillok*, 14:16b.
197. *Ibid.*, 26:65a–b.
198. *Hyojong sillok* in *Chosŏn wangjo sillok*, 15:2b–3a; *Sukchong sillok* in *Chosŏn wangjo sillok*, 5:6a.
199. *Sejong sillok*, 52:40a.
200. *Ibid.*, 38:3b.
201. During the summer months, wine was replaced by tea. *Ibid.*, 52:44a–b.
202. *Ibid.*, 52:35b.
203. His establishment was referred to as the *Tonggung* (the East Palace) and consequently he was sometimes referred to as *Tonggung*.
204. *Kyŏngguk taejŏn*, vol. 2, pp. 189–91. *Taejŏn hoet'ong*, p. 592.
205. *Kyŏngguk taejŏn*, vol. 2, pp. 17–21. *Taejŏn hoet'ong*, p. 372.
206. Kim Yongsuk, "Yijo kungjung p'ungsok ŭi yŏn'gu," in *Yijo yŏryu munhak mit kungjung p'ungsok ŭi yŏn'gu* (Seoul: Sukmyŏng yŏja taehakkyo ch'ulp'anbu, 1970), pp. 343–65. See also Prince Sado's wife Lady Hong's account of her marriage in *Hanjungnok*, pp. 14–45, 111, 113.
207. *Kyŏngguk taejŏn*, vol. 1, p. 18. *Taejŏn hoet'ong* p. 23.
208. *T'aejong sillok*, 3:24a–b; 3:35a–36b.
209. *Chungjong sillok*, 23:20a; 27:59a; 31:9a–10a.
210. *Chungjong sillok*, 26:40a; 32:16a–b.
211. *Sejong sillok*, 83:16b–18b.
212. Kim Yongsuk, "Yijo kungjung p'ungsok," pp. 316–17.
213. A child fathered by Yŏngjo was conceived during the mourning period for

his mother. Min Chinwŏn, *Tanam mallok* in *P'aerim* (Seoul: T'amgudang, 1970), 2:12a (9:161).

214. For the Yi sumptuary laws, see Kim Tonguk, *Yijo chŏn'gi poksik yŏn'gu* (Seoul: Han'guk yŏn'guwŏn, 1963).
215. *Hanjungnok*, p. 209.
216. *Ibid.*, p. 45, p. 113.
217. Records of these notes of greeting, which were obligatory, are found at the beginning of daily entries in the *Records of the Royal Secretariat (Sŭngjŏngwŏn ilgi)*.
218. E.g., *Kyŏngjong ch'un'gung ilgi* (Sigangwŏn, 1690–1760, Mss., Kyujanggak), *Changhŏn seja tonggung ilgi* (Sigangwŏn, 1738–62, Mss., Kyujanggak), *Chŏngjo tonggung ilgi* (Sigangwŏn, 1762–76, Mss., Kyujanggak).
219. E.g., *Chungjong sillok*, 45:2a.
220. *Yŏlsŏngjo kye kang ch'aekcha ch'aje.*
221. See above, note 218.
222. E.g., *Hanjungnok*, pp. 103–11.
223. Kim Yongsuk, "Yijo kungjung p'ungsok," pp. 279–310.
224.. *T'aejong sillok*, 10:22a.
225. *Ibid.*, 11:17a.
226. E.g., *ibid.*, 25:7a.
227. *Ibid.*, 14:29a–b; 15:13a–17b.
228. *Ibid.*, 25:19a–b.
229. *Ibid.*, 24:27a; 25:4b–5a; 25:2b–3a.
230. *Ibid.*, 33:10a–12b.
231. Yangnyŏng was one of the renowned calligraphers of his time.
232. *T'aejong sillok*, 35:46b–49a.
233. *Ibid.*, 35:49a–b; 35:53a–54a; 35:56a.
234. *Ibid.*, 35:61a–63a.
235. *Ibid.*, 35:63a–64a.
236. *Ibid.*, 35:64b–65a. Yangnyŏng was put on a regular prince's stipend and Yŏri was returned to him. *Ibid.*, 35:69b–71a.
237. JaHyun Kim Haboush, "A Heritage of Kings: One Man's Monarchy in the Confucian World" (Ph.D. diss., Columbia University; Ann Arbor, Mich.: University Microfilms, 1978), pp. 166–267.
238. *Hanjungnok*, pp. 143–92.
239. *Ibid.*, pp. 97–101.
240. Haboush, "Heritage," pp. 393–408.
241. They are known as the *Muo sahwa* and the *Kapcha sahwa*. See *Yŏnsan'gun ilgi*, 30:3b–27a; 55:21a–56:25b. See also Wagner, *The Literati Purges*, pp. 42–69.
242. *Yŏnsan'gun ilgi*, 57:12b.
243. *Ibid.*, 57:19b–20a; 57:20b.
244. *Ibid.*, 62:14a.
245. *Ibid.*, 56:32a; 62:8b.
246. *Ibid.*, 54:24b–25a.

247. Haboush, "Heritage," pp. 86–105.
248. *Yŏnsan'gun ilgi*, 63:20b.
249. Min Chinwŏn, *Tanam mallok*, 1:47b–48a (9:151).
250. *Yŏnsan'gun ilgi*, 63:20a–b.
251. Haboush, "Heritage," pp. 47–60.
252. *Ibid.*, pp. 61–72.
253. Munro, *The Concept of Man*, pp. 81–116.
254. Ping-ti Ho, *The Ladder of Success in Imperial China* (New York: Columbia University Press, 1962), pp. 1–52.
255. *Kyŏngguk taejŏn*, pp. 137–50.

Sa-Soon Youn

T'oegye's Identification of "To Be" and "Ought": T'oegye's Theory of Value

I

IT MAY BE said that Confucianism aims more at the perfection of ethical consciousness than at any other pursuit. As plain evidence for its pursuit of moral perfection, it may be pointed out that originally instruction in ritual or decorum was identified with Confucian teaching. Like the other branches of Confucianism, Neo-Confucianism also retains this thorough moral sense, for it was formed in an effort to make more rational and to deepen, on the basis of metaphysics, Confucianism's original ethical point of view.

Yi T'oegye (Yi Hwang, 1501–70) was a great master of Neo-Confucianism. From the standpoint of Chu Hsi, he arranged and systematized historically and theoretically the Neo-Confucianism of the Sung, Yüan, and Ming periods. He not only consolidated earlier Neo-Confucian theories but also extended, through his own speculation, their most profound doctrines. His effort was crystallized in such works as *Record of the Learning of Principle in the Sung, Yüan, and Ming (Songge Wŏn Myŏng ihak t'ongnok)* and *Ten Diagrams of the Sage Learning (Sŏnghak sipto)*. Therefore it may safely be said that a thorough study of Toegye's works will lead us to understand one of the ethical viewpoints of Confucianism that he intensified to the highest degree on the plane of metaphysics.

II

In Neo-Confucianism ethical behavior is termed *i-li chih hsing*, which means "righteous" or "virtuous" behavior performed in accordance with reason. T'oegye distinguished *i-li chih hsing* from instinctive and emotional action, or in his own words "*hsing-ch'i chih so wei*," for he regarded the latter not as a behavior of moral significance but as a meaningless action. He refuted Wang Yang-ming's doctrine of the inseparability of knowledge and practice in terms of *hsing-ch'i chih so wei*.[1] T'oegye thought that moral behavior, unlike purposeless action, should imply the practice of righteousness.

It may not be far-fetched to say that the ultimate purpose of learning for T'oegye was to seek out some standard of judgment by which we can determine or verify, in the light of "ethical behavior" *(i-li chih hsing)*, the ethical value of an act. For he did not think that knowledge is one thing and practice another. On the contrary, he maintained that knowledge and practice are coexistent and cooperative *(chihaeng pyŏngjin sŏl)*. In other words, knowledge and practice are in such a close relationship that they can be compared to "two wheels of a wagon," or "two wings of a bird." On this basis T'oegye refuted Wang Yang-ming's doctrine of the inseparability of knowledge and practice. T'oegye thought that knowledge should refer not only to an abstract understanding but also to a wisdom translatable into practice. Having realized that there is no necessary or inevitable oneness of knowledge and practice (as held by Wang Yang-ming), he seems to have emphasized the mutual dependence of the two. Thus, it may safely be said that his ethical point of view was formed on the basis of the interdependence of knowledge and practice. From his emphasis on the interdependence of the two, we can imagine his consistent and positive will to realize "righteous behavior." It may be regarded as another evidence of this will to righteous behavior that he had much trouble choosing his career: throughout his whole life, he took much pains to refuse offers of a government post that he considered compromising in this respect.[2]

T'oegye's tenacious pursuit of ethical behavior, however, is evidenced not only in his choice of career but also in his belief in the traditional ethical constants of Confucianism, widely known as the Five Relations *(wu-lun)*, namely, the five moral obligations of human relationship between sovereign and subject, parent and child, husband and wife, the young and the old, and friends. Needless to say, the fulfillment of these obligations in practice would lead one ultimately to the highest ethical behavior.

There is one thing at this point that we should not overlook; that is, T'oegye believed that the practice of the Five Relations was essential not only for maintaining social order but also for conforming to the natural order. The works of Mencius and the *Mean* also elucidate this conformity: "Wherever the superior man passes through, transformation follows. Wherever he abides, his influence is of a spiritual nature. It flows abroad, above and beneath, like that of Heaven and Earth" (*Mencius* 7A, 13), or "able to give its full development to his own nature, he can assist the transforming and nourishing powers of Heaven and Earth" (the *Mean* 22). In this context T'oegye also said: "Virtuous deeds in accordance with an ethical code may lead us into the blessed state of the union of man and nature."[3] He believed the state of Heaven and man joined as one *(t'ien-jen ho-i)* to be the ultimate stage. It is certain, therefore, that his pursuit of righteous behavior extended ultimately to the state of the harmonization of man and nature.

The fact that T'oegye regarded the harmonization of man and nature as the inevitable consequence of righteous behavior means that he accepted the following teaching in the *Mean*: "What is given by Nature is called human nature, and to follow human nature is called moral."[4] In other words, he admitted that the ultimate purpose of ethical practice lies in the realization of an *a priori* endowment of human nature. His attitude is made clearer in the following remarks: "Humanity, righteousness, decorum, and wisdom are the highest virtues of human nature. These virtues appear in man as the Four Beginnings according to his response to given situations. Sometimes they appear as affection toward parents, . . . and sometimes respect towards elders."[5] He also thought in accordance with the doctrine of Chu Hsi or Ch'eng I that nature is principle[6] and that the ways of the Five Relations are the same as those of the Five Constants *(wu-ch'ang)*.[7] Accordingly, it follows that "ought" as normative law is not different from "be" as natural law as far as its fundamental nature is concerned. That is, T'oegye's view implies that "ought" is one with "to be," for what "ought" seeks after is "to be," namely, human nature.

Since T'oegye in accordance with the traditional idea of Confucianism identified "to be" with "ought" or "should," I would like to focus my discussion on his identification as such. I also want to continue my discussion under the subtitle "T'oegye's Theory of Value." For T'oegye's ethical point of view cannot be considered only within the scope of normative principle, of which the main concern rests with the ethical behavior of man. In other words, as his viewpoint implies a cosmological or ontological metaphysics in its background, it should be examined within the broader scope of a theory of value.

III

In Neo-Confucian terms natural law, as it relates to questions of "being," is called the law of "what is so" *(so-i-jan)*, while normative law concerning questions of "ought" is called "what should be so" *(so-tang-jan)*. Of course, there may arise a question as to whether the Chinese "what is so" and "what should be so" can be equated with the "be" and "ought" of German philosophy (there really are differences of nuance between them). However, they agree on the fundamental principles they imply. Therefore, the question of the union of "be" and "ought" can safely be explicated in Neo-Confucianism in terms of "what is so" and "what should be so."

T'oegye came to be deeply concerned with this subject when Ki Taesŭng (Kobong, 1527–72) and Chŏng Yuil (Munbong, 1533–76), after an inconclusive argument between them, asked T'oegye about this matter.[8] While Ki Taesŭng thought that "what is so" refers to principle *(li)*, and "what should be so" to instances *(shih)*, Chŏng Yuil insisted that both of them refer to the same principle. With their opposite views, they finally asked T'oegye about this matter.

T'oegye answered that though "what is so" and "what should be so" can be viewed separately as principle and facts or instances, they can be said ultimately to represent the same principle. To conclude the matter he said that "what should be so" as well as "what is so" can be equated with principle. In this context he expressed the normative laws and the physical laws of things in terms of both principle and "what should be so": "That ships should sail on the sea, and wheels should roll on the earth is principle. . . . That kings should show benevolence, subjects respect, fathers benignity, and sons piety, all these refer to principle."[9] T'oegye thought that the above-mentioned obligations were not only the principle of "what is so" but also the principle of "what should be so." Here we can perceive the basis of T'oegye's identification of "what is so" and "what should be so."

T'oegye pointed out that instances of "what should be so" contain the quality of principle innate in human beings. He quoted Chen Te-hsiu (Hsi-shan, 1178–1235) to explain this problem:

It is only right if, for example, a sovereign and his ministers maintain their relationship on the basis of benevolence and respect. If not, it is wrong. Thus such obligatory behavior is called "what should be so." However, it can also be called "what is so," for human nature such as benevolence or respectfulness is not taught but given by nature or by Heaven. To know "what should be so" is to know human nature *(hsing)*, and to know "what is so" is to know Heaven or the original source of principle.[10]

Chen Te-hsiu called instantiation *(shih)* or realization in practice, such as benevolence or respectfulness, "what should be so" because instantiation or realization in this case is in accordance with reason, that is, it is reasonable. The rationality of "what should be so" explains in itself the reason why it can be called "principle." Furthermore, if we regard "what should be so" as practice or instantiation, the practice or instantiation is not taught but given by nature. This inborn ability to practice is called principle. Principle, which is given by Heaven, is in human nature explained as the imperative of Heaven *(T'ien-ming)* in the *Mean*. In short, Chen Te-hsiu thought that practice or instantiation of "what should be so" is the manifestation of human nature, and human nature in turn is principle as "what is so." Therefore, he believed that "what should be so" and "what is so" refer to principle as if they were two sides of the same coin.

We can take as examples of the manifestation of human nature Mencius' Four Beginnings, especially the feeling of pity and shame. If a child is seen falling into a well, everyone will feel a spontaneous outflow of pity for the child. This is an example of the manifestation of human nature, the sense of commiseration. If a beggar is given something with abuse heaped upon him, he will, quite naturally, feel shame. This too is an example of the manifestation of human nature, giving actual expression to the sense of what is right, fitting, or proper.

T'oegye regarded the manifestation of the Four Beginnings as practical evidence of the inborn ability of realizing human nature. Thus, he believed that principle as human nature is a natural disposition. It would not suffice to say at this point that principle as a natural disposition remains in his philosophy only a "possibility." Ultimately T'oegye's principle can be said to mean the Reality often called the Supreme Ultimate or the original ground of the universe. Thus, T'oegye regarded the "spontaneous manifestation" of human nature (principle) as "something active," not as "something passive." His attitude as such is reflected in his interpretation of the Four Beginnings in connection with "the issuance of principle." In the Four-Seven Thesis he emphasized the spontaneity or active manifestation of principle in terms of nonartificial principle and artificial issuance (fa). According to him the Four Beginnings refer to the issuance of principle, and the Seven Emotions to the issuance of material force (ch'i).[11]

Then, can it be said that "be" and "ought," that is, the "what is so" and "what should be so" of human nature, are always in accord with each other? Did T'oegye believe that these two are never in discord? As was discussed, T'oegye distinguished ethical behavior from instinctive action. Doesn't this distinction itself provide the evidence of a discordance between "what is so" and "what should be so"? Discordance between the "what is so" and "what should be so" of human nature means man's inability perfectly to achieve righteous behavior, that is, practice or instantiation of "what should be so." In a word, it refers to a case in which a man does not practice virtuous deeds but commits misdeeds. Admitting the possibility of man's misdeeds, T'oegye explained the occurrence of such cases: "In consequence of failing to achieve the issuances of principle, and being veiled by material force, man is subject to misdeeds. . . . If material force is in excess so as to obscure principle, misdeeds prevail."[12] The above statement means that misdeeds prevail when the proper manifestation of nature is hindered by the material force of the physical disposition (ch'i-chih), or when the way of "what should be so" fails to be realized because material force does not attain due measure and degree. In short, according to T'oegye evil is due to material force or the physical disposition.

Like Chang Tsai, T'oegye made a distinction between human nature as having a direct relation to material force or physical disposition, that is, the physical nature (ch'i-chih chih hsing), and that which had no relation to it, namely the original nature (pen-jan chih hsing).[13] The latter refers to the rational nature which aims at the achievement of goodness, whereas the former refers to the emotional nature which leads to misdeeds. To put his classification in terms of "what is so" and "what should be so," original nature can be said to refer to the nature where the two are in accord, while the physical or material nature refers to where they are not in accord. Therefore, so long as he acknowledges the possibility of human misdeeds and two natures, his view of identifying "what is so" and "what should be so" could not be maintained. To make his view reasonable, he had to present a theory overcoming the problem presented by the two natures and by the fact of misdeeds.

IV

As discussed earlier, T'oegye's ethical point of view does not remain only within the scope of normative principle. It should be examined in the broader scope of cosmology or ontological metaphysics. Therefore, in dealing with the problems of evil or human nature, T'oegye, like the other Neo-Confucian scholars, did not establish separate categories of learning concerning human nature, cosmology, and ontology. Rather, Neo-Confucian scholars in general, including T'oegye, were inclined to grasp human nature on an ontological basis. For the sake of convenience, however, we will examine this subject by dividing it into the categories of human nature and cosmology (or ontology).

As we have seen, T'oegye frequently affirmed that, "The occurrence of evil is due to material force or physical nature."[14] This statement can be explained in two ways. First, in view of material force, it can be interpreted as meaning that material force does not operate in accord with "what should be so." Secondly, in view of physical or material nature, it can mean that action resulting from material nature such as emotion and instinct gets out of the control of reason as original nature and becomes unreasonable. Therefore, the operation of material force can be said to be the cause of evil occurrences not only in man but in all things in general. Only when evil occurs in man can we ascribe the cause to material nature. Accordingly, we should examine T'oegye's theory of overcoming evil phenomena by dividing them into those occurring in man and in things in general.

First, let us examine the occurrence of evil in man. T'oegye thought that the original nature can and does ultimately overcome the obstacles caused by the emotional (or instinctive) needs of material nature. His belief is expressed in the following remarks:

The *Ting-hsing shu* teaches us, "Wrath can easily be aroused and is the least controllable of human feelings. However, the fact that we can easily calm our wrath and judge right and wrong according to reason proves that the temptations of our external surroundings themselves are not a sufficient cause for stimulating evil." This teaching shows that we can control material force with principle.[15]

The feeling of wrath will be aroused when the material nature hinders the proper issuance of the original nature. However, man can finally calm the feeling of wrath that may result in unreasonable deeds, and can judge right and wrong in view of "what should be so." When T'oegye said, "We can control material force with principle,"[16] he expressed his belief that the original nature can overcome the hindrances of material nature.

T'oegye also explained this triumph of original nature over material nature in the terms of Chu Hsi: "To get rid of human desire and to preserve Heaven's principle" *(T'ien-li).*[17] Here he called the desire of material nature human desire, and the original nature, Heaven's principle. Sometimes he called human desire the human mind (in the sense that the human mind and heart are the origin of human desire), and the mind in pursuit of Heaven's principle he called the "Way-mind" *(tao-hsin).* Accordingly, like the other scholars of the Ch'eng-Chu school, T'oegye said "The human mind should always follow the direction of the Way-mind."[18] In this connection he asserted that what the cultivation of human nature finally aims at is "to discard human desire as the material nature and to preserve Heaven's principle as the original nature."[19]

However, here a question arises: doesn't his statement imply that overcoming material nature can only be achieved by conscious (i.e., artificial) or nonnatural means? Unlike the case wherein he cited the issuance of original nature in the form of the Four Beginnings, he does not seem here to believe that material nature can be overcome by spontaneous or natural means. Rather, he seems to suggest here that material nature is to be overcome by means of conscious effort. For his statements, such as "The human mind should always follow the direction of the Way-mind" or "Get rid of human desire," imply that he acknowledged conscious effort for the issuance of original nature.

In fact, T'oegye did think that conscious, artificial effort is required to overcome the hindrance of material nature. According to him, before making such an effort we should recognize Heaven's principle as the original nature and human desire as material nature. Such being the case we need to distinguish Heaven's principle from human desire. T'oegye distinguished between them in the way human needs are satisfied, that is, what is in accord with Heaven's principle is good and allowable in the satisfaction of human needs, while improper satisfaction is called "human desire." In this sense he affirmed that Heaven's principle and human desire result from different "self-controlling abilities of mind."[20] Therefore, T'oegye thought that Heaven's principle and human desire cannot be recognized and distinguished outside one's mind; more specifically, the distinction can be recognized only when mind is in the state of "refined singleness" (ching-i) or reverent seriousness (ching). He explained this state by giving as an example a psychological state Mencius recommended earlier: "Don't let up in your efforts—there is always more to do; one should neither forget the practice of what is right nor push it too fast."[21] He thought that one could recognize the distinction between Heaven's principle and human desire when one attains "an alert and faithful state of mind" by concentrating one's consciousness.[22]

Let us summarize at this point T'oegye's ways of overcoming the hindrance, and avoiding the misdeeds, of material nature. First, one should make a conscious effort to keep an alert and faithful state of mind. Then one should be able to recognize the difference between Heaven's principle and human desire. Finally, one should endeavor to give up human desire upon one's recognition of the difference. It can safely be said that in T'oegye's philosophy the significance of education lies in stimulating such an effort as mentioned above.

It seems to be in line with such an effort that T'oegye, in "The Four-Seven Debate," emphasized the issuance of principle: that is, he wanted to convince people of the propriety and spontaneity of one's original nature which enable one to overcome the possible hindrance of material nature.

To say that misdeeds resulting from material nature can be overcome by conscious, artificial effort may be interpreted to mean that "what is so" and "what should be so" are identified by artificial means. If so, is this not in direct contradiction to T'oegye's aforementioned theory that "what is so" and "what should be so" can be identified by the natural manifestation of the original nature as is shown by the nonartificial, spontaneous issuances of the Four Beginnings? At first thought, it may seem so. However, T'oegye might well have thought that the artificial effort to overcome the handicap of material nature can be made not by heteronomy but by autonomy. In view of this autonomous effort, he seems to have identified the "what should be so" and "what is so" of human beings. Therefore, it would be unreasonable to assert that his identification of "what is so" and "what should be so" is not workable only because he emphasized the artificial means of overcoming hindrances of material nature.

Now, let us examine T'oegye's theory of overcoming the evil phenomena in things in general which arise when material force operates against "what should be so." T'oegye recognized that discordances between "what is so" and "what should be so" sometimes arise in the phenomena of the universe or nature. Such a discordance is due to the "distorting of principle." Evil occurs when principle, riding on material force, becomes distorted when it meets biased "distorted material force" *(p'ien-ch'i)* instead of a perfectly balanced material force *(ch'üan-ch'i)*. T'oegye compares distorted principle to water: "Cleanliness is the nature of water. Distorted principle can be compared to muddy water that has lost its cleanliness."[23] Thus, distorted principle can be said to be another expression of material nature, and the evil phenomena of the universe and nature or things in general can be explained in view of distorted principle insofar as it denotes the discordance between "what should be so" and "what is so."

T'oegye explained the good and evil in things in general: "Good occurs if principle manifests itself and material force follows, while evil occurs if material force veils principle and principle recedes."[24] That is to say, good occurs when material force follows the direction of "what should be so" and principle thereby achieves the way of "what should be so." In contrast to this, evil occurs when the functioning of material force does not attain due measure and degree and principle consequently does not manifest the way of "what should be so." Accordingly, it may be said that in the case of good phenomena T'oegye's identification of "what should be so" and "what is so" is applicable, while it is not applicable in the case of evil phenomena. Consequently, in order to apply his identification of "what is so" and "what should be so" even to the case of evil phenomena in things in general, T'oegye needed to establish some other theory to render his application plausible.

To examine how T'oegye demonstrated the applicability of his identification, let us note his statement as follows: "If material force operates against principle, principle becomes hidden. But the withdrawal of principle is not because of weakness. It is due to circumstantial forces" *(shih)*.[25]

According to the above statement, the functioning of material force contrary to "what should be so" is of course the cause of evil phenomena where principle becomes hidden. Basically, however, they can be ascribed to external circumstantial forces called *shih*, rather than to any weakness or deficiency of principle in a given instance.

To put the matter the other way around, if there is no external influence from circumstantial forces, the material force inherent in a thing may operate along the line of the "what should be so" of principle; in short, there may be no evil except through the operation of circumstantial forces. Therefore, evil phenomena, T'oegye thought, should be understood in view of outer conditions or in the relation of one thing to another.

As T'oegye explained the identification of "what is so" and "what should be so" using a ship and a wagon as metaphors, let us compare the evil aspects of a thing or event to the movement of a ship. A ship can move on the water because it is made to float on the water. That a ship is made to float on water is the "what is so" of a ship, and that it moves on water is its "what should be so." The fact that "a ship moves on the water" denotes that the "what is so" and "what should be so" of a ship are accomplished at the same time. However, when a ship is driven ashore because of an external circumstantial force such as a typhoon, this ship can be said to be contrary to what it should be, though it still retains its "what is so." This is the case when the "what should be so" of the principle inherent in a ship is not in evidence.

If we accept the circumstantial force as an outer condition, the evil aspects of a thing or event, resulting from the effacing of "what should be so," should not be ascribed only to material force in the thing. It should be explained in connection with external things, and ultimately, with all objects in the universe. Therefore, it may be said that T'oegye ultimately took the whole universe into consideration when he regarded the principle of a thing as its original nature, and the operation or functioning of a thing as "what should be so." What then is the basis on which the identification of "what is so" and "what should be so" can be extended to the whole universe? To suggest a clear answer to this question is in fact to demonstrate T'oegye's theory of identification.

V

In order to render reasonable the identification of "what is so" and "what should be so," we should demonstrate, in view of our previous discussion, the absence of the influence of circumstantial forces on the formation of the universe. Therefore, to manifest the basis on which the theory of identification can be applied to the universe is no other than to prove the absence of circumstantial forces in the formation of the universe. Here a problem arises: Could T'oegye really confirm the absence of circumstantial forces in the universe? We can find, it would appear, the answer to this question in his following remarks:

In the case of an individual thing, there surely appears some deviation of principle. To extend the matter to things in general, however, principle remains in an undifferentiated state *(hun-lun)*. Why? Because principle in its essence cannot be qualified by material force or objects. Therefore, an individual thing's deviation cannot disturb the perfect balance *(ta-ch'üan)* of the undifferentiated state.[26]

The deviation of principle, or a discordance between "what is so" and "what should be so," resulting from the operation of material force, is possible only in an individual thing, not in the universe as a whole. In the whole universe principle is mixed with material force to form the state of perfect balance. For principle in its essence cannot be qualified by material force or by objects.

Here "principle" in its essence seems to denote the intangible, extrasensory quality of principle. However, as long as we think that it means only that quality, we may come to be concerned simply with the inactivity of principle and should therefore accept in reality only the operation or function of material force. Such being the case, we should regard "principle in its essence" as denoting "the quality of principle including its extended meaning." Then, what is the extended meaning of "principle in its essence" in the larger context of the universe? The Supreme Ultimate *(t'ai-chi)* is the answer to this question. For *t'ai-chi* refers to principle as the basis of the universe.

At this point let us pay attention to T'oegye's explanation about the Supreme Ultimate and its relation to all the objects of the universe: "If the same principle is distributed uniformly to every object, each comes to have its own nature. Though each object has a different material force, principle does not disappear regardless of the functioning of material force.

Therefore, everything can be said to have one Supreme Ultimate."[27] So long as the premise, "the nature is principle," is acknowledged, the Supreme Ultimate may be said to denote the "original nature" of things in general as well as the principle of the whole universe. The Supreme Ultimate as such is the primordial principle of the universe, as Chu Hsi defined it as "the sum total of the principles of everything."[28] T'oegye conformed not only to Chu Hsi's definition of Supreme Ultimate, but also to his theory that "everything retains the great Supreme Ultimate."[29] That is, he believed in the theory of "principle is one; its particularizations are diverse" (li-i fen-shu).

What theory will result therefrom? If all the objects retain one Supreme Ultimate, the universe, the assemblage of everything, may be said to be "a system of the same principle(s)." In other words, it can hold good that the universe is "a certain state of harmonization" which can be grasped in the light of the system of the same principle(s). Here we are led to think that T'oegye's cosmology is concerned with "the harmonious creation of the universe." Therefore, we can conclude that his view of the Supreme Ultimate, so far as the whole universe is concerned, does not admit of any disharmony from the deviation or distortion of principle by circumstantial forces.

His thought as such is also expressed in the following statement:

The Supreme Ultimate moves of itself if it moves, and Heaven's Imperative, likewise flows of itself if it flows at all. How can there be an outer influence that makes them move or flow? . . . On the whole an object is made by a mysterious function by means of which principle and material force are combined. There is no such thing that makes heaven's Imperative flow. For the principle of Heaven's Imperative is the highest form that always orders without being ordered.[30]

The point of this statement is that in whatever terms the formation of the universe is explained (for example, the movement of the Supreme Ultimate, or the flow of Heaven's Imperative), it is not the result of any other function than that of principle. In this sense the universe can be said to be formed by the spontaneous and mysterious function of principle. This may safely be affirmed because principle by nature only orders without being ordered. In other words, if there can be found a cause in the phenomena manifested by principle, it is the cause arising of itself. If the whole universe is the system of one principle, the Supreme Ultimate or Heaven's Imperative, then ultimately everything in the universe, T'oegye believed, may be formed by the force inherent in principle. Thus in the harmonious formation of the universe there cannot be any operation of circumstantial forces as distorted or deviated principle. Here we can perceive that T'oegye's identification of "what is so" and "what should be so" implies an idea about the harmony of the universe.

At this point however we should acknowledge that T'oegye's theory is only a logical and abstract justification. It is not a practical demonstration of the harmonious formation of the universe. Though its logic seems to be reasonable, it may not be persuasive enough to be accepted wholeheartedly if there is no practical suggestion about how the function of material force operates in the formation of the universe. Thus, T'oegye's view of identification should be supplemented by the explication of the functioning of material force.

As was already explained in the example of the ship, the law of "what is so" is applicable when a thing can be formed necessarily (or naturally) while that of "what should be so" is applicable when a thing is formed intentionally. So, a thing must be formed necessarily (naturally) and intentionally in order to satisfy the conditions of both these laws. This is the condition under which the identification of "what is so" and "what should be so" can actually be maintained. Therefore, in order to apply T'oegye's theory to the whole universe, we should demonstrate that the universe is formed in the same way an individual is formed.

As already mentioned, in Neo-Confucianism the universe containing everything is regarded as the aggregation of material force. Like Ch'eng-Chu, T'oegye thought that one of the characteristics of material force is its capacity for generation and destruction *(sheng-mieh-hsing)*, and that the universe, as the aggregation of material force, is a living entity, or a kind of "organism."

In the *Changes*, from which Neo-Confucians like T'oegye derive the conception of Supreme Ultimate, the universe is described as a living entity: "Life itself can represent the virtue of the universe."[31] In the light of such a viewpoint, T'oegye emphasized "the mobility of principle" *(li tung)* to justify "the formation of primordial material force" and applied the concept of the substance and functioning of principle *(t'i-yung)* to justify the mobility of principle.[32]

Furthermore, in the *Changes* change or the ceaseless flux of life is termed *i*. The notion implicit in this view of change as the ceaseless flux of life is that the universe is a kind of organism. Therefore, Neo-Confucianists after Ch'eng-Chu, including T'oegye, interpreted the four qualities of starting, flourishing, reaping, and preserving *(yüan heng li chen)* in connection with the organic view.[33] That is, they interpreted the four qualities of starting, flourishing, reaping, and preserving in terms of the stages of growth of an organism. T'oegye must have kept in mind the organic view of the universe, and in this light thought about the vitality and mortality of material force and the changes of things.

What does change in an organism mean? It appears at first sight to be something resulting from necessity or with no purpose. But it can also be spoken of as changing according to some purpose. For instance, we can say that a flower blooms naturally and purposelessly while at the same time it blooms for the purpose of fruition. Each leaf grows by itself but its growth is connected with the growth of the whole tree. In this way the change of each part of an organism proceeds inevitably (or naturally), while at the same time it does so purposefully because it is associated with the change of the whole. Thus no change in an organism can be explicable only in terms of "what is so [of itself]." In other words, it can be said that there is no phenomenon of circumstantial force such as distorted principle *(p'ien-li)* in the change of an organism. After all, the view of the universe as an organism may prove T'oegye's true theoretical basis on which the identification of "what is so" and "what should be so" is seen as rational. In other words, his view of the universe as such, together with his view of human nature, can be said to support his assertions of moral behavior conforming to nature, or ethical behavior conforming to original nature when "what is so" and "what should be so" are identified.

VI

Even though T'oegye, identifying "what is so" and "what should be so" rationalized moral behavior based upon nature, his theory is still subject to some dispute.

In the first place, if the organic view of the universe is really founded on the basis of the material force's being subject to generation and destruction, there should be a fundamental explanation of this characteristic in material force. In this respect, though it may seem far-fetched, there should also be presented some theory of life itself.

Secondly, the attitude of attempting to explain, in view of the emotional aspect of nature expressed in the Four Beginnings, all of moral conduct such as "propriety" or "righteousness" formulated categorically in the "Five Moral Constants," cannot avoid the kind of vulnerability to which psychologism or emotionism is generally exposed. Since each individual has different degrees of feeling, this theory may be said to be liable to the fallacy of making absolute what is a relative moral reality. Thus if the true meaning of "propriety" itself is not clearly understood, this theory may fall into the kind of formalism which exacts blind obedience to and acceptance of the established order or system. This possibility is rendered all the more likely by the fact that Ch'eng-Chu Neo-Confucianism is much more formalistic than the Confucianism of the pre-Ch'in and Han-T'ang periods. This formalistic attitude may be said to be a general tendency of Neo-Confucianism. However, considering that it is a tendency all the more striking in a Neo-Confucianism stressing principle and order, this tendency cannot indeed be treated lightly in the case of T'oegye.

The theory of the issuance of principle *(li-fa-shuo)*, which emphasizes the manifestation of human nature in terms of the phenomena of Four Beginnings, has as many problems as the theory of the mobility of principle *(li-tung-shuo)*. T'oegye's theory of the issuance of principle is based on the concept of the substance and function of principle, which ultimately claims that substance and function are of one source.[34] Therefore, different interpretations of the idea that substance and function are of one source may lead to corresponding controversies. If it is understood to mean that substance and function are indistinguishable because they are of the same source, it cannot be thought to support the theory of the issuance of principle. For it might have brought confusion to T'oegye, who firmly believed in the dualism of principle and material force.

There remains also a problem in T'oegye's thought that human nature as Heaven's principle, which T'oegye recommended be preserved and cultivated, should be grasped in the scope of the whole universe. If human nature is understood in this way, it must be very difficult for us ordinary people to embody it in real life, as well as to grasp its meaning thoroughly. If the human will has no role in the formation of the universe, the mystery of the universe itself, the reason why man exists and acts in it, cannot be unraveled thoroughly. Then it becomes almost impossible to accomplish what T'oegye has recommended: the realization of the original nature in actual life. With the theory of cosmic harmony, it is hard to distinguish clearly and thereby practice good and evil, for the theory itself is tinged with a sort of fatalism. After all we can say that owing to the fatalistic tendency in a Neo-Confucianism stressing principle and order, it gives the impression of retaining a conservative and formalistic character. This can be confirmed in the history of Neo-Confucianism, especially in the latter period of the Yi dynasty.

But we cannot say that T'oegye's sense of value should be estimated lightly. The ultimate aim of his sense of value is to help man return to his true self through the recognition of his nature. It is a kind of humanism which enables man to be relieved from moral degradation, to act out righteous behavior, to recover the true self, and thus to establish man's proper position and dignity in the whole universe. Therefore, even if a theory such as the issuance of principle is in fact problematic, it can be accepted in terms of the theory of value. That is, it can be accepted as an expression for the spontaneous and self-governing manifestation of human reasoning power called nature. In other words, "the cultivation of self-governing human beings" through the recognition of reason is the basic intention of this theory. Furthermore, this theory seems to have arisen from the painful effort to establish and theorize a system of order by using the capacity of reason. Thus, as long as the cultivation of self-governing human beings through the capacity of reasoning, and the establishment of social order thereby, are required in human life, his ethics founded on the theory of the issuance of principle cannot be neglected even today. Rather, it should be considered as a legacy to be conserved.

T'oegye's other theory stressing the priority of principle and order is often criticized on the ground that it may, because of its conservative character, encourage anachronistic thinking. However, it may be quite natural to say that the evolution and development of a civilization must be considered and estimated ultimately in terms of its defense of humanity. Can senselessness and disorder be permitted in the name of the evolution and development of human history? Though the pursuit of progress itself may be important, it cannot be blind but should be predicated on preserving a sensible stability and order. If the contemporary task is to establish new value and order in the face of absurdity and confusion, though T'oegye's theory of value involves some problems as mentioned above, it is still worthy of being examined and studied further. In fact, for example, though the attitude of scholars upholding the priority of principle and order in the latter period of the Yi dynasty had the drawbacks attached to a conservative tendency, at the same time these scholars had a sublime value-oriented spirit of self-sacrifice for the realization of perfect virtue. Moreover, even the formalistic tendency of Neo-Confucianism represents the rationalistic character inherent in Neo-Confucianism. Therefore it can be said that it is in accord with the modern spirit which pursues rationalism. Thus, it is characteristic of T'oegye's theory of value that he tried to find out the ultimate moral value on the basis of the rationalism inherent in Neo-Confucianism.

We should return at this point to Chu Hsi's theory of cosmic harmony already mentioned. This theory is reminiscent of the Monadology of Leibniz (1646–1716),[35] but in fact it has its source in the Flower Garland Scripture *(Hua-yen-ching)* of Buddhism.[36] Therefore we can say that it can appropriately be examined in view of comparative philosophy. Although we cannot deny that it has been elaborated and developed under the influence of Buddhism, it is also based on the naturalistic view of nature implicit in Confucianism. In the Confucian view, nature is seen as the object which man is to adjust himself to and to be in harmony with. As was mentioned at the beginning of this essay, T'oegye thought that the state of morality is ultimately "Heaven and man joined as one" *(T'ien-jen ho-i)*. Thus, even if Buddhist philosophy had some influence upon T'oegye's view of the universe, e.g., in the doctrine of the Supreme Ultimate or Heaven's principle, fundamentally, his view remained consistent in that it regarded the universe as an object man should adjust himself to and be in harmony with. His identification of "what is so" and "what should be so" also implies the harmonious union of man and nature.

T'oegye's doctrine of the Supreme Ultimate might give one the impression that his view of this harmonious union means the union of man with an abstract nature. This, however, is incorrect. His own poems offer contrary evidence. That is to say, he confessed in many of his poems that he was so deeply in love with nature that he acquired the habits of a nature-devotee. In one poem he sings that he feels, surrounded by nature and standing aloof from human concerns, a sublime paradisal happiness.[37] In another he presents himself as glorified through devotion to nature.[38] In this way, T'oegye, before developing his theory of the universe, sought with a sincere and humble attitude for a harmonious union with the actual nature. Considering his love of nature, we can say that T'oegye's idea of the harmonious union of man and nature is not an abstract idea but a practical one.

NOTES

1. T'oegye's refutation of Wang Yang-ming is recorded at *Chŏnsŭmnok non-byŏn* in *T'oegye chŏnsŏ* (Seoul: Taedong Cultural Institute, 1958), vol. 1, pp. 922–25.
2. Consult T'oegye's *chronological history* in *T'oegye chŏnsŏ*, vol. 2, pp. 733–72, or his letter in vol. 1, pp. 402–3.
3. *T'oegye chŏnsŏ*, vol. 1, p. 198.
4. The *Mean*, 1.
5. *T'oegye chŏnsŏ*, vol. 1, p. 201.
6. *Ibid.*, vol. 1, p. 204.
7. *Ibid.*
8. *Ibid.*, vol. 2, pp. 185–86. But this problem was presented for the first time in *Ta-hsüeh huo-wen*.
9. *Ibid.*, p. 702.
10. *Ibid.*, p. 185.
11. *Ibid.*, vol. 1, pp. 405–30.
12. *Ibid.*, p. 205.
13. *Ibid.*, p. 809.
14. *Ibid.*, p. 600.
15. *Ibid.*, p. 420.
16. *Ibid.*
17. *Ibid.*, p. 849.
18. *Ibid.*, p. 816.
19. *Ibid.*, p. 824.
20. *Ibid.*, p. 816.
21. *Mencius*, 2A:2.
22. *T'oegye chŏnsŏ*, vol. 1, p. 824.
23. *Ibid.*, vol. 2, p. 160.
24. *Ibid.*, vol. 1, p. 600.
25. *Ibid.*, p. 354.
26. *Ibid.*, p. 808.
27. *Ibid.*, p. 897.
28. *Chu Tzu yü-lei* (Seoul: Cho Youngsung, 1977), vol. 1, p. 21.
29. *Ibid.*
30. *Ibid.*, p. 354.
31. *I-ching* (Seoul: Iihoe, 1982), p. 1075.
32. T'oegye discussed the "mobility" of principle in his theory of the formation of the universe, the "issuance" of principle in the "Four-Seven Debate," and the "attainment" of principle in relation to the "investigation of things," i.e., Confucian epistemology. In order to rationalize or justify such an operation of principle, he employed the concept of substance and function. The present writer gave a detailed explanation of this matter in *T'oegye ch'ŏrhak ŭi yŏn'gu* (A Study on T'oegye's Philosophy) (Seoul: Korea University Press, 1980).

33. *T'oegye chŏnsŏ*, vol. 1, pp. 911–16.
34. *Ibid.*, p. 918.
35. Consult David E. Mungello, *Leibniz and Confucianism: The Search For Accord* (Honolulu: The University Press of Hawaii, 1977).
36. Consult Fung Yu-Ian, *A History of Chinese Philosophy* (Hongkong: Taipingyang tushukungssu, 1959), pp. 902–3.
37. *T'oegye chŏnsŏ*, vol. 1, pp. 47–162.
38. *Ibid.*

Tomoeda Ryūtarō

Yi T'oegye and Chu Hsi: Differences in Their Theories of Principle and Material Force

PREFACE

IN THE DEVELOPMENT of Neo-Confucianism in East Asia, Yi T'oe-gye (1501–70) played an important part by reformulating Chu Hsi's philosophy as it was passed on from China to Japan. He was born about three hundred years after the death of Chu Hsi (1130–1200), and contributed to the establishment of a golden age in Korean Neo-Confucianism. Before his time, Lo Ch'in-shun (Cheng-an, 1465–1547), Wang Yang-ming (1472–1528), and Wang Ting-hsiang (1474–1544) were active under the Ming dynasty. After his time, Fujiwara Seika (1561–1619), Hayashi Razan (1583–1657), and Yamazaki Ansai (1618–82) became founders of Neo-Confucianism in Edo period Japan.

Yi inherited Chu Hsi's philosophy and adhered to it in strict detail, but in the intervening three hundred years new developments necessitated a clarification of certain issues which gave rise to differences in their views. In this paper I shall try to clarify the differences in their views on principle and material force *(li-ch'i)*.

1. CHU HSI'S THEORY
OF PRINCIPLE AND MATERIAL FORCE

For Chu Hsi, his theory of principle and material force is first of all a theory about the relation between the Supreme Ultimate *(T'ai-chi)*, the ground-providing principle, and yin-yang (positive and negative aspects of material force). Chu defined the Supreme Ultimate as metaphysical principle, and yin-yang as physical or vital force.

Chu established his theory of the Supreme Ultimate after he was forty years old. He thought that the human mind and consciousness converged on, diffused into, or circulated between the manifest *(i-fa)* and unmanifest state *(wei-fa)*, just as Heaven, Earth, and nature converged upon, diffused into, and circulated between quiescence *(yin-ching)* and movement *(yang-tung)*. The Supreme Ultimate controlled the quiescence and movement of nature and the manifest/unmanifest phases of the human mind and consciousness. It was the ground-providing principle of man and nature which maintained their orderly and harmonious movement. That is why he said: "The Supreme Ultimate is the principle of movement-quiescence, and of the manifest and unmanifest"[1] and he also called it "the pivot of creation and ground of all things."[2]

Can we perhaps say that the Supreme Ultimate, which is called the "ground and pivot," is one thing which exists prior to the transformation of the yin and yang? *Shu-niu* (pivot) means a central point on which something turns, *ken-ti* (ground) means a base and a foundation. In his *Classified Conversations (Chu Tzu yü-lei)*, Chu Hsi said that the heavens revolved around the line between the South and North Poles. So he called that line "the axis of Heaven."[3] And in his *Collected Commentaries on the Analects (Lun-yü chi-chu)* he called the North Star *(pei-chen)* "the pivot of Heaven."[4] In my opinion the heavenly bodies could not have been produced from the pivot of the Heavens *(pei-chen)* or the North-South axis *(Nan-pei-chi)* of Heaven. So yin-yang could not have been formed from the principle of the Supreme Ultimate.

Chu Hsi says:

The Supreme Ultimate is the reality by which yin is still and yang moves, but it cannot exist apart from yin-yang. The Supreme Ultimate points to the reality of yin-yang. It is expressed in conformity with yin-yang but without mixing into yin and yang.[5]

I think he used the word Supreme Ultimate to point to the ground and pivot of the actual world of yin-yang, and so it is undoubtedly a misunderstanding for Lo Ch'in-shun and Tai Chen (Tung-yüan, 1723–77) to regard it as something which exists prior to yin-yang.

Chu Hsi wrote a poem:

> Yin and yang never cease to function.
> Cold and heat alternate with each other.
> One principle (li) harmoniously controls them,
> A principle not obscure but clear.[6]
>
> Look at the transformation of yin and yang.
> Upward and downward through Heaven and Earth.
> Look to where there is no beginning.
> Look to where there is no ending.
> The finest principle exists there.
> The present is eternal.[7]

The Supreme Ultimate is the one principle and the finest principle in the unending movement of yin-yang, cold and heat. And it is the pivot of the actual world. Thus, the present actual world, having this fine pivot, is eternal. In these poems, Chu Hsi does not say that principle produces yin-yang, cold and heat. He does say in the postscript to his Diagram of the Supreme Ultimate Explained (T'ai-chi-t'u chieh):

We cannot say that there are two principles between yin-yang and the Supreme Ultimate, but the Supreme Ultimate is formless, while yin-yang has material force (ch'i), therefore there is a difference between the metaphysical and physical. If we speak of principle, we are first of all indicating substance and secondly function because when substance is mentioned function's principle is inherent in it, so that substance and function have the same origin. If we speak of things and affairs (shih), we express phenomenon (hsien) first and noumenon (wei) second; because whenever there is a phenomenon the substance of principle is inherent there, so that there is no gap between phenomenon and noumenon.[8]

There is a dialectic relationship between the Supreme Ultimate and yin-yang, principle and material force, which is neither separate nor mixed (pu-li pu-tsa), neither one nor many (pu-i pu-erh). It is certain that there is no one thing which precedes yin-yang, material force, or things and affairs. This postscript to the Diagram was written when he was forty-four years old, and the two poems were probably written at about the same time.

When fifty-nine years old, Chu Hsi sent a letter to Lu Hsiang-shan (1139–1192). He said:

What is the meaning of the Supreme Ultimate in the Great Appendix *(Hsi-tz'u-chuan)* to the *Book of Changes?* It means the principle of the two modes *(liang-i)*, four signs *(ssu-hsiang)*, and eight trigrams *(pa-kua)* is self-existent, and yet inheres in the two modes, four signs, and eight trigrams.

Why does Chou Tun-i (Lien-hsi, 1017–1072) speak about *wu-chi?* It is because the Supreme Ultimate occupies no place and has no shape; it exists where there is nothing and where there is something; it is everywhere, yet is essentially imperceptible to the senses.[9]

The Supreme Ultimate is transcendent and yet immanent in yin-yang and all things. This means there is a dialectical relationship between principle and material force. It is not possible for the Supreme Ultimate to produce yin-yang and all things. Nor can it be that yin-yang and all things emanate from the Supreme Ultimate. Chu Hsi's theory is rather one concerning the structure of the Supreme Ultimate and yin-yang.

This theory of the dialectical and structural relationship between principle and material force is one derived from the concept of the four realms of truth *(ssu fa-chieh)* of Hua-yen Buddhism. The four realms are as follows:

1. *shih-fa-chieh*—the realm of differentiated fact or phenomena.
2. *li-fa-chieh*—the realm of undifferentiated principle or noumena which underlies or stands behind the realm of differentiated phenomena.
3. *li-shih wu-ai fa-chieh*—the realm in which principle and fact, or differentiated phenomena and undifferentiated noumena, do not exclude each other; the world where there is no conflict between principle and fact.
4. *shih-shih wu-ai fa-chieh*—the realm in which principle is absorbed into the realm of fact, the realm in which no phenomenon excludes another.

The concepts of principle (noumenon) and fact (phenomena) already appeared in this theory of the four realms. The theory of principle and material force in the Ch'eng-Chu school was established by accepting the realm in which principle and fact do not exclude each other, and then using the traditional concept of material force in place of fact or thing. This was because the Ch'eng-Chu school thought that in the realm in which no fact excludes another, the norms of human relations and the laws of nature were lost. The standpoint of the Ch'eng-Chu school is a philosophy of reason. By contrast, that of Wang Yang-ming is a philosophy of life similar to the realm in which phenomena do not exclude one another.

Ch'eng I (I-ch'uan, 1033–1107) read the *Flower Garland Sutra (Hua-yen-ching)* and noted three views: (1) the view of true emptiness and non-appearance *(chen-k'ung chüeh-hsiang kuan)*; (2) the view of principle and fact *(shih-li wu-ai kuan)*; and (3) the view of one fact not excluding another *(shih-shih wu-ai kuan)*, then he said: "If we cover it in one phrase, we can say that many principles return to one principle."[10]

Here he uses principle, so he accepts the view in which principle and fact do not exclude one another. Chu Hsi takes up this point and asserts that principle and material force are neither separate nor mixed. In the Hua-yen view of principle and fact not excluding one another it is not maintained that principle produces fact; similarly with the Ch'eng-Chu school's theory of principle and material force. It is a structural theory of existence.

Ch'eng's theory of substance and function having one source *(t'i-yung i-yüan)* and of there being no separation of the manifest and hidden *(hsien-wei wu-chien)* in the preface of his *Commentary on the Changes (I-chuan)* adopts the same standpoint as principle and fact not excluding one another. And he maintained that one principle contains many principles *(i-li wan-li)* or principle is one and its particularizations are diverse *(li-i fen-shu)*. Chu Hsi adopts this theory and asserts the doctrine of *so-i-jan chih ku* and *so-tang-jan chih tse*. "So-i-jan chih ku" means the basic principle of all things and their laws, that is, the Supreme Ultimate. "So-tang-jan chih tse" means the principles for what things and affairs should be. The former is Ch'eng I's one principle, the latter is his many principles. In the theory of investigating things and extending knowledge *(ko-wu chih-chih)*, Chu Hsi says that our knowing investigates the many principles of all things and affairs, and then, on awakening, our wisdom grasps one principle. This is the dual character of principle. One principle in the noumenon appears as many principles in phenomena.

Chu Hsi's theory of the Supreme Ultimate and yin-yang is a dialectical and structural theory. The characteristic of his theory is that principle (reality) is established and then function *(yung)* carries on, as he set it forth in the postscript to his *Diagram of the Supreme Ultimate Explained*.

In his *Questions and Answers on the Mean (Chung-yung huo-wen)*
he says:

From the standpoint of things and affairs *(shih)*, of course, there are scholars who
think that first there exists principle and then there exist facts. Even from the
standpoint of principle, they do not think that there exists only principle and no
facts. But our way of expressing this is not perfect, so that students have some
doubts about it. If we say directly, from the standpoint of facts, that principle
inheres in facts, it could be perfect.[11]

He also says in *Questions on the Great Learning (Ta-hsüeh huo-wen)*:

Heaven's way (principle) flows and everything grows. The things by which everything is created are yin-yang and the five powers *(wu-hsing)*. In what is called yin-
yang and the five powers, principle necessarily exists, and then there exists material force. When material force produces things, material force necessarily con-
denses, and then it assumes form or shape. Thus man and things are created; they
necessarily acquired this principle and then possessed their natures *(hsing)*: the
so-called firmness *(chien)*, docility *(shun)*, humaneness *(jen)*, righteousness *(i)*,
decorum *(li)*, and wisdom *(chih)*. Just as surely they acquire material force and
then form their selves consisting of the so-called soul *(hun-p'o)*, five organs *(wu-
tsang)*, and hundred bones *(pai-hsieh)*. This is the meaning of Master Chou's
expression "the reality of the nonfinite *(wu-chi)* and essence of yin-yang and the
five forces both coalesce harmoniously."[12]

In these statements, Chu Hsi defined man and other things under
the aspects of both principle and material force, therefore we can say that
his theory of principle and material force is a structural theory of existence. Creation and production are the function of material force. The
nonfinite principle that has no place or shape is only riding on and controlling man and other things that are the development of material force,
yin-yang, and the five powers.

However, as I state above, Chu Hsi says that there exists principle
and then there exists material force or factual existence. I think this
expression means that reality is established and then function comes into
operation. But it is doubtful whether his expression means that principle
(reality) has priority over material force (function) in respect of value, or
that between principle and material force there is an order of existential
priority. Considering that in Chu Hsi's *Classified Conversations* many
questions arose in the minds of his disciples, I am sure that many points
in it still remained unclear.

II. LATER VIEWS OF PRINCIPLE AND MATERIAL FORCE IN THE MING DYNASTY

Huang Kan (Mien-chai, 1152–1221), Chu Hsi's son-in-law, says: "The Supreme Ultimate does not exist before yin-yang. . . . It is impossible that one comes into being first and the two next."[13]

Ch'en Ch'un (Pei-hsi, 1157–1222) says:

The Supreme Ultimate only expresses the totality of principles in Heaven, Earth, and all things. You must not speak about the Supreme Ultimate apart from Heaven, Earth, and all things. If you do, the Supreme Ultimate and Heaven, Earth, and all things will immediately be cut in two.

In short, principle must exist before Heaven, Earth, and all things exist but that does not mean it is hanging out in space waiting. Where principle exists, material force exists. Where material force exists, principle exists in it. Where principle and material force fuse, there is no gap between them. How can I separate them as if one were first, the other second?[14]

Later Hsüeh Hsüan (Ching-hsien, 1389–1464) said:

"Nonfinite and yet the Supreme Ultimate" have never been separate from yin-yang. If you consider that one thing exists outside yin-yang and define this one thing as the Supreme Ultimate, then your idea is wrong.[15] Principle and material force must not be discussed in terms of priority and posteriority.[16]

The above three successors of Chu Hsi uphold the dialectical theory of principle and material force.

Lo Ch'in-shun in the Ming dynasty, who took issue with Chu Hsi, believed that Chu Hsi's original and yet not fully defined theory, formulated when he was thirty-seven years old, was right. That theory is in short that the operation of yin-yang never ceases, being either yin or yang, and that it is at once the whole substance. He criticized Chu Hsi's so-called "definitive view" because it gives the impression that principle and material force can be separated into two, and he arrived at his own view that principle and material force are fused into one. He also rejected Chou Tun-i's assertion that the reality of the nonfinite (wu-chi) and the essence of yin-yang and the five forces both coalesce harmoniously, and also Ch'eng I's assertion that principle is the ground of the functioning of yin-yang. He approved Ch'eng Hao's (1032-85) statement that concrete things are the Way and the Way is concrete things (ch'i-i-tao, tao-i-ch'i). He said:

Material force is originally one. It moves and then is quiet, comes and goes, closes and opens, goes up and down, and never ceases to circulate. . . . Many and complex are the rules and laws, but they do not interfere with one another. I cannot understand why this is so, but it is the case and that is principle. It is not true that a substantial principle exists prior to material force, or that it operates by riding on material force.[17]

He thought that principles are not affected by changes in the development of the manifold aspects of material force. His principle is mainly Chu Hsi's principle for what a thing should be (*so-tang-jan chih tse*) and there is little room for Chu's reason for a thing being what it is (*so-i-jan chih ku*). His principle is nothing but material force and there is no gap between them. Principle and material force are just one thing. Chu Hsi's "principle prior to material force" (*li-hsien ch'i-hou*) does not appear in his theory. His theory of principle and material force is simple and not dialectical. Moreover, he is in error in taking Chu Hsi's *Supreme Ultimate* as a substantial thing which exists prior to material force.

Wang Yang-ming's thought assimilated Chu Hsi's principle for what a thing should be and the reason for being what it is. For him, self-knowledge (*chih*) is the subjective intention of practice (*hsing*) and practice is the exercise of self-knowledge.[18] He dispenses with Chu Hsi's investigation of things and extension of knowledge and he asserts that man should evolve his innate knowing (*liang-chih*) and ability (*liang-neng*).[19] Therefore it can be said that his standpoint is similar to the view of one fact not excluding another in Hua-yen philosophy.

Wang T'ing-hsiang rejected Chu Hsi's Supreme Ultimate and asserted his theory of primal material force,[20] but his theory was not well known in Yi dynasty Korea or Tokugawa Japan.

III. YI T'OEGYE'S THEORY OF PRINCIPLE AND MATERIAL FORCE

Yi T'oegye's acceptance of Chu Hsi's thought is connected with his own experience in regard to the philosophy of mind-and-heart. It is revealed in a poem[21] he wrote in his youth, in his life-long respect for the *Heart Classic, Supplemented and Annotated* (*Hsin-ching fu-chu*), in his publication in Korea of Chu Hsi's *Dialogues with Yen-p'ing* (*Yŏnp'yŏng tammun*), and in his work the *Essentials of Master Chu's Letters* (*Chujasŏ chŏryo*).

At the age of fifty-three, he revised Chŏng Chiun's (Ch'uman, 1509–

61) *Old Diagram of Heaven's Imperative (Ch'ŏnmyŏng kudo)* and drew up his own *New Diagram of Heaven's Imperative (Ch'ŏnmyŏng sindo)*. His theory of principle and material force is shown in this diagram.

Chou Tun'i's *Diagram of the Supreme Ultimate (T'ai-chi-t'u)* has five stages: the Supreme Ultimate, yin-yang, the five powers *(wu-hsing)*, the transformation of material force *(ch'i-hua)*, and the differentiation of forms *(hsing-hua)*. But Chŏng Chiun's and T'oegye's Diagrams do not have these five stages.

Within a big circle, they draw alternations of yin-yang, wood *[mu (yüan)]*, fire *[huo (heng)]*, metal *[chin (li)]*, and water *[shui (chen)]*. And in a square in the center are shown humanity, righteousness, decorum, wisdom, the Four Beginnings *(ssu-tuan)*, Seven Emotions *(ch'i-ch'ing)*, and so on. On this point, T'oegye says:

Chou Tun-i clarifies the origin of principle and material force and the subtle workings of the creative process. If he had not divided this into five stages, he could not have made people understand it. This diagram is drawn up in accordance with the characters and tempers of man and things, looking to the combination and growth of principle and material force. If we do not combine them into one, they cannot take a suitable position.[22]

Chou Tun-i's *Diagram of the Supreme Ultimate* presents an emanational theory of existence from the Supreme Ultimate down to man and things. By contrast, T'oegye's *New Diagram* is a structural theory, as he says that principle and material force combine with each other and that this compound forms man and things.

Chu Hsi too interprets the *Diagram of the Supreme Ultimate* as a structural theory of principle and material force. T'oegye inherits Chu Hsi's standpoint; therefore the five stages of Chou's Diagram are regarded as one. Yi says:

Do you think that there are three stages of the Supreme Ultimate, yin-yang and the five powers, and that the transformation of material force and differentiation of forms represent two stages beyond the three stages? The five powers are one yin-yang. Yin-yang are one Supreme Ultimate. The mixing of two things (yin and yang) is a function of one *(T'ai-chi)*. So we speak of the whole as just one Supreme Ultimate.[23]

This is the theory of principle and material force according to the school of Chu Hsi and Yi T'oegye. It can be said that the value of Chu Hsi's theory is demonstrated in T'oegye's *New Diagram*.

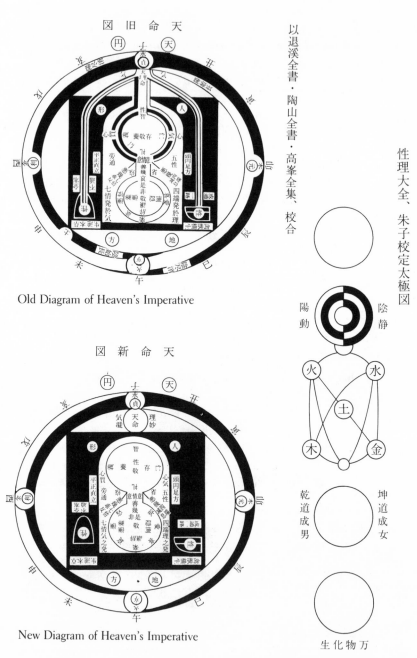

図旧命天

以退渓全書・陶山全書・高峯全集、校合

性理大全、朱子校定太極図

陽動　陰静

火　水

土

木　金

乾道成男　坤道成女

万物化生

Old Diagram of Heaven's Imperative

図新命天

New Diagram of Heaven's Imperative

Diagram of the Supreme Ultimate

In regard to the revision of the *Old Diagram*, the difference between the old and the new diagrams is that T'oegye added "the wondrous coalescence of principle and material force" (*li-ch'i miao-ning*) on top of the square in the big circle. He says:

The *Diagram of the Supreme Ultimate* begins from the Supreme Ultimate, next there is yin-yang and the five powers, and then the circle of wondrous coalescence. The circle of wondrous coalescence is that of Heaven's imperative (*T'ien-ming*), which is shown in this diagram.

Chu Hsi says "In the Supreme Ultimate there is movement and quiescence, this is the flowing forth of Heaven's imperative." How true are these words! When one diagrams Heaven's imperative, it should begin with the Supreme Ultimate. Then why does it begin here with wondrous coalescence (*miao-ho erh ning*)? From the world where man and things have already come into being, I have inferred the structure of them and reached the point of wondrous coalescence. It is a culmination. So I set it at the upper part of this circle and in contact with the imperative of Heaven.

The circle of Heaven's imperative is what Chou Tun-i describes as the reality of the nonfinite, and the refined essence of the two and five (*erh-wu*) wondrously coalesce and harmonize.[24]

The *Diagram of the Supreme Ultimate* starts from the upper white circle which represents the Supreme Ultimate. Chu Hsi thinks of it as pure principle. However, T'oegye's *New Diagram* starts from the wondrous coalescence of principle and material force in the *Diagrammatic Treatise on Heaven's Imperative (Ch'ŏnmyŏng tosŏl)*. Here principle and material force are dialectical and opposed to each other. Within a big circle, T'oegye depicts the exchange of yin-yang, wood, fire, metal, and water which appear in Chu Hsi's theory of humaneness and his lecture at Yü-shan. Chu Hsi and T'oegye thought that wood, fire, metal, and water were material force, while starting (*yüan*), flourishing (*heng*), reaping (*li*), and preserving (*chen*) were principle. Principle and material force have a dialectical relationship. T'oegye says:

Between Heaven and Earth are principle and material force. Wherever principle exists at all there also material force exists. Likewise wherever any material force exists at all, there also principle exists. . . . Material force does not exist outside of principle and principle does not exist outside material force. Of course they are inseparable from each other, but the distinction between them should not be blurred.[25]

This follows Chu Hsi's theory of "neither separate nor mixed." In T'oegye's *New Diagram* principle and material force are wonderfully har-

monized in a dialectical relation. Thus, when fifty-three years old, T'oegye approved Chŏng Chiun's saying that "the Four Beginnings issue from
principle and the Seven Emotions issue from material force."[26]

In a heated debate with Ki Taesŭng (Kobong, 1527-72), T'oegye revised this to say that the Four Beginnings came from principle only, so
they are good, and the Seven Emotions come from principle and material force, so they can be either good or evil;[27] then he revised it again to
assert that principle and material force dominated in turn in the dialectical process.[28] At the age of sixty, he revised this a third time and stated
that the Four Beginnings issued from principle, and material force followed principle, whereas the Seven Emotions issued from material force,
and principle rode on them.[29] These discussions constitute the problem
of "principle dominant" (chu-li) and "material force dominant" (chu-ch'i)
in T'oegye's dialectical theory. Many editions of the New Diagram carry
a mistake on this point, and it is necessary to revise "the issuance of principle" (li chih fa) to read "principle issues forth and material force follows
it" (li-fa erh ch'i sui chih) and "the issuance of material force" (ch'i chih
fa) to read "Material force issues forth and principle rides on it" (ch'i-fa
erh li ch'eng chih). Also, within the upper little circle in the square, the
two characters "ts'un-yang" are often left out; these should be filled in in
accordance with the same diagram in the Kobongjip.[30]

At the age of sixty-one, T'oegye sent a letter to Chŏng Yuil (Munbong, 1533–76) which said: "When principle moves, material force comes
into being. When material force moves, principle becomes manifest."[31]
This is the same way of thinking as "the issuance of principle" (li-fa) and
the "issuance of material force" (ch'i-fa).

How did T'oegye understand the problem of Chu Hsi's "principle
prior, material force posterior (li-hsien ch'i-hou)"? Of course, as he said,
"principle issues and material force issues" and "principle moves and material force moves" (li-tung, ch'i-tung); this means there was no existential priority for principle over material force. He also says, however:
"Principle is the leader of material force and material force is the follower
of principle."[32] "Heavenly principle itself flows naturally without being
commanded by anything. This principle is most valuable and has nothing to compare with it, because it orders man and things rather than being
ordered by them."[33]

T'oegye found the value of principle to be manifested at the point
where principle and material force become conjoined in the working out

of Heaven's imperative. He thought that principle controlled material force, that material force obeyed principle, and that the relation between principle and material force was like that between master and follower. He states more clearly than Chu Hsi had that principle has priority over material force in respect to value.

On Chu Hsi's view of "principle as prior, material force as posterior," T'oegye asserted clearly that principle had no existential priority over material force but it has priority in terms of ethical values. His contribution in clarifying this obscure part of Chu Hsi's theory is superior to that of Hsüeh Hsüan.

IV. T'OEGYE'S CRITIQUE OF LO CH'IN-SHUN AND WANG YANG-MING

From T'oegye's standpoint, which accepted that of Chu Hsi in regard to principle and material force, he refuted Lo Ch'in-shun and Wang Yang-ming, who had taken issue with Chu Hsi on the question of whether principle and material force were separable or distinguishable.

In demonstrating that principle and material force are not one thing, T'oegye says:

Because the Way cannot be found separate from material force Ch'eng Hao (Ming-tao, 1032–85) states that "concrete things are the Way." These words do not mean however that concrete things are directly identical with the Way. Because material force cannot exist apart from the Way, he says that the Way is concrete things. But this does not mean that the Way is directly identical with concrete things. [34]

Lo Ch'in-shun understood that concrete things were directly identical with the Way and the Way was directly identical with concrete things, and he asserted that principle and material force are one thing. [35] Against this, T'oegye comments on Chu Hsi's letter to Liu Shu-wen:

In his everyday discussions of principle and material force Chu did not say that principle and material force were just one thing. Then, in his letter, he said plainly that principle and material force were definitely two things, and he also said that even if principle exists in material force, the latter is material force in and of itself; the two were not mixed together and we should not think of the clear part of material force as one's nature or the rough part of one's nature as material force. [36]

T'oegye also criticizes Lo Ch'in-shun on the ground that he only understood part of Chu's theory but mistakenly regarded principle and material
force as one thing.[37]

As I stated earlier, Lo Ch'in-shun rejected the views of Chou Tun-
i, Ch'eng I, and Chu Hsi on this matter and went along with Cheng
Hao's opinion that principle and material force were one thing. Thus it
was natural that T'oegye should have rejected Lo's position.

T'oegye also rejected Wang Yang-ming's view. Discussing *Instructions for Practical Living (Ch'uan-hsi lu)*, he criticized four points. The
first three were based on positions Chu Hsi had also held, but the last
one was his own opinion. Against Wang Yang-ming's view of the unity
of knowing and acting *(chih-hsing ho-i)*, T'oegye says:

Generally speaking, the mind that issues from our physical form *(hsing-ch'i)* knows
everything without learning and knows how without making any effort. What we
like or dislike is the same whether inside or outside of the mind. When we see a
beautiful color, we recognize its beauty and really like it from the heart. When
we scent a bad smell, we recognize that it is bad and really hate it from the heart.
It may thus be said that action lodges in knowing. On the other hand, when our
mind knows principles and laws, it is different. If we do not learn, we cannot
know. If we do not make an effort we cannot act. Outward actions are not always
true to our inner feelings. It may be that even if we see someone doing good, we
may not necessarily recognize it as good, and even if we recognize it as good, we
may not always like it in our heart. We cannot say that when we see good being
done it is something we have already liked in our heart, or that seeing evil being
done the same things cannot be said about it.[38]

Wang Yang-ming thinks that his theory of the unity of knowing and
acting is applicable to both the emotional and rational sides of the human
mind. On the contrary, says T'oegye, Yang-ming's theory is applicable to
the emotional side, but not to the rational.

T'oegye's critique of Yang-ming corresponds to his theory of principle and material force, in which principle is not mixed with material force
and the Four Beginnings are not mixed with the Seven Emotions.

At the age of sixty-one, in his *Tosan'gi*, he wrote:

In a quiet room, with piles of books by the four walls, I sit silently at a reading
desk and keep my mind concentrated and investigate [principles]. Whenever I
understand a problem, I forget about eating out of the joy of learning. When I
do not understand it, I consult with a friend, and when I still cannot understand
it, I exert myself further. But if I cannot understand it in a natural unforced man-

ner, then I set aside the problem for a while and pick it up again later, reflecting on it with an open (empty) mind, and wait for the problem to be solved naturally.[39]

T'oegye's method of sitting silently, keeping his mind concentrated, investigating principles, and meditating with an open mind are characteristic of his philosophy. These derive from the method of Li T'ung (1093–1163) and Chu Hsi, and differ widely from that of Wang Yang-ming.

It is from this point of view that T'oegye rejected Yang-ming's theory. We can say that this is clearly a further development of Neo-Confucian thought in Korea.

CONCLUSIONS

1. Chu-Hsi's theory of principle and material force derives from Ch'eng I's, which in turn goes back to the view in Hua-yen Buddhism of principle and fact as not excluding one another. His theory is a dialectical and structural theory of existence, in which it is not possible for principle to produce material force or for there to be an existential order of priority between principle and material force. Chu Hsi's expression "there exists principle and then material force comes into existence" does however suggest an existential priority of principle over material force, which betrays the influence of Chou Tun-i's five stages in the *Diagram of the Supreme Ultimate*. This left a question for Chu Hsi's disciples to ponder over.

2. T'oegye revised Chŏng Chiun's *Old Diagram of Heaven's Imperative* and thereby developed his theory of principle and material force. His central idea is the coalescence of principle and material force, and he states "when principle issues forth, material force follows; when material force issues, principle rides on it; when principle moves, material force appears; when material force moves, principle appears." For him, the relation between principle and material force is dialectical from beginning to end. He asserts that principle is the leader and material force the follower. He states more clearly than Chu Hsi that principle has priority over material force in respect to value. Thus Chu Hsi's dialectical and structural theory of existence was clarified by T'oegye.

3. T'oegye rejected Lo Ch'in-shun's and Wang Yang-ming's theo-

ries, which were opposed to Chu Hsi's. He asserted a consistent dialectical and structural theory against both of their views, each of which differs from the other. This is a remarkable achievement for Neo-Confucianism in Korea.

NOTES

1. *Chu Tzu wen-chi* (SPTK ed.), 42:14a.
2. *T'ai-chi-t'u chieh* in *Chou Lien-ch'i chi*, *Kuo-hsüeh chi-pen ts'ung-shu* (Shanghai: Commercial Press, 1937), p. 4.
3. *Chu Tzu yü-lei*, Fuku seika ed. in Nihon Naikaku bunko, 2:6b.
4. *Lun-yü chi-chu*, Wu Chih-chung ed. (Taipei: I-wen yin-shu-kuan, 1978), 1:8a.
5. *T'ai-chi-t'u chieh* in *Chou Lien-ch'i chi*, p. 2.
6. *Chu Tzu wen-chi*, 4:10a.
7. *Ibid.*, 4:10b.
8. Postscript to *T'ai-chi-t'u chieh* in *Chou Lien-ch'i chi*, p. 27.
9. *Chu Tzu wen-chi*, 36:9a–10b.
10. *Ch'eng-shih i-shu* in Erh ch'eng ch'üan-shu (Chin-ling, 1871), 18:16a.
11. *Chung-yung huo-wen*, Kinsei kanseki sōkan, shisō sanpen (Kyoto: Chūbun shuppansha, 1977), 5:11b.
12. *Ta-hsüeh huo-wen*, Kinsei kanseki sōkan, shisō sanpen (Kyoto: Chūbun shuppansha, 1977), 5:3a.
13. *Mien-chai wen-chi* in *Sung Yüan hsüeh-an* (Taipei: Kuang-wen shu-chü, 1971), 63:13b.
14. *Hsing-li tzu-i*, Kinsei kanseki sōkan, shi sōhen (Kyoto: Chūbun shuppansha, 1972), 8:hsia:1a-b.
15. *Tu-shu lu*, Kinsei kanseki sōkan, shisō-zokuhen (Kyoto: Chūbun shuppansha, 1975), 6:3:2a.
16. *Ibid.*, 2:25b.
17. *K'un-chih chi*, Kinsei kanseki sōkan shisō-zokuhen (Kyoto: Chūbun shuppansha, 1975), 8:shang:6a.
18. *Ch'uan-hsi lu* in *Wang Wen-ch'eng-kung ch'üan-shu* (SPTK ed.), 1:7a.
19. *Ibid.*, 2:21a.
20. *T'ai-chi pien* in *Wang-shih chia-ts'ang-chi*, (Taipei: Wei-wen t'u-shu ch'u-pan-she, 1976), 33:1a (3:1473).
21. *T'oegye yŏnbo* in *T'oegye chŏnsŏ* (Seoul: Sŏnggyun'gwan taehakkyo, Tae-dong yŏn'guwŏn, 1971), 3:57b.
22. *T'oegye chŏnsŏ*, 2:322.
23. *Ibid.*
24. *Ibid.*, 2:323–24.
25. *Ibid.*, 2:141.
26. *Ibid.*, 2:325.
27. *Ibid.*, 1:402.
28. *Ibid.*, 1:405–6.
29. *Ibid.*, 1:417, 419.
30. *Kobong chŏnjip* (Seoul: Sŏnggyun'gwan taehakkyo, Taedong yŏn'guwŏn, 1976), p. 288.
31. *T'oegye chŏnsŏ*, 2:18.

32. *Ibid.*, 3:141.
33. *Ibid.*, 1:354.
34. *Ibid.*, 2:331.
35. *K'un-chih chi, shang:* 6a, *hsia:*8a.
36. *T'oegye chŏnsŏ,* 2:331.
37. *Ibid.*, 2:332.
38. *Ibid.*, 2:334.
39. *Ibid.*, 1:101.

Tu Wei-ming

Yi T'oegye's Perception of Human Nature: A Preliminary Inquiry into the Four-Seven Debate in Korean Neo-Confucianism

IN THE SPRING of 1559, Yi Hwang (T'oegye, 1501–70), one of the most influential thinkers in Korean Neo-Confucianism, commonly referred to as the Chu Hsi of Korea, began a scholarly communication on the so-called "Four-Seven" issue with his friend, Ki Taesŭng (Kobong, 1527–72).[1] The initial correspondence may have appeared to Master T'oegye no more than a matter of clarification. Specifically, it involved the *Old Diagram of the Heaven's Imperative (Ch'ŏnmyŏng kudo)* composed by Chŏng Chiun in which the "Four Beginnings" *(ssu-tuan)* mentioned in the *Mencius* are shown to have emanated from principle *(li)* and the "Seven Emotions" *(ch'i-ch'ing)* mentioned in the *Doctrine of the Mean* are shown to have emanated from *ch'i* (material force, or vital force).[2] In response to doubts about the feasibility of separating the "Four Beginnings" and the "Seven Emotions" in such a clear-cut dichotomy, T'oegye modified Chŏng's explanatory note to suggest a way out: "the Four Beginnings are issued from the principle and therefore cannot but be good; whereas the Seven Emotions are issued (not only from the principle but also) from the material force and therefore can be either good or evil." The response prompted Kobong to send a thorough critique of the dichotomous tendency implicit in T'oegye's mode of thinking. T'oegye's defense further enabled Kobong to elaborate on his challenging criticisms.

The exchange reached a compromise when Kobong sent a conciliatory
letter to T'oegye in 1562, which was enthusiastically endorsed by the
Master.[3]

The communication on the "Four-Seven" issue is unquestionably
one of the most important intellectual events in Korean Confucian thought.
Indeed, it symbolizes a major landmark of philosophical sophistication in
the tradition of East Asian Confucianism; and in several ways, it can very
well be compared with the celebrated Goose Lake Temple Debate between Chu Hsi (1130–1200) and Lu Hsiang-shan (1139–93) in 1175.
While the Chu-Lu Debate was a dramatic "encounter of two sharply different ways of life—one for 'honoring the moral nature' and the other for
'following the path of inquiry and study,' "[4] the Yi-Ki exchange was a
penetrating inquiry into one of the most intriguing problems in Neo-
Confucian psychology and anthropology. The former may have been instrumental in differentiating the Neo-Confucian heritage in China into
the School of Principle (li-hsüeh) and the School of Mind (hsin-hsüeh);[5]
the latter, by probing the underlying structure of the Confucian perception of human feelings, created an authentic possibility for the development of the School of Material Force (ch'i-hsüeh), which was to become
a unique feature of Korean Neo-Confucianism. Furthermore, the "Four-
Seven" Debate, far beyond being an encounter of two brilliant minds,
provided a model of scholarly communication for generations of subsequent followers of the Sagely Way in Korea.[6] The seriousness and open-
mindedness with which T'oegye entertained Kobong's pointed questions
set a high standard of inspiration for those who assumed responsibility for
elucidating the classics through demonstration and argumentation.

The historical significance of the "Four-Seven" Debate was greatly
enhanced when another towering Confucian thinker, Yi I (Yulgok, 1536–
84), reopened the issue through a series of correspondences with a devoted follower of T'oegye, Sŏng Hon (Ugye, 1535–98), more than a decade after the Yi-Ki exchange and two years after the death of Master
T'oegye.[7] Yulgok was obviously sympathetic with Kobong's attempt to go
beyond the dichotomy of principle and material force in understanding
the origins of the Four Beginnings and Seven Emotions. For him, a solution to the problem was to classify the Four as a subset of the Seven.
In other words, the Four Beginnings are the good elements within the
Seven Emotions which signify a more comprehensive category of human
feelings. Since human feelings necessarily involve material force as well

as principle, the Four and the Seven must contain both. Yulgok maintains that material force initiates all feelings, without which neither the Four nor the Seven can be issued forth. Principle, on the other hand, is the original reason that feelings are manifested: it provides the ultimate ground for material force to function in such a way that feelings can be expressed according to the order of things decreed by Heaven.[8]

THE CLASSICAL CONTEXT

The *locus classicus* for the idea of the Four Beginnings is the *Mencius*:

A man without the feeling of commiseration is not a man; a man without the feeling of shame and dislike is not a man; a man without the feeling of deference and compliance is not a man; and a man without the feeling of right and wrong is not a man. The feeling of commiseration is the beginning of humanity; the feeling of shame and dislike is the beginning of righteousness; the feeling of deference and compliance is the beginning of propriety; and the feeling of right and wrong is the beginning of wisdom. Men have these Four Beginnings just as they have their four limbs. Having these Four Beginnings but saying that they cannot develop them is to destroy themselves.[9]

The Mencian assumption of the Four Beginnings is predicated on the belief that "humanity, righteousness, propriety, and wisdom are not drilled into us from outside. We originally have them with us."[10] Mencius' insistence upon the "internality" *(nei)* of these moral qualities, clearly shown in his well-known debate with Kao Tzu, is an integral part of his general theory of human nature: "If you let people follow their feelings (original nature), they will be able to do good. This is what is meant by saying that human nature is good, if man does evil, it is not the fault of his natural endowment."[11] The feelings of commiseration, shame and dislike, deference and compliance (or respect and reverence), and right and wrong are therefore defining characteristics of human nature. We are human beings because we naturally and necessarily possess these feelings. So far as the ultimate justification for being human is concerned, the Four Beginnings have ontological status.[12] The Neo-Confucians in general accept this interpretive position as self-evidently true. The central concern then is to demonstrate, in practical living, how this truth ought to be realized.

Although the terms for the Seven Emotions are mentioned in the

Book of Rites, which states that joy, anger, sorrow, fear, love, hatred, and desire are basic human feelings and that they are not acquired through learning from the outside,[13] the *locus classicus* for the Neo-Confucian appreciation of the idea is the first chapter of the *Doctrine of the Mean:*

Before the feelings of pleasure, anger, sorrow, and joy are aroused it is called equilibrium (*chung*, centrality, mean). When these feelings are aroused and each and all attain due measure and degree, it is called harmony. Equilibrium is the great foundation of the world, and harmony is its universal path. When equilibrium and harmony are realized to the highest degree, Heaven and Earth will attain proper order and all things will flourish.[14]

Obviously the Seven Emotions also have metaphysical, if not ontological, significance. To be sure, they are psychological states but they are framed in a cosmological context. The firmament in which the constellation of basic human feelings is displayed, as it were, is the universe as a whole. To understand this fully we need to probe the underlying philosophy of mind and its ultimate metaphysical justification.

Historically there is no evidence that, in formulating the idea of the Four Beginnings, Mencius was aware of the idea of the Seven Emotions referred to in the *Doctrine of the Mean*.[15] However, since it was taken for granted by the Neo-Confucians that the Mencian line of Confucian thought originated from Confucius' grandson, Tzu-ssu, the alleged author of the *Mean*, the Mencian interpretation of human nature was thought to have been a further refinement of Tzu-ssu's original formulation, namely "what Heaven (*T'ien*, Nature) imparts to man is called human nature. To follow our nature is called the Way (Tao). Cultivating the Way is called education."[16] Of course, it can very well be argued that the conception of human nature as endowed by Heaven provides a metaphysical justification for the thesis that human nature is intrinsically good. But this does not preclude the possibility that the Emotions in the *Mean* and the Beginnings in the *Mencius* may still point to separate realms of human affectivity. For instance, the Emotions may simply refer to common feelings understood in a naturalistic sense, whereas the Beginnings are particularly conceived as indications of the human potential for moral self-cultivation. Surely there is likely a meaningful connection between the two realms. The whole intellectual enterprise of the "Four-Seven" debate, after all, was to define precisely what the connection is. Presumably, the shared orientation of the two classical traditions can provide the background for locating the point of convergence between them. Yet modern scholarship on the subject suggests that the *Mean* seems to have evolved from symbolic resources later than and significantly different from those that Mencius tapped for articulating his philosophical anthropology.[17] Therefore, the Four Beginnings and the Seven Emotions, despite the assumption of the Neo-Confucians, do not necessarily operate in the same intellectual discourse.

The matter is further complicated by the systematic effort of Chu Hsi to present a coherent interpretation of the Confucian heritage as a whole. As is well known, the central piece of Chu Hsi's interpretation, or more accurately his re-presentation, is the Four Books. According to his preferred pedagogical sequence, the *Mencius* and the *Doctrine of the Mean*, which follow the *Great Learning* and the *Analects*, provide respectively a broadening and a deepening appreciation of the Confucian Way. All the central concerns in them, on this view, are integral parts of a holistic vision. The assumptive reason can be summed up as follows: (1) the sages may have responded to changing circumstances in different ages with various instructions, but their intention to enlighten us is universal; (2) although the classics have come into existence through many historical eras, they are symbolizations of the sagely intention; (3) we may never understand the deep meaning of the classics by adhering to their words because literal fundamentalism fails to take into account the situational contexts in which the sagely intention is articulated, but the authentic way of grasping the subtlety of the sagely intention is through the correct interpretation of the classics; (4) it is conceivable that there is a multiplicity of valid interpretations of a given classical text and that these interpretations are complimentary to each other, but irreconcilable conflict of interpretation is not allowed because the sagely intention always unfolds in human rationality.[18]

Accordingly, to find the linkage between the Four Beginnings and the Seven Emotions is not only desirable but also necessary. Furthermore, it can point to a concrete way of understanding the sagely intention in regard to the critical issue of the role of human feelings in self-realization. Paradoxically, however, Chu Hsi's strenuous effort to comprehend the state of the mind before the emotions are aroused, which is commonly known as his meditative thinking on "centrality" and "harmony," led him to define the classical insight in a new light. As a result, his understanding of self-cultivation was a departure from rather than a confirmation of the Mencian project.[19] For one thing, the critical issue of how to realize the full potential of one's mind through a direct appeal to one's basic feelings was relegated to the background. Intent on formulating a balanced approach to self-education, Chu Hsi decided to make the parallelism in Ch'eng I's (1033–1107) thought his pedagogical focus: "Self-cultivation requires seriousness; the pursuit of learning depends on the extension of knowledge."[20] Therefore, the dispositional state of being serious or reverent and the active participation in the quest for the underlying principle in things, often through book learning, took precedence over an experiential understanding of the affective contents, the various states of the mind after it has been aroused.

T'OEGYE'S *PROBLEMATIK*

The question why the Korean Neo-Confucians, notably T'oegye, were particularity fascinated by the issue of human feelings *(ch'ing)* is of great cultural and historical significance. It is not satisfactory simply to note that T'oegye was led to a general reflection on the issue mainly because Kobong's critique had prompted him in that direction. The debate may have been occasioned by an historical accident, but the way it was framed and the manner in which the priority of values was identified indicate a mode of questioning which must have had deep roots in Korean culture.[21] Needless to say, a topic of this magnitude requires a separate monographic study. Suffice it here to mention that despite T'oegye's articulated purpose to formulate an interpretation of the "Four-Seven" issue in the spirit of Chu Hsi, the problem that he chose to respond to, the procedure by which he made his strategic moves, and the solution he arrived at had no clear precedents in Chu Hsi Confucianism. In other words, even though the classical context may provide us the background understanding of the Debate, the newness of the questioning and the originality of the response must be sought in T'oegye's central *Problematik* which compelled him to undertake the whole intellectual enterprise.

As I have noted in my preliminary study on T'oegye's perception of the mind, his deliberate attempt to align himself with Chu Hsi's School of Principle must be understood in the light of his own spiritual quest for self-knowledge through an experiential reading of the *Heart Classic*, edited by Chen Te-hsiu (1178–1235).[22] Because the *Heart Classic* had been

a continuous source of inspiration for him ever since his first enlighten-
ing encounter with it in his youth, his appreciation of Chu Hsi's project
may have been preconditioned by what he had learned from the *Heart
Classic* as, in his view, the repository of the root ideas of learning to be
human. Since practical living, rather than theoretical consistency, was
the main concern of the Neo-Confucians, T'oegye was primarily interested in the problem of the mind as a lived reality. Thus, in addition to
the construction of a speculative system in which the multidimensional
nature of the mind can be specified in a logical fashion, his primary purpose was to demonstrate the validity of his insight in daily human existence. The real challenge to him then was not only intellectual sophistication but also common sense and readily understandable good reason.

Part of the complexity of T'oegye's *Problematik* lies in this twofold
methodology: to make it perfectly clear what the structure of the mind in
the Mencian tradition is, and to demonstrate that this structure is grounded
in ordinary human experience and hence is accessible to the sensory perceptions of those who are willing to reflect upon their own processes of
personal knowledge. His penchant for diagrammatical representations of
the sagely intention, notably the *Ten Diagrams on Sage Learning*, strongly
suggests the optimism in translating subtle instructions of the sages from
time immemorial into pictorial signs readily comprehensible to those who
have received a rudimentary education in Confucian classics.[23] The confidence in giving an account of the principal ideas of the sagely teaching
in precisely formulated symmetrical relationships and the desire to show
that these relationships are experientially verifiable were further complicated by T'oegye's fidelity to his mission of upholding as "orthodoxy" Chu
Hsi's synthesis of the classical Confucian tradition, particularly the assumption that the *Doctrine of the Mean* and the *Mencius* symbolize the
unfolding of a coherent anthropocosmic vision.

Although Chu Hsi made extensive comments on the relationship
between "centrality" and "harmony" in his landmark correspondence with
Chang Shih (Nan-hsüan, 1133–80),[24] he hardly ever discussed the Seven
Emotions in reference to the Four Beginnings. His isolated statement that
the Four Beginnings are issued forth *(fa)* by the principle and the Seven
Emotions are issued forth by the material force does not seem to have
been an attempt to present a systematic analysis of their precise relationship.[25] The statement is actually predicated on Chu Hsi's perception of
the mind. Following Chang Tsai's (1020–77) observation that the mind

"commands" and "combines" *(t'ung)* nature and feeling,[26] Chu Hsi seems to have taken the mind to be "the dynamic agent whereby feelings are properly regulated so that they can be gathered, as it were, into a harmonious manifestation of true human nature."[27] Since the mind is itself a combination of principle (human nature) and material force (feelings), it is conceivable that the mind can be the manifestation of either principle or material force. Thus, it seems reasonable to assume that the manifestation of principle in the mind is symbolized by the Four Beginnings and the manifestation of material force in the mind is symbolized by the Seven Emotions.

An unresolved problem in this dualistic approach to the structure of the mind is the ontological status and experiential basis of the Four Beginnings. First of all, are they feelings? If so, how can they be separate from material force? If they are inescapably manifestations of material force, in what sense can they be defined as "transcendental"? In the Mencian tradition, it should be reiterated, the Four Beginnings are defining characteristics of human nature. We may recall that the precept that human nature is principle *(hsing chi li)* is universally assumed in Neo-Confucian thought. On this view, the Four Beginnings must also be conceived as principle. Yet, in Chu Hsi's philosophical system, it is not at all clear whether principle is mere reason or it is also an activity. In the Mencian conception of human nature, however, the Four Beginnings are obviously dynamic experiential categories:

When I say that all men have the mind which cannot bear to see the suffering of others, my meaning may be illustrated thus: Now, when men suddenly see a child about to fall into a well, they all have a feeling of alarm and distress, not to gain friendship with the child's parents, nor to seek the praise of their neighbors and friends, not because they dislike the reputation (of lack of humanity if they did not rescue the child). From such a case, we see that a man without the feeling of commiseration is not a man.[28]

The dilemma for T'oegye then was to formulate a correct interpretation of the Mencian idea of human nature in the light of Chu Hsi's concept of mind. If there was a perceived conflict between the two orientations, his task was to see to it that it be satisfactorily resolved.

KOBONG'S CHALLENGE

On the surface, Kobong's insistence that the Four Beginnings and the Seven Emotions are basically all human feelings signifies a monistic attack on T'oegye's implicit dualism. The real challenge, in the light of our discussion of T'oegye's *Problematik*, is the ontological status of the Four Beginnings. Kobong, in his first letter to T'oegye, proposes that instead of differentiating the Four and Seven according to the binary system of principle and material force, the Four should be understood as a subset, namely the pure and good feelings, of the Seven. In other words, the Four Beginnings are deliberately "singled out" by Mencius to convey the idea that human nature is good. Specifically, Kobong suggests that the Four are the "roots" of those feelings in the Seven that are eventually harmonizable. Since principle is the master of material force and material force is the stuff of principle, even though they are distinguishable conceptually, they are inseparable in the concrete thing. While the mind in the state of centrality before the feelings are aroused is absolutely pure and good, the mind in the state of harmony is an achievement. The harmonized feeling, as an achievement, cannot be said to be automatically pure and good.[29]

Implicit in Kobong's line of reasoning is that the Four Beginnings, like the Seven Emotions, are basic human feelings and thus the incipient manifestations of the mind after arousal. The reason that they are specified as good by Mencius is in fact an *a posteriori* assertion that they can be eventually harmonized. Chu Hsi's intention of stressing the Four Beginnings as the Four Virtues in his discourse on the intersection of human nature and feelings, Kobong further suggests, was basically heuristic. It was meant to be a cautionary note against the mistake of identifying human nature with material force. The Four Beginnings are simply harmonized good feelings; the Seven Emotions, if "all attain due measure and degree," can also become good. So far as feeling is concerned, it necessarily involves both principle and material force.

In response to Kobong's preliminary query, T'oegye points out the importance of analyzing the divergence as well as the convergence of the Four and Seven. It is true that they, in terms of their consequential developments, cannot but involve both principle and material force. Yet, their origins are significantly different. The Four are initiated by inborn moral qualities of the mind such as humanity, righteousness, propriety, and wisdom, whereas the Seven are stimulated by complex processes involving both internal and external conditions. Only in this particular sense are the Seven said to have been dominated by a combination of principle and material force and the Four dominated by principle alone. The danger of failing to recognize the critical distinction between the Four and the Seven lies in confusing human desires with the Heavenly Principle.[30] T'oegye's first strategic move to meet Kobong's challenge can thus be summed up as follows: (1) the Four and Seven are both feelings, but they refer to different realms of experienced truth; (2) the Four refer to the "original state" (pen-jan) rather than the "physical endowment" (ch'i-chih) of human nature; (3) despite the mutual dependence of principle and material force, human feelings like human nature are expressed by either principle or material force; (4) the Four, expressed by principle, are purely good and the Seven, expressed by material force, can be good through deliberate harmonization; (5) failure to perceive the difference in origins of the Four and the Seven, even though they are both legitimate human feelings, may lead to the unhappy consequence of misidentifying desires aroused by external stimuli with inner urges generated by the moral sense.

In the summer of 1560, more than a year after he had sent the preliminary query, Kobong formulated a twelve-point critique of T'oegye's first response. The strategy employed in the critique involves three interrelated tactics. First, Kobong notes that an appeal to orthodox interpretation of the original meaning of the classical texts, including the authority of Chu Hsi, must be supplemented by personal understanding. For one thing, our intellectual predecessors themselves may have difficulty in reaching a consensus. In the case of Chu Hsi, it is well known that his early and later views on "centrality" and "harmony" are significantly different.[31] Second, Kobong further notes the necessity of determining beforehand what the debate is really about. The Four-Seven Debate, he contends, is primarily about mind, human nature, and feelings. The issue of the moral implications of principle and material force is not central to the debate.[32] Third, Kobong suggests that divergent ways of addressing the same reality can simply be a matter of emphasis. The Four and Seven do not seem to refer to two discrete realities. They probably refer to the same reality from two mutually complementary perspectives.[33]

The thoroughness with which Kobong criticized T'oegye's first response prompted T'oegye to modify his position and reformulate his argument. As an appreciation for Kobong's point-by-point analysis of his first response, T'oegye rewrote it and sent the revised version together with his second response to his challenger in the fall of 1560, three months after he had received the thorough critique. T'oegye made seven corrections in his revised version of the first response.[34] He deleted a passing reference to Lo Ch'in-shun (1465–1547), acknowledging that he was mistaken in assuming that Kobong actually advocated a theory of collapsing principle and material force into an undifferentiated whole reminiscent of Lo's monistic attack on Chu Hsi's alleged dualism.[35] He also made three editorial changes in order to give more preciseness to his argumentation. A noticeable concession was his more positive view on the Seven Emotions. In the original version, the moral status of the Seven Emotions is "uncertain;" the emphasis is that they must be cultivated to become harmonious. In the revised version, the Seven Emotions are said to be "originally good," although they are prone to depart from the accepted norms of proper expression and thus become evil.[36] However, despite T'oegye's willingness to accommodate some of Kobong's insights, his original position that the Four Beginnings and the Seven Emotions are qualitatively different and that the category of principle and material force can be meaningfully applied remains intact.

True to Kobong's thoroughness, T'oegye adopted the same style of communication in his second response. He rearranged the twelve-point critique into five sections: (1) a line he misread in Kobong's first letter to him and was misinterpreted by him in the first response; he simply apologizes for the oversight; (2) four statements he believed to have been true but, through Kobong's instructions, he now admits are inadequately expressed; (3) thirteen observations that are basically compatible; only a matter of clarification is required; (4) eight items of dispute that originally seemed resolvable to him which he now finds incompatible; and (5) nine problem areas in which fundamental disagreement still remains.[37] Understandably, T'oegye's second response focuses its attention on categories (4) and (5). Among the eight items of dispute, the issue most challenging to T'oegye's interpretive position is Kobong's claim that just as the Seven Emotions necessarily involve principle, the Four Beginnings necessarily involve material force. Similarly, among the nine problem areas, Kobong's criticism that T'oegye, intent on according a special status to the Four Beginnings as feelings, bifurcates morality into two separate forms of goodness, seems most threatening to his intellectual enterprise.[38]

MIND-HEART, HUMAN NATURE AND FEELING

T'oegye readily accepted Kobong's criticism that the Seven Emotions do not refer to material force alone and that they are not just aroused by stimuli from the outside. Yet, he contended that to accept that the Seven Emotions necessarily involve principle and that they are inherent in the mind does not lead to the conclusion that they are defining characteristics of human nature. Accordingly, T'oegye could have further argued, they can still be clearly differentiated from the Four Beginnings in terms of origin and priority. After all, the Four Beginnings are natural, spontaneous, and autonomous manifestations of the mind-heart. They are irreducible qualities of human nature, indeed the very reason that human nature is good. On the other hand, even though the Seven Emotions are "human, all too human," they are not, in the Mencian sense, roots of morality. Furthermore, while the dynamic process of learning to be human entails the growth and development of the Four Beginnings, it does not depend upon the unrestrained expression of the Seven Emotions. In fact, as the Mencian idea of "making the desires few"[39] amply suggests, the cultivation of the mind necessitates a measure of control over the Seven Emotions. The concern for the Four Beginnings is that they may not have enough supply to carry one very far. Like the spring that is about to issue forth or the fire that only starts to burn,[40] we have to nourish our Beginnings so that they can overcome the dehumanizing tendencies from within as well as without. On the contrary, the problem with the Seven Emotions is excessiveness. The purpose of self-cultivation in this particular connection is either to return to a prior state of tranquility or to attain a state of harmony after they have been aroused. To express one's Seven Emotions according to proper measure and degree is therefore to channel them through a ritualized form so that their excessiveness can be adequately dealt with. In other words, the concern for deficiency in commiseration and deference and the fear for surplus in anger and joy belong to two qualitatively different moral realms.

Although T'oegye did not argue exactly along the lines just mentioned, it is not difficult to show that he was critically aware of the Mencian project and that his insistence on a clear separation of the Four and Seven was predicated on similar assumptive reasoning. The complexity of his interpretation arose from his fidelity to Chu Hsi's philosophy of mind, which he took to be an orthodox explanation of what must have been implied in Mencius' theory of human nature. The problem of feeling came to the fore of the discussion because as we have already alluded, Chu Hsi, in formulating his great synthesis, took as a basic precept Chang Tsai's assertion that "the mind commands human nature and feelings." Commenting on this precept, Wing-tsit Chan states:

This is a simple saying but the doctrine became a major one in Neo-Confucianism because it not only restores feeling to a position of equality with nature; it also makes the mind the master of a person's total being. What is more, Neo-Confucianists were very insistent that reality and function, and in this theory substance (nature) and function (feelings), are harmonized by the mind.[41]

It should be noted that the term *t'ung*, rendered as "command" here, also conveys meanings of "master," "synthesize" and, in our earlier reference, "combine." The four-character precept, *hsin t'ung hsing ch'ing*, can thus be understood as follows: the mind, in mastering (embodying and harmonizing) human nature and feelings, synthesizes and combines two distinctive features of human reality into a coherent, dynamic whole.

Whether or not Chu Hsi deliberately chose a more complex mode of perceiving the relationship between mind and human nature than the *Mencius* warrants, his tripartite division demands two parallel operations in the art of self-cultivation. The mind does not "command" human nature in the way it "commands" feelings. Human nature as principle is the ultimate reason for a thing (including the mind as a thing) to be a thing. Although the mind potentially contains all the principles in its internal structure, it needs to be purified and informed through physical as well as mental discipline to make itself a worthy agency in allowing the principles to fully manifest themselves. That the mind "commands" principle, in this sense, seems to mean that principle can be realized through the proper self-activation of the mind. By contrast, feelings are inevitable expressions of the mind. To attain the so-called "centrality" before the feelings are aroused requires self-cultivation as a daily ritual. To command feelings, so conceived, is to harmonize them. Underlying this precept then is the assumption that although the mind contains principle, it is itself a refined manifestation of material force. The mind must constantly try to bring the principles to bear on practical living, lest they should forever remain unrealized possibilities. The harmonization of feelings cannot automatically bring about the idea of the profound person. The project of learning (all the disciplines implied in the "investigation of things") is absolutely necessary, which clearly indicates the recognition that empirical knowledge is crucial to moral self-development.

Chu Hsi's teaching on self-cultivation is obviously more elaborate than the Mencian instruction that "learning consists in nothing other than the search for the lost mind."[42] It is difficult to ascertain, however, whether Chu Hsi's intended elaboration on the Mencian theory of human nature broadened the scope or actually restructured the character of the original project. The fruitful ambiguity in Chu Hsi's concept of mind, formulated in terms of a tripartite division of mind, human nature, and feelings, may have been a significant departure from the Mencian perception of the inseparability of mind and human nature. Chu Hsi was critically aware of the far-reaching implications of introducing a more complex analysis of human nature into the original project. The category of "physical nature," which was not systematically explored in the Mencian theory, certainly broadened the scope of the Mencian insight that human nature is good. An unintended consequence, however, was a significant reorientation of the original project in the idea of "moral nature" as principle. Mencius tried to demonstrate that the moral propensity of the mind, concretely manifested in the incipient activations of the Four Beginnings, proves that the creative power of self-realization is inherent in human nature. It is in this specific sense that human nature is said to be good. If moral nature is defined as principle and if it is problematical whether principle is mere reason or can also be a form of activity, the center of moral creativity inevitably shifts to the indeterminate character of the mind. As a result, even though human nature is potentially and originally good, there is no ontological guarantee that the moral propensity inherent in the mind will necessarily reveal itself.

T'OEGYE'S RESPONSE

In our discussion of T'oegye's *Problematik*, we identified as one of the central issues the ontological status and experiential basis of the Four Beginnings. The main reason that the precise nature of the Four Beginnings, the sources and roots of morality in Mencius become somehow problematical was, as we have already noticed, Chu Hsi's tripartite division of mind, human nature, and feelings in his philosophical psychology. Since T'oegye was committed to the learning of the mind in the tradition of Mencius and at the same time committed to Chu Hsi's elaborate interpretation of the Mencian project as self-evidently true, his task was to demonstrate how the apparent conflict can be resolved. Kobong's challenge impelled T'oegye to address the issue in the dichotomous terminology of principle and material force. The ingenuity of T'oegye's response, philosophically speaking, lies in his ability to establish the claim that the Four Beginnings are initiated by principle and thus purely good, whereas the Seven Emotions are initiated by material force and thus can be either good or evil. To be sure, in Chu Hsi's *Classified Conversations*, some comparable statement is made and there is reason to believe that Chu Hsi may have a similar idea in mind in making such a statement. Nevertheless, T'oegye, by formulating his understanding of Chu Hsi's intention in the spirit of Mencius, made an original contribution to Ch'eng-Chu Neo-Confucian thinking.

To appreciate the profound significance of this seemingly simplistic assertion, it is vitally important to ask what sort of feelings the Four Beginnings really are. As a preliminary step in our inquiry, it may be helpful to distinguish feelings from emotions. Although the Chinese character *ch'ing*, as in the Seven Emotions *(ch'i-ch'ing)*, can be rendered as feeling, affection, sentiment, love, or passion, as well as emotion, the distinction between feeling and emotion in the English language can be useful for identifying more sharply what the Four Beginnings purport to convey. While emotion suggests "a moving, stirring, agitation and peturbation,"[43] feeling refers to "the 'sense of touch' in the looser acceptance of the term, in which it includes all physical sensibility not referable to the special senses of sight, hearing, taste, and smell."[44] Emotion is an excited mental state, often the result of a disturbance of the mind; feeling, as a "physical sensation or perception through the sense of touch or general sensibility of the body," connotes "susceptibility to the higher and more refined emotions."[45] Despite the overlapping of the two terms, they point to rather different realms of human experience. Feeling seems to be deeper, emotion stronger. Feeling came from the verb "feel," emotion derived from the original meaning of "migration" and "transference from one place to another."[46] A feeling person is sensitive and intuitive, an emotional person often yields to uncontrollable passions. Feeling can be a constant state, emotion is often short-lived. In sum, we can feel (or sense) what is within us without expressing it but our emotions cannot but show upon our countenances.

T'oegye maintained that the Four Beginnings are initiated by principle for the sake of establishing, from the outset, the claim that, unlike emotive states such as joy and anger, they are inherent in human nature. Furthermore, while emotions are aroused or agitated by external conditions, the Four Beginnings as feelings are natural and spontaneous expressions of the mind. In ordinary English usage, emotions are distinguished from the other classes of mental phenomena such as cognitive or volitional states of consciousness.[47] Feeling as sensibility, in the case of "knowing by a feeling experience,"[48] is intertwined with cognition and volition. The Four Beginnings—commiseration, shame and dislike, deference and compliance, and right and wrong, are, strictly speaking, not only feeling but also knowing and willing. Indeed, the Four Beginnings are not *mere reasons* because they generate energy to perform transformative acts. To say that they are somehow energized by material force in the same manner that emotions are energized is misleading. The Four Beginnings, for one thing, have autonomy, internality and self-direction, whereas the Seven Emotions do not have these qualities in their original states. The analogy of a man riding a horse, which Chu Hsi was fond of using in explaining the relationship between principle and material force, inspired T'oegye to articulate the following thesis: the Four Beginnings are initiated by principle but material force follows them, whereas the Seven Emotions are initiated by material force but principle rides on them.[49]

The main problem with Kobong's definition of the Four Beginnings as a subset of the Seven Emotions is, in T'oegye's view, his failure to understand that the Four Beginnings are not emotions harmonized but the subtle, incipient activations of the mind; not simply as responses to external stimuli but as authentic manifestations of what human nature originally is. To grasp T'oegye's mode of thinking, we may borrow an analogy from the modern Confucian philosopher Hsiung Shih-li (1885–1968): the relationship between the Four Beginnings and the original state of the mind is like that of the waves and the ocean.[50] As the ocean naturally manifests itself in waves, the mind spontaneously expresses itself in the Four Beginnings. Every human being is capable of these feelings and it is inconceivable that a single member of the human community is, in principle, incapable of showing them. The principle of being human is such that "a man without the feeling of commiseration is not a man."[51] To say that the feeling of commiseration is initiated by principle is therefore to underscore the ontological status of the Four Beginnings. This line of reasoning is predicated on the assumption that principle, like the man on horseback, is in command. As it wills, controls, and directs, material force, like the horse, follows. There is the possibility that the horse may disobey what the rider orders. But to say that the rider does not know where he wants to go is not permissible in the Mencian grammar of action. It is true, T'oegye contends, from a synthetic point of view, that the Four Beginnings and the Seven Emotions involve both principle and material force. Analytically, however, it is of paramount importance to note the difference in origin and priority.[52]

Human nature, according to the *Doctrine of the Mean*, is decreed by Heaven; the Four Beginnings as defining characteristics of human nature must also be endowed by Heaven. They are, therefore, primordial and, indeed, transcendental. The Seven Emotions, by contrast, are not integral parts of our primordial and transcendental nature, which T'oegye referred to as the "original state" of our nature. Rather, they are conditional expressions of our physiological and psychological states, which T'oegye referred to as one's "physical nature."[53] To say that the Seven Emotions are initiated by material force is certainly not to deny the relevance of principle to the harmonization of these powerful human feelings. There are proper ways to be joyful, angry, sorrowful, fearful, loving, hating, and wanting. To express these strong feelings according to a measure and degree of appropriateness requires ritual practice. The body as well as the mind must learn to express itself through a disciplined form. Once these emotions come into existence, presumably by some complex psychosomatic mechanism, conscious effort will be required to guide them to flow properly through the channels. The dramatic idea that, after the emotions are aroused, principle will ride on them is precisely to convey this sense of resuming control at the right moment.

T'oegye acknowledged that it is in the interaction of principle and material force that human feelings, including the Four Beginnings and the Seven Emotions, come into existence as experienced realities. However, it is one thing to notice the inseparability of principle and material force in a synthetic apprehension of human affectivity but quite something else to argue that the harmonized emotions such as anger and joy are in some way comparable to the feelings of commiseration and deference. The significance of T'oegye's analytical distinction lies in its "special pleading" for the Four Beginnings. A natural consequence of this is a more dynamic and creative interpretation of principle as a form of transformative activity. It is well known that the problem of whether or not principle "moves" *(tung)* is highly controversial in Chu Hsi's philosophy of mind.[54] T'oegye, in response to Kobong's challenge, interpreted principle to be a generative power inherent in the mind which not only defines human nature but also guides us to realize it according to its own directionality. Thus, the transcendent dignity of man, which seems problematical in Chu Hsi's seemingly empiricist definition of the mind,[55] is fully restored in T'oegye's philosophical anthropology.

EPILOGUE

T'oegye seems to have had the last word in his debate with Kobong. He was overjoyed to have received a conciliatory letter from his junior friend and greatly heartened to find that Kobong's "Summary Statement" *(tsunglun)* is virtually a representation of his own ideas. For T'oegye and Kobong, the Four-Seven Debate was brought to completion on a mutually beneficial basis. However, from the perspective of Korean Confucian thought in the Yi Dynasty, the friendly note in support of T'oegye's interpretive position symbolizes only the conclusion of the first half of this historical debate. The exchange between Yulgok and Ugye was an entirely different matter.[56] Had T'oegye been informed of the thrust of the Four-Seven Debate in the Yulgok and Ugye correspondence, he would have been deeply concerned. To speculate on how he might have responded to the probing questions that Yulgok raised, which seem to have disarmed much of Ugye's defensive tactics, can be intriguing and interesting. An attempt to address such a philosophically significant issue would require a comprehensive analysis of T'oegye's intellectual enterprise.

The Four-Seven Debate may have been occasioned by the Yi-Ko exchange in response to deep-rooted cultural and psychological assumptions in Korean Confucian thought. Indeed, it has been characterized by traditional as well as modern interpreters as a distinctive feature of the intellectual history of the Yi dynasty. However, since the exchange addresses vital issues in the Confucian tradition as a whole and since the problem of feelings and emotions in moral self-cultivation is a perennial human concern, the Four-Seven Debate deepens and broadens our understanding of the Neo-Confucian agenda in East Asia. Our preliminary inquiry simply shows how rich and complex the agenda is.

NOTES

1. For a general account of the debate in English, see Munsang Seoh, "The Ultimate Concern of Yi Korean Confucians: An Analysis of the *i-ki* Debates," *Occasional Papers on Korea*, 5 (Joint Committee on Korean Studies of the ACLS and the SSRC, March 1977): 20–66.
2. For a brief description of Chŏng Chiun's Diagram, see *ibid.*, pp. 32 and 59n23.
3. Some key documents for this exchange, including Kobong's letters, are found in T'oegye's collected works. See *T'oegye chŏnsŏ*, 4 vols. (enlarged ed.; Seoul: Sŏnggyun'gwan University Press, 1978), vol. 1, 16:8a–17:30a (pp. 405–42).
4. For a short note on this dramatic encounter between Chu Hsi and Lu Hsiang-shan, see Wing-tsit Chan, *A Source Book in Chinese Philosophy* (Princeton: Princeton University Press, 1969), pp. 583–84.
5. It should be mentioned that the traditional practice of "differentiating the Neo-Confucian heritage in China into the School of Principle and the School of Mind" has been seriously challenged by modern scholarship. See Mou Tsung-san, *Hsin-t'i yü hsing-t'i*, 3 vols. (Taipei: Cheng-chung Book Co., 1969), vol. 1, Prolegomenon.
6. See Munsang Seoh, pp. 31–56. Also see Takahashi Tōru, "Richō jugakushi ni okeru shuriha shukiha no hattatsu," in the *Chōsen Shina bunka no kenkyū* (Tokyo, 1929), pp. 141–281.
7. For a discussion of this exchange, see Chai-sik Chung, "Studies in Korean Confucian Tradition," pp. 51–62 (unpublished manuscript). For a systematic inquiry into Yi Yulgok's philosophical anthropology, see Yong Chan Ro, "The Anthropology of Yulgok: A Non-dualistic Approach to the Mind and the Problem of *Li* and *Ch'i*" (Ph.D. diss., University of California, Santa Barbara, 1982), chap. 2.
8. Ro, *Anthropology of Yulgok*, pp. 55–62.
9. *Mencius*, 2A:6. For this translation, see Wing-tsit Chan, *A Source Book*, p. 65.
10. *Mencius*, 6A:6. See *A Source Book*, p. 54.
11. *Ibid.*
12. For a discussion on this issue, see Tu Wei-ming, "On the Mencian Perception of Moral Self-Development," *The Monist* (January 1978), 61(1):72–81.
13. See the "Li-yün" chapter of the *Li-chi*; James Legge, trans., *The Chinese Classics* (reprint, Hong Kong: Hong Kong University Press, 1970), vol. 1, p. 379.
14. *The Doctrine of the Mean*, chap. 1; *A Source Book*, p. 98.
15. For a brief discussion on the text of *Chung-yung*, see Tu Wei-ming, *Centrality and Commonality: An Essay on Chung-yung* (Honolulu: University of Hawaii Press, 1976), pp. 1–28.
16. *A Source Book*, p. 98.
17. For a significant contribution to our understanding of this, see A.C. Graham, "The Background of the Mencian Theory of Human Nature," *The Tsing*

Hua Journal of Chinese Studies, new series (December 1967), 6(1–2):215–74.

18. For a succinct discussion of Chu Hsi's method of interpreting the classics, see Ch'ien Mu, *Chu Tzu hsin hsüeh-an*, 5 vols. (Taipei: San-min, 1971), vol. 4, pp. 231–300.

19. For a philosophical analysis of the issue, see Mou Tsung-san, *Hsin-t'i yü hsing-t'i*, vol. 3, chaps. 1–2.

20. *Erh-Ch'eng I-shu*, in *Erh-Ch'eng ch'üan-shu* (SPPY edition), 18:5b. For this translation, see *A Source Book*, p. 562. It should be mentioned that the term *"ching,"* rendered as "seriousness," is also translated as "reverence" or "respect."

21. For background understanding, see Park Chong-hong (Pak Chonghong), "Philosophical Foundation of Korean Civilization and Course of Its Development," part 1, *Korea Journal* (March 1963), 3(3):23–27; Kim Hyong-hyo (Hyŏnghyo), "Confucian Thought in Korea," *Korea Journal* (September 1977), 17(9):42–52; Kim Doo-hun (Tuhŏn), "Confucian Influences on Korean Society," *Korea Journal* (September 1963), 3(9):5–11, 41; Lee Sang-eun (Yi Sangŭn), "On the Criticism of Confucianism in Korea," *Korea Journal* (September 1967), 7(9):4–18; Hong I-sop (Isŏp), "Political Philosophy of Korean Confucianism," *Korea Journal* (September 1963), 3(9):12–16, 37; Park Chong-hong (Pak Chonghong), "T'oegye and his Thought," *Korea Journal* (March 1971), 11(3):19–23; Martina Deuchler, "Neo-Confucianism in Early Yi Korea: Some Reflections on the Role of Ye," *Korea Journal* (May 1975), 15(5):12–17; Lee Chong-young (Yi Chongyŏng), "Yi Dynasty and its Confucian Culture," *Korea Journal* (July 1964), 4(7):19–25; and Michael C. Kalton, "An Introduction to Silhak," *Korea Journal* (May 1975), 16(5):29–46.

22. Tu Wei-ming, "Yi Hwang's Perception of the Mind," *T'oegye hakpo* (October 1978), 19:455–67. See also, Wm. T. de Bary, *Neo-Confucian Orthodoxy and the Learning of the Mind-and-Heart* (New York: Columbia University Press, 1981), pp. 73–91.

23. See T'oegye's memorial to the emperor in presenting the Diagram, *T'oegye chŏnsŏ*, vol. 1, 7:4b–35b (pp. 195–211).

24. Ch'ien Mu, vol. 2, pp. 123–82.

25. See the conclusion of Chu Hsi's commentary on the Four Beginnings in the *Chu Tzu yü-lei* (1876 ed.), 53:20a–b. For T'oegye's reference to this, see his first response to Ki Kobong, *T'oegye chŏnsŏ*, vol. 1, 16:12a (p. 407).

26. *Chang Tzu ch'üan-shu* (SPPY edition), 14:2a. For a discussion, see *A Source Book*, p. 517.

27. Tu Wei-ming, "Yi Hwang's Perception of the Mind," p. 457.

28. *Mencius*, 2A:6. For this translation, see *A Source Book*, p. 65.

29. Kobong's letter to T'oegye, in *T'oegye chŏnsŏ*, vol. 1, 16:12b–14b (pp. 407–8).

30. *Ibid.*, 16:12a (p. 407).

31. This claim can be easily substantiated by Chu Hsi's critical reflection on his early views on "centrality" and "harmony." For a philosophical discussion on

this important issue, see Mou Tsung-san, *Hsin-t'i yü hsing-t'i*, vol. 3, chaps. 1–2.

32. See Ki Taesŭng, *Kobong chŏnjip* (reprint, Seoul: Sŏnggyun'gwan University, 1976), p. 247.
33. *Ibid.*
34. *T'oegye chŏnsŏ*, vol. 1, 16:19a–24a (pp. 411–13).
35. *Ibid.*, 16:23a–b (p. 413).
36. *Ibid.*, 16:21b (p. 412).
37. *Ibid.*, 16:25a–28a (pp. 414–15).
38. *Ibid.*, 16:28a–39a (pp. 415–21).
39. *Mencius*, 7B:35. Cf. D. C. Lau's translation of the passage: "There is nothing better for the nurturing of the heart than to reduce the number of one's desires. When a man has but few desires, even if there is anything he fails to retain in himself, it cannot be much; but when he has a great many desires, then even if there is anything he manages to retain in himself, it cannot be much." See D. C. Lau, trans., *Mencius* (Middlesex, England: Penguin Classics, 1970), pp. 201–2.
40. *Mencius*, 2A:6. See *A Source Book*, p. 66; D. C. Lau, p. 83.
41. *A Source Book*, p. 517.
42. *Mencius*, 6A:11. Cf. D. C. Lau, p. 167.
43. *The Compact Edition of the Oxford English Dictionary*, E, 124, 2 under Emotion (p. 853).
44. *Ibid.*, F, 135, 2 under Feeling (p. 978).
45. *Ibid.*, 2b and 5 under Feeling.
46. *Ibid.*, E, 124, 1 under Emotion (p. 853). For a general discussion on "emotion" in modern scientific literature, see *Encyclopedia Britannica*, 6:757–66.
47. *Oxford English Dictionary*, E, 124, 4b under Emotion (p. 853).
48. *Ibid.*, F, 136, 3 under Feeling (p. 978).
49. *T'oegye chŏnsŏ*, 16:36a (p. 419).
50. Hsiung Shih-li, *T'i-yung lun* (reprint, Taipei: Hsüeh-sheng, 1976), p. 28.
51. *Mencius*, 2A:6.
52. *T'oegye chŏnsŏ*, 16:32a–33a (pp. 417–18).
53. *Ibid.*, 16:30a–31a (pp. 416–17).
54. For a discussion on this, see Ch'ien Mu, vol. 1, pp. 249–51.
55. See T'ang Chün-i, "Chu Tzu chih li-ch'i hsin-hsing lun," in his *Chung-kuo che-hsüeh yüan-lun yüan-hsing p'ien* (Hong Kong: New Asia Research Institute, 1968), pp. 358–411, particularly pp. 392–99.
56. See Munsang Seoh, pp. 37–41.

Wing-tsit Chan

How T'oegye
Understood Chu Hsi

THE PRESENT BRIEF study is an attempt to find out how T'oegye (Yi Hwang, 1501–70) understood Chu Hsi (1130–1200). Perhaps I should have waited to examine T'oegye's complete works as well as the many studies on him by Korean and Japanese scholars before making the attempt, but that is a task I have not been able to perform. In the meantime, an examination of some of his works can be very revealing. The works I have chosen are three, namely, his *Annotation of the Biographical Account of Master Chu (Chuja haengjang chipchu)*, which deals chiefly with his life, his *Essentials of Master Chu's Letters (Chujasŏ chŏryo)*, which deals chiefly with his doctrine, and his *General Records of the Learning of Principle (Ihak t'ongnok)*, which deals with his pupils.

The primary source for the study of Chu Hsi, as every student of Neo-Confucianism knows, is the *Chu Tzu hsing-chuang*,[1] written by Chu Hsi's longtime pupil and son-in-law, Huang Kan (Mien-chai, Chih- ch'ing, 1152–1221). It was written twenty years after Chu Hsi's death, thus affording a proper perspective and profound reflections. It is generally accepted as the most authentic, impartial, and understanding account of the philosopher's career and thoughts. The only annotation of it that has come to my attention is that by T'oegye, and Professor Yamazaki Michio has written an excellent article on it. According to Professor Yamazaki, the *Hsing-chuang* was used as a text in family academies, Asami Keisai (1652–1732) lectured on it at least four times, and his pupil, Wakabayashi Kyōsai (1679–1732), included it in his curriculum.[2] So far as I know, the *Hsing-chuang* has neither been annotated nor used in the curriculum in China. Does this mean that Korea and Japan have taken the *Hsing-chuang* more seriously than China? Not necessarily. As Professor Yamazaki has pointed out, Hu Chü-jen (Ching-chai, 1434–84) often urged his students to read it.[3] Since there were always teachers available, no annotation was needed, and there were too many classics and other texts to be included in the curriculum. The fact that T'oegye saw fit to annotate it not merely as a study aid but to make significant comments merits our attention.

Contrary to ordinary annotations, T'oegye's is brief and selective. There are no comments on the long memorials quoted in the *Hsing-chuang*, for example, but only a note here and there to show why or how they were written. According to T'oegye's own preface, because the biography in the *History of the Sung Dynasty* is too brief and both the chronological account *(Nien-p'u)* by Chu Hsi's pupil, Li Fang-tzu (Kung-hui, Kuo-chai, 1214 cs) and the records of words and deeds *(Huang-ch'ao tao-hsüeh ming-ch'en wai-lu)* by Li Yu-wu were in places brief or detailed, T'oegye has added what the *Hsing-chuang* has left out with materials from these three sources. But as Profrssor Yamazaki has pointed out, T'oegye has utilized many more sources, such as Li T'ung's (Yen-p'ing, 1093–1163) answers to Chu Hsi's questions *(Yen-p'ing ta-wen)*, the *Supplement to the General Mirror for Aid in Government (Hsü Tzu-chih t'ung-chien)*, etc.[4] T'oegye's work was published in 1576 by his pupil Cho Mok (Wŏlch'ŏn, 1524–1606) and others. Originally it was ch. 1 of the *Ihak t'ongnok*, but has been regularly circulated as an independent work.

T'oegye's most direct and obvious contribution to the study of the *Hsing-chuang* is the supply of certain information. Invariably, for places important in Chu Hsi's life, T'oegye would indicate the location. For example, Ch'ung-an County, where Chu Hsi lived in the earlier part of his life, was 240 *li* north of Chien-ning prefectural capital (2a).[5] and P'ing-shan (Mount P'ing) was southeast of the county capital (2a). We learn from T'oegye that Chien-yang County, where Chu Hsi lived from 1191 until he died, was 120 *li* north of the Chien-ning prefectural capital (2b), and that K'ao-t'ing, ("ancestors' pavillion"), a name later identified with Chu Hsi himself, was west of the county capital in San-kuei ("three cassias") village, which was founded by an imperial censor of the T'ang dynasty to sacrifice to his ancestors (2b). We learn, too, that Yün-ku ("cloud valley"), which Chu Hsi also adopted as his name, where he built a small hut in 1175 called Hμi-an, another name by which he has been most commonly known, was on top of the Lu Mountain 70 *li* northwest of the Chien-yang capital (8b), and that the Wu-i Study, which he built in 1183, was in Wu-i Mountain 30 *li* south of Ch'ung-an (22a). (Actually, the present map shows that the mountain is northwest of Ch'ung-an.) Where the *Hsing-chuang* said that Chu Hsi was appointed imperial compiler in 1191., T'oegye has added that it was at the recommendation of Shih Hao (1106–94) (36b). None of this information is found in Tai Hsien's (1496 cs) *Authentic Records of Master Chu*, (*Chu Tzu shih-chi*, 1513), which collected important information from various sources and is the most important source for Chu Hsi's biography before T'oegye's time, and Wang Mou-hung's (1668–1741) *Chronological Biography of Master Chu* (*Chu Tzu nien-p'u*), the most authoritative biographical material after T'oegye's time. T'oegye was the first to name the prime minister and the high official who recommended Chu Hsi for the imperial audience in 1194 (38b). He also explained that Hsin-an, which Chu Hsi often called his native place, was the name in the Chin period (264–420) for Hui-chou, where his ancestors lived (1b); that "ministers grabbing power" in Chu Hsi's memorial to the emperor referred to Han T'o-chou (1151–1202) (47a); that those who sought the Way but went too far meant Lu Hsiang-shan (Chiu-yüan, 1139–93) and his Kiangsi school of sudden enlightenment; and that those whose doctrines bent too low meant Ch'en Liang (T'ung-fu, 1143–94) and his Chekiang school of practical results (60b).

The above may be mere identifications and throw no special light on Chu Hsi. With reference to Chu Hsi's teacher Liu Tzu-hui (P'ing-shan, 1101–47), however, Tai Hsien has quoted from Chu Hsi's own essays and concluded that "This is briefly what he had learned from Liu." T'oegye, quoting from the same essays at greater length, concluded that "This is all he had learned from Liu." This brief statement means that Chu Hsi had learned no more from Liu. This is important because Chu Hsi himself said that learning no more from Liu and other teachers was the turning point in his career of study. In the *Classified Conversations of Master Chu* (*Chu Tzu yü-lei*) we read that at first he studied under Liu and Hu Hsien (Chi-hsi, 1086–1162); that Hu was fond of Buddhism and Taoism, that he felt he understood very little of the Way; and that was why he went to Li T'ung, who, all scholars agree, directed him back to Confucianism.[6] P'ing-shan had taught him the doctrine of *fu* (to return) in the *Book of Changes*[7] to emphasize the importance of returning to the source, and the doctrine of self-examination[8] and self-renewal.[9] These injunctions are contained in the essays quoted. These are good, traditional Confucian teachings. But since Liu and Hu taught no more than these traditional values, Chu Hsi was not satisfied and, therefore, sought new light from Li T'ung.

Of equal significance is T'oegye's selection of Chu Hsi's poem commenting on Hu Hsien. According to Li Fang-tzu's *Nien-p'u*, Hu had retired from minor government service and had for two decades devoted his
life to studying and teaching, but in 1159, at the advanced age of over
seventy, he had accepted an appointment as collator in the imperial library. In the Confucian tradition it is perfectly honorable to advise a ruler,
as did the eighty-year-old fisherman giving counsel to King Wen. To accept an appointment in old age, after having held no office for a long
time, however, would give rise to the suspicion that one was compromising himself in order to fulfill unsatisfied ambitions for wealth or fame.
This may be an unfair suspicion but the Confucian sense of integrity was
so strong that most scholars would decline such an invitation. When Hu
Hsien was invited, Chu Hsi was only thirty. He wrote a poem to say fare-
well to Hu in which he said that the teacher was not interested in fame
and only had service to the people in mind, but faced the prospect of
returning "with his hands inside his sleeves," that is, having done nothing. Later he sent a poem saying that the blue mountain remained blue.
It was generally understood that Chu Hsi was satirical. Therefore, Hu
Hung (Wu-feng, 1105–55) wrote a poem to say that the blue mountain
never got old, his purpose being to offer an explanation to save Hu Hsien
from the satire. It is interesting to note that Tai Hsien quoted all three
poems in his *Chu Tzu shih-chi* and added the remark that "We can to
some extent see how serious Chu was in regard to taking up the responsibility of upholding the Way."[10] In his *Chu Tzu nien-p'u*, Wang Mou-
hung omitted the poems altogether but in his *K'ao-i* (Research Notes)
supplementing the *Nien-p'u*, he asked whether the inclusion of the poems
was not intended to show why Chu Hsi himself declined the imperial
summons to the temporary capital at Lin-ch'uan (present Hangchow). But
he thought Hu Hung's poem was pointless.[11] In T'oegye's annotation, only
the verse saying that the blue mountain remains blue is quoted, without
any comment (3b). It is easy to understand why the verse about the sleeves
is omitted, because that is obviously critical and T'oegye probably wanted
us to forget it. But why keep the verse about the blue mountain remaining blue? Had he lived later than Wang Mou-hung, he might have shared
Wang's viewpoint, but he lived a century and a half earlier. I am inclined
to believe that T'oegye wanted to show that Chu Hsi was convinced of
the integrity of his teacher.

Another important episode occurred in 1188. Chu Hsi had had an audience with the emperor and offered various counsels to him, but because he disagreed with powerful officials, he was appointed in the eighth month to an office outside the capital. In the eleventh month he sent the emperor a sealed memorial urging him to give the crown prince able assistance, to select ministers carefully, to promote high moral standards, to effect social reforms, to undertake economic developments, and to improve the military situation.[12] In his earlier memorials, he had always made a central point of refusing to make peace with the invading Chin but rather resisting them, and it was his opposition to making peace that led him into political trouble more than once. But in this long memorial of more than 11,000 words, this note is not made. Had he changed his policy, or had he weakened his opposition? T'oegye quoted Chu Hsi's pupil Yang Fu who, having recited from the memorial that "When the great foundation is established and the (six) urgent measures enacted, if the Central Plain will not be recovered and the enemy not destroyed, I shall kneel to be executed," asked, "When did our Teacher forget the moral principle of revenging the enemy?" T'oegye is not unique in quoting Yang Fu. Both Tai's Shih-chi and Wang's Nien-p'u quote him. What is unique with T'oegye is that his comment on this matter is the longest in his annotation. Obviously, he wanted to leave the strong impression that Chu Hsi was a man of great integrity and unflinching convictions.

In this connection, what T'oegye did about Chu Hsi's commentary on the Elegies of Ch'u (Ch'u-tz'u) should be noted. In 1195, when Chu Hsi was virtually dismissed from the government, he wrote the commentary. His pupil, Yang Chi (1142–1213), had this to say:

One could see from his expression that our Master was worrying about the conditions of the time. One day he suddenly showed us students his annotation on the Elegies of Ch'u. After I had bowed out, I thought that ordinarily, in teaching students, our Teacher began with the Four Books of the Great Learning, the Analects, the Mencius, ant the Doctrine of the Mean, then the Six Classics,[13] and then the histories and biographies. As to literary works after Ch'in and Han times, he would comment on them as matters of secondary importance. Then why had he now engaged in explaining the Elegies of Ch'u? The Master never told us and we dared not ask.

Tai Hsien quoted Yang Chi in his Chu Tzu shih-chi because, he said, Yang's words are gentle and deep.[14] T'oegye quoted the same words but made no comment (49b). Students of Chinese literature all know that Ch'ü Yüan (343–277 B.C.?) wrote the Elegies of Ch'u to express his sor-

row for the sad condition of the state. There is no doubt that T'oegye
quoted from Yang Chi, as Tai Hsien did before him, to show that Chu
Hsi was much concerned with the state of public affairs practically to the
end of his life.

There is very little in the *Hsing-chuang* about Chu Hsi's religious
life. Tai Hsien noted that after burying his mother in Chien-yang in 1170,
Chu Hsi went home to Ch'ung-an on the first and fifteenth day of every
month to perform sacrifices to his ancestors,[15] but the *Shih-chi* paid more
attention to Chu Hsi's compilation of ritual texts to which Chu Hsi devoted a number of years toward the end of his life. Wang Mou-hung
omitted this account from his *Nien-p'u* and merely noted the fact in his
research notes but then went on at great length to Chu Hsi's compilation
of ritual texts.[16] In sharp contrast, T'oegye dismissed the compilation in
three words, thus concentrating on Chu Hsi's religious life (8a). To me
this is a real insight absent in practically all other biographies.

The above comments deal with Chu Hsi's feelings. Generally speaking, T'oegye's annotation is not much involved with philosophical matters. In commenting on Chu Hsi's relation with Li T'ung, he quoted from
one of Chu Hsi's letters and his conversations as well as Li T'ung's answers to his questions, all on the main doctrine that he learned from Li,
namely, to be one's own master in quietude and to observe the disposition before the feelings are aroused. This is the theme emphasized in both
the *Shih-chi*[17] and the *Nien-p'u*.[18] In addition to this, however, T'oegye
also quoted Li T'ung's injunction to Chu Hsi that while principle is one,
one must understand that its manifestations are many (54b). This doctrine of *li-i fen-shu* is one of the basic tenets of Neo-Confucian thought.
In a recent study, I have tried to show that Chu Hsi did not turn to Ch'eng
I (I-ch'uan, 1033–1107) after Li T'ung directed him away from Buddhism but that he was attracted to Ch'eng I from childhood and that the
doctrine that Li T'ung taught him and that made the greatest impression
on him was not the doctrine of observing the state before the feelings are
aroused but the doctrine of *li-i fen-shu*. I pointed out that in Li T'ung's
conversations with Chu Hsi, *li-i fen-shu* was more often talked about than
the doctrine of quietude and the longest conversation concerns *li-i fen-
shu*.[19] T'oegye must be given much credit for recognizing this line of
transmission.

While T'oegye was sure about Chu Hsi's convictions and what he
learned from Li T'ung, he was not at all dogmatic. Both Tai Hsien and

Wang Mou-hung said that after the emperor read Chu Hsi's memorial in 1180, he was very angry.[20] T'oegye, however, having quoted from Li Fang-tzu's *Nien-p'u* that the emperor was not offended, remarked that the two accounts differed and he did not know which was right (14b). In 1181, Chu Hsi was appointed to be superintendent of ever-normal granaries, tea, and salt in the Kiangsi area. According to the *Hsing-chuang*, at first he was to be sent to Szechuan, but the emperor did not want him to be too far away and that was why he was given a post in nearby Kiangsi (14b). This is the version accepted in both the *Shih-chi* and the *Nien-p'u*. T'oegye, however, quoting from the *History of the Sung Dynasty*, offered an alternative explanation for the reader to consider—that the appointment was made following the recommendation from a high official that Chu Hsi's talents should be utilized (14b). About his appointment as prefect of Changsha in 1193, both the *Shih-chi* and the *Nien-p'u* accepted the explanation that when a captive returned and reported that the Chin enemy had inquired about Chu Hsi and that the captive had replied that Chu Hsi was in a high post in the government, Chu Hsi was immediately appointed to the post.[21] To T'oegye, there was another reason. He quoted from the *History of the Sung Dynasty* that prime minister Liu Cheng (1129–1206) felt that Chu Hsi was too strict and was afraid that he would create trouble in the capital. If the two earlier alternative explanations tend to be in Chu Hsi's favor, this explanation is surely not flattering. All this goes to show that T'oegye, while he adored Chu Hsi, remained objective.

I have noticed a few errors in T'oegye's annotation. When Chu Hsi's grandfather died in 1165, his father, having retired as a magistrate in Fu-kien, was too poor to take his family back to Hui-chou in Anhui, and therefore the family settled in Fukien, where Chu Hsi was born. Li Fang-tzu's *Nien-p'u* said that it was due to Fang La's rebellion that the family could not return to Hui-chou. The *Shih-chi* accepted this account but added that it was also due to the family's poverty (1a). T'oegye accepted the account of the rebellion but not that of poverty (2a). The *Nien-p'u*, however, allowed only the explanation of poverty because he found that Fang La's rebellion took place in 1060–61.[22] To overlook the poverty in Chu Hsi's family is certainly a serious oversight on T'oegye's part, for poverty was an outstanding fact in Chu Hsi's life.

Following the *Shih-chi*,[23] T'oegye said that Chu Hsi visited Li T'ung in 1160 and stayed in the Hsi-lin Hall for a month (3b). But Chu Hsi

himself said that he stayed there for several months,[24] a fact noted in the
Nien-p'u.[25] To mention the Chu-lin Study under the year 1192 (36b) is
at least misleading, for that study was not built until two years later.

In 1195, after he was let off from the government and returned home,
Chu Hsi composed a memorial in more than 10,000 words to urge the
emperor to avoid wicked officials. His pupils, sensing the great risk involved, asked for divination. The Hsing-chuang said that in the divination the 33rd hexagram, tun (retirement), was followed by the 13th hexagram, t'ung-jen (companions). Thereupon, Chu Hsi withdrew in silence
and burned the draft of the memorial. According to the Shih-chi, however, the hexagram tun was followed by the 37th hexagram, chia-jen
(family).[26] T'oegye chose to follow the Hsing-chuang rather than the Shih-
chi (48b). Wang Mou-hung has argued that if the second hexagram had
been t'ung-jen instead of chia-jen, only the lower half of the hexagram
would have been divined. He therefore concluded that t'ung-jen was a
misprint.[27] The difference between t'ung-jen and chia-jen is that if it were
the former, it would have meant it was good to be on the same level and
therefore to challenge the officials, but in a family it is the duty of a subordinate to obey. Therefore, Chu Hsi withdrew and called himself Old
Man in Retirement.

Turning to the Chujasŏ chŏryo, we shall be dealing with Chu Hsi's
teachings. This compilation was completed in 1558 when T'oegye was
fifty-eight. According to his preface, he was not aware of the Collected
Literary Works of Master Chu (Chu Tzu wen-chi) until 1543. When he
compared Chu's letters with his other works, he felt that the latter were
either too general or, like the recorded conversations, not by the Master
himself, whereas the letters were all his own writing and geared to specific individuals and particular situations. What is more, they served as
the starting points of one's learning process and were particularly stimulating. Therefore, he selected about a third of Chu Hsi's letters to make
the Chujasŏ chŏryo in fourteen chapters (now divided into twenty chapters).

T'oegye was not the first to make such a selection. According to the
preface, Wang Po (1197–1274) had made one, but it has been lost. A
postscript to T'oegye's work by Hwang Chunnyang dated 1561 tells us that
Wu Ssu-an had made another selection, but that presumably has been
lost too. Thus, T'oegye's work is virtually original and, so far as I know,

the only such selection in existence. He followed the order of the letters in the *Chu Tzu wen-chi*. Only a small number of correspondents are omitted. At the beginning of each chapter, he has provided a list of the names of the correspondents and a brief biographical sketch. In the selections, he has added notes here and there to identify people, places, and dates, to explain archaic terms or literary and historical allusions, and to give the background of the letter. Curiously, in a few cases, where the *Wen-chi* has given the private name of the correspondent or the date of the letter, T'oegye has omitted it (7:23b, C36:49a, 11:41a, C48:30a).[28] In the letters, Chu Hsi added some notes or comments. T'oegye has included many of these, but he has omitted some of them. In one case the omission is serious. In his letter to his pupil Ts'ao Chien (Li-chih, 1162–91), he said that Lu Hsiang-shan's pupil Pao Yang (Hsien-tao) had declared that reading and study would be a disaster because they block the path to humanity and righteousness and added the note that he heard Pao's remark at Nan-feng[29] from Yang Tzu-chih (Fang) (C51:29b). Book-reading is a central issue of dispute between the Chu Hsi school, which laid emphasis on "following the path of inquiry and study," and the Lu school, which stressed almost exclusively "honoring the moral nature."[30] This is an issue, though exaggerated, that has sharply divided the two rival schools. Chu Hsi added the note to show that the remark was not his own invention. Unfortunately, T'oegye somehow deleted it (12:26a). Such omissions are, however, very few. In most cases, he has included Chu Hsi's notes, including the very important one on the Ch'eng brothers. In a letter to his good friend Chang Shih (Nan-hsüan, Ching-fu, 1133–80), Chu Hsi noted that Ch'eng Hao's (Ming-tao, 1032–85) perfection came by nature and required no human effort, while his younger brother I-ch'uan's efforts reached the highest peak and could win over the skill of Heaven (C31:7a). This comparison of the two brothers is not found anywhere else in Chu Hsi's writings and has been hailed as the best appraisal of them. Happily, T'oegye has retained the note (3:21b).

T'oegye also made some comments of his own, sometimes supplying background information (11:37b), sometimes discussing an item (8:18a), sometimes pointing out the objective of the passage (3:12a), sometimes raising a doubt (1:5b, 3:27b, 4:5a), and sometimes even correcting Chu Hsi (7:30b). It is difficult to find fault with his notes or comments. In one case, however, I feel T'oegye's note is inadequate. On Chu Hsi's letter to his son-in-law Huang Kan in 1120, T'oegye simply noted that it was in the third month (2:31b). He could have been more precise, and added that it was the eighth day, the day before Chu Hsi passed away.

In the earlier chapters of the book, T'oegye underscored some sentences that he considered important by adding dots on the side. An examination shows that his choices are all on moral cultivation. To this end, sometimes only one out of several letters to the same person or only one sentence out of a long passage is selected (2:20b, 4:5a, 4:11a, 19:22a). T'oegye adhered firmly to his central objective of moral motivation and stimulation. It must be from this point of view that the work is evaluated.

One could argue that by confining oneself to Chu Hsi's letters and thus excluding his memorials where he urged upon the emperor certain moral values, political documents where he explains why he accepted or declined an office, the essays on *jen*' (humanity, humaneness) and seriousness *(ching, reverence),*[31] or poems where he expressed his deep feelings, the reader might miss out on Chu Hsi's strong convictions on when to serve or not to serve and his teachings on how to practice humaneness and seriousness. However, it is unfair to judge what one does by what one has not done, like criticizing a pianist for not playing golf. The question is whether his moral teachings in general are covered in the selections of his letters. By and large, they are.

But how is one going to appraise the selections themselves? The *Chu Tzu wen-chi* contains 2,000 letters written to over 500 people. It would be pointless and impossible to examine each letter. I have, therefore, chosen to examine several groups on certain subjects, and try to see if these subjects are well handled. Among the most famous of Chu Hsi's letters are those he sent Lu Hsiang-shan in a debate on the Great Ultimate. The *Wen-chi* contains eleven letters to the Lu brothers—two to Chiu-ling (Tzu-shou, 1132–80), three to Chiu-shao (Tzu-mei, fl. 1150), and six to Chiu-yüan (Tzu-ching). T'oegye chose the second of the two letters to Tzu-shou on religious rites (5:1a–2b, C36:1a–3a). Of the two letters to Tzu-mei, only the first is used, in which Chu Hsi defended Chou Tun-i's (Lien-hsi, 1017–73) statement of "The Ultimate of Non-being" *(Wu-chi)* and also the "Great Ultimate" *(T'ai-chi)*[32] by saying that without the Ultimate of Nonbeing, the Great Ultimate would be just one of the things and could not itself function as the root of things, and without the Great Ultimate the Ultimate of Nonbeing would be empty and would not be capable of being the root of things (5:2b, C36:3b). The debate ended in displeasure on both sides. Later, in 1188, Lu Hsiang-shan took up the debate and wrote a long letter of 2,000 words to challenge Chu Hsi.[33] In a reply the same year, Chu Hsi refuted Lu. Lu had argued that *Wu-chi* is a Taoist term never used by Confucian sages, that *chi* means *chung* (central) and not a metaphysical entity, and that Master Chou had made *Wu-chi* and *T'ai-chi* into two different things. In rebuttal, Chu Hsi said that just as Confucius was the first to use the term *T'ai-chi* (in the *Book of Changes*), so it was all right for Master Chou to be the first to use the term *Wu-chi*; that the Great Ultimate has been described as central but not centrality itself, and that the Ultimate of Nonbeing is simply the Great Ultimate in its indescribable form but not a separate thing (5:4b–5b, C36:8a–9b). This is the only letter to Lu Hsiang-shan used by T'oegye, yet all the basic arguments on Chu Hsi's side are represented. I wish two more letters, the second and the third (C36:6a–7a), had been included also, for here Chu Hsi criticized Lu for neglecting daily affairs in search of abstract and mysterious ideals.

An almost equally famous debate took place in 1184–85 between Chu Hsi and Ch'en Liang. Of the thirteen letters to Ch'en Liang (C36:16a–32b), five are concerned with the debate (4th, 6th–9th), and they are the longest. Chu Hsi strongly attacked Ch'en Liang's theory that righteousness and profit can go together and a kingly ruler and the lord of hegemony are the same, and that the Principle of Heaven and evil human desires can operate simultaneously. He insisted that the accomplishments of the Han and T'ang rulers, which Ch'en Liang highly praised, should be condemned because their motives were evil. T'oegye's selection of the 4th, 6th, 8th, and 9th (5:8b–17b) is more than adequate to record the controversy. In fact, proportionately, the selection of letters to Ch'en Liang is fuller than that of anyone else. I wish another letter (Supplement, 7:7b–8b), had been included. In this letter Chu Hsi recalled his son's intelligence as a child, the son's death and burial, his poverty-stricken state, and the gift of a pad of white wool to Ch'en. This would show that it was characteristic of Chu Hsi to be very severe and strict in matters of ideas, yet courteous and warm in personal relations.

This warmth in personal feelings is no better expressed than in his letters to Chang Nan-hsüan. There are altogether fifty-four letters to Chang[34] over the course of some twenty years. They cover all kinds of subjects—political, personal, textual, philosophical. There are two dominant themes, namely, those of centrality and harmony *(chung-ho)*, and of humanity. In his middle age, Chu Hsi wrestled for several years with the problem of how to attain centrality and harmony in one's nature and feelings before and after the feelings are aroused, as taught in the *Doctrine of the Mean*.[35] At first he adhered to his teacher Li T'ung's theory that centrality is to be sought before the feelings are aroused, chiefly through quiet sitting. Gradually he felt that the mind is a state in which feelings are already aroused, a position close to that of the Hunan School of which Chang Nan-hsüan was the leader. So in 1167 he visited Chang in Changsha and stayed for two months, discussing the problem most of the time. After he returned home, he sent Chang the first letter on *chung-ho* (C30:19a–b), setting forth the idea that the mind is an aroused state. Before long he discarded the idea and sent Chang the second letter on *chung-ho* (C30:19a–b), saying that the mind is both unaroused and aroused, that is, both substance and function. But then he felt this letter was even more mistaken because it was too general and abstract, so he wrote Chang the third letter on *chung-ho* (C32:4a–5a), emphasizing the point that one must be his own master in dealing with various psychological situations. However, Chu Hsi had yet to come to a concrete means of attaining centrality and harmony. He therefore had to write the fourth letter on *chung-ho* to stress the point that they are spontaneous and uninterrupted, and that substance and function are naturally a unity. After a year's thinking and two more letters on *chung-ho*, he finally declared all previous letters to be "old theory" and wrote his "first letter" on *chung-ho* in 1169 to the several gentlemen of Hunan (C63:28b–29b). In this letter he said that the cultivation of seriousness and study must go hand in hand so the substance of the mind attains centrality in its state of tranquility, and its functions, that is, the feelings, attain harmony in their expressions. This synthesis of "honoring the moral nature" and "following the path of inquiry and study," of the states before and after the feelings are aroused, and of substance and function, has remained central to the moral philosophy of the Chu Hsi school.

Of these letters on *chung-ho*, T'oegye omitted the first two letters on the ground that Chu Hsi himself had rejected them (3:26b). To be consistent, he should have excluded the fourth too. However, he has selected the third, the fourth (3:26ab–27b), the sixth (3:30b–33a), and the "first letter" to the Hunan gentlemen (18:22b–23b), and these cover the essential ideas completely. This part of the selection can very well be considered the best in T'oegye's whole work.

The same cannot be said about his selection on the subject of humanity. More than ten of Chu Hsi's letters (C32:16b–21b) deal with this concept, four on Chu Hsi's "Treatise on Humanity" (C67:20a–21b) alone. T'oegye included only one of them (3:29b–30b, C32:19–ab), leaving out three of Chu Hsi's cardinal ideas: that *jen* means the character of the mind and the principle of love; that *jen* comes from the mind of Heaven and Earth to create; and that Hsieh Liang-tso's (Shang-ts'ai, 1050–1103) theory that *jen* is consciousness and Yang Shih's (Kuei-shan, 1053–1135) theory that *jen* means forming one body with Heaven and Earth and all things, are both unsound. Instead, T'oegye devoted more space to Chu Hsi's criticism of Chang Nan-hsüan's proposed collection of sayings by Confucius and Mencius on *jen* (3:19b–22b), a subject hardly comparable in historical or philosophical significance.

Nan-hsüan was one of Chu Hsi's best friends. The other was Lü Tsuch'ien (Tung-lai, Po-kung, 1137–81). They were intimate and full of mutual respect and affection, although they represented three incompatible lines of thought. In a way, he had more to do with Tung-lai. He sent his son to study with him. Tung-lai visited him in 1175, joined in compiling the *Chin-ssu lu*,[36] and arranged for him and Lu Hsiang-shan to meet at the Goose Lake Temple. Chu Hsi's letters to Tung-lai number 106 (C25:14a–16a, 21a–22a; C33:1a–35:11a; Supplement C1:1ab). They may be grouped under three headings: (1) those on his son, (2) those on the concept of *jen*, and (3) those on Lu Hsiang-shan and his brothers. Of these, T'oegye's selections only cover the Lu brothers adequately (4:17a, 19b, 20b). Chu Hsi had told Tung-lai that he wanted to meet Hsiang-shan (C33:17a), that the Lu brothers had confessed their mistakes (C34:4b), that Hsiang-shan's pupils began to realize their teacher's errors (C34:17ab), that Hsiang-shan finally taught people to read books (C34:23b), that Hsiang-shan still retained his old views (C34:26a), that Lu planned to visit a mountain with Chu Hsi (C34:28a), that Tzu-shou had passed away (C34:30a), that Hsiang-shan had requested a tomb inscription for his mother (C34:32a), that Lu had come to visit him for a few days (C34:33a), and that his former disposition still remained with him (C34:34a). T'oegye has covered the most important of these points.

As to letters to his pupils, they are also equally divided into those on moral endeavor and personal affairs, on the one hand, and philosophical and textual discussions on the other. Perhaps the best illustrations are those to Huang Kan (his son-in-law), Ts'ai Yüan-ting (Chi-t'ung, 1135–98), and

Ch'en Ch'un (Pai-hsi, 1153–1217), who were among the most prominent. Letters to Huang Kan are many (C29:22b–23a, C46:30a–35b,
Supplement C1:1a–22a Separate, C2:1ab). They deal with personal and
family affairs, discussions on the Great Ultimate, rites, etc. In T'oegye's
selections (2:31b–32a, 11:20a–21b, 19:1a–12b), I do miss the note in which
Chu Hsi regretted that he could not afford a dowry for his daughter (Supplement C1:10a), but I am particularly happy that T'oegye has included
the letter Chu Hsi wrote Huang Kan the day before he died, in which he
said he had no more worry because he was confident that the pupil could
carry on the Way (2:31b–32a, C29:22b–23a).

T'oegye seems to be uninterested in textual matters. In Chu Hsi's
letters to Ts'ai Yüan-ting, of which there are more than one hundred letters and excerpts (C44:1a–16b, Supplement C2:1a–3:6b, Separate C2:2a–
3a), much space is devoted to the discussion on various texts, including
the *Book of Changes*, of which Yüan-ting was an expert. He was the one
who suggested the use of divination in 1195. For years Yüan-ting assisted
the Teacher on ritual texts. He was a highly regarded specialist on mu-
sical pipes, and there is much deliberation in the letters on the subject.
T'oegye has ignored almost all of these in favor of concern with moral
matters (10:1a–6b, 19:13a–21b, 21:7a).

This is also true of his selection of letters to Ch'en Ch'un. Since
Ch'en Ch'un did not study with Chu Hsi until his last decade and personal contact lasted for only seven months, their discourses were mostly
by mail. The six surviving letters are therefore very long (C57:10b–43a).
Ch'en was the most philosophical among Chu Hsi's pupils. Consequently, most of the discussions are on philosophical concepts. Happily
T'oegye has included Ch'en's long question on the distinctions between
what should be, what is, and what must be (15:19a). Still, his emphasis
lies in personal conduct (15:15a–18b).

T'oegye's preference for passages on personal cultivation instead of
those on book study or philosophical investigation was definitely by choice.
Some deletions of philosophical passages are striking. In the letter to Yang
Chih-jen, the very important paragraph on whether principle *(li)* or material force *(ch'i)* exists first is not used (16:6a, C58:10b). Two letters to
Ch'eng K'o-chiu on the Great Ultimate are excluded (6:18b, C. C37:31b–
33b). Two letters to Ho Shu-ching on *jen* and the mind of Heaven and
Earth (8:13b, C40:29a–30a) are passed over. In the letters to Lin Tse-
chih (Yung-chung) passages on *jen* (9:31b, C43:27b–28b) are not in-

cluded. The long and very important letter on the Great Ultimate sent to Yang Fang (10:18b; C45:11a–12b) will surely be missed by those interested in his central Neo-Confucian subject. All this has been done to provide space for teachings on preserving the nature, nourishing the vital force, recovering the original mind, etc. In T'oegye's eyes, Chu Hsi was primarily a great teacher, like Confucius, whose aim was to direct and help people to attain sagehood.

It may be interesting to compare T'oegye's work with the *Essentials of Master Chu (Chu Tzu chieh-yao)* by Kao P'an-lung (Ching-i, 1562–1626). In many ways, the two works are not comparable. P'an-lung drew material from both the *Chu Tzu wen-chi* and the *Chu Tzu yü-lei*, while T'oegye drew only from the *Wen-chi* and then only the letters in it. P'an-lung has followed the arrangement of the *Chin-ssu lu* and divided the book into fourteen chapters on as many subjects. He has made use of less than thirty letters, while T'oegye has used hundreds. In fact, P'an-lung depended chiefly on the recorded conversations. And yet the titles of the two works are almost the same. T'oegye's compilation was done in 1534 but not published until 1572, while P'an-lung's anthology was compiled in 1602. In terms of time, they are not really too far apart. Neither scholar, however, was aware of the other.

An examination of P'an-lung's selection of letters reveals a surprising fact. With the exception of the letter to Lin Sung-ch'ing on life and death in ch. 1, all the rest are devoted to moral cultivation, including the several letters to Chang Nan-hsüan and the letter to the several gentlemen of Hunan. Of course, since the first chapter of the book is on the substance of Tao, there is bound to be discussion on metaphysics, as there are necessarily passages on intellectual pursuit in the second chapter on how to study. But the whole book, consisting mostly of recorded conversations, is permeated with the spirit of moral endeavor. Both T'oegye and P'an-lung seem to want the same lessons from Master Chu, whom they regarded primarily as a great teacher. Shall we not say that the two intellectual giants in China and Korea in the late sixteenth century were thinking alike?

The same moral concern dominates T'oegye's third work under consideration, the *Ihak t'ongnok*. It is a record of Chu Hsi's 411 pupils, Nan-hsüan's 8, and 26 of their indirect disciples. In the introduction, T'oegye says, "The students of Confucius and Mencius attained the Way to a greater or smaller degree and they were in some ways right and in other ways wrong. They all found their answers in the nuances of their Master's teachings. This should serve as the model for the pupils (of Chu Hsi)." For this purpose, T'oegye has divided the account of each pupil into three parts: biography, conversations with Chu Hsi, and Chu Hsi's letters. His sources were the *History of the Sung Dynasty*, the *Chu Tzu shih-chi*, the *Ta-Ming i-t'ung chi* (General Records of the Great Ming Dynasty), the *Chu Tzu yü-lei*, and the *Chu Tzu wen-chi*. For the biographies, he also used other sources, and thus was able to provide more information on names and places (3:21a, 4:33a, 5:28a, 6:8a, 8:43a, etc.). Although he relied chiefly on the *Shih-chi* and has perpetuated some of its errors (6:56a, 7:6b, etc.), in a few places he has corrected its mistakes (3:20a, 42a, 6:38a, 7:12a).

In resorting to the *Yü-lei* and the *Wen-chi*, T'oegye was pioneering, for the *Shih-chi* is confined to biographies plus a few of the Master's complimentary remarks on certain pupils. Eight years before the publication of the *Ihak t'ongnok* in 1576, there had been published in China in 1568 the *K'ao-t'ing yüan-yüan lu* (Records of the Source of the Chu Hsi School) compiled by Sung Tuan-i (1447–1507) decades earlier. But T'oegye was not aware of this. While the *Yüan-yüan lu* is long on biography and short on recorded conversations and letters from Chu Hsi, the *Ihak t'ongnok* is the reverse.

In the use of the *Yü-lei*, T'oegye went far beyond the *Yüan-yüan lu*. T'oegye's selections are ample and carefully made. He must have studied the *Yü-lei* very closely, at least chs. 113–21, which contain Chu Hsi's instructions to his pupils. T'oegye's effort has led him to identify at least seven people as Chu Hsi's pupils (7:25b, 26a, 34a–1, 37a–2, 37b, 42a–a, 8:31b). None of these has been identified in the *Shih-chi* before or in any later work. He has found evidences in the *Yü-lei*. Also, in some other cases, he has been the only one to cite from the *Yü-lei* to support the claim that the scholars were pupils (7:36a, 38a–1, 38b–1, 38b–2, 39b–1&2, 41a).

Similar thoroughness can be seen in the selections from letters in the *Wen-chi*. Generally speaking, the selections were made from his *Chujasŏ chŏryo*, with the same emphasis on moral training and the same disinterest in philosophy and books. Unfortunately, the letter Chu Hsi wrote to his son-in-law the day before he died expressing confidence that Huang Kan would carry on the Way has been omitted, but fortunately,

Chu Hsi's own note in a letter about Pao Yang's remark against book-learning, which was omitted in the *chŏryo*, is here restored (8:15a).

In the *Wen-chi* there is a letter criticizing a pupil for his explanation of the *Book of Odes* as farfetched.[37] The *Shih-chi* overlooked the criticism and quoted only Chu Hsi's complimentary remark that the pupil's purpose was deep (8:12a). There is no question that Tai Hsien in his *Shih-chi*, like Sung Tuan-i later in his *K'ao-t'ing yüan-yüan lu*, deliberately distorted in order to exaggerate the virtues of Chu Hsi's followers. T'oegye quoted the *Shih-chi* (7:9a) without question. Whether he was aware of Tai Hsien's deception, he certainly followed the *Shih-chi* too extensively. The purpose of both the *Shih-chi* and the *K'ao-t'ing yüan-yüan lu* was to glorify the Chu Hsi School and their compilers therefore included many prominent people as pupils of Chu who had corresponded or exchanged poems with him or accompanied him on a tour. T'oegye has adopted many such people from the *Shih-chi* and added some of his own. Most of the 146 people in ch. 8 of the *Ihak t'ongnok* belong to this category.

This high enthusiasm for the Chu Hsi School is understandable for it is characteristic of practically all books on Chu Hsi's pupils. Chu I-tsun's (1623–1709) *Ching-i k'ao* (Investigation into the Meanings of the Classics) puts the number of pupils to whom Chu Hsi "transmitted the classics" at 139.[38] In his *Ju-lin tsung-p'ai* (Schools of Confucianism) Wan Ssu-t'ung has increased the number to 433.[39] Huang Tsung-hsi's (1610–95) *Sung Yüan hsüeh-an* (Case Studies of Sung and Yüan Confucians), amended by Ch'üan Tsu-wang (1705–55), is more selective and critical, and has reduced the number to 224.[40] The *Sung Yüan hsüeh-an pu-i* (Supplement to the *Sung-Yüan hsüeh-an*), however, has more than doubled the number to 552.[41] Many with only a tenuous relation with Chu Hsi are counted as pupils.

In the case of the *Ihak t'ongnok* this defect is more than offset by the careful study of the *Yü-lei* and the *Wen-chi*. It has many distinct contributions. The fact that T'oegye alone identified a number of Chu Hsi's pupils has already been noted. The *Shih-chi*, the *K'ao-ting yüan-yüan lu*, and the *Ju-lin tsung-p'ai* all give one name as Ting Yao. In the *Wen-chi*,[42] there are Ting Yao, Ting K'e, and Ting Fu-chih. T'oegye, departing from the *Shih-chi*, chose to call him Ting K'e. This choice is sound because in the *Analects* it is said, "To master (*k'e*) oneself and return (*fu*) to propriety is humanity."[43] Thus there is a definite connection between

k'e and *fu* but hardly any between Emperor Yao and the concept of returning. The *Sung Yüan hsüeh-an pu-i* finally corrected the misprint in
the *Wen-chi* which the several books had perpetuated.[44] If the *Ihak t'ongnok* had been consulted, China would not have had to wait almost a century for the correction to be made. I believe the *Ihak t'ongnok* has not
been studied outside of Korea, nor was it even known in China. Neither
were the two other works we have discussed or his *Chujasŏ chŏryo kiŭi*
(Record of Doubts Concerning the *Chujasŏ chŏryo*) in five chapters. All
these deserve our attention and respect. In fact, any work by T'oegye deserves our attention and respect.

NOTES

1. *Huang Mien-chai chi* (Collection of Literary Works of Huang Kan), *Cheng-i-t'ang ch'üan-shu* (Complete Library of the Hall of Rectifying the Way) edition, ch. 8, or *Mien-chai chi, Ssu-k'u ch'üan-shu chen-pen* (Treasured Works of the Four Libraries) edition, ch. 36.
2. Yamazaki Michio, "Shushi gyōjō T'oegye shūchū no igi," *T'oegye hakpo* (August 1978), 19:132, 402.
3. *Ibid.*, p. 412.
4. *Ibid.*, p. 406.
5. This and the following references are to the undated Japanese edition of T'oegye's work published by Asakura Gisuke in Kyoto.
6. *Chu Tzu yü-lei*, ch. 104, sec. 37 (Taipei: Cheng-chung, 1970), p. 4164.
7. Hexagram no. 24, *fu* (to return).
8. *Analects*, 1:4.
9. *The Great Learning*, ch. 2.
10. *Chu Tzu shih-chi*. (Taipei: Kuang-wen, 1972), p. 91. Hereafter cited as *Shih-chi*.
11. *Chu Tzu nien-p'u. Ts'ung-shu chi-ch'eng* (Collections Series) edition, pp. 15, 248–49. Hereafter cited as *Nien-p'u*.
12. This memorial is found in the *Chu Tzu wen-chi* (Collection of Literary Works of Master Chu), *Ssu-pu pei-yao* (Essentials of the Four Libraries) edition entitled *Chu Tzu ta-ch'üan* (Complete Literary Works of Master Chu), 11:17a–37b.
13. The *Book of Odes*, the *Book of History*, the *Book of Changes*, the *Book of Rites*, and the *Spring and Autumn Annals*. Originally there was also the *Book of Music*, but it was lost before the third century B.C. and in Sung times it was replaced by the *Rites of Chou*.
14. *Shih-chi*, p. 197.
15. *Ibid.*, p. 100.
16. *Nien-p'u*, pp. 42, 262–65.
17. *Shih-chi*, pp. 84–86.
18. *Nien-p'u*, pp. 249–50.
19. "Patterns for Neo-Confucianism: Why Chu Hsi Differed from Ch'eng I?" *Journal of Chinese Philosophy* (1978), 2:101–4.
20. *Shih-chi*, p. 122; *Nien-p'u*, p. 291.
21. *Shih-chi*, p. 173; *Nien-p'u*, p. 191.
22. *Nien-p'u*, pp. 1, 242.
23. *Shih-chi*, p. 91.
24. *Chu Tzu wen-chi*, 2:11a, "T'i Hsi-lin K'o-shih Ta-kuan hsüan" (On the Broad View Studio of Priest K'o-shih in Hsi-lin Hall).
25. *Nien-p'u*, p. 15.
26. *Shih-chi*, p. 196.
27. *Nien-p'u*, p. 335.

28. These are examples. References without the letter C are to the *Chajasŏ chŏryo*, *Kinsei kanseki sōkan*, and those with the letter are to the *Chu Tzu wen-chi*.
29. Nan-feng is a county in Kiangsi.
30. *Doctrine of the Mean*, ch. 27.
31. For memorials, see the *Chu Tzu wen-chi*, ch. 11–14. For documents concerning political appointments, see ch. 22–23. For the essay on *jen*, see 67:20a–21b; for regulations at the White Deer Grotto Academy, see 74:16b–17b; for the lecture at Yü-shan, see 74:18a–22a; and for the admonition on *ching*, see 85:5b–62.
32. The beginning sentence of the *T'ai-chi-t'u shuo* (Explanation of the Diagram of the Great Ultimate) at the start of the *Chou Tzu ch'üan-shu* (Complete works of Master Chou).
33. This letter is found in the *Hsiang-shan ch'üan-chi* (Complete Collection of Literary Works of Lu Hsiang-shan), *Ssu-pu pei-yao* ed. 2:42–7b.
34. *Chu Tzu wen-chi* 24:27b, 25:1a–7b, 30:17a–32:26b.
35. *Doctrine of the Mean*, ch. 1.
36. I have translated the *Chin-ssu lu* into English as *Reflections on Things at Hand: The Neo-Confucian Anthology* (New York: Columbia University Press, 1967).
37. *Chu Tzu wen-chi*, 39:23a, to Ch'en Ch'i-chung.
38. *Ching-i k'ao*, ch. 283–85.
39. Wan Ssu-t'ung, *Ju-lin tsung-p'ai*, (Chekiang Library ed., 1911), 9:1a–10b; 10:1a–9b.
40. *Sung Yüan hsüeh-an*, ch. 49, 69.
41. Compiled by Wang Tzu-ts'ai (1792–1851) and Feng Yün-hao (1834 *cs*), ch. 49, 69.
42. *Chu Tzu wen-chi*, Separate Collection, 7:10a, 84:29b.
43. *Analects*, 12:1.
44. *Sung Yüan hsüeh-an pu-i*, 69:194.

Julia Ching

Yi Yulgok on the "Four Beginnings and the Seven Emotions"

YI YULGOK (Yi I, 1536–84) and Yi T'oegye (Yi Hwang, 1501–70) stand together as two of the greatest minds of traditional Korea. They are frequently mentioned together, the latter as the more senior, the more revered, and the former sometimes as the more independent and original thinker. Both were followers of Neo-Confucian philosophy as taught by the great Chinese philosopher Chu Hsi (1130–1200), whose teachings became nearly sacrosanct in Korea even though they were at times criticized in China, especially in the fifteenth and sixteenth centuries. Each was in turn involved in a philosophical discussion and debate over the relationship between the Four Beginnings of Virtue and the Seven Emotions, the so-called "Four-Seven Debate," but represented the opposite sides of opinion on this question. In this paper, I propose to focus on Yulgok's discussions of the Four Beginnings and the Seven Emotions, because I believe this will offer us an appropriate entry into his deeper insights, laying bare his differences from Chu Hsi and from T'oegye, as well as revealing the wider implications of his philosophy of human nature.

As the names of Yulgok and T'oegye are so frequently mentioned together, a few facts about the life of each may be useful, showing how their paths in life met. T'oegye lost his father early in life, before he was twelve years old, while Yulgok mourned his mother's death at the age of fifteen, subsequently entering a Buddhist monastery for one year, where he studied Buddhist scriptures and learned the art of meditation. At the age of twenty-three, Yulgok visited T'oegye at Tosan for about two days. That same year, he passed his civil examinations with a treatise entitled *Treatise on the Way of Heaven (Ch'ŏndoch'aek)*. He was a brilliant scholar, attaining first place nine times in a series of examinations. Like T'oegye also, Yulgok was to hold public offices. But while T'oegye was mainly proccupied with lecturing and writing, Yulgok held important positions, such as that of envoy to China (1568), governor of Hwanghae Province (1574), and minister of the Board of War (1582). He predicted a Japanese invasion of Korea—which took place under Hideyoshi in 1592—and suggested measures of military training and defense. Unfortunately for Korea those measures were not carried through by the government. While T'oegye lived to the age of sixty-nine (1570), Yulgok died comparatively young, in his forty-ninth year. If T'oegye is honored frequently as "Korea's Chu Hsi," Yulgok gained enough respect among Chinese envoys to Korea to have been addressed by them as *Fu-tzu* (Master), after K'ung Fu-tzu (Confucius) himself. T'oegye became identified with the Yŏngnam school of thought, which he founded; Yulgok became leader of the Kiho School.[1]

THE FOUR-SEVEN DEBATES *(SACH'ILLON)*

The Ambiguous Legacy

The *locus classicus* for the Four and the Seven is respectively the *Mencius* (2A:6) and the chapter on the Evolution of Rites in the *Book of Rites*. The Mencius passage offers us his belief in the original goodness of human nature; he proposes here that the seeds of goodness are to be found in human nature. He refers specifically to the "mind-and-heart" *(hsin)* of commiseration, shame, modesty, and moral discernment as the Beginnings of the Four Virtues of Humanity, Righteousness, Propriety, and Wisdom.[2] The human mind-and-heart is thus presented as the source of virtue, a point that Yi Yulgok would emphasize. The Seven Emotions as enumerated in the *Book of Rites* include joy, anger, sadness, fear, love, repulsion, and desire, and are said "to belong to men without their having to learn them."[3] As this list is a little long, the first four, singled out by the *Mean (Chung-yung)* (ch. 1), are often cited to represent all seven. This was done by both T'oegye and Yulgok.

Reading the *Mencius* by itself, one might initially have difficulty understanding why the Four Beginnings are singled out for honorable mention, and why they should all be regarded as belonging to the same class, particularly since the discernment between right and wrong does not appear to have that much in common with commiseration, an obvious "feeling." But then, while the context in which they appear, as well as the example Mencius gives—of the rise of commiseration in one's heart when the person sees a child falling into a well—would describe all Four Beginnings as feelings, let us not forget that Mencius refers to them in terms of the mind-and-heart *(hsin)*. He talks about the "mind-and-heart" of commiseration, of discerning between right and wrong, and so on. He may be understood as trying to go to a level deeper than feelings in general—to *moral* intuitions, which have an emotive dimension, or to *moral feelings*. But herein lies another ambiguity: what does Mencius think of feelings in general, and what would he regard to be the relationship between "moral" feelings, and feelings in general? The *Mencius* is quite silent on this subject.[4]

Another area of ambiguity in Mencius is the distinction between human nature *(hsing)*, considered as originally good, and the human mind-and-heart, to which the Four are referred. To make up here for his silence, Chang Tsai and Chu Hsi supply the explanation that the mind-and-heart *(hsin)* is that active agent which is "in control of nature and the feelings *(hsin t'ung hsing ch'ing)*.[5] According to them and to the Ch'eng brothers, mind-and-heart is active while nature is passive. Furthermore, if innate moral feelings are presented as the ground of human perfectibility, feelings themselves are also given as having the power to lead men astray, giving rise to moral evil.

To explain the possibility of evil, another philosophical distinction is proposed, between human-nature-in-its-original state *(pen-jan chih hsing)* and human nature incorporated into its physical endowment *(ch'i-chih chih hsing)*[6]—while the former in itself is "all good," the latter, or human-nature-as-we-find-it, is capable of either good or evil. This distinction is based on Chu Hsi's philosophy of *li* and *ch'i*, the "moral" and the "physical" principles which make up all things, for physical endowment in human nature is especially conditioned by our *ch'i*, which in turn explains the rise of feelings.

Chu Hsi clearly acknowledges that the Four Beginnings also belong to the order of feelings or emotions. But he makes the distinction between the Four and the Seven by saying that "the Four Beginnings manifest *li* and the Seven Emotions manifest *ch'i*."[7] The Chinese word *fa* (manifest, or "issue" from) is ambiguous, so that the same statement might be translated in another way as "the Four Beginnings issue from *li*, the

Seven Emotions issue from *ch'i.*" While such a statement seems to put greater distance between the Four and the Seven—and indeed, between *li* and *ch'i*—Chu Hsi continues by saying that he sees a real similarity between the emotions and the virtues.[8]

The question which may arise in our minds in this case is: why make any distinction between the Four and the Seven, if they are all feelings? Are the Four superior to the Seven—or is the distinction between them, purely arbitrary and textual?

This question saw little discussion in China but very much in Korea—lasting several centuries. Speaking in general, some thinkers insisted on a stricter separation between the Four and the Seven and others saw more of a continuum.

T'oegye versus Kobong

The debates actually predated T'oegye, having attracted attention on account of Sŏ Kyŏngdŏk (Hwadam, 1489–1546). Sŏ spoke of a monism of *ch'i* as the Great Harmony *(T'ai-ho)* or the Great One *(T'ai-yi)* which further manifests itself in the two modes of *yin* and *yang*. His language was reminiscent of Chang Tsai and even of Shao Yung (1011–77). For him, *li* is nothing other than the form of *ch'i*.[9] So he diverges from Chu Hsi, who sees *li* and *ch'i* as coordinates, with a logical priority given to *li*.

T'oegye sought to follow Chu Hsi closely, repeating the statement that the Four Beginnings manifest *li* while the Seven Emotions manifest *ch'i*. He says that the distinction is between nature *(hsing)* as endowed by Heaven, which contains the Four in the form of *li*, and the physical or sensual nature, which, as the source of the Seven, brings with them occasions for good or evil. He was resisted by Ki Taesŭng (Kobong, 1527–72) who emphasizes that the Seven in a state of harmony *(ho)* are no different from the Four.[10]

At issue of course is the metaphysical question of the exact status of *li* and *ch'i* and their reciprocal relationship. If the two are inseparable, how can either be regarded as an autonomous principle or source for either Four or Seven? And, should they be regarded as autonomous, would not Chu Hsi's entire philosophical system, based as it is on their coordination, be put in danger? What are the consequences for human nature of separating the Four and the Seven? Would this not confuse the ontological character of feelings in general, by claiming that Four of them are always good, while Seven others are sometimes good, sometimes evil?

THE THEORY OF ALTERNATING MANIFESTATION (HU-FA)

In the T'oegye-Kobong debate, T'oegye eventually softened his position by attempting to recognize more of a continuum between the Four and the Seven. But he did so by introducing new notions into the interpretation of li and ch'i. He speaks of li, which is always regarded as a passive principle by Chu Hsi and others, in dynamic terms as possessing the ability to manifest itself in response to our efforts of investigating things. And he speaks of the relationship between li and ch'i as one of hu-fa.[11] Literally, these two words might be taken to mean "reciprocal manifestation" or even "calling each other into being." But he adds that in the case of the Four, li becomes manifest and ch'i follows, while, with the Seven, ch'i becomes manifest and li "rides" it.[12] Thus it appears that he means by the term (1) both li and ch'i have the active power of manifesting themselves, and (2) they do not manifest themselves at one and the same time, although they involve each other in some way or other. In this context, I shall translate hu-fa as "alternating manifestation," and this seems to be what T'oegye means especially with reference to the difference between the Four and the Seven. With this theory, the T'oegye-Kobong debates came to a halt, but it could not settle the philosophical issues, which soon reemerged. Besides, it marked an important difference between T'oegye and Chu Hsi, a difference clearly acknowledged, which cannot escape note.

Although Yulgok had met T'oegye personally, he never discussed with him the problem of the Four and the Seven.[13] As it reemerged, with added complexity on account of the hu-fa theory, Yulgok declared himself to be more on Kobong's side,[14] although he furthered the arguments with his own ideas. Thus the new debate between Yulgok and Ugye brought to a climax the Four-Seven controversy.

Yulgok versus Ugye

Yulgok's ideas on the Four and the Seven are found especially in his correspondence with Sŏng Hon (Ugye, 1536–98), a scholar who had studied

T'oegye's writings privately and who tended to agree with T'oegye with certain reservations. He was a close friend of Yulgok's, and wrote to ask for clarification especially regarding the *hu-fa* theory.[15] In doing so, he would initiate a wide-ranging discussion and debate covering the whole ground that T'oegye and Kobong had traversed, while introducing also new arguments based on the relationship between the mind of man, or human mind (*jen-hsin*), and mind of *tao*, or moral mind (*tao-hsin*).

The principal exchanges between Yulgok and Ugye took place in 1572, when Yulgok was thirty-seven years old and Ugye thirty-eight. They extend to six queries-and-responses, of which some are especially lengthy. The arguments are not systematic, since most of the issues are discussed over and over again; after all, many of them are interrelated.

The Mind of Man and Mind of Heaven: Jen-hsin versus Tao-hsin?

The terms *jen-hsin* and *tao-hsin* come from a passage taken out of a chapter of the *Book of Documents*—a chapter allegedly transmitted to posterity in the pre-Ch'in "old" script, but which has been proved spurious in origin. All complete in sixteen Chinese characters, this cryptic passage, adopted by Chu Hsi and others as a short "creedal" formula of Neo-Confucian philosophy, may be translated this way:

> The human mind is error-prone (*wei$_1$*);
> The moral mind is subtle (*wei$_2$*).
> Remain discerning and one (*yi*):
> Keep steadfastly to the Middle (*chung*).[16]

As it stands, this formula is difficult to understand and even harder to translate. Because of its proven spurious origin, it is impossible, among other things, to establish the intended meaning of its real author. We could, however, examine the Neo-Confucian interpretation, which has given it such prominence. In this case, it is interesting to note that while the word "mind" (*hsin*) occurs twice, each time in a different context or with a different adjective, the exhortation of the third line carries the unmistaken word for "one" or "oneness." Besides, the last word in the entire formula, the "middle," is usually identified by Neo-Confucians with the doctrine of harmony in the *Mean*. Such an interpretation, while arbitrary, becomes especially significant in discussions on the human mind and human nature, and the place of human feelings or emotions.

Ugye started the discussions by asking Yulgok for an explanation about the presence of the two terms for mind, human and moral.[17]

The mind *(hsin)* is one in its vacuous spirituality and consciousness. But why have we the two terms of "human mind" and "moral mind"? [Because] one is born of the partialness *(ssu)* of our physical being *(hsing-ch'i)* and the other takes its origin from the correctness of our nature and destiny[18] *(hsing-ming)*. As *li* and *ch'i* differ in manifestations *(fa)*; the human mind and the moral mind also differ in their functions *(yung):* one is error-prone, the other is subtle. And so we have two names.

Thus his question turns out in part to be rhetorical. He has also offered his own explanation. Ugye seems to say here that while the mind is ontologically one, it may be morally two, on account of the difference between *li* and *ch'i*, which becomes manifest in the distinction between our "correct" nature, and our "partial" nature, which in turn is source respectively for our "moral" or "human" mind. Then he brings in a proposed correlation between the moral and human mind, and the Four and the Seven, admitting a definite nuance in such a correlation:

Now it is all right to call the moral mind the Four Beginnings, but it is not correct to call the human mind the Seven Emotions. Besides, the Four Beginnings and the Seven Emotions refer to what nature *(hsing)* manifests; the human mind and the moral mind refer to what the mind manifests. Their names and meanings are not quite the same.[19]

Ugye then asks Yulgok's help, explaining that he himself sees nothing wrong in opposing the Four and the Seven, assigning the Four to *li* and the Seven to *ch'i* as their respective "manifestations" *(fa)*. However, he acknowledges that both Four and Seven are emotions, although the Seven might lead to evil when they are not in "equilibrium," on account of certain excesses or deficiencies of *ch'i*. He also sides with T'oegye on the proposition of the "alternating manifestation" *(hu-fa)* of *li* and *ch'i*, although he considers what T'oegye says about "*li* manifesting and *ch'i* following" and "*ch'i* manifesting and *li* 'riding' on it" cumbersome and unduly complicated.[20]

Yulgok's reply shows again a dialectical turn of mind. He says:

The mind is one. To call it "moral" and "human" is to distinguish between nature and destiny on the one hand and physical shape on the other. Emotions also belong to one [and the same] order. To call them Four or to call them Seven is to speak only of *li*, or to speak also of *ch'i*. Hence the human mind and the moral mind are different but intertwined; the Four Beginnings cannot include the Seven Emotions but the Seven Emotions include the Four Beginnings.[21]

He then explains what he means by the human mind and the moral mind being "intertwined"—or, literally, being "each other's beginning or end": that one might be initially well-intentioned, thus "beginning with the moral mind" and fall into selfishness or the "human mind," or begin with an ill intention "with the human mind" and then decide for self-control or the "moral mind." [22] However, he says, the human mind and the moral mind refer to both emotions and intentions, and are not the right parallels for the Four and the Seven. Besides:

What Chu Hsi says about manifesting *li* and manifesting *ch'i* is meant only in a general sense. How would he know that others later would separate [*li* and *ch'i*] too much? Scholars should read the text dynamically. Besides, Master T'oegye first reserves good to the Four Beginnings, and then says that the Seven Emotions are not without good. In that case, there are good emotions outside of the Four Beginnings. Where do these emotions come from? [23]

Ch'i versus Li?

According to Yulgok, *ch'i* is what manifests (*fa-che*), *li* is what causes it to manifest (*so-yi-fa-che*). When what is manifest accords with *li* with no disturbance by *ch'i*, it is the moral mind, and shows the good present in the Seven Emotions. When *ch'i* is already at work at the moment of "manifestation," we have the human mind, which shows the Seven Emotions as containing both good and evil. But the human mind may either obey the moral mind or follow the impulse of passions and become prone to error. He concludes by saying that the proposition of alternating manifestation (*hu-fa*) opposes *li* to *ch'i*, giving each too much autonomy, while the suggestion Ugye makes, that the Four and the Seven come from nature while the moral mind and the human mind issue from mind, tends also to divorce mind and nature. "Nature is the *li* of the mind, and mind is the container holding nature. How can there be any difference between what comes from nature and what comes from mind?" [24]

In his second letter on the subject, Yulgok includes a diagram [25] of his own showing how nature and mind belong together, in the same large circle, with an explanation that nature is originally good before the rise of emotions, with no admixture of evil, while mind refers to what is conditioned by physical endowment, with various gradations of "purity." He regards the feelings as coming from *hsin*, and taking on manifestations of either good or evil. As good, the Seven Emotions also serve as the Four Beginnings. As evil, the Seven Emotions are still considered as "originating" in the goodness, although they end up serving diametrically opposite ends, thus doing injury to the virtues represented by the Four Beginnings.

Ugye was not easily persuaded. He insists that if one could speak of nature as *li* (original nature), or as *ch'i* (physical nature), one should also be able to speak of emotions as *li* or *ch'i*.[26] To this, Yulgok gives the following reply, in their third exchange of letters, on the subject of the Four and the Seven:

Li is master of *ch'i*; *ch'i* is what gives movement to *li*. Without *li*, *ch'i* has no root; without *ch'i*, *li* has nothing to depend on. They are neither two things nor one thing. Not being one thing, they are one-yet-two; not being two things, they are two-yet-one. Why are they not one thing? Because *li* and *ch'i* are inseparable, yet in their mysterious unity, *li* is *li* and *ch'i* is *ch'i*, they are interrelated without one being prior and the other posterior.[27]

For Yulgok, *li* is a universal principle, unconditioned and indeterminate except when conditioned and determined by *ch'i*, an individuating principle always in motion and of various grades of purity.

Although *li* is one, it takes on myriad variations when conditioned by *ch'i*. Thus, in Heaven and Earth, it becomes the *li* of Heaven and Earth; in the myriad things, it becomes the *li* of the myriad things; in us, it becomes our *li*. What is different and unequal comes from *ch'i* . . . but since *li* functions as the controlling principle (*chu-tsai*) it is also the reason behind such inequality. . . . But the *li* of Heaven and Earth is also the *li* of the myriad things, which, in turn, is also our *li*. This is what is called the one universal *T'ai-chi*. And yet, while it is the same one *li*, human nature is different from the nature of things, and the dog's nature is different from the cow's. This is what is meant by each having its own nature. Fundamentally speaking, *li* and *ch'i* are the father and mother of Heaven and Earth, while Heaven and Earth are the father and mother of human beings and things.[28]

Obviously, he is giving a philosophy of *T'ai-chi* based on Chou Tun-yi's exposé on the *Diagram of the Great Ultimate*. He goes on to explain, in the same context, how human beings receive the best of *ch'i*, with a wide range covering various grades of "purity." The sage is endowed with the purest of *ch'i*, and serves as the norm of all others, in the same way as Heaven and Earth serve as the norm for the sage. "The transformations of Heaven and Earth do not take rise from two different roots; and the manifestations (*fa*) of our mind do not come from two different sources."[29] The desires for virtuous behavior—for humanity, righteousness, propriety, the thorough investigation of *li*, loyalty, faithfulness, filial piety, and the rest—result from the moral mind *(tao-hsin)* and are its responses to external stimuli. Although the behavior depends on physical cooperation, the movements come straight from the Four Beginnings and have *li* as principal backing, without obstruction on the part of *ch'i*. On the other hand, our physical desires for the fulfillment of basic needs such as hunger, thirst, shelter, and the rest stem from what is called the human mind. Although these also derive fundamentally from the same Heaven-endowed nature, they manifest as the specific and partial needs of our body and its senses, with *ch'i* as principal backing.[30]

The moral mind's manifestations are as difficult to discern as the kindling of a flame and the source of a spring, for which reason it is described as "subtle." The human mind's manifestations are as difficult to control as a liberated eagle and an unbridled horse, for which reason it is described as "prone to error." Although they have two names, they constitute in principle only one mind. . . . The names come strictly from their manifestations. Should *li* and *ch'i*, on the other hand, manifest themselves alternately *(hu-fa)*, as your letter claims, then *li* and *ch'i* would be two things each with its own root and [ontological] ground.[31]

FOUR VERSUS SEVEN

Yulgok reasons that by separating *li* and *ch'i*, the theory of *hu-fa* leads to the supposition that we each have two minds. He sets forth his own views on the Four-Seven relationship in the following words:

The Four Beginnings are the good side of the Seven Emotions; the Seven Emotions are what comprehend the Four Beginnings. How can we oppose one side to the whole?[32]

He ventures his own interpretation of Chu Hsi's statement concerning the Four and the Seven manifesting *li* and *ch'i*:

Chu Hsi means only that the Four Beginnings refer especially to *li*, while the Seven Emotions refer also to *ch'i*. He does not say that in the case of the Four Beginnings, *li* is first manifest, and in the case of the Seven Emotions, *ch'i* is first manifest.[33]

Given these explanations, Yulgok says he disapproves of T'oegye's theory that in the case of the Four, *li* is manifest and *ch'i* follows along, since it would establish an order of sequence which does harm to their intrinsic inseparability. But he approves of the other half of the theory, that in the

case of the Seven—and he would add, in the case of the Four as well—
ch'i is manifest and *li* is conditioned by it.[34]

The Seven Emotions already include the Four Beginnings. Do you not see this
already? With human emotions, we are joyous when there is cause for joy, sorrowful on account of bereavement; we rejoice in seeing those we love, and desire
to investigate and possess *li* when we see it, and to emulate the worthy when we
meet one. All this is the beginning for [the virtue of] humanity. When we are
angry with just cause, or dislike something for a just reason, there is the beginning of righteousness. When we fear our elders and betters, there is the beginning
of propriety. To know when one ought to have joy, anger, sorrow, and fear, at
the moment that we have these feelings, and to know when we ought not have
joy, anger, sorrow, and fear, is the beginning of wisdom. . . . If we are to assign
the Four Beginnings to the Seven Emotions more specifically, then commiseration belongs to love, the feeling of shame and disgust belongs to dislike, respect
and reverence belong to fear, the discernment of right and wrong belongs to wisdom. . . . Outside of the Seven Emotions, there are no Four Beginnings. The
Four Beginnings refer to the moral mind in particular; the Seven Emotions refer
to the human mind and the moral mind together as a whole. Is not this [expla-
nation] quite different from separating the human mind and the moral mind from
each other, and opposing them to each other?[35]

Pursuing the argument, Yulgok faults Ugye for allying original nature only
to *li*, and physical nature only to *ch'i*, since this gives the impression also
that there are two human natures in the same human being. He insists
that what Chu Hsi means by *"li* and *ch'i* are definitely two things"[36] is
that *li* and *ch'i* are distinct, but not that one comes first, and the other
comes afterwards. With great confidence, he appeals to Ugye to reread
Ch'eng Hao's letter on calming one's nature,[37] and Chu Hsi's *Chin-ssu
lu*,[38] as well as the beginning passage in the *Doctrine of the Mean*,[39] and
meditate on these texts until he reaches the same conclusions.

These arguments did not however win over Ugye, who remained attached to T'oegye's theories on *li* and *ch'i*. He reiterates the old parable,
already used by T'oegye and Kobong, about horse and rider, to illustrate
what the relationship of human mind and moral mind means to him.[40]

In this, their fourth exchange, Yulgok returns once more to the basics:
the dialectical unity of *li* and *ch'i*, each belonging distinctively to a different order, that beyond shapes and that within shapes, and yet bound
together in their inseparability and oneness of function or manifestation.
He insists that *"li* is passive and *ch'i* is active,"[41] that the theory of each
having its own power of manifesting would mean that their movements

might not always coincide, and the cosmic process would have to be understood in a thoroughly dualistic way, with *yin* and *yang* gaining for each an independent origin, rather than serving as two modes of *ch'i*.

Even good and evil, which are two different things, are not independent of each other and cannot be described as each generating itself. How much more so is this true of *li* and *ch'i*, in their inseparable togetherness? How can they be said to have the power each inherently to manifest itself in opposition to the other? Should Chu Hsi really consider that *li* and *ch'i* each have such powers . . . , then Chu Hsi is also wrong, and how can he be given so much respect as Chu Hsi?[42]

Taking up the parable of the horse and rider, Yulgok further explains the interrelationship between the original nature and the physical nature in man, and the importance of having *li* in control of *ch'i*:

The nature of the horse may be either tame or untame, according to its endowment of *ch'i*, whether that is clearer or more turbid. When one goes out riding, either the horse follows the man's wishes, or the man has to follow the horse's lead. When the horse follows the man's wishes, man is in control, as in the case of the moral mind [being in control]. When the rider follows the horse's lead, the horse is in control, as in the case of the human mind [being in control]. . . . The sage is like the ordinary man, being made also of blood and *ch'i*. He is in need of food when hungry, of drink when thirsty . . . and is not without the human mind. . . . When the horse follows the man's wishes without need of control, and truly goes on the right path, it is like the sage who follows the desires of his heart [without transgressing what is right (*Analects*, 2:4)]. Here the human mind becomes also the moral mind. . . . But if we follow the theory of alternating manifestation (*hu-fa*), it is like the horse and the man remaining separate first, and then the man sometimes riding the horse, or the man moves first and the horse follows, or the horse moves first and the man follows.[43]

These arguments encountered the same resistance from Ugye, who repeated the same hesitations as before. In their fifth exchange, Yulgok sends a poem to Ugye to explain his understanding of *li* and *ch'i*:

> The primal *ch'i*—where does it take origin?
> The invisible is found in the visible.
> The source, when found, turns out to be one,
> The variations are only along the way.
> Water takes the shape of square or round utensils,
> Air makes itself small or big in the bottles.
> Let not the seeming duality confuse you:
> In silence, reflect that feelings belong to nature.[44]

He adds that as there is only one human nature, although there are such terms as original nature and physical nature, emotions also cannot be separated into two kinds, one as manifesting *li*, the other *ch'i*.[45]

Remaining unconvinced, Ugye finds Yulgok misinterpreting T'oegye by saying that the latter's theory separates *li* and *ch'i*. He too insists:

You are convinced that there is no other way than *ch'i* manifesting itself and *li* being conditioned by it. But I insist that at the moment before [the emotions are] aroused *(wei-fa)*, there is not yet a divergence between *li* and *ch'i*, but when the intention moves, one may speak of either *li* or *ch'i* being in control. It is not as though each comes forth independently. . . . . This is what T'oegye means by *hu-fa*.[46]

THE WORKINGS OF *CH'I*

Ugye's persistence initiated the final major exchange of correspondence on the subject of Four and Seven. Yulgok's reply gives his clearest and strongest presentation of *li* and *ch'i*: that one is invisible and the other visible, that one is passive and the other active, that one is universal or "penetrating" *(t'ung)* and the other particular or limited *(chü)*: "*Li* has neither beginning nor end, nothing before it and nothing following it."[47] And besides:

[*Li*] relies upon the process "circulation" *(liu-hsing)* of *ch'i*, uneven as this may be. Its original excellence is everywhere, unlimited by the partiality of *ch'i*. And yet, it also takes the lead of *ch'i* as a particularizing [principle]. What is particular is due to *ch'i*, not *li*. When *ch'i* is complete, so too is *li*. What is complete is *ch'i* not *li*. *Li* is everywhere present, even in . . . dregs, ashes, excrement, and dirt. It is the reason for each having its own nature. Yet *li* suffers no injury in its original excellence. This is what is meant by *li* being universal. But what is the meaning of *ch'i* being particular? *Ch'i* is the visible and has its beginning and end, with something prior to it, and something posterior. *Ch'i* is originally one and clear and pure. How can we speak [in this first instance] of the *ch'i* of . . . dregs and excrement and dirt? But since it moves without cease, ascending and descending, it becomes uneven and produces myriad changes. [And such things come about] . . . as clear *ch'i*, which is different from turbid *ch'i*, and even the *ch'i* of . . . dregs and excrement and dirt.[48]

He goes on to explain what he means by *li* relying on *ch'i* manifesting itself, by speaking of the two modes of *ch'i*: yin and yang. Yin is by nature quiet and still, while yang is by nature active. When *li* relies on *ch'i* manifesting itself, it may be conditioned by the activity or tranquillity of yang or yin, without being itself agent of activity or tranquillity.[49]

This sixth communication appears to conclude Yulgok's discussions with Ugye about *li* and *ch'i*, the Four and the Seven, without Ugye having expressed complete agreement. Their correspondence continued, and Yulgok would discuss more general questions regarding the quest of sagehood. For example, he speaks of three grades of scholars: those who read the books of sages and worthies and acquire a literal meaning, those who read the books, get the literal meaning, meditate further and acquire real insights, and those others who not only understand and have insights, but also put these teachings into practice. It is like mountain climbing. When one ascends the mountain, one sees a view which is not the same as hearing about it from others, and even more, when one reaches the peak, one commands the entire view, and becomes completely liberated from the partial or erroneous reports of others.[50] After all, sages and worthies have certain intended meanings in their teachings. "Not to seek these [intended] meanings, but to become trapped in their words, is to do injury to their basic doctrine."[51]

CONCLUSIONS

There are interesting historical differences between the T'oegye-Kobong debate and the Yulgok-Ugye debate. In the first case, T'oegye was by far Kobong's senior: he was fifty-nine when the latter was thirty-three, while Yulgok and Ugye were about the same age, although Yulgok enjoyed a greater reputation. In the second case, and in spite of age difference, Kobong's letters to T'oegye were real challenges: the language was direct and the arguments clear, putting T'oegye very much on the defensive, indeed, leading him to rewrite and reformulate his own thinking. Ugye's letters, on the other hand, were repetitious if persistent, while Yulgok wrote with far greater confidence and authority.

In both cases, however, the arguments tend to be made on textual grounds, to resolve a problem which is posed in textual terms. To the extent that feelings are an important part of the human experience, experience itself is not neglected as a tribunal. Only on this account would each man dare to differ from the authority of the texts which is especially the authority of Chu Hsi. But here, if T'oegye departs from Chu Hsi, he does so in order to take into account what he considers as Kobong's arguments, while Yulgok makes a conscious appeal to his own understanding, and comes up with his own interpretation not only of the texts but of the issues themselves.

To return to the philosophical issues, I shall offer an evaluation of the positions of T'oegye and Yulgok (Ugye's and Kobong's are generally not that different from those of the two better known thinkers). I shall deal first with the *hu-fa* theory of alternating manifestation, and then proceed to the Four and the Seven, analyzing the understanding of each and measuring it against Chu Hsi's known position. I shall conclude by drawing out some of the wider implications of their philosophical differences, in order better to answer the fundamental question regarding the significance and relevance of the Four-Seven discussions.

I find that in advancing his arguments Yulgok chooses to attack with greater vehemence the theory of "alternating manifestation" *(hu-fa)* of *li* and *ch'i* as well as the interpretation derived therefrom that, in the case of the Four Beginnings, "*li* is manifest and is followed by *ch'i*." He contends that no suggestion of sequential order may be applied to the *li-ch'i* relationship. In doing so, however, he is simplifying his opponent's position, as Ugye points out. The latter insists that T'oegye sees the divergence between *li* and *ch'i* as occurring not from "the very beginning," but only with the movement of the intention, when one may speak of "either *li* or *ch'i* being in control." Here, Yulgok appears to overlook some important nuances, and does not give sufficient attention to Ugye's claim that T'oegye is not advocating any independent "issuance" or "manifestation" (*fa*) of *li* and *ch'i.*

From the viewpoint of doctrinal orthodoxy, it is safe to attack the theory of "alternating manifestation," which is a clear innovation. From the viewpoint of philosophical interpretation, however, one should make some allowance for T'oegye's innovative attempt, based as this is on his understanding of *T'ai-chi,* the fullness of *li* as a self-determining principle capable of both activity and tranquillity. It also serves clearly to set *li* before *ch'i,* the moral order before the natural order, the realm of virtuous behavior represented by the Four before the realm of natural emotional responses, in excess or defect of harmony or due proportion, as represented by the Seven.

Whether taken with or without the theory of "alternating manifestation," T'oegye's position tends to be dualistic, preferring to oppose *li* to *ch'i*, the Four to the Seven. But the dualism comes from Chu Hsi himself, who has sought to maintain a dialectical unity between the dual principles but has left behind a legacy of ambiguity giving rise to understandable debates and controversies. Even T'oegye's innovation is made with the purpose of better defending the differences between *li* and *'ch'i*, the Four and the Seven, as he purports to see them in Chu Hsi. Once the innovation is made, however, T'oegye finds himself contradicting other tendencies in Chu Hsi's thought—those moving more in the direction of dialectical unity.

Yulgok, on the other hand, clearly rejects the theory of "alternating manifestation." He has done so not just by appealing to Chu Hsi's authority, but especially by appealing to the philosophical meaning of the interrelationship of *li* and *ch'i* as these are discussed in Chu Hsi's system. This shows that T'oegye's theory is not only an innovation, a departure from orthodoxy, but a philosophically confusing innovation, since it confuses the categories of *li* and *ch'i*, giving *li* the dynamism which is reserved in Chu Hsi only to *ch'i*, until the distinction becomes almost meaningless.

And then Yulgok gives his own analysis of the Four and the Seven, agreeing with T'oegye and Ugye that they both refer to feelings, but rejecting their attempt to associate one set to *li* and the other set to *ch'i*. Like Kobong, he sees rather the Four as a subset of the Seven, the "good side" of the Seven, which are themselves also potentially good but may turn to evil by excess or defect.

And how about Yulgok's position? Yulgok has protected the fundamental inseparability of *li* and *ch'i* as well as their distinctive functions as passive and active principles. He has gone on from this to show the *nuanced* relationship between the Four and the Seven, not as simply allied to either *li* and *ch'i*, but as involving in each case the manifestation of *ch'i* as a conditioning of *li*—to use the one-half of T'oegye's statement about *li* and *ch'i*. The Four differ from the Seven as being the "good" manifestations of *ch'i*, or even better, as being the Seven manifested as good. But the Seven may also be manifested as less than good, that is, evil—by excess or defect of the emotions,[52] which causes us to "miss" the Mean of psychic harmony *(chung)*.

In offering his explanations, Yulgok has made a real contribution to Neo-Confucian philosophy, on an issue that Chinese thinkers have not settled clearly. He has removed certain ambiguities present in Chu Hsi's statements, especially regarding *li* and *ch'i*: that these are "two things," and yet must remain inseparable. On the other hand, he has done so by emphasizing the role of *ch'i* in the rise of emotions both good and bad, thus affirming the positive character of *ch'i* itself as well as of emotions themselves, both the Four and the Seven. Obviously, Yulgok realizes that he is drawing certain implications from Chu Hsi's thought that are not acceptable to those who prefer other implications, such as the dominance of *li* or a stricter duality between *li* and *ch'i*. As it relates to the Four-Seven debate, Yulgok has shown, in demolishing T'oegye's arguments, that Chu Hsi's own philosophy harbors certain ambiguities that could lead to serious inconsistencies. For this reason his final appeal is not to Chu Hsi's authority but to his own philosophical ground.

On balance, Yulgok skillfully shows the *basic incongruity* of any Four-Seven distinction based on the theory of "alternating manifestation." But he has not settled the controversy, which will remain so long as Chu Hsi's ambiguous legacy remains. And if T'oegye has erred in the direction of preferring *li* to *ch'i*, Yulgok has also erred—from the viewpoint of doctrinal orthodoxy—in deciding for a certain subtle primacy of *ch'i*. For he too has made an innovation, albeit a quiet one.

The Four-Seven debates have a certain relevance, not merely in trying to draw out the implications of Chu Hsi's thought, but also because of the emotions themselves, which are an important part of human experience in need of cultivation and control. The seemingly hair-splitting textual discussions hide a more profound exercise, that of searching for meaning and understanding in regard to the proper role of emotions in human life. Yulgok is aware of this, as is T'oegye. Both insist on the proper cultivation of the due harmony of the emotions. But their ideas on this subject lie beyond the scope of this paper.[53]

NOTES

1. For the lives of the two men, I have consulted their chronological biographies in the collected works ascribed to each. In writing this paper, I have used the Sŏnggyun'gwan University editions of *T'oegye chŏnsŏ* and *Yulgok chŏnsŏ*, prepared by the University's Institute of Eastern Studies, and published in 1978 and 1958 respectively. Other works consulted include: Abe Yoshio, ed., *Chōsen no Shushigaku*, in *Shushigaku taikei*, vol. 12a (Tokyo: Meitoku shuppansha, 1977), Chang Chiyŏn, *Chosŏn yugyo yŏnwŏn* (Seoul, 1923), Yi Pyŏngdo, *Charyo Han'guk yuhaksa ch'ogo* (mimeographed version, Seoul, 1959)—the latter two being works in Chinese by Korean scholars. I wish to thank Dr. Fang Chaoying of Columbia University for passing on to me the rare copy of Dr. Yi Pyŏngdo's work. I was fortunate to have met Dr. Yi Pyŏngdo myself at Seoul, in September 1980, during the Asian Studies Conference (II) organized by Sŏnggyun'gwan University, where I presented a preliminary paper on "Yi Yulgok on Human Nature." The present paper has been completely rewritten after the Bellagio conference of July 1981. For Korean history in general, I consulted W.E. Henthorn, *A History of Korea* (New York: Free Press, 1971). Where transliterations are concerned, I usually keep to Chinese transliterations in the case of technical philosophical terms, while romanizing Korean names according to Korean pronunciations.

2. See James Legge, tr., in *The Chinese Classics* (Oxford: Clarendon, 1892), vol. 2, pp. 202–3.

3. See James Legge, tr., *Li Ki* (Sacred Books of the East series, comp. by Max Müller, vol. 27), p. 379.

4. In this study, I am using the two English words, "feeling" and "emotion" interchangeably, while I am aware that there may be a difference of nuance in their meanings. As for the *Mencius*, there is little that is substantial in discussions of feelings outside of the discussion of the Four Beginnings.

5. *Chu Tzu yü-lei* comp. by Li Ching-te (1270), Ming ed. (1473), (reprint, Taipei: Cheng-chung shu-chü, 1970), 5:9a. Chu Hsi shows here his full agreement with Chang Tsai on this subject.

6. *Ibid.*, 4:12b–13b. Chu Hsi speaks of "original nature" also as the nature endowed by Heaven *(T'ien-ming chih hsing)*.

7. *Ibid.*, 53:17b.

8. *Ibid.*

9. Yi Pyŏngdo, *Charyo Han'guk*, part 3, chap. 2.

10. For the T'oegye-Kobong debate, see *T'oegye chŏnsŏ*, 16:1–17:6.

11. For the *hu-fa* theory, see *T'oegye chŏnsŏ*, 16:30b.

12. *Ibid.*, 16:36a–b.

13. There exist five letters from Yulgok to T'oegye in *Yulgok chŏnsŏ*, ch. 9. 2a–14b. Yulgok admits to Ugye that he had refrained from questioning T'oegye on his theory of *li* and *ch'i* because he(Yulgok) considered himself too young then.

14. There exists one letter from Yulgok to Kobong, in *Yulgok chŏnsŏ*, 9:14b–17a. In it, Yulgok challenges Kobong on his interpretation of the "highest good," disagreeing with his limiting the highest good to the realm of action, and not extending it also to that of knowledge. In discussions with Ugye, however, Yulgok gives Kobong credit for his clear arguments and fluent expressions in the T'oegye-Kobong debate, criticizing T'oegye for being repetitious and lacking in clarity. He also acknowledges that he is mainly following Kobong's arguments. See also 10:8b.

15. Ugye's letters of query are included in *Yulgok chŏnsŏ*, usually following Yulgok's responses.

16. English translation is my own. See for reference, James Legge, tr., *The Chinese Classics*, vol. 3, p. 61.

17. *Yulgok chŏnsŏ*, 9:37a.

18. Ugye is referring to Chu Hsi's words. See Chu's preface to the Doctrine of the Mean, in *Ssu-shu chi-chu*, SPPY ed. Preface to *Chung-yung*, p. 1.

19. *Yulgok chŏnsŏ*, 9:37a–b.

20. *Ibid.*

21. *Ibid.*, 9:34b.

22. *Ibid.*, 9:34b–35a.

23. *Ibid.*, 9:35b.

24. *Ibid.*, 9:36b.

25. *Ibid.*, 9:38b.

26. *Ibid.*, 10:10a–b.

27. *Ibid.*, 10:2a–b.

28. *Ibid.*, 10:2–3.

29. *Ibid.*, 10:3b–4a.

30. *Ibid.*

31. *Ibid.*, 4a–b.

32. *Ibid.*, 10:5a.

33. *Ibid.*

34. *Ibid.*, 10:5b.

35. *Ibid.*, 10:7a–b.

36. See Chu Hsi's letter to Liu Shu-wen, in *Hui-an hsien-sheng Chu Wen-kung wen-chi*, Prefaced 1532 (Japanese ed., 1711; reprint, Taipei: Chūbun shuppansha, 1972). This belongs to the series entitled *Chin-shih Han-chi ts'ung-k'an, Kinsei kanseki sōkan* compiled by Okada Takehiko. See 46:26a. While Chu begins this letter by claiming that *li* and *ch'i* are "two things," he also insists on their inseparability.

37. See *Erh-Ch'eng ch'üan-shu*, SPPY ed., *Ming-tao wen-chi* 3:1a–b. English translation in Wing-tsit Chan, *A Source Book in Chinese Philosophy* (Princeton: Princeton University Press, 1963).

38. English translation by Wing-tsit Chan, *Reflections on Things at Hand* (New York: Columbia University Press, 1967).

39. Doctrine of the Mean, ch. 1. "What Heaven endows is called nature."

40. *Yulgok chŏnsŏ*, 10:18a–b.

41. *Ibid.*, 10:12a.
42. *Ibid.*, 10:12b.
43. *Ibid.*, 10:15b–16a.
44. *Ibid.*, 10:22a.
45. *Ibid.*, 10:22b.
46. *Ibid.*, 10:31a–b.
47. *Ibid.*, 10:25b–26a.
48. *Ibid.*, 10:26a–b. In his discussions of *li* and *ch'i*, Yulgok shows his indebtedness to Hua-yen philosophy, as does Chu Hsi himself.
49. *Ibid.*, 10:26b–27a.
50. *Ibid.*, 10:34–35.
51. *Ibid.*, 10:35a.
52. The Neo-Confucian idea that moral evil appears on account of "excess or defect" of the emotions is reminiscent of Aristotle's ideas. In both cases, virtue lies in the "Mean," between excess and defect. However, the theory that *ch'i* is active and *li* passive is the exact opposite of Aristotle's interpretation of matter and form.
53. For Yulgok's ideas on spiritual cultivation and political ethics, see his *Sŏnghak chibyo* in *Yulgok chŏnsŏ*, ch. 19–26. It also contains a short summary of his views on the Four and the Seven. *Yulgok chŏnsŏ*, 20:55–60.

Sakai Tadao

Yi Yulgok
and the Community
Compact

I

THE COMMUNITY COMPACT *(hyangyak)* in Korea, which reflected
the influence of the community compact in China, was introduced to the
Korean peninsula in the early sixteenth century. In 1517, Kim Imbŏm
presented a memorial to the king Chungjong (r. 1506–44), petitioning
him to adopt the community compact system as originally proposed in
The Community Compact of the Lü Family (Lü-shih hsiang-yüeh) by Lu
Ta-fang and his brothers in eleventh-century Sung China. For this Kim
received royal sanction. In the next year, Kim An'guk (1478–1543), Third
Minister without Portfolio and Governor of Kyŏngsang Province, is said
to have published an edition of the *Lü Family Community Compact* in
the Korean vernacular.[1] However, the "Articles of the Community Compact" *(Hyangnip yakcho)* which was compiled by Yi T'oegye (1501–70)
for his home region in 1556, is said to be the first community compact
which was actually put into practice.[2]

The "Articles of the Community Compact" is a simple version, attached to T'oegye's "Preamble to the Articles of the Community Compact" *(Hyangnip yakcho sŏ).*[3] According to the explanation given in the
"Preamble," Master Nongam, who was the leader of his local community, had once hoped to establish such a compact in order to rectify wrong
customs, but did not achieve his purpose. However, when Yi T'oegye fell
ill and went home to recover from his illness, the people in his home

Editor's note: This paper is a revision of Sakai Tadao, "Ri Rikkoku to kyōyaku," in *Higashi
Ajia shisō to bunka*, Tokyo, September 1974.

province asked him and a few others to fulfill Master Nongam's wish, so they conferred together and wrote up the "Articles of the Community Compact." Nongam is none other than Yi Hyŏnbo (1467–1555).[4] The compact enumerates "violations of rites and mores that do harm to local customs," with a view to punishing them on the basis of the following three categories.[5]

I. Disobeying parents.
    Quarreling with brothers.
    Disrupting the peace and order of the family.
    Interfering with official business and meddling in village affairs.
    Arrogating the power to usurp public functions and pursue private gain.
    Insulting village elders.
    Seducing, threatening, defiling, or corrupting virtuous widows.

The foregoing to be punished in the highest degree.

II. Impairing good relations among relatives.
    Displacing legal wives.
    Causing disharmony among neighbors.
    Beating or reviling fellow workers.
    Shamelessly corrupting the mores of gentlemen.
    Relying upon coercion to intimidate the weak, that one might bilk and blackmail them.
    Ganging up with vagabonds to commit perverse and violent acts.
    Criticizing those who govern in public or private assemblies.
    Fabricating evidence and fictitious stories to slander others and incriminate them.
    Idly sitting back and refusing assistance to those in misfortune, even when able to do so.
    Exploiting the departure and replacement of officials to invent official pretexts for committing misdeeds.
    For no good reason failing to attend marriages, funerals, and sacrifices.
    In disregard of basic principles, failing to respect village ordinances.
    Refusing to submit to the village consensus and, instead, harboring resistance and resentment.
    Entering into and participating in village activities with ulterior motives of selfish gain.
    Failing to attend, for no good reason, farewell feasts for departing officials.

The foregoing to be punished in the second degree.

III. Arriving late for public meetings.
     Sitting in a disorderly manner and violating decorum.
     Being noisy and argumentative at meetings.

Leaving one's seat at will.
Leaving early for no good reason.

The foregoing to be punished in the lowest degree.

Enumerated also, but without specified punishment, are:

I. Villainous village functionaries and their underlings abusing the people.
Withholding and hoarding produce subject to levy for the purpose of manipulating prices.
Commoners being disrespectful of the gentry.

As indicated in Yi T'oegye's "Preamble," after drafting of the compact by a select number of people, the general contents were to be set before the people of the village, who were asked for their opinion. Only then was a definitive version finally promulgated.

After the end of the Koryŏ dynasty rapid social changes had taken place in the Korean peninsula. This was especially true in T'oegye's home region, one of the most advanced in the peninsula. Therefore he and others must have wanted to buttress social order in the region, with leadership centering on the *yangban* class. Such words as village ordinance (hyangnyŏng) and village consensus *(hyangnon)* are used in the compact, similar to the usage in the compacts found in China. In China, however, the village ordinances *(hsiang-li, hsiang-ling)* evolved and changed into the community compact. The *Lü Family Compact* had been devised on the basis of this tradition of village ordinances. About the historical uses of the village ordinances in China, we can find many historical materials[6] from the T'ang dynasty on. Abundant historical documentation for the community compact as it was carried out in rural Yüan-Ming society is found in the *Popular Encyclopedia for Daily Use*[7] (*Jih-yung lei-shu*). One of these encyclopedias, *Wan-yung cheng-tsung*, in the Hōsa Library (see note 7), used the word *hsiang-yüeh* as a synonym for *hsiang-li*. The term *hyangnyŏng* in T'oegye's "Preamble" to *Hyangnip yakcho* has the same sociohistorical meaning as *hsiang-li* in China, and is similar to the *hyanggyu* (local statutes of local *yangban*) which are actually a kind of Korean-type community compact.

In Korea during the Yi dynasty, village statutes were established through associations for communal discipline *(Yuhyangso)* composed of local *yangban* such as scholars with official ranks *(p'umgwan)* and local families *(sajok)*, so that the local statutes for every community would have some connection with a covenant association *(kye)* [8] of *yangban* in the local community. Therefore it is possible that social practices similar to those in China had already existed there, to which the word village ordinance became applicable. This would mean that a new meaning of community compact could possibly be uncovered through the historical study of communities in the Korean peninsula.

Even during the time of Yi Hyŏnbo the matter of the compact was viewed as a problem still needing to be solved. It is clear that T'oegye, who succeeded Yi Hyŏnbo, wanted to put the compact into practice only after conferring with villagers *(hyangin)* and with the support of a village consensus. [9] This strikes us as an interesting point. Such being the circumstance, the specific items in the compact came to be drafted in keeping with the actual conditions of his home province. Around 1556, when the compact was drafted, T'oegye must have known about *Master Chu's Revision of the Lü Family Community Compact (Chu Tzu tseng-sun Lüshih hsiang-yüeh)* because the *Great Compendium of Master Chu's Collected Works (Chu Tzu ta-ch'üan wen-chi)*, which contained this compact, was published by Chungjong's order in 1542, when T'oegye first came to know about it and himself bought the book. [10]

Prior to this, *The Community Compact of the Lü Family* contained in the *Great Compendium of Human Nature and Principle (Hsing-li ta-ch'üan)*, [11] as distinct from *Master Chu's Revision* contained in the *Great Compendium of Master Chu's Collected Works*, was brought from China, and the *Great Compendium of Master Chu's Collected Works* must have been presented by the Ming dynasty to the Yi dynasty around 1403. [12] Based upon these books, Kim An'guk wrote a colloquial version of Chu's "Revised Version," entitled *Vernacular Version of Proper Customs (Chŏngsok ŏnhae)* in 1518, and published it. It is quite possible that T'oegye saw this colloquial version.

As the representative scholar of the Chu Hsi school, T'oegye could not have been unaware of Chu's "Revised Version," and yet his "Articles of the Community Compact" are noteworthy for the fact that the distinctive features of *The Community Compact of the Lü Family*, the four principles of (1) mutual encouragement of virtuous deeds and duties *(tŏgŏp sanggwŏn)*; (2) mutual regulation of errors and omissions *(kwasil sanggyu)*; (3) reciprocity in rites and customs *(yesok sanggyo)*; and (4) mutual aid in difficulties and misfortunes *(hwannan sanghyul)*, are not to be found therein. This may be due to T'oegye's own originality as a *yangban* scholar, since his learning is not merely limited to collecting and tidying up Chu Hsi's theories, and since he was original enough as a scholar of Chu's philosophy to make his own epoch-making mark on history.

In any case, there is no positive proof to show that this compact was in practice in T'oegye's lifetime. However, among the successors of T'oegye there were some who preached the four principles of *The Community Compact of the Lü Family*. For instance, although much later the village compact *(tongyak)* of Pu Indong in the period of Yŏngjo (r. 1724–76) was based upon *The Community Compact of the Lü Family*, the content of his "mutual regulation of errors and omissions" *(kwasil sanggyu)* was different from *The Community Compact of the Lü Family*, and instead adopted T'oegye's compact just as it was.[13]

II

After Yi T'oegye, Yi Yulgok was the next famous scholar to devise a community compact in Korea during the Yi dynasty. Yulgok wrote *The Community Compact of Sŏwŏn (Sŏwŏn hyangyak)*[14] when he was magistrate in Ch'ŏngju in 1571. According to the explanation given in the "Preamble" *(ibŭi)* at the beginning of this work,

In the Ch'ŏngju area, there was already a community compact drafted by the two gentlemen, Yi Chŭngyŏng and Yi In. However, because Yi In was replaced as the official in charge of this region and was reassigned to the central government, the people in the region were discouraged and the compact became mere words on paper. Yulgok, succeeding to the wish of the two gentlemen and adopting the preceding compact [as written by them], consulted *The Community Compact of the Lü Family* and composed the "Articles of the Community Compact" *(Hyangyak choyak)*, omitting some and adding some clauses.

According to this explanation, before Yulgok wrote his compact, there was already a community compact written by these two predecessors, and Yulgok wrote a new one incorporating elements from the preceding compact, referring to the *Lü Family Compact*, and making some insertions and excisions of his own. Therefore, it may be safe to assume that the "preceding compact" did not refer to the *Lü Family Compact*. It is the same as the "Articles" of T'oegye in this regard. Also it says, "In consulting the village elders about the way to choose the right path, the vil-

lagers all considered it best to have a clearly stated community compact."
Just as in the case of T'oegye, Yulgok must have had discussions with the
people in the region beforehand and then wrote up the compact. It can
be presumed also that the people in the region already had very much in
mind the need for "a clearly stated compact" *(sinmyŏng hyangyak)*.

According to a provision in *The Community Compact of Sŏwŏn*, the
compact was administered by four covenant directors *(togyejang)*, twenty-
five covenant unit chiefs *(kyejang)*, one covenant unit chief for each of
the twenty-five units *(chang)* in Ch'ŏngju, twenty-five officers for the
guidance of young people *(tongmong hunhoe)*, and twenty-five administrative officers *(saekchang)* (possibly one guidance officer and one administrative officer for each of twenty-five units in Ch'ŏngju), and also one
administrative aide *(pyŏlgŏm;* for every village *(i)*. Over the unit *(chang
myŏn)*,[15] which was the lower organization of the local administrative
system, and the village, administrative officers and aides were set up and,
superimposed on these basic units, was the covenant association organized by the community compact.

This covenant association was a community organization which was
artificially created in order to carry out the community compact above
the natural, lower-level administrative and cooperative organizations at
the community level. The administrative officers, as the lower officers of
the convenant, were supposed to choose the leaders who were "hard working
and righteous, irrespective of whether they belonged to the upper or lower
classes." Among the articles of the compact is the statement, "When an
entire family, stricken by disease or misfortune, is forced to abandon
farming, then the rest of the hamlet is to pool its resources and till the
land for those stricken." Moreover, since the natural village cooperatives
were composed mainly of peasants, the community compact was organized and conducted in accordance with the existing social divisions of
the covenant associations, such as the *yangban*, commoners *(sangmin)*,
and low-born *(ch'ŏnmin)*. According to the rules of the "Protocol for
Readings of the Pact at Meetings of the Association" *(Hyanghoe togyakpŏp)* of the *Sŏwŏn Compact*, at the time of meetings people from all walks
of life gather together, but "Commoners and those beneath them shall
occupy the south row. Commoners with association posts shall occupy
the front row in their quarter. Illegitimate offspring of the *yangban* should
be all in one row. Commoners with no occupation, and private slaves,
shall form the last row." Thus in meetings of the compact, the seating

arrangement was strict, made in accordance with one's position in life.

According to *The Community Compact of Sŏwŏn*, ledgers of good and bad deeds *(sŏnakchŏk)* were set up and disciplinary actions were meted out. Under the heading of "good deeds" about half of the actions corresponded to those of *Master Chu's Revision of the Lü Family Community Compact*, but under the heading of "evil deeds" they were, with few exceptions, different from those stipulated in Chu Hsi's version and T'oegye's Community Compact. For example, good deeds were listed as:

Effectively showing filiality toward parents, effectively showing affection for siblings, effectively showing friendliness to relatives and acquaintances, effectively instructing the sons and youngsters of the family that they may be guided to righteousness; effectively maintaining one's honesty and integrity, extending charity, guiding others to become good, disentangling people from quarrel and combat, helping those in difficulty and misfortune.

Evil deeds:

Indulging in drinking and gambling, delighting in dispute and taking pleasure in combat, fabricating rumors and falsely implicating others.

These were similar to what is found in Chu Hsi's version, and all the rest were dissimilar. As compared with T'oegye's "Articles," the "evil deeds" were expressed in a more formalized manner, reflecting changes in society.

From these observations, it may be seen that Yulgok's *Community Compact of Sŏwŏn* was oriented toward actual practice much more than T'oegye's "Articles." Also the relationship between the Compact and the administrative organization and natural communities was much more concretely spelled out. It is noteworthy that the covenant associations embraced the constituents of local society, irrespective of class distinctions such as *yangban*, commoners, and low-born and that such lower posts as administrative officers and administrative aides, etc. of the Compact were chosen irrespective of their social position. On the other hand those who gathered at a community compact meeting were seated strictly in accordance with such class distinctions as *yangban*, commoners, and low born. *The Community Compact of Sŏwŏn* makes more reference to *Master Chu's Revision of the Lü Family Community Compact* and is more influenced by it than was T'oegye's "Articles," and this is another point which makes Yulgok's Compact different from T'oegye's "Articles."

III

Yulgok went back to Sŏktam, in Haeju, in 1576, and there wrote up a community compact in the next year, 1577.[16] This version is known as *The Community Compact of Haeju (Haeju hyangyak)*. To summarize the differences between the Sŏwŏn and Haeju compacts, in the Haeju version, such posts as director of the compact association *(toyakchŏng)*, deputy director of the compact association *(tobuyakchŏng)*, officers of the compact association *(yakchŏng)*, etc., were created instead of director of the covenant association and unit chief as in the Sŏwŏn version, and although there was no mention of it in the *Sŏwŏn Compact*, there is a new provision in the Haeju version to the effect that meetings of the compact were to be held at the local academy *(sŏwŏn)*, and that they were to be carried out in conjunction with the communal granary systems *(sach'angpŏp)*. It is not clearly shown in the *Haeju Compact* what subordinate posts were created under the director and officers, nor is the relationship between the *yangban*, commoners, and the low-born within the compact. However, according to the provisions, etc., in the Covenant Association of the Communal Granary *(sach'anggye)*, which was integrated with the compact, there were similar subordinate positions and similar relationships between the *yangban* and commoners as in the *Sŏwŏn Compact*.

After the Organizational Guide *(ibyak pyŏmnye)* of the *Haeju Compact*, *Master Chu's Revision of the Lü Family Community Compact* is attached, and in the beginning the four basic principles of the *Lü Family Compact* are enumerated. It is thus clear that the *Haeju Compact* referred to the *Lü Family Compact*, but did not specifically attribute these four principles to it. The *Haeju Compact* carried the text of *Master Chu's Revision of the Lü Family Community Compact* and states that it was generally written on the outline of the *Lü Family Compact* without copying it in detail. And this was exactly right because under the heading of "mutual encouragement of virtuous deeds and duties," virtuous deeds *(tŏk)* and duties *(ŏp)* are differentiated, and under each heading sub-items are specifically enumerated, including such items as "regulation of errors and omissions," "reciprocity in rites and customs," and "mutual aid in difficulties and misfortunes," while each of the sub-items under the four principles adopt almost the same sub-items as in *Master Chu's Revision of the Lü Family Community Compact*, the only difference being the explanation given to the arrangement of the sub-items. In differentiating virtuous deeds from duties and enumerating each sub-item under them, some sub-items under virtuous deeds in *Master Chu's Revision of the Lü Family Community Compact* are transferred to the sub-heading of duties. In the beginning of the chapter explaining the content, the first sub-item mentioned is "loyalty to the state" *(ch'ung yŏ kukka)*, which is not found in Chu Hsi's version. This may reveal a special characteristic of the Korean situation.

Such posts as compact director, deputy director, officer, secretary *(chigwŏl)*, in the *Haeju Compact* have been transferred from Chu Hsi's version just as they were, with the exception of treasurer *(sahwa)*. According to the *Organizational Guide*, a man of knowledge and virtue would be made compact director, and two men of knowledge and virtue made deputy directors:

Members of the Association shall assume the duties of clerk-recorder and treasurer by turns. Only those who have slaves able to assist them may serve as secretary. Whosoever serves as treasurer is to be a scholar enrolled in the Academy.

Except in unforeseen circumstances the director and deputy directors would not be replaced. The secretary was to be rotated monthly, but the treasurer was to be alternated every year. Scholars in the academy who became treasurer would not necessarily come from the *yangban;* those from the common people could also assume the post. The secretary was to be from the class of big landholders who owned servants and slaves. The titles of officers of the *Haeju Compact* were modeled after those of *Master Chu's Revision of the Lü Family Community Compact* and even though they were established in view of the actual conditions existing then in the Korean peninsula, and were based upon the *yangban,* the upper class of society, some common people were assigned to subordinate posts. However, in looking through the *Organizational Guide,* the Text of the Compact *(hyangyangmun),* and the "Protocol for Readings of the Pact at Meetings of the Association" *(hoejip togyakpŏp)* in *The Community Compact of Haeju,* there is no close relationship between the compact and the administrative organization and natural community in Korea such as can be found in the *Sŏwŏn Compact* previously described. It is also difficult to find any such relationship in the organization of the local academies, which were the base for carrying out the *Haeju Compact.* Something of this can be seen, however, in the provisions of the communal granary with which the execution of the *Haeju Compact* was closely integrated.

In late Ming China of the sixteenth and seventeenth centuries, the community compact and community granary were actually carried out in such an integrated manner in the context of a local society led by local elites such as the "gentry" (*hsiang-shen*) and licentiates (*shih-jen*). This then is something that Yulgok must have introduced to Korea. After Yulgok, Kim Seryŏm (1593–1646)[17] put into practice the above-mentioned late Ming type of community compact introduced from China, including the Six Edicts (*liu-yü/yukyu*) instead of the Lü Family's four principles.

As to the relationship between the compact and the local academy, there is some such definite relationship between the compact and the community school (*hsiang-chiao/hyanggyo*) to be found in *Master Chu's Revision of the Lü Family Community Compact*. However in the *Haeju Compact*, the relationship existing between the local academy and community compact could not have been directly influenced by the relationship between the community school[18] and community compact in China as described in Chu Hsi's version.

The community school of the Southern Sung dynasty was changed into the local school (*she-hsüeh*) of the Ming dynasty. In the Haeju case the academy founded by Yulgok was one of those used by the *yangban* as centers for scholars living in their home communities. The community school mentioned in *Master Chu's Revision of the Lü Family Community Compact* differs from the local academy of Yulgok's time. It is more like the local school of late Ming China, which was combined with the community compact and communal granary, than like the community public school of Yi dynasty Korea, which ceased to function effectively in the sixteenth century with the rise of the local academy. The local academy as referred to in the *Haeju Compact*, like the other academies of the time, constituted a base for the activities of the *yangban* and scholars in their home communities. Therefore, the official posts in the academies were held by the *yangban* and discussions (*kangnon*) and readings (*toksŏ*) held there were conducted under *yangban* guidance.

A concrete example of the type of academy Yulgok referred to can be seen in the *School Regulations of the Ŭnbyŏng Academy*, which was drafted in the year 1578.[19] In these regulations it was prescribed that the most senior scholar, chosen from among those who could enter the academy (*chŏngsa*), should hold the post of headmaster (*tangjang*). Among his fellow scholars, the one who was the most learned was made the discussion leader *(changŭi)*, and two were selected to be clerks *(yusa)*. Two more were chosen from among the scholars, each taking turns, to serve as secretary. Except for some extraordinary occurrence, the headmaster, discussion leader, and clerks were not replaced, but the secretaries changed from month to month. These posts would correspond to those in the community compact and communal granary, but those of the residential academy and the local academy tended to be occupied more by the *yangban*. However, those who could enter *(ipchae)* Yulgok's academy included not only the *yangban*, but also the common people. According to the *School Regulations of the Ŭnbyŏng Academy*, those who could enter the school were supposed to have been persons who wished to learn, irrespective of such class distinctions as that between *yangban* and commoners. At this academy the local compact was discussed, the "ledger of good and evil deeds" of the participants in the compact *(ibyakcha)* was dealt with as prescribed in the Organizational Guide, and the discussion of the compact *(kangyak)*, as found in the Method of Reading the Pact in General Assembly, was carried out. Thus there was discussion of the text of the compact, interpretation of the compact, and recording and punishment of the actions, good and bad, of participants in accordance with the provisions of the compact. These were all carried out at the academy. Since the beginning of the sixteenth century in Korea the *yangban* in each community established academies for the education of the coming generations in that region. Educational activities were carried out by the academy centering around the aristocracy and scholars in the community, and social education by means of the community compact, as well as social welfare and relief activities by means of the communal granary, developed. The fact that the community compact was carried out with Yulgok's academy as its center and base is a concrete example of this development.

At these academies, established by aristocrats and scholars, it was mostly the children of aristocrats who were enrolled, but children of the common people could enter also, as stated above. Since the compact was an undertaking of the local community, even though of a type guided by the aristocracy, it goes without saying that the aristocracy and common people of the community were included in it. In the text of the *Lü Family Compact* revised by Chu Hsi, as it is included in the *Haeju Compact*, there is an article entitled "Reciprocity in Rites and Customs" which says, "In general, seating arrangements shall be determined by age. Illegitimate

offspring *(sŏŏl)* and those not of the *yangban (pisajok)* shall be seated separately." Also under the heading of "Mutual Aid in Difficulties and Misfortunes," it is written "When an entire family, bedridden with illness, is
unable to farm, then the members of the assocation should help with their
slaves and oxen to till the land of those stricken." This shows plainly that
common people who were engaged in agriculture, and not the *yangban,*
constituted the majority of the members.

The term "nonaristocracy" *(fei-shih-tsu)* is also found in the original
text of *Master Chu's Revision of the Lü Family Community Compact.*
However, the description found in the text of the *Haeju Compact* must
have been based upon the actual conditions in Korea, as is obvious from
the use of such expressions as "illegitimate offspring and those not of the
yangban," meaning that the children born of concubines of the aristocrats were also included. The phrase "those unable to farm because of
illness" is also found in the above *Sŏwŏn Compact,* but is not found in
the original text of *Master Chu's Revision of the Lü Family Community
Compact.* Therefore, this must have been inserted in accordance with actual conditions and customs existing in Korea. In short, the *Haeju Compact,* with its execution centering around the local academy, shows no
close relationship with the administrative units and natural groupings in
Korea such as is seen in the *Sŏwŏn* Compact, except for the two cases,
stipulated in the foregoing passages of the Organizational Guide, the text
of the *Revised Compact of the Lü Family,* and the Method of Reading
the Compact in the General Assembly. This is seen in the provisions for
the integration of the communal granary operation with the conduct of
the compact, as found in the *Haeju Compact.* The *Haeju Compact,* which
was carried out more in actual practice than were the concrete contents
of the *Sŏwŏn Compact,* had these three elements of the academy, the
compact, and the communal granary, about which it also contained more
details.

IV

It is clear that the communal granary, a constituent of the *Haeju Compact,* was fully integrated in the workings of the compact by virtue of the
commitments of the communal granary system based on the four basic
principles of the compact, namely: "mutual encouragement of virtuous

deeds and duties," "regulation of errors and omissions," "reciprocity in rites and customs," and "mutual aid in difficulties and misfortunes." It is only natural that the relationship of the communal granary with administrative units and natural groupings is concretely shown in the cooperative and mutual aid organization of the community. Yulgok indicates this in the articles of the commitments of the Communal Granary Association which is divided into three parts; Organizational Guide, Commitments, and Communal Granary System. The Covenant Association of the Communal Granary shows that a covenant association was established, as an artificial joint group, in order to carry out the communal granary, based upon the local administrative units and the natural groupings. In the concrete content of the commitment, the word "covenant association" is often mentioned. According to the Preamble and Introduction of the communal granary covenant, there were such posts as one chairman (yakchang), one vice-chairman (puyakchang), two clerks (yusa), one administrative assistant (changmu), two warehouse stewards (kojik), four orderlies (saryŏng), and a number of five-family foremen (ojang). The chairman was the one who was recommended by all the members of the association (yakchung) and his assistant was the vice-chairman. Except for some extraordinary contingency, the director and the assistant director were not replaced. Under these two there were to be two supervisors who were replaced every year, each taking turns, and they were to be of a caliber that could bear the responsibility of the post. The posts of administrative assistant, warehouse steward, and orderly were to be held by "commoners or the low-born who are capable of discharging the requisite responsibilities." Of them, the administrative assistant and orderlies were those who administered the orders of the two supervisors and were replaced each year. The warehouse steward was "the one in charge of public grain stores" (ch'angyŏk) and was replaced every three years. The five-family foreman was the chief of the organization consisting of five families, and was to be replaced every year. The posts subordinate to the administrator under the chairman, which were responsible for the practical business of the communal granary, were to be chosen from among the commoner and low-born classes. Since it says in the Organizational Guide that "each year, in the spring and in the autumn, association membership, both high and low, shall meet to discuss awards and penalties levied by the association," it is clear that the members of the communal granary covenant association consisted of both upper and lower classes. The "high" *(sangin)* must have meant the aristocrats, and "low" *(hain)* those who are lower than common people. These terms must have been in daily use among the people. In the covenant, in referring to membership the word *yangban* is used often, distinguishing them from the "low," and in describing regulations governing penalties *(pŏlch'ŭk)* the *yangban* are again distinguished from the lower classes in the application of penalties. It states that "The scholar-officials shall decide upon teaching and instruction. They shall teach and instruct local commoners and slaves about phrases which they do not understand and codes of which they are ignorant." This is in keeping with the fact that according to the provisions of the compact the officers met at the academy, and centering around the director, officers, and the secretary, the business of the compact was carried out. The members of the communal granary association contributed "one bushel of unthreshed rice" *(chomi iltu)* in the case of aristocrats, and "five pecks" *(osŭng)* in the case of members of the lower class. Under the supervision of the supervisor and administrative assistant, the warehouse steward was responsible for storing the rice in the communal granary which was to be used for aid in emergency cases.

In the covenant association of the communal granary, as in the text of the community compact, the four basic principles of the *Revised Compact of the Lü Family* are adopted. While the text of the *Haeju Compact* adopted the contents of *Master Chu's Revision of the Lü Family Community Compact* in many details, the covenant association of the communal granary in explaining the basic principles other than "mutual encouragement of virtuous deeds and duties" gives very concrete descriptions which are in keeping with the actual conditions of the administrative organization and natural groupings of society. Especially under the heading of "regulation of errors and omissions," the regulations concerning penalties are divided into those for the gentry and the lower-class members of the community, stipulating things in detail. Even in respect to "mutual encouragement of virtuous deeds and duties," the items listed as "virtuous deeds," although similar to *Master Chu's Revision of the Lü Family Community Compact,* have explanatory comments giving many concrete details, appropriate to the circumstances of commoners and the low-born, as well as of the lowest class of people, according to the actual conditions of Korean society.

The *Haeju Compact* of Yulgok was put into practice by coordinating the three elements of the compact, academy, and communal granary. The compact was carried out by such officers as director, deputy director, officer, secretary, and treasurer. The academy had such officers as headmaster, discussion leader, clerk, and secretary. The granary was managed by a chairman, vice-chairman, supervisor, administrative assistant, warehouse steward, and orderly of the communal granary, and for the treasurer of the compact, these posts were held by officials *(kwanin)* and *yangban* in the community. The system was guided by the *yangban* and administered to maintain order and stability in the indigenous society *(hyangt'o)*, under the leadership of the Korean elite.

Yi T'oegye also established an academy (later the Tosan Sŏwŏn) and a community compact. He took a stronger posture than Yulgok in trying strictly to maintain the duties of the class system. It is true that Yi T'oegye, in adapting to the actual conditions of a changing society, did not provide for a communal granary and did not include provision for not discriminating between the *yangban* and the common people. Both he and Yi Yulgok had the same strong consciousness of class distinction. As *yangban* and scholars, both maintained a belief in a social order governed by the *yangban* class. They were ready to defend this belief even in an age when society was changing as a consequence of improved agricultural productivity based on developments in agricultural technology, and of improvement in the position of farmers.

As seen in his compact, Yulgok was a little more progressive, positive, and pragmatic in trying to cope with the changing society than was Yi T'oegye, and that is why he drafted the concrete provisions for the communal granary. In Yulgok's time the social change was more intense, as seen in the frequent incidence of literati purges *(sahwa)* and in the struggles between traditionalists and progressives among the elite. Perhaps the times were already ripe for Korea to be influenced by the changes which had occurred in Chinese society and culture after the beginning of the sixteenth century.

V

In the *Sŏwŏn Compact* it speaks of "reading and discussing the meaning of the articles of the pact," and in the "Protocol for Readings of the Pact" of the *Haeju Compact* it says "read the pact at the academy," so that after reading the text aloud the deputy director may "interpret and explain its meaning." In the Organizational Guide of the communal granary it is written, "the members of the upper class should instruct the commoners and lower-class people in the neighborhood who do not read or understand the law, and interpret the compact for them so that they would understand the law, getting them together in the morning for the purpose." In Yulgok's *Life Chronology* (*yŏnbo*) it says that "when the members of the clan meet on the New Year's Day, the laws of the compact are to be taught to their maids, servants, and slaves in the Korean vernacular."[20] It is said that in the early seventeenth century, after the officially edited book of compacts appeared, such methods of interpretation as phonetic inscription (*kugyŏl*), transliterations into the Korean alphabet (*ŏnt'o*), and local dialect (*pangŏn*) were to be called "Korean translation" (*ŏnhae*) in general.[21] The interpretation of Yulgok's compact would have been given in colloquial language, especially when it was given to "commoners and the low-born." It is in this connection that such words as "to read" (*kang*), "to interpret and explain" (*ch'usŏl*), and "to elucidate" (*haesŏk*) are used in the text of Yulgok's compact.

It was in the middle of the fifteenth century that the Korean alphabet (*Hunmin chŏngŭm*) had been created by Sejong (r. 1418–50) and his scholars. Thereafter, it was disseminated among the common and lower-class people. In the 1520s, various kinds of educational books and glossaries using the Korean alphabet were published. Yi T'oegye wrote *Three Classics Interpreted* (*Samgyŏng sŏgŭi*), contained in the fifth book of the *Complete Works of Yi T'oegye* (*T'oegye chŏnsŏ*). Yu Hŭich'un (1513–77) wrote *The Book of Odes Interpreted* (*Sisŏ sŏgŭi*) in the vernacular. These books are interpretations of the Confucian classics in colloquial language.

When Kim An'guk published the colloquial version of the *Lü Family Compact* in 1518, it became very popular. As stated before, Yulgok's compact added to and deleted somewhat from *Master Chu's Revision of the Lu Family Community Compact* so as to be in keeping with the actual conditions of the society at the time. When it was interpreted for the sake of the common and lower-class people, a colloquial version different from the Korean (*ŏnmun*) version of Kim An'guk must have been in use. Moreover, when Yulgok set up his compact, although Kim An'guk's colloquial version of *The Community Compact of the Lü Family* was in circulation, he did not choose to use it. A colloquial version of Yulgok's text was used when the text was interpreted for the common and lower-class people, but when it was published, the colloquial version was apparently not printed together with the text.

However, the fact that Yulgok interpreted the compact to the common and lower-class people, and gave guidance to the maids and servants of the clan in dialect and colloquial language, goes to show that he was adaptable to the new age, understanding how a member of the elite should deal with that class of people in order to make them understand. He showed this adaptability also by writing *Collected Notes on the Elementary Learning (Sohak chipchu)*, and *Notes on the Elementary Learning Explained (Sohak chusŏl)*, and by disseminating later the *Great Compendium on the Reading and Meaning of the Elementary Learning (Hunŭi Sohak taejŏn)* with Korean notation and explanation of the text.

It would not be amiss to consider Yulgok's attitude toward the common and lower-class people, revealed in his teaching to them in dialect and colloquial language, as it bears on the nature of his learning itself. Yulgok, when he was young, studied at a Zen temple, acquiring a knowledge of Buddhism, of the Buddhist scriptures, and of Buddhist-Taoist books. He was well-versed in various magical techniques of the Taoist cult of immortality and knew something about the *Taoist Concordance to the Book of Changes (Chou-i ts'an-t'ung-ch'i)*. Not only did he know about the Lao Tzu, Chuang Tzu, Lieh Tzu, the Taoist immortals, and the Huang-po teachings of Taoism, but he also studied the Wang Yang-ming school of China at the time. It is said that Yulgok owes something to the philosophy of Chuang Tzu for his ideas.[22] Yulgok's teaching was inherited by Kim Changsaeng (1548–1631) and Song Siyŏl (1607–89), and Song Siyŏl's criticism of Yi T'oegye was based upon Yulgok's views. These things are recorded in Yulgok's *Life Chronology*, his *Recorded Conversations (Ŏrok)*, and in the accounts of later scholars contained in the *Complete Writings of Master Yulgok (Yulgok sŏnsaeng chŏnsŏ)*. Yulgok was conversant with the lore of the yin-yang system, divination (*poksŏ*), prognostication and physiognomy (*chŏmsang*), and medical arts (*ŭibang*), also.[23] Of these four, he regarded the medical arts as most important, saying "it is especially important for its daily applications and it cannot be neglected." Thus Yulgok's learning was formulated after he had digested and evaluated many elements.

Yulgok was also aware of the teachings of Wang Yang-ming (1472–1529) which swept through the scholarly world of China at the time. Once a disciple asked Yulgok about the teaching of Hsüeh Hsüan (1389–1464), Lo Ch'in-shun (1465–1547), and Wang Yang-ming.[24] (Hsüeh and Lo were scholar-officials identified with the Ch'eng-Chu School, and the latter had criticized Wang Yang-ming.) Yulgok, after giving an evaluation of these two scholars, and understanding clearly both that Wang Yang-ming had been critical of some doctrines of the Chu Hsi School, and that Yang-ming had been esteemed in China so much that he was enshrined in the Confucian Temple, nevertheless said that one should not fail to study whatever sort of learning was held to in China (i.e., nothing should be ruled out as heterodox).

In the questions and answers preceding this dialogue, Yulgok had answered as follows when he was asked about the learning of Korea at the time during the Yi dynasty:

The rise of Neo-Confucianism began with Cho Chŏngam [Kwangjo, 1482–1519]. After T'oedo [T'oegye], it appeared that Confucianism achieved a certain maturity. However, T'oedo merely followed and carried out the teachings of the sages and wise men without perceiving that each had his own point of view. Hwadam [Sŏ Kyŏngdŏk, 1489–1546] did have his own ideas but he saw only one small corner of things.

These two dialogues took place in the year 1579, after he had returned to Sŏktam, in Haeju, and put into effect the *Haeju Compact* discussed above. What he told his disciples was that "the basis of Neo-Confucianism in Korea was established and perfected by T'oegye's teachings of the Chu Hsi philosophy, but his learning merely kept to what had been said by former sages and worthies and lacked originality. Sŏ Kyŏngdŏk had some original ideas in some part of his learning." Yulgok must have criticized the rigidity of T'oegye's Chu Hsi philosophy when he said that T'oegye merely followed the sages and worthies of the past and lacked originality.

This criticism probably arose not from any doctrinal difference, etc., between the learning of T'oegye and Yulgok, but from the difference in their outlook on the social changes taking place in Korea. Yulgok's learning drew upon Sŏ Kyŏngdŏk's, which emphasized ether or material force (*ch'i*). Yulgok tried to develop and perfect the theory of principle (*li*) and material force based on the primacy of material force. In his criticism of Sŏ above, Yulgok showed himself conscious of the fact that his own philosophy of material force was not just copying Sŏ but had its own originality, reflecting his personal experience in trying to cope with the actual conditions of his own time, and his realism in adapting his compact to the actual circumstances he found.

This new realism in his approach to the new lower-class people at the time seems to have been in keeping with a philosophy which stressed material force, i.e., concrete reality. Also, his insistence that one should have one's own point of view shows something in common with the pragmatic stand of Wang Yang-ming. That is why Yulgok could take an objective position in answering the question concerning Wang Yang-ming. Nevertheless, while Yulgok was receptive to the various religions and ideologies of China, including the teachings of Lu Hsiang-shan (1139–93) and Wang Yang-ming, he sought to integrate them into his own brand of Chu Hsi philosophy, different from Yi T'oegye's.

In the postscript he wrote in 1581[25] for the Hsüeh-pu t'ung-pien, written in 1548 by Ch'en Chien, a Chu Hsi scholar of the Ming dynasty, Yulgok agreed with the views expressed in the Hsüeh-pu t'ung-pien which denounced the theories of Lu and Wang, attacked Lao Tzu, Chuang Tzu, Yang Chu, and Mo Tzu as heretics, and criticized the Ch'an sect of Buddhism. To the question, "Scholars in China are very much tainted by the Lu school and yet we in Korea have not heard of it. How has it come to pass that the correctness of mind of people in Korea has come to surpass the correctness of mind of people in China?" Yulgok answered, "Untainted by the Lu school and wholeheartedly devoted to the Chu Hsi school, we are able to understand and practice it well. Thus indeed we are superior to China." This shows that his basic standpoint was that of the Chu Hsi school, which was the official teaching of the Yi dynasty in Korea at the time. His criticism of the Lu-Wang teaching had become sharper in his "Postscript to Hsüeh-pu t'ung-pien" (Hakpu t'ongbyŏn pal) which was written two years after he made his evaluation of Hsüeh Hsüan, Lo Ch'in-shun, and Wang Yang-ming. This may have been influenced by his reading of the Hsüeh-pu t'ung-pien.

In sixteenth-century China, during the same period when T'oegye and Yulgok were adapting Master Chu's Revision of the Lü Family Compact and carrying it out in keeping with the conditions in Korea, the compact was undergoing change from the Lü Family's version to one based on the Six Edicts of the Ming Emperor T'ai-tsu. Already in Wang Yang-ming's Nan-kan Compact there was the beginning of this change to a compact based on T'ai-tsu's Six Edicts, and the full-fledged change took place from about 1529–30.[26] In Korea, in the Yi dynasty of the sixteenth century, as Wang Yang-ming's influence was largely excluded, and the position of Chu Hsi was confirmed, *Master Chu's Revision of the Lü Family's Community Compact* was generally put into effect. A compact based on the Six Edicts was eventually carried out by Kim Seryŏm in the 1640s.

In Japan, the Chu Hsi school developed as a teaching officially encouraged by the Edo Shogunate in the seventeenth century. It had originally been brought over to Japan from Korea in the early Yi dynasty. The Wang Yang-ming school was also brought from China in the seventeenth century. The social movement based on the community compact of China, which after the sixteenth century adopted the Six Edicts rather than the *Lü Family Compact*, reached Japan subsequently with the introduction of the *Extended Meaning of the Six Edicts (Liu-yü yen-i)*, a work of the late Ming dynasty. In the early eighteenth century, this was adopted by the Chu Hsi scholars of the Kyoto school, and came to be incorporated in the Shogunate's national educational policy. Thus there was not much influence of the *Lü Family Compact* or Chu Hsi's revision of it, in contrast to the situation in Korea during the Yi dynasty. As to the communal granary system, this was practiced in Japan independent of the compact, although in the *Haeju Compact* the communal granary system was an integral part of the compact system. That is to say, the communal granary system was introduced to Japan earlier than the *Extended Meaning of the Six Edicts*, beginning with the publication of *Master Chu's Communal Granary System (Shushi shōsōhō)* by Yamazaki Ansai (1618–82), a Chu Hsi scholar of the Nangaku school, at the end of the seventeenth century. In eighteenth-century Japan, such feudal domains as Aizu, Okayama, and Hiroshima adopted it.

Thus there was a clear-cut difference between the Korean kingdom and Japan of the Edo period in their reception of the community compact and communal granary movement which had originated in China. This must be due to the difference between the political and social orders in the two countries. The community compact and granary movement in China, which in the sixteenth century was carried out in close coordination with the *pao-chia* security sytem and the communal schools, was handed down to the Ch'ing dynasty. The *pao-chia* system can be considered equivalent to the community compact (as exemplified in the "Community Compact" and the "Sai-yü" of Yin Keng during the Chia-ching period). During the Ch'ing dynasty, the *pao-chia* system played a large role together with the Six Edicts and community compact based on the Imperial Edicts (Sheng-yü hsiang-yüeh). Neither in Yi dynasty Korea nor in Japan was the *pao-chia* system,[27] so prevalent in China after the sixteenth century, taken up to the same extent as the community compact and granary system. This also must be due to differences in political and social conditions which existed in China at the time, in Korea during the Yi dynasty, and in Japan during the Edo period, when the *gonin-gumi* (five-family neighborhood unit) system was in effect. And the enforcement of the *gonin-gumi* system reflects an indifference toward the Chinese *pao-chia* system. It is an important problem for us to explore the differences between China, Korea, and Japan, as shown by the comparison between the community compact which was autonomously carried out among agrarian villages, the village rules (*muraokite*) of Japan, and similar voluntary agreements in Korea on the one hand, and the compact which was carried out under the direction of the Yi dynasty and the *yangban* elite in Korea.

When aspects of a foreign culture are introduced to another country, naturally the conditions existing on the receiving side become a problem. In the case of Yi dynasty Korea, it was only natural that the government should want to take and promote the Chu Hsi philosophy as its official line, in order to maintain its political and social regime under *yangban* leadership. That is why historical figures like Yi T'oegye and Yi Yulgok played their roles as representative scholars from the *yangban* elite, which was the leading class in the political and social systems in the Korean peninsula. In the philosophies of both Chu Hsi and Wang Yang-ming it is not surprising that the community compact and granary systems became highly important as instruments of administration to provide for the welfare of the common people. The reason why the compact and communal granary system outlined in Chu Hsi's writings became important in Korea is that both the political and social systems had a stronger need for them than was the case in China and Japan.

In Korea under the Yi dynasty, the influence of Chu Hsi's revision of the *Lü Family Compact* as seen in the works of T'oegye and Yulgok, continued for some time. Kim Seryŏm, as stated above, introduced to Korea the late Ming compact in the form of the Six Edicts instead of the Lü Family's four principles. But in Korea the Compact of the Lü Family prevailed over the Six Edicts version. At the end of the eighteenth century (1797), the *Combined Compendium on Community Rituals (Hyang-*

nye happy'ŏn) was edited, printed, and distributed by royal order. In this matter Song Siyŏl, a disciple of Yulgok, was involved. This collection of community compact materials did not include the Community Compact Based on the Six Edicts. The *Combined Compendium on Community Rituals* incorporates material concerning community rituals *(hyangnye)* and family rituals *(karye)*. Among the former are included the community wine drinking ritual *(hyangŭm churye)* and *Master Chu's Revision of the Lü Family Community Compact.* The family rituals include the *Ceremonials of the Ssu-ma Family (Ssu-ma shih shu-i)* and the *Family Ritual of Master Chu (Chu Tzu chia-li).*[28] Of the ten volumes of *Ssu-ma Family Ceremonial Texts,* one is devoted to capping ceremonies, two to wedding ceremonies, and six to mourning rituals.

In this way Korean scholars showed their adherence to earlier Neo-Confucian models and refused to accept in their stead later systems adopted by the Ming and Ch'ing dynasties.

NOTES

1. There are several versions of *Master Chu's Revision of the Lü Family Community Compact* (*Chu Tzu tseng-sun Lü-shih hsiang-yüeh*) with its supplementary notes by Kim An'guk in Chinese and Korean vernacular translation closely related to the texts. When one compares the *Lü Family Compact*, published by the Institute of Orientology at the Tan'guk University in September 1976, with *Master Chu's Revision of the Lü Family Community Compact* included in vol. 74 of the *Great Compendium of Master Chu's Collected Works* (*Chu Tzu ta-ch'üan wen-chi*), one finds that the former is based on the latter with supplementary notes in Korean and Chinese as well as with Korean vernacular translations. *Master Chu's Revision of the Lü Family Community Compact* included in the *Great Compendium of Master Chu's Collected Works* incorporated a number of materials based on the four principles of the *Lü Family's Compact* at Lan-t'ien, to which Chu added ideas of his own to meet the actual situation he faced. Furthermore Chu added the ritual of "Reading the Compact at Monthly Meetings" (*Yüeh-tan chi-hui tu-yüeh*) which he himself compiled. It provides for the ritual of Reading the Compact to be performed at the community school, something lacking in the *Lü Family Compact* of the Northern Sung period but added by Chu Hsi in order to adapt to the actual circumstances of the village community in the early Southern Sung.

   In the Korean translation by Kim An'guk this community school is discussed in relation to the counties of the Yi Dynasty, with a view to instituting and conducting the compact in conjunction with the county schools of that time in Korea. In the latter half of the sixteenth century, much after Kim An'guk's time, the community compact came to be conducted in conjunction with local private academies presided over by the *yangban*, as seen in the *Haeju Compact* of Yi Yulgok, to be discussed later.
2. Cf. Matsuda Kō, "Richō jidai no kyōyaku" in *Zoku Nissen shiwa*, vol. 3 (Seoul: Chōsen sōtokufu, 1931). Dr. Tabana Tameo, in his *Chōsen kyōyaku kyōkashi kenkyū*, (Historical Section) (Tokyo: Meihōsha, 1972), pp. 194–97, fails to include the *Hyangnip yakcho* on the ground that it is not part of the Family Compact. Since *hyangyak* originally meant community consitution or regulations, it goes without saying that the "Articles of the Community Compact" belong among the traditional local constitutions of a community in Korea. The only thing to be noted is that it is free from the influence of the *Lü Family Compact* derived from China. Like Dr. Tabana, Dr. Tagawa Kōzo and others do not regard the "Articles of the Community Compact" and the Community Compact of Yi Yulgok (discussed later) as Community Compacts but as Community Regulations (Tagawa Kōzo, "Richō no kyōki ni tsuite," in *Chōsen gakuhō* (July 1975), 76:35–72. These community regulations (*hyanggyu*) should be regarded as representative of the traditional community constitutions of Korean society. A comparative study of com-

munity constitutions in China, Korea, and Japan would inevitably lead to the comparative study of Chinese *hsiang-li* and *hsiang-yüeh*, the Korean *hyangnyŏng* and *hyanggyu*, and the Japanese *muraokite*.

3. *Chŭngbo T'oegye chŏnsŏ*, 5 vols. (Seoul: Sŏnggyun'gwan taehakkyo, Tae-donga munhwa yŏn'guwŏn, 1971), 42:8b–12b (2:352153).

4. Yi Hyŏnbo, *cha*: Paejung. He passed the preliminary examinations in 1495 and the civil examination *(munkwa)* in 1498. During the time of King Yŏn-san (r. 1476–1506) he was in official disfavor, but later held successive governmental posts. For details see Sakai, "Ririkkoku to kyōyaku," in *Higashi Ajia no shisō to bunka* (Tokyo: Kankoku kenkyūin, 1980), p. 150.

5. The language of the original text does not distinguish between the violation and the violater. In English we resolve the ambiguity by identifying the act, not "he who" or "those who" commit it (ed. note).

6. Cf. Tadao Sakai, "Pang no minshū no ishiki" in *Tōyōshi kenkyū* (September 1972), 31(2):98–101.

7. (a) *Shih-lin kuang-chi* (1340 ed. in the Archive of the Japanese Imperial Household Ministry), *Wu chi*, "Kung-li . . . chuang-shih."

   (b) *Wan-yung Cheng-tsung* (1599 ed. in the Hōsa Library, vol. 27, *Min yung men*, "Hsiang-yüeh t'i-lei."

   (c) *Wen-lin kuang-chi* (1607 ed. in the Archive of the Imperial Household Ministry), vol. 26, *Hsin-tseng pien-yung ko-shih*, "Hsiang-yüeh."

   (d) *Wan-pao ch'üan-shu* (1614 ed. in the Imperial Household Ministry), vol. 9, "Ti-fang yeh-yüeh."

8. The Korean people have the customary practice of forming covenant associations *(kye)*. The members of the *kye* used to regulate one another according to the statutes (see *Sŏnjo sillok*, 7:32b–33b; Yi Sugwang, *Chibong yusŏl*, kw. 2, "Chegukpu p'ungsok." Also see Kim Yongdŏk, *Hyangch'ŏng yŏn'gu* (Seoul: Han'guk yŏn'guwŏn, 1978), pp. 29–43, 120–24, 181–207. Local covenant associations were formed within the framework of the village community. Community regulations were based on the statutes of the local association of *yangban* aristocrats *(hyangan)*. Yi Yulgok's *Sŏwŏn Compact*, the communal granary, and the later Community Compact of An Chŏngbok (1712–91) regulated by the Six Edicts, were carried out on the basis of a covenant association. For different concrete examples of *kye* in the Yi dynasty, one may refer to Shikata Hiroshi, "Richō jidai ni okeru kei-kiyaku no kenkyū" in Shikata, *Chōsen shakai keizai-shi kenkyū* (Tokyo: Kokusho kankōkai, 1976), pp. 69–121. The *kye* is very similar to the *she* in China, a society specially formed for a specific purpose, such as has existed since the Six Dynasties. The other is a society based on the village community *li-she*, which has been known since ancient times, and has come to have *hsiang-li* as its community regulations since the T'ang period. In general the Korean *kye* could be formed within any social class (for example the commoner class or *yangban*), and the interrelationship among its members was comparatively horizontal, just like the *she* in China. The key members, originally belonging to one class, later belonged to several classes, as seen in the *Communal Granary Cove-*

nant of Yi Yulgok. In this case the interrelationship among the members is not horizontal, and the upper class *(yangban)* among those classes comprising the *kye* has come to assume the leadership of the *kye*.

9. Cf. Tabana Tameo, "Kyōyaku kyōho to dōgi kyōyaku" in *Chōsen gakuhō* (October 1953) 5(10):127–54, and "Richō Jinso ōdai no kyōyaku kyōka" in *Chōsen gakuhō* (January 1975), 48:169–80, also Tagawa Kōzo, "Richō no kyōki ni tsuite" (parts 1, 2, 3) in *Chōsen gakuhō* (July 1975), 76:35–72; (January 1976), 78:45–87; (October 1976), 81:179–209. In the first of Dr. Tagawa's articles T'oegye's "*Hyangnip yakcho*" is referred to and in the third, Yulgok's compact.

10. Yi T'oegye, Preface to *Chujasŏ chŏryo* in *Chŭngbo T'oegye chŏnsŏ*, 42:2b–52, 2:348–50.

11. The officially compiled *Hsing-li ta-ch'üan* was commissioned by the emperor during the Yung-lo reign (in 1415), and was subsequently available in Yi dynasty Korea. A Korean edition was printed at the end of the fifteenth century.

12. *T'aejong sillok*, 6:23a.

13. Cf. Matsuda Kō, "Richō jidai no kyōyaku" as in note 2 above.

14. *Yulgok chŏnsŏ* (Seoul: Sŏnggyun'gwan taehakkyo, 1971), 16:2a–7a (1:340–42).

15. In the articles of the *Sŏwŏn Compact* it is written "within each unit *(chang)*, one covenant unit chief is to be appointed" and "once each year the covenant director is to assemble the *myŏn* unit chiefs and clerks in one place to discuss the compact system (laws)." In the "Protocol for Reading the Community Compact in General Assembly," the terms "each *myŏn* unit chief" and "such *myŏn* unit chiefs" appear. Judging from these examples we may conclude that the *chang* unit and *myŏn* unit are equivalent.

16. *Yulgok chŏnsŏ*, 34:5a–6b, Life Chronology, part 2, 2:308–9.

17. Cf. Tabana Tameo, *Chōsen kyōyaku kyōkashi no kenkyū*, Historical Section, chap. 4, pp. 395–405.

18. The *Hsiang-hsiao*, as found in Chu Hsi's supplementary comments attached to the *Lü Family Community Compact*, refers to local public schools, prefectural schools *(fu-hsüeh)*, subprefectural schools *(chou-hsüeh)*, and county schools *(hsien-hsüeh)*, and to small private schools established by scholars in their localities. It was a general term for local primary schools which were concerned with popular education and were related to the lower educated class. In Chu Hsi's comments it probably corresponded to the *hsiang-hsiao* mentioned in the Confucian classics. I do not think that a public system of local schools was actually carried out in the Sung period. Community schools in Korea were first established in the Koryŏ period around the beginning of the twelfth century, and became prevalent in the Yi dynasty as local public schools under the local administrative system. Therefore they are equivalent to the Chinese system of schools known as the prefectural schools, subprefectural schools, and county schools in the Ming-Ch'ing period.

19. *Yulgok chŏnsŏ*, 15:46b–47b, *Ŭnbyŏng chŏngsa hakkyu*, 1:336.

20. *Ibid.*, 34:5a (2:308).

21. "Kyōsho genkai," in Maema Kyosaku, *Kosen sappu* (Tokyo: Tōyō bunko, 1944), Book One, p. 389.

22. An Pyŏngju, "Explanatory Introduction to Sŏ Hwadam and Yi Yulgok" in *Shushigaku taikei* (Tokyo: Meitoku shuppansha, 1977), vol. 12, p. 15.

23. *Yulgok chŏnso*, "sūbyu," 6:3a–9b (2:564–67).

24. *Ibid.*, 31 (*Ŏrok*, part 1):60a (2:258).

25. *Ibid.*, 13:32a–34a (1:272–73).

26. Sakai Tadao, *Chūgoku zensho no kenkyū* (Tokyo: Kokusho kankōkai, 1972), chaps. 1 and 7. Since the publication of the *Lü Family Compact*, many Confucian scholars, including Chu Hsi in the Southern Sung dynasty, endorsed and explained the *Lü Family Compact* at least in their scholarly works. This concept became so prevalent that it was introduced even in the *Popular Encyclopedias for Daily Use* in the Yüan and Ming periods (refer to the 1280 ed. of the *Shih-lin kuang-chi, wu chi*).

27. Later in Yi Korea one notices the influence of the *pao-chia* system and the community compacts of the Ming dynasty in the clauses concerning military duty (*pangyŏk*) contained in the village compacts and community compacts written by An Chŏngbok. Cf. Tabana Tameo, "Kyōyaku kyōhō."

28. See the *Ssu-k'u ch'üan-shu tsung-mu t'i-yao*, vol. 22, *li-lei, tsa-li-shu* (assorted ritual texts). Such popular books of the Yüan-Ming and Ch'ing dynasties as *Chü-chia pi-yung shih-lei ch'üan-chi* of the late Yüan dynasty (part 2, vol. 3) and *Hsün-su i-kuei* (vol. 1) in Ch'en Hung-mou's *Wu-chung i-kuei* of the Ch'ing dynasty, included Ssu-ma Kuang's *Wen-kung chü-chia tsa-i*. The *Tsuan-t'u tseng-lei shih-lin kuang-chi* (part 2, vol. 1) included the *Wen-kung chia-i*. The text therein is similar to that of *Wen-kung chü-chia tsa-i* quoted above. The latter and the *Wen-kung chia-i* are probably extracts from the *Ssu-ma shih shu-i* or documents closely related to it. Also in the original late Yüan edition of the *Hsin-p'ien shih-wen lei-yao ch'i-cha ch'ing-ch'ien*, vol. 6, Special Supplement (formerly owned by Lord Mori of the Tokugawa feudal domain) there is a reference to what may be an extract from the *Ssu-ma shih shu-i*, identified in the table of contents as *Wen-kung chia-i* and in the main text as *Wen-kung chia-li*.

Han Young-woo

Kija Worship
in the Koryŏ
and Early Yi Dynasties:
A Cultural Symbol
in the Relationship
Between Korea and China

1. INTRODUCTION

WRITINGS ABOUT KIJA (Chi Tzu), reputedly a Shang refugee who
has been worshipped as a patriarch of ancient Koreans, pose one of the
more important questions in the study of Korean ancient history and intellectual history. Records of Kija's personality and achievements are found
in profusion in a variety of Chinese classics such as the *Analects (Lun-
yü)*, the *Documents (Shu-ching)*, the *Changes (I-ching)*, the *Tso Commentary (Tso-chuan)*, the *Records of the Grand Historian (Shih-chi)*, the
History of the Han Dynasty (Han-shu), the *History of the Later Han Dynasty (Hou-Han-shu)*, the *Commentaries on Canons of Yao and Shun
(Shang-shu ta-chuan)*, the *Memorable Events of the Wei Dynasty (Wei-
lüeh)*, the *History of the Three Kingdoms (San-kuo-chih)*, the *Comprehensive Institutes (T'ung-tien)*, the *Bamboo Annals (Chu-shu chi-nien)*, the
Universal Encyclopedia (San-ts'ai t'u-hui), and so on. At the same time,
the tomb of Kija and remains of the well-field system, thought to have
been introduced into Korea by Kija, are alleged to have been found in
the P'yŏngyang area. Kija was worshipped by such Korean clans as the
Hans, the Kis, and the Sŏnus as their patriarch.

The accounts concerning Kija are based on legends and one can hardly accept them as facts. Yet, Kija had already become an object of reverence in the Three Kingdoms period, and in the ensuing Koryŏ and Yi periods not only was he regarded as a historical personage but Kija worship played an important role in political ideology and scholarship. This became especially pronounced in the Yi dynasty. From the beginning of the dynasty, Kija Chosŏn was included as a historical dynasty in the official historiography. Some of the later Yi historiographical works represented Kija Chosŏn as the first legitimate state in Korean history.[1] These works, written under the influence of Neo-Confucian concepts of legitimacy, sought to establish the legitimacy of successive dynasties by tracing them to an appropriate antecedent. Kija Chosŏn was chosen as this antecedent, ininitiating a new historiographical tradition. Kija worship reached its climax at the founding of the Great Han Empire (Tae Han cheguk) in 1897; Kija was honored as the Great Progenitor, the Sage King of Civilization (T'aejo Munsŏngwang), and historical works published in this period contained detailed accounts of Kija and his successors.[2] The name of the empire, the Great Han, seems to have been closely associated with Kija worship. The Kija worshipped during this period was the one who had fled China, proclaimed his independence, and become king of Korea—he was not the Kija protrayed as a vassal of King Wu of the Chou dynasty. Thus, Kija worship had a distinct connotation of independence from China.

During the Japanese occupation of Korea, some Japanese historians interpreted Kija Chosŏn as a Chinese colony, thus implying colonial beginnings for Korea. To counter this, Korean nationalistic historians either denied the theory of Kija's immigration into the peninsula or interpreted Kija Chosŏn as one of the feudal vassals of Tan'gun Chosŏn.[3] During the Japanese colonial period, caught between these opposing views of Kija, Kija worship rapidly disappeared in favor of Tan'gun, the legendary father of the Korean people.

Most modern Korean historians do not accept the theory of Kija's immigration to the east and interpret the so-called Kija Chosŏn as an internal change in the ruling class in ancient Korean society.[4] More recently, a new interpretation has emerged viewing the immigration of Kija not as that of one individual but as that of a "Kija tribe," which is seen as one of the Tung-i (Eastern bowmen or Eastern barbarians) people of the Shang race.[5] Another recent theory sees Kija Chosŏn as a group of

Tung-i people who were part of the bronze and plain pottery culture.[6] No definitive theory has been established but a general consensus is emerging which accepts the immigration of a Kija tribe and which views it as a branch of the *Tung-i* people.

There are two ways to study the question of Kija. One is to investigate the existence of Kija Chosŏn and its historical character; this properly belongs to the domain of ancient history. The second is to examine how Kija and Kija Chosŏn were viewed at various stages of Korean history; this is a question of historiography and intellectual history. It is to the latter question that this paper will be addressed. I will examine the process of change and transformation in the image of Kija from the Three Kingdoms period, when the first records of Kija worship appear, through the middle of the Yi dynasty, that is, the sixteenth century, when Kija worship became linked to Neo-Confucianism.[7]

2. THE IMAGE OF KIJA DURING THE KORYŎ PERIOD

Descriptions of Kija began to appear in Korean records during the reign of King T'aejo (r. 918–43), founder of the Koryŏ dynasty. But there are Chinese source materials dating from earlier periods that describe Kija worship. According to the *Old T'ang History (Chiu-T'ang-shu)*, the so-called *yin-ssu* belief (deity worship), for instance, prevailed in Koguryŏ where people worshipped the Sun, the Stars, Kagan, and Kija as deities.[8] *Yin-ssu* meant deity worship, which was of course heathenish from the Confucian viewpoint. The Chinese record relates that Kija was worshipped as a deity in Koguryŏ, where Confucianism had not yet taken root.

That the Chinese viewed Kija worship as a pagan belief indicates that Kija was worshipped as an ancestral deity rather than as a submissive vassal of King Wu of Chou or as a Confucian sage. The deity Kagan worshipped with Kija seems to indicate the "God of Chumong," the founder deity of Koguryŏ. Following Koguryŏ's transfer of its capital to P'yŏngyang, the Kija deity is believed to have become a part of the national set of Koguryŏ's beliefs.

There is no mention of Kija worship in records dating from the unified Silla period, because P'yŏngyang was at best a peripheral concern of the

unified Silla Kingdom. Kija worship, being the belief of the northern Koguryŏ people, was not a matter of great interest to the southern people of
Silla.

Kija became an object of interest with the founding of the new Koryŏ
Dynasty. In the sixteenth year of the reign of King T'aejo, (933), a diplomatic delegation of the Later T'ang paid a call on the Koryŏ king with
a letter from the emperor. Praising the brilliant achievements of King
T'aejo, the letter stated that the Koryŏ ruler ascended to the throne in the
spirit of Ko Chumong, and that he administered his country peacefully
and wisely in Kija's footsteps.[9] That is, the T'ang emperor viewed the
founder of the Koryŏ dynasty as the successor of both Ko Chumong and
Kija.

That the founders of the Koryŏ claimed to be successors to Koguryŏ
is apparent in the name of the dynasty they adopted. Whether or not they
wanted to claim the Kija heritage as well is uncertain. If they did, they
most likely saw Kija as an ancestral deity, in accordance with the Koguryŏ view, rather than as a Chinese feudal lord. The Chinese at this
time portrayed Kija as a Chinese feudal lord and a civilizer of Korea, and
at the same time they linked the founding of the Koryŏ dynasty to the
Kija Chosŏn. There is no evidence, however, that the Koryŏ court accepted this new image of Kija endorsed by the Chinese.

Only in 1102, during the reign of King Sukchong (r. 1095–1195),
did the Koryŏ court display an interest in Kija. In the tenth month of
1102, the Ministry of Rites *(Yebu)* proposed that Kija's tomb be found
and that a shrine be built and dedicated to him in P'yŏngyang. The stated
reason for this proposal was that Korean culture and civilized life began
with Kija. There was no reference to the theory that Kija had been a
Chinese feudal lord.[10] This recommendation was made during Sukchong's tour of the western capital (Sŏgyŏng, better known as P'yŏngyang), where he held a banquet for the local civil and military elites, granted
an amnesty to criminals, and took measures to encourage commercial activity in the area. The decision to build a shrine to Kija was reached during this stay at P'yŏngyang. During his reign, Sukchong made two long
trips to P'yŏngyang. The first was from the seventh to tenth months of
1102, during which the construction of a Kija shrine was decided upon.
He went back to P'yŏngyang in the eighth month of 1105 and on this
occasion attended a sacrifice at the shrine of Ko Chumong, the founder
of the Koguryŏ dynasty.

Sukchong's trips to P'yŏngyang were based on geomancy, according to which P'yŏngyang was considered an auspicious place. Soon after Sukchong's accession in 1096, a geomancer, Kim Wije, citing the *Record of Tosŏn (Tosŏn'gi)*, a prophetic work by a Buddhist monk, Tosŏn (827–98), recommended to the king that he should move the capital to the southern capital (Namgyŏng), now Seoul, and that he should pay special attention to P'yŏngyang. According to Kim Wije, the *Record of Tosŏn* predicted that if the king resided in the middle capital (Kaegyŏng) from the eleventh to second month, in the southern capital from the third to sixth month, and at the western capital from the seventh to tenth month, the Koryŏ house would receive tribute from thirty-six countries. The *Record of Tosŏn* is also said to have forewarned that the Koryŏ capital should be moved to Seoul 160 years after the founding of the dynasty.[11] Accepting Kim's recommendation, Sukchong prepared to move the capital to Seoul, while making visits to P'yŏngyang. The Kija shrine was built under these circumstances.

Consequently, Kija worship during Sukchong's reign was related to a movement to restore importance to P'yŏngyang, and in the process the local cult of Kija in the P'yŏngyang area became a national cult. But in addition, Kija was transformed from an ancestral or tribal deity to a civilizer who initiated civilization and rites in Korea. While this suggests that Koryŏ partly accepted the Chinese view of Kija, there is no evidence that it also accepted the theory that Kija had been a vassal of the Chou king. Moreover, when one considers that the movement to restore P'yŏngyang was rooted in the policy of northern expansion and the hope of recapturing from China territory that had belonged to the Koguryŏ kingdom, it is highly unlikely that Kija worship in this period entailed the idea that Kija had been a vassal of the Chou king. It is more logical to see Kija worship as a desire to enhance national prestige by asserting the long cultural tradition of P'yŏngyang. It is recorded that the Koryŏ court in its early years compiled the *Old History of the Three Kingdoms (Ku Samguksa)* which contained a section on Tan'gun. This already shows a historiographical consciousness in that the legitimate succession was considered a process beginning with Tan'gun and continuing through Koguryŏ to Koryŏ. But this was a purely ancestral or political succession, and it is doubtful whether the Koryŏ people regarded Tan'gun as the originator of civilization or rites. Especially in the early eleventh century Tan'gun was worshipped either as a creator or as a progenitor of the Korean race, not as a civilizer.[12] The

Koryŏ dynasty seems to have turned to Kija, whose concrete accomplishments were recorded in Chinese records, in order to establish their cultural identity. In other words, the Koryŏ court seems to have used Tangun and Ko Chumong as their ancestral sages, in order to emphasize the homogeneity of the Korean race, while it used Kija to assert their cultural distinctiveness. And with these two, they pursued a balance between the policy of northern expansion and the policy of maintaining diplomatic relations with China.

The image of Kija went through a drastic transformation in the *Historical Records of the Three Kingdoms (Samguk sagi)* compiled by Kim Pusik (1075–1151) in 1145. Kim Pusik was a Confucian scholar from Kyŏngju, the old capital of the Silla dynasty. He was the leader of a group which came to power under King Injong (r. 1122–46) after thwarting the Myoch'ŏng (?–1135) group which attempted to move the capital to P'yŏngyang. Not surprisingly, the *Historical Records of the Three Kingdoms* is written in a Silla-centered historiographical tradition. It makes no mention of Tan'gun Chosŏn, which was associated with P'yŏngyang, and places the founding of the Koguryŏ dynasty at a later date than that of the Silla dynasty. Changes in the image of Kija in the *Historical Records of the Three Kingdoms* were made in this context.

There are various references to Kija in the *Historical Records of the Three Kingdoms*. The first occurs in the preface to the chronological table:

There had been a state in Korea for a long time when Kija was enfeoffed by the Chou court. At the time of the early Han dynasty in China, Wiman came to power and there was a change of dynasties [in Korea]. Since these events occurred long ago and the records are incomplete, it is not possible to ascertain the details.[13]

In the section on sacrifice *(chesa)* in the "Miscellaneous Chapter" *(chapchi)*, obviously quoting from the *T'ang History (T'ang-shu)*, the book mentions that Kija was offered a sacrifice as a deity during Koguryŏ.[14] The most comprehensive discussion of Kija's accomplishments is included in Kim Pusik's comments at the end of the chapter on Koguryŏ. It says that from the time that Kija was enfeoffed in Korea, he taught the people decorum, farming, and sericulture, and instituted the Eight Prohibitive Injunctions *(p'alcho kŭmpŏp)*. He thus succeeded in propagating benevolence and wisdom, and this caused Confucius to say that he would have been glad to go there, even by sailing on driftwood, to live.[15] This comment seems to have been written more in explanation of why Koguryŏ was destroyed than in praise of Kija. That is, the territory that Koguryŏ occupied had previously belonged to Kija Chosŏn, which was a state of high civilization, but Koguryŏ had neither been dutiful to its great neighbor (China) nor benevolent to its people, thus inviting self-destruction. Kim Pusik was in fact implying that the culture of benevolence and righteousness introduced by Kija Chosŏn had not been carried on by Koguryŏ.[16]

The composite picture that emerges in the *Historical Records of the Three Kingdoms* is that Kija was a Chinese vassal who established the first state in Korea and who succeeded in creating such a high degree of civilization that it was even admired by Confucius. What is new in this is twofold: that Kija, who established the first Korean state, had been enfeoffed by the Chou court and that Kija Chosŏn's admirable cultural tradition was not inherited by Koguryŏ. In this sense, the Kija of the *Historical Records of the Three Kingdoms* became a symbol, not of the policy of northern expansion but rather of the policy of promoting the relationship with China (Sung dynasty). Likewise, Kija was worshipped not as a deity but as a Confucian sage. And unlike the image of Kija which had been constructed in the main from legends and artifacts of the P'yŏngyang area, it was based exclusively on Chinese documents.[17] At the root of this change was Kim Pusik's China and Silla-oriented historiographical posture.

The concept of the Koryŏ dynasty as a successor to the Koguryŏ dynasty was revived during the military regime which came to power in the late twelfth century and lasted for about a century. *On King Tongymyŏng (Tongmyŏngwang p'yŏn)*, written by Yi Kyubo (1168–1241) in 1193, is representative of this historiographical trend which harked back to the early Koryŏ, ascribing a higher culture to Koguryŏ.[18] But this work makes no reference to the tradition linking Koguryŏ to either Tan'gun or Kija. The reason for this is not clear, but it probably has something to do with the fact that the work was written, not to promote the restoration of P'yŏngyang as capital or the policy of northern expansion but, on the one hand, to display Koryŏ's cultural superiority to the Liao and the Chin dynasties, and on the other, to oppose those who promoted the rhetoric of a Silla restoration. The relative inattention to Kija during this period, however, can best be explained perhaps by the tense international situation. As may be inferred from a diplomatic letter from the Chin ruler to King Sinjong (r. 1197–1204), the Chin court, which constantly threatened Koryŏ and pressed for its submission, had used Kija's vassal status as ground for demanding Korean capitulation.[19] No wonder, then, that the military regime placed so little emphasis on Kija.

During the periods of Mongol intervention (between the latter half of the thirteenth and the latter half of the fourteenth centuries), there was a certain convergence between the concept of Kija associated with Koguryŏ and the concept of Kija as a vassal of King Wu. This ideological conflux would seem to have been rooted in sociopolitical conditions; the preservation of Koryŏ's independence, threatened by the Mongol invaders, demanded a consensus among intellectuals. That is, identification with China in the face of the Mongol threat brought about a convergence of two ideologies, one which took pride in Koryŏ's status as the successor to Koguryŏ, and another which defined Koryŏ's cultural achievement by labeling it a "Small China" (Kim Pusik's version). The changes in the Korean cultural and historical consciousness during the period of Mongol intervention is reflected in two historical works, the *Remaining Records of the Three Kingdoms (Samguk yusa)* (1281) written by Iryŏn (1206–89), and the *Records of Emperors and Kings (Chewang un'gi)* (1287) by Yi Sŭnghyu (1224–1300).

Quoting from such documents as the *Old Records (Kogi)*, the *Biography of Tang Paegu (Tang Paegujŏn)*, the *History of Wei (Wei-chih)* in the *History of the Three Kingdoms (San-kuo-chih)*, the *Remaining Records of the Three Kingdoms* deals with the rise and fall of Kija Chosŏn. It makes three assertions: (1) When Kija became a vassal in Korea (Chosŏn) under King Wu of Chou, Tan'gun left for Changdanggyŏng; (2) Koryŏ (Chosŏn) was originally the state of Kojukkuk (now Haeju) and King Wu of Chou made Kija the King of Chosŏn; and (3) As Wiman attacked Kija Chosŏn, King Chun of Kija Chosŏn moved to the south and established the Mahan state.[20]

The *Remaining Records of the Three Kingdoms* agrees with the *Historical Records of the Three Kingdoms* in that it states that Kija was enfeoffed by King Wu of the Chou dynasty, but it sets forth a new theory, claiming that Tan'gun had existed prior to Kija and that the last king of Kija Chosŏn, pressed by Wiman on the north, moved to the south and established the state of Mahan. Unlike the *Historical Records of the Three Kingdoms*, the *Remaining Records* makes no reference to Kija's cultural accomplishments. This probably reflected Iryŏn's cultural and world views. Though he was a Buddhist monk, he was conversant with Confucianism and folk religions, and while he, as a Kyŏngju Kim, held to a Silla-centered historical view, he had a broad knowledge of ancient Korean history and legends such as those about Tan'gun, Kija, Puyŏ, Mahan, etc.[21] Consequently, the image of Kija reflected in the *Remaining Records* is not that of a cultural progenitor but merely that of an historical ruler of ancient Korea. This view of Kija Chosŏn probably corresponded to the political and social composition of the Koryŏ ruling group of the time. Unlike the early twelfth century, which had been dominated by old Silla families, or the military regime, in which groups claiming descent from Koguryŏ and Paekche were in power, the late thirteenth and the fourteenth centuries witnessed a balance of power between these groups.

The *Records of Emperors and Kings* of the same period portrays a new image of Kija and also places Kija Chosŏn firmly in the chronological history of Korea. It dates the founding of Kija Chosŏn 160 years after the demise of Tan'gun Chosŏn. Moreover, it states that Kija was the founder of the later Chosŏn, not a conquerer of Tan'gun Chosŏn. Furthermore, Kija's relationship to King Wu of the Chou dynasty is recorded in detail. Kija fled to Korea and independently founded his state, and only later accepted enfeoffment from King Wu. On a courtesy call to the Chou court during the reign of King Wu, Kija lectured to King Wu on the Nine Divisions of the "Great Plan" *(Hung-fan chiu-ch'ou)*. This is based on the *Documents*, which had not hitherto been quoted. By asserting that Kija had established his state prior to his acceptance of enfeoffment by Wu, Yi Sŭnghyu makes him a person of substantial independence. Furthermore, Yi does not refer to the theory that Kija was a Shang refugee, thus not acknowledging him as a Chinese. In addition, one senses a certain pride in his description of Kija, a Korean King, lecturing on the "Great Plan" to a Chinese ruler. Finally, the *Records of Emperors and Kings* states that Kija Chosŏn lasted 928 years and that its last ruler, King Chun, moved the capital to Kŭmmagun and continued to rule. It does not say, however, what happened to King Chun and his new state, or how it was related to any of the later Korean states.[22]

There are two interesting aspects of this new image of Kija portrayed in the *Records of Emperors and Kings*. First, as it is constructed on the basis of the *Documents*, Kija was now revered as the transmitter of the Nine Divisions of the "Great Plan." Second, Kija's independent founding of a state is emphasized. That is, for the first time, Kija was protrayed as having been an independent founder of a Korean state who subsequently accepted the status of feudal lord from King Wu. This suggests several trends in the thought of the author and the outlook of the period. This view is closely related to an emerging historiographical consensus which saw Korean history as beginning with Tan'gun. It also reflects the syncretic outlook of the author, Yi Sŭnghyu. Yi was definitely a Neo-Confucian but he also tried to formulate a syncretic theory incorporating Neo-Confucianism, Buddhism, and Taoism or folk religion. What he was really aiming for was a position which would permit the Koryŏ state to maintain a subordinate relation to the Yüan dynasty while simultaneously promoting a spirit of independence and self-will in the Koryŏ state. In other words, Yi Sŭnghyu's view of Tan'gun and Kija was rooted in Confucian-nationalistic duality. Such a view was inherited by the Confucian scholars of the early Yi dynasty.

3. THE IMAGE OF KIJA IN THE FIFTEENTH CENTURY

Kija was first discussed at the Yi court in the eighth month of 1392, soon after the new dynasty was founded. As part of the process of Confucianizing national sacrifices and rites, the Yi court accepted a proposal of Cho Pak, Minster of Rites, suggesting that national sacrifices be offered to Tan'gun and Kija in P'yŏngyang.[23] The rhetorical justification for this acceptance was based on a belief that Tan'gun was the first Korean ruler and that he had received his Mandate *(myŏng)* while Kija was the ruler who had initiated Korean culture. In other words, Tan'gun became the symbol of the Korean race and state while Kija became a symbol of Korean culture. This was the first time that Tan'gun was worshipped in national rites along with Kija. During the Koryŏ dynasty, Kija and Ko Chumong had been the objects of national worship but now the era of Tan'gun and Kija worship began.

The rites in honor of Tan'gun and Kija indicate a national acknowledgment of Tan'gun Chosŏn and Kija Chosŏn in the early Yi period. In view of this, the possibility of renaming the new dynasty was considered. In the second year of T'aejo's reign, the new dynasty was named "Chosŏn."[24] "Chosŏn" and "Hwaryŏng" (the hometown of Yi Sŏnggye) had been proposed as possible names for the new dynasty in a meeting of ranking officials held in the eleventh month of the first year. "Chosŏn" was chosen as the name of the dynasty at the suggestion of the Ming Emperor, who favored the name because it was "rich in tradition and most beautiful." Probably he thought it beautiful in association with Kija Chosŏn.

Chŏng Tojŏn (1342–98), who played a crucial role in devising the Yi government structure, concurs, in his *Statutes for the Governance of the State of Chosŏn (Chosŏn kyŏnggukchŏn)*, that Chosŏn was chosen in homage to the Kija tradition and cites two reasons for its adoption. The first was that among the three dynastic founders, Tan'gun, Kija, and Wiman, only Kija was enfeoffed in Korea by King Wu of the Chou dynasty. In the same breath, Chŏng points out the similarity to Yi T'aejo's relationship with the Ming emperor. The second reason Chŏng cites is Kija's admirable cultural accomplishments. Kija transmitted the "Great Plan" to King Wu of the Chou dynasty and he instituted the Eight Injunctions in Korea. Chŏng was the first person to attribute both the Great Plan and the Eight Prohibitive Injunctions to Kija, implying equal levels of cultural accomplishment for the Chou dynasty and Kija Chosŏn. Chŏng also advocated that the Yi court's service to the Ming dynasty, like Kija's service to King Wu of Chou, should be predicated upon cultural equality between the two countries. Quoting Confucius, he expresses a certain pride and a sense of mission in his committment to make Korea into the Chou of the east,[25] the ultimate symbol of civilization.

Though the Ming Emperor and Chŏng Tojŏn shared the same view— that the new dynasty was the successor to Kija Chosŏn—it is difficult to believe that the Yi government adopted the name of the dynasty for its association with Kija Chosŏn alone. For now that Tan'gun was worshipped along with Kija, the name of Chosŏn did not exclusively symbolize Kija Chosŏn. Hanyang (Seoul), for instance, was chosen as the capital of the new dynasty according to a prophecy of Sinji, the legendary immortal of Tan'gun's time who thought that Hanyang would be an auspicious site for the capital. Chŏng Tojŏn was an eminent Neo-Confucian scholar who held great respect for Chou China. In designing the Yi government structure, for instance, he took his inspiration from the *Rites of Chou (Chou-li)*.[26] Nevertheless, he accepted this prophecy which proposed Hanyang as an auspicious site for the new capital and foretold the crowning of a member of the Yi clan as king. In the seventh year of T'aejo's reign, he even urged the king to launch an expedition to conquer the

Liao-tung peninsula to reclaim old Koguryŏ territory, referring to the *Tung-i* kings' past conquest of China.[27] At the time of the so-called *p'yojŏnmun* (a diplomatic paper sent to the Ming Emperor) incident, the Ming Emperor accused Chŏng Tojŏn of being "the root of the evil troubling Korea" and attempted to drive him from power in fear of his planning to attack Liao-tung.[28]

In considering Chŏng's activities, we can not dismiss him as a mere admirer of Kija or as a Neo-Confucian moralist. As far as his learning is concerned, he was an ardent advocate of Neo-Confucianism, an admirer of Chinese culture and of Kija. As an official, however, he committed himself to such ideas as folk beliefs and the rule of might to promote national enrichment and strength. Here we recognize his intellectual duality and his eclecticism. He knew of the existence of Tan'gun Chosŏn as well as of Kija Chosŏn. It would be appropriate to surmise that he associated the name of the dynasty with Kija as a symbol of amity to win the approval of the Ming court.

As an expedient, in order to adopt both Tan'gun and Kija as national deities, Tan'gun was enshrined with Kija in the Kija shrine in 1412.[29] Tan'gun had already been worshipped during the time of King T'aejo. But Tan'gun and Kija had been separately worshipped under the auspices of the city of P'yŏngyang. The enshrinement of Tan'gun in the Kija shrine in P'yŏngyang was designed to acquaint Chinese diplomats with Tan'gun as the patriarch of Koreans, for it was customary for visiting members of Chinese diplomatic missions to pay homage at Kija's shrine. This idea had been proposed by Ha Yun (1347–1416),[30] a renowned Confucian scholar-official and T'aejong's confidante. In 1402, Ha Yun had, together with Kwŏn Kūn (1352–1409), compiled the *Short History of the Eastern Nation (Tongguk saryak)*. This work orders the chronology of ancient Korean states from Tan'gun Chosŏn through Kija Chosŏn to Wiman Chosŏn.[31] This was the first inclusion of Tan'gun and Kija in state-commissioned official historiography. It is not surprising that Koreans made an effort to establish Tan'gun as a figure of veneration in this way, thereby serving notice to the visiting Chinese of his undisputed official status.

In 1413, the sacrificial rites offered to Kija and Tan'gun were elevated to the same status as those dedicated to King T'aejo of Koryŏ.[32] But since Kija was enshrined on the altar on the northern side, while Tan-gun's altar was on the eastern side, the status of Kija was slightly higher than Tan'gun's. An attempt to elevate the status of Tan'gun was made during the reign of Sejong (r. 1418–50). In 1425, a decision was made to construct a shrine devoted to Tan'gun alone and it was finished in 1429. But sacrifices were also offered to Ko Chumong at this shrine.

The separation of Tan'gun's shrine from Kija's shrine was originally advocated by Chŏng Ch'ŏk (1390–1475). He contended that Tan'gun should be higher than Kija in status, for Tan'gun not only founded his state 1,230 years earlier than Kija, but in addition, unlike Kija who was enfeoffed by King Wu, he became an independent ruler. "It is absurd to enshrine Tan'gun in the Kija shrine," he remarked. "A shrine, therefore, should be built exclusively for Tan'gun."[33] He argued for the superiority of Tan'gun over Kija from the viewpoint of national independence and seniority in time.

During the reign of Sejong, meanwhile, there was a move to stress the independence of Kija from China. In 1428, for instance, the king had Pyŏn Kyeryang (1319–1430), an eminent Confucian scholar-official, write the text of an inscription to be carved on the monument to Kija. The point of the inscription is as follows: (1) Kija, one of the three eminent Shang sages, was appointed a vassal by King Wu of Chou, but he refused to serve the Chou court; (2) Kija propagated Confucian ethics for the first time by drafting the "Great Plan" for the Chou court and brought to Korea the well-field system and the Eight Injunctions, which made Korea a culturally advanced country like China.[34] He gave an interpretation of Kija as a pioneer of Confucianism and emphasized his independence from the Chou court.

A disciple of Chŏng Mongju (1337–92), usually viewed as the founder of Korean Neo-Confucianism, Pyŏn Kyeryang was one of the prominent scholars of the Chu Hsi school. For this reason, he seems to have evaluated the achievements of Kija highly as an advocate of Confucianism. But at the same time, he emphasized his independence from the Chou court. On the occasion of a debate over the matters related to the Korean king's performing sacrifices to Heaven in 1416, Pyŏn Kyeryang insisted on the validity of the rites in spite of the Confucian rule according to which the emperor of China alone was qualified to offer such ritual services. He contended that upon descending from Heaven, Tan'gun independently founded his country and the ritual offerings to Heaven had been held for over 1,000 years. "We cannot therefore abolish this time-honored ritual system," he said.[35] To him, Tan'gun as the symbol of national independence was compatible with Kija as the symbol of Confucian culture.

The independent nature of Kija was emphasized in a memorial written by the governor of P'yŏngan Province in 1428. "Kija never was a vassal of King Wu," he insisted. "His name stands for 'the viscount of the Ki state.' It is therefore contradictory to have his title on his memorial tablet read 'Kija, the marquis of Chosŏn' *(Chosŏnhu Kija)*." He proposed to replace the title "the marquis of Chosŏn" with "the great Shang teacher" *(Ŭn t'aesa)* and to add to it other honorific titles.[36] A similar opinion regarding Kija's title was voiced in the same year by Sin Sang (1372–1435), Minister of Rites.[37]

Eventually, in 1430, the old title written on his memorial tablet was replaced by a new one reading "Kija, the founder of Later Chosŏn" *(Hu Chosŏn sijo Kija)*.[38] The independent nature of Kija was officially acknowledged with the elevation of his status from that of marquis to patriarch. At the same time, the title of Tan'gun reading *"Chosŏnhu Tan'gun chi wi"* (Tan'gun, the marquis of Chosŏn) was replaced by *"Chosŏn Tan'gun"* (Tan'gun of Chosŏn), and thereby his status was also elevated.

The image of Kija in the Sejong period is reflected in the *Verse History of the Eastern Nation (Tongguk senyŏn'ga)* (1436) compiled by Kwŏn Che (1387–1445). The book deals with the history of Korea covering the period between Tan'gun Chosŏn and the end of Koryŏ. Written in verse, it is similar in content to the *Records of the Emperors and Kings (Chewang un'gi)*. The two books agree that Kija founded his state in Korea 164 years after Tan'gun went to Asadal and became a mountain god. They also agree that Kija became a vassal to King Wu after drafting the "Great Plan" for the Chou ruler.[39] The *Records of Emperors and Kings*, however, stresses that Kija became a feudal lord after founding his state in Korea, whereas the *Verse History of the Eastern Nation* indirectly denies Kija's submission to the Chou court by stating: "Kija's name is Sŏyŏ; 'Ki' is the name of his state and 'Ja' means his title."[40]

It must be noted that this view of Kija was closely related to the policy enunciated in this period, to develop the northern province with P'yŏngyang as its center. As a measure to fortify the border neighboring the Khitans, the government promoted the settlement of the northern area and established the so-called *t'ogwan* (lit., native officials) responsible for the care of new settlers in P'yŏngan Province, Hamgyŏng Province, and other northern areas.[41] Among them the one in P'yŏngyang was the largest. Memorial services held at the Kija and Tan'gun shrines in P'yŏngyang as well as those for King Tongmyŏng were supposed to boost the morale of people of the northern province.

During the Sejong period, Tan'gun and Kija were worshipped as two independent national founders. This reflects the cultural traits of this period, the pursuit of harmony between internationalism and nationalism. That is, while positively accepting Chinese culture by strengthening friendly ties with China, the government sought to enhance the spirit of national identity.

The equal status of Kija and Tan'gun was affirmed during Sejo's (r. 1455–68) reign. In 1456, Tan'gun, Kija, and Tongmyŏng were honored with new tablets. The title "Chosŏn Tan'gun" was replaced by "Chosŏn sijo Tan'gun chi wi" (Tan'gun, the founder of Chosŏn); Kija's title "HuChosŏn sijo Kija" (Kija, founder of Later Chosŏn) by a tablet inscribed "HuChosŏn sijo Kija chi wi"; and the title "Koguryŏ sijo" (the founder of Koguryŏ) by a tablet reading "Koguryŏ sijo Tongmyŏngwang chi wi" (King Tongmyŏng, the founder of Koguryŏ).[42] When he offered memorial services for Tan'gun, Kija, and Tongmyŏng in 1460, Sejo sat between the tablets of Tan'gun and Tongmyŏng and expressed his respect for King Tongymŏng by saying that "Koguryŏ was the most powerful of the Three Kingdoms in Korea."[43] Thus Tan'gun was firmly established as the prime patriarch of Korea.

Historians of Sejo's reign were represented by Yang Sŏngji (1415–82) and Kwŏn Nam (1416–65). Affiliated with the Hall of Worthies (Chiphyŏnjŏn), Yang Sŏngji was also a Confucian scholar. He won the king's confidence for his efforts to promote Confucianism and national development. He revered Kija from a Confucian point of view and took pride in Korea as a "Small China." On the other hand, he also revered Tan'gun and insisted that Korea should preserve its indigenous ways and customs. Seeing his country as a "nation extending over ten thousand *li* in width," he emphasized the national interests in the northern area, Liaotung.[44]

Kwŏn Nam was the son of Kwŏn Che, the author of the Verse History of the Eastern Nation and the History of the Koryŏ Dynasty, and the grandson of Kwŏn Kŭn, author of the Short History of the Eastern Nation. Influenced by his family traditions, he showed a great interest in history. He is known for his work, Commentaries on Ŭngje si (Ŭngje siju), commentaries on his grandfather's work. The book is not a historical work in the strict sense. It nevertheless contains new information on Korean history, including ancient anecdotes and legends. In this work, he systematized two different Tan'gun legends contained in the *Records of Emperors and Kings* and the *Remaining Records of the Three Kingdoms*. He showed some originality in his approach by stating that the four Han-Chinese colonies had been in Manchuria; he also considered the eastern and western parts of the Liao-ho River as Liao-tung, and said that the Liao-tung peninsula, not the P'yŏngyang area, was the territory of Kija.[45] His view was associated with the idea of searching for the center of ancient Korea in Manchuria, specifically in the Liao-tung peninsula. At the same time, it reflects the cultural trends of Sejo's reign. At the time Koreans thought their country was over ten thousand *li* wide, and if we examine maps of Korea made during Sejo's reign we find that Manchuria was included as part of Korean territory.

During Sejo's reign, concern centered more upon the location of Kija Chosŏn than on its cultural achievements, while the focus of interest was more on the Tan'gun myth. We need only consider Sejo's proclivity for Buddhism, Taoism, and shamanism to explain the decline of interest in Kija. Since Sejo was a usurper—he had deprived his nephew, Tanjong (r. 1452–55), of the throne—he was not in a position to justify his position on a Confucian basis. He seems to have sought to legitimize himself by brandishing the image of an ancient ruler associated with the concept of Heaven. He sought to establish a new view of his country's history by compiling *A Comprehensive Mirror of the Eastern Nation (Tongguk t'onggam)*. This work however was not completed during his reign.

An interest in Kija reemerged during the reign of King Sŏngjong (r. 1469–94). Under his policy of promoting Confucianism, he reinstated in power the *sarim*, young Neo-Confucian scholars who had been set aside during Sejo's reign. The view of Kija in this period is to be found in the *Condensed History of the Three Kingdoms (Samguksa chŏryo)* (1476) and the revised edition of *A Comprehensive Mirror of the Eastern Nation* (1485).

A chapter in the *Condensed History of the Three Kingdoms* devoted to Kija points out that : (1) King Wu of Chou gave the country of Chosŏn as a fiefdom to Kija; (2) Kija established the Eight Injunctions in the P'yŏngyang area and civilized the people; (3) The descendants of Kija once attempted to attack the state of Yen on behalf of the Chou court; (4) Kija Chosŏn suffered an attack from the army of Ch'in K'ai, a Yen general, and Mahan was founded by Ki Chun, the 41st ruler of Kija Chosŏn.[46] These accounts were taken mainly from various Chinese historical works. It must be noted that this book does not mention Kija's achievements such as the "Great Plan" and the well-field system. It, however, acknowledges that succession to Kija was inherited by Mahan. This theory of the Kija-Mahan succession first appeared in the *Remaining Records of the Three Kingdoms* by quoting from the *Memorable Events of the Wei Dynasty* and also the *Short History of the Eastern Nation* but it was conspicuously absent in the *Verse History of the Eastern Nation*. This theory heightened the importance of the historical position of Kija Chosŏn and provided the basis for the so-called "theory of legitimacy of Mahan" that emerged in the late Yi period. At any rate this work is more concerned with Kija Chosŏn's position in Korean history than Kija's own activities.

In addition to what is discussed in the *Condensed History of the Three Kingdoms*, *A Comprehensive Mirror of the Eastern Nation* contains information on Kija: (1) Before coming to Korea, Kija was a relative of the tyrant Chou, the last ruler of the Shang dynasty. As Chou grew outrageous, however, Kija rebelled against him. He then came to Korea after presenting the Nine Divisions of the Great Plan to King Wu and became his vassal. (2) Kija brought to Korea some 5,000 Chinese and taught Chinese literature, etiquette, music, arts, and the five moral relations to Koreans. He also taught the Eight Injunctions and promoted the concepts of faith, loyalty, righteousness and Confucian ethics. (3) Kija rejected warfare and tyranny and upheld rule by virtue. As a result, Korean culture and institutions became the same as those of China and Koreans came to respect literature, humanity, and righteousness.[47]

The image of Kija portrayed in *A Comprehensive Mirror of the Eastern Nation* was similar—Kija was a man of integrity who refused to remain loyal to a tyrant like Chou, and he made Korea a Confucian country like China. During Sejong's period Kija's disloyalty to King Wu and his spirit of independence had been stressed, but during Sŏngjong's period the emphasis was placed on his protest against the tyranny of King Chou and his spirit of righteousness.

Why did *A Comprehensive Mirror of the Eastern Nation* suddenly emphasize Kija's sense of righteousness? One reason is that the book was written with reference to materials contained in classics like the *Record of the Grand Historian* and *Han hsü Tzu*. But we must consider the political and ideological background of the book. That is, the so-called *sarim* scholars, who greatly valued the moral concept of righteousness and loyalty under the influence of Neo-Confucianism,[48] also participated in the compilation of the book. The *sarim* scholar-officials were disciples of Kim Chongjik (1431–92) who regarded themselves as the heirs of the school of Chŏng Mongju, the eminent Neo-Confucian loyalist who died for the Koryŏ dynasty opposing the foundation of the new dynasty. They were critical of King Sejo, who usurped the throne from his nephew, and were sympathetic with the six loyalists who were killed while attempting to reinstate Tanjong, the boy king who had been forced to abdicate. Their loyalty to moral principle and renewed interest in Kija as a man of integrity and righteousness was a form of criticism of Sejo and his supporters, the so-called *hun'gu p'a*, who helped him to take the throne by force (according to a rather well-founded view in Confucian scholarship). This *sarim* attack on the *hun'gu* was consonant with King Sŏngjong's plan to strengthen his power by controlling the *hun'gu*.

Since A *Comprehensive Mirror of the Eastern Nation* was compiled jointly by *hun'gu* officials and *sarim* scholars, it did not reflect the viewpoint of the *sarim* group alone. But when one compares it to the *Short History of the Three Kingdoms*, which, as might be expected of a book written exclusively by members of the *hun'gu p'a*, does not mention Kija's rebellion against the tyrant Chou, one immediately feels the influence of the *sarim* point of view. In this sense, A *Comprehensive Mirror of the Eastern Nation* reflects a transition in historiography between the period during which the *hun'gu* were in control and the period dominated by the *sarim*. As this work represents the most influential official historiography of the early Yi period, the exalted position that Kija and Kija Chosŏn were accorded in it paved the way for the Kija-centered historiography that was to emerge in the seventeenth and eighteenth centuries.

4. THE *SARIM*'S UNDERSTANDING OF KIJA DURING THE SIXTEENTH CENTURY

The conflict between the idealist Confucian *sarim* scholars and realist *hun'gu* group grew more intense during the sixteenth century, the period between the reigns of Yŏnsan'gun (r. 1494–1506) and Sŏnjo (r. 1567–1608), in which scholar-officials of the *sarim* were continually purged by the *hun'gu* group in power. The *sarim* group, however, did come to power toward the end of the sixteenth century.

Unlike the *hun'gu* group of the fifteenth century, the *hun'gu* group of the sixteenth century showed little interest in history. On the other hand, the *sarim* scholars produced various historical works. The two most representative works of the first half of the sixteenth century are the *Short History of the Eastern Nation (Tongguk saryak)* written by Pak Sang (1474–1530) and the *Topical Short History of the Eastern Nation (P'yoje ŭmju Tongguk saryak)* by Yu Hŭiryŏng (1480–1552). Neither of these works was officially sponsored, however, and the historiographical views represented in them were those of private scholars. Consequently, the Kija images presented in them differed from the official version in the inscription written by Pyŏn Kyeryang in 1428.[49] Except in carrying out sacrifices to the Kija shrine according to the prescribed manner, the Yi court paid little attention to Kija in this period. After devoting a chapter to Tan'gun, the *Short History of the Eastern Nation* describes Kija. It states that Kija was enfeoffed by King Wu after coming to Korea with 5,000 Chinese, that he taught the people decorum, morality, farming, and sericulture and promulgated the Eight Injunctions, and that he transformed the people through the rule of benevolence and wisdom. It refers neither to Kija's alleged rebellion against King Chou of the Shang dynasty nor to his supposed lecture to King Wu of the Chou dynasty on the Great Plan. What it presents as the most important accomplishment of Kija is that he transformed the people through the rule of benevolence and wisdom.[50] This emphasis can perhaps be explained by the fact that the author was a member of the *sarim* group from the Kiho region. Unlike the Yŏngnam group, which stressed loyalty above all else, the Kiho group regarded the political realization of the Kingly Way *(wangdo)* as the primary task of Confucians. That the *Short History of the Eastern Nation* portrayed Kija as someone who realized the culture of benevolence and wisdom seems to reflect this commitment to the Kingly Way.

The *Topical Short History of the Eastern Nation* repeats the same description of Kija as that contained in the *Short History of the Eastern Nation* but it adds more information. In fact, divided into seven topical headings, its description of Kija is the most detailed up to that time. After following the same views on Kija's arrival in the east and his accomplishments in Korea as the *Short History of the Eastern Nation*, it adds that the people were so overjoyed that they compared the Taedong River (which flows through P'yŏngyang) to the Yellow River and composed a song in his praise.[51] The additional information includes an analysis of Kija's name, his successful adoption of the well-field system, the location of his tomb, his lament on the fall of the Shang dynasty, a description of several of Kija's descendants' rules, and the assertion that King Chun, the last ruler of the Kija Chosŏn dynasty, established the new state of Pyŏnhan in the south.

The main focus on Kija in this work is upon his activities in Korea. It also tries to portray Kija and his descendants as politically independent from China. It acknowledges that Kija was enfeoffed by King Wu but it stresses that it happened after Kija had fled China of his own will. As for Kija's descendants, it omits the customary term for them, rejecting the concept that Kija Chosŏn was a vassal state to China. Moreover, the phrase "the costumes and clothes and the system [of Korea] became the same as [those in] China," which appeared in the *Short History of the Eastern Nation*, is conspicuously absent. Yu Hŭiryŏng's portrayal of Kija should be understood in the context of his historical view of Korea as politically independent and culturally distinct. He pays a great deal of attention to Tan'gun Chosŏn. In discussing the Three Kingdoms' period, he places Koguryŏ before Silla, departing from the Silla-centered historiographical tradition which had been accepted since the *Historical Records of the Three Kingdoms*.[52] Yu's views might have been influenced by the tradition of his family, whose ancestor had been a meritorious minister of King Sejo. They may, however, just as well reflect the emerging intellectual trends of the mid-sixteenth century, which tended to place Kija in the context of independent Korean history.

Perhaps as the result of stabilized diplomatic relations with China on the one hand and a deepening understanding of Neo-Confucianism on the other, the *sarim* scholars displayed a heightened interest in Kija in the latter half of the sixteenth century. *The Records on Kija (Kijaji)* compiled by Yun Tusu (1533–1601) in 1580 was a collection of source materials on Kija and it was to be used as a reference on the question of Kija to prepare diplomats for dealings with China. On his trip to China as a member of an ambassadorial entourage in 1577, Yun was asked many questions concerning Kija by the Chinese but he was unable to answer them satisfactorily. This is said to have been his motive for compiling the *Records on Kija*.[53] In any case, Yun Tusu gathered information and references from all the available sources—the classics, historical works, private collected works, and poems, both Chinese and Korean—and arranged them under nine categories.

Thorough as the *Records on Kija* was in collecting materials on Kija, it was basically a reference book and thus it did not express a unifying historiographical view of the author. Moreover, arranged according to classifications of the genre of the original sources, rather than chronologically, it was difficult for readers to formulate a coherent image of Kija. Yi Yulgok (1536–84) wrote the *Real Records of Kija (Kija silgi)* to remedy these disadvantages.[54] Written in the year of publication of the *Records on Kija*, the *Real Records of Kija* draws its material from the *Records on Kija*, and it shows that Yulgok had access to it prior to its publication. Unlike the *Records on Kija*, however, Yulgok arranges pertinent information on Kija and Kija Chosŏn in chronological order.

The *Real Records of Kija* begins with a description of Kija prior to his departure from China. He was a member of the Shang royal house and held the office of Great Teacher. But Kija was imprisoned and enslaved as a result of his admonishment of King Chou for licentiousness and tyranny. After King Wu of the Chou dynasty destroyed the Shang dynasty, he released Kija from prison and visited him in person. First King Wu explained to Kija why he had to destroy the Shang and kill King Chou and he asked his opinion as to whether what he did was the right thing. Kija did not answer. Upon being asked how to rule in accordance with the Way of Heaven (*ch'ŏndo*), however, Kija explained to King Wu the Nine Divisions of the Great Plan. Moreover, he emphasized impartiality as the most important quality for the ruler to pursue in order to govern according to the Kingly Way.[55]

Then Yulgok clarifies the relationship of Kija to King Wu. Kija preferred not to serve under King Wu, who also saw that it was not wise to force him to do so. In order to avoid living in China, Kija came to Korea. Upon hearing of this, King Wu enfeoffed him.[56] In other words, Kija is presented as a feudal lord who declared his independence of King Wu. Here Yulgok is clearly rejecting the theory that Kija served King Wu.

As for the Kija's accomplishments in Korea, Yulgok lists such things as instruction in decorum, farming, sericulture, and the well-field system, promulgation of the Eight Injunctions, etc. As a result, Confucian ways became widespread in Korea, Korean clothes and customs became the same as those of China and, transformed by the rule of benevolence and wisdom, Korea became a country of high culture and civilization. The people's admiration of Kija and Kija's sadness over the fall of the Shang were also mentioned.

In assessing the history of Kija Chosŏn, Yulgok more or less adopts

the views presented in A *Mirror of the Eastern Nation*. The only departure was that Yulgok used *hyung* (an honorific term meaning "to die,"
reserved for rulers) for all the descendants of Kija, a gesture of the highest
respect.

Perhaps Yulgok's view of Kija is best summarized in his concluding
comments *(ch'an)*. He surmises that the Korean people had existed since
time immemorial, certainly as long as the Chinese. He also accepts Tan-
gun as the first Korean sagely ruler but he concludes that, due to paucity
of records, nothing can be ascertained about his rule. Then he attributes
to Kija a high level of Korean civilization and culture, which, in his view,
was as high as that of China. It was Kija who transformed Korea into a
state equivalent to Lu (Confucius' home state) and Ch'i (Mencius' state).
Kija transmitted the Great Plan to King Wu in China and established
civilized customs and life in Korea. His descendants ruled the country for
a thousand years, upholding his teachings. This definitively shows that
Kija was a great sage. But the people of Ch'i know only Kuan Tzu and
Yen Tzu, which shows their limited outlook, while the Shantung Confucians only pursue the hidden truth of Confucius, and the scholars of
the Loyang and Fukien schools hold only to the Ch'eng and Chu teachings respectively. Perhaps this is inevitable. Koreans, on the other hand,
are so deeply indebted to Kija that they should not only praise him but
make every effort to become more familiar with all of his accomplishments.[57]

Yulgok is clearly stating that Kija was as great a sage to the Koreans
as Kuan Tzu, Yen Tzu, Confucius, the Ch'eng brothers, or Chu Hsi
were to the Chinese. But this respect was due to him not as a politician
or a founder of a dynasty but as a sage who practiced the Kingly Way. It
should be noted that Yulgok put Kija's relationship to King Wu of the
Chou dynasty in a cultural context through his transmission of the Great
Plan, while he made him politically a Shang loyalist.

Yulgok's view of Kija as the originator of government by the Kingly
Way in Korea was already expressed in his *Questions and Answers at the
Eastern Lake (Tongho mundap)*.[58] This was written eleven years prior to
the *Real Record of Kija*. In the *Real Record of Kija*, this idea was developed in more specific detail. Yulgok defines the ideological basis of Kija's
Kingly Way in the Great Plan and illustrates his practical accomplishments with the promulgation of the Eight Injunctions, the well-field system, etc. In Yulgok's philosophy of the Kingly Way, Kija, as its origina-

tor in Korea, became the great sage whose stature equalled that of
Confucius, Mencius, the Ch'eng brothers, and Chu Hsi.

CONCLUSION

I have discussed the changes which the image of Kija underwent from
the Koguryŏ period, when he was worshipped as an ancestral deity, to the
sixteenth century, when he was presented as a great Confucian sage in
Korea. These changes were partly due to the differing sources, mostly
Chinese in origin, available in each period. How one interpreted and ac-
commodated the various oral and folk traditions surrounding Kija which
had sprung up in Korea had much influence on how one viewed him.
The major factor, however, which accounted for the changing images of
Kija was how the historical and cultural consciousness of each era was
reflected in the way available sources were interpreted. Generally speaking, depending on the political and intellectual inclinations of the author
and his period, Kija was projected as a symbol of either political independence or subservience to China, on the one hand, and as a symbol of
either cultural distinctiveness or uniformity with China on the other. In
Yulgok, however, Kija became the ultimate cultural hero who raised the
level of Korean culture to that of Chinese culture by the standard of the
universal norm of benevolence and wisdom. He further came to symbolize a person of the highest political integrity and independence, who
nevertheless maintained a polite relationship with China.

NOTES

1. Hong Yŏha, in his book *Tongguk t'onggam chegang* (1672), recognized for the first time Kija Chosŏn as first in the chronological series of legitimate states in Korean history. In the *Tongsa kangmok* (1778), An Chŏngbok followed suit. Both Hong and An belonged to the Namin faction (Southerners). See Yi Usŏng, "Ijo hugi Kŭn'gi hakp'a e issŏsŏ ŭi chŏngt'ongnon ŭi chŏngae" (Development of the Historical Concept of Legitimacy among the Kŭn'gi School in the Late Yi Period), *Yŏksa hakpo* (1966) 31:174–79.
2. See Han Young-woo, "Hanmal ŭi Sin Ch'aeho ŭi yŏksa insik" (Sin Ch'aeho's View on History at the End of Yi Dynasty), in *Tanjae Sin Ch'aeho wa minjok sagwan* (Seoul: Hyŏngsŏl ch'ulp'ansa, 1980), pp. 152–54.
3. One of the most nationalistic works produced in this period is *Tan'gi kosa* (Ch'ŏngju: Sanggo munhwasa, 1907). This work denies the theory of Kija's migration to the east and insists that the Kija who founded Kija Chosŏn was Tan'gun's descendant. Ch'oe Namsŏn, An Chaehong, and Chŏng Inbo also followed this line.
4. Yi Pyŏngdo was the first historian who put forth this hypothesis. He conjectured that Kija Chosŏn was in fact a Korean dynasty ruled by the Han family line. See Yi Pyŏngdo, *Han'guk kodaesa yŏn'gu* (Seoul: Pagyŏngsa, 1976).
5. Ch'ŏn Kwanu, "Kija ko" (On Kija) in *Tongbang hakchi* (1974), 15:1–72.
6. Kim Chŏngbae, *Han'guk minjok munhwa ŭi kiwŏn* (Seoul: Korea University Press, 1973).
7. For a study of changing images of Kija from the Koryŏ dynasty to the end of the Yi dynasty, see Pak Kwangyong, "Kija Chosŏn e taehan insik ŭi pyŏnch'ŏn" (The Changing Images of Kija Chosŏn) in *Han'guk saron* (1980) 6:252–96.
8. *Chiu-T'ang-shu*, in *Chōsenshi* (Keijo: Chosēn sōtokufu, 1933), 1(3):132.
9. *Koryŏsa* (Seoul: Yŏnsei taehakkyo tongbanghak yŏn'guso, 1960), 2:3b.
10. *Ibid.*, 63:22b–23a.
11. *Koryŏsa chŏryo* (Seoul: Tongguk munhwasa, 1960), 6:29a–b (p. 153).
12. Kang Man'gil, "Yijo sidae ŭi Tan'gun sungbae" (Tan'gun Worship During the Yi Dynasty) in *Yi Hongjik paksa hoegap kinyŏm Han'guksa nonch'ong* (Seoul: Sin'gu munhwasa, 1969), p. 260.
13. Kim Pusik, *Samguk sagi* (Seoul: Minjok munhwa ch'ujin wiwŏnhoe, 1973), p. 206.
14. *Ibid.*, p. 292. Quotation is from the *T'ang-shu* in *Chōsenshi*, 1(3):171.
15. *Samguk sagi*, p. 171.
16. *Ibid.*
17. The portrayal of Kija in the *Historical Records of the Three Kingdoms* was based on the sources selected from the *Old T'ang History* (*Chiu-T'ang-shu*), the *New T'ang History* (*Hsin-T'ang-shu*), the *History of the Former Han Dynasty* (*Ch'ien-Han-shu*), the *History of the Later Han Dynasty*, and the *Rec-*

ords of the Grand Historian. The information on Kija in these works is not necessarily consistent.

18. Yi Kyubo's *Tongmyŏngwang p'yŏn*, written in 1193, is the representative work which reflects nationalistic sentiment during the reign of the military officials. See Yi Usŏng, "Koryŏ chunggi ŭi minjok sŏsasi—*Tongmyŏngwang p'yŏn* kwa *Chewang un'gi* ŭi yŏn'gu" (Nationalistic Epics Written in the Middle of the Koryŏ Dynasty—A study of *Tongmyŏngwang p'yŏn* and *Chewang un'gi*) in *Han'guk ŭi yŏksa insik* (Seoul: Ch'angjak kwa pip'yŏngsa, 1976), pp. 148–90.

19. *Koryŏsa*, 21:8a–b.

20. *Samguk yusa* (Seoul: Minjok munkwa ch'ujin wiwŏnhoe, 1973), Kii Ko-Chosŏn 1:2a–b, Mahan 1:4a.

21. Nationalist historians like Sin Ch'aeho and Ch'oe Namsŏn pointed out that the *Samguk sagi* and the *Samguk yusa* were Silla-centered history books. Recently Professor Kim Ch'ŏlchun presented a similar argument. Dr. Koh Byong-ik, however, argues that these popular views were incorrect. See his article, "*Samguk sagi* ŭi yŏksa sŏsul" (Historiography of *Samguk sagi*) in *Han'guk ŭi Yŏksa insik*, pp. 31–63.

22. *Chewang un'gi* (Seoul: Chosŏn kojŏn kanhaenghoe, 1939), *Tongguk kaeguk yŏndae, ha*:2b.

23. *T'aejo sillok* (Seoul: Kuksa p'yŏnch'an wiwŏnhoe, 1955), 1:51b.

24. *Ibid.*, 3:3b.

25. *Sambongjip* (Collected Writings of Chŏng Tojŏn) (Seoul: Kuksa p'yŏnch'an wiwŏnhoe, 1961), p. 205.

26. Han Young-woo, *Chŏng Tojŏn sasang ŭi yŏn'gu* (A Study of the Thought of Chŏng Tojŏn) (Seoul: Seoul taehakkyo ch'ulp'ansa, 1978), p. 277.

27. *T'aejong sillok*, 9:25b.

28. See Pak Wŏnho, "Myŏngch'o Chosŏn ŭi Yodong kongbŏl kwa p'yojŏn munje" (The Yi Court's Planned Conquest of Liao-tung Peninsula and the Problems of Diplomatic Documents Between the Yi and Ming Courts in the Early Ming Dynasty) in *Paeksan hakpo* (1975) 19:105–36.

29. *T'aejong sillok*, 24:3b.

30. *Ibid.*, 23:38b.

31. See Chŏng Kubok, "*Tongguk saryak* e taehan sahaksajŏk koch'al (A Historiographical Inquiry into the *Short History of the Eastern Nation*) in *Yŏksa hakpo* (1975), 68:12–4.

32. *T'aejong sillok*, 26:36a–b.

33. *Sejong sillok*, 29:29a–b.

34. *Sejong sillok*, 40:7b–8a.

35. *T'aejong sillok*, 31:44a–45b.

36. *Sejong sillok*, 41:9a–b.

37. *Ibid.*, 41:15b.

38. *Ibid.*, 48:3b, 49:13a.

39. Han Young-woo, *Chosŏn chŏn'gi sahaksa yŏn'gu* (A Study on Historiography

of the Early Yi Dynasty) (Seoul: Seoul taehakkyo ch'ulp'anbu, 1981), pp. 36–39.

40. *Yŏktae senyŏn'ga* (Seoul: Kyujanggak 5, 1981), *Tongguk senyŏn'ga*, 1:1a.
41. Yi Chaeryong, "Chosŏn ch'ogi ŭi t'ogwan e taehayŏ" (On the Native Officials of the Early Yi Dynasty) in *Chindan hakpo* (1966), 29/30:117–28.
42. Kang Man'gil (see note 12), pp. 255–56.
43. *Sejo sillok*, 22:10b.
44. See Han Young-woo, *Chosŏn chŏn'gi sahoe sasang yŏn'gu* (Social Thought of the Early Yi Dynasty) (Seoul: Jisik sanŏpsa, 1983), pp. 161–228.
45. Han, *Sahaksa yŏn'gu*, pp. 53–59.
46. *Samguksa chŏryo* (Seoul: Asea munhwasa, 1973), pp. 11–12.
47. Han, *Sahaksa yŏn'gu*, pp. 188–89.
48. *Tongguk t'onggam* was jointly compiled by both *hun'gu* and *sarim* officials. While Sŏ Kŏjŏng, Yi Kŭkton, and Chŏng Hyohang belonged to the former, P'yo Yŏnmal, Ch'oe Po, and Yu Inhong, three students of Kim Chongjik, were members of the latter.
49. *Myŏngjong sillok*, 28:12b.
50. See Han, *Sahaksa yŏn'gu*, pp. 225–37.
51. *P'yoje ŭmju Tongguk saryak* (Sŏngam mun'go, private collection), *kwŏn* 1.
52. See Han, *Sahaksa yŏn'gu*, pp. 238–50.
53. *Kija silgi* in *Yulgok chŏnsŏ* (Seoul: Taedong munhwa yŏn'guwŏn, 1971), *pp.* 290–92.
54. *Ibid.*, p. 292.
55. *Ibid.*, p. 290.
56. *Ibid.*
57. *Ibid.*, p. 291.
58. *Tongho mundap*, in *Yulgok chŏnsŏ*, 15:9b (1:317).

Martina Deuchler

Reject the False
and Uphold the Straight:
Attitudes Toward
Heterodox Thought
in Early Yi Korea

THE FOUNDING OF the Yi dynasty in 1392 ended the mutual tolerance between Confucianism and Buddhism that had been characteristic
during the Koryŏ period (935–1392). With a holistic conception of their
mission, the Neo-Confucian scholar-officials began to claim, beyond the
traditionally Confucian domain of state affairs, authority over the spiri-
tual-religious sphere of life hitherto monopolized by the Buddhists. Conflict between Confucianism and Buddhism, therefore, was inevitable.[1]

In his sharply formulated polemics against Buddhism, one of the intellectual founders of the new dynasty, Chŏng Tojŏn (1342–98), put this
confrontation in words and introduced into Korea for the first time the
concept of "heterodox thought" *(idan)*.[2] He thus took up the Confucian
tradition of drawing a clear distinction between "right learning" *(chŏnghak)* and "aberrant concepts" *(idan)*, begun by Confucius (551–479 B.C.)
and strengthened by Mencius (371–289 B.C.).[3] At the same time Chŏng's
colleague, Kwŏn Kŭn (1352–1409), prepared the ground for Confucians
to assert themselves in spiritual matters. In his *Diagrammatic Treatise for
Entering upon Learning (Iphak tosŏl)*, Kwŏn presented a sweeping picture of the interconnection between the realm of Heaven and the realm
of human affairs and opened up a religious dimension by affirming the
immortality of man through his descendants.[4]

The characterization of the difference between Confucianism and
Buddhism remained a pervasive theme. An interesting example is pro-

vided by the Confucian scholar, Kim Koengp'il (1454–1504). Kim stated: "The ways of Confucianism and Buddhism are not the same; their literature is not the same; their laws are not the same; their behavior is not the same." After discussing each assertion in detail, Kim pointed to the most decisive difference between the two creeds: the difference in their respective understanding of self. The Confucian self, if properly developed, casts off its selfishness and becomes public-oriented. Because it is rational by nature, it can be disciplined and polished by scholarship. In contrast, the Buddhist self is fixed on "nothingness" and thus, lacking rationality, falls into selfishness. It was obvious for Kim that Confucianism had to be pursued as "right" *(chŏng)* and "straight" *(chik)* and Buddhism had to be rejected as "false" *(sa)* and "crooked" *(kok)*.[5]

Intellectually, then, the Yi dynasty started on quite a different note from the Ming (1368–1644) a few decades earlier.[6] From the beginning the Neo-Confucians were in control and fully committed to transforming Korea into a Confucian state in which the legacy of Sung (960–1279) Neo-Confucianism would be properly preserved. The development of Neo-Confucian orthodoxy *(chŏnghak)* gained momentum through its contest with heterodoxy *(idan)*. First used to denote the Buddhist challenge, "heterodox thought" came to include certain tendencies within Confucianism as well. The intensification this term underwent over time reflects the growing intolerance of the guardians of orthodoxy to intellectual diversity.[7] A study of this process thus throws light upon the nature of Korean Neo-Confucianism.

THE FORMATION OF A CONFUCIAN SELF-IMAGE

Neo-Confucian orthodoxy in Korea developed in relative isolation. Despite the frequent exchange of embassies, political issues clouded the early Ming-Yi relations, and consequently the intellectual interaction between the two countries was not as intensive as it had been between Yüan and Koryŏ. The early Ming emperors deigned to send to Korea their official versions of Neo-Confucian orthodoxy, the complete collected commentaries on the Five Classics and the Four Books by Chu Hsi (1130–1200) and other Sung Confucians, and the monumental compendium of Sung philosophy, the *Hsing-li ta-ch'üan*. They refused, however, to grant the Korean request of 1433 to send Korean students to China to study at the very source of orthodoxy.[8] Unofficially, editions of the works of Chu Hsi's successors of the late Sung, Yüan, and early Ming found their way into the hands of the Korean scholars. It was an immensely taxing task for the Koreans to find their way through the complexities of this literature without direct Chinese assistance and to establish their own point of view.

The creation of the Korean version of Neo-Confucian orthodoxy was therefore a long and complicated process.[9] This process, extending from the beginning of the dynasty to the last decades of the sixteenth century, was difficult because of the different demands that had to be satisfied by the new creed. As the political philosophy of the dynastic founders, the practical aspects of Neo-Confucianism—one spoke of "substantial learning" (sirhak)—were emphasized and utilized for the building of a Confucian state and society. Concomitantly, the Neo-Confucian canon became the foundation of the civil service examination system. The idealistic components of Neo-Confucian thought, the cultivation of self and the moral education of men, although centering on the individual, were equally put to the service of the state. The early Yi strategists were thus heirs to both traditions of Sung thought: the reformist activism and the call for seeking sagehood. The welding of these two elements into one harmonious pattern provided the formation of the Korean Neo-Confucian orthodoxy with its inner momentum. The double responsibility to scholarship and to government service put enormous demands on scholar-bureaurats, and the history of Korean Neo-Confucian orthodoxy reflects the tumultuous course of events at the beginning of the dynasty.

The full commitment to the heritage of the Ch'eng-Chu school became the basis of Yi Confucianism, and the Koreans eventually came to see themselves as the natural guardians of this tradition.[10] This nascent self-image is clearly reflected, for example, in the statements of Ch'oe Pu (1454–1504), a Korean official who was shipwrecked on the Chinese coast in 1487 on his way back from Chejudo. Ch'oe said to his Chinese interrogators, "Our Chosŏn, now, has exposed heresies and respects the Confucian Way." Or, "The gentlemen of my country consider study of the classics and the probing of principles to be their concern." Or, "My country respects the Confucian practices. . . . There are Buddhists, but people do not esteem them. There is no Taoism."[11] These pronouncements have a tone of self-righteousness and pride that remained audible even later.

The Yi Koreans were conscious of the fact that they derived their Confucianism directly from the Sung sources—without the intermediation of the Ming. Although the Confucians of the sixteenth century had to admit that their contemporary social and political situation did not fully correspond to the ideal order as described in the classics, they explained such discrepancies in terms of local and timely variability sanctioned by Neo-Confucian doctrine. They were ready to grant the same allowance to the Ming Chinese.[12] They did not, however, tolerate deviations from the scriptural basis of the Ch'eng-Chu school. It is a remarkable circumstance that the deepened knowledge of the "learning of principle" *(ihak)* on the one hand provided the Koreans with a heightened awareness of their own national identity—making them distinctly non-Chinese—and on the other hand encouraged them to adhere to the minutiae of the orthodox Sung tradition—making them suspicious of philosophical developments in Ming China.

ADVANCES INTO NEW INTELLECTUAL TERRITORY

The political events at the end of the fifteenth and the beginning of the sixteenth centuries—the literati purges of 1498, 1504, and 1519—seriously disrupted but did not permanently halt the development of the "learning of principle." While Cho Kwangjo's (1482–1519) concerns were still primarily centered on problems of state and rulership, Confucian thought eventually began to detach itself from daily political and social affairs and turn to the investigation of the metaphysical components of Neo-Confucian philosophy. This change of direction, perhaps partly accelerated by a sense of political failure, did not, however, signal a general abandonment of worldly affairs. Rather, it indicated an increased familiarity with the intricacies of the Ch'eng-Chu tradition and a maturing understanding of fundamental Neo-Confucian concepts—the first outlines of which had been staked out at the very beginning of the dynasty by such outstanding scholars as Chŏng Tojŏn and Kwŏn Kŭn.

A first representative example of this new trend was the *Sŏngniyŏnwŏn ch'waryo* (Selected Source Materials on Nature and Principle) by Yu Sungjo (1452–1512). Yu submitted it with his work on the *Great Learning*, the *Taehak samgang p'almok cham* (Admonitions on the Three Main Points and Eight Items of the *Ta-hsüeh*), to royal inspection in 1511. The *Sŏngniyŏnwŏn ch'waryo* is a compilation of quotations from the classics and from pertinent commentaries by Chu Hsi, scholars of the immediate post-Chu era such as Ch'en Ch'un (1153–1217) and Chen Te-hsiu (1178–1235), and scholars of the Yüan period such as Ch'eng Fu-hsin (1257–1340). Yu opened his work by presenting definitions of key Neo-Confucian concepts (a lengthy initial part is devoted to the Great Ultimate), briefly dealt with Buddhism, Taoism, and the two "villains," Yang Chu and Mo Ti, and then launched himself on the topic obviously closest to his interests: human nature (sŏng). Yu's works were the result of his reputed erudition and did not reflect particular originality, but they nevertheless designated the two areas in which research was intense and debate heated throughout the sixteenth century and beyond: the strategies of the *Great Learning* and the question of human nature.[13]

The vitality of this unprecedented take-off into hitherto unexplored areas of classical scholarship and philosophical speculation is evidenced by the appearance of a number of discourses that explored transmitted Neo-Confucian wisdom and, by placing willful accents and adding unconventional ideas, at times provided fresh insights and interpretations.

A representative of this new preoccupation with the "learning of principle" was Pak Yŏng (1471–1540). Although of military background, Pak reportedly was well versed in the classics and history. "There was no book he had not read." He also had such intimate knowledge of the "learning of principle" that "the people of his time submitted [to his authority]." Despite the respect he paid to Confucius and Mencius and to Neo-Confucian scholarship he seems to have been primarily concerned with finding in himself (chadŭk) the right approach to true learning. He arranged the contents of the *Great Learning* in two charts that center on "rectifying the mind-and-heart" (chŏngsim). This is the link between knowledge and action. Knowledge, Pak thought, derives from "the effort (kongbu) in the mind itself" and is thus the sum of such mental activities as the investigation of things, the extension of knowledge, and the making sincere of one's thoughts. This knowledge is the basis of action that is in fact the direct outcome of the rectification of the mind. Pak thus postulated, on the authority of the *Great Learning*, an intimate relationship between knowledge and action and the moral mind. He stated: "Outside the mind there is no principle; outside principle there are no affairs (sa). Knowledge is lodged in myself and principle in things. Therefore the investigation of things is identical with the extension of knowledge, and knowledge means the spiritual substance of the mind." Pak seems to have given a special activist twist to the problem of knowledge and action and revealed an independence of mind that made him suspect to scholars of later generations.[14]

Pak's slightly younger contemporary, Sŏ Kyŏngdok (1489–1546), advanced, with his fascination for cosmogony, to purely speculative realms. Turning his back upon the political world and hiding away in a small place near Kaesŏng, Sŏ was especially attracted by Chang Tsai's (1020–77) concept of the "Great Void" *(T'aehŏ)*. In a few short treatises he set out his own bold ideas about the genesis of the universe and the function of material force *(ki)* in this process. He differentiated between two stages of the universe: the one prior to the process of creation *(sŏnch'ŏn)*, characterized by its total emptiness and shapelessness, and the one after the creational process sets in *(huch'ŏn)*. Sŏ maintained that creation is initiated by material force; principle *(i)* that cannot exist outside material force fulfills the supportive role of guide. With the mind of a natural scientist, Sŏ's foremost interest was in the workings of material force; he paid no attention to the moral dimensions of the dichotomy of principle and material force and its implications for human nature. This inclination was apparently visible early on. When, at the age of eighteen, Sŏ read about "the extension of knowledge through the investigation of things," he reportedly exclaimed with indignation: "To read books without first investigating things, of what use can this be for learning?" He then wrote the names of all "the ten thousand things between Heaven and Earth" on his walls and absorbed himself daily in investigating them. Perhaps because of his dislike of bookish learning, Sŏ's philosophical works are few, but even his later critics could not deny his originality of mind.[15]

The most versatile and comprehensive scholar active during the first half of the sixteenth century was Yi Ŏnjŏk (1491–1553). In contrast to Sŏ Kyŏngdok, Yi had a long, if stormy, official career and left a copious oeuvre. His interests ranged from the nature of the Great Ultimate—expressed in his correspondence with Cho Hanbo on this subject—to classical scholarship. He labored over textual problems of the *Great Learning*, elaborated on the nine rules governing state and society as outlined in chapter 20 of the *Mean* in his *Chungyong kugyŏng yŏnŭi* (Extended Meaning of the Nine Rules of the *Chung-yung*), and in his *Kuillok* (Record in Search of Humaneness) collected and commented upon quotations on the theme of humaneness *(in)*. The scope of Yi's scholarship became the platform from which later scholars took off.[16]

Pak Yŏng, Sŏ Kyŏngdŏk, and Yi Ŏnjŏk advanced, each in his own

way, Neo-Confucian scholarship in Korea during the first half of the sixteenth century. They pursued their interests in a remarkable spirit of independence and thus often deviated from conventional interpretations.
Although their inquiries did not focus on a common theme, the problem
of human nature and humaneness seems to have been—perhaps with the
exception of Sŏ Kyŏngdŏk—uppermost in their minds. The subsequent
evaluation of their contributions to the learning of principle became part
of the process of defining the Korean version of Confucian orthodoxy.

THE INFILTRATION OF ALTERNATIVE THOUGHT

The advances of scholarship just described were the result of the intellectual challenge inherent in the Neo-Confucian philosophy; they were not
motivated by fresh impulses received from contemporary Ming China.
During the first half of the sixteenth century there were frequent com-
plaints about the lack of books, and at the very end of 1514 the Chon-
gyŏnggak, the library of the Royal Confucian College (Sŏnggyun'gwan),
caught fire, a catastrophe that was interpreted as a sign from Heaven
warning against the low literati mores and the unsophisticated state of
classical scholarship in Korea. The books that could not be replaced from
Korean sources, it was urged, should be purchased again in Peking.[17]

The purchase of books by Koreans in Peking, however, was not easy.
Some differences between Chinese officials and Korean embassy members in the early 1520s had led the Chinese to guard the gates of Jade
River House (Yü-ho kuan), the Korean headquarters in Peking, so that
the Koreans were unable to move around freely and browse through the
markets for books.[18] Although this ban was lifted in 1537, the acquisition
of books continued to depend on gifts of the Chinese government and on
random purchases made by the Koreans. In 1533, for example, the career
official So Seyang (1486–1562) was ordered to buy books during his mission to the Ming capital. He came home with some classic literature and
a collection of Chu Hsi's poetry.[19]

By 1541, the collecting of books had become such a critical issue
that the problem was discussed in the highest government circles. It was
decided that book buying could no longer be left to the discretion of sub-
altern officials, and the eminent scholar-official, Kim An'guk (1478–1543),
was directed to prepare a purchasing list. On the basis of Chinese biblio-

graphical works, Kim discovered that the Korean holdings were very incomplete and recommended that works dealing with classical scholarship
and Neo-Confucianism *(isŏ)* be given priority. He also put the titles of
some Yüan and Ming works on his list. When he returned from Peking
in 1542, Kim brought back a wide selection of Chinese books he recommended for printing in Korea.[20]

Despite the tenuous communications between Yi Korea and Ming
China, information about developments outside the Ch'eng-Chu school
and about the contemporary Chinese intellectual scene eventually began
to be discussed inside and outside the Korean government. There is no
evidence to determine the exact dates when the works of such alternative
Confucian thinkers as Chu Hsi's rival, Lu Hsiang-shan (1139–93), and
Lu's Ming successor, Wang Yang-ming (1472–1529), reached Korea.
Hearsay seems to have preceded the actual transmission of their works.

From the 1510s occasional references to "learning of the mind-and-
heart" *(simhak)* appear in court discussions. The term may have become
fashionable through the influence of the *Sheng-hsüeh hsin-fa* (The System of the Mind-and-Heart in the Learning of the Sage), the Ming Emperor Ch'eng-tsu's (r. 1402–24) voluminous work for the instruction of
rulers and ministers, that was first brought to Korea in 1499 (and again
in 1521) and was recommended as critical reading for the Korean king.[21]
Deploring the depressed state of scholarship—the result of the literati purges
at the turn of the century—officials used the new term to refer, in contrast to literary styles and classical scholarship, to a more penetrating and
sophisticated understanding of Ch'eng-Chu thought. "Learning of the mind-
and-heart" thus was used synonymously with "learning of principle," the
designation for all those who engaged in the kind of scholarship that de-
noted at the beginning of the sixteenth century intellectual advancement
as well as potential political danger. The term, in short, did not refer to
the alternative thought of Lu-Wang origin.[22]

One of the first references to Lu Hsiang-shan in the official records
is found in a review of the development of Neo-Confucianism in China
in 1517. While the "learning of nature and heavenly decree" *(sŏngmyŏng
chi hak)* was, it is stated, extremely subtle and "entering upon the correct
way" *(chŏngdo)* was difficult, Lu Hsiang-shan's appearance was ascribed
to the rise of some literary trends. "He [Lu] could not become a genuine
Confucian *(chinyu)*. Real Confucianism cannot be obtained through
words."[23] It cannot be known what information the Korean discussant

based this opinion on, yet he put Lu firmly outside mainstream Confucianism.

In 1542 the Minister of Rites, Kim An'guk, came back from Peking with a copy of Lu Hsiang-shan's collected works. In his report to the throne, Kim briefly commented on it as follows:

The *Hsiang-shan chi* is the work of the eminent Sung Confucian, Lu Chiu-yüan. Lu and Chu Hsi concentrated their minds at the same time on "honoring virtuous nature" *(chondŏksŏng)*, and they exchanged discussions on it. Although he differed from Chu Hsi, he nevertheless clearly explained the "learning of the mind and nature" *(simsŏng chi hak)*. [Our] scholars revere the Ch'eng-Chu teachings, [yet] to consult this work is not without benefit.[24]

Recognizing that Chu Hsi's contemporary was heading in a different intellectual direction, Kim thought that this contrast between the two scholars could be put to use for the propagation of the Ch'eng-Chu traditon. He therefore recommended the work for printing and distributing. As Kim used the term, "learning of the mind and nature" clearly indicated alternative thought.

There is no evidence that knowledge about Wang Yang-ming reached Korea during his lifetime. News about the Ming philosopher gradually seeped into the Korean peninsula. It can be assumed that So Seyang, while in Peking in 1533, learned about Wang from his Chinese discussion partner who happened to be a younger brother of Huang Wan (1477–1551), a close friend and disciple of Wang Yang-ming. Being a man of limited intellectual range, So did not perhaps grasp the importance of the information and therefore did not leave details about his conversations in his diary.[25]

A brief passage in the preface Yi Ŏnjŏk wrote in 1549 to his version of the *Great Learning*, the *Taehak changgu poyu* (Commentary to the *Ta-hsüeh*) is intriguing. He wrote: "In recent years one hears about a great Confucian *(taeyu)* in China who got the missing passages in the text and rearranged the sections and phrases. I wish I could see it, but I cannot get it."[26] There can be little doubt that Yi was referring to Wang Yang-ming's version of the *Great Learning* that was published in 1518 and widely discussed and criticized thereafter. Yet, since Yi's own version later came under severe attack as offending Ch'eng-Chu tradition—it almost ruined his chances for canonization—Yi's admirers had to belittle this allusion to Wang by interpreting it as referring to some earlier Chinese scholars.[27]

This is almost certainly a willful distortion that has found its way into modern scholarship.

The exact date when Wang Yang-ming's works were brought to Korea is unknown. The well-known scholar-official Yu Sŏngyong(1542–1607) claimed the first introduction of Wang's works to Korea for himself. In a brief reminiscence written for his descendants in 1593, Yu wrote that when he stayed with his father, who was the magistrate of Ŭiju, he discovered a copy of Wang's works in the luggage Sim T'ongwŏn, the head of the returning winter solstice mission of 1556–57, had to leave behind on the bank of the Yalu.[28] This account may be correct as far as Yu's personal experience is concerned, but copies of Wang's works were circulating before that time even among scholars living outside the capital.

On July 20, 1553, the widely learned Hong Inu (1515–54) noted in his diary:

The previous night I heard through Mr. Kyŏngho [Yi Hwang] of Wang Yang-ming's *Ch'uan-hsi lu*. I acquired and read it [and found that] his teachings generally have a liking for the unorthodox. In particular, he holds that the one mind (*sim*) is interior, while Heaven, Earth, and the ten thousand things are exterior. He considers the investigation [of things] and the extension [of knowledge] as wrong and the short cut method as right.

Shortly thereafter Yi Hwang (T'oegye, 1501–70) sent Hong a letter in which he warned Hong and his companions of Wang Yang-ming's captivating rhetoric.[29] This is evidence enough to indicate that around the middle of the sixteenth century the works of Wang Yang-ming were available and studied in certain scholarly circles in Korea.

YI HWANG: THE DEFINITION OF "RIGHT LEARNING"

The mid-sixteenth century was intellectually a turbulent period. It was marked by a brief revival of Buddhism under the energetic and influential monk, Pou (1515–65)—a revival that briefly reactivated the Buddhist-Confucian controversy.[30] Moreover, contemporary Ming thought in the form of Wang Yang-ming's idealistic emphasis on the mind began to attract Korean attention. Also, it was the time when Yi Hwang's scholarship reached maturity. His intellectual authority became the touchstone for evaluating his predecessors and the guidepost for future generations of scholars. Yi Hwang was one of the principal formulators of Korean Neo-

Confucian orthodoxy and he also became an outspoken critic of "aberrant thought." It is therefore important to consider Yi's concept of "right learning."

Yi Hwang saw himself as direct successor of Chu Hsi. Although he recognized that there were "many scholars in China," he looked up to Chu Hsi with full and unqualified admiration. For Yi, Chu Hsi had once and for all determined the right meaning of the classics and given the Neo-Confucian wisdom in his commentaries its final and unalterable form. Chu's philosophy is what Yi Hwang called "completely centered and absolutely straight" (taejung chijŏng), the essence of the "right learning" or the "right Way," an intellectual entity that was perfect in itself and therefore did not need any additions or amendments. "Right learning" had to be coupled with moral nature (tŏksŏng), a combination as essential as "two wheels for the driving of a cart or two wings for the flying of a bird." This union, Yi Hwang stated, was at the heart of Chu Hsi's teachings, indeed was the basis of Confucianism itself.[31]

Yi Hwang's predilection for Chu Hsi's school is well expressed in his biographical work of Neo-Confucianism, the Songgye Wŏn Myŏng ihak t'ongnok (Record of the Learning of Principle in the Sung, Yüan, and Ming Dynasties). The whole first chapter consists of Huang Kan's (1152–1221) biography of Chu Hsi, the Chu Tzu hsing-chuang, to which Yi Hwang supplied some additional information from other sources. The following seven chapters enumerate a great number of Chu's direct and indirect disciples. A further chapter lists the names of Confucians of the late Sung period, and the last chapter gives information about Confucian scholars of the Yüan period. The section on the Ming lists a few names, but refers to a Ming source for detailed information. The only Ming scholar treated at some length is Ch'en Hsien-chang's (1428–1500) disciple, Ho Ch'in (1437–1511). Yi Hwang was unable to complete this work. As his disciple, Cho Mok (1524–1606), remarks in a postface of 1576, Yi left an unfinished Oejip (Appendix) and notes on two Ming scholars, Ts'ao Tuan (1376–1434) and Lo Ch'in-shun (1465–1547). He had apparently also intended to include some Yi dynasty scholars.[32]

What Yi Hwang thought of the state of scholarship in Korea is revealed in the brief exposé of Korean Confucianism he gave to two Chinese envoys who visited Korea in the fall of 1567. In reply to the envoys' inquiry about the "learning of the mind-and-heart" in Korea, Yi outlined Korea's intellectual development from the times of the legendary Kija to

the end of Koryŏ when the works of the Ch'eng-Chu school were gradually transmitted to Korea. He mentioned U T'ak (1263–1342) and Chŏng
Mongju (1337–92) as the first practitioners of the "learning of nature and
principle" (sŏngnihak) in Korea and enumerated the names of those scholars
who were in his own days being considered for official recognition as the
transmitters of orthodox Confucianism in Korea: Yun Sang (1373–1455),
Kim Koengp'il, Chŏng Yŏch'ang (1450–1504), Cho Kwangjo, and Yi
Ŏnjŏk. He also mentioned Sŏ Kyŏngdŏk. Yi added that although the lit-
erati-officials (sa), selected on the basis of the Four Books and the Three
Classics, were reciting the words of Confucius, Mencius, and the Ch'eng-
Chu school, their understanding was either hampered by routine or clouded
by undue ambitions. The fact that he had only mentioned the names of
dead scholars he apologetically explained with the temporal and geo-
graphic distance that removed the Koreans from the teachings of the sages
and worthies. As if in self-defense, Yi concluded rhetorically: "Is a life-
long commitment not sufficient to become a follower of the 'learning of
the mind-and-heart'?"[33]

Although Yi Hwang acknowledged no Korean scholar as his intellectual mentor and teacher and was generally critical of the quality of
scholarship in Korea, he found praise for Cho Kwangjo and Yi Ŏnjŏk.
Cho, Yi felt, had defended the Way in a difficult period of time, and Yi
Ŏnjŏk had reached scholarly eminence without the benefit of a teacher
and had left a great number of works to future generations.[34] In contrast,
Yi found fault with Sŏ Kyŏngdŏk's thought. Although he could not overlook Sŏ's contribution to scholarship—he mentioned him to the Chinese
envoys—Yi censured Sŏ's emphasis on material force as a one-sided
interpretation that came dangerously close to confounding material force
with principle. Yi was also irritated by the veneration Sŏ received from
his many disciples who compared their teacher to Chang Tsai. Yi considered this comparison an exaggeration because he found fault with all
of Sŏ's treatises. Yi extended his disapproval to Sŏ's most prominent disciple, Yi Ku (?–1573).[35]

For Yi Hwang, "right learning," thus, was a full commitment to the
Ch'eng-Chu school that set absolute standards for scholarly pursuits. This
demand for strict adherence to fixed, tradition-bound intellectual models—
so impressively followed by Yi Hwang's own scholarly self-discipline—
naturally resulted in viewing any deviation or innovation as "abnormal"
and subversive and therefore subject to censure.

YI HWANG: THE REFUTATION OF "HETERODOX THOUGHT"

His own faithfulness to the Ch'eng-Chu school obliged Yi Hwang to be alert to and critical of any deviations from "right learning." He made himself guardian of the Ch'eng-Chu legacy and continued the Confucian tradition of condemning "aberrant concepts." Yi reportedly worried constantly that his stand against heterodoxy might not be firm enough. Heterodoxy in traditional terms meant Buddhism, and Yi Hwang, paraphrasing a passage of the *Reflections on Things at Hand (Chin-ssu lu)*, warned that Buddhism, like "licentious songs and beautiful women," be kept at a distance. He admonished his students not to read Buddhist literature, but to concentrate on the books of the sages and worthies.[36] Yet, although Yi Hwang witnessed a Buddhist revival during the 1550s, he did not launch a systematic attack on Buddhism. In his judgment, the real danger to "right learning" lurked in a different mode of thinking.

Yi Hwang considered the most dangerous challengers to be those crypto-Buddhists who outwardly presented themselves as Confucians, yet in reality had succumbed to the pernicious influence of Buddhist teachings. Lu Hsiang-shan was a representative example, and as a warning to his students Yi Hwang compiled a *Oejip* to his *Songgye Wŏn Myŏng ihak t'ongnok* in which he listed the names of potential enemies, starting with Lu Hsiang-shan and his brother and Lu's disciple, Yang Chien (1141–1226).[37]

Not surprisingly, Yi felt that all Ming scholars, with the exception of Hsüeh Hsüan (1389–1464), exuded "the smell of the Onion Range," that is, had Buddhist inclinations.[38] He even had reservations about Ch'eng Min-cheng (1445–99+), the Ming editor of Chen Te-hsiu's the *Classic of the Mind-and-Heart (Hsin-ching)*, the book he revered as much as the Four Books and the *Reflections on Things at Hand*. It was in Ch'eng's version, the *Additional Commentaries to the Hsin-ching (Hsin-ching fu-chu)*, that Yi Hwang became acquainted with this work. In an epilogue (*huron*) of 1566, Yi suspected Ch'eng of attempting to convert the whole world to the thinking of Lu Hsiang-shan. Yi received supporting evidence for his suspicion from Ch'en Chien (1497–1567), who in his A *General Critique of Obscurations to Learning (Hsüeh-pu t'ung-pien)* criticized Ch'eng for constructing total agreement between Chu Hsi and Lu Hsiang-shan. Asked whether Ch'eng's aberrations were damaging the authority of the book, Yi answered that Ch'eng's failings could not detract from the teachings of the sages and the commentaries of the worthies contained in the *Hsin-ching*.[39]

While Yi Hwang repeatedly warned his followers against the Buddhist tendencies of Lu Hsiang-shan, he reserved his most detailed and systematic criticism for Wang Yang-ming and Ch'en Hsien-chang (1428–1500), the two scholars who shifted Ming Confucianism away from Ch'eng-Chu orthodoxy to an idealism that centered on the moral mind *(hsin/sim)*. It is not clear how and when Yi got hold of Wang's *Instructions for Practical Living (Ch'uan-hsi lu)*—even he complained about the limited supply of Chinese books arriving in Seoul[40]—but it must have been before the summer of 1553 when he introduced it to Hong Inu. Although undated, his refutation, entitled *Discourse on the Ch'uan-hsi lu (Chŏnsŏmnok nonbyŏn)*, presumably was written shortly thereafter. It deals only with the first four sections of the work because this selection, a brief introductory note suggests, is indicative of the rest.[41]

Yi Hwang's objections begin with Wang's replacement of the characters "to renovate the people" *(hsin-min)* with "to love the people" *(ch'in-min)* in the opening phrase of the *Great Learning*. With this change Wang intended to express his full commitment, which ranged from the perfection of self to loving all people through moral cultivation.[42] Yi, on the other hand, interpreted this passage as an appeal to the educated. Scholarship, Yi stated, is the means through which man brightens his own virtue and, as the next step, makes all people partake in his scholarship to "renovate their own virtues." In Yi's interpretation, then, the passage did not mean, as it did for Wang Yang-ming, an emotional embracing of all humanity as a manifestation of clear virtue, but a transformation of the people guided by the scholar.

It is in this vein of argument that Yi also rejected Wang's assertion that the highest good must be sought in the mind. For Yi, this was a confusion of the normal sequence of acquiring the highest good: the "effort *(kung-fu)* of investigating the principle" has to precede the "effect of realizing the acquired knowledge." For the same reason that he could not accept Wang's emphasis on the mind as the starting-point of all intellectual endeavor and moral pursuit, Yi considered absurd Wang's elimination of "all things and affairs" as objects of investigation. This was proof, Yi felt, that Wang's pronouncements against Buddhism served the sole purpose of covering up his own Buddhist inclinations. Such an elimination would mean the denial of the omnipresence of principle *(li)* in all things and therefore would limit the field of action in the search for total truth.

Yi's most vigorous attack was directed against Wang's concept of the unity of knowledge and action. He found Wang's exposition superficial, even if cleverly worded. Since he could not accept Wang's premise that "the source of all being and virtue lies in *hsin*," he was equally critical of Wang's combining knowledge and action into one integral entity. The basic error of Wang's doctrine, Yi thought, lay in his way of reducing all actions to reactions of the instinct, to the exclusion of rational judgment. Yi granted that as long as the mind is thought to be shaped by material force, the liking of beautiful colors upon seeing them and the hating of bad odors upon smelling them are automatic and spontaneous and do not need any learning. Such a view, however, completely ignores the other component of the mind, that part which is connected with the rational principle *(ŭiri)*, and therefore denies the rational capability of man. Action cannot but be secondary to knowledge that must be cultivated by learning. Through the extension of knowledge man is able to differentiate between good and evil so that action is the result of a conscious act of judgment. Yi Hwang therefore insisted on the *coordination* of knowledge and action and firmly rejected their unity.

Wang's doctrine, Yi further objected, disregards the moral dimensions of the problem of knowledge and action. By paying sole attention to the mind-and-heart, Wang does not interact with external affairs and things *(samu)* as the sages and worthies have done. If one loves the good, Yi demanded, it is not enough to like it merely with one's mind-and-heart; it is necessary to pursue it in one's activities. In the same way, it is not enough to hate the bad; one must eradicate it in one's dealings. Action therefore must be guided by a moral commitment that eliminates the possibility of misdirected action such as merely covering up bad smells instead of washing them off.

Yi Hwang's refutation of Wang Yang-ming's philosophy ended on a social rather than a philosophical note. Exclaimed Yi:

If we call being hungry and cold action *(haeng)*, then what acts is the mind of man *(insim)* and not the mind of Tao *(tosim)*. To recognize *(chi)* being in pain as pain and being cold and hungry as coldness and hunger, even the man in the street, the beggar, and the wild animals are capable of this! If this can be called knowledge and action, of what use is scholarship?

For Yi, knowledge meant more than the mere recognition of a state of being on the basis of an intuitive and therefore physical impulse. Knowledge had to be the result of scholarship, and action was consequently the controlled and therefore moral outcome of knowledge.[43]

In a second treatise dedicated to Ch'en Hsien-chang's poetic work and Wang Yang-ming's *Ch'uan-hsi lu*, Yi Hwang summed up his assessment of the two men. Although he disliked Ch'en as a Confucian renegade, he greatly admired Ch'en's poetic talents. Because Ch'en had not completely abandoned the books of the sages and worthies, a selective and critical perusal of Ch'en's work was still permissible.[44] In contrast, Wang was the more dangerous of the two. Yi thought that he could discover a certain development in Wang's thinking. At first Wang wanted only to discard the external affairs and things without intending "to destroy human relations and to cut himself off from things," as the Buddhists do. But afterwards Wang created his theory that the mind is identical with principle and argued that the world's principle is lodged in man's mind. Thus, all the students had to do was to preserve their minds to the exclusion of all external things and affairs, even the five human relationships. This, Yi judged, was completely Buddhist. Worse yet, Wang was an iconoclast who dared change the meaning of the teachings of the sages and worthies in support of his own "false views" (*sagyŏn*). Yi worried about Wang's adverse influence on "this Way" (*sado*) and on the Confucian world and feared that it might be worse than Ch'in Shih Huang-ti's burning of the books.[45]

While Yi Hwang directed the full force of his criticism at Wang Yang-ming, he was not less disapproving of Wang's contemporary, Lo Ch'in-shun. Lo's work, *Notes on Knowledge Painfully Acquired (K'un-chih chi)*, was transmitted to Korea in the early 1550s and may have been printed in Korea for the first time around 1560.[46] Yi regarded this work with suspicion. He felt that although Lo professed to reject heterodox thought, he was in fact turning things inside out and thus committing inexcusable offenses against the Ch'eng-Chu tradition. Yi agreed with the critique Ki Taesŭng (1527–72) presented, allegedly with Yi's collaboration (although this is not noted), in his *Non Konjigi* (Discussion of the *K'un-chih chi*). Lo's teachings, Ki stated, come right out of Ch'an Buddhism. Yet Lo disguises this by adorning them with words from the sages and worthies so that his deceptive and false arguments get even worse. If Mencius came to life again, he would certainly expose Lo's errors and vigorously refute them in order to set the people's hearts straight and stop their anxiety.

Putting himself in Mencius' place, Ki identified Lo's worst errors as his statements on human nature and human feelings, his *ch'i* monism, and his assertion that "innate knowledge" *(yangji)* was not part of the heavenly principle. Ki especially felt that Lo's one-sided emphasis on material force was a direct outgrowth of his Buddhist inclinations and the main source of his aberrations. By finding fault with the classical tradition, Lo was in fact accusing himself.[47]

Because Lo's Buddhist proclivities were so obvious, Yi Hwang and Ki Taesŭng rated Lo as much less dangerous than Wang Yang-ming. Yi was deeply offended by Wang's thought because it compromised the most central elements of his own philosophy: priority of principle over material force, the rational property of human nature, the moral basis of action, and the emphasis on scriptural evidence. Moreover, Yi Hwang's dissatisfaction with Wang undoubtedly had an additional social dimension. Although Yi Hwang rarely spoke out on contemporary social issues and did not allude directly to the implications of Wang's philosophy for society, Yi must certainly have been aware of the potential challenge Wang's thought posed to the Korean social structure. In an argument delivered in 1553 when he was serving as a first deputy commander *(sanghogun)* in Seoul, Yi forcefully defended Korea's hierarchical social order which was built, he stated, upon the differentiations between primary and secondary descent lines *(chŏk, sŏ)* and between high and low social status. Although Yi granted that Heaven creates talents in every generation without regard to social origin, Yi maintained that it was not permissible to weaken the "social bulwark" *(taebang)* by admitting secondary sons *(sŏŏl)* to government positions, even at the risk of wasting a few talents.[48]

Yi's view of the hierarchical structure of society was thus founded on the strong hierarchical emphasis evident in his philosophical value system. Scholarship, and by extension government service and political power, had to be the unassailable privilege of the rationally well-endowed upper class. Clearly, Yi Hwang must have interpreted Wang Yang-ming's elimination of the rational aspect from action and the consequent devaluation of scholarship as frontal attacks against his own social credo. Alarmed at the philosophical as well as the social implications of Wang Yang-ming's thought, Yi Hwang therefore used all his authority to expose Wang's errors and block their dissemination in Korea.

YI I: IN FAVOR OF AN INDEPENDENT EFFORT

For Yi Hwang's younger contemporary, Yi I (Yulgok, 1536–84), the issue of orthodoxy and heterodoxy was intimately linked to the varying degrees of understanding of Confucian truth. Such understanding ranged from merely grasping the literal meaning of the scriptures to comprehending and actualizing their innermost significance. The highest level of understanding was to go beyond the written word and formulate an individual opinion—a creative and independent act of scholarship.

Yi I illustrated his view with the image of a mountain and postulated three categories of prospective mountaineers. To the first belong the people who do not themselves climb the mountain and thus are entirely dependent on informants to learn about it. The same is true for understanding the classics. Those who have to rely on somebody else's interpretations, which are either right or wrong, may miss their essence completely. Another category of people, upon learning the whereabouts of the mountain through others, actually gets to see its beautiful scenery and is no longer swayed by false reports. Indeed, because some delight in what they see, they may even want to climb the mountain. Others, satisfied with merely bragging about their discovery, make no attempt to go up. This is still only a partial view of the mountain. The third category consists of people who are so intrigued with what they see from afar that they make an all-out effort to climb the mountain. But the way is long and energies are limited so that only a few reach and explore the top. Moreover, there is considerable variation depending on the direction from which the mountain is viewed or the climbing started: those viewing or climbing it from the west may have a "western bias," those viewing or climbing it from the east an "eastern bias." Only a few succeed in taking in the full view of the mountain.

There is also a temporal aspect of understanding. Some know of the mountain's whereabouts before they have seen it. They climb it and reach its top in a short time. Because feet and eyes reach the summit at the same time, the mountain becomes the climber's possession. Such a climber was Confucius' pupil, Tseng Tzu (505–c.436 B.C.). Others find the mountain path by chance, without any prior knowledge of the mountain. Although they may be able to go up, they actually know little about the mountain, the more so since they have not seen it from a distance. Such people, exemplified by Ssu-ma Kuang (1019–86), are in the end unable to reach the top.

Using this scenario to evaluate the performances of his contemporaries, Yi I was openly pessimistic about the intellectual state of his time. He regretted that Korean scholars were only following the beaten path, and even this not without error. Among the Chinese Confucians who reached the top of the mountain, Yi I reserved special respect for Chu Hsi who, at sixty, exclaimed: "Now, finally, I have no [more] doubts!" Such words, Yi felt, could only be uttered by someone who had seen the whole mountain with his own eyes (ch'in'gyŏn). Ch'in'gyŏn was for Yi I synonymous with the Mencian expression chadŭk, "to obtain [the truth] through one's own efforts," the greatest accomplishment of a Confucian.

Understanding, however, may not only be incomplete; it may also be misled. "Aberrant thought" is misguided understanding that does not focus on this, i.e. Confucian, mountain, but on that, i.e. Buddhist, mountain. Especially sensitive to this issue because of his own Buddhist experiences in his youth,[49] Yi felt that those with only a partial view of this mountain, although not themselves on the wrong track, can with their confused statements misdirect others toward that mountain. The danger of erring from the right path, thus, was inherent in a partial understanding of the Confucian message.

For Yi I, the first demand of learning was the full and complete comprehension of the orthodox tradition. Yet, learning had to be more than mere passive reception; it had to be a creative process that would lead to independent insights—the scholar's contribution to established wisdom. Conceptualized in the formula "to obtain truth through one's own efforts" (chadŭk), Yi made this personal contribution the principal criterion by which he judged the works of his Korean and Chinese contemporaries.

Yi ranked them as follows: Lo Ch'in-shun, Yi Hwang, Sŏ Kyŏng-dŏk. Only Lo and Sŏ deserved in Yi's judgment the attribute chadŭk. Yi Hwang, he found, adhered too closely to Chu Hsi's words. Yi I admired Lo Ch'in-shun as one of the outstanding Confucians of his time. Lo, Yi felt, had taken in the full view of the Confucian mountain and with his lofty ideas had been unwilling to follow Chu Hsi's lead. Yi defended Lo against the criticism that he had taken principle for material force. But because his pronouncements were not always clear, he might have given rise to doubts.[50]

Whereas Lo's errors lay in the realm of semantics, Yi considered Yi Hwang's shortcomings more serious because they were philosophical. Although in his debates with Ki Taesŭng on principle and material force Yi Hwang's argumentation was detailed and subtle, it lacked clarity in Yi's opinion and, because of its metaphysical bias, left the ground of reality (*chŏksil*). Yi Hwang was an extraordinarily conscientious and dedicated scholar, but because of his excessive dependence on Chu Hsi his opinions lacked originality, and his arguments were narrow and pedantic.

In contrast, Yi regarded Sŏ Kyŏngdŏk as a scholar who, with his outstanding intelligence, was able to detach himself from the written word and search for the truth independently. The result of this search—the identification of material force with principle—was erroneous, however, and Yi was grateful to Yi Hwang for exposing Sŏ's errors and thus saving future scholars from the same pitfalls.[51]

Admitting that Confucian learning had many facets, Yi I did not find an easy characterization of "right learning." Learning cannot be completely "correct," *(chŏng)* without any flaws *(sa)*, and therefore Yi could not define absolute standards. But even though he regarded independent effort as a critical constituent of "right learning," he insisted that classical scholarship had to be taken as the common foundation and point of departure. He himself contributed to the solidification of the scriptural basis by compiling the *Sŏnghak chibyo* (Essentials of the Learning of the Sage).[52] To put the acquisition of an individual point of view ahead of Confucian training—an offense he accused Pak Yŏng of—could easily result in being misled by "heterodox learning" *(ihak)*.[53] One condition of "right learning," therefore, had to be constant vigilance against aberrant thought.

"Right learning" had always had its challengers, but, Yi thought, this challenge had become more perfidious in the course of time. During the declining years of the Chou dynasty even Mencius could not stop Lao Tzu, Chuang Tzu, Yang Chu, and Mo Ti from spreading their false doctrines *(sasŏl)*. Yet, the falseness of their arguments was so evident that scholars could stay clear of such men. In subsequent times heterodox thought became more subtle so that it appeared correct on the surface, while it was false underneath. The culmination of this transformation was reached with the emergence of Ch'an Buddhism during the T'ang dynasty when even bright scholars were deceived by it. To their merit, the Ch'eng brothers and Chu Hsi forced Buddhism into decline, but after they died teachings that appeared to be Confucian, yet really were Buddhist, reappeared. These frequent recurrences of false doctrines showed the difficulty of suppressing them permanently.

Yi I does not seem to have concerned himself with studying Wang Yang-ming's thought closely. He praised, however, Ch'en Chien, the author of the Hsüeh-pu t'ung-pien,[54] for exposing the deviousness of Wang Yang-ming and Lu Hsiang-shan at a time when China seemed to come completely under the sway of their teachings. There even was a move to enshrine Wang in the Shrine of Confucius, which, Yi feared, would permanently damage the chance of checking heterodoxy.

Yi felt, however, that China's slow decline into heterodoxy should not give Korean scholars, ignorant of Lu Hsiang-shan, an unwarranted sense of superiority. The Chinese scholars were at least serious and dedicated regardless of whether or not they admired Chu or Lu, whereas the Koreans studied neither Chu nor Lu and only cared for routine matters that would lead to profit and advancement. Disenchanted with the intellectual milieu of his own country, Yi regarded the abandonment of the Way in pursuit of personal aggrandizement just as much a form of heterodoxy as the teachings of the Buddhists, Taoists, and Lu. Selfless and uncompromising dedication, then, lay at the bottom of any scholarly endeavor—even if it should conflict with "right learning."[55]

Yi I was undoubtedly a more flexible thinker than Yi Hwang. Flexibility, however, did not make him compromise with the fundamental Confucian truth. Rather, it led him to realize that the Ch'eng-Chu legacy was the inspirational source of diverse thought. "Right learning" could not be monolithic; it thus contained the potential of internal conflict. Yi was working with all his authority for harmony when during the last years of his life the first signs of such conflict appeared—a personal effort that did not, however, succeed in preventing eventual division within Korean orthodoxy.[56]

THE RISK OF DIVERSITY

The key figure in the distribution of knowledge about Wang Yang-ming was Hong Inu, who in 1553 had become acquainted with Wang's Ch'uan-hsi lu through Yi Hwang. Hong seems to have been aware from the outset of the controversial nature of the work, for he noted in his diary that Lo Ch'in-shun had written the *K'un-chih chi* with the intention of refuting Wang's errors. Hong did not hesitate, however, to share his discovery with his younger friend and brother-in-law, Nam Ŏn'gyŏng (1528–94).[57] Hong had met Nam first in 1551 and was deeply impressed by Nam's scholarship and commanding personality. Nam had received his first intellectual formation from Sŏ Kyŏngdŏk and, through Hong, was introduced to the most prominent representative of mainstream Confucianism of his day, Yi Hwang, and also, virtually at the same time, to the work of the major challenger, Wang Yang-ming.

Nam seems to have become an avid reader of Wang's work, a fact that displeased Yi Hwang, who recognized Nam's unusual scholarly abilities. Nam visited Yi Hwang occasionally to debate his ideas and also sent him a few letters. Judging from Yi's answers—the only extant part of this correspondence—the main subject of their exchanges was the thought of Sŏ Kyŏngdŏk. Yi relentlessly pointed to what he considered Sŏ's aberrations and at the same time warned Nam against becoming enthralled by Wang Yang-ming's philosophy.[58]

Because no work in his name is preserved,[59] the contours of Nam's thought emerge only from fragmentary references in contemporary sources. A key term Nam seems to have used at an early stage was quiescence (*chŏng*). The importance he attached to this concept was evidenced by his making it the name of his study as well as his first pen name (*chŏngjae*). In 1553 he asked Yi Hwang to write a short piece on this theme. In response to this request—and surely as a sign of his esteem for Nam—Yi wrote the *Chŏngjaegi* (Note for the Quiescence Study). At considerable length Yi elaborated on the duality and complementarity of quiescence and movement (*tong*) and unmistakably cautioned Nam against the Buddhist and Taoist implications of a one-sided emphasis on quiescence.[60] Nam's erudition, however, was not one-sided. Besides being well-read in Buddhist and Taoist literature, he was equally recognized for his extensive knowledge of the Confucian classics. Moreover, Nam had scholarly exchanges with many of his contemporaries, including Yi I. Due to his broad scholarship—and perhaps despite his by then well-known predilection for Wang Yang-ming—Nam was, on the occasion of a special search for talents in 1566, recommended to the king and subsequently appointed to a local post.[61]

When, upon his appointment, he was received in audience by King

Myŏngjong (r. 1545–67), Nam was asked to comment on the rule of the sage rulers of antiquity. In his elaboration, Nam mentioned the "preservation of the mind" *(chonsim)* as the first condition for good rule. All human beings, sage rulers as well as ordinary men, are endowed with a mind that contains the heavenly principle of pure nature untarnished by external things. Because ordinary men have lost this pure mind through the influence of material force and the emotions, the sage rulers devised for them the method of "rectifying the mind" to regain their original nature. This argument, supported from the *Great Learning* and other sources, reveals Nam's preoccupation with the nature of the human mind.[62] Earlier he had reportedly developed a theory according to which good and evil coexist in the mind *(sim)*, an assertion that drew Yi Hwang's criticism. Yi called such a theory a "grave error" because the mind-and-heart, Yi insisted, is at its earliest stage without any evil.[63]

The fragmentary transmission of Nam's thought makes it impossible to assess the degree of his absorption of Wang Yang-ming's philosophy.[64] That a scholar of Nam's intellectual caliber was attracted by Wang, however, alerted Yi Hwang, and it may not be too farfetched to suggest that Nam's incurability eventually compelled Yi to write his critique of Wang Yang-ming's *Ch'uan-hsi lu*. Nam played not only the involuntary role of catalyst in the movement against heterodox thought, he was also an active teacher.[65] It was one of his reportedly numerous disciples, Yi Yo (n.d.),who once positively identified Nam as a practitioner of the "learning of the mind."[66] Even if Nam is at times called "the first follower" of Wang Yang-ming in Korea, there were in the second half of the sixteenth century quite a few scholars who studied Wang Yang-ming. Yet, it was rarely judicious to espouse openly one's sympathies for the Chinese heretic.

A similar preoccupation with the "preservation of the mind" is found in the thought of Nam Ŏn'gyŏng's contemporary and colleague, No Susin (1515–90). Although he spent close to twenty years in remote exile, No seems to have been well acquainted with the intellectual trends of Ming China. He acquired a copy of Lo Ch'in-shun's *K'un-chih chi* and assessed its value in a postface dated 1560, *Konjigi pal* (Postface to the *K'un-chih chi*): "Its wording is upright and subtle; it develops as yet undeveloped points and thus has great merits for the Ch'eng-Chu school."[67] That No read Lo's work with great care is apparent in his study on human nature in which he not only quoted Lo at length, but also adopted some of Lo's concepts, especially the unconventional duality of the mind of Tao *(tosim)* as substance *(ch'e)* and of the mind of man *(insim)* as function *(yong)*. No's work, entitled *Insim tosimbyŏn* (Discourse on the Mind of Man and the Mind of Tao) and dated 1559, drew critical reactions from such diverse thinkers as Yi Hwang, who reprimanded No severely, and Nam Ŏn'gyŏng, who raised some questions of interpretation.[68]

No was a scholar of broad interests. Presumably through contacts with Hong Inu he became familiar with Wang Yang-ming's work. During a royal lecture in the summer of 1574 he startled his audience with remarks that were unmistakably inspired by Wang. Knowledge and action, No said, do not constitute two different things, and all men have to do is to preserve their mind. To underscore the importance he attributed to the mind, No maintained that once the classics and the commentaries are committed to the mind they become useless.[69] Reliance on the mind and disregard for the written word, so characteristic of Wang Yang-ming, may have been for No a means of intellectual survival as much as a personal form of protest.

No Susin's self-reliance is also visible in the postface he wrote to Yi Ŏnjŏk's *Taehak changgu poyu* in 1584. No pondered over the various interpretations of the *Great Learning* by Chinese scholars and ventured some doubts about Chu Hsi's arrangement of the text. He admired Yi Ŏnjŏk for the independence of mind that had led Yi to contradict Chu's version, and he concluded that the elucidation of the classics could not be the concern of one single school. No asked rhetorically: "Does a compromise or a small difference harm the Way?"[70]

Chang Yu (1587–1638), known for his diplomatic skills as well as for his admiration of Lu Hsiang-shan, whom he considered superior to Wang Yang-ming, reflected a few decades later on the question No had raised earlier. Chang was impressed with the diversity of thought in China where Confucians, Buddhists, and Taoists coexisted, and he deplored the situation in Korea where all scholars, regardless of the degree of their sophistication, adhered so strictly to the Ch'eng-Chu tradition that no other branch of learning was cultivated. Echoing an opinion Yi I had first expressed some fifty years earlier, Chang did not think that such conformity indicated Korea's greater "wisdom" *(hyŏn)*. On the contrary, Chinese scholars pursued their own intellectual inclinations and thus produced diverse and often original works. In Korea the submission to the Ch'eng-

Chu school stifled not only originality but also scholarly advancement within the bounds of orthodoxy.[71] Although Chang did not offer an explanation of this phenomenon, he might have agreed to the proposition that in Korea the pursuit of diversity was riskier because by the end of the sixteenth century Yi Hwang's legacy of recognizing the Ch'eng-Chu philosophy as the only permissible version of orthodoxy had itself become part of this orthodoxy.

DEFENDING THE WAY AGAINST CHINESE SUBVERSION

During the last two decades of his life and even after his death, Yi Hwang's authority as the guardian of "right learning" was unassailable. He was praised for having achieved a synthesis of Neo-Confucian thought and for having defended the Ch'eng-Chu tradition against heterodox ideas. Indeed, his outstanding merits for Neo-Confucianism were easily summed up in the formula: reject the false and uphold the straight.[72] Yi Hwang's defense of the right Way was continued by his numerous disciples who faithfully preserved their master's credo and Korea's reputation as the land of orthodoxy in the face of what they considered China's deepening intellectual crisis in the last decades of the sixteenth century.

Koreans who went to Peking during this period often engaged Chinese officials and scholars in heated debates that highlighted the almost missionary zeal with which the Koreans tried to argue their partners out of their adherence to the Lu-Wang school. In 1566, Yun Kŭnsu (1537–1616), a disciple of Yi Hwang, accompanied a Korean embassy to Peking and conducted a lengthy exchange of ideas with a Chinese scholar-official, Lu Kuang-tsu.[73] Thoroughly familiar with the main points of his master's critique of Wang Yang-ming, Yun chided Lu for his assertion that Wang was, after Lu Hsiang-shan, the only representative of the Mencian tradition and pointed to the Buddhist orientation in Wang's equation of the learning of the Way (tao-hsüeh) with man's mind-and-heart (jen-hsin). Yun contested most vigorously Lu's statement that the human mind was, to the exclusion of the investigation of principle, the only standard for judging the appropriateness of human emotions such as pleasure, anger, sorrow, or joy. Moreover, Yun felt, the "extension of innate knowledge" overemphasized the singularity of each individual's mind and also discarded scholarship. Yun was not happy with the result of his oral exhanges with Lu and in a letter demanded further clarifications. But their points of view were, of course, irreconcilable, and Yun received no satisfaction from Lu's written replies. Nevertheless, Yun's encounter with an educated Chinese was later rated by Yi Hwang as a rare opportunity for a Korean scholar to counteract the pernicious influence of Lu Hsiang-shan's Ch'anism in China.[74]

On a later occasion, in 1569, Yi Hwang's disciple Yu Sŏngyong was in Peking where he received a large student delegation from the Confucian Academy. His question as to who was the present leader of the "learning of the Way" (*tohak*) in China, Yu recalled later, drew embarrassed looks and the hesitant answer: Wang Yang-ming and Ch'en Pai-sha. Yu's suggestion that the students take Hsüeh Hsüan as their leader was apparently welcomed by only one single scholar who praised Yu for his determination to "refute heresies."[75]

In a similar vein, Hŏ Pong (1551–88), who went to Peking as the secretary of a special mission in 1574, seized every opportunity to discuss the intellectual differences between Korea and China, even before he reached the Chinese capital. He seemed to offend his Chinese audiences by suggesting that the disappearance of the Way in China was due to the flourishing of "false doctrines" (*sasŏl*). Despite Chinese insistence to the contrary, Hŏ accused Wang Yang-ming of disrupting the orthodox line of transmission from the Ch'eng-Chu school to the Ming through his adherence to Lu Hsiang-shan. Hŏ maintained that Wang rebelled against the Way by openly declaring that he would not believe anybody's statements that did not tally with his own convictions, even if they came from Confucius himself. The ultimate proof of Wang's rebellion was his rearrangement of the *Great Learning*. Hŏ's advice that the works of Hsü Heng (1209–81) be studied, he remembered regretfully, did not meet with approval.[76]

The alarming trends the Koreans identified in China's intellectual life were confirmed in the changes the Chinese made in the Shrine of Confucius, a visit to which was a customary part of any sight-seeing program in Peking. Yun Kŭnsu recalled years later the disgust he felt in 1566 when he discovered the tablet of Lu Hsiang-shan, who had been enshrined in 1530.[77] The famous classicist, Yu Hŭich'un (1513–77), interpreted Lu's canonization as certain evidence of China's betrayal of the Ch'eng-Chu orthodoxy. When rumors of an impending enshrinement of Wang Yang-ming reached Seoul in the early 1570s, Yu was up in arms and contemptuously repudiated the Chinese arguments that Wang had been Lu Hsiang-shan's disciple and that there were no significant differences between the teachings of Lu and Chu Hsi.[78]

After Wang was canonized in 1584, Yun Kŭnsu drew some satisfaction from the report that Wang's enshrinement was not the result of a unanimous decision but had been forced through by the numerically stronger southern faction. This fact, Yun felt, freed the Koreans from any moral obligation to follow the Chinese example, and Yun pleaded therefore against hasty changes in the Shrine of Confucius (Munmyo) in Seoul.[79]

The adulteration of the Ch'eng-Chu legacy in Peking committed the Koreans to giving Confucian orthodoxy a permanent abode in Seoul. Yu Hŭich'un, disturbed by the developments in China, became a principal promoter of the canonization of the Korean transmitters of the Way— Kim Koengp'il, Chŏng Yŏch'ang, Cho Kwangjo, Yi Ŏnjŏk, and Yi Hwang.[80] The enshrinement of these five worthies in 1610, then, not only testified to the Koreans' fidelity to "right learning,"[81] it also became an institutionalized safeguard against further subversion from China.

CONCLUSIONS: KOREA THE LAND OF ORTHODOXY

A well-known saying has it that the Korean Neo-Confucians used to study Chu Hsi's works on their desks, those of Wang Yang-ming underneath. This statement, although an obvious exaggeration, nevertheless suggests that Wang's thought was a more pervasive undercurrent in Korea's intellectual life than the records reveal. The inconspicuous transmission of his work into the country, his immediate stigmatization as heterodox, and the consequently rare open discussions of his major ideas transformed Wang Yang-ming into a scholar of shady credentials. The Koreans' initial response to Wang Yang-ming, and conversely Wang's fate in Korea, were conditioned by the particular stage of development Korean Neo-Confucianism had reached by the middle of the sixteenth century.

Wang Yang-ming's work appeared in the peninsula at a time when Korean Neo-Confucian orthodoxy was receiving its final historical and philosophical shape. The Koreans had been from the inception of the dynasty alert to the necessary correlation between historical legitimation and intellectual credibility. The determination of the rightful transmitters of the Way was therefore of crucial importance. The early Yi Neo-Confucians acknowledged their intellectual indebtedness to their immediate predecessors and teachers, most of whom had studied in Yüan China and had become, through their teaching activities, the actual transmitters of the Way in its Yüan configuration. By the middle of the sixteenth century, however, this perspective was considerably amended. Yüan China was no longer recognized as the land of original instruction, and the Neo-Confucian scholars of the late Koryŏ period were ignored as the actual transmitters. The roots of Korean Neo-Confucianism were boldly traced back directly to Sung China, with Chŏng Mongju as the sole intellectual and historical intermediary. As Song Siyŏl (1607–87) summed it up: "From afar he [Chŏng Mongju] took up the Way of the teacher of Yin [Kija]; from nearby he observed the rules of Chu Hsi." The two components—Korea's link to Chinese antiquity and the Neo-Confucians' ties with Sung orthodoxy—were thus amalgamated into one tradition that construed Chŏng Mongju as its "middle ancestor" *(chungjo)*. The line of transmission after Chŏng was then completed with a roster of Korean candidates.

Wang Yang-ming did not fit into this scheme. No Korean regarded the Sung tradition, and by extension its Korean successor, as a synthesis that in the past had absorbed a variety of thought and in the course of time became susceptible to new influences. Wang—and with him most of his Ming contemporaries—was therefore not welcomed as a further development of this tradition. On the contrary, he was rejected because he was found to have deviated from this very tradition under the influence of Buddhism.

The central theme of Korean Neo-Confucianism is the structure and the quality of human nature as the principal determinants of moral behavior. From the beginning of the dynasty, every Neo-Confucian grappled with these concepts, and around the middle of the sixteenth century Yi Hwang attempted a final definition. Judging from the timely circumstances, it is likely that the arrival of Wang Yang-ming's work accelerated this process. Directly, Wang challenged Yi Hwang to take issue with his major ideas; this resulted in Yi's refutation of Wang. Indirectly, Wang prompted Yi Hwang to produce his own unassailable formulation of "right learning"; this may have contributed to the initiation of debates between Yi and Ki Taesŭng about the relative significance of principle and material force in the formation of the Four Beginnings *(sadan)* and the Seven Emotions *(ch'ilchŏng)*. By staking out the terrain of inquiry and supplying the appropriate terminology, these debates, continued by successive generations of scholars, had a profound influence on the tenor and direction of Korean Neo-Confucianism.

Woven into the theme of human nature was a strong emphasis on morality, the property that connected the philosophical discussion with the sociopolitical reality. The definition, exercise, and control of morality vested the ruling elite with a high measure of authority. This very authority would have been endangered if Wang Yang-ming's egalitarian claims of intuitive knowledge and spontaneous action had been allowed to take root in Korea. Only a strong reaffirmation of the rational component of human nature as the basis of moral action could ward off the onslaught of the irrational and save the hierarchical principles of Korean society.

In sum, then, a variety of factors combined to prevent Wang Yang-ming's official integration into Korea's intellectual and social life.

In the land of orthodoxy, which institution or individual was responsible for watching over the purity of "right learning"? In the sixteenth century this question was repeatedly debated, and it was generally recognized that the state and the Confucians (*yusaeng*) had two distinct, yet complementary assignments. While the state provided teaching and administered the examinations, the thinking had to be done in private academies (or in the solitude of exile). The relationship between state and scholarship was even more complex because official and scholar formed a nearly inseparable entity. The examinations scrutinized "bureaucratic learning" (*kwanhak*) and thus were not, as often charged, the proper vehicle for promoting the "learning of principle." But they were an important means of official legitimation—if not a scholarship then of social and political status. Yet, scholarship was also dependent on state authority for receiving final endorsement. The enshrinement of a scholar's tablet in the Shrine of Confucius was a state affair. The choice of an appropriate candidate, however, was the result of a usually drawn-out process during which state concerns (for example the imitation of Chinese precedents) were carefully balanced with the demands of the scholarly world. State orthodoxy and intellectual orthodoxy reinforced each other for the benefit of both.

In the case of Wang Yang-ming, the guardians of "right learning" decried him as heterodox and effectively excluded him from the mainstream of Korean Neo-Confucianism. The state, in a demonstration against Ming China, did not canonize him. Was it therefore unnecessary to ban Wang's works or to put them on an index? The books that were burned in 1703—the only book-burning in Yi Korea—were not Wang's works, but the writings of a rebel from within, Pak Sedang (1629–1703), who dared question Chu Hsi's textual authority. In contrast, Wang Yang-ming, the rebel from without, continued to lead an as yet unexplored underground existence until the end of the dynasty.

NOTES

The research upon which this work is based was made possible by a grant from the Swiss National Science Foundation. I am grateful for the many useful comments I received from the members of the Conference on Korean Neo-Confucianism held in Bellagio in August 1981.—M.D.

1. For a discussion on the Confucian polemics against Buddhism, see Martina Deuchler, "Neo-Confucianism: The Impulse for Social Action in Early Yi Korea," *Journal of Korean Studies* (1980), 2:75–79.
2. There is no mention of *idan* in the *Koryŏsa*. *Idan* in the *Chŭngbo munhŏn pigo* means mainly Buddhism. There are a few references to shamanism; 85:1–15; 206:14–17b.
3. *Lun-yü* 2:16; James Legge, *The Four Books* (reprint without date), p. 19; *Mencius* 3B:9; Legge, *Four Books*, pp. 678–80; Chŏng Tojŏn, "Pulssi chappyŏn," *Sambongjip* (Writings of Chŏng Tojŏn) (Seoul: Kuksa p'yŏnch'an wiwŏnhoe, 1961), pp. 273–79.
4. Michael C. Kalton has discussed Kwŏn Kŭn's views on the interconnection between Heaven and man in an unpublished paper entitled "Early Yi Dynasty Neo-Confucianism: An Integrated View."
5. *Sŏngjong sillok* (Seoul: Kuksa p'yŏnch'an wiwŏnhoe, 1955–1963), 118:13–15.
6. The intellectual milieu at the beginning of the Ming dynasty is discussed in Wm. Theodore de Bary, *Neo-Confucian Orthodoxy and The Learning of the Mind-And-Heart* (New York: Columbia University Press, 1981), pp. 153 ff.
7. The establishment of Confucian orthodoxy in Korea is discussed in Martina Deuchler, "Self-Cultivation for the Governance of Men: The Beginnings of Neo-Confucian Orthodoxy in Yi Korea," *Asiatische Studien* (1980), 34(2):9–39. Two articles by the late Yun Namhan were of special relevance for the present study: "Yijo Yangmyŏnghak ŭi chŏllae wa suyong ŭi munje" (Problems Concerning the Transmission and Reception of Wang Yang-ming in the Yi Dynasty), *Chungang saron* (December 1972), 1:1–18, and "Chungjong tae ŭi tohak kwa simhakhwa undong" (The Learning of the Way and the Movement Toward the Learning of the Mind in Chungjong's Reign), *Sachong* (October 1977), 21/22:459–95. A convenient survey of relevant source materials is given in Yi Nŭnghwa, "Chōsen jukai no Yōmei gakuha" (The Wang Yang-ming School in the Confucianism of the Chosŏn Period), *Seikyū gakusō* (August 1936), 25:105–42.
8. *Sejong sillok*, 61:51b–52, 55b–56b; 62:26a–b, 28; 69:18b–19; *Ming hui-yao* (Relevant Source Materials on the Ming) (Shanghai: Chung-hua shu-chü, 1957), vol. 2, p. 1493.
9. For details, see the two above-mentioned articles by Martina Deuchler.
10. The Korean Neo-Confucians did not feel compelled to make allowances for a native creed as the Japanese Neo-Confucians did for native Shintō. For a

discussion of the Japanese case, see Kate Wildman Nakai, "The Naturalization of Confucianism in Tokugawa Japan: The Problem of Sinocentrism," *Harvard Journal of Asiatic Studies* (June 1980), 40(1):157–99.

11. John Meskill, *Ch'oe Pu's Diary: A Record of Drifting Across the Sea* (Tucson: The University of Arizona Press, 1965), pp. 83, 92, 107, 120.

12. For details, see Deuchler, "Neo-Confucianism," pp. 96–97.

13. Yu Sungjo's two works, with some scattered materials collected after his death, were reprinted by Asea munhwasa, Seoul, in 1973. His version of the *Ta-hsüeh* was considered so important that it was reproduced in toto in the *Chungjong sillok*. The *Sŏngniyŏnwŏn ch'waryo* was found to be too long for the same honor. *Chungjong sillok*, 13:28b–33; 15:13; 27:35b, 37; 67:5b.

14. For a short study of Pak Yŏng's thought, see Yun Namhan, "Chungjong tae ŭi tohak kwa simhakhwa undong," pp. 484–90. In this article Prof. Yun tries to establish the intellectual background against which the reception of Wang Yang-ming's thought should be seen. He therefore insists that people like Pak Yŏng were expounding ideas of "learning of the mind" *(simhak)*. Since there is not enough evidence for such a view, I cannot agree with Prof. Yun on this point. A prominent disciple of Pak was Yi Hang (1499–1576) who postulated a monistic theory of principle and material force.

15. Sŏ Kyŏngdŏk's short treatises can be found in his collected works, *Hwadamjip, kw* 2. For a short sketch of Sŏ's life and thought, see Yi Pyŏngdo, "Sŏ Hwadam kŭp Yi Yŏnbang e taehan sogo," (A Short Study of Sŏ Kyŏngdŏk and Yi Ku), *Chindan hakpo* (April 1936), 4:122–26.

16. For a brief article on Yi Ŏnjŏk's life and work, see Yi Pyŏngdo, "Yi Hoejae wa kŭ hangmun" (Yi Ŏnjŏk and His Scholarship), *Chindan hakpo* (November 1936), 6:132–47. Also Deuchler, "Self-Cultivation," pp. 28–29.

17. *Chungjong sillok*, 13:55b; 21:29, 30, 31.

18. *Ibid.*, 44:2; 76:44b–46b. For details, see Yun Namhan, "Chungjong tae ŭi tohak kwa simhakhwa undong," pp. 478–80.

19. *Chungjong sillok*, 76:47; 77:24–26b; *Chōsenshi* (Keijo: Chōsen sōtokufu, 1936), 4(7):455.

20. *Chungjong sillok*, 95:56; 96:1a–b, 5–6; 98:20a–b; Kim An'guk, *Mojaejip* (Collected Works of Kim An'guk) (1687 ed.; Kyujanggak) 9:35b–39.

21. *Yŏnsan'gun ilgi*, 35:1; *Chungjong sillok*, 41:31. For a discussion of the *Sheng-hsüeh hsin-fa*, see de Bary, *Neo-Confucian Orthodoxy*, pp. 159–64.

22. *Chungjong sillok*, 29:47b, 52b–54; 50:3.

23. *Ibid.*, 29:53b–54.

24. *Ibid.*, 98:20; Kim An'guk, *Mojaejip* 9:37b.

25. So Seyang's diary, *Yanggok pugyŏng ilgi* (So Seyang's Diary of a Trip to Peking) is reproduced in *Seikyū gakusō* (August 1930), 1:192, 195–96; Julia Ching, *To Acquire Wisdom* (New York: Columbia University Press, 1976), pp. 189–90.

26. Yi Ŏnjŏk, Introduction to *Taehak changgu poyu* in *Hoejae chŏnsŏ* (Collected Works of Yi Ŏnjŏk) (Seoul: Sŏnggyun'gwan taehakkyo, Taedong munhwa yŏn'guwŏn, 1973), p. 553; *Sŏnjo sillok*, 175:3b. Yi I discussed some of Yi Ŏnjŏk's work on the *Ta-hsüeh* in *Yulgok chŏnsŏ* (Collected Works of Yi I)

(Seoul: Kyŏngin munhwasa, 1971), "Hoejae Taehak poyu huŭi," 14:36–38.

27. The scholars usually mentioned as those to whom Yi Ŏnjŏk is supposed to have referred are Tung Huai of Sung (1213 cs), Wang Po (1197–1274), and Fang Hsiao-ju (1357–1402).

28. Yu Sŏngyong, Sŏae sŏnsaeng munjip (Collected Works of Yu Sŏngyong) (Seoul: Sŏnggyun'gwan taehakkyo, Taedong munhwa yŏn'guwŏn, 1958), "Sŏ Yangmyŏngjip hu," 18:5b–6. For Sim T'ongwŏn's mission, see Myŏngjong sillok, 21:15b, 46a–b, 48–50.

29. Hong Inu, Ch'ijaejip (Collected Works of Hong Inu) (n.d.), "Ch'ijae yugo," 2:26; Yi Hwang, T'oegye chŏnsŏ (Collected Works of Yi Hwang) (Seoul: Kyŏngin munhwasa, 1971), 13:5b–6 (letter to Hong Inu).

30. For the Buddhist-Confucian controversy around Pou, see the many entries in Myŏngjong sillok, kw 9–17.

31. Yi Hwang, T'oegye chŏnsŏ, 10:7b (letter to No Susin); 11:9; 41:11b, 13b.

32. Cho Mok's Postface is in Songgye Wŏn Myŏng ihak t'ongnok, 11:1–3.

33. Yi Hwang, T'oegye chŏnsŏ, "Ŏnhaengnok," 5:31b–33; Sŏnjo sillok, 1:2a–b.

34. Yi Hwang wrote biographies of Cho Kwangjo and Yi Ŏnjŏk. See T'oegye chŏnsŏ, 48:28–38; 49:1–14.

35. Yi Hwang, T'oegye chŏnsŏ, "T'oegye sŏnsaeng ŏnhaengnok," 5:13b; 14:7b–9b; 25:20b–21; 41:22a–b.

36. Yi Hwang, T'oegye chŏnsŏ, "T'oegye sŏnsaeng ŏnhaeng t'ongnok," 2:40a–b; Wing-Tsit Chan, Reflections on Things at Hand (New York: Columbia University Press, 1967), pp. 283, 285.

37. Yi Hwang, T'oegye chŏnsŏ, "T'oegye sŏnsaeng ŏnhaeng t'ongnok," 2:40; Postface by Cho Mok to Songgye Wŏn Myŏng ihak t'ongnok, 11:1–3.

38. Yi Hwang, T'oegye chŏnsŏ, "T'oegye sŏnsaeng ŏnhaeng t'ongnok," 2:40b.

39. Yi Hwang, T'oegye chŏnsŏ, "Simgyŏng huron," 41:11b–16; de Bary, Neo-Confucian Orthodoxy, pp. 176–77.

40. Yi Hwang, T'oegye chŏnsŏ, 10:16a–b (letter to No Susin).

41. The Chŏnsŭmnok nonbyŏn can be found in Yi Hwang, T'oegye chŏnsŏ, 41:23b–29b.

42. Wing-Tsit China, Instructions for Practical Living (New York: Columbia University Press, 1963), pp. 5–6; Julia Ching, To Acquire Wisdom, pp. 131–35.

43. Yi Hwang, "Chŏnsŭmnok nonbyŏn," 41:23b–29b; Yi Sangŭn, T'oegye ŭi saengae wa hangmun (The Life and Work of Yi Hwang) (Seoul: Sŏmun mun'go no. 83, 1973), pp. 155–79; Chan, Instructions, pp. 3–12; Julia Ching, To Acquire Wisdom.

44. Yi Hwang, T'oegye chŏnsŏ, "T'oegye sŏnsaeng ŏnhaeng t'ongnok," 2:40b; 13:6; 14:14. For a detailed study of Ch'en Hsien-chang's life and thought, see Jen Yu-wen, "Ch'en Hsien-chang's Philosophy of the Natural" in de Bary, ed., Self and Society in Ming Thought (New York: Columbia University Press, 1970), pp. 53–92.

45. Yi Hwang, T'oegye chŏnsŏ, "Paeksa sigyo Chŏnsŭmnok ch'ojŏn insŏ kihu," 41:29b–31b.

46. Hong Inu, Ch'ijaejip, kw 2, "Ch'ijae yugo," p. 26. For a general study on

Lo Ch'in-shun and his influence on Japanese Neo-Confucian thinkers, see Irene Bloom, "On the 'Abstraction' of Ming Thought: Some Concrete Evidence from the Philosophy of Lo Ch'in-shun," in de Bary and Bloom, eds., *Principle and Practicality* (New York: Columbia University Press, 1979), pp. 69–125. Yun Namhan mentions 1560 as the possible date of the first Korean printing of Lo's work. But he does not give any evidence for this assertion. See his "Yijo Yangmyŏnghak," pp. 2, 6. Abe Yoshio mentions a Korean edition which was printed in Sŏngju and was later taken to Japan. He gives no date. See Abe Yoshio, *Nihon Shushigaku to Chōsen* (Japanese Neo-Confucianism and Korea) (Tokyo: Tokyo daigaku shuppankai, 1965), pp. 514–20.

47. Ki Taesŭng, *Kobong munjip* (The Collected Works of Ki Taesŭng) (Seoul: Sŏnggyun'gwan taehakkyo, Taedong munhwa yŏn'guwŏn, 1976), 2:45–49b; Yi Hwang, *T'oegye chŏnsŏ*, "T'oegye sŏnsaeng ŏnhaeng t'ongnok," 2:40b; 13:5b.

48. *Myŏngjong sillok*, 15:38a–b.

49. Yi I confessed his transgression into Buddhism in a memorial he submitted upon his appointment as fifth counselor *(kyori)* of Hongmun'gwan in 1568. *Sŏnjo sujŏng sillok*, 2:6a–b.

50. Yi I, *Yulgok chŏnsŏ*, 10:8b, 13b, 37a–b; Hŏ Pong, *Hagok sŏnsaeng choch'ŏn'gi* (Hŏ Pong's Diary of a Trip to Peking) in: *Yŏnhaengnok sŏnjip* (Collection of Peking Diaries) (Seoul: Sŏnggyun'gwan taehakkyo, Taedong munhwa yŏn'guwŏn, 1960), A:3b.

51. Yi I, *Yulgok chŏnsŏ*, 10:2–9, 11–18, 34–38b (correspondence with Sŏng Hon, 1572); 29:63b–64b.

52. Yi I submitted the *Sŏnghak chipyo* in 1575. Yi I, *Yulgok chŏnsŏ*, "Yŏnbo," 33:55b–56; *Sŏnjo sillok*, 9:29b; *Sŏnjo sujŏng sillok*, 9:12–13.

53. Yi I, *Yulgok chŏnsŏ*, "Kyŏngmongp'yŏn pal," 13:31–32.

54. *Sŏnjo sillok*, 7:13b, 19. Ch'en Chien quoted many of Wang Yang-ming's poems to demonstrate the extent of Buddhist influence on his thought. Julia Ching, *To Acquire Wisdom*, p. 160.

55. Yi I, *Yulgok chŏnsŏ*, "Hakpu t'ongbyŏn pal," 13:32–34; for Yi's views on the Way in Korea, see "Tongho mundap," 15:8b–9b; "Ŏrok," 31:60.

56. Yi I protested vigorously against Yi Chun'gyŏng's (1499–1572) deathbed prediction that there would be factional groups. *Sŏnjo sujŏng sillok*, 6:4–5b.

57. Nam Ŏn'gyŏng's life and thought are studied in Yun Namhan, "Nam Ŏn'gyŏng ŭi saengae, sasang mit Yangmyŏnghak munje" (The Life and Thought of Nam Ŏn'gyŏng and Problems Concerning Wang Yang-ming), *Chungang saron* (June 1975), 2:29–63. I am greatly indebted to Prof. Yun's careful research.

58. Yi Hwang, *T'oegye chŏnsŏ*, 14:7b–9b, 13b–15.

59. Prof. Yun suggests that despite the fact that Nam Ŏn'gyŏng had many friends and acquaintances, references to his thought in their collected works were dropped because of Nam's "scholarly deficiences." Yun Namhan, "Nam Ŏn'gyŏng," p. 50. Nam's own work was burned during the Manchu invasions.

60. Yi Hwang, *T'oegye chŏnsŏ*, 42:20b–25b.

61. *Myŏngjong sillok*, 32:76b, 77b; 33:5b, 7, 10b.

62. *Ibid.*, 33:44–45.

63. Yi Hwang, *T'oegye chŏnsŏ*, 13:6b–8 (letter to Hong Inu).

64. Nam Ŏn'gyŏng's official career, during which he was recommended for promotion by Yi I, No Susin, and others, ended in 1589 when he lost his office as the result of one of the first factional struggles. Although he had tried to stay neutral, his sympathies were on Yi I's side. During the Japanese invasions he regained some prominence as a leader of a righteous army unit *(ŭibyŏng)*, but died early in the campaign in 1594. For details of Nam's life, see Prof. Yun's study.

65. Prof. Yun studied Nam's disciples and concluded that the majority came from the lower levels of the aristocracy or even from commoner background. Among Nam's teachers there were some of secondary son origin. See Yun Namhan, "Nam Ŏn'gyŏng," pp. 43–48.

66. *Sŏnjo sillok*, 53:19. Yi Yo, a member of the royal clan, lectured about the "learning of the mind" to King Sŏnjo in 1594 when the king solicited opinions about solving the Japanese crisis. The king was severely reprimanded by an official of the Hongmun'gwan for lending his ear to the wild talk of "a madman" like Yi Yo. *Sŏnjo sillok*, 53:16–17, 17b–20, 24b–25b. It is interesting to note that many of the early followers of Wang Yang-ming were related to each other by marital ties. Yun Namhan, "Nam Ŏn'gyŏng," pp. 41–42.

67. No Susin, *Sojaejip* (The Collected Works of No Susin) (date uncertain; Kyujanggak), 7:16a–b.

68. No Su-sin, *Sojae sŏnsaeng naejip*, hap'yŏn, "Kusaerok," part 2, 8:1–7, 20b–21b; Yi Hwang, *T'oegye chŏnsŏ*, "Ŏnhaengnok," 2:40b.

69. *Sŏnjo sillok*, 8:32b, 38a–b.

70. Yi Ŏnjŏk, *Hoejae chŏnsŏ*, "Taehak changgu poyu pal," 1–2 (No Susin's postface).

71. Chang Yu, *Kyegokchip* (The Collected Works of Chang Yu) (1643 ed.; Kyujanggak), "Manp'il chasŏ," 1:24a–b, 35.

72. *Sŏnjo sillok*, 10:4b–5; Yi Hwang, *T'oegye chŏnsŏ*, "Ŏnhaengnok," 1:19a–b; Cho Mok, *Wŏlch'ŏnjip* (Collected Works of Cho Mok) (date uncertain; Kyujanggak), 3:3.

73. Lu Kuang-tsu's biography is in *Ming-shih*, "Biographies," *chüan* 224. There are no dates for his life. He passed the *chin-shih* examination in 1547.

74. Yun Kŭnsu, *Wŏlchŏng sŏnsaeng pyŏlchip* (Additional Collected Works of Yun Kŭnsu) (1773 ed.; Kyujanggak), 1:1–14; Yi Hwang, *T'oegye chŏnsŏ*, 35:16b.

75. Yu Sŏngyong, *Sŏae munjip*, "Yŏnbo," 1:5b.

76. Hŏ Pong, *Hagok sŏnsaeng choch'ŏn'gi*, A and B, entries throughout diary; Cho Hŏn, *Choch'ŏn ilgi* in *Chungbong sŏnsaeng munjip* (Collected Works of Cho Hŏn) (Ch'ŏngju, Ch'ungbuk taehak, 1973), *kw* 10.

77. See note 74.

78. *Sŏnjo sillok*, 5:9–10; 6:24b–25. During the *chia-ching* period (1522–66) several earlier Confucians were replaced with such eminent names of the late

Sung as Hu An-kuo (1073–1138), Lu Hsiang-shan, and Chen Te-hsiu, and with the first Ming scholar, Hsüeh Hsüan. The Korean government apparently wanted to follow suit, but Yi Hwang cautioned against hasty changes. Similar later requests were rejected. *Chŭngbo munhŏn pigo* (Enlarged and Supplemented Encyclopedia) (Seoul: Tongguk munhwasa, 1957), 204:3b.

79. Yun Kŭnsu asserted that the Koreans followed the changes in the Chinese Shrine of Confucius on the basis of the entries in the *Ta-Ming hui-tien*. *Wŏlchŏngjip* (Collected Works of Yun Kŭnsu) (1651 ed.; Kyujanggak), 4:21–24; 5:42–43 (letter to Chang Yu).

80. Cho Hŏn, who accompanied Hŏ Pong to Peking in 1574, pleaded in his report about recent changes in the Chinese Shrine of Confucius for the speedy enshrinement of Korean Neo-Confucians. *Sŏnjo sujŏng sillok*, 8:28b–30b, 39b. Cho Hŏn apparently also asked for following the Chinese changes. See *Chŭngbo munhŏn pigo*, 204:3b, 10–11b.

81. Deuchler, "Self-Cultivation," p. 31.

Miura Kunio

Orthodoxy and Heterodoxy in Seventeenth-Century Korea: Song Siyŏl and Yun Hyu

1. INTRODUCTION

THE TERM I refer to here as "heterodoxy is *i-tuan* in Chinese, which literally means "aberrant outgrowth" or "deviation." It was not originally used in opposition to *cheng-t'ung*, "legitimate succession," a political-historical term which had its own antonym in *jun-t'ung*, "interim control." Rather the "deviation" of *i-tuan* was understood to be a departure from the Way (Tao), known in Confucianism as the "Way of the Duke of Chou and Confucius," in Taoism as the "Way of Lao Tzu" and in Chinese Buddhism as the "Way of Buddha." Mencius was the first Confucian to distinguish between the Way of Confucius and the "heretical doctrines" *(hsieh-shuo)* of Yang Chu and Mo Tzu,[1] but during the long period of Confucian dominance in the Han, and the subsequent rise of Neo-Taoism and Buddhism in the medieval period, no such distinction was emphasized. Chu Hsi (1130–1200) later described this as a period in which the Way was lost. In this Middle Age the controversy about orthodoxy and heterodoxy was between Buddhists and Taoists,[2] and the Confucians, with a few exceptions like Han Yü (768–824), remained impassive observers of the controversy which was going on.

It was left to the Ch'eng brothers in the Sung, who in the name of the Learning or School of the Way *(tao-hsüeh)* proclaimed the orthodoxy of Confucianism to level sharp attacks on Buddhism and Taoism as heretical.[3] Chu Hsi of the Southern Sung, a follower of the Ch'eng brothers, carried on their fight against heresy, aiming especially at Zen Buddhism, the School of Lu Hsiang-shan (1139–93), Taoism,[4] and the School of Utilitarianism *(shih-kung-p'ai)* of the Che-chiang, Yung-chia and Yung-k'ang schools. As the School of the Way became established, Neo-Confucianism was adopted as the official ideology of the Mongol dynasty, but it was still not until the time of Wang Yang-ming (1472–1529) in the Ming dynasty that Neo-Confucianism really developed a heresy within it.

The Western notion of orthodoxy vs. heterodoxy involves a conflict between opposing things, each of which belongs to the same category or claims a common ground.[5] That is to say, heretics were not pagans, yet this makes it all the more significant that the purported defenders of orthodox Christianity aimed their attacks at heresies within Christianity. In China, Buddhism or Taoism are to Confucianism what paganism was to Christianity in Europe. Their only parallel in China to the European case of orthodoxy vs. heterodoxy is the controversy between the Chu Hsi School of Neo-Confucianism and the Wang Yang-ming School. But we should note that the Wang Yang-ming School, even though attacked as heterodox Neo-Confucianism,[6] was not subjected to official persecution. Nor was there serious repression of Taoism and Buddhism. Religious Taoism had penetrated extensively among the people, and Buddhism had broad social support, so the so-called "three teachings" had learned to live together without serious conflict. In fact, during the Ming the trend of the times was toward coalescence, and to what was called the "Unity of the Three Teachings." Thus in China there was not an atmosphere of intolerance and repression in which a man who stood outside of orthodoxy might be put to death.[7]

In Korea, I think there was definitely a tendency toward intolerance: toward the view that only one orthodox teaching should be allowed to exist. That one orthodox doctrine was, of course, Neo-Confucianism.[8] In the earlier days of the Yi dynasty students of Neo-Confucianism sometimes had suffered repression, namely, in the political purges known as *sahwa* (1498–1545), but by the time of the two great Neo-Confucian scholars, Yi T'oegye (Yi Hwang, 1501–70) and Yi Yulgok (Yi I, 1563–84), Neo-Confucianism had secured a position of indisputable preeminence. Other teachings had no solid ground on which to stand against it. Buddhism had yielded its place as the guiding principle of the society to Confucianism immediately after the political change from Koryŏ to the Yi dynasty. Taoism had no power or influence worthy of notice at that time. And the Wang Yang-ming School, though transmitted to Korea, had immediately become stigmatized as heresy. Thus there was none of the kind of controversy that had arisen between the Chu Hsi and Wang Yang-ming schools of Neo-Confucianism or between Confucianism, Buddhism, or Taoism in China. Conflict, if any, could only arise on rather narrow grounds within Neo-Confucianism. The controversy over the Four Beginnings and Seven Emotions *(sadan ch'ilchŏng)* is an example of this. The tragic dispute which arose between Song Siyŏl (1607–89) and Yun Hyu (1617–80) over orthodoxy and heterodoxy within Neo-Confucianism is another case.

In China, Neo-Confucianism had come to hold the position of orthodoxy as the established teaching in the bureaucratic examination system. It was necessary for one to master Neo-Confucian texts if he wished to enter into the ranks of the government officials, but outside that system there was still a good measure of freedom of thought. A man who studied Buddhism, Taoism, or the Yang-ming philosophy might be criticized as a heretic, but was rarely subjected to actual persecution. In Japan, Neo-Confucianism had been recognized as the legitimate teaching by the Tokugawa shogunate, but in the absence of an examination system, mastery of Neo-Confucian texts was not a sine qua non for entering into the ranks of officials. Furthermore, institutionally speaking, Confucians were independent of the governing *samurai* class so that they were free to study without bearing a direct political responsibility. Many of the distinguished thinkers in the Edo period, such as Itō Jinsai (1627–1705) and Ogyū Sorai (1666–1728), began as students of Ch'eng-Chu Neo-Confucianism, but ended up as its critics. We can say, then, that Neo-Confucianism in Japan was only a symbolic orthodoxy. In Korea, by contrast, Neo-Confucianism dominated not only the bureaucratic system, but even the daily life of the people (concretely in the form of the *Family Ritual of Master Chu [Chu Tzu chia-li]*) and their spiritual life as well. How then do we account for this difference?

For an adequate answer to this question one would have to approach it from several angles, including the sociological, economic, or historical points of view. But, for my part, I shall discuss it from the standpoint of the consciousness of Korean intellectuals. In a word, it is in terms of how they identified themselves. They had a sense of inferiority about their own country, which they thought of as an outlying country and as a country of "barbarians to the east of China" *(tongi)*.[9] In order for a country on the frontier to associate with China, a minimum requirement was the reforming of its "barbarian" manners and customs to conform to Confucian decorum, and a maximum requirement was to adopt the orthodox teaching of China. Neo-Confucianism fulfilled just these requirements because it possessed a coherent body of ritual literature, as represented by the *Explanatory Guide to Classics and Commentaries on Ceremonies and Rituals (I-li ching-chuan t'ung-chieh)* by Chu Hsi and Huang Kan (1152– 1221) and by Chu's *Family Ritual*.

Korean Neo-Confucianism had not only its metaphysical superstructure, but, so to speak, a solid body of ritual in the regulations governing the scholar-officials' daily life, to which much more importance was attached in Korea than in China. This is far different from the case with Neo-Confucianism in Japan, where the metaphysics was readily adopted but for the most part, aside from a few real enthusiasts among the Confucians, people proved inhospitable to the *Family Ritual*. That is why it was said that Confucianism came to Japan not as a religion but as a form of learning.[10]

Cho Hŏn's (1544–92) memorial to King Sŏnjo (r. 1567–1608) is a typical example of how eagerly the Koreans adopted the Neo-Confucian ritual. Here is revealed the consciousness of a Korean scholar-official:

The Chinese system of dress and headgear is generally simple and easy to provide. Now there is unified rule over the whole land and all of the peoples share the same writing system. In regions of Yün-nan and Kuei-chou over ten thousand *li* from the capital, the people once rolled their hair on a pin like barbarians, and spoke in words beyond our understanding, but now they follow only Chinese institutions. On the other hand, our Korea, needless to say, less than four thousand *li* from the capital, and comparable to the five feudal domains of the capital region, nonetheless exhibits so many shameful customs in regard to the people's style of dress and headgear. Why should this be?[11]

The Neo-Confucian ritual was nominally adopted at the founding of the Yi dynasty. The *Family Ritual* was propagated by Chŏng Mongju (1337–92) as early as the fourteenth century, but its spread was hampered by the so-called "Eastern customs" (*tongsok*). Although by the seventeenth century Korea had won the admiration of the Chinese as a "land of courtesy and decorum," in the age of Song Siyŏl many obstacles remained to be overcome. Therefore even in the lifetime of Song Siyŏl, a disciple of Kim Changsaeng (Sagye, 1548–1631) who was known as "a great scholar of rites in the East," there was still conflict between the Confucian ritual and the "customs of the East." In fact, Song's collected works, the *Compendium of Master Song's Work (Songja taejŏn)*, is filled with questions and answers, exchanged between him and his disciples, as to how the regulations stated in the *Family Ritual* should be observed in their daily life.

Suzuki Mitsuo has asserted that Neo-Confucianism was originally an expression of the self-assertion of the Han Chinese living on the southern frontier.[12] (Chu Hsi was born and brought up in the border area of Chung-yüan, Fukien Province.) However, the relationship between Neo-Confucianism and Korean Confucians living on the far eastern edge of the Chinese world was even closer and more important as the basis of the scholar's identity than was that between the central culture of China and Chu Hsi. Thus it was natural for Korean Confucians to feel extreme discomfort at the thought that the philosophy of Wang Yang-ming should have come to displace Chu Hsi's teaching in the homeland of orthodox Neo-Confucianism. They must have felt a threat to their own insecure position more strongly than Chinese scholars, who did not face this problem of cultural identity. At the same time it should not be overlooked that they acquired a sense of mission and derived some pride from the fact that the integrity of the orthodox teaching should be defended nowhere else so well as in "this eastern country of ours." For instance, Sŏng Hon (Ugye, 1535–98) sent this letter to the Chinese Yüan Huang, who respected the teachings of Wang Yang-ming while rejecting the Neo-Confucianism of Chu Hsi in the mid-Ming period:

Our people study only the Confucian classics, the commentaries on them, and the works of the learning of human nature and principle that your country sent us. And they think that there is no other principle of the Way than the one found in these doctrines.[13]

This attitude became even more firmly entrenched after the Manchu invasions of 1627 *(chŏngmyo horan)* and 1636 *(pyŏngja horan)*, and after China herself had experienced the catastrophe of 1644—the fall of the Ming dynasty and the domination of the barbarian Manchus. Koreans despaired over the fact that it should not be the Han race but hateful barbarians who now reigned over the China they had so respected. But, on the other hand, this aroused a sense of responsibility for protecting the orthodox tradition, in this far "eastern country of ours." No other scholar-official embodied this sense of pride and zeal more than did Song Siyŏl. And if anyone should dare to appear before him and misread a line of

Master Chu's commentaries or try to explain some mistaken theory of ritual, he could expect to be subjected to a withering fire of criticism in the name of "rejecting heresy and respecting orthodoxy" *(pyŏksa wido)*.[14]

2. CHU HSI AND NEO-CONFUCIANISM IN SONG SIYŎL

Not for his systematic thought, but for his fanatic devotion to Chu Hsi, is Song Siyŏl remembered, with a special aura about him, in the history of East-Asian Confucianism. His worship of Chu Hsi was directed not only to Chu's doctrine but also toward his every action and gesture, as if with the fond gaze of a lover. Indeed in no other country—Japan, Vietnam, or even China—has there appeared such an enthusiastic and wholehearted admirer of Chu Hsi's teaching, understood here not only as a system of philosophy, but as all that Chu Hsi stood for in personal behavior; in sum, the whole being of Chu Hsi. Does this not express in a special way the attitude of Koreans who were trying to establish their own identity in difficult circumstances on the frontier of Chinese civilization? It was Song Siyŏl who preeminently embodied this attitude.

Song's philosophical world view is set forth in relatively well-ordered fashion in, for example, his *Reading Notes (Kansŏ chamnok)*,[15] but he had no original philosophy which went beyond the bounds of Chu's Neo-Confucianism. For him even a slight deviation from the track of Chu Hsi was an unpardonable crime, so that to construct a philosophical edifice of his own never would have occurred to him. For him Chu Hsi was an infallible guide. He said, "The man of whom it could be said that all his words are correct, and all of his conduct proper, is Master Chu."[16] Song also said, "Master Chu's every word and phrase is most reasonable and authoritative."[17]

Song believed that the truths of Neo-Confucianism transcended time and space, and were therefore valid norms not only for China five hundred years before but for Korea in his own time. He told King Hyojong (r. 1649–59) that Chu Hsi's precepts were not less practicable in the present than in the past.[18] Thus he could do no better than to expound as thoroughly as possible what Chu Hsi had already taught.[19] The exposition of Neo-Confucianism and the worship of Chu Hsi in themselves constituted Song's philosophy.

Next to Chu Hsi, Song Siyŏl honored Yi Yulgok partly as a matter of his own relation to the succession of Neo-Confucian teaching (i.e., Yulgok was the master of Song Siyŏl's master Kim Changsaeng), and partly also because he believed that Yulgok represented the legitimate succession to Chu Hsi's doctrine in the east.[20]

Here we cannot overlook a certain partisanship in Song's pressing the claims of the school of Kiho against the school of Yŏngnam, which claimed succession to Chu Hsi's doctrine for Yi T'oegye. Song Siyŏl compiled "Yulgok's life chronology" *(Yulgok yŏnbo)* and often expressed admiration for Yulgok in his letters and official utterances. This expressed his own protest against what he considered to be a wrongful estimate of Yulgok in the learned and political circles of his time. By contrast, Song Siyŏl maintained an ambivalent attitude toward Yi T'oegye. In those days this leader of Korean Confucianism had won a respect among scholars that crossed party lines and Song Siyŏl too at times paid unusual tribute to this great thinker. But at other times, while taking care not to provoke the Yongnam school, he expressed some disapproval of T'oegye's philosophy and conduct.[21]

Returning now to the matter of Song Siyŏl's devotion to Chu Hsi, he said, "Hanhwŏn [Kim Koengp'il, 1454–1504] respected the *Elementary Learning (Hsiao-hsüeh)*, Chŏngam [Cho Kwangjo, 1482–1519] respected *Reflections on Things at Hand (Chin-ssu lu)*, T'oedo [Yi T'oegye] respected the *Heart Classic (Hsin-ching)*, Yulgok respected the *Four Books (Ssu-shu)*, and Sagye respected the *Elementary Learning* and *Family Ritual of Master Chu*."[22] Here I would like to add that Song Siyŏl respected the *Great Compendium of Master Chu's Work (Chu Tzu ta-ch'üan)* and *Classified Conversations of Master Chu (Chu Tzu yü-lei)*. The reason Song always kept these two books close at hand was that, while Chu's *Commentaries on the Four Books (Ssu-shu chi-chu)* contained the marrow of Master Chu's philosophy, these two collections were alive with the flesh and blood of his thought—vibrant with the processes of his own thinking and questioning, expressions of the delicate shades of his feelings, and the accounts of his behavior—that is, with the person Chu Hsi himself was. To Song these books were Scriptures *(Ching)*. The *Compendium of Master Chu's Work* was even more sacred a text than the *Classified Conversations*, and Song went so far as to criticize Yi T'oegye for profaning this "scripture" by punctuating it with a lot of dots in the text of his *Essentials of Master Chu's Letters (Chujasŏ chŏryo)*, a selection of Chu Hsi's letters.[23]

Song's respect and affection for Chu's *Compendium* led him to produce his *Critical Notes on the Compendium of Master Chu's Work (Chuja taejŏn ch'aŭi),*[24] the first and most complete book discussing the entirety of the *Compendium* in all of East Asia. Though Yi T'oegye had already written expositions on some part of the *Compendium* in his *Essentials of Chu's Letters* and *Commentary on the Essentials of Chu's Letters (Chujasŏ chŏryo kiŭi),* Song Siyŏl took over this project and succeeded in completing this laborious work in the midst of cutthroat partisan strife during the last days of his life.[25]

In classical Chinese terms this work would have qualified as a commentary *(chuan)* on a classic *(ching),* that is on the *Compendium,* but Song Siyŏl hesitated to have his work called a *chuan*[26] (commentary), partly because he was concerned about the claims of the Yŏngnam school to T'oegye's having produced a commentary in the form of *Essentials of Chu's Letters (chŏryo)* and *Commentary on the Essentials of Chu's Letters (kiŭi),* and partly because it seemed to him too great an honor to accord his own effort the venerable status of *chuan* (commentary). This is why he chose the more modest title of *Critical Notes (ch'aŭi).*

Incidentally, Song Siyŏl's Critical Notes were supplemented later by the *Questions on the Critical Notes (Chuja taejŏn ch'aŭi munmok)* written by Kim Ch'anghyŏp (1651–1708), Song's disciple, which was further augmented in the Supplement, *Chuja taejŏn ch'aŭi munmok p'yobo* written by Kim Maesun (1776–1840) Ch'anghyŏp's descendant. Finally the long history of exposition on the *Compendium* reached its culmination in the *Chuja taejŏn ch'aŭi chippo* written by Yi Hangno (1792–1868), an advocate of "Defend Orthodoxy and Reject Heterodoxy" *(wijŏng chŏksa)* in the final period of the Yi dynasty. In East Asia this may be the only example of a man's scholarly work gaining as much respect as a classic does and thus attracting the supplementary annotations of successive scholars through four hundred years. Can this perhaps be seen as a distinctively Korean phenomenon?

Now let me set forth more concretely the ways in which Song Siyŏl expressed his devotion to Chu Hsi. Reflecting on his own past, Song once said, "My whole life has been spent in reading the *Compendium* and *Classified Conversations of Master Chu."*[27] The "reading" he refers to is not the kind that could be done in the solitude of one's study. As a faithful follower of Chu Hsi who recognized the need to combine the "fathoming of principle" *(ch'iung-li)* with "actual practice" *(shih-hsien),* what

Song meant by "reading" was to live up to the norms of word and deed that Chu Hsi had set forth in these works. In fact he lived all of his life in that way.

He derived great satisfaction from modeling himself as closely as possible on Chu Hsi both in politics and in everyday life. Concerning the former, we know something about his activities on behalf of the communal granary system *(sach'angpŏp)* which he tried to put into practice in two places in Ch'ungch'ŏng Province. He was not of course the only scholar who tried this in Korea. According to his own account of the system *(Sach'anggi)* contained in his *Compendium*, a good many scholar-officials seemed to have made such an attempt in those days.[28] His sworn enemy Yun Hyu also "studied Master Chu's communal granary system with members of his village and, by adding here and subtracting there, established such a system in the village [of Igang]."[29] Since Song had "put it into practice in strict accordance with Master Chu's provisions for the communal granary,"[30] if he had heard of Yun Hyu's modifications he would no doubt have been angered at the thought that Yun should have dared to add or subtract anything from Chu Hsi's system! Furthermore, he recommended the adoption of Master Chu's famine relief policies *(Chiu-huang-ts'e)*,[31] supplemented a book on agricultural policies written by Sin Husok (1600–61), then magistrate of Kongju by adding Chu Hsi's "Essay on the Encouragement of Agriculture" *(Ch'üan-nung-wen)*,[32] and advised King Sukchong in political matters by presenting his annotations on Chu Hsi's memorials,[33] which constituted a section of his *Critical Notes*.

As for ritual, I have already noted that Song Siyŏl was foremost in putting Chu Hsi's *Family Ritual* into thoroughgoing practice, hoping thereby to reform "the customs and manners of the East." Korean Confucians had already devoted much study to Chu's *Family Ritual* by this time, and there is abundant evidence in the collected literary writings of Korean scholars that Song's predecessors had struggled mightily to convert Koreans from their barbarian customs and manners to the Confucian ritual.[34] This is found in the *Manual for Mourning Services (Sangnye piyo)* written by Sin Ŭigyŏng (fl. 1610) and expanded by Kim Changsaeng, *Questions and Explanations on Doubtful Points in Ritual (Ŭirye munhae)* and *Comprehensive Examinations of the Family Ritual (Karye chimnam)* compiled by Kim to elucidate the Way of Ritual. In the same age as Song Siyŏl, Yu Kye (1607–64) edited the *Source and the Branches of the Family Ritual (Karye wŏllyu)* and later Yi Sŏnjo (fl. 1800) edited the

Supplementary Explanations on the Family Ritual (Karye chŭnghae), which brought together the views on ritual of Confucians up to that time. But customs and manners are the most obstinate and conservative elements in human behavior, and to change their direction is far less easy than to change from one system of metaphysics to another. Furthermore, the *Family Ritual* was not just a simple routine, but involved many different instrumentalities of foreign provenance, so that problems arose one after the other in their practical implementation. Even Kim Changsaeng at the end of his life expressed the thought, "I have studied the *Family Ritual* all my life, but I still cannot understand all of it."[35] It was by performing these ceremonial practices according to the *Family Ritual* that Confucians were supposed to identify themselves as such. Yet, in describing his predecessors' conduct of life or writing their epitaphs, for example, Song Siyŏl often made mention of their following the *Family Ritual* as a point of special distinction. For this to be so means conversely that many scholar-officials of those times did not measure up to the same standard in their observance of the *Family Ritual*.

In the area of family ritual Song Siyŏl wrote *Questions and Answers on Doubtful Points in Ritual (Yeŭi mundap)*, but he was by no means merely a scholar who pursued his researches on ritual within the privacy of his study. We can see what great pains he took to practice the rituals himself from his disciples' testimony that their master "constantly was trying to transform our own manners and customs to accord with the institutions of China."[36] And it was just like him to have said just before he took a cup of poison in his place of exile that his funeral should be performed mainly according to the *Family Ritual*, but if there were anything lacking in it, reference should be made to the *Manual for Mourning Services*.[37]

These are only a few instances among many which might be cited of his devotion to the ritual cult of Chu Hsi. His aim was not merely to give concrete embodiment to the teachings of Chu Hsi, but to experience for himself what Chu Hsi had experienced, so to speak to breathe the same air as Chu Hsi. So for him, the well-known slogan that "A man can learn to become a sage" must have meant "A man can learn to become a Master Chu." The following are a few episodes which illustrate this point.

In order to cure the piles from which he suffered in his declining years, he adopted a prescription Chu Hsi had given to his disciples.[38] Song also had eye trouble just like Chu Hsi, who almost lost his eyesight in later life, but Song rather thought it a great honor to have the same experience as Chu Hsi, even if it meant suffering such an ailment.[39]

Moreover he gave his grandchild a courtesy name, Muwŏn (Wu-yüan), after the name of Chu Hsi's native town.[40] In 1667 (when Siyŏl was sixty-one years old), a ship carrying ninety-five merchants from Ch'üan-chou and Chang-chou in China to Japan was shipwrecked on the coast of Cheju Island. A little while after the accident, Song Siyŏl heard the news that the passengers' heads were not shaven in accordance with the Manchu practice, and moreover were dressed in the style of Ming. He was greatly pleased to learn that people of the Great Ming still lived, but at the same time, hearing that they had been returned to China, he felt sorry that he could not have seen and asked them about historic spots associated with Chu Hsi (Chu Hsi had served as a public official in Ch'üan-chou and Chang-chou).[41]

It was in imitation of Chu Hsi's action that he sent back a birthday present that had been sent to him.[42] When one of his granddaughters, born in the cyclical year of kyesa, died young, he sent a letter to her betrothed, a man named Cho Pokhyang, saying that Chu Hsi's daughter, born in the same cyclical year, also had died young just after being engaged to a man of the same name—Chao in Chinese—and completing the payment of dowry.[43] Another time, when Song intended to submit a memorial to the king, he had divination performed according to the Book of Changes by his friend Min Chŏngjung (1628–92), so as to ascertain whether or not it was propitious to pursue his intention. The answer was negative: chŏmgwae (chien-kua). So he gave it up, and burned the draft of his memorial to ashes.[44] In this instance he was following Chu Hsi's example on a similar occasion involving tun-kua[45] in the Book of Changes.

There are many other examples which could be given to show Song Siyŏl's worshipful emulation of Chu Hsi, such as letters to his disciples written in rhetoric reminiscent of Chu Hsi's letters (and T'oegye's rhetoric too was somewhat in the same vein). Often after having fully presented his views, he would say: "This is not my opinion, but Chu Hsi's." Moreover, in his speech and letters he often used Chu Hsi's words and phrases.

3. SONG SIYŎL AND YUN HYU

Song's idolization of Chu Hsi grew the more intense as he became involved in a confrontation with Yun Hyu. The more he became con-

vinced of Yun's heresy, the more he felt called upon to defend orthodoxy.

Song Siyŏl and Yun Hyu, in youth, had been intimate friends. But
when Yun Hyu revised Chu Hsi's *Commentary on the Mean (Chungyong
changgu)* at about the age of thirty-six,[46] Song threw at him the bitter
epithet "a rebel who destroys Confucian culture" *(samun nanjŏk)*.[47] Yet
he continued to hold some friendly feelings toward him, hoping still to
lead him back to the right way. Thus it was not until Song was fifty years
old that he began to criticize Yun Hyu openly. We can see this in a letter
he wrote in 1656 in which he began to attack Yun Hyu in something of
the fiery tone which became so characteristic later:

> Igong [Yun Hyu] comes up with more and more novel ideas. Now he criticizes
> Master Chu, saying that his interpretation of the *Book of Odes* loses its true spirit.
> How dreadful! Yet the more novel his view becomes, the more people are misled.
> Who is there to take a stand against this menace, which threatens disaster like a
> flood. How lamentable it is![48]

The rites dispute of 1659 *(kihae yesong)*, three years later, made them
part from one another in political as well as philosophical matters. Then
the rites dispute of 1674 *(kabin yesong)* led to the irreparable break between them. And this was followed by the political upheaval of 1680 during which the Namin (Southerners) were ousted from power by Song's
faction, the Sŏin (Westerners), and Yun Hyu, a Namin, lost his life.

In the meantime, Song Siyŏl had become intensely angry when he
heard that Yun Hyu had trapped Yulgok and Sŏng Hon in collusion with
the school of Yŏngnam; that Yun prided himself on having made a contribution greater even than the achievements of the sage-king Yü by de-
nouncing Chu Hsi; and that he had said it was not necessary to read any
of the commentaries of Chu Hsi, and that Confucius could be named
directly without regard to taboos.[49] The intensity of his anger can be seen
in the following words: "I will never repent of having condemned Yun
Hyu, even if it should bring upon me a disaster like the "burning of the
books and condemning of the Confucians" *(fen-shu k'eng-ju)*.[50] He also
said: "If I were to be killed by Yun Hyu, I would be glad to die the most
glorious death."[51]

The *Compendium of Master Song's Work* is filled with Song Siyŏl's
reproaches of Yun Hyu. What he could not possibly tolerate was Yun's
denunciation of Chu Hsi's whole theory rather than simply pointing to

differences in their interpretation of ritual. (It seemed to Song to be a more severe denunciation than the actual facts warranted.) Even in the practice of ritual, Song thought Yun was deliberately challenging Chu Hsi, saying "Yun does not observe the regulations of mourning dress as Chu Hsi prescribed and disrupts the canonical order."[52]

Song Siyŏl continued to accuse Yun Hyu of being hostile to Chu Hsi and went so far as to call him "a man beyond all reason" (ioe chi in).[53] This is more than heresy, which according to the classical definition is a diversion from the main current but still in the same stream of basic principles. "A man beyond all reason" is rather close to being a pagan. In fact, Song Siyŏl went so far as to say, "A man who does not believe in Chu Hsi is a barbarian."[54] One cannot help thinking that such fierce denunciations made Yun Hyu appear to be a traitor to the nation.[55]

However, Song Siyŏl's fanaticism could not fail to call forth his second enemy: Yun Sŏn'gŏ (1610–69) and his son Yun Chŭng (1629–1714). Yun Sŏn'gŏ and Song Siyŏl had studied under the direction of the same teacher, Kim Chip (1574–1656) (Siyŏl's second master), but Yun highly appreciated Yun Hyu's scholarship and, even after the relationship between Song Siyŏl and Yun Hyu had broken up, continued to keep up a friendship with Yun Hyu and often defended him from Song Siyŏl's attack. This attitude made Sŏn'gŏ look like a traitor in the eyes of Song, and soon he too became an enemy of the latter. After Yun Sŏn'gŏ had died, his son Chŭng incurred the antagonism of Song Siyŏl in the same way. Song Siyŏl, late in life denounced this father and son more furiously even than he had Yun Hyu, and from this fierce attack arose the bitter factional struggle between the two factions, the Noron (Old Doctrine) and Soron (Young Doctrine).

For their part, the two Yuns wished to stand aloof from factional strife and, in fact, did not denounce Song Siyŏl on behalf of Yun Hyu's partisans. In this respect, we must say that they fell innocent victims to the factional strife, since in the end they were driven into a corner and had to join the opposing faction in resistance to Song Siyŏl's intransigence.[56]

One of the reasons Song Siyŏl felt he had to denounce heretics was that he had his own doubts about the scholar-officials of his day.[57] He deeply deplored the decline of the School of the Way in China[58] and the neglect of Chu Hsi's books there.[59] In that situation, if heretics like Wang

Yang-ming were to take the place of orthodox Chu Hsi scholars, the whole world would surely descend to the condition of barbarians and beasts.[60] Therefore, it is no wonder that he was driven to say:

> If I were not here [to defend him] Master Chu would not be a sage second only to the Great Sage of the East (Confucius) nor would Yulgok be able to uphold the orthodox succession to the Way; on the contrary, Yun Hyu would appear to be a true Confucian, and the King of the Manchus would appear to be the legitimate ruler of the world.[61]

Song's passion for "attacking heterodoxy and defending the Way" was more intensively and exclusively directed at the idolization of Chu Hsi in his stormy later years. After he survived his defeat in the rites dispute of 1674 at the age of sixty-eight, he succeeded in purging Yun Hyu and the Namin in 1680. But, a decade later, in 1689, he was pushed into a corner and finally met death at the hands of the remnants of the Namin and Soron. It was these fifteen years of adversity that made Song Siyŏl feel very close to Chu Hsi personally because the struggle which he experienced for the protection of orthodox scholarship in the period reminded him of the persecution which Chu Hsi had experienced in the period of the proscription of false learning (*wei-hsüeh-chin*) by the Southern Sung dynasty.

In 1674, when the Namin brought about his downfall, Song wrote a letter as follows:

> Master Chu said: "It is a great honor to have my name put on the blacklist in the last days of my life." Now if the honorable Sir Nam [Nam Kuman, 1629–1711] does so to me, it would be a double honor.[62]

The quotation is from an ironical remark made by Chu Hsi during the proscription of "false learning." Song Siyŏl often mentioned this phrase in order to comfort himself in the midst of severe factional strife.

The year of 1675, when he was condemned to exile, was a turning point in Song's political life. Only then did he become alive to the dangerous threat represented by his antagonists. We have seen his reference to the danger of burning books and burying Confucians alive in his letter of that year.[63] And he compared his *ŭlmyo* (1675)) and *pyŏngjin* (1676) years to Chu Hsi's *wu-wu* (1198) and *chi-wei* (1199).[64] In the years of *ŭlmyo* and *pyŏngjin*, Song Siyŏl was sixty-nine and seventy years old, and in the years of *Ch'ing-yüan wu-wu* (1198) and *chi-wei* (1199) Chu Hsi, at the same age, saw his life at stake, confronted by the false learning proscription at its height.

After Song Siyŏl was exiled, he became even more absorbed in reading Chu's *Compendium* than before. That autumn he wrote to Min Yujung (1630–87): "Now, if we threw away this book, where would it end?"[65]
In his period of exile he had completed his *Critical Notes on the Compendium of Master Chu's Work* as mentioned before. At the age of seventy, also, he stated that though, after the false learning proscription, Master
Chu had made frequent use of the word "laugh" *(hsiao)* in his letters,
only now could he understand its real significance.[66] This reflects his intensive reading of the *Compendium* in order to encourage himself in adversity.

In the summer of 1680, upon hearing that Yun Hyu had been put
to death on his way home after being discharged from his post, Song Siyŏl trembled in astonishment and terror, and then made the following
prophecy to his grandson Song Chusŏk (1650–92):

In the future the disasters befalling scholar-officials will become more frightful
than before. Sooner or later it will be asserted that Yun Hyu was falsely charged.
Then another disaster will befall scholar-officials. It will be Yun Chŭng taking
revenge for Hyu.[67]

And he gave his son this admonition:

My family had better act as if it were not involved in the present case [of Yun
Hyu and other Namin leaders being put to death]. In the time of Chŏng Yŏrip
(?–1589) some people expressed their delight too freely. As a result the disaster of
1591 was precipitated. We are not without a precedent in a former age.[68]

We can guess from these words that when the Namin faction was
purged, rather than taking an optimistic view Song anticipated disaster in
the future. In fact it was not only the remnants of the Namin but a new
antagonist in the person of Yun Chŭng who openly began to denounce
Song. Their influence grew stronger day by day. Nevertheless in response
to this, Song only grew more passionate, despite his advanced age, in
"defending Master Chu's Way and opposing the wrong way."[69]

At the age of 81 he said: "If Master Chu's Way could be extended
to our East, I would be glad to make any sacrifice for it and even die by
the Iron Ring."[70] But we cannot fail also to note that at the same age he
said: "I could cut myself off from this confused world, withdraw into the
mountains with Master Chu's books, and die in a cave."[71] To engage in
factional strife and the denunciation of heretics was not his deepest intention.

In the spring of his eighty-third year Song Siyŏl incurred King Sukchong's (r. 1674–1720) wrath by making representations against an early decision on who should be crown prince. Seizing on this opportune moment, the Namin began a campaign to incriminate this formidable foe of theirs and Song was condemned to exile on Cheju Island. In the third month of the same year, he felt the end of his life approaching and wrote to his favorite disciple Kwŏn Sangha (1641–1721) from Cheju Island:

One day Ch'angju [Kim Ikhŭi, 1610–56] said to me: "Since you did not learn from T'oegye but from Master Chu, your life will come to no good end." Now I can understand well what he meant. However, I do not repent the choice by which I might bring ruin on myself because I have greatly benefited from Master Chu. It is as the old saying has it: "If one hears the Way in the morning, he can die [without regret] in the evening."[72]

In those days, Song Siyŏl presented a disciple of his with a saying by Chu Hsi: "Stand like a towering rock."[73] This saying as well as the above-mentioned "great honor in the last days of my life" was one of is favorite mottos. But, it is worth noting that Yun Hyu also had alluded to those sayings.[74]

Following is part of the memorial address which he dedicated to his disciple Song Sangmin (1621–79), a month before he was ordered by the king to take poison:

Again I am a solitary prisoner on a floating isle in the ocean, and there is rumor abroad that I shall be killed. My life at morning may not last until evening. If my lord is to take away my life, I would be glad to have a good time with you there, and then travel with you on foot as far as Yün-ku and K'ao-t'ing [Chu Hsi's last living place in Fukien Province] so as to ask Master Chu questions about his *Compendium* and *Classified Conversations*. What a pleasure that would be![75]

In this way Song Siyŏl's enthusiastic idolization of Chu Hsi found its opposite in the persons of Yun Hyu and Yun Chŭng, whose attack on him in turn only caused him to identify with Chu Hsi all the more. If so, it might not be wrong to say that Song Siyŏl died for Chu Hsi. In fact Song Siyŏl himself wrote half in jest:

Chu Hsi's Way brought calamity on the people of his day in that Chu Hsi's friends and disciples died in the proscription of "False Learning," and his writings have brought disaster upon people today, too.[76]

In this way Song showed a calm consciousness and foresight into his own impending catastrophe. Truly he was an unusual person who not only wrote a great commentary expounding on Chu Hsi's *Compendium*, but also lived his own life as an exposition of Chu Hsi's life.

4. CHU HSI AND NEO-CONFUCIANISM IN YUN HYU

We now turn to the question: Was Yun Hyu really such a "subverter of the Way" that he deserved to be attacked so fiercely by Song Siyŏl?

The Yun family of Namwŏn[77] had not produced any great scholars or bureaucrats, nor had it, on the other hand, any "heretics" among its ancestors. Rather, it was a family which had inherited the orthodox Korean Confucianism of the school of Cho Kwangjo. Yun Hyojŏn (?–1619), Yun Hyu's father, was a genuine Confucian bureaucrat who had been a student of Min Sŭpchŏng, a disciple of So Kyŏngdŏk (1489–1546), and had been a friend of Chang Hyŏn'gwang (1554–1637) and Chŏng Ku (1543–1620). The latter had paid tribute to the memory of Hyojŏn at his death:

He devoted himself to Neo-Confucianism and spoke of nothing but the two Ch'engs, Chang Tsai and Chu Hsi. Above all he practised the ritual conscientiously, fearing lest he should fail to observe it all faithfully.[78]

As for Yun Hyu, he had been taught for a while in his boyhood by Yi Min'gu (1589–1670) (Yi Sugwang's [1563–1628] son and Yi Sŏnggu's [1584–1644] younger brother) but, unlike Song Siyŏl, who had Kim Changsaeng as his honored teacher, he seems to have had no definite teacher. As for his party affiliation, his father had belonged to the Sobuk (Small Northerners), but Yun Hyu was regarded as a Sŏin because of his friendship with Song Siyŏl and Min Chŏngjung, until he clearly declared himself later to be one of the Namin.

If one took Song Siyŏl's charge of his "subverting the Way" at its face value, one would be surprised to discover in Yun Hyu's *Complete Works (Paekho chŏnsŏ)* a true Confucian. His basic way of thinking did not extend beyond the framework of Neo-Confucianism. It is said that when, for example, he taught children, he first instructed them in the *Elementary Learning*, the Inner Rules (Nei-tse) Chapter of the *Book of Rites (Li-chi)*, the *Classic of Filial Piety (Hsiao-ching)*, the poems of Chu Hsi *(Chu Tzu kan-hsing shih)*, the *Regulations of the White Deer Hollow (Pai-lu-tung hsüeh-kuei)*, and the Chou-nan and Chao-nan sections in the *Book of Odes (Shih-ching)*. However he would not teach them the poems of literary men lest it have an overpowering effect on their youthful sentiments.[79]

He also often quoted Chu Hsi's views as authority for his own views, though not so often as did Song Siyŏl. He said in a certain passage that:

This is just that my Lord has a great sense of the need to fear Heaven and serve the people, to complete human affairs and respond to an unusual change in Heaven. Master Chu said, "There is no limit to the good things that arise from prudence and industry, but there is also no limit to the evils that descend from negligence." This remark has much charm.[80]

However, unlike Song Siyŏl and many other Confucians of those times, he did not take Chu Hsi's views as definitive, and he was frank and brave enough to express whatever doubts he felt. This was the basis of his widely recognized originality. He did not think of this as fighting against Chu Hsi, but following his teachings, as is shown in the conclusion to his preface to *Chungyong Chuja changgu porok*. This text is a commentary on the *Mean* (*Chung-yung*) by Yun Hyu himself, which was later criticized by Song Siyŏl together with Yun's *Chungyong changgu ch'aje*, a revision of Chu Hsi's *Sentences and Phrases of the Mean* (*Chung-yung chang-chü*).

Here I have done nothing but note what I have heard and seen and found suggestive among the hidden implications of Chu Hsi's commentaries. I called it *Supplement to Master Chu's Sentences and Phrases in the Mean* (*Chuja changgu porok*) because I wanted to express my intention of perpetuating the doctrines of the ancient sages and to discuss them with the same intention. I hope my colleagues will forgive my egregious folly, and will discuss the strong and weak points of this work together, for this was the very purpose of Chu Hsi's saying: "Moral principles belong to all the people of the world, so they should discuss them together."[81]

This saying of Chu Hsi, "Moral principles belong to all the people of the world," as well as his words, "There is no limit to the moral principles of all in the world," in Chu's *Compendium*, were believed in by Yun as basic precepts. He read the classics with this same conviction. He had to accept the usual restrictions of time and space and of conditions under the Yi dynasty in the seventeenth century, but he was free from any limits imposed by Chu Hsi. In what follows I will give a few examples of how he criticized Chu Hsi's theories.

Yun had also made a sweeping revision of Chu's *Sentences and Phrases of the Mean* and added his own commentary to it. Regarding the *Great Learning* as a guide to the understanding of the Six Classics and as vital to the understanding of. the sacred learning, and attaching great importance to it along with the *Classic of Filial Piety*, he was dissatisfied with Chu Hsi's *Sentences and Phrases of the Great Learning* (*Ta-hsüeh chang-chü*).[82] He insisted that the original text of the *Great Learning* must not be discarded,[83] and also that, without the old texts of ancient writings, we could not understand the process of their discussion by ancient Confucians.[84] Thus he dared to use the original text (the old text of the *Great Learning* before Ch'eng I [1033–1107] revised it) and added his own commentary. What is remarkable about his interpretation is that in his commentary on "*tsai-ch'in-min*" he used an explanatory comment quoted from Wang Yang-ming's *Ta-hsüeh-wen*, referring to it only as "a certain person said."[85] Song Siyŏl apparently did not detect this, for had he known of it he would undoubtedly have made it a target of attack.

What is even more remarkable is his criticism of Chu Hsi's supplementary comment on the investigation of things *(ko-wu pu-chuan)*. This was a natural consequence of his having adopted the original text, and there he uses a peculiar logic of his own to demonstrate the fallacy of Chu Hsi's commentary. According to his logic, the reason why *ko-wu chih-chih* was not interpreted in the original Commentary is that it is in keeping with Confucius' words "I would prefer not to speak" *(wu yü wu yen)*, which is a method of suggesting a deep truth by keeping silence.[86]

For the interpretation of "investigation" *(ko)*, Yun presented a new explanation. We can see it in detail in his *Explanation of the True Aim of the Great Learning (Taehak chŏnp'yŏn taeji ansŏl)*, which is the key text for understanding how he interpreted the Confucian classics. He did not accept Chu Hsi's explanation that *ko* means *chih* "to arrive at" but he offered a new interpretation that it means "to reach" or "move" *(kant'ung)*, and every time the word *ko* is used in the Confucian classics it means the same thing.[87] Furthermore, he used the word *ko* in the same sense in his other writings, too. In a certain memorial to the Throne, for example, we must read the word *ko* with the meaning of "move" or as in the following: "My way is not enough to move Heaven, and my loyalty is not enough to be trusted by the Throne."[88]

In this manner he undertook a reexamination of the Confucian classics, keeping some distance between himself and the dogma of Neo-Confucianism. His unique method of interpreting the classics is this: on the premise that each of the classics is closely related to the others in its organic function, he attempted to synthesize all the separate contexts into a system. For instance, he read the *Mean* in terms of the *Great Learning*,[89] and stated that the *Great Learning*, the *Mean*, the *Classic of Filial Piety*, and the Inner Rules chapter of the *Book of Rites* are complementary to one another.[90]

Actually this had been the methodology of the Han commentator Cheng Hsüan (127–200) and of Chu Hsi as well.[91] However, the Korea of the seventeenth century did not allow Yun enough time to build up the kind of systematic scholarship that Cheng Hsüan and Chu Hsi had accomplished earlier using the same methodology.

How was it then that he was able, not only to develop a new interest in the science of "barbarian" Europe,[92] but also to keep himself aloof from the contemporary trend towards acceptance of Neo-Confucianism as virtually sacrosanct? In my opinion, the explanation lies in Yun Hyu's respect for Heaven. I think his reliance on the absolute authority of Heaven (*T'ien*) as superior even to Chu Hsi gave him the leverage with which to evaluate even Chu Hsi.

Reading his poetry we find that it expresses a distinctive sentiment of cosmic grandeur. This may reveal the influence of Shao Yung's (1011–77) *Huang-chi ching-shih-shu*, which he had read with pleasure since his early days.[93] In fact, the word Heaven appears frequently in Yun Hyu's *Complete Works (Paekho chŏnsŏ)* where he often expressed a sense of reverent awe toward Heaven. There is this statement in his diary at the age of twenty-four (here the Lord-on-High [*Shang-ti*] is synonymous with Heaven [*T'ien*]):

Ancient people experienced fear and trembling, and were uneasy in mind; they behaved prudently as if they were being watched from above or on all sides,[94] and used to speak of "the Lord-on-High" in everything. When they performed their tasks, they said, "By command of the Lord-on-High." And when something was wrong, they said, "Prohibited by the Lord-on-High."[95]

It is not difficult to find mention of "wei T'ien" (reverent awe of Heaven) in his *Complete Works*. Here are a few examples among many.

When I was sick, I wrote a reminder on the wall of my study as a caution. It was: "A wise man said, 'Never stop learning.' " But, what should we learn? The first thing is "To be in awe of Heaven." The second is "Be kind to people" *(ch'in-min)*; the third, "Aim high!" *(shang-chih)*; the fourth, "Do good" *(ch'ü-shan)*.[96]

Even in his interpretation of the *Mean*, Heaven was given a higher position than it had in Chu Hsi's interpretation: "The *Mean* teaches the way in which we must obey Heaven, and the *Great Learning* defines detailed rules as to the application of the Way."[97] For example:

We can call a person a noble man *(chün-tzu)* who holds a reverent awe toward Heaven. Besides holding a reverent awe toward Heaven, he can strike the mean as the occasion demands. The small man *(hsiao-jen)*, because he does not know that the imperative of Heaven must be revered with awe, tries to satisfy his desires at will and thus goes wrong.[98] Why must Heaven be revered with awe? Because Heaven not only creates all things and watches over them from above, but "produces principle and is a deep source of the Way."[99] Therefore, it is small wonder that "an ancient sage attributed the fate of the Way and human movements to Heaven."[100] The principles that Heaven produces are called "principles of Heaven" *(T'ien-li)*. Universal among these principles are the three bonds *(san-kang)* and the five norms *(wu-ch'ang)* [the three major human relationships and the five constant virtues of Confucianism]. All things possess this Heaven-endowed "natural law" *(tzu-jan chih tse)*.[101] To stand in reverent awe of Heaven is nothing but to conduct oneself in accordance with Heavenly principle. With respect to the ruler, if his conduct does not accord with Heaven's principles, Heaven manifests abnormal phenomena in the world of nature, but if it does, Heaven responds favorably and bestows good fortune on the nation.[102]

The will of Heaven, he thought, was entrusted to the sages:

Heaven creates all things and entrusts them to the sage. While the sage is human, he cooperates with Heaven. When he institutes "things or affairs" *(shih)* in accordance with his own will, the Way exists in these things and affairs.[103]

"Things" here means, to be concrete, "ritual, music, punishments, and administration *(li-yüeh-hsing-cheng)*." The following passage gives fuller details of the above:

The Way of Heaven *(T'ien-tao)* returns blessings to the good and misfortunes to the wicked. During the period of the three dynasties, the Hsia, Shang, and Chou, these principles of the Way *(tao-li)* remained inviolate. Thereafter things got turned around. But how could that have happened? For blessings to be returned to the good and misfortunes to the wicked is the correct principle of Heaven. That is, it accords with the human mind's seeking to do good and avoid evil, and it can be practised in all situations. But impelled by *ch'i-shu* [the irresistible fate arising from *ch'i*], man upset this and the governance of Heaven could not prevail. The sages, taking account of these circumstances, established rites, music, punishments, and administration. Three hundred standard rules and three thousand detailed regulations do no more than support these principles and make up for anything needed to complete Heaven's creation.[104]

It is in the Confucian classics that the rites, music, punishments, and administration of the sages are to be found:

The ancient sages wrote the classics and revealed them to the world. There can be no imperfection in them. The principles of all-under-Heaven and the grandeur of kingly rule find complete expression in the classics.[105]

Yun Hyu's worshipful attitude toward antiquity is tied up with this reverent awe of Heaven, the sages, and the classics in the belief that the rites, music, punishments, and administration of the sages had always found practical realization in ancient times. Thus his adoration of antiquity was not a devotion to things classical simply for their own sake, but was reinforced by his interest in the concrete designs of statecraft. His work entitled *Konggo chikchang tosŏl* is a good example of this.[106] He engaged in serious study of ancient institutions. He would reform, he thought, evils in the present which stood in sharp contrast to the ideal institutions of ancient times. He was early recognized as a Confucian who observed carefully the trends of his own times,[107] and submitted a concrete plan of reform, covering government organization, financial affairs, and a military administration. This was an expression of his passionate desire to achieve a classical Utopia in his own times.[108]

At this point it may be helpful to take a look at Song Siyŏl's view of Heaven. He also spoke of it often. And he, like Yun Hyu, thought that strange occurrences were Heaven's way of warning the ruler, and admonishing him to correct his mistakes.[109] But, unlike Yun Hyu, Song Siyŏl had no wholehearted belief in or reverent awe of Heaven, and never hesitated to express his doubts about Heaven. In Song's case *ch'i-shu*—the irresistible fate arising from *ch'i*— takes the place of Heaven.

The word *ch'i-shu* is found only a few times in Yun's *Complete Works*,[110] while it is found far more frequently in the works of Song than the word "Heaven" is. The word *ch'i-shu* had already appeared in the literature of the Six Dynasties period, but it was Chu Hsi who used it as a technical term in the philosophy of history.[111] According to Chu Hsi, both the power of nature and the power of man move history forward; within nature herself, there is a conflict between the power which moves history in the direction of goodness (principle, that is, Heaven) and the power which tends to prevent it *(ch'i, that is, ch'i-shu)*. And Chu thought that, ever since the times of Yao and Shun, the *ch'i-shu* had been increasing in power. It was under the influence of Chu Hsi's pessimistic philosophy of history that Song Siyŏl so often expressed the idea that "Heaven is not omnipotent,"[112] and Heaven is oppressed by *ch'i-shu*.[113]

I return now to Yun Hyu, who believed that, although the classics had been written by the sages, their authority was vouched for by Heaven, not by Chu Hsi as Song Siyŏl thought. To Yun's mind, Chu Hsi ought simply to be regarded as an expounder of the sages' teaching. Thus for

Song Siyŏl's simple schema in which the classics were equated with Chu Hsi (or the sage), Yun substituted the more hierarchic schema descending from Heaven to the sage, to the classics, to Chu Hsi (which, incidentally, resembles the thought of Kaibara Ekken (1630–1714) in Japan). The tradition of Confucianism from ancient times had a higher authority for him than did the newer tradition of Neo-Confucianism.

Nevertheless Chu Hsi was seen by Yun as an epoch-making "Great Confucian," as shown by references to himself as one who lived "three thousand years after Confucius, and five hundred years since Chu Hsi."[114] For him, however, to study Chu Hsi's learning was not to obey Chu Hsi without question, but to take a step forward from Chu Hsi. He thought that to do so was to serve as a witness of the "Neo-Confucian conscience,"[115] and to safeguard Confucian tradition.

5. THE CONFLICT BETWEEN SONG SIYŎL AND YUN HYU

As stated in the preceding section, Yun Hyu was beyond doubt a Confucian, and what was more, regarded himself as an authentic Neo-Confucian. In this respect he too drew a sharp line between orthodoxy and heterodoxy. Following Ch'eng I and Chu Hsi, he identified as heterodoxies: the egoism of Yang Chu, the all-embracing love of Mo Tzu, the denial of self by Lao-Chuang, the utilitarianism of Kuan Tzu, the juxtaposition of names and actualities by Shen Pu-hai and Shang Yang, and the teaching of Nirvana by the Buddha.[116]

His criticism of Buddhism may be found in his *Record of An Excursion to Mt. P'ungak (P'ungangnok)*,[117] which contains an exchange between himself and a Buddhist priest on the merits of Confucianism and Buddhism. This book is an account of a trip to Diamond Mountain, which he climbed at the age of fifty-six. At this time he met a Zen priest in the mountains and criticized Buddhism to his face. I regret that I cannot set forth here some of this interesting dialogue. But, it is worth noting that his tone was peremptory. Confident that Confucianism was superior in all respects to Buddhism, he unhesitatingly admonished the monk to defect from Buddhism.

Yun's criticism of Taoism we can see, at least in outline, from his letter in answer[118] to a certain Min who had read the *Chuang Tzu*. In this letter he rebuked Min for reading the *Chuang Tzu* instead of the *Elementary Learning, Great Learning,* and the works of Ch'eng-Chu.

On the other hand, he wrote a "Preface to the *Lao Tzu Tao-te-ching*" *(Noja Todŏkkyŏng sŏ),*[119] in which, while he allowed that some of the teachings of Lao Tzu had "a certain significance," it did not alter the position of Confucianism in his mind. He said that "Lao Tzu's Way was one end, and the sages' another," yet he also asserted that there was in Lao Tzu "something impure" that "despised humaneness and righteousness, and ignored human obligations."

Such being Yun Hyu's view, it must have outraged him to be accused of heresy by Song Siyŏl. Naturally he did not feel obliged to remain silent in the face of such an attack. Moreover, he was a self-reliant, uncompromising, and aggressive man, who observed of himself, "I have a fault in my desire to win and have my way at any cost."[120]

From the extant text of his complete works his criticisms of Song Siyŏl appear to have increased in number after the rites dispute of 1674. Here is an example, a paragraph from a memorial submitted in 1675, in which he declared Song Siyŏl's views to be heretical:

Song Siyŏl and his group have controlled the Government at will for more than ten years, insisting on their own views, spreading heresy throughout society, flaunting their crimes and misdeeds, and finally destroying the moral fabric of the world and corrupting the minds of the people. The damage is far worse a calamity than anything caused by a flood or beasts.[121]

Yun also submitted a memorial in the year before he was ordered by the ruler to take his own life, at the age of 63. At this time, Song Siyŏl was in exile on a distant island. The memorial said:

Didn't Siyŏl [in the rites disputes of 1659 and 1674 concerning Hyojong's (r. 1649–59) mourning period] take the lead in advancing the theory of succession to the throne by the son of a legal wife? This theory that slights the ruler and departs from Truth disturbs the times and causes people's hearts to fall into evil ways. In the long run it has become an excuse for rebels to rise and come to shake the Government. Whose crime is this? We ought to throw Siyŏl into the King's prison and conduct an inquiry into his guilt. If he is not involved in any crime, and shows repentance, we should banish him to the ends of the sea, there to rule over evil spirits in accordance with the statutes [that the Sage-king Yao] applied to the four rowdies. If he is stubborn, and not compliant, and has in fact committed inexcusable crimes, we ought to execute him in the city, throw him to the crowd, and make an object lesson of him to the nation.[122]

While Yun Hyu, however, impeached Song severely like this, he was not altogether lacking in tolerance, as was Song Siyŏl, who recognized in Yun Hyu no good whatever. For example, Yun spoke as follows in a letter to Hŏ Mok (1595–1682):

> In the views of "the guest of Changi" [Song Siyŏl] there is some good and some bad. The theories of "mourning for a year" and "succession to the throne by the son of a legal wife," for instance, should be subjected to all-out attack. But, there is, indeed, something righteous in the fact that he did not forget about avenging and clearing [the honor of martyred ministers] and commemorated Sŏng [Sammun, 1418–56] and Pak [P'aengnyŏn, 1417–56][123] in his writing. . . . We should not sacrifice this belief out of association with his other views.[124]

Furthermore when Yun Hyu was sixty-three years of age, the case of Song Sangmin[125] arose, and a demand for punishing Song Siyŏl was pressed at court. This was because Siyŏl had sent a memorial from his place of exile which said that after the persecution of Confucius and Yen Hui at K'uang, Sangmin was the only one who still guarded the learning of Confucianism. What was more, out of deep respect for this disciple of his, he even addressed him as "Master Sŏkkok," contrary to common practice. At that time Yun Hyu was opposed to punishing Siyŏl, and became a target for criticism by his own party for protecting an enemy.[126]

As stated above, Yun had characterized Song Siyŏl's views as heretical. On what basis then did he judge these views as heretical? In Song's case the criterion of orthodoxy had been fidelity to the teachings of Chu Hsi, but for Yun it was more important whether or not one held the correct view of ritual. It is a complicated question,[127] but simply put, the core of Yun Hyu's argument was that Song Siyŏl had confused the ritual of the king with that of the scholar-official (sadaebu). After the rites dispute of 1674, Yun Hyu submitted a memorial which said in part:

> What we call the state ritual system is delineated in the Five Rituals and Ceremonies of the Dynasty (Kukcho oryeŭi). The Five Rituals and Ceremonies prescribe the system of mourning dress for the ruling house (kukhyul pokche). The system of dress falls into two kinds—trimmed and untrimmed. Those who go into mourning for the King are to follow the specification of untrimmed mourning dress (ch'amch'oe), and those in mourning for the Queen follow those of trimmed mourning dress (chaech'oe). For the classes below this, there are other regulations for the five forms of dress for mourning of the scholar-official. These regulations are prescribed in the Ritual Canon (Yejŏn), currently represented by the Great Statutes for the Governance of the State (Kyŏngguk taejŏn). Between the two a sharp distinction should be made. Nobody should confuse them.[128]

According to Yun this failure led Song Siyŏl to mistakenly prescribe the ritual of a second son for the eldest son and to cause the royal family to observe the customs of the common people.[129]

Thus he directed his criticism of Song Siyŏl at his views on ritual. However, he could not be expected to keep silent over Song Siyŏl's charge of his being a traitor to the school of Chu Hsi. As we have seen, Yun thought that his criticizing a part of Chu Hsi's theory did not mean he was against Neo-Confucianism. In the extant text of his *Complete Works* there is no direct refutation to the charge of heresy. It may be a fact, as Haje (his second son) put it, that "Yun Hyu does not care. He laughed it off."[130] But the following is worth noticing:

There are some people who even go so far as to say that those who do not follow Chu Hsi's commentaries are barbarians or beasts, and have no qualms about doing anything, no matter how wrong it is, and so on. Now, I happened to get two commentaries in the city, one by Minister Song[Song Siyŏl] and another by Pak Hŏn, who talked like this. I read them repeatedly and know their views in detail. I deeply regret that what has been done cannot now be undone. What they think of as Chu Hsi's views are not, in truth, those of Chu Hsi himself; they contravene the classics and are contrary to ritual. This point ought to be brought to light.[131]

I am prepared to acknowledge that Yun Hyu was quite conceited and even thought of himself as a true successor to Chu Hsi. There is a passage in the extant text of his *Complete Works*, in a letter to Yun Sŏn'gŏ written the year after the rites dispute of 1659, in which he refers to "false scholars of Ch'eng-Chu learning." These must be Song Siyŏl and his followers. By implication Yun means conversely that, "We are the persons who truly understand Chu Hsi, not Song Siyŏl and his followers, who have a blind faith in Chu Hsi." "When you associate with false scholars of Ch'eng-Chu learning, can you explain to the world why you always respect and admire the two wise men (Master Ch'eng and Master Chu)?"[132]

When Yun Hyu, imitating Chu Hsi, proudly called his group "our party" (*odang*) and its doctrine "our Way" (*odo*) (and Song Siyŏl, too, often used these expressions), there can be no doubt that they invoke the authority of Chu Hsi and Neo-Confucianism. This is just the way Chu Hsi spoke[133] when he was compelled to fight hard against his enemies. Hearing about the death of Kwŏn Si (1604–72) Yun said: "Now that he has died our Way stands more and more alone."[134] When Yun Sŏn'gŏ died, he said: "That Kilbo should have suddenly come to this! How poorly Heaven has taken care of our party!"[135]

It is a curious fact that, when Yun was attacked by Song Siyŏl and his company, he also identified himself with Chu Hsi's sufferings from the Proscription of False Learning, readily identifying his opponents with Han T'o-chou (1152–1207) or Hu Hung (1106–62), both of whom suppressed the school of Chu Hsi. For example, when he was impeached by Cho Kasŏk (1634–81), Yun remarked as follows:

Now I have heard the contents of Cho Kasŏk's memorial. He heaps abuse on me, and makes false charges against high ministers. Even Kung Wen-chung's (1037–87) specification of misdeeds by the "five spirits" [attack on the Ch'eng brothers], Hu Hung's impeachment [of Chu Hsi] for ten crimes in the service of the devil, and Hwang Kyeok's memorial for the execution of Cho Kwangjo did not go so far.[136]

Yun Hyu and his sympathizers thought that they carried on the orthodox tradition of Chu Hsi. This is clearly expressed in memorial addresses by his disciples requesting the reburial of Yun Hyu in 1692, three years after he had been exonerated through the political change of 1689.

The reputation of our teacher spread throughout the country from the time he was a youth. His literary works have followed the ancient literature of Ch'in-Han, and his scholarship has carried on the orthodox tradition of Kuan and Min [Ch'eng-Chu learning].[137]

As the spring of a stream flows out from the past to the future, the transparent stream of Igang [the home of Yun Hyu] has now revived itself, and the peak of the School of the Way rises high.[138]

In conclusion, let me review the record of conflict between Song Siyŏl and Yun Hyu. The germ of mutual antagonism had first sprouted out from differences in their understanding of Neo-Confucianism when they were young,[139] but it was at the time of the rites dispute of 1659 that it assumed visible form. At that time, Song Siyŏl shifted the point of dispute from their views on ritual and he extended his battle lines to the field of Neo-Confucianism. On grounds of defending orthodoxy (Neo-Confucianism) against heterodoxy (anti-Neo-Confucianism), he aimed not just to bury Yun Hyu's theory of ritual but to cut the ground from under its whole existence.

It seems obvious, however, that the charges of "heretical views" and "traitor fo Confucian culture" (samun nanjŏk) were simply rhetorical fabrications. Song Siyŏl criticized only Yun Hyu's revised interpretation of the Mean and did not go into the question of the Great Learning or

Classic of Filial Piety at all. And indeed even in the case of Yun Hyu's exposition of the *Mean*, Song seems not to have made any detailed inquiry into its contents. He did not, and would rather not, see his opponent as he really was. The mere thought of anyone revising Chu Hsi's comments aroused his total opposition and led him to exaggerate the threat represented by such an enemy. With the termination of direct communication between the two after the rites dispute of 1659, there was nothing left but the allegation of blasphemy and treason: "Traitor to 'Confucian culture.' "

On the other hand, though he at first tried to limit the area of contention to ritual, Yun Hyu could not help defending himself and justifying his own orthodoxy, even in the field of Neo-Confucianism, against an opponent who took his revision of Chu Hsi's commentary as evidence of heresy. Since the line which Yun Hyu drew between orthodoxy and heterodoxy was the one between Confucianism (including Neo-Confucianism) and anti-Confucianism, Yun, on his own terms, clearly could not be branded as heretical.

In this way, the conflict took the form of a dispute over ritual on its surface, but was implicitly tied to the issue of Neo-Confucian orthodoxy. It became a struggle between an absolutist and relativist interpretation of Chu Hsi. However, as both Song and Yun were active in the center of politics, the struggle on orthodoxy became a scramble for political power, which involved them in the harsh logic of politics, "an eye for an eye," and struggle to the death. Hence, it failed to develop into a fruitful intellectual controversy. Moreover, after the dispute over orthodoxy-heterodoxy had come to an end, with each leader granted an honorable death by the king, the words "traitor to 'Confucian culture' " written in blood, hung over the heads of scholar-officials, dampening any spirit of liberal and life-giving criticism within Neo-Confucianism.

NOTES

1. Mencius 3:9, "T'eng-wen-kung" (Sage Emperors Cease To Arise).
2. See Seng-yu, *Hung-ming chi* in *Taishō daizōkyō* (Yokyo: Taishō daizōkyō kankōkai, 1927), 52:1–96; Tao-hsüan, *Kuang-hung-ming chi* in *Taishō*, 52:97–361; Tao-hsüan, *Chi-ku-chin fu-tao lun-heng* in *Taishō*, 52:363–97, etc.
3. Ch'eng I spoke of his elder brother Ch'eng Hao as follows: "When Master Ch'eng appeared he upheld the Sages' learning and explained it for men so as to distinguish it from heterodoxy *(i-tuan)*, and drive out heresy *(ya-shuo)*." *Ming-tao hsien-sheng mu-piao,* in *Erh Ch'eng ch'üan-shu* (Ssu-pu pei-yao ed., Taiwan: Chung-hua shu-chü, 1966), 7:7b. This seems to be the earliest use of the words "heterodoxy" and "heresy" together.
4. Chu Hsi insisted outwardly on the exclusion of Taoism, but really felt, I think, a secret sympathy for it. Cf. Miura Kunio, "Chu Tzu to kokyū," in *Chūgoku ni okeru ningensei no tankyū* (Tokyo: Sōbunsha, 1983), pp. 499–521.
5 Horigome Yōzō, *Seitō to itan* (Tokyo: Chūō kōronsha, 1964), p. 30.
6. Chang Ling, for example, wrote the *I-tuan pien-cheng*. The ostensible point of dispute in this book is whether Confucianism has been infected with Zen, but underlying this is the question of Wang Yang-ming's philosophy.
7. See Mencius 7:29, "Chin-hsin" (Those Who Are Fleeing from the Errors of Mo Tzu Naturally Turn to Yang). Also Chu Hsi's note on this. *Meng Tzu chi-chu* (Taipei, I-wen yin-shu-kuan, 1969), 14:9a. We can see here some attempt to understand one's opponent. In Chu Hsi there is not, ontologically speaking, a final opposition but rather an implied synthesis in the Supreme Ultimate *(T'ai-chi)* between yin (heterodoxy) and yang (orthodoxy). Furthermore, the yin or yang itself is a union combining the yin and yang in opposition. It seems that while Confucianism, Taoism, and Buddhism are opposed to one another, there is some ontological basis for the union of the three teachings.
8. I do not mean to say here that Korean thought is limited to Neo-Confucianism.
9. In modern times Chang Chiyŏn stated proudly in his preface to the *Chosŏn yugyo yŏnwŏn* that the character for "*i*" in "Eastern barbarian," consisting of "bow" and "man," differentiated the Koreans from other barbarians. Paradoxically this may be taken to express a sense of inferiority. *Chang Chiyŏn chŏnso* (Seoul: Tan'guk taehak tongyanghak yŏn'guso, 1979) 1:449.
10. Tsuda Sōkichi, *Jukyō no jissendōtoku* (Tokyo: Iwanami shoten, 1938), p. 189.
11. *Songa taejŏn* (Seoul: Han'guk samun hakhoe photo reproduction, 1971) (complete in 7 vols. including *Songja taejŏn* in 215 vols.; Appendix, in 19 vols.; *Songsŏ sŭbyu* in 9 vols.; *Songsŏ soksŭbyu* in 2 vols.), 207:8a.
12. Suzuki Mitsuo, "Aru sōshinkai no tanjō" in *Han* (1979) 85:299.
13. Yi Chŏnggwi, "Sŏng Hon Haengjang," in *Chōsen jinmei jisho* (Kyoto: Linsen shoten, 1972), p. 418.
14. *Songja*, 36:14b.

15. *Ibid.*, 131:1a–24a.
16. *Ibid.*, Appendix, 17:27b.
17. *Ibid.*, 7:3a.
18. *Ibid.*, *Songsŏ sŭbyu*, 7:11b.
19. Cf. *ibid.*, Appendix 18:29a.
20. Cf. *ibid.*, 100:22a.
21. *Ibid.*, 93:26b; 90:20b; 129–19a, etc.
22. *Ibid.*, Appendix 15:31a.
23. *Ibid.*, 51:21a.
24. For further details see Miura Kunio "*Chuja taejŏn ch'aŭi* o megutte" in *Mori Mikisaburō hakase shōju kinen tōyōgaku ronshū* (Kyoto: Hōyū shoten, 1979), pp. 723–40.
25. In the second month of the year when Song Siyŏl was eighty-three years of age, he wrote a preface to this book in his place of exile on Cheju Island. But he was deeply conscious of its still being incomplete.
26. *Songja*, 92:20a.
27. *Ibid.*, 89:26b.
28. *Ibid.*, 142:20a.
29. *Paekho chŏnsŏ* (Taegu: Kyŏngbuk University Press, 1974) (complete in 3 vols.), Appendix 2:1914.
30. *Songja*, 47:4a.
31. *Ibid.*, 80:17a and others.
32. *Ibid.*, 137:1a.
33. *Ibid.*, 18:21b.
34. See collected works of Yi Ŏnjŏk, *Hoejae sŏnsaeng munjip*; Kim Inhu, *Hasŏ sŏnsaeng munjip*; Yi T'oegye, *T'oegye chŏnsŏ*; Ki Taesŭng, *Kobong sŏnsaeng munjip*; Yi Yulgok, *Yulgok chŏnsŏ*; Sŏng Hon, *Ugye sŏnsaengjip*; Chŏng Ch'ŏl, *Songgang sŏnsaengjip*; Song Ikp'il, *Kwibong sŏnsaengjip*; Chŏng Ku, *Hangang sŏnsaeng munjip*; Yu Sŏngnyong, *Sŏae sŏnsaeng munjip*; Chŏng Kyŏngse, *Ubok sŏnsaeng munjip*; Chang Hyŏn'gwang, *Yŏhŏn sŏnsaeng munjip*.
35. *Songja*, 79:21b.
36. *Ibid.*, Appendix, 18:40b.
37. *Ibid.*, Appendix, 11:26b.
38. *Ibid.*, 76:24b.
39. *Ibid.*, 64:18b.
40. *Ibid.*, 128:40b.
41. *Ibid.*, 80:24b; Appendix 17:11a.
42. *Ibid.*, 82:18a.
43. *Ibid.*, 81:12a.
44. *Ibid.*, 58:25b; "*Songja taejŏn such'a*" (A Commentary on All Volumes of *Songja taejŏn*) 6:31a. I cannot see why he refrained from submitting the memorial on account of *chien-kua* (symbol of going forward). Perhaps it was because he thought *chih-kua* (*kua* that has changed) was bad.
45. When the proscription of False Learning was at its height, Chu Hsi wanted

to impeach Han T'o-chou and his followers, but his disciples opposed this. Then he inquired about the propriety of this through divination, and got *tun-kua* (the symbol of retiring). So he felt compelled to give it up and burn the draft to ashes. Huang Kan, *Chu Tzu hsing-chuang*, in *Chu Tzu hsing-chuang chi-chu* (1665 Japanese ed.), 39a.

46. Yun Chŭng, *Myŏngjae yugo* (1732 ed.), 20:15a.
47. *Songja*, Appendix, 2:32a.
48. *Ibid.*, 40:14a.
49. On the question of Master Chu's notes and a posthumous name for Confucius there survives a refutation by Yun Hyu in *Paekho*, Appendix, 3:1971.
50. *Songja*, 106:16b. The words "a disaster of Fen-shu k'eng-ju" are Chu Hsi's. *Chu Tzu ta-ch'üan* (Ssu-pu t'sung-kan ed.), 52:23b.
51. *Songja*, 59:29a.
52. *Ibid.*, 70:16b.
53. *Ibid.*, 131:31a.
54. *Ibid.*, 116:2b.
55. *Ibid.*, 53:20b.
56. Pak Sech'ae (Hwasuk, 1631–95) was caught in the conflict. He tried but failed to mediate between the two, and then went over to the Soron. Min Chŏng-jung, in contrast to Pak, broke with Yun Hyu, and took sides with Song Si-yŏl.
57. Yun Hyu also felt as uneasy as he. *Paekho*, 2:1104.
58. *Songja*, 49:16b.
59. *Ibid.*, 76:31b.
60. As for his feeling of uneasiness, see also *Songja*, 4:76b; 53:20a; 68:54b, and so on.
61. *Songja*, 60:38b.
62. *Ibid.*, 45:9b.
63. *Ibid.*, 105:18a.
64. *Ibid.*, 60:21a.
65. *Ibid.*, 63:16b.
66. *Ibid.*, 84:22a.
67. *Ibid.*, 78:37a, and so forth.
68. *Ibid.*, 125:18b.
69. *Ibid.*, 56:20b.
70. *Ibid.*, *Songsŏ sŭbyu*, 4:15b.
71. *Ibid.*, 96:17a.
72. *Ibid.*, 89:19a.
73. *Ibid.*, 85:33b.
74. *Paekho*, 2:1380.
75. *Songja*, 153:36b.
76. *Ibid.*, 53:41a.
77. On Yun Hyu's family line, relationships, and friendships see Han Woo-keun, "Paekho Yun Hyu yŏn'gu," *Yŏksa hakpo* (September 1961), 15:1–29; Han Yŏngguk and Yi T'aejin, "Paekho chŏnso haeje" in *Paekho* 3:2179–92.

78. *Paekho*, Appendix, 2:1884.
79. *Ibid.*, 3:1916.
80. *Ibid.*, 1:499.
81. *Ibid.*, 3:1462. "The moral principles belong to all the people of the world." *Chu Tzu ta-ch'üan*, 54:86–9a. "The moral principles of all in the world are limitless." *Chu Tzu yü-lei* (Kyoto: Chūbun shuppansha, 1970), 9:8a.
82. *Paekho*, 1:310.
83. *Ibid.*, 3:1524.
84. *Ibid.*, 3:1501.
85. *Ibid.*
86. *Ibid.*, 3:1515; 1524.
87. *Ibid.*, 3:1517.
88. *Ibid.*, 1:322.
89. *Ibid.*, 3:1466.
90. *Ibid.*, 3:1515.
91. On Cheng Hsüan, see Yoshikawa Kōjirō, *Shinajin no koten to sono seikatsu* (Tokyo: Iwanami shoten, 1944), pp. 316 ff. On Chu Hsi see Yoshikawa Kōjirō and Miura Kunio, *Shushi shu* (Tokyo: Asahi shinbunsha, 1976), p. 129.
92. *Paekho*, 2:1382.
93. *Ibid.*, Appendix; Song Siyŏl preferred *I-ch'uan chi-jang chi*, which is a collection of Shao Yung's poetical works.
94. These are Chu Hsi's words. *Chu Tzu ta-ch'üan*, 14:26a.
95. *Paekho*, 2:1346.
96. *Ibid.*, Appendix, 3:1891.
97. *Ibid.*, 3:1893.
98. *Ibid.*, 3:1465.
99. *Ibid.*, 2:1193; 3:1480.
100. *Ibid.*, 1:326.
101. *Ibid.*, 2:1203.
102. This so-called thought of *chaei* often appears in his memorials; e.g., *Paekho*, 1:264.
103. *Paekho*, 3:1662.
104. *Ibid.*, 2:1172.
105. *Ibid.*, 3:1686.
106. *Ibid.*, 2:1177–1271.
107. *Ibid.*, Appendix, 3:2137.
108. For his statecraft, see Han, "Paekho Yun Hyu yŏn'gu," 2,3.
109. See, for example, *Songja*, 8:6a.
110. I cannot go into this problem here, but it is not true that Yun Hyu had no regard for *ch'i*.
111. See Yoshikawa and Miura, *Shushi shu*, pp. 411 ff.
112. *Songja*, 74:21b.
113. See, for example, *Songja*, 49:23a; *Chu Tzu ta-ch'üan*, 76:8a.
114. *Paekho*, 1:75.
115. See "Paekho chŏnsŏ haeje," p. 2191.

116. *Paekho*, 2:1227; 3:1661.
117. *Ibid.*, 2:1385–1426.
118. *Ibid.*, 1:722.
119. *Ibid.*, 1:991–1022.
120. *Ibid.*, 1:545.
121. *Ibid.*, 1:556. The phrase "a disaster caused by a flood or beasts" is Chu Hsi's. *Meng Tzu chi-chu*, 6:13a.
122. *Paekho*, 1:476.
123. Sŏng Sammun and Pak P'aengnyŏn were two of "six martyred ministers" *(sayuksin)* who were killed by King Sejo (r. 1455–68) for attempting to restore Tanjong (r. 1452–55) to the throne. Sejo had usurped the throne from his young nephew, Tanjong. Song Siyŏl wrote eulogies in praise of their loyalty. See "Hoedŏk Paksŏnsaeng yuhŏbi" *(Songja*, 171:24a), "Hongju Sŏngsŏnsaeng yuhŏbi" *(Songja*, 171:25a), "Yŏnsan Sŏngsŏnsaeng yuhŏbi" *(Songja*, 171:26a).
124. *Paekho*, 1:618.
125. Song Sangmin wrote the "Chongjŏk t'ongdosŏl" and sent it to the king for the purpose of exculpating his master, Song Siyŏl, from a false charge. For this, however, he incurred Sukchong's anger and was beaten to death with the heavy bamboo.
126. *Paekho*, Appendix, 3:2084; 3:2168.
127. For further particulars see Kang Sangun, "Yesong kwa No-So pundang" in *Asea hakpo* (June 1968), 5:88–117.
128. *Paekho*, 1:369; 3:2168.
129. *Ibid.*, 1:243.
130. *Paekho*, 1:894; Appendix, 3:1879.
131. *Ibid.*, 2:1077.
132. *Ibid.*, 1:700.
133. *Chu Tzu ta-ch'üan, hsü-chi*, 1:1a.
134. *Paekho*, 1:42.
135. *Ibid.*, 1:717. We can find similar words of Chu Hsi in the *Chu Tzu ta-chüan, hsü-chi* 7:7a.
136. *Paekho*, 1:355.
137. *Ibid.*, Appendix, 3:1852.
138. *Ibid.*, Appendix, 3:1849.
139. When Song Siyŏl was thirty-four years of age, he criticized Yun Hyu's theory of *li-ch'i*. See *Songsŏ sŭbyu*, 2:6a. For Yun Hyu's theory of Four-Seven, see Han Woo-keun, "Paekho Yun Hyu ui sadan ch'ilchŏng, insim tosimsŏl" in *Yi Sangbaek paksa hoegap kinyŏm nonch'ong* (Seoul: Ŭryu munhwasa, 1964), pp. 237–48. For Yun Hyu's theory of *li-ch'i*, see Song Kŭngsŏp, "Paekho Yun Hyu igi ch'ŏrhak yŏn'gu sŏsŏl" in *Ch'ŏrhak yŏn'gu* (1969), 11:123–57.

Daniel Bouchez

Buddhism and Neo-Confucianism in Kim Manjung's *Random Essays (Sŏp'o manp'il)*

THE SUBJECT OF this paper is a collection of essays composed, in the words of the title, "as the brush goes," by Sŏp'o, that is, by Kim Manjung (1637–92). He is well known as the author of a masterpiece of Korean fiction, the novel *Nine Cloud Dream (Kuunmong)*. He is also credited with another novel, less famous but not less interesting, the *Record of a Southern Journey (Namjŏnggi)* which is especially well documented and on which I have already published several articles.[1]

The Buddhist inspiration of the former of the two works of fiction had already been pointed out by a contemporary, Yi Chae (1680–1746), the very man through whom we know of Kim Manjung's authorship. Here is what Yi, who was twelve years old at the time the writer died, had to report on the matter: "Among the works of fiction *(p'aesŏl)*, there is the *Nine Cloud Dream*, which was written by Sŏp'o. Its main theme is that merit, fame, wealth, and honors are like a springtime dream. . . . As a child, I used to listen to that story, which was looked on as a Buddhist parable *(Sŏkka uŏn)*."[2] The spring dream metaphor is not really Buddhist, but the belief in the evanescence, even the unreality, of the best things in life is no doubt at the very heart of that religion. Besides, the term "Buddhist parable" shows well what contemporaries thought the real source of its inspiration was.

In spite of this unmistakable testimony, a few scholars have striven to find in the *Nine Cloud Dream* Confucian and Taoist elements too, even holding to the view that the underlying religious standpoint of the novel was the syncretist idea of the unity of the three doctrines *(samgyo hwahap non)*. To counter this, Professor Chŏng Kyubok, in an article published in 1967,[3] demonstrated that the main inspiration of the work was Buddhist, even if the novel as a matter of fact bore with it many Confucian and Taoist elements. He even determined that the main theme was actually emptiness *(śūnyatā)* as taught by *The Diamond Sūtra (Vajracchedikā-prajñāpāramitā sūtra)*, the scripture that, in the novel, the master of the young hero had brought with him from India to China as his only baggage, and that, in the end, before returning to the West, he bequeathed to his disciple. In a very thorough study, published in 1972,[4] Sŏl Sŏnggyŏng demonstrated that the very structure of the *Nine Cloud Dream*, as shown in the distribution of time between dream and real life, reflected the thought and even the structure of that sutra. Thus one may consider it an established fact that Kim Manjung's novel was of Buddhist inspiration.

The other novel known to be by the same author is of another sort. It features a virtuous wife, Lady Hsieh, whose unjust repudiation by her husband is invested with a double allegorical significance. On the one hand she represents Queen Min, dethroned and repudiated in 1689 by King Sukchong; on the other she stands for the author, banished from the Seoul court for opposing that action of the King. The novel is reminiscent of the poet Ch'ü Yüan (c. 343–c. 277 B.C.), whom later Confucian tradition cast in the role of the loyal counselor unjustly exiled. Although basically unlike the *Nine Cloud Dream*, it contains a puzzling detail, which I have noted elsewhere,[5] in which the high-ranked scholar-official seems to commit himself to the compassion of the Bodhisattva Kuan-yin (Avalokiteśvara). Kim Manjung had been exiled to the island of Namhae, on the South coast of Korea, which local legend regarded as the Korean Potalaka, the abode of the great Kuan-yin in the South Sea (Namhae). Now, in his novel, Kim has Heaven put the estranged wife, who represents himself, under Kuan-yin's protection, the bodhisattva being for the occasion designated by the unusual appellation, Immortal of the South Sea *(Namhae toin)*. This is certainly a devotional touch, surprising in a supposedly Confucian *yangban*. Nothing we know about Kim Manjung explains this. But still more puzzling is the deep impregnation of Buddhist thought in the *Nine Cloud Dream*, which remains a riddle to modern historians of Korean literature.[6]

The family Kim Manjung came from, the man he called his master, the public offices he held—everything about him should have combined to inspire in him an aversion for this religion. The clan he belonged to, the Kim of Kwangsan, was one of the pillars of the Confucian faction known as the "Westerners," the Sŏin. His great grandfather was Kim Changsaeng (Sagye, 1548–1631), the scholar whose commentaries on the family rites, *Karye chimnam* (Comprehensive Examinations of the Family Ritual), and on the funeral rites according to Chu Hsi, *Sangnye piyo* (Manual for the Mourning Services), were considered authoritative. Kim Changsaeng had been the master of Song Siyŏl (1607–89), of whom Kim Manjung would call himself[7] a disciple and in the shadow of whom Kim would remain all his life. Song Siyŏl was, among the Westerners, the founder of the hard-core subfaction called Noron, which, after a short eclipse at the time of the exile and death of Song Siyŏl and Kim Manjung, was to hold almost undivided power until the end of the dynasty in 1910.

Concerning the public career of Kim Manjung, begun in 1655 when he was twenty-six years old, we should take note of the nature of certain offices that were entrusted to him. These would lead one to think that he had a reputation, not only as a man of learning, but also as a staunch Confucian. Some of the public offices held by Kim Manjung were, according to Korean custom, held concurrently with the office of lecturer on the classics to the King (*siganggwan* or *sidokkwan*). The conduct of the Royal Lectures (*Kyŏngyŏn*) was a function of the Office of the Special Counselors (*Hongmun'gwan*), to which Kim Manjung was to be reassigned several times as he rose to higher rank in the hierarchy: first counselor (*pujehak*) in 1680 and 1682, director (*taejehak*) in 1683 and 1686. The latter title placed him at the head of that same organ in charge of the storage of classical and historical books, and made him counselor and tutor to the king. The mere suspicion of harboring some sympathy towards Buddhism would have been enough to disqualify him from holding such offices.

Even the setbacks which Sŏp'o experienced in his career, which was interrupted four times, were in no way attributable to liberties he might have taken with the regnant orthodoxy. The first time, in 1668, it was due to his stubbornness in a small matter of etiquette.[8] The second time, in 1673, he had harshly criticized[9] Hŏ Chŏk (1610–80), a respected figure of the opposing faction, the Southerners (Namin), whose appointment at the top of the hierarchy had served the policy of King Hyŏnjong (r. 1659–74) to maintain a balance between the factions. The same partisanship and dogmatic rigidity are noticeable in the fierce attack led by Kim Manjung[10] in 1675 against another Southerner, Yun Hyu (1617–80), one of the few nonconformists of the time.[11] In particular Kim rebuked him for having proposed to do away with the reading of Chu Hsi's commentaries during the Royal Lectures. Finally, in 1687, while Kim as Director of the Office of the Special Counselors was commenting upon the classics in the presence of King Sukchong (r. 1674–1720), he incurred the royal anger for having brought up rumors related to the entourage of the new favorite, Lady Chang. In so doing he was only following the lead of his old master, Song Siyŏl, who was also the head of his faction.

Kim Manjung's political behavior was, as far as one can see, that of a man who apparently had fully assimilated the dominant Neo-Confucianism and did not deviate from pursuing the narrow interests of his clan. Nothing in the record leads one to suspect an inner evolution in his thinking such as is suggested by his novels. Current attempts to explain this refer to the disappointments and the sufferings Sŏp'o went through at the end of his career. Exiled to Sŏnch'ŏn, near the Chinese border, in the ninth month of 1687, he was called back in the eleventh month of 1688, only to be subjected to interrogation with his son in Seoul. In the third intercalary month of 1689, he barely escaped a death sentence. Instead the harshest form of banishment was inflicted upon him—exile to an island, and confinement to a small fenced-in cottage, *chŏlto wiri anch'i*.[12] He stayed there for three years before passing away at fifty-five, probably from a lung disease he had contracted long before.[13]

Exile was made more painful by the death, in the twelfth month of 1689, of his mother, of whom he was, after his elder brother's death, the only support. The influence of his mother, to whom he was deeply attached, is also cited to explain Sŏp'o's attraction toward Buddhism. The posthumous son of a father who had perished during the Manchu invasion in 1637, Manjung had been, as he tells it,[14] entirely educated by his mother, too poor to pay for the lessons of a master from outside. Korean women, then as now, had remained more susceptible than men to the attractions of Buddhism. Yi Chae's text, quoted above,[15] reports that Sŏp'o had written the *Nine Cloud Dream* in order to console his aged mother.[16] If this is true, there must have been a secret understanding between mother and son concerning their shared interest in Buddhism.

Confronted by this unusual phenomenon, historians of Korean lit-

erature have not been able to offer any other explanation than these political setbacks and the maternal influence. Some, however, do recall that
in the random notes left by the author, the *Random Essays of Sŏp'o*, there
are many passages dealing favorably with Buddhism. These had at the
time caused some lifting of eyebrows, as reported in the Preface by the
author's grandnephew, Kim Ch'unt'aek (1670–1717). First readers had
been of the opinion that the *Random Essays of Sŏp'o* "at places strayed
away from the forefathers of Confucianism and showed the heavy influence of Buddhism."[17] This is no doubt the reason why, in spite of the
author's fame, the book was never printed. In modern times, it has not
yet been given the attention it deserves. Scholars generally quote only one
or two sentences to establish, as one puts it,[18] that Kim Manjung "had a
deep interest in Buddhism." But the analysis, to my knowledge, has hardly
been carried further. Still less has the philosophical thought of the author
ever been subjected to overall analysis. My own purpose here is not to
undertake such a large project. It is, more modestly, to present the texts
of the *Random Essays of Sŏp'o* concerned with Buddhism, and expose
their rationale and the problems they raise. Their study, I believe, should
throw some light on the real feelings of this great writer and dignitary of
the Confucian regime toward the supposedly despised religion. It should
also, I hope, contribute to the reconstruction of his thought, which is a
task that will have to be grappled with some day.

A manuscript of the *Random Essays of Sŏp'o*[19] was reproduced pho-
tographically and published in 1971 in Seoul,[20] in a volume where it occupies pages 375 to 658, that is, 143 leaves with 11 columns on each face
and 22 characters in each column. Before this, in 1959, a mimeographed
edition[21] had come to light. Comparison with the 1971 facsimile shows
considerable differences in the sequence of essays, and reveals many important lacunae. The 1971 text, however, corresponds to other manuscripts examined,[22] with the exception of a few negligible variants, and it
is the one I shall refer to here. As to ascertaining in which period of his
life Kim Manjung jotted down the notes from which this book was compiled, I hope that this study may make some contribution toward dealing
with this matter of chronology.[23]

Of the various essays in the *Random Essays of Sŏp'o*, the ones dealing with Buddhism directly, indirectly, or by way of allusion are about
fifty in number, scattered throughout the book. The longest one has about

1,300 characters and the shortest only 63. It is in a rambling style, with a quality of spontaneity, allusive in expression and at times enigmatic. If one tried to follow every turn in Kim's thought, one would soon get lost. Some sorting out and rearrangement are therefore needed. I have selected those texts which refute the anti-Buddhist arguments of Chu Hsi's school and, secondly, those which draw a parallel between Buddhism and Neo-Confucianism and emphasize the dependence of the latter upon the former.

Before coming to the heart of the matter, I wish first to take up what an esteemed scholar, the late Pak Sŏngŭi, wrote in 1972 in a book which attracted some attention.[24] After quoting several texts, which according to him showed that Sŏp'o upheld the idea of the harmony of the Three Teachings, he added: "From the examples quoted above, it would seem that Sŏp'o was a supporter of Buddhism. The following shows that he was nothing of the sort."[25] Then, to back his denial, Professor Pak quotes two texts, one dealing with the prohibition of Buddhist rites, the other with a poem Sŏp'o had composed years before.

The first passage[26] refutes an opinion expressed by Ssu-ma Kuang calling for the prohibition of Buddhist ceremonies in funeral rites for the purpose of supporting Confucian doctrine (*ŭijae pugyo*). Sŏp'o remarks that the classics themselves are full of stories of spirits, similar to the ones propagated by Buddhists. Nor do they lack a theory of retribution after death: a good man's *ch'i* ascends to Heaven, a bad man's becomes an evil spirit, *yŏgwi*. There are prayers also to plead for the remission of sins committed by the deceased during his life. Now, Sŏp'o observes, in such cases prayers to Heaven are addressed to the Heaven of the Chinese, which is no other than the Tengri of the Northern Barbarians.[27] In the past, even the Emperor Shun could not change an evil father when he was alive; how much less could prayers addressed to a barbarian god, *hosin*, on behalf of a deceased parent, be effective? Sacrifices to ancestors have no other goal than to release their spirits' energy (*ch'i*) and express the sincerity of the offerer. What use then to add foreign rites?[28]

Professor Pak's commentary on this is: "Kim Manjung defends the sacrificial rites of Confucianism and rejects the Buddhist ones. He calls the Buddha a 'barbarian god' and Buddhist ceremonies 'barbarian rites.' He thus holds that religion in contempt. He hints that offerings to Buddha are meaningless and ineffective. He seems to share the mentality of the ordinary scholar; respect for Confucianism and rejection of Buddhism (*sungyu ch'ŏkpul*)."

If I am correct, my summing up of Sŏp'o's text shows on the contrary that Professor Pak oversimplifies and distorts what the author is trying to say. Also he misinterprets the term *hosin*, which does not refer to Śākyamuni but to the Chinese Heaven. As a matter of fact what Sŏp'o means is that prayers addressed to the latter are no more effective than the ones to the Buddha. Either way sacrificial rites have an effect only on the mind of the living and, as far as the deceased are concerned, on their *ch'i*. Consequently it is useless to borrow new rites from foreigners and add them to ours. The writer thus makes the agnosticism of the Confucian tradition his own and draws a bold parallel between the Heaven of Confucius and the Tengri of the Mongols. Far from vilifying Buddhism, he insinuates that arguments used against it can be turned round against those who use them.

The second text put forward by Professor Pak[29] begins by observing that Taoism and Buddhism are often treated alike and branded as *idan* (heresy). There is, however, a poem by Chu Hsi where he appears to be biased in favor of Taoism against Buddhism. This is also the case with the preface he wrote for Wei Poyang's Taoist work of the Han period, the *San-t'ung-ch'i*. Kim Manjung expresses doubts about Chu Hsi's authorship of both. Then he relates that having received the latter work from Nam Kuman (1629–1711), he had thanked that gentleman by writing a long poem in verses of five feet, which was a fierce attack against Buddhism. In it the Emperor Ming's famous dream was said to be a bad omen, the introduction of Buddhism into China a running stain, and the suppression of 845 a just punishment from Heaven, which unfortunately had not burned out all the weeds. Chu Hsi came at last, and finally rid us of it. Quoting his poem, Professor Pak concludes that Kim Manjung, as a true disciple of Chu Hsi, felt nothing but contempt for Buddhism. Here we have a good illustration of the danger of abridged editions. The cuts Pak makes in his quotation of the text correspond to the ones noticed in the 1959 mimeographed edition,[30] which he should not have trusted. Thus misled, Professor Pak misunderstands the reason why the author recalls this episode. Sŏp'o is not boasting about having composed such a virulent poem against Buddhism. In the unexpurgated text, he says that the addressee of the poem, Nam Kuman, had been shocked by his lumping together Chu Hsi and the persecutors of Buddhism, the emperors Wu of T'ang and Hui of Sung. Upon receiving that rebuke from an elder, Sŏp'o had torn his draft to pieces. Writing it out here from memory does not mean, Kim says, that he wants to vindicate himself. On the contrary, he is admitting that he made a mistake (*o kwa i i*).[31]

Professor Pak also fails to say that the poem is dated. It had been offered to Nam Kuman when he was appointed governor *(kwanch'alsa)* of Hamgyŏng Province in 1674. This dating is one of the few landmarks we have for determining the chronology of the *Random Essays of Sŏp'o*. The contrast between the poem of 1674 and the kind remarks about Buddhism strewn throughout the later book throws a striking light on the long path the author has traveled.

There are many passages approving of Buddhism, but none of them is quoted by Professor Pak. Let us mention a few here for the record. One[32] expresses the author's admiration for the way in which the prophecies of the Buddhist scriptures have come true. He is referring to the three periods that are supposed to mark the evolution of the Buddhist teaching: the period of true dharma (rectitude, C. *cheng*), the period of the counterfeit dharma (C. *hsiang*), and the period of the decay of the dharma (C. *mo*). Sŏp'o proceeds to the countdown, on the basis of the chronology taught in the *Sūtra of the Great Compassion (Mahākarunā Sūtra)* and taking as his starting point the year 1009 B.C., which he considers to be that of Śākyamuni's entrance into Nirvana: one thousand years of true dharma lead up to the Emperor Kuang-wu of Han; another thousand covers the coming of Buddhism to China, the six patriarchs, and the five families of Ch'an Buddhism. As for the last period of decay, which started with the Sung dynasty and must last ten thousand years, we shall see later the unexpected manner in which it is characterized by Sŏp'o. Buddhism is strange and mysterious, he concludes.

Elsewhere[33] Sŏp'o engages in a long discussion of the arguments put forward by Chinese Buddhists to prove the antiquity of their religion on Chinese soil. Sŏp'o is conversant with most of the accounts related to Buddhism during the Han period, which are examined by E. Zürcher in his master work.[34] These are the Emperor Ming's dream according to the *Hou-Han-shu*, quotations from the Preface to the *Lieh-hsien chuan*, the oral transmission of Buddhism by a Yüeh-chih envoy according to the *Wei-lüeh*, interpretation of the golden statue of the Hsiung-nu king in the *Shih-shuo hsin-yü*, and Tung-fang Shuo's reply to the Emperor Wu about the mysterious black substance of Lake K'un-ming. In regard to the Buddhist scriptures allegedly seen by Liu Hsiang under the reign of the Emperor Ping, Sŏp'o refers to a note by a commentator on Han Yü quoting the *K'ai-huang li-tai san-pao chi* of the Sui dynasty, which asserted that those scriptures were circulated in China as early as the Chou period. Sŏp'o also mentions the Great Sage of the West in the *Lieh Tzu* and, from the same work, the magicians who had come from the far West.

To all the claims thus advanced, Sŏp'o at first expresses a thorough scepticism, taking note of contradictions, showing improbabilities, and exposing suspect testimony. But in the end he concludes that, despite the great distances to be traveled and formidable natural obstacles to be overcome, there must have been some connection between India and China at a very early period through the peoples of Central Asia,[35] in particular through the Hsiung-nu, who were so powerful during the Ch'in and Former Han dynasties. Only such contacts, he writes, could have made possible Chang Ch'ien's mission to the Yüeh-chih kingdom. They would also explain the presence of Buddhism in China under Emperor Wu, which is something Sŏp'o holds as certain, although he admits that the first pieces of information that were passed on must have been very scanty. Sŏp'o's conclusion is concerned with the slowness in the propagation of a religion. In short, without succumbing to the excessive claims of the apologists, he is willing to acknowledge the antiquity of the Buddhist religion in China.

In another essay,[36] Sŏp'o expresses his admiration for the clarity and depth of certain Buddhist concepts, such as *chŏnghye* (C. *ting-hui*) and *pŏmmun* (C. *fa-men*). As we shall see later, he has difficulty finding their equivalents in Neo-Confucianism.

Regarding his own country, Korea, Sŏp'o reminds us that Chinese writing had been brought in by Buddhist missionaries.[37] At the inception of Korean literature, he goes on, there is Sŏl Ch'ong, whom he names after Śākyamuni's son, Rahu, because that great writer was the son of the Buddhist master, Wŏnhyo (617–86). "As for that great man of letters, Ch'oe Ch'iwŏn (857–?), was he not in China reputed to be a Vimalakīrti in his ten-square-foot cell?"[38] It was not before the end of the Koryŏ period that the Koreans came back to Confucianism. But, as far as the earlier period is concerned, the contributions of Buddhism to education are beyond question. Elsewhere[39] Kim Manjung calls attention to the sacrifices offered in Korea at the royal tombs, in which only vegetarian food is used. He pours ridicule on the excuses offered by those ashamed of a custom so similar to the rites of the religion they despise. As a matter of fact, it is, Sŏp'o says, a legacy from the Koryŏ dynasty. In other words, it is actually to Buddhism and its prohibition on killing and eating meat that one must look for the origin of that ritual prescription.

The author's good will towards Buddhism is evident. Far from despising that religion, as Professor Pak would have it, he holds it in undeniable esteem. It is no surprise, then, to find him, in the texts I am going to examine now, sifting arguments against Buddhism tediously repeated by his masters and friends, the literati of Korea and China. By refusing to accept them at face value, he shows his independence of mind from the tradition he has been brought up in.

One of the objections to Buddhism circulating in Confucian circles had been borrowed from Han Yü's (768–824) famous *Memorial on the Bone of the Buddha*[40] and taken up in Korea by Chŏng Tojŏn (1342–98) in his *Pulssi chappyŏn*.[41] Buddhism, they said, had brought bad luck to the emperors who patronized it and shortened their reign. Kim Manjung makes short work of this in a text[42] where he likens it to what Chu Hsi wrote[43] about the setbacks experienced by the two last emperors of the Northern Sung. The Master attributed them to a violation of the rules of geomancy perpetrated in the wrong orientation of a tomb. Sŏp'o has no difficulty in bringing examples, from the T'ang to the Ming, to prove the ineptitude of such an explanation. Since Hsien-tsung died a little after the reception of the bone relic at court, people inferred that Han Yü's warning was well-grounded. What to say, then, Sŏp'o remarks, of the tragic death of many persecutors of Buddhism? Life and death, riches and honors are in the hands of destiny; they are no more affected by the vicissitudes of the Buddhist religion than by the orientation of a tomb.

Sŏp'o devotes two other notes to defending against Chu Hsi the authenticity, that is, the Indian origin, of some Buddhist scriptures. The Master had unceasingly denounced in the foreign religion what he judged to be stealthy borrowings from pure Chinese, especially Taoist, tradition. In his *Shih-shih lun* (Treatise on Buddhism)[44] Chu found fault with the stanzas, *gāthās*, attributed by *The Transmission of the Lamp (Ch'uan-teng lu)*[45] to the twenty-eight Ch'an patriarchs. He scoffed at Yang I (974–1020) and Su Ch'e (1039–1112), who had been unable to detect the imposture which, he thought, conformity to Chinese prosody sufficed to prove. Recalling Chu Hsi's text, Sŏp'o[46] also begins by suspecting the authenticity of the stanzas, but on different grounds. In China, he observes, close to nothing has come down to us from the teachings of the ancient Sages. Is it reasonable to think that the words of those of India have been transmitted for several thousand years just as they were pronounced? Of course not. This does not mean, however, that he finds some merit in Chu Hsi's argument. Any Korean scholar versed in translation from his tongue into Chinese knows very well that it is up to the translator to follow the rules of Chinese grammar or prosody, giving the final text a Chinese flavor, without losing too much of the original. Neither respect for Chinese rules of meter, rhyme, and number of words, Sŏp'o writes, nor the fitness of the vocabulary, can in themselves be taken as proof that a poem is not a translation. The Chinese, he remarks after recalling an example drawn from Korean experience, are ignoramuses in the matter of foreign languages. This applies even to Master Chu.

The following article[47] is in the same vein. It answers a charge of plagiarism. "There are today among the Ch'anists," Chu Hsi had said,[48] "ideas that do not come from the Buddhist patriarchs. . . . Let us see what the *Yüan-chüeh ching* (Sūtra of Perfect Enlightenment) says: 'When the four elements are dispersed, where is the illusory body?' This is borrowed from the *Lieh Tzu*, which says: 'Bones and flesh return whence they come, the spirit enters through its own door; where then is the Ego?' "[49]

It is not plagiarism at all, Sŏp'o retorts, appealing again to the experience of the Korean scholar who is skilled in translation. Taoism and Buddhism have it in common to value the spirit and to ignore the body. No wonder that translators, aware of similarities between the two, used a formulation close to that of *Lieh Tzu* in order to render the words of the Sūtra into Chinese.

Sŏp'o also remembers having read in Chu Hsi that the only sūtra in the Chinese Canon to have come from India, and therefore the only genuine one, was the *Szu-shih-erh chang ching* (Sūtra-in-forty-two articles).[50] Sŏp'o's refutation is based once again upon experience from Korean life. After the invention of the Korean alphabet, in 1446, he recalls, translation into the vernacular began with the easiest works, such as the *Elementary Learning (Hsiao-hsüeh)*, and only later went to harder books such as the *Book of Changes (I-ching)*. Likewise, on the Buddhist side, they did not get around to translating the *Sūramgama Sūtra* (Sūtra of the Heroic March) or the *Yüan-chüeh-ching* before the T'ang dynasty.

Finally, concerning the *Vimalakīrti nirdeśa sūtra* (Sūtra Spoken by Vimalakīrti), Sŏp'o blames Chu Hsi[51] for having said it was a Chinese forgery of the time of the Northern and Southern dynasties (317–589). To counter this, he quotes the words of Yin Hao (A.D. ?–356) and of Wang T'an-shih (4th century), recorded in the *Shih-shuo hsin-yü*, according to which the work was already widely circulated at the time of Eastern Chin (316–420). He points also to the frescoes painted at the same time by Ku K'ai-chih, representing Vimalakīrti's avatar, Chin-su.

Sŏp'o defends the Buddhists against attack on still another front: respect for life and abstinence from meat. Confucian tradition is ambiguous in this regard, he remarks.[52] On one side, there is Chang Chiu-ch'eng, who would refrain even from eating crab, and Mencius, who would not eat the flesh of an animal he had seen alive and who recommended to good Confucian gentlemen that they keep away from the kitchen. On the other hand, Yang Shih has reminded us that the Duke of Chou hunted wild beasts and slayed barbarians. Fu Hsi practiced net fishing but Ch'eng T'ang used to loosen three of the four sides of his net. As for Confucius, he practiced angling but not netting. Which one should we take as a model? As a matter of fact, Sŏp'o writes, there is no golden mean in this matter. The Buddha's position is the only consistent one.[53] That it could not be laid down as a rule for everybody does not detract from its validity. After all, did not Ch'eng I tolerate his niece's remarriage, going counter to his own teaching, and did he not receive Chu Hsi's approbation on this score? It is the same with Śākyamuni's prohibition on killing. It cannot be denied that it is a virtue, *in* (C. *jen*). You say that it is carried to an extreme? All right. But, in the Chinese tradition, men like Po I and Chan Huo too went further than the Sages, the former in purity, the second in mildness. As for Śākyamuni, it is only in respect to compassion *(che/cha)* that he went to an extreme. Even as regards Confucian virtue, lack of restraint is assuredly a fault. Why then deplore and hate it only in Śākyamuni?[54]

To reject oversimplified arguments, to demand fairness in judgments and insist on seriousness in philological criticism, these could characterize Kim Manjung's approach to the texts so far examined. In others, Sŏp'o goes still further and turns against Chu Hsi and his disciples the very objections they raised against Buddhism. We saw him before[55] dealing with funeral rites and pointing to things in Confucian tradition that the Confucians themselves had held against Buddhism: retribution after death or prayers for remission of sins committed by a deceased person.[56] In the same way, there is another note in the *Random Essays of Sŏp'o* in which Kim Manjung turns on Chu Hsi a rebuke he had administered to Buddhism and hits him on a distinction essential to his thought.

The Master had written several times that "the mind of man" (*jen-hsin*) should follow the "mind of the Way" (*tao-hsin*). This is a strange splitting of the mind, Sŏp'o says,[57] commenting upon Chu's preface to his commentary on the *Mean* (*Chung-yung*). This is not to say that he does not understand what Chu Hsi means, since he explains it immediately, using the Master's own terms. But he adds the following: "This is exactly the Buddhist theory of the mind looking at the mind (*hsin kuan hsin/sim kwan sim*), already refuted by Chi Hsi himself. . . . I cannot see any difference."

The Master of Neo-Confucianism had often accused the Buddhists of concocting a second mind, through which man would look at himself.[58] "The mind should not be split into two," he would say.[59] "It is as if men would look at their eyes with their own eyes." This argument, Sŏp'o thinks, can be turned against the man who put it forward. Does he say this because he does not accept the distinction made by Chu Hsi? Is he of Lu Hsiang-shan's opinion, i.e., that it leads to a dualistic view of the human mind which is not allowable? One is left to wonder. Sŏ'po's text is too brief, too allusive to allow us to answer this with certainty. It seems to me however that this is not what he thinks. He does say at the beginning of this essay that the sentence quoted from Chu's preface is "hard to read (*nandok*)" and he makes fun of it. But next he gives a plausible explanation of it: "What comes from physical forces (*hyŏnggi*) must never refuse to follow reason (*ŭiri*)." To which he adds that Chu Hsi's distinction is mainly a manner of speaking, convenient and easy to understand. He refrains from making it into a dichotomy of reality itself. Maybe this is only to suggest that the same is true of the so-called splitting of the mind criticized by Chu Hsi in Buddhism. If this is the case, what it means here is that Chu Hsi should show towards Buddhism the same forbearance which his own interpreters are asked to show to him.

Whatever the meaning of this particular text, it implies a certain parallelism, or better a deep similarity, between Buddhism and Neo-Confucianism, beneath the surface of polemical controversy. This was the case with the beliefs implied by the funeral rites,[60] and also with Buddhist compassion and Confucian humaneness. So it is now with the wonderful Buddhist concepts like *chŏnghye* and *pŏmmun*. Of the first one,[61] which evokes a recollectedness and luminous certitude of the spirit, Sŏp'o offers as a Confucian equivalent *hamyang* (C. *han-yang*), which may be translated as "self-control and self-nurturing." He pairs the second, *pŏm-mun*, gateway to wisdom, together with the Confucian "extension of knowledge," *(chih-chih/ch'iji)*. He concedes however that these terms are not to be found in the classics.

Sŏp'o elaborates in other texts on the parallelism he sees between the two doctrines. In one text,[62] he finds it in the historical evolution of both teachings. In Confucianism, Mencius' theories of the goodness of human nature or of the *ch'i* were not found in Confucius. Nor can one find in the Ch'eng brothers anything close to the *Hsün-meng-shu* (Instructions) attached by Chu Hsi in front of the *Mean* or to the first chapter of the *Chin-ssu lu*. The explanation of this fact is simple. What a master confidentially commits to his disciples become basic assumptions taken for granted and repeated as clichés by succeeding generations.[63] Let us pause to consider the two terms chosen to express such an oral tradition inside Confucianism. They are actually Buddhist. The first one, *milbu* (C. *mi-fu*), is used by the Ch'anists to mean the direct passing on of truth, from heart to heart, between master and disciple. The second, "singular transmission" *(tan-ch'uan/tanjŏn)*, refers to the fact that the Buddhist patriarch, Bodhidharma, did not rely on the written word in imparting his teaching.[64] A similar oral tradition is also at work inside Confucianism, Sŏp'o believes, going beyond what has been put into writing. It accounts for the differences among the great thinkers.

Similarly, discrepancies among the masters of Buddhism, pointed out by their Confucian opponents, are but the inescapable consequences of the same situation. Accepting the traditional division of Buddha's life into periods, as popularized by the *Lotus Sūtra*, Sŏp'o notes that Śākyamuni himself, in his teaching, took his time and was careful not to rush things. True there has been a written tradition after him. But with Bodhidharma's coming to China and with his successors, it was direct oral tradition again, from master to disciple. Admittedly each one had his own method: Bodhidharma sat nine years facing a wall; Tao-hsin did not lie down for thirty years; Hui-neng would strike whomever he would see seated but still he taught principles like "think neither good nor evil." Yet Tao-i (Ma-tsu) saw all these things as hindrances and to awaken his disciples he would resort to insoluble riddles. Any oral tradition, Sŏp'o says, involves such variations.

And so Sŏp'o then draws up a comparative list of the Sages of the two traditions, showing the parallelism between their respective historical evolutions: Bodhidharma is Mencius' counterpart. Seng-ts'an, Hui-k'e, Hung-jen, and Tao-hsin were to Buddhism what Chou Tun-i, Chang Tsai, and the Ch'eng brothers were to Confucianism. Chu Hsi is the Confucian Hui-neng. The list goes on down to Lu Hsiang-shan and Wang Yang-ming on one side and Tao-i and I-hsüan on the other. Among the Buddhists, from the founder down to the last names, change had come about little by little (chŏm), through a slow process. The author implies that the evolution of Confucianism, so strangely parallel, developed in the same way.[65]

Is such a parallelism rooted at a deeper level, in a similarity of doctrine itself between the thinkers mentioned on both sides, Mencius and Bodhidharma, Seng-ts'an and Chou Tun-i? The text, which proceeds by way of cryptic allusions, does not say as much. However another essay[66] notes analogies at the very heart of both systems. This is the text most often quoted by modern scholars who wish to illustrate either the interest in Buddhism taken by the writer of the Nine Cloud Dream or his tendency toward syncretism. Unfortunately they content themselves with a paraphrase of the first part of the text and do not take into account its conclusion. The text ends with a quotation from a letter by Chu Hsi to Lo Po-wen.[67] Referring to the contents of a previous letter, Chu Hsi makes the following remark, quoted in full by Kim Manjung:

This matter, after all, is like the relationship between the Ch'an and the School [of Confucius], which are quite similar to each other and are only quarreling over trifles. Nevertheless it is precisely these trifles that occupy an important place, for it was already true that the School did not know the Ch'an; now Ch'an does not know the School either. They fight without succeeding in hitting the critical spots. How ridiculous!

This quotation contains three different statements: the similarity between Buddhism and Confucianism; the importance of the slight differences that separate them; and their lack of knowledge about each other. But the two examples cited by Sŏp'o in his conclusion do not go into the slight differences. They relate only to the two systems being similar to each other and to their mutual blindness about one another.

The first example is Chou Tun-i's Diagram of the Supreme Ultimate (T'ai-chi-t'u shuo). The second, which I shall examine first, refers to a writing with a close connection to it, dealing with the nature of quiescence and movement. It is Ch'eng Hao's famous letter to Chang Tsai on "stabilizing the nature" *(Ting-hsing shu)*.[68] In a comment made by Chu Hsi on this letter, Sŏp'o ironically discovers an instance of the very blindness with regard to Buddhism which is deplored elsewhere by the same Chu Hsi. The Master had remarked one day[69] that in the letter Ch'eng Hao had used the word *hsing* (nature) wrongly where *hsin* (mind) should have been used. He probably meant that Nature, an immutable metaphysical reality, could not be altered by a psychological action, such as the one designated by the term *ting*. To that, Sŏp'o observes that in Buddhist writings the word *hsing* (K. *sŏng*) has the meaning of *tso-yung* (K. *chagyong*), function or operation. "I suspect," he says, "that in Ch'eng and Chang the phrase *ting-hsing* actually came from Ch'an and that they were using it by force of habit."

Another similarity to Buddhism appears in a passage as fundamental to Neo-Confucianism as the first sentence of Chou Tun-i's *Diagram of the Supreme Ultimate*, first mentioned by Sŏp'o at the beginning of the same article. In Buddhist writings, he says at the outset, there are plenty of tedious repetitions. But the main point is contained in the four characters "absolute emptiness / spontaneous existence" *(chen-k'ung miao-yu/chinkong myoyu)*.[70] These four terms had been commented upon by the fifth patriarch of the Hua-yen sect, Tsung-mi, in two statements that defy any effort at translation: "The truth of emptiness does not contradict the unreality of phenomenal existence; the deep reality of phenomenal existence does not contradict the truth of emptiness."[71] This abstruse statement is what Sŏp'o compares to Neo-Confucianism. He likens it to the "without limit and yet the Supreme Ultimate *(Wu-chi erh t'ai-chi)*" of Chou Tun-i. But doesn't the similarity reside in the same paradoxical balance of antithetical and apparently contradictory terms, a balance intended to suggest transcendence? Or does it only express the desire, new to Confucianism, to put in words what is beyond words? Perhaps, on the contrary, the similarity lies in the contents of the two philosophies. Sŏp'o does not tell us. But what he does say leads one to believe that the analogy is rooted at this deeper level.

After having quoted the *Diagram of the Supreme Ultimate* and Ch'eng Hao's letter, in which the term *ting-hsing* seems borrowed from Ch'an, he refers to the *gāthā* composed by Wo-lun and amended by Hui-neng, as reported in *The Platform Sūtra*.[72] The paradoxical way of expressing the absolute is the same: "I, Hui-neng, know of no technique. My thoughts are not being suppressed. The objective world excites my mind forever.

What need to make illumination ripen?" Sŏp'o's commentary on this is: "It is nothing else than the *ting-hsing* of Chang and Ch'eng,"[73] which itself is so close to the first sentence of the *Diagram of the Supreme Ultimate*. The implicit conclusion is, as suggested before, that the concept had really been borrowed from Ch'an by the two Neo-Confucian philosophers.

The similarity between the opposing sides is no accident. On the contrary, as hinted in this latter essay, it is the result of the influence of one upon the other. Sŏp'o develops this idea in other essays, which I shall now examine.

A disciple does not always put his master's lessons to the use intended by the latter. This need not mean denying his debt to him. Such is the significance of the defense of the mirror-polisher as related by Sŏp'o.[74] "Suppose someone is learning how to polish a mirror; his master polishes it and puts it back in its case. But the apprentice uses it to set his dress straight and see how he looks." The pupil in this case is Hsieh Liang-tso, whose rule to keep constantly awake was inspired by the "wake up, wake up" of the Ch'an monks. Chu Hsi admits that the words are the same in each case,[75] but, he says, the method *(kung-fu)* needed to attain the goal, illumination, is totally different. Hence Chu Hsi refuses to acknowledge that the phrase has been borrowed from the Buddhists. Thus he refuses to recognize the fact, for even a change in the way the formula is used afterwards does not change the fact of borrowing itself.

There was "no one among the disciples of the Ch'eng brothers who was not tinged with Buddhism," Sŏp'o writes,[76] including Lü Yu-shu (Lü Ta-lin, 1046–92), who was nevertheless praised by Chu Hsi, Yu Kuang-p'ing (Yu Tso, 1053–1123), as well as the other two of the "four masters," Yang Shih and Hsieh Liang-tso. The Ch'eng brothers themselves were no exception. It is true that, to Chu Hsi's eyes, the Buddhist elements found in their *Conversations (Yü-lu)* are interpolations by Yu Tso's hand. But, even in their *I-shu* (Surviving Writings), the Ch'engs acknowledge that there is in Buddhism what they call the "seriousness to straighten the inner self *(ching erh chih nei)*." "I would say myself," Kim Manjung writes, "that the Loyang School could not at first keep from borrowing from Buddhism. The tide being about to overflow, they tried to dam it up. But the disciples were much too used to borrowing and did not comply. In the last period, the situation had become unmanageable and led to men like Heng-p'u (Chang Chiu-ch'eng) and Chin-hsi (Lu

Chiu-yüan)." The struggle to check the penetration of Buddhism into Sung Neo-Confucianism might be compared, according to Sŏp'o, to the efforts made by the Chinese emperors to hold back the barbarians, who finally succeeded in invading China.

Buddhist influence upon the two Ch'engs had been admitted by Chu Hsi himself, Sŏp'o reminds us.[77] In a letter to Ch'eng Yün-fu (Ch'eng Hsün) he wrote that they had been "sick and then cured," as compared to the Su brothers, who had on the contrary gone from good health to sickness.[78] "They must have had contact," Sŏp'o remarks, "at the time they became contaminated, with some people who had studied Buddhism." Yet, in his *Classified Conversations*, Chu Hsi strenuously[79] denies the visit that, according to Hsieh Liang-tso, young I-ch'uan had paid to a monk[80] as well as the fact that he had been in correspondence with another monk named Ling-yüan.[81] His wrath might have been aroused by Hsieh's statement that the young man had "pilfered" the monk's teaching. But, by defending I-ch'uan as he does and by looking for excuses, Chu Hsi only adds to the suspicion, Sŏp'o says. In the latter's view, there must have been many other instances of intercourse between the two Ch'engs and Buddhist believers.

Chu Hsi himself, according to Sŏp'o, did not escape their influence. Another essay in the *Random Essays of Sop'o*[82] quotes a Ming author, Wang Yuan-mei (Wang Shih-chen, 1526–93), who, having studied Buddhism late in life, had heard his master saying: "Lu (Hsiang-shan) is actually Ch'an. As for Chu (Hsi), he had no right to blame him for that."[83] To explain this insinuation, Sŏp'o echoes a tradition saying that the young Chu Hsi had taken lessons from a monk called Tao-ch'ien.[84] So, he goes on, what the Master said on the theory and practice of the mind actually came from Southern Ch'an, while his concept of "preserving and nurturing" *(ts'un-yang)* came from Hui-neng. Elsewhere[85] Sŏp'o takes note of Chu Hsi's efforts to replace the Buddhist term *ting-hui* by *chi-kan*, which he takes as another sign of Buddhist influence on Chu's thought.

This must have seemed quite irreverent in Yi dynasty Korea, coming from a high-ranking scholar-official. Sŏp'o realized of course that his words might scandalize. So, after having mentioned the assumed relationship between Chu Hsi and Tao-ch'ien,[86] he makes a remark on the independence of the Chinese from Master Chu's authority. "Chu Hsi's refutation of Ch'an and Lu [Hsiang-shan]," he writes, "was extremely severe. Besides, on account of I-ch'uan, he disliked Tung-p'o (Su Shih). Yet, under the Ming, for three hundred years, those who have discussed philosophy follow the Kiangsi school, men of letters have adhered to Mei-shan [Su Shih], and those who have laughed at Hui-an [Chu Hsi] were legion."[87] Sŏp'o's point is made clear by the conclusion: "As a matter of fact 'killing one's master,' as the saying goes, is no crime, stamping on him is not forbidden." In other words, China pays no attention to the taboos of Korea. To shake off a hardened local tradition by appealing to one of a greater, more prestigious, and idealized country is typical behavior among nonconformists of that small country. Three hundred years later, reformers were to act in the same way to break the crust of conservatism and promote Western-style modernization.

"Under the T'ang," another essay[88] begins, "many cultivated people studied Buddhism." They differed in their personalities and what they gained from it also varied. But, among all those listed by Sŏp'o down to the Sung dynasty, the main thing they got was *suddhā, ch'ing-ching,* purification from blemishes and illusions. Thanks to Buddhism, they attained strength in the expression of their ideas and in the management of public affairs, which other people lacked. In the first rank of the latter is Han Yü, who had not benefited any less than the others from Confucian tradition and yet, from his place of exile, Ch'ao-chou sent lamentations that later became an embarrassment to his admirers. "It was because he had not studied Buddhism," Kim Manjung is not afraid to say.[89] In other words, a better knowledge of the foreign religion, so fiercely criticized by Han Yü, would have helped him to become a better Confucian.

Among those named by Sŏp'o in this note, none had an exclusive interest in Buddhism. On the contrary, this doctrine was but a complement to what remained their main source of inspiration, Confucianism. Such is, in medical treatment, the function of the refreshing powder, *ch'ŏngnyangsan,* which one takes at evening in a drink, after having had in the morning a hot soup of bitter herbs. These men made no secret of their studying Buddhism but did not confound it with their Confucianism. In contrast to them, Sŏp'o goes on, the Ch'engs, as well as their disciples, mixed the hot soup with the cool drink and then claimed to have rediscovered the recipe of ancient medicine.[90] They forgot, however, that the ancients knew nothing of the refreshing powder that Buddhism represents. Lu Hsiang-shan and Yang Chien (1141–1226) made the same concoction but at least they were candid and made no secret of it.

To combine without mixing, to differentiate without opposing. These seem to constitute the basic tendencies in Kim Manjung's thought. Though it is the legitimate complement of ancient Confucian wisdom, Buddhism should still not be confounded with it. "Since the theories of Lao Tzu and Śākyamuni are in circulation," Sŏp'o says also, "we Confucianists have been standing on the side, making our choice and using one or the other."[91] The term "using," *yong*, is worth noting. Confucianism, in practice, *uses* Buddhism, which remains something alien to it, and the mind, for its part, must take care not to confound what ought to be kept distinct. Thus we return in the end to the words with which Kim Ch'unt'aek, in the Preface, characterized Sŏp'o's approach: "To look for sources and to discriminate currents."[92] This is actually what Sŏp'o does in the texts just examined.

Such a characterization, as well as the pharmacological comparison quoted above, throw some light on two passages in which Sŏp'o goes so far as to say that Sung Neo-Confucianism *was* actually Buddhism. The first one occurs at the end of an essay quoted above, in which Sŏp'o admires the accuracy of Buddha's prophecies about the vicissitudes of his doctrine down the road of history.[93] Coming to the third and last predicted period, *malpŏp*, he writes: "From the Sung, the Law of Buddha started to decay. Undergoing change, Ch'an has become Confucianism.[94] Yu Tso, Hsieh Liang-tso, Chang Chiu-ch'eng, and the rest represent the 'decline of the Law' *(mo-fa)!*" The second text goes still further.[95] Comparing the School of the Ch'engs with the reforms of Wang An-shih, which obtained results opposite to those intended, it adds: "Ch'eng I-ch'uan developed the study of the Way in order to drive Ch'an out of the Empire. He wanted to make Confucianism succeed but what he did was on the contrary to eliminate Confucianism and promote the study of Ch'an." Confronted with these two peremptory assertions, one has to make allowance for hyperbole as well as for the exaggeration of polemics. The author is irritated at the oversimplifications or distortions of many arguments against Buddhism put forward under the cover of Chu Hsi's authority. As he writes, he has in mind those self-appointed "old masters" *(nosa)* and "scholars of long standing" *(sugyu)*, mentioned by Kim Ch'unt'aek in the Preface of the *Random Essays of Sŏp'o*,[96] who do not know the first word about the religion they vilify. To them, Sŏp'o takes a malicious pleasure in showing that their Confucianism, from the Sung period on, has been inextricably mixed up with Buddhism. He is not averse to shocking them by his sharp wording.

Even though, in this case, his rhetoric is somewhat extreme, the essential meaning of these two texts is nevertheless that Confucianism has inherited the gist of the Buddhist tradition and that in return has itself been modified by this development while the Buddhist tree itself has been withering away. The metaphor of the two potions, one to be taken in the morning and the other in the evening, shows that Sŏp'o does not deplore the use of both medicines by the same person. On the contrary, he recommends it and praises the great T'ang scholars for having taken both. This, he says, is in conformity with the Confucian tradition itself, which grows by absorbing external elements. What Sŏp'o finds reprehensible is the intellectual admixture of the two, especially when it is done on the sly. He wants to expose in Neo-Confucianism what are unconscious, unadmitted, or disguised borrowings. He wants also to denounce the hypocrisy of vilifying a religion one has fed on for so long and feasted on so abundantly, seeing it as very close actually to repudiating oneself. A critical but hospitable mind, lucid but tolerant—such appears to be, at the end of this study, the mental outlook of the author of the *Random Essays of Sŏp'o.*

The texts presented here raise questions concerning both the history of literature and history of thought. To the first kind belong the problem of chronology. These writings might have been composed over a long period of time and been collected later by the writer or, after his death, by pious hands. As far as Buddhism is concerned, however, the very strangeness of the ideas expressed in these various essays, as compared to the then accepted opinions, leads one to think that they were the result of a long evolution in Kim Manjung's thinking. The little chronological evidence we have also corroborates the supposition that these writings were of relatively late date.

Sŏp'o elsewhere[97] mentions a conversation he had with an old Buddhist monk, when he was, as he puts it, at the Western frontier *(sŏsae).* According to the only historian who has dealt with this problem of chronology, Professor Kim Mujo,[98] this geographical term designates a place called Kŭmsŏng, to which Kim Manjung had been banished for six months, in 1673–74, when he was thirty-seven. Kŭmsŏng, however, is not located west of Seoul but at about 120 km, as the crow flies, northeast of Seoul. We do well to remember in this respect that it was customary in old Korea to call west what is actually northwest. China was said to be west of Korea, which was the "Eastern Country," Tongguk. "Sŏsae" must be near the western border with China and cannot possibly mean

Kŭmsŏng. Therefore it must mean Sŏnch'ŏn,[99] where Kim Manjung was banished much later, from the ninth month of 1687 to the eleventh month` of 1688. The note mentioning the encounter with the monk might have been jotted down when Kim was in Seoul, just back from Sŏnch'ŏn. But he stayed in the capital only five months, during which he was constantly subjected to questioning.[100] Therefore the text is more likely to have been written during the last exile, at Namhae, between 1689 and the death of the author, in 1692.

Another evidence in favor of a later date has already been mentioned above: Sŏp'o's recalling of a poem composed in 1674.[101] The contrast between its contents, a diatribe against Buddhism, and other texts from the *Random Essays of Sŏp'o*, in which that religion is dealt with respectfully and sympathetically, enables one to estimate the distance covered. In 1674, Kim Manjung had only eighteen years more to live, and yet such a profound change in outlook must have taken many years to develop. The texts on Buddhism must consequently have been written in the very last years of his life.

In this respect comparison of Buddhism with the refreshing powder one takes in the evening is also suggestive. One would suppose that it must have some application to the writer himself. Would he have used the metaphor if he had not himself, in the evening of his life, taken comfort from this light potion, which offsets the effects of the more solid medicine absorbed in the morning?

Another question: from which sources did Sŏp'o draw his knowledge of the Buddhist religion? In the *Random Essays* he quotes from several Buddhist scriptures and mentions many more. Which of them had he read and applied to himself? The importance of *The Diamond Sūtra* in the novel *Nine Cloud Dream* suggests that Sŏp'o had really read it and meditated upon it. The only Buddhist work that, in the *Random Essays of Sŏp'o*, he says he has read is the collected writings of the Korean monk Hyujŏng (1520–1604).[102] On this he observes scornfully that there is nothing new in it compared to the letters of the Sung master Ta-hui, which had been edited in one volume in Korea, or to the *Sŏnyo* (The Main Points of Dhyāna) by the Korean master Kobong, alias Pŏpchang (1351–1428). It can be inferred from this that Sŏp'o had also read these latter works.

The mere mention of the title of a book or its date, or even a general reference to its contents, does not necessarily mean that one has read it.

As a matter of fact, in the *Random Essays* many Buddhist writings are referred to indirectly, in connection with quotations from other authors. In this way *The Teaching of Vimalakīrti* is mentioned once, in order to refute the accusation by Chu Hsi[103] of its being a later forgery.

Sometimes, however, quotations are textual. So it is with *The Platform Sūtra*, the *Commentary* by Tsung-mi on the *Yüan-chüeh-ching*, and *The Transmission of the Lamp*. Lastly, in Kim Manjung's collected writings, the *Sŏp'ojip*, there is a quatrain in seven-foot verses[104] in which the author, who is in exile, complains about having nothing to read and asks a monk to lend him a few Buddhist books. It is followed by another poem thanking the same person for sending the *Śūramgama sūtra* and the *Yüan-chüeh-ching*, two titles also mentioned in a passing way in the *Random Essays of Sŏp'o*.[105] These two poems can be dated from the winter spent at Sŏnch'ŏn in 1687–88.[106] They indicate that Kim Manjung had these two Buddhist scriptures available at a time of forced leisure, conducive to meditation. How many Korean scholar-officials had read this kind of book? Short of actual investigation, one can guess that there were not many. Kim Manjung's knowledge of Buddhist literature must have been quite exceptional.

Kim's attitude towards Buddhism also raises questions related to the history of thought. First of all, there is one concerning the originality of his views. Was Kim Manjung a maverick among Korean Neo-Confucians? Or were there others who saw things as he did? What he says about the heavy influence of Buddhism upon Neo-Confucianism is relatively common knowledge today. Was it known to the Korean readers of his time? Was it known but thought to be better left unsaid, or was it upheld by some and denied by others? In this respect, the fact that, in spite of Sŏp'o's fame, the book was never printed is no doubt significant.

As for the reasons behind the evolution, political misfortune and maternal influence are only partial answers. His relationship to Lu Hsiang-shan will surely have to be investigated, as will the ones he might have had with the Ming thinkers his own thought is apparently so close to. If such influences can be detected, the question will rise again whether they reached him only through their own writings or whether it was through the medium of other scholars in Korea.

NOTES

1. Daniel Bouchez, "Le roman *Namjŏng ki* et l'affaire de la reine Min," *Journal asiatique* (1976), 264: 405–51; "*Namjŏng ki* e taehan il koch'al," *Asea yŏn'gu* (January 1977), 20(1):189–211; "Les propos de Kim Ch'unt'aek sur le *Namjŏng ki*," *Mélanges de coréanologie offerts à M. Charles Haguenauer* (Paris: Collège de France, 1979), pp. 1–43.
2. *Samgwan'gi* in *P'aerim* (Seoul: T'amgudang, 1970), vol. 9, p. 338.
3. "*Kuunmong* ŭi kŭnbon sasang ko," *Asea yŏn'gu* (December 1967), 10(4):65–88.
4. "*Kuunmong* ŭi kujojŏk yŏn'gu," Part I in *Inmun kwahak* (1972), 27/28:231–76; Part II in *Ŏnŏ munhwa* (December 1974), 1:73–103; Part III in *Kugŏ kungmunhak* (December 1972), 58/60:291–319.
5. D. Bouchez, "*Namjŏng ki*," pp. 437–39.
6. "Riddle" is the very term used in a recent History of Korean Literature: Kim Tonguk, *Kungmunhaksa* (Seoul: Ilsinsa, 1976), p. 180.
7. *Sukchong sillok* in *Chosŏn wangjo sillok*, 49 vols. (Seoul: Kuksa p'yŏnch'an wiwŏnhoe, 1955–1963), 4:14b: "Since Song Siyŏl was indicted, the King says, Kim Manjung has been claiming *(ka ch'ing)* to be his disciple."
8. *Hyŏnjong sillok*, 18:50ab.
9. *Ibid.*, 27:26a.
10. *Sukchong sillok*, 4:30ab.
11. In the Preface to *Sŏp'o manp'il*, Kim Ch'unt'aek mentions Yun Hyu's name in order to illustrate the fact that others than Kim Manjung took liberties with the teaching of the great Neo-Confucianists: *Sŏp'ojip Sŏp'o manp'il* (abbr. SPMP), introduction by Chŏng Kyubok (Seoul: T'ongmun'gwan, 1971).
12. *Sukchong sillok*, 20:34a.
13. *Ibid.*, 24:14b. In a letter written by Kim Manjung to his nephew Chin'gwi and quoted by Professor Chŏng Kyubok (*Kodae sinmun*, no. 602), he says: "As for blood spitting, there is no aggravation."
14. "Sŏnbi chŏnggyŏng puin haengjang," *Sŏp'ojip Sŏp'o manp'il*, pp. 360–61 (*Sŏp'ojip*).
15. See above, note 2.
16. See glossary at *Yo i wi sŏk*.
17. See glossary at *Si yŏ sŏn yu*.
18. Chŏng Pyŏnguk, ed., *Kuunmong* in *Han'guk kojŏn munhak taegye* (Seoul: Minjung sŏgwan, 1972), vol. 9, p. 18.
19. This undated manuscript belongs, as Professor Chŏng Kyubok was kind enough to advise me, to Mr. Im Ch'angsun.
20. It is the book (abbr. SPMP) referred to above, note 11.
21. *Sŏp'o manp'il* in *Kungmunhak charyo* (Seoul: Mullimsa, 1959).
22. Bibliographical references concerning the two manuscripts I have compared to the 1971 facsimile: (1) *Mansong Kim Wansŏp mun'go mongnok* (Seoul:

Koryŏ University, 1979), p. 253; (2) *Kyujanggak tosŏ Han'gukpon ch'ong-mongnok* (Seoul: Seoul National University, 1965), p. 556 (7353).

23. Another edition of *Sŏp'o manp'il*, coupled with a translation into Korean, has come out lately: *Han'guk ŭi sasang taejŏnjip* (Seoul: Tonghwa, 1977), vol. 18, Korean translation by Sŏng Nakhun, pp. 287–368, Chinese text, pp. 426–43. I regret having to advise caution in using this edition, from which many parts of the text have been cut out without any indication of it. Comparison with my own translations below will also show that I do not always agree with the Korean translator.

24. Pak Sŏngŭi, *Han'guk munhak paegyŏng yŏn'gu* (Studies on the Background of Korean Literature) (Seoul: Hyŏnamsa, 1972), pp. 762–65.

25. *Ibid.*, p. 449.

26. *Ibid.*; see SPMP, 502:6–504:3.

27. Like the supreme deity of the Mongols, the Chinese one is a Sky-god designated by the very term for "sky." Modern scholarship confirms the parallel drawn by Kim Manjung. See Mircea Eliade, *Patterns in Comparative Religion*, tr. from the French by R. Sheed (New York: Sheed and Ward, 1958), pp. 58–64.

28. See glossary under *U an yong ch'a*.

29. Pak, *Paegyŏng*, p. 450.

30. *Kungmunhak charyo*, vol. 2, p. 22.

31. The fault for which Sŏp'o accepts the blame is not, as one would have supposed, that he vilified Buddhism, but rather, if I understand correctly, that he had been disrespectful to Chu Hsi by comparing him with emperors who had gotten bad marks from official historians. It remains true, however, that Sŏp'o, a few years later, would not have spoken of Buddhism in such a disparaging way.

32. *SPMP*, 513:2–8.

33. *SPMP*, 543:2–548:7.

34. E. Zürcher, *The Buddhist Conquest of China* (Leiden: Brill, 1959), vol. 1, pp. 18–43.

35. Cf. *ibid.*, vol. 2, p. 325, note 30.

36. *SPMP*, 585:11–586:5.

37. *SPMP*, 516:2–7.

38. See glossary under *Ch'oe Munch'ang i*.

39. *SPMP*, 575:8–576:6.

40. Han Yü, *Ch'ang-li hsien-sheng wen-chi* (SPTD ed.), 39:26–46.

41. Chŏng Tojŏn, *Pulssi chappyŏn* (Arguments Against Mr. Buddha), in *Sambongjip*, kw. 9 (Seoul: Kuksa p'yŏnch'an wiwŏnhoe, 1961), pp. 254–79.

42. *SPMP*, 541:9–543:1.

43. "Shan ling i chuang," in *Chu Tzu ta-ch'üan*, ch. 16.

44. *Chu Wen-kung pieh chi*, ch. 8; Chinese text and French translation in G. E. Sargent, *Tchou Hi contre le Bouddhisme* (Paris: Imprimerie nationale, 1955), pp. 142–48. See also *Chu Tzu yü-lei*, Li Ching-te ed. (reprint, Taipei: Chung-wen shu-chü, 1979), 126:4817; Sargent, *Tchou Hi*, p. 58.

45. *Ching-te ch'uan-teng lu,* Taishō 2076. Quoting from memory, Kim Manjung is mistaken. These *gāthā* are to be found in *Ch'uan-fa cheng-tsung chi,* Taishô 2079, as Chu Hsi has it correctly.
46. *SPMP,* 505:1–506:4.
47. *SPMP,* 506:5–507:8.
48. *Chu Tzu yü-lei,* 126:4817; Sargent, *Tchou Hi,* pp. 55–59.
49. *Lieh Tzu,* ch. 1.
50. This is not exactly what Chu Hsi says when he explains once again (*Chu Tzu yü-lei,* 126:4818–19) that, in his view, Buddhism is but a collection of old theories stolen from the Taoists: "At first there was only the *Sūtra-in-forty-two articles,* which was not much." Chu Hsi held this work to be one of the few genuine sūtras, one of the first anyhow to have been introduced into China, but not as the only one. See Sargent, *Tchou Hi,* pp. 62–63.
51. *Chu Tzu yü-lei,* 126:4852.
52. *SPMP,* 501:3–502:5.
53. "Whoever wants to examine this matter thoroughly cannot stop before he has reached the Buddha's [position]. [Otherwise], it would be as if, aiming to seize the golden mean, one went only halfway up and then fell back." *SPMP,* 501:10–11.
54. See glossary at *Yŏn ha p'il tok.*
55. See above, pp. 450–52.
56. *SPMP,* 503:4, where Sŏp'o quotes and refutes a sentence from Chŏng Tojŏn's *Pulssi chappyŏn* regarding the Buddhist underworld: "How is it that before the introduction of Buddhism in China there was no one risen from the dead to report that he had seen King Yama?" (See *Sambongjip,* p. 264).
57. *SPMP,* 459:10–460–69.
58. *Chu Wen-kung pieh-chi,* ch. 8; Sargent, *Tchou Hi,* p. 138.
59. See Sargent, *Tchou Hi,* p. 140.
60. *SPMP,* 502:6–504:3.
61. *SPMP,* 585:11.
62. *SPMP,* 482:11–484:3.
63. See glossary at *Tae chŏ chŏn in.*
64. In his article, "Chu Hsi's completion of Neo-Confucianism," Professor W. T. Chan denies any influence of the Buddhist idea of transmission through the patriarchs upon the Confucian concept of the *tao-t'ung* (Tradition of the Way): Françoise Aubin, ed., *Études Song–Sung Studies, In Memoriam Etienne Balazs* (Paris: Mouton, 1973), Series 2, no. 1, pp. 78–81.
65. In *SPMP,* 648:9–649:7, Kim Manjung brings up the same idea again.
66. *SPMP,* 485:2–486:1.
67. *Chu Wen-kung hsü chi,* ch. 5, "Ta Lo ts'an i."
68. *Ming-tao wen chi,* ch. 3.
69. *Chu Tzu yü-lei,* 95:3876.
70. See glossary under *Pul sŏ su pŏn.*
71. See glossary under *Chin kong cha pu.*
72. *Liu-tsu t'an ching* (The Platform Sūtra), 7, Taishō 2008, 48:358.

73. See glossary under *Ch'a chuk Chang Chŏng.*
74. *SPMP*, 559:5–9.
75. *Chu Tzu yü-lei*, 126:4851–2.
76. *SPMP*, 486:2–487:3.
77. *SPMP*, 482:4–5.
78. *Chu Tzu ta-ch'üan, wen chi*, ch. 41, "Ta Ch'eng Yün-fu" (answer to Ch'eng Hsün).
79. *Chu Tzu yü-lei*, 126:4872–73.
80. Chu Hsi *(ibid.)* says he had read it in a work by Yeh Meng-ting (Shih-lin, d. 1278), called *Kuo-t'ing lu*, a title written *Pi-shu lu* in Kim Manjung's quotation.
81. See Tokiwa Daijō, *Shina ni okeru Bukkyō to Jukyō Dōkyō, Tōyō bunko ronsō*, no. 13 (Tokyo: Tōyō bunko, 1930), pp. 301–4.
82. *SPMP*, 487:4–10.
83. Translation *ad sensum*. In fact Sŏp'o uses a phrase borrowed from Mencius (1:1:3): "Chu Hsi is like [a soldier who fled only] fifty paces and who laughs at [another who fled] one hundred paces."
84. The story of the relationship, mentioned here, between Chu Hsi and the Buddhist monk Tao-ch'ien comes, according to Tokiwa who accepts its veracity (pp. 381–82), from a defense of Buddhism written by a Ming author, Hsin T'ai, and entitled *Fo fa chin t'ang pien (Zoku Daizōkyō*, vol. 148, p. 484). It is in fact a quotation from a Yüan book, *Li-tai shih-shi tzu-chien*, 12 ch., by Hsi Chung, ch. 11 *(ibid.*, vol. 132, p. 118a). G. E. Sargent distrusts this tradition because of the lack of earlier sources.
85. *SPMP*, 585:11–586:6.
86. *SPMP*, 487:5.
87. See glossary at *Chiang hsüeh che.*
88. *SPMP*, 549:10–551:5.
89. See glossary under *Cho chu ae myŏng.*
90. See glossary under *Chŏng mun che kong.*
91. *SPMP*, 495:2–9.
92. *SPMP*, 377:2. See glossary under *Ku wŏn i pyŏn ryu.*
93. *SPMP*, 513:2–8. See above p. 452.
94. See glossary under *Cha Song i hu.*
95. *SPMP*, 570:10–571:2.
96. *SPMP*, 376:10.
97. *SPMP*, 519:6.
98. Kim Mujo, *Sŏp'o sosŏl yŏn'gu* (A Study of Sŏp'o's Novels) (Seoul: Hyŏngsŏl, 1976), p. 65.
99. In the Northern part of P'yŏngan Province.
100. *Sukchong sillok*, 20:14 ff. (*CWS*, 39:157).
101. See above, pp. 451–52 and *SPMP*, 596:10–597:11.
102. *SPMP*, 507:6.
103. *SPMP*, 507:6.
104. *Sŏp'ojip Sŏp'o manp'il*, p. 179.

105. *SPMP*, 458:11 *(Śurangama sūtra)* and 506:5, 507:5 *(Yüan-chüeh ching)*.
106. The title of the poem is: "Request for Buddhist Books Following the Rhyme Proposed by Sŏltong, Monk at Pogwang." The *Sinjŭng Tongguk yŏji sŭngnam* (Geography of Korea, new enlarged ed.), dated 1530, does mention, *kw.* 53, a monastery called Pogwang in the Sŏnch'ŏn district. Reference in the poem to snow covering the bushes suggests that the poem was written in winter.

Peter H. Lee

Versions
of the Self in the
Storytellers' Miscellany
(*P'aegwan chapki*)

I

ONE OF THE curious literary phenomena of the Yi dynasty was a flourishing of anecdotes, observations, and comments on various subjects. Works of this kind, written in Chinese and bearing in their titles such words as "miscellaneous," "random," "unofficial," constituted a distinct literary genre for nearly five hundred years.[1] The author of such jottings, which ran from one sentence to several pages in length, was typically a man of letters and affairs who was often involved in the major events of his day. A student of the humanistic tradition, he espoused the tenets of Confucian morality and political philosophy. He relished rules, categories, and typology. His interests were encyclopedic, and his habits of mind were such that his fondest hope was to while his time away among cultured companions. He demonstrated a keen sense of analogy, a penchant for quotations, and a reverence for authority, and he expected his reader to follow all his allusions and references. He was, or hoped to be, a critic both of life and literature. He knew that he was initiating no new fashion in writing, but was in fact following one. He often used the first person pronoun or its equivalent to add a note of intimacy. He was usually casual and familiar, chatty, and relaxed; but he could also be humorous, pointed, or ironic.

Ŏ Sukkwŏn (fl. 1525–54) was one such writer of the sixteenth century. An illegitimate son, Ŏ passed the examination in the documentary style and became an instructor of it (1525) in the Office of Diplomatic

Correspondence. He went to Peking seven times as an interpreter (II,42). He was an assiduous scribbler (he kept a diary whenever he could; II,77), an industrious researcher, and a zealous scholar. His works reveal in varying degrees an unquenchable curiosity of mind. He is remembered chiefly for his *Kosa ch'waryo* (1554),[2] an encyclopedic handbook. Our concern here is his second book, the *Storyteller's Miscellany (P'aegwan chapki)* (hereafter *The Miscellany*),[3] a collection of Ŏ's random jottings on a wide range of topics and a representative collection of this sort from the Yi dynasty. Ŏ greatly expanded the possibilities of the genre, but he also inherited many of the strong points and shortcomings of earlier examples.

Such earlier specimens as the *P'ahanjip* (pub. 1260),[4] the *Pohanjip* (1254),[5] and the *Nagong pisŏl* (or *Yŏgong p'aesŏl*) (1342)[6] display some basic features of the genre. These works, compiled mainly to preserve certain poems for posterity, abound in quotations and terse comments on particular lines from the poems. The works debate pro and con regarding the use of certain words, phrases, allusions, and rhymes, as well as providing information about the circumstances under which a given poem was written. Thus major portions of these three works (about half of the first, two-thirds of the second, and less than one-third of the third) are devoted to poetic criticism, and they therefore recall the method and tone of the Chinese *shih-hua* (remarks on poetry). The remainder of the works consist of reflections on behavior in public and in private, often illustrated by anecdotes describing a person's habits of thought or his behavior. This gallery of often pointed and clever portraits resembles the early seventeenth-century English character books, though with some differences in approach and aims.

The writers who created Theophrastian characters in England meant to portray general human types by recounting the characteristic behavior of individuals that exemplify specific vices or virtues.[7] Sir Thomas Overbury's "a very very woman," "a nobel and retired housekeeper," "an almanac maker," and "an affected traveler," John Hall's "the malcontent," "the flatterer," "the superstitious," and "the humble man," or John Earle's "the young and raw preacher," "the precise hypocrite," "a downright scholar," "the sordid rich man"—all these characters were meant to represent universal types. Although the habit of seeing men as types was firmly established in the East Asian mind by classical education, our examples usually do not deal with personified abstractions ("He is the sort of man who . . ."), but rather with historical figures ("Song Ch'ŏnhŭi was resolute and unyielding"; II, 19).

Korean portraits were not always psychological or moral in intent. The writer could seek particularizing details or topoi, parallels or contrasts, in the classics, histories, or mirror literature. But if he was to achieve brevity in depiction, he should discover some telling detail of word, deed, or gesture. He was not writing a biography, but he still had to sum up his subject's character. Generally, the writer was not a taxonomer of social types, nor a moralist out to assail vice. He might voice moral indignation, but he usually refrained from overt disapproval, biting irony, or pungent satire.

The subjects of earlier specimens therefore comprise some poetic criticism, some character sketches, and some miscellanea. Like later examples of the genre, these earlier works resemble the essay in their informal tone and emphasis on personal taste and judgment. But seldom do these examples achieve the status of a treatise or an essay in the Western sense. To produce a more formal and tightly knit discussion, writers could turn to other genres, such as the *lun* (disquisition), the *wen*, or the *shuo*. And if we compare these pieces with the essays of Bacon, Montaigne, or Lamb, we will find few "dispersed meditations."

What led to the efflorescence of such collections in the Yi dynasty? More widespread literacy, an increase in the number of men of letters, a wider circle of cultivated readers, greater leisure for the lettered classes, and the position of the writer in the bureaucracy and in society as a whole were contributing causes. Let us consider briefly the writer, his audience, and the general cultural milieu of the time.

The majority of writers in Ŏ Sukkwŏn's time were governmental functionaries recruited from the literati; indeed, Ŏ mentions more than a hundred of these. Comparison with the origins of some English writers reveals some differences: Chaucer was the son of a vintner; Spenser, of a tailor; Marlowe, of a cobbler; and Herrick, of a goldsmith. In Korea, writers of humble origin were few. The civil service examination system set the mode of life for the literati. From childhood, virtually all aspirants to public service were trained in and read the same, primarily Chinese, works. Upon passing the examination, a candidate received a political appointment that carried immense social prestige. From early in life he learned that the art of statesmanship and that of literature went hand in hand. The predominance of writers at court provided the courtier with constant encouragement, though it was at times a source of rivalry as well. It provided him with opportunity to talk with and observe a variety of men who had achieved distinction in politics and literature. Such observation of the varied hu-

man scene provided insight into human nature. Sharing intellectual pride
and literary talent, those at court could exchange erudite views concerning every major event. Apart from time spent on courtly functions and
official duties, they found the opportunity to write in verse and prose.
Poems were produced on every conceivable occasion; the courtiers must
have thought in verse. In fact, numerous poems were actually inspired
by dreams. In such a cultural setting, none could dispute the place of
literature in society and culture, and even a brutal ruler like Yŏnsan'gun
(r. 1494–1506), who delighted in butchering the innocent, left scores of
poems behind. Although some rigid moralists saw literature as a vehicle
of Neo-Confucianism and called poetry frivolous, few spoke out against
it. Censorship, and the climate of opinion of the lettered class, had to be
taken into account. Still, most writers knew how to avoid such controversial issues as the province of majesty, and could thus avert official
sanction.

Who comprised the audience of the early Yi dynasty writer? First
there was the circle of the author's close friends, among whom manuscripts (or transcriptions) were circulated. Intractable allusions, quotations, puns on persons' names, numerous poems of friendship, com-
mendatory verse, prefaces, epilogues, "appreciations" of individual
collections: all of these attest to the intimate nature of the group. Here
the literati wrote about the literati for the literati. He was presumed to be
as knowledgeable as the writer, and was expected to follow all allusions
and quotations.

Literary patronage, a topic hitherto little explored, existed in various
forms. Such an enlightened monarch as Sejong (r. 1418–50) set the model
through the example of his munificence. In 1420 he established the
Academy of Worthies (Chiphyŏnjŏn), a royal research institute, and as-
sembled young scholars there.[8] Both symbol of enlightenment and the
intellectual and cultural center of the nation, the academy nurtured a
number of brilliant scholar-statesmen of Early Yi. In 1426, he established
the Hall of Reading, where the virtuous and talented were given a leave
of absence to devote time to reading and writing.[9] The institution per-
sisted, with some interruptions, down to the early seventeenth century.
When King Sejong learned that one member of the academy, Sin Sukchu (1417–75), had pored over rare books while on night duty and dozed
off only at dawn, he himself went to have Sin covered with a sable robe.[10]
Such a touching episode as this illustrates the generosity of the throne

toward men of letters, who in turn offered their lord genuine affection. A roll of silk, a basketful of tangerines, a flagon of wine, or a bouquet of chrysanthemums bestowed upon a favorite writer inspired more gratitude than sinecures or pensions. There also existed a sort of informal private patronage, though the Korean writer was less fortunate in this than his counterpart in England, where "every writer before 1475 [or perhaps 1500] had a patron."[11] The best form of patronage was of course an official appointment, the highest recognition a man of letters could receive. Such an appointment did not guarantee uninterrupted literary activity, but this was irrelevant. Poetic talent was presumed to ensure political advancement, and most of the literati combined writing with their official duties. The relative lack of mercenary flattery or fawning is refreshing as compared, for example, with Elizabethan England.[12] This may also explain why comparatively few works were dedicated to patrons (although dedication was no proof of patronage). No one wrote for pecuniary gain, and no one made a living by writing, ghost writing excepted. Yet few forsook literature, nonetheless.

Literary and rhetorical skills were called for on various occasions: deliberations on state affairs, missions to foreign lands, writing of missives, and production of literary works. East Asia has little rhetorical theory to speak of, partly because of the relative unimportance of oratory,[13] except for "private-speaking" in the form of advice to, remonstration with, and persuasion of a ruler, a patron, or a friend. By rhetoric, then, I mean not the art of persuasion as practiced by Western orators, but the art of discourse, written and occasionally spoken, the aim of which was to influence the viewpoints of readers and listeners in various forms. East Asian history is replete with speeches of all kinds, and rhetorically minded historians ascribe speeches, dialogues, or summaries of speeches to rulers and ministers. The oldest history in China, the *Book of Documents* (the *Shu-ching*, or *Shang-shu*), consists almost exclusively of speeches—pronouncements, declarations, or injunctions—although it is uncertain whether they were actually delivered in specific instances. The Confucian classics and later histories abound in speeches, as delivered or reconstructed, the incorporation of which was a historiographic convention. Accusations, defenses, exhortations, and pleas, although not intended as orations, aim to produce verbal effects. The arrangement of the material in such speeches along with their citing of historical precedents and classical allusions, parallelism, sententiae, subtlety of approach, anticipatory refutation, and other devices to heighten the emotional tone, indicate that they were scrupulously prepared. Actual delivery of speeches was not part of the traditional curriculum of the Korean Royal College, though candidates for the civil service examination were asked to publicly present exegeses of classical texts.

Rhetorical consciousness is present, therefore, in all forms of writing, and all use rhetoric effectively. If the law courts were "the primary scene of ancient oratory in the West,"[14] the equivalent in East Asia was the royal court, where policies were deliberated daily and where men of letters assumed various roles. Education in East Asia was not intended primarily to train public speakers, and no East Asian man of letters would view himself primarily as a "patron," in the Western sense, an orator called upon to defend his clients' interests.[15] In the West, training in rhetoric was essential to success in public office, "where all transactions are conducted through the medium of language."[16] In East Asia, a broad grounding in the liberal arts was the prerequisite to public service. A statesman would use rhetorical devices, which he learned from past examples, in the exposition of his political, historical, philosophical, and literary ideals. The skillful organization and presentation of ideas was not viewed as a distinct skill, but was integrated with other "components of human learning."[17] The typical writer in public service was proficient in writing and delivering speeches, in private or in public. He was at once a man of action and of words, and his duties required skill in persuasion.

Parallelism was the foremost rhetorical device used in official documents of all kinds in East Asia (I, 11, 12). We may well pity those whose job it was to draw up such documents in the Office of Royal Decrees, the Office of Special Counselors, or in the Office of Diplomatic Correspondence. However, many writers felt at home in more than one style. Ŏ Sukkwŏn used at least three: parallel prose; a kind of institutional style (*imun*, or documentary style); and the plain style, which he used in the *Miscellany*. Probably no style is more suitable for expressing one's view on contemporary issues, morals and manners, or scholarship and literature. More to the point, it expresses well the writer's attempts to understand himself and the world that he inhabits, resembling as it does the language used when jotting down random thoughts or favorite passages from a poem in a notebook. Eloquence is a hindrance to the plain style, and the association of the miscellany (*chapki*) with plain style is no accident.

It is a relief for the modern reader to turn from the labored and ornate official style to a plain style that allows the writer's thoughts to develop naturally in writing. The transition resembles that from the oratorical Asiatic to the plain style. Symmetry, parallelism (balance and antithesis), and luxuriance were characteristic of the official style. Note, for example, the memorial to the Ming emperor, which read in part: "The sun sheds light everywhere; even its least beam thoroughly brightens the obscure and small. Your vast kindness pervades all; its least wavelet thoroughly cleanses the false and the oppressed. Your benevolence covers both the living and the dead. Your kindness extends to both the dead and the living" (I, 11). Every word of such turgid passages as this had to be carefully weighed (a lack of decorum or the egregious inclusion of tabu words would cost the writer his life), every clause balanced, and every cadence measured. The writer strained after "ingenious hints and mysterious allusions." By contrast, the *chapki* was characteristically loose and choppy in style, but natural and rapid in movement. The difference in style also affects the relation of thought to form. While the movement of parallelism is spatial, that in the looser mode of structure is linear. One is built upon correspondence, another upon addition.[18] As the Ciceronian and the Senecan are combined in the composite style of seventeenth-century English prose, so the florid and the plain are often mixed in Korea.

Ŏ Sukkwŏn uses verbal skills to produce rhetorical effects. Some arguments resemble the enthymeme, moving either from the premise to the conclusion (e.g., I, 18; 21, 49; II, 6) or from the conclusion to the premise (I, 38). In such an abbreviated argumentative syllogism, the obvious (usually the major premise) is omitted to quicken the flow of the discourse and to hold the reader's interest. Ŏ successfully defines himself to the reader as a man of sound sense, judicious temper, high moral character, and requisite erudition. When his subjects are scholarly or literary, he establishes an effective ethos by his reputation as interpreter, his competence in spoken and written Chinese, the popularity of his subjects, and his citations of authorities (the topic of testimony). This last in particular identifies him as one who shares the interests and tastes of the literati, and his views are lent force by the esteem in which his society holds the classics, histories, and other literature that he cites. Sensitive and candid, he presents himself as a casual essayist whose approach is tentative and exploratory and whose concern is to inquire and probe. He is often willing to concede points to the opposition. The postures Ŏ adopts are more or less the same as those assumed by writers of the *chapki* and *pi-chi*.

Ŏ also makes extensive use of direct address, exclamations, rhetorical questions, and other devices that impart an exhortatory and rhetorical character to his work. The exclamation *(ecphonesis; exclamatio)* [19] in particular defines his stance. Appearing in the conclusions of an episode and addressed to an absent person, it is an appeal to pathos. For example, "This was a terrible error indeed!" (I, 21), "This is ridiculous!" (I, 43), "How regrettable!" (II, 33), "How pitiable!" (II, 88), "This is terrifying!" (IV, 71), or "How strange!" (IV, 73).

The writer may use rhetorical questions at appropriate spots to induce a calculated response in the reader. The answer to a rhetorical question *(erotesis; interrogatio)* is presumed to be evident from the question itself: "Kim's Chinese saved the lives of two hundred men. Who could ridicule such a man?" (I, 16); "Had not the tradesmen taught the Japanese silver smelting, how could evil and corruption have become so widespread?" (I, 17); "Is this not fate?" (II, 52); "If this is not idiotic, what is?" (II, 71); "How can this be considered a trivial matter?" (II, 84); or "What will they think of this?" (IV, 47). The unconsenting reader is challenged. If he does not answer in the affirmative or the negative, the writer will have failed to induce the appropriate response.

Ŏ uses another argumentative figure, the aphorism, to "generalize a particular truth." [20] For example: "Ninety *li* is only half of a hundred. This illustrates the difficulties that attend the last phase of man's career" (II, 34); "They could be described as tending to their duties while drawing their salaries" (II, 50); "It is in the nature of the cock to crow" (in a poem by Yi Pyŏl; II, 60); or "to catch a tiger with a straw net" (III, 13).

Epigrammatic and pithy, proverbs and folk sayings invest the discourse with "moral character," as Aristotle pointed out long ago. Such is Ŏ's use of argumentative and stance figures, as well as the logical, the ethical, and the emotional modes of appeal. He seldom uses tropes or indulges in defective pathos, [21] however. His skillful adaptation of the means to fit his subject, the occasion, and his audience clearly reveals the workings of rhetoric.

II

The salient feature of such literary miscellanies as Ŏ Sukkwŏn's is their emphasis on portraits of others together with portraits of the author himself. The penetrating observations of human conduct and motives, observations not only of what one is but of what one *does*, set the literary miscellany apart from biographical writing of the traditional sort. Early East Asian characterization tended to be by types, with comparatively little attention paid to the subject's external appearance,[22] garb, or habits. Specifically contemporary details are also rare. Biography in the Confucian tradition, including some celebrated narrative passages in the *Shih-chi*, has produced a series of representative personality types in the form of standard anecdotes used for characterization.[23] Likewise, anecdotes from the lives of eminent men are presented as examples of Confucian conduct. They assume "an ultraindividual significance"[24] and serve to perpetuate the Confucian ethical norm. Paradigms are repetitive and backward-looking, directed as they are toward praxis. With virtually no information given about a figure's private life, it does little to illuminate or renew our image of man. Contrarily, the portrait in the literary miscellany endeavors to go beyond the conventionalized behavior of the public self and reveal the individual.

Literary characterization assumes the fundamental consistency of personality. Confucian thought upheld those who strove to maintain their identities. The demands made upon the Confucian gentleman were exhausting and exacting, but the biographer does not tell us how he maintained continuity and coherence in his personality to become an idealized exemplar of the tradition. The way in which Confucian values were absorbed varied from age to age, but the process of internalization of enduring values emphasized by Neo-Confucians was seldom depicted in biographies. The portraits in the *chapki*, we recall, do not always include a moral or present any psychological analysis. Some sketches recapitulate familiar types, while others vividly depict individual qualities.

Ŏ Sukkwŏn's sketches of Kwŏn Talsu (1469–1504) (II, 28) and Kwŏn Kyŏngu (fl. 1470–98) (II, 29), for example, are based on Confucian principles. The choice of details is intended to exemplify Confucian ideals of conduct, moral courage, and adherence to principles in particular. Sometimes a person reveals his character in his writing, as does Yi Sukcha (II, 53). The portraits of An Chungson (II, 59) and Yi Pyŏl (II, 60) both recall the traditional recluse who has renounced the world, delights in simple rural retirement, and finds joy in communion with nature. An Chungson's candidness is illustrated by an episode in which he is visited by his superior: "An was in the fields but he returned home in a reed hat and short breeches, a plow slung over his shoulder. Sitting before his gate, he called for unstrained wine and offered it to the guests."

Depiction of laudable moral individuals was a convention rooted deeply in tradition, and writers of the *chapki* often employed the method and style of classical examples. Some resembled catalogues of virtues, while others merely repeated platitudes, formulaic diction, and detail devoid of distinguishing features. The realistic narrative came late in Korea, and the contributions to the novel by the *chapki* writers may lie in their relatively more accomplished portraits of individuals.

In the *Life of Herbert*, which is praised as a "masterpiece" and "the most lyrical of all English biographies,"[25] Izaak Walton (1593–1683) writes: "Of the three Sisters I need not say more, than that they were all married to persons of worth, and plentiful fortunes; and lived to be examples of *vertue*, and to do good in their generations."[26] The sisters might well be characters in a fairy tale, so much does even Walton rely on platitudes in describing them.

A number of Ŏ Sukkwŏn's portraits demonstrate his superior technique and unusual insights. He had a keen eye for the single act that reveals the essence of an individual. Chŏn Im (d. 1509), a military man who became magistrate of Seoul is "rude and fierce in character" (IV, 5).

Once, he noted that the horse he rode had boils on its back. He then cut into the back of his aged servant, saying, "You did not protect the horse from boils; now feel its pain." Later, when he became critically ill, he arose and became violent. He stared and bent his bow, yelling angrily, "What ghosts are you that dare kill me?" He stomped with rage for a long while thereafter.

The improvident and sluggish Yu Kŭn, a lecturer in the Royal College, is portrayed in IV, 6:

When his superior summoned his subordinates for promotion or demotion, Yu arrived around noon. When his superior asked him why he was late, Yu replied, "I was at home having a snack."

Disgraced by his superior, the incorruptible Sŏl Wi "threw away his official baton and left," leaving a poem on his desk, in which he compares himself to Po Ya (IV, 26), who broke his zither when his best friend Chung Tzu-ch'i died because he no longer had a friend who really understood his music. Kim Suon (1409–81) studies behind closed doors (IV, 28):

One day he stepped out into the courtyard to urinate. Only then did he notice fallen leaves and realized that autumn had come. Later, when he was gravely ill and about to die, Kim told his juniors, "All of you should take heed not to study the *Doctrine of the Mean* and the *Great Learning*. I'm in agony, for I see only phrases from these two books."

"To spend too much time in studies," Bacon says in "Of Studies," "is sloth." Is it because he felt that he had not attained the wisdom of a sage? Or because he found out belatedly that his passion for knowledge was misdirected? The frugality of Cho Wŏn'gi (1457–1533) is illustrated by a single episode (IV, 65):

He once asked a furrier to make him a cape. Usually, tailors use the thicker fur to make the outside, and the thinner fur to line the interior. On seeing this Cho remarked, "What an unskilled worker you are. The reason we have capes is to keep warm. Now you sew the thin fur in the inner side and thick fur in the outer. This is no way to keep warm." He then ordered the procedure reversed.

Finally, there is a sketch of the iconoclastic behavior of Kim Sisŭp (1435–93), used to hide his brilliance (IV, 29): When an old man from a rich family gave him a cassock of white satin he wore it to the capital, where he took it off and threw it away after rolling in filthy water dozens of times. Later, when King Sejo invited him to the festival of land and water, Kim, "appeared in a tattered cassock, carrying a bundle of herring. Kim left the fish partially exposed throughout his audience with the king. Sejo thought him mad." Ŏ Sukkwŏn does *not* think Kim mad; only Sejo the usurper does.

In his portraits, Ŏ Sukkwŏn chose essential personality traits that could be illustrated by anecdotes. He did not seek to treat his subject in great detail, but rather to touch upon such essential manifestations of the subject's personality as his distinctive way of speaking or his personal views and idiosyncracies. In this sense, Ŏ Sukkwŏn could be termed a biographer of the moment. Much of the liveliness in the sketches, however, comes from vivid glimpses they give of an individual, without a word of overt approval or disapproval. Each is an arresting, graphic piece that captures a man's mind and character. Ŏ is in perfect control of his ma-

terial, and his style never obscures his subject. The sketches whet the curiosity of the reader, and he is impelled to find more about the lives of
the interesting individuals they portray.

The traditional Confucian hierarchical society was comprised not only
of the literati, who prided themselves in their knowledge and supplied
talented candidates for public service, but also of slaves, merchants, doctors, monks, female entertainers, actors, and shamans, all of whom receive some attention in the *Miscellany*. The Three Bonds and the Five
Relations were constantly preached and upheld in Confucian society, and
the inculcation of social virtues to the unlettered masses was a perennial
concern of the government. The gates of filial children or chaste wives
were customarily marked as a measure to encourage virtuous behavior (II,
32). Despite such efforts on the part of the establishment, rapacious and
corrupt officials at all levels disrupted the moral and social order. Ŏ's observation on officials, illegitimate children, slaves, filial sons, widows, and
merchants are not intended to explore the value system or social features
of sixteenth-century Korea. Yet his perceptions of special social phenomena are an index of his social consciousness.

Ŏ's protest against corruption and extortion takes various forms. The
subject of a folk play presented at court is a greedy official who is finally
apprehended and punished. "Indeed the actors could impeach a corrupt
official" (II, 6). In other instances, in a satiric poem pasted to the coffin
of a cruel magistrate, an anonymous village poet compares the dead man
to Hell's five hungry demons (II, 7). The subject of another poem is the
forced collection of fruit by harsh officials, in consequence of which the
people are constrained to fell their trees (II, 36):

> When the people's bellies are filled with rice,
> The officials' mouths water, and their anger is aroused.
> When the people are warm in fur coats,
> The officials would as soon seize them by the arms and peel off their skins.

Ŏ Sukkwŏn, himself an illegitimate son, is critical of discrimination.
The fact that he ended up as an instructor in documentary style and interpreter indicates that he bore a social stigma. Unlike China, where no
law restricted the rise of illegitimate children, Korea had stringent statutes
to keep even the most talented of them from high offices: "Even when
they had outstanding talents, [illegitimate sons] have been thwarted in their

aspirations and have usually died in obscurity" (II, 88).[27] Chŏng Pŏn, who passed the examination in 1523, is dismissed by the Censor-General due to his low origins. Chŏng submits a memorial that obtains him a position as a documentary-style instructor, and he receives unusual royal favors. But the censorate is determined to oust him, and he dies in poverty (II, 52). Ŏ comments again elsewhere: "In Korea . . . because of its small size, people pay heed to trifling matters. Koreans' discussion of one's character usually centers around one's lineage. Few who are not descendants of the literati will be drawn to belles-lettres, let alone merchants, workmen, and other common folk" (IV, 17).

Concerning the institution of slavery,[28] Ŏ presents contrasting examples of inhuman and magnanimous treatment. One rebelling slave is buried alive, while another who has done wrong is pardoned by his master (II, 58). A third bribes officials to obtain the praise due a filial son; but once redeemed, he proves to be corrupt (II, 36). One filial son becomes a toady to an evil minister (II, 34), while Pak Hŭimun is praised by Ŏ for slicing the flesh from his thigh to serve his mother. Even after her death, Pak scrupulously observes mourning and begs for rice to offer her spirit. If people ask him to show the scars on his thigh, he willingly displays them. Some deride Pak, thinking that he had exaggerated the incident to glorify himself. "How could slicing one's thigh be a hypocritical deed?" Ŏ asks. He concludes that indiscriminate and jealous people discourage goodness in others (II, 31).

In spite of the fact that there are more women than men in Korea (III, 17), an official's widowed daughter should not remarry (IV, 34), says Ŏ. In fact, a certain Chŏng who had his young widowed daughter remarry was dismissed from office. The sons and grandsons of women who remarried were usually banned from high official careers beginning in the late fifteenth century; they were barred from the civil service examinations. This measure served to maintain the stability of the family system and to limit the number of officials. At the same time, in a society where every learned man aspired to the privileges of high rank, to be denied the opportunity to take the civil service examination while those from lower classes were not,[29] was a great blow to the unfortunate children of second marriages. Therefore Ŏ condemns the practice of pressing the wives of transported criminals to remarry butchers or official slaves. "If a widow cannot be made chaste or constant by force, how can one bear to undermine her determination and make her remarry?" (II, 33). In matters of economic disruption, Ŏ cites merchants who illegally trade silver (I, 17) or who circulate bad cloth for quick profit and thereby cause inflation (II, 85).

Ŏ upholds orthodoxy and scorns all forms of heterodoxy, such as folk beliefs in the spirits of smallpox and sores (II, 83); the worship of local tutelary spirits, at whose "objectionable shrine" the ignorant squander their money (II, 84); the worship of a wooden idol (II, 18); a fraudulent shaman who calls himself a Buddha (I, 35); or other legends connected with places (II, 19). Ŏ inherits this critical spirit from his great-grandfather, Ŏ Hyoch'ŏm (1405–75), who opposes geomancy (I, 29), allows no shamans or wizards into his house (I, 29), and forbids the practice of officials, including those in the Office of Inspector General, to offer the sacrifices to *pugun* shrines with votive paper money (I, 30).[30] Ŏ spoofs the hallowed tradition of the Ko clan of Cheju Island, whose members believe that their ancestors gushed forth from a cave north of Mount Halla.

During the era of *cheng-te* (1506–21), one Ko filled a post in the Palace Guard. When a certain military official named Yi returned from a trip to Cheju, Ko asked him if he had seen the cave. Yi replied, "I saw it and urinated into it." Ko was speechless. (III, 12)

In all likelihood, Ŏ also opposed Buddhism. He cites a story of the banishment of a Confucian student because he proposed the erection of monasteries (II, 9). Another episode in II, 70 bears quoting:

Buddhists have chosen the way of compassion and nonviolence. Once a mendicant monk in Hwanghae Province encountered mounted hunters pursuing a boar. The animal was enraged. The monk confronted the animal saying, "Poor thing, poor thing." Then he pointed to the south with his stick and said, "Run quickly to the south." However the boar attacked the monk and gored him.

Ŏ is not wholly consistent, however, when he tells of dream prognostications. Sŏ Kŏjŏng's filial devotion is revealed by his correct interpretation of a dream (a lunar eclipse, a symbol of death)[31] that tells of the death of his mother while he is on his way to China (I, 31). Sometimes the poet dreams of a poem (I, 27, 34; III, 5) that foretells his success, banishment, or death. Sometimes, a spirit instructs a writer to choose as his polite name or pen name certain logographs that portend his death (IV, 1). Ŏ also tells of a diviner who seeks to predict who will place first in the civil service examination (II, 69) by divining the hidden meanings of certain characters in a person's name, or dividing a character into its components. A popular song widespread prior to a historic confrontation (and undoubtedly fabricated by a partisan to the dispute) is said to have predicted the fate of the loser (IV, 19). And the collapse of the platform at a reception ceremony for Chinese envoys, like that of the portico at Aachen foreshadowing the imminent death of Charlemagne, is said to have foretold the king's early demise (II, 91). Although Ŏ seems to question the prophecy ("The people rumored that this was a bad omen"), in the end he confirms it, "Injong died within four months (1545)." Dream visions, onomancy, and prophecies of various kinds were part of the daily life of people, including the lettered, and Ŏ Sukkwŏn was no exception.

In addition to a masterful control of his prose and his vivid descriptions of scenes, situations, and characters, Ŏ Sukkwŏn has a strong sense of the past and of his own identity. The pronoun "I" appears some thirty times in the *Miscellany*, often in passing: "When I spoke to Chŏng Saryong and Yi Hŭibo about this (Huang T'ing-chien's poem), they agreed with my interpretation" (I, 40); "One day I called on Yi Hŭibo" (I, 41); "I have seen several such cases (of dying from eating ginko nuts)" (I, 45); "On my way home (from Peking) I observed the behavior of the castaways and found it to be exactly as Yang had described" (II, 43).

It was used to introduce lengthier, more intimate glimpses as well:

I have been to Peking on official duty seven times in all. The Liao-tung (Military Commission) and the Ministry of Rites however never betrayed any signs of misunderstanding when reading letters from Korea. . . . When a carter stole the interpreter Yi Sunjong's luggage, I was asked to write a letter to be presented to the Provincial Commander. When Li T'ang read the letter, he praised it. "Excellent," he exclaimed many times. . . . These are two instances from my own personal experience. It is indeed hard to credit the statement that the documentary style of Korea is difficult to understand. (II, 42)

I was the youngest and least learned of my [fellow documentary style instructors]. Still, Ch'oe Sejin dealt leniently with my errors and unceasingly advised and encouraged me. (II, 51)

I lodged in the same inn with Interpreter Hong Kyŏm and called for a lamp so that I could write in my diary. . . . The following day I asked Kung Yung-ch'ing about this and ascertained that Hong was telling the truth. (II, 77)

In the year *hsin-ch'ou* of *Chia-ching* (1541), I accompanied our envoy to Peking to present birthday felicitations to the emperor. Early one morning I sat for a while outside the gate and observed the majority of the court officials as they sat beneath the eaves of the palace. One clerk asked Interpreter Hong Kyŏm whether he could compose a poem. . . . Hong then pointed to me and replied, "He too can write. Ask him." I wrote the following. . . . (II, 90)

I once traveled along the shores of the Yellow Sea for half a year. Later I joined my elder brother in the capital. Hwang Hyohŏn sent us the following poem. (III, 3)

When I was young I had three tubercles on my neck. One doctor saw them and remarked, "If you do not cure them now, you will not be able to later." Grieved and alarmed, I could not put the matter out of my mind. I would often touch the sores to see whether they had changed size. For six or seven years I applied raw lead and ten-fragrance plaster, but the sores not only became larger every year, but a smaller one began to appear. One day I suddenly admonished myself, "Death and life are preordained. Why should I be obsessed with remedies and torture my mind?" I then discarded the medicine and discontinued the treatment. One year later the tubercles disappeared of themselves. It has been more than thirty years now, and only one remains, its form barely discernible. (II, 81)

These are based on his memory and imagination. Ŏ tells us what has happened to him, and private or public records may corroborate him. However his predilection for autobiography and his accurate reporting engender a sense of immediacy and authenticity.[32] In a society where fiction was subordinate to history, the first examples of the former appeared in the guise of chronicles, journals, letters, memoirs, and biographies. Fiction evinced the influence of historiography in its outward form, possibly in order to "pass itself off as literature so as not to seem like 'literature' in the pejorative sense."[33]

Autobiographical sketches by Ŏ Sukkwŏn show that he is an autobiographer of the moment. The author of such a sketch tended to deduce the existence of the self and then verify it through a review of his actions. The reader accepts his version of the author's past as a genuine record of his identity, though the account is in fact devoid of detail. The reader is left with the task of discerning a pattern in the account that will allow him to arrive at his own understanding of the author's character. Yet he still cannot know how much of what he reads is fact, and how much is fiction.

To tell stories about oneself automatically commits the teller to the vices of immodesty, affectation, and vanity. Presentation of the self to an audience, imagined or real, is always display. Commitment to truth may be the writer's justification, but the reader suspects that a difference may exist between what the writer understands of his past and what he tells, and between his need for self-assertion and his desire for self-concealment through conformity. Also, the past events have no real existence and must be recreated by the experiencer as act of the imagination. Indeed, fictionality is inherent in man's relation to time.[34]

Writings like Ŏ Sukkwŏn's *Miscellany* have been called "unofficial histories" (perhaps because they often expose the lies of official histories) or as "small talk" (*sosŏl*), as Ŏ himself styled these notes. Such works contain, among other things, legends, myths, wonder tales, romances, and satires of social and professional groups like female entertainers, the blind, monks, and shamans.[35] A history in the accepted sense is written not by its own dramatis persona, but by a court-appointed committee. The unofficial history is written by an individual who is an eyewitness to, and participant in, the events he is recording. One such history may be written in the third person, while another is written in the first. In the latter instance, the narrator also records stories heard secondhand, freely shifting his stance from that of eyewitness to that of historian.[36] He enjoys the freedom to present a personal eyewitness account in his own name or a fictional account in the name of one of his characters (especially in portraits). In such instances the writer takes pains to stress that he is presenting true events rather than fiction. If his stance is not quite that of a realistic novelist, it is because of his culture's insistence on historicity, and because of the tyranny of historiography. In fact, the rigid society of Ŏ's Korea, which masked reality with a veneer of culture in the name of order and continuity, could not tolerate the creation of alternative realities in overtly fictional form.

Therefore the *chapki* could not escape the domination of historiography. Note, for example, the beginnings of the portrait (a sensitive and detailed account of the subject's personal experiences presented for its dramatic appeal) in the *chapki* and the biography in official history. Both begin with a formulaic introduction giving the character's name, lineage, social position, and some characteristic traits. The temptation to fictionalize is especially strong in the portrait, the veracity of which the reader is helpless to assess. But like a historian who is fond of moralizing, the writer might on occasion stoop to editorialize, as in the portrait of Kim Suon ("Our elders studied as diligently as he did"; IV, 28) and elsewhere (e.g., II, 10, 20). A writer such as Ŏ Sukkwŏn has not yet fully reconciled the conflicting claims of history and fiction, but by his sophisticated critical stance, his emphasis on personal experience and concrete details, and his adoption of the first-person, eyewitness narrative, he has moved one step closer to the art of fiction.

III

Ŏ Sukkwŏn portrays a society that upheld the importance of order and degree and saw the fulfillment of mutual duties and responsibilities as essential to the established order. The balance of power between the king and bureaucracy was delicate and complex and could be upset by any disturbance. The literati *(yangban)* who occupied the highest social class monopolized education and access to the examinations. In principle, the *yangban* consisted of civilian and military branches, but power was in fact concentrated in the hands of a small group of high civil officials. Also, the examination system was not what it purported to be. It was not open to all qualified candidates, and success in it was based less on an individual's learning or talent than on his pedigree and his ancestor's social status. It was required of every candidate, for example, to record at the head of the examination paper the names and ranks of his father, grandfather, and great-grandfather, and the name, title, and clan home site of his maternal grandfather. Because of his origin, a man like Ŏ Sukkwŏn could not reach the rank of the *yangban*. He belonged to the middle class *(chungin)*, consisting of lower-ranking administrators and independant skilled workers like doctors (II, 79, 81, 82) and artisans (II, 80). A member of the *chungin* could not be promoted beyond a certain rank or hold a post slated for the ruling class. Stories of Cho Sin, an illegitimate son who became an interpreter (II, 6, 47; IV, 25, 27), Ŏ Mujŏk, an official slave turned poet (II, 26), or Yi Sangjwa, a private slave who excelled in painting (II, 57) show that some from the middle and lower classes did win recognition, yet such cases were exceptional. There were also nonconformists like Kim Sisŭp, who in Ŏ's account laments the moral disruption caused by Sejo's usurpation and abandons the world (II, 33); recluses like Yi Pyŏl (II, 60) and Pak Kyegang (IV, 17); or a prince of the blood like Chean (1466–1526), the second son of King Yejong (r. 1468–69), who feigned idiocy in order to survive. "Some say that the prince was not truly an idiot," Ŏ comments. "Being a descendant of the royal line he might have come to harm if he had distinguished himself too brilliantly, and he therefore disguised his talents" (II, 71).

In the face of a Confucian ideology that urges the maintenance of order, obedience to the state, and the dominance of a factious nobility, Ŏ espouses the traditional system of values. Central to this system is authority in its various forms. Ŏ accepts the authority of the monarch as the metaphorical father of the state. However, the Korean monarch historically owes his legitimacy and authority not only to his own people, but also to China's emperor. That is, the Chinese emperor was the father of the Korean king, who was in turn the father of the Korean people. Ŏ Sukkwŏn's *Miscellany* is the first work of the *chapki* genre to begin with a genealogy of the Ming dynasty rulers. (It may be a parody of history, or a subtle way of showing its own conventionality or of claiming the privileged status of his own work.) By placing at the head of his work the genealogy of the Ming emperors, Ŏ accepts the father figure of the Confucian ecumene who elicits loyalty and fealty. Nowhere does he question the figure of the king in a monarchical state, the only form of government he knows, or the source of his authority, or the way in which he uses it. From the classics and histories he has learned the requirements for, and attributes of, kingship. As he accepts the king-subject relationship, so does he accept the father-child relationship within the family. In more than ten episodes he affectionately tells about his ancestors, who were all members of the ruling class. And Ŏ is proud of being a descendant, albeit an illegitimate one, of a distinguished family that has produced a number of scholar-statesmen. A struggle between father and son is unthinkable. The past, whatever the strengths and weaknesses of its legacy, always bears on the present. The father protects, inspires, and guides the son, as the king does his subjects.

Another feature of the *Miscellany* is its adherence to the norm. Any deviation from conventional behavior on the part of anyone, king or slave, violates the norm. The tyrant Yŏnsan'gun, who took cruel pleasure in inflicting unjust punishments, represents the antithesis of the virtuous ruler of a harmonious society, the defender of the established order. Yŏnsan-gun not only goes astray himself, but also corrupts others and defies the traditional principles of Confucian rule (II, 30; IV, 10, 49). Such ministers as the greedy Kim Allo (1481–1537) (IV, 12) or Im Sahong (1455–1506), who falsely accuses and kills his impeacher (IV, 20), and other greedy magistrates (II, 6, 7) are represented as corrupt men who abuse their position. Ŏ constantly questions the validity of beliefs, and especially of all forms of heterodoxy. He even turns to the animal world to

describe the weird behavior of dogs, or a horse that gives birth to a human being (IV, 2). In the realm of language and literature, he laments
the general lack of style in writing or the ignorance of current Chinese
usage. In a society in which success for the educated man hinged upon
his mastery of Chinese verse and prose, the assimilation of conventions
"constitutive of literature as an institution"[37] was a prerequisite of a writer.
Ŏ's interpretations of a variety of literary elements demonstrate that he
was a competent reader who was conversant with tradition and convention. His criticism is usually aimed at the reader who cannot cope with
literary texts.

Lastly, what strikes the modern reader is Ŏ Sukkwŏn's loyalty to the
privileged status of language and literature. The power of the written word
in traditional Confucian society is well-known. The Korean literati, while
they spoke Korean, wrote mostly in Chinese. Most works of history and
literature were in Chinese, which was also the language of administration
and diplomacy.

Language was also a means of protest and denunciation, of "converting passion into a privilege."[38] How the logos is a substitute for praxis
is illustrated in poems satirizing maladministration. From the literati's
viewpoint, language transcended its cognitive and communicative functions. The skillful use of written Chinese, the supreme cultural creation,
was a status symbol whose value was seldom questioned. If a soldier,
merchant, or slave is mentioned in the *Miscellany*, for example, it is because of his ability to write poetry in Chinese (IV, 17). Chinese as the
only means of cultured expression by the educated in Korea recalls a similar belief in England, where English was sometimes considered "gauche
and parvenu,"[39] as compared to Latin and French. For example, John
Skelton (1460?–1529) writes:

> Our natural tongue is rude
> And hard to be ennuede
> With pollyshed termes lustye
> Oure language is so rustye
> So cankered and so ful
> Of frowardes and so dul
> That if I would apply
> To write ornatly
> I wot not where to finde
> Termes to serue my mynde,

Or Waller (1606–87) in "Of English Verse":

> Poets that lasting marble seek,
> Must carve in Latin, or in Greek. . . .[40]

Given the importance of Chinese to the Korean literati, it is no wonder that to be known in China was the highest honor a writer could hope for. Ŏ mentions a number of Korean writers who have won international fame. The favorite pastime of Chinese envoys and Korean receptionists was to exchange verses, each trying to outdo the other. Some imprudent Koreans, anxious to have their talent recognized, awaited every opportunity to submit their works to the envoys. For example, the *Miscellany* tells of the unfortunate monk Sŏrong who is punished for showing a mediocre poem to the Chinese envoy T'ang Kao (IV, 76). The written word has a still deeper significance to Koreans of Ŏ's day, however: it served to arrest the flow of time.

In converting his life into a story, the writer seeking to verify his own existence falls back on his memory, by which he recaptures his past. Whether the idea of selfhood exists in the memory alone or also exists in the imagination requires study. The sense of continuing identity is a product of our consciousness, which consists in a series of experiences of the moment. These moments are stabilized and given permanence in the literary portrait. Indeed, the literary miscellany represents a significant response on the part of the Confucian humanist to the Confucian age in Korean history. It was an age of instability and impermanence owing to factionalism and other evils endemic to Confucian systems. Ŏ Sukkwŏn is painfully aware of the tension between ideology and actuality, demand and desire, and of his search for self-knowledge and his submission to the flux of life. In spite of the demand of conformity and commitment, he wishes to probe the man's inner being as he criticizes and evaluates his own being and becoming. His jottings are the products of the tension he experiences as he looks within himself and outward upon the world. The literary miscellany is probably the only adequate literary form for a Confucian gentleman like Ŏ Sukkwŏn as he attempts in this way to define himself and assert his identity. The portrait "saves individual identity from pure subjectivity by converting human beings into objects for public contemplation,"[41] enjoyment, and judgment. Moments of life are removed from the temporal frame, although the act of reading occurs in time.

By creating versions of the self and images of personality, Ŏ Suk-kwŏn affirmed the significance of memory and imagination, the power of language to create a sense of identity in objectified form, and the communicability of that identity through selection and evocative writing.

NOTES

1. A mid-seventeenth-century collection comprises 53 titles, the early nine-teenth-century collection, 143, and the late-nineteenth-century collection, 96. Min Pyŏngsu, "P'aegwan munhak e taehayŏ," *Kojŏn munhak yŏn'gu* (1971), 1:163–71. For a comprehensive survey of the miscellany, see Kim Kŭnsu, ed., *Yasa ch'ongsŏ ŭi ch'ongch'ejŏk yŏn'gu* (Seoul: Hangukhak yŏn'guso, 1976), which lists a total of some 560 titles.
2. There are two modern photolithographic editions, 1941 and 1974.
3. Also known as *P'aegwan sorok* in *Kimyorok poyu*. References to *P'aegwan chapki* will hereafter be cited in the text.
4. Sŏ Susaeng, *Koryŏjo hanmunhak yŏn'gu* (1971), pp. 11–108.
5. Ch'a Chuhwan, "Ch'oe Cha ŭi sip'yŏng," *Tonga munhwa* (1970), 9:1–57; Ch'oe Sinho, "Ch'ogi sihwa e nat'anan yongsa iron ŭi yangsang," *Kojŏn munhak yŏn'gu* (1971), 1:117–36.
6. Sŏ Susaeng, *Koryŏjo*, pp. 201–55.
7. Benjamin Boyce, *The Theophrastan Character in England to 1642* (Cambridge, Mass.: Harvard University Press, 1947); *The Polemic Character 1640–1661* (Lincoln, Nebraska: University of Nebraska Press, 1955); and W. J. Paylor, *The Overburian Characters* (Oxford: Blackwell, 1936), pp. v–xxxi.
8. See my *Songs of Flying Dragons: A Critical Reading* (Cambridge, Mass.: Harvard University Press, 1975), p. 7, n. 7.
9. Kim Sanggi, "Toksŏdang ŭi yurae wa pyŏnch'ŏn," *Hyangt'o Seoul* (1958), 4:13–39. See *Yongjae ch'onghwa*, 4, 14 (pp. 94–99), for the linked verse composed by scholars at the Chin'gwan monastery on Mount Samgak in 1442.
10. Kim Allo, *Yongch'ŏn tamjŏkki* (Chōsen kosho kankōkai ed., 1910), p. 250; also in *Hŭiraktang ko*, 2 vols. (1974 reprint, Kŏn'guk University Press), vol. 2, p. 8.
11. J. W. Saunders, *The Profession of English Letters* (London: Routledge & Kegan Paul, 1964), p. 28.
12. Phoebe Sheavyn, *The Literary Profession in the Elizabethan Age*, ed. J. W. Saunders (Manchester: Manchester University Press 1967), chap. 1; Saunders, *The Profession*, chaps. 2 and 3; Edwin H. Miller, *The Professional Writer in Elizabethan England* (Cambridge, Mass.: Harvard University Press 1959), chap. 4.
13. J. I. Crump, Jr., *Intrigues: Studies in the Chan-kuo Ts'e* (Ann Arbor: University of Michigan Press, 1964), p. 99.
14. George Kennedy, *The Art of Rhetoric in the Roman World*, 300 B.C.–A.D. 300 (Princeton: Princeton University Press, 1972), p. 434.
15. *Ibid.*, p. 215.
16. Donald Lemen Clark, *Rhetoric in Greco-Roman Education* (New York: Columbia University Press, 1957), p. 58.
17. *Ibid.*, p. 263.
18. George Williamson, *The Senecan Amble: A Study in Prose Form from Bacon*

to *Collier* (London: Faber & Faber, 1959), p. 52. For Attic prose, see Morris W. Croll, *Style, Rhetoric, and Rhythm*, ed. J. Max Patrick (Princeton: Princeton University Press, 1966), Essay 2.

19. I.e., figures of attitudinizing. "All discourse reflects, and depends on, a particular attitude toward its subject, a stance, and very often it involves some sort of definition of the writer as well," says William J. Brandt, *The Rhetoric of Argumentation* (Indianapolis: Bobbs-Merrill 1970), p. 153.

20. *Ibid.*, p. 125.

21. Pathos is almost always defective "when it intrudes itself into the body of the speech or essay." The mark of defective pathos is "a cluster of response-demanding figures—the exclamation, the apostrophe, and the rhetorical question." Brandt, *Rhetoric*, pp. 224–25.

22. Generally, man's external aspect is neglected in the *chapki*. For example, except in 4, 3 (p. 86) and 8, 25 (p. 294), *Yongjae ch'onghwa* offers few external features. Neither does Kenkō's *Tsurezuregusa* (c. 1330–32), except in episodes 42 and 175.

23. Joseph Roe Allen III, "An Introductory Study of Narrative Structure in the *Shi ji*," *Chinese Literature, Essays, Articles, Reviews* (January 1981), 3(1):31–66.

24. Claudio Guillen, *Literature as System* (Princeton: Princeton University Press, 1971), p. 212.

25. Vivian de Sola Pinto, *English Biography in the Seventeenth Century* (London: Harrap, 1951), pp. 38, 39.

26. *Ibid.*, p. 49.

27. *Han'guksa* (1974), 10:607–11; Yi Sangbaek, *Han'guk munhwasa yŏn'gu non'go* (1954), pp. 173–204.

28. *Han'guksa*, 10:662–93.

29. Yi Sangbaek, *Han'guk*, pp. 207–48.

30. His "Accounts of Conduct" *(haengjang)* proudly mentions the fact. Also a number of other works repeat the same, for example, *P'irwŏn chapki*, 2, 34 (pp. 349–350), and *Yongjae ch'onghwa*, 9, 29 (p. 243).

31. Shakespeare, Sonnet 107, ll. 5–6: "The mortal moon hath her eclipse endur'd,/ And the sand augurs mock their own presage."

32. Tzvetan Todorov, in "The Origin of Genres," *New Literary History* (Autumn 1976), 8(1):168, comments: In autobiographical discourse, when the author, the narrator, and sometimes the main character are identical, "the identity of the author and narrator separates the 'referential' or 'historical' genres from all the 'fictional' genres."

33. Robert Alter, *Partial Magic* (Berkeley: University of California Press, 1975), p. 241.

34. An East Asian contemplating his own spiritual autobiography, Buddhist or Confucian, a story of the cultivation of ideal universals, must contend with paradoxes intrinsic to the genre of autobiography. The changes he undergoes are predetermined and paradigmatic, a design and meaning imposed from without. Thus his story has a plot known in advance. It is a success story at

that, a record of sanctioned change in the service of accepted goals. Patricia Meyer Spacks, *Imagining a Self: Autobiography and Novel in Eighteenth Century England* (Cambridge, Mass.: Harvard University Press, 1976), p. 268. See also Burton Pike, "Time in Autobiography," *Comparative Literature* (1976), 28:326–42, esp. 337–38.

35. Earlier *chapki* (e.g., *Yongjae ch'onghwa*) contain episodes on social types, which resemble the medieval West's invectives against the special evils of every calling.

36. Robert Scholes and Robert Kellogg, *The Nature of Narrative* (New York: Oxford University Press, 1966), chap. 7.

37. Jonathan Culler, *Structuralist Poetics: Structuralism, Linguistics, and the Study of Literature* (London: Routledge & Kegan Paul, 1975), p. 50.

38. Roland Barthes, "Racinian Man," in *European Literary Theory and Practice*, ed. Vernon W. Gras (New York: Dell, 1973), p. 340.

39. Saunders, *The Profession*, p. 19.

40. *Ibid.*, pp. 19, 38.

41. Spacks, *Imagining a Self*, p. 300. For this and the next paragraph I am indebted to her book.

Glossary

Abe Yoshio 阿部吉雄
Aizu 会津
Ajia-teki nōgyō to nōgyō shakai アジア的
　農業と農業社会
Amano Motonosuike 天野元之助
An Chaehong 安在鴻
An Chijung 安之中
An Chin 安震
An Chŏngbok 安鼎福
An Ch'uk 安軸
An Chungson 安仲孫
An Hyang 安珦
An Po 安輔
An Pyŏngju 安炳周
An Ugi 安于器
Anbyŏn 安邊
Andong 安東
Anhŭngsa 安興寺
Anŭm 安陰
Aru sōshinkai no tanjō 或子宗親会の
　誕生
Asadal 阿斯達
Asakura Gisuke 朝倉儀助
Asami Keisai 淺見絅齋
Asea yŏn'gu 亞細亞研究
Bukkyō no shisō 佛教の思想
cha 慈
Ch'a Chuhwan 車柱環
Ch'a chŭk Chang Chŏng ... 此即張程
　性之旨也
Cha Song i hu ... 自宋以後佛法始衰

而禪變爲儒
chadŭk 自得
chaech'oe 齊衰
chaei 災異
ch'aengmun 策文
chaksŏng 作聖
ch'amshoe 斬衰
Ch'an 禪
ch'an 贊
Chan Huo 展獲
Chan Ling 詹陵
Chan Wing-tsit 陳榮捷
Chang (Lady) 張
chang 掌
Chang Chaesik 張在軾
Chang Chiyŏn 張志淵
Chang Chiyŏn chŏnsŏ 張志淵全書
Chang Ch'ien 張騫
Chang Chiu-ch'eng 張九成
Chang-chou 漳州
Chang Hyŏn'gwang (Yŏhŏn) 張顯光,
　(旅軒)
Chang Liang 張良
Chang Shih (Nan-hsüan, Ching-fu)
　張栻 (南軒, 敬夫)
Chang Shih-ch'eng 張士誠
Chang Tsai 張載
Chang Tzu ch'üan-shu 張子全書
Chang Yu 張維
Changdanggyŏng 藏唐京
Changgi 長鬐

Ch'anggok 倉穀

Changhŏn seja tonggung ilgi 莊獻世子東宮日記

changju 章奏

changmu 掌務

changŭi 掌議

Ch'ao-chou 潮州

Chao Fu 趙復

Chao Meng-fu 趙孟頫

Chao-nan 召南

chapchi 雜志

Chaphak 雜學

chapki 雜記

chapkwa 雜科

chapsa 雜祀

Charyo Han'guk yuhaksa ch'ogo 資料韓國儒學史草稿

Che-Chiang 浙江

Chean (prince) 齊安大君

Chegukpu p'ungsok 諸國部風俗

Cheihoe Tongyang munhwa kukche haksul hoeŭi nonmunjip 第二回東洋文化國際學術會議論文集

Cheju (do) 濟州(島)

chekwa 制科

Chen-kuan cheng-yao 貞觀政要

chen-k'ung chüeh-hsiang kuan 眞空絕相觀

Ch'en Ch'i-chung 陳齊仲

Ch'en Chien 陳建

Ch'en Ch'un (Pei-hsi) 陳淳(北溪)

Ch'en Fu 陳敷

Ch'en Hao 陳澔

Ch'en Hsien-chang 陳獻章

Ch'en Hung-mou 陳弘謀

Ch'en Liang (T'ung-fu) 凍亮(同甫)

Ch'en Pai-sha 陳白沙

Chen Te-hsiu 眞德秀

cheng 正

ch'eng 成

ch'eng 誠

Cheng-ching 政經

Ch'eng-Chu 程朱

Cheng-chung 正中

Ch'eng Fu-hsin 程復心

Ch'eng Hao (Ming-tao) 程顥(明道)

Cheng Hsüan 鄭玄

Ch'eng Hsün 程洵

Ch'eng I (I-ch'uan) 程頤(伊川)

Cheng-i-t'ang ch'üan-shu 正誼堂全書

Ch'eng K'o-chiu 程可久

Cheng-meng 正蒙

Ch'eng Min-cheng 程敏政

Ch'eng-shih i-shu 程氏遺書

Ch'eng T'ang 成湯

cheng-tao 正道

Ch'eng-tsu 成祖

cheng-t'ung 正統

cheng-tung-hsing chung-shu-sheng ju-hsüeh t'i-chü 征東行中書省儒學提舉

Ch'eng Yün-fu 程允夫

cheŏn 提堰

chesa 祭祀

chesul 製述

Chewang un'gi 帝王韻記

chi 知

chi 記

chi 極

Ch'i 齊

ch'i 氣

ch'i-chih 氣質

ch'i-chih chih hsing 氣質之性

ch'i chih fa 氣之發

ch'i-ch'ing 七情

ch'i-fa 氣發

ch'i-fa erh li-ch'eng chih 氣發而理乘之

ch'i-hsüeh 氣學

ch'i-hua 氣化

ch'i-i-tao, tao-i-ch'i 器亦道, 道亦器

chi-kan 寂感

Chi-ku-chin fu-tao lun-heng 集古今佛道
論衡

ch'i-shu 氣數

Chi Tzu 季子

Chi Tzu 箕子

chi-wei 己未

Chia-ching 嘉靖

chia-jen 家人

Chia-li 家禮

Chiang hsüeh che ... 講學者宗江西,
文章之士附眉山譏侮晦菴者所成羣

Chibong yusŏl 芝峰類說

chien 健

Ch'ien Mu 錢穆

Chien-ning 建寧

Ch'ien-tzu-wen 千字文

Chien-yang 建湯

chigwŏl 直月

chih 至

chih 知

chih 智

chih-hsing ho-i 知行合一

chih-k'o 制科

chii 智異

Ch'ijae yugo 恥齋遺稿

Ch'ijaejip 恥齋集

ch'iji 致知

Ch'ijŏn 治典

chik 直

ch'ilchŏng 七情

Chin 金

Ch'in-Han 秦漢

Chin-hsi 金谿

Ch'in K'ai 秦開

Chin kong cha pu ... 眞空者不違有
之空也妙有者不違空之有也

chin kong myo yu 眞空妙有

chin (li) 金(利)

ch'in-min 親民

chin-shih 進士

Chin-shih han-chi ts'ung-k'an 近世漢籍
叢刊

*Chin-shih ju-hsüeh yü T'ui-ch'i-hsüeh
kuo-chi hui-i lun-wen-chi* 近世儒學與
退溪學國際會議論文集

Chin-ssu lu 近思錄

Chin-ssu lu chi-chu 近思錄集註

Chin Su 金粟

Chindan hakpo 震檀學報

ching 經

ching 敬

ch'ing 情

Ching Chia-yi (Julia) 秦家懿

ch'ing-ching 清淨

ching erh chih nei 敬而直內

Ching-i kao 經義攷

ching-shih chih yung 經世致用

Ching-te ch'uan-teng-lu 景德傳燈錄

ching-tso 靜坐

ch'ing-yüan wu-wu 慶元戊午

chin'gukkong 鎭國公

Chin'gwan (sa) 津寬寺

Chin'gwi (Kim) 鎭龜(金)

ch'in'gyŏn 親見

Chinju 晉州

chinsa 進士

chinyu 眞儒

Chiphyŏnjŏn 集賢殿

Chiu-huang-ts'e 救荒策

Chiu-T'ang-shu 舊唐書

ch'iung-li 窮理

Cho chu ae myŏng ... 潮州哀鳴大不
滿人意者以無佛學故也
Cho Chun 趙浚
Cho Ch'ŏngse 趙靖世
Cho Chwaho 曹佐鎬
Cho Hanbo 曹漢輔
Cho Hŏn 趙憲
Cho Inok 趙仁沃
Cho Kan 趙簡
Cho Kasŏk 趙嘉錫
Cho Kwangjo (Chŏngam) 趙光祖(靜庵)
Cho Mok (Wŏlch'ŏn) 趙穆(月川)
Cho Myŏnggi paksa hwagap kinyŏm
nonch'ong 趙明基博士華甲記念論叢
Cho Pak 趙璞
Cho Pokhyŏng 趙復亨
Cho Sin 曹伸
Cho Wŏn'gi 趙元紀
Ch'oe Cha ŭi sip'yŏng 崔滋의詩評
Ch'oe Ch'iwŏn 崔致遠
Ch'oe Hae 崔瀣
Ch'oe Munch'ang i ... 崔文昌以文室
之維摩大鳴中華
Ch'oe Namsŏn 崔南善
Ch'oe Pu 崔溥
Ch'oe Sejin 崔世珍
Ch'oe Sinho 崔信浩
Ch'oe Sŭngno 崔承老
Ch'oe Ŭi 崔竩
Ch'oe Yŏng 崔瑩
Ch'ogi sihwa e nat'anan yongsa iron
ŭi yangsang 初期詩話에나타난用
事理論의樣相
Chogye Sŏn 曹溪禪
chŏk 嫡
chŏksil 的實
Chŏlla (do) 全羅(道)
chŏlto wiri anch'i 絶島圍籬安置

chŏm 漸
chomi iltu 造米一斗
chŏmkwe (Ch. chien-kua) 漸卦
chŏmsang 占相
Chŏn Im 田霖
Ch'ŏn Kwanu 千寬宇
ch'oṅbang 川防
Ch'ŏndo 天道
Ch'ŏndoch'aek 天道策
chondŏksŏng 尊德性
chŏng 正
Chŏng Chaesik 鄭載植
Chŏng Chiun (Ch'uman) 鄭之雲(秋巒)
Chŏng Ch'ŏk 鄭陟
Chŏng Ch'ŏl 鄭澈
Chŏng Inbo 鄭寅普
Chŏng Ku (Han'gang) 鄭逑(寒岡)
Chŏng Kubok 鄭求福
Chŏng Kyŏngse 鄭經世
Chŏng Kyubok 丁奎福
Chŏng Mongju 鄭夢周
Chŏng mun che kong ... 程門諸公則
不然, 旣合溫涼之劑從而大言於人
日古方本如此
Chŏng Pŏn 鄭蕃
Chŏng Pyŏnguk 鄭炳昱
Chŏng Saryong 鄭士龍
Chŏng Sŭbin 鄭習仁
Chŏng Sunmok 丁淳睦
Chŏng Tojŏn 鄭道傳
Chŏng Tojŏn sasang ŭi yŏn'gu 鄭道傳思
想의硏究
Chŏng Tojŏn sŏngnihak ŭi t'ŭksŏng
kwa kŭ p'yŏngka munje 鄭道傳性
理學의特性과그評價問題
Chŏng Yŏch'ang 鄭汝昌
Chŏng Yŏrip 鄭汝立
Chŏng Yuil (Munbong, Chajung)

鄭惟一(文峯, 子中)
chŏngdo 正道
Ch'ŏnggye pacsŏngso 清溪拜星所
Chonghak 宗學
chŏnghak 正學
Chŏnghŭi 貞熹
chŏnghye 定慧
Chongji 宗之
Chŏngjo 正祖
Chŏngjo tonggung ilgi 正祖東宮日記
Chongjŏk t'ongdosŏl 宗嫡統圖說
Chŏngjŏn 政典
Chŏngjong 定宗
Ch'ŏngju 清州
chŏngjwa 靜坐
Chŏngmyo horan 丁卯胡亂
chŏngsa 精舍
chŏngsim 正心
Chŏngsokpy'ŏn 正俗篇
Chon'gyŏnggak 尊經閣
ch'ŏngnyangsan 清涼散
chŏnin 町人
ch'ŏnmin 賤民
Ch'ŏnmyŏng kudo 天命舊圖
Ch'ŏnmyŏng sindo 天命新圖
Ch'ŏnmyŏng tosŏl 天命圖說
chonsim 尊心
Chŏnsŭmnok nonbyŏn 傳習錄論辨
chŏpkyŏng 帖經
Ch'ŏrhak yŏn'gu 哲學研究
chŏrŭi 節義
Chōsen gakuhō 朝鮮学報
Chōsen jinmei jisho 朝鮮人名辞書
Chōsen jukai no Yōmeigakuha
　朝鮮儒界の陽明学派
Chōsen kyōyaku kyōkashi no kenkyū
　朝鮮郷約教化史の研究
Chōsen no Shushigaku 朝鮮の朱子学

Chōsen nōgyōshi-jo ni okeru jūgo seiki
　朝鮮農業史上における十五世紀
Chōsen rekishi ronsō 朝鮮歴史論叢
Chōsen shakai keizai-shi kenkyū 朝鮮社
　会経済史研究
Chōsen shisō 朝鮮史叢
Chōsenshi 朝鮮史
Chosŏn 朝鮮
Chosŏn ch'ogi ŭi kisulgwan kwa kŭ
　chiwi 朝鮮初期의技術官과그地位
Chosŏn ch'ogi ŭi t'ogwan e taehayŏ
　朝鮮初期의土官에對하여
Chosŏn ch'ogi ŭi hyanggyo 朝鮮初期
　의鄉校
Chosŏn chŏn'gi hyangch'on chilsŏ
　朝鮮前期鄉村秩序
Chosŏn chŏn'gi sahaksa yŏn'gu 朝鮮前期
　史學史研究
Chosŏn hugi nongŏpsa yŏn'gu 朝鮮後期
　農業史研究
Chosŏn kyŏnggukchŏn 朝鮮經國典
Chosŏn pulgyo t'ongsa 朝鮮佛教通史
Chosŏn sijo Tan'gun chi wi 朝鮮始祖
　檀君之位
Chosŏn Tan'gun 朝鮮檀君
Chosŏn wanjo sillok 朝鮮王朝實錄
Chosŏn yugyo yŏnwŏn 朝鮮儒教淵源
Chosŏnhu Kija 朝鮮侯箕子
Chosŏnhu Tan'gun chi wi 朝鮮侯檀
　君之位
Chou 紂
Chou 周
Chou-hsüeh 州學
Chou-i 周易
Chou-i ts'an-t'ung-ch'i 周易參同契
Chou-li 周禮
Chou Lien-hsi chi 周濂溪集
Chou-nan 周南

Chou Tun-i (Lien-hsi) 周敦頤（濂溪）

Chou Tzu ch'üan-shu 周子全書

chu 州

chü 局

chu-ch'i 主氣

Chü-chia pi-yung shih-lei ch'üan-chi 居家必用事類全集

chu-ching 主靜

chü-ching ch'iung-li 居敬窮理

Ch'u Chŏk (Nodang) 秋適（露堂）

Chu Hsi 朱熹

Chu I-tsun 朱彝尊

chu-li 主理

Chu-Lu 朱陸

ch'ü-shan 取善

Chu-shu chi-nien 竹書紀年

chu-tsai 主宰

Ch'u-tz'u 楚辭

Chu Tzu chi-chu 朱子集註

Chu Tzu chia-li 朱子家禮

Chu Tzu chieh-yao 朱子節要

Chu Tzu chih li-ch'i hsin-hsing lun 朱子之理氣心性論

Chu Tzu ch'üan-shu 朱子全書

Chu Tzu hsin-hsüeh-an 朱子新學案

Chu Tzu hsing-chuang 朱子行狀

Chu Tzu kan-hsing-shih 朱子感興詩

Chu Tzu nien-p'u 朱子年譜

Chu Tzu shih-chi 朱子實紀

Chu Tzu shu 朱子書

Chu Tzu ta-ch'üan 朱子大全

Chu Tzu ta-ch'üan wen-chi 朱子大全文集

Chu Tzu to kokyū 朱子と呼吸

Chu Tzu tseng-sun Lü-shih hsiang-yüeh 朱子增損呂氏鄉約

Chu Tzu wen-chi 朱子文集

Chu Tzu yü-lei 朱子語類

Ch'ü Yüan 屈原

chuan 傳

chüan 卷

ch'üan-ch'i 全氣

Ch'üan-chou 泉州

Ch'uan fa cheng-tsung-chi 傳法正宗記

Ch'uan-hsi lu 傳習錄

Ch'uan-nung-wen 勸農文

Ch'uan-teng-lu 傳燈錄

ch'üan-t'i ta-yung 全体大用

Ch'üan Tsu-wang 全祖望

Chuang Tzu 莊子

Chūgoku keizaishi kenkyū 中国経済史研究

Chūgoku nōgyōshi kenkyū 中国農業史研究

Chūgoku tetsugaku kenkyū 中国哲学研究

Chūgoku zensho no kenkyū 中国善書の研究

ch'ŭgŭn 惻隱

Chuja changgu porok 朱子章句補錄

Chuja haengjang chipchu 朱子行狀輯注

Chuja taejŏn 朱子大全

Chuja taejŏn ch'aŭi 朱子大全箚疑

Chuja taejŏn ch'aŭi chippo 朱子大全箚疑輯補

Chuja taejŏn ch'aŭi munmok 朱子大全箚疑問目

Chuja taejŏn ch'aŭi munmok p'yobo 朱子大全箚疑問目標補

Chuja taejŏn ch'aŭi o megutte 朱子大全箚疑をめぐって

Chujasŏ chŏryo 朱子書節要

Chujasŏ chŏryo kiŭi 朱子書節要記疑

Chun 準

Ch'un-ch'iu 春秋

chün-tzu 君子

chung 中

ch'ung 思

Ch'ung-an 崇安

Chung Chai-sik, see Chŏng Chaesik

chung-ho 中和

Chung-kuo che-hsüeh shih 中國哲學史

Chung-kuo che-hsüeh yüan-lun yüan-hsing p'ien 中國哲學原論原性篇

Chung-kuo tzu-hsüeh ming-chu chi-ch'eng 中國子學名著集成

ch'ung yŏ kukka 忠於國家

Chung-yang yen-chiu yüan 中央研究院

Chung-yüan 中原

Chung-yung 中庸

Chung-yung chang-chü 中庸章句

Chung-yung huo-wen 中庸或問

Chungang saron 中央史論

Chŭngbo munhŏnbigo 增補文獻備考

Chŭngbo T'oegye chŏnsŏ 增補退溪全書

Chungbong sŏnsaeng munjip 重峯先生文集

Chungbu haktang 中部學堂

chungin 中人

Chungjo 中祖

Chungjong 中宗

Chungjong sillok 中宗實錄

Chungjong tae ŭi tohak kwa simhakhwa undong 中宗代의道學과心學化運動

Ch'ungju 忠州

Ch'ungnyŏl (wang) 忠烈(王)

Ch'ungnyŏng 忠寧

Ch'ungsŏn (wang) 忠宣(王)

Ch'ungsuk (wang) 忠肅(王)

Chungyong changgu 中庸章句

Chungyong changgu ch'aje 中庸章句次第

Chungyong kugyŏng yŏnŭi 中庸九經衍義

Chungyong Chuja changgu porok 中庸朱

子章句補錄

chuiron 主理論

ch'usŏl 推說

chwaju munsaengje 座主門生制

chwau chŏngja 左右正字

chwau munhak 左右文學

chwau p'ilsŏn 左右弼善

chwau pin'gaek 左右賓客

chwau podŏk 左右輔德

chwau sa 左右師

chwau sagyŏng 左右司經

daimyō 大名

Erh Ch'eng ch'üan-shu 二程全書

Erh-Ch'eng i-shu 二程遺書

erh-wu 二五

fa 發

fa-che 發者

fan-li 凡例

Fan-t'ai-shih chi 范太史集

Fan Tsu-yü 范祖禹

Fang Chaoying 房兆楹

Fang Hsiao-ju 方孝孺

Fang La 方臘

fen 分

fen-shu k'eng-ju 焚書坑儒

Feng Yün-hao 馮雲濠

Fo-fa chin-t'ang-pien 佛法金湯編

fu 復

Fu Hsi 伏羲

fu-hsüeh 府學

Fu-tzu 夫子

Fujiwara Seika 藤原惺窩

Fukien 福建

Fung Yu-lan 馮友蘭

gakkō 学校

Gendai no jugaku kyōiku 元代の儒学教育

gonin-gumi 五人組

Pang no minshū no ishiki 帮の民衆の
意識

Ha Yŏn 河演

Ha Yun 河崙

Haeju 海州

Haeju hyangyak 海州鄉約

haeng 行

Haengdan 杏壇

haengjang 行狀

haesŏk 解釋

Hagok sŏnsaeng choch'ŏn'gi 荷谷先生朝
天記

hai-t'ang 海塘

hain 下人

hakchang 學長

hakkung 學宮

Hakkyo mobŏm 學校模範

Hakkyogo 學校考

Hakpu t'ongpyŏn pal 學部通辨跋

Haktang 學堂

Hamgyŏng 咸鏡

Hamhŏ 涵虛

Hamhŏ Hwasang Hyŏnjŏngnon 涵虛和
尙顯正論

hamyang 涵養

han 藩

Han 韓

Han Ch'ang-li hsien-sheng wen-chi 韓昌
黎先生文集

Han hsü Tzu 涵虛子

pan-jih ching-tso, pan-jih tu-shu 半日
靜坐, 半日讀書

Han shu 漢書

Han T'o-chou 韓侂冑

Han Ugŭn 韓㳓劤

Han Woo-keun, see Han Ugŭn

*Han Ugŭn paksa chŏnguyŏn kinyŏm
sahak nonch'ong* 韓㳓劤博士停年紀

念史學論叢

Han Yŏngguk 韓榮國

Han Yŏngu 韓永愚

Han Young-woo, see Han Yŏngu

Han Yü 韓愈

Han'gang sŏnsaeng munjip 寒岡先生文集

Hangnyegang 學禮講

Han'guk e issŏsŏ Chujahak ŭi suyong
kwajŏng 韓國에 있어서 朱子學의
受容過程

Han'guk kodaesa yŏn'gu 韓國古代史
研究

Han'guk koinshoe kisulsa 韓國古印刷技
術史

Han'guk kojŏn munhak taegye 韓國古典
文學大系

Han'guk minjok munhwa ŭi kiwŏn 韓國
民族文化의起源

Han'guk munhak paegyŭng yŏn'gu 韓國
文學背景研究

Han'guk munhwasa yŏn'gu nongo 韓國
文化史研究論攷

Han'guk ŭi kwagŏje wa kŭ t'ŭksŏng
韓國의科擧制와그特性

Han'guk ŭi sasang taejŏnjip 韓國의思想
大全集

Han'guk ŭi yŏksa insik 韓國의歷史認識

Han'guksa 韓國史

Han'guksaron 韓國史論

Hanmal ŭi Sin Ch'aeho ŭi yŏksa insik
韓末의申采浩의歷史認識

Hanyang 漢陽

hao 號

hap 合

Hasŏ sŏnsaeng munjip 河西先生文集

Hatada Takashi 旗田巍

Hayashi Razan 林羅山

Heng-p'u 橫浦

Hideyoshi 秀吉

Higashi Asia no shisō to bunka 東アジア
の思想と文化

Hiroshima 広島

ho 號

Ho Ch'in 賀欽

Hŏ Chŏk 許積

Hŏ Pong 許篈

Ho Shu-ching 河叔京

Hoeam 檜巖

Hoedŏk hyŏn 懷德縣

Hoedŏk Paksŏnsaeng yuhŏbi 懷德朴
先生遺墟碑

hoegang 會講

Hoehŏnjip 晦軒集

Hoejae chŏnsŏ 晦齋全書

Hoejae sŏnsaeng munjip 晦齋先生文集

Hoejae Taehak poyu huŭi 晦齋大學補
遺後議

hoejip tokyakpŏp 會集讀約法

Hoguk chi sin 護國之神

Hogukpaek 護國伯

Hong Inu 洪仁祐

Hong Isŏp 洪以燮

Hong Kyŏm 洪謙

Hong Yak 洪瀹

Hong Yŏha 洪汝河

Honggŏnjŏk 紅巾賊

Hongju Sŏngsŏnsaeng yuhŏbi
洪州成先生遺墟碑

Hongmun'gwan 弘文館

Hŏnjŏn 憲典

Horigome Yōzō 堀米庸三

hosin 胡神

Hou-Han-shu 後漢書

Hsi Chung 熙仲

Hsi-lin 西林

Hsi-ming 西銘

Hsi-shan wen-chi 西山文集

Hsi-tz'u-chuan 繫辭傳

Hsia 夏

hsiang-li, hsiang-ling 鄉例, 鄉令

Hsiang-shan chi 象山集

Hsiang-shan ch'üan-chi 象山全集

hsiang-yüeh 鄉約

hsiao 笑

hsiao 孝

Hsiao-ching 孝經

Hsiao-hsüeh 小學

hsiao-hsüeh 小學

hsiao-jen 小人

hsiao-ti chung-hsin 孝悌忠信

Hsiao-tsung 孝宗

hsieh 邪

Hsieh (Lady) 謝

Hsieh Liang-tso (Shang-ts'ai) 謝良佐
（尚蔡）

hsieh-shuo 邪說

hsien 顯

hsien-hsüeh 縣學

hsien-wei wu-chien 顯微無間

hsin 心

Hsin-an 新安

hsin chih t'i-yung 心之體用

Hsin-ching fu-chu 心經附註

hsin-fa 心法

hsin-hsüeh 心學

hsin-min 新民

*Hsin-p'ien shih-wen lei-yao ch'i-cha
ch'ing-ch'ien* 新編事文類要啓箚
青錢

Hsin T'ai 心泰

Hsin-T'ang-shu 新唐書

Hsin-t'i yü hsing-t'i 心體與性體

hsin t'ung hsing-ch'ing 心統性情

hsing 性

hsing 行

hsing chi li 性即理

hsing-ch'i 形氣

hsing-ch'i chih so-wei 形氣之所爲

hsing-chuang 行狀

hsing-erh-hsia 形而下

hsing-erh-shang 形而上

hsing-hua 形化

Hsing-li ching-i 性理精義

hsing-li hsüeh 性理學

Hsing-li ta-ch'üan 性理大全

Hsing-li tzu-i 性理字義

hsing-ming 性命

hsiu-chi chih-jen 修己治人

hsiu-shen chih-kuo 修身治國

Hsiung-nu 匈奴

Hsiung Shih-li 熊十力

Hsü Heng 許衡

Hsü Lu-chai hsin-fa 許魯齋心法

Hsü Tzu-chih t'ung-chien 續資治通鑑

Hsüan-tsung 宣宗

Hsüan-tsung 玄宗

hsüeh 學

Hsüeh Hsüan (Ching-hsien) 薛瑄
   (敬軒)

Hsüeh-pu t'ung-pien 學蔀通辨

hsüeh-sheng 學生

Hsün-meng-shu 訓蒙書

Hsün-su i-kuei 訓俗遺規

Hu An-kuo 胡安國

Hu Chosŏn sijo Kija 後朝鮮始祖箕子

Hu Chosŏn sijo Kija chi wi 後朝鮮始
   祖箕子之位

Hu Chü-jen (Ching-chai) 胡居仁 (敬齋)

hu-fa 互發

Hu Hsien 胡憲

Hu Hung (Wu-feng) 胡宏 (五峰)

Hu San-sheng chu Tzu-chih t'ung-chien

胡三省註資治通鑑

Hu Yüan 胡瑗

Hua-yen 華嚴

Hua-yen-ching 華嚴經

Huamsa 厚岩寺

Huang-ch'ao tao-hsüeh ming-ch'en wai-lu
   皇朝道學名臣外錄

Huang-chi ching-shih-shu 皇極經世書

Huang Kan (Mien-chai, Chih-ch'ing)
   黃榦 (勉齋, 直卿)

Huang Mien-chai chi 黃勉齋集

Huang-po 黃白

Huang Tsung-hsi 黃宗羲

Huang Wan 黃綰

huch'ŏn 後天

Hui (ti) 徽 (帝)

Hui-an 晦菴

*Hui-an hsien-sheng Chu Wen-kung wen-
   chi* 晦菴先生朱文公文集

Hui-chou 徽州

Hui-k'e 慧可

Hui-neng 慧能

Hui-shih 會試

Hŭiraktang ko 希樂堂稿

Hullyŏn'gwan 訓鍊觀

hun-lun 渾淪

hun-p'o 魂魄

Hung-fan 洪範

Hung-fan chiu-ch'ou 洪範九疇

Hung-jen 弘忍

Hung-ming chi 弘明集

hun'gup'a 勳舊派

Hunmin chŏngŭm 訓民正音

Hunŭi Sohak taejŏn 訓義小學大全

huo (heng) 火 (亨)

huron 後論

Hwadamjip 花潭集

Hwang Chunnyang 黃俊良

Hwang Hyohŏn 黃孝獻
Hwang Kyeok 黃季沃
Hwanghae (do) 黃海(道)
hwannan sanghyul 患難相恤
Hwaryŏng 和寧
hyangan 鄉案
Hyangch'ŏng yŏn'gu 鄉廳研究
hyangdo 香徒
hyangdoyŏn 香徒宴
hyanggyo 鄉校
hyanggyu 鄉規
Hyanghoe tŏkyakpŏp 鄉會讀約法
hyangin 鄉人
hyangni 鄉吏
Hyangnip yakcho 鄉立約條
Hyangnip yakcho sŏ 鄉立約條序
hyangnon 鄉論
hyangnye 鄉禮
Hyangnye happ'yŏn 鄉禮合編
hyangnyŏng 鄉令
hyangsadang 鄉射堂
hyangsarye 鄉射禮
Hyangsi 鄉試
hyangt'o 鄉土
Hyangt'o Seoul 鄉土서울
hyangŭm churye 鄉飲酒禮
hyangyak 鄉約
Hyangyak choyak 鄉約條約
hyangyangmun 鄉約文
hyoin yeŭi 孝仁禮義
Hyojong 孝宗
Hyojong sillok 孝宗實錄
hyŏn 賢
Hyŏnjong 顯宗
hyŏng-i-ha 形而下
hyŏng-i-sang 形而上
hyŏnggi 形氣
Hyŏnjong 顯宗

Hyŏnjong sillok 顯宗實錄
Hyŏnjŏngnon 顯正論
Hyujŏng 休靜
hyung 薨
i 夷
i 義
i 理
I bungakushi ikō 尹文學士遺槀
I-ching 易經
I-chuan 易傳
I-ch'uan 伊川
I-ch'uan chi-jang chi 伊川擊壤集
I-ch'uan wen-chi 伊川文集
i-fa 已發
i-gi 理氣
I-hsüan 義玄
i-li chih hsing 義理之行
I-li ching-chuan t'ung-chieh 儀禮經傳
　通解
i-li wan-li 一理萬理
i-pen wan-shu 一本萬殊
I-shu 遺書
i-tuan 異端
I-tuan pien-cheng 異端辯正
ibŭi 立議
ibyak pyŏmnye 立約凡例
ibyakcha 入約者
Ich'ŏn 利川
idan 異端
Igang 驪江
Igong 驪公
ihak 理學
Ihak t'ongnok 理學通錄
ijang 里長
Ijo 吏曹
ijŏng 里正
Ikchu 益州
Ikeda Shizuo 池田龍夫

Im Kkŏkchŏng 林巨正

Im Kkŏkchŏng no hanran to sono shakai-teki kaikei 林巨正の反乱とその社会的背景

Im Pak 林樸

Im Sahong 任士洪

imsinja 壬申字

imun 吏文

Imwŏn simyukchi 林園十六志

in 仁

Injong 仁宗

Inmul Han'guksa 人物韓國史

Inmun kwahak 人文科學

Inmun sahoe kwahak 人文社會科學

insim 人心

Insim tosimbyŏn 人心道心辨

ioe chi in 理外之人

ipchae 入齋

ipchi 立志

Iphak tosŏl 入學圖說

iphak ŭi 入學儀

Iryŏn 一然

isa 里社

isŏ 理書

Itō Jinsai 伊藤仁齋

jen 仁

jen-hsin 人心

jen-tao 人道

Jen-tsung 仁宗

Jih-yung lei-shu 日用類書

Ju-chia 儒家

Ju-lin tsung-p'ai 儒林宗派

Jukyō no jissendōtoku 儒教の実踐道徳

jun-t'ung 閏統

Kabin yesong 甲寅禮訟

kabinja 甲寅字

kaeguk kongsin 開國功臣

Kaegyŏng 開京

Kagan 河汗

kahun 家訓

K'ai-huang li-tai san-pao-chi 開皇歷代三寶記

Kaibara Ekken 貝原益軒

Kamata Shigeo 鎌田芝雄

Kamsa yoyak 監司要約

kan-t'ung 感通

Kanan 家難

Kanaya kyōju taikan kinen ronbunshū 金谷教授退官記念論文集

kang 講

Kang Inbu 姜仁富

Kang Man'gil 姜萬吉

Kang Sangun 姜尙雲

Kang Sinhang 姜信沆

kanggyŏng 講經

kanghakpŏp 講學法

kangmu 講武

kangnon 講論

Kangwŏn (do) 江原(道)

kangyak 講約

Kankoku ni okeru Shushigaku no juyō katei 韓國における朱子学の受容過程

Kansŏ chamnok 看書雜錄

K'ao-i 考異

Kao P'an-lung (Ching-i) 高攀龍(景逸)

K'ao-t'ing 考亭

K'ao-t'ing yüan-yüan lu 考亭淵源錄

Kao Tzu 告子

kapchinja 甲辰字

Karye 家禮

Karye chimnam 家禮輯覽

Karye chŭnghae 家禮增解

Karye wŏllyu 家禮源流

Karye wollyu songno 家禮源流續錄

Keisho genkai 經書諺解

ken-tı 根柢

ki 氣

ki 記

Ki 奇

Ki no shisō 氣の思想

Ki no tetsugaku 氣の哲學

Ki Taesŭng (Kobong) 奇大升（高峰）

Kiangsi 江西

Kihae yesong 己亥礼訟

Kiho 畿湖

kihwa 已和

Kija 箕子

Kija Chosŏn 箕子朝鮮

Kija Chosŏn e taehan insik ŭi
    pyŏnch'ŏn 箕子朝鮮에대한認識의
    변천

Kija ko 箕子攷

Kija silgi 箕子實紀

Kijaji 箕子志

Kil Chae 吉再

Kim Allo 金安老

Kim An'guk 金安國

Kim Changsaeng (Sagye) 金長生（沙溪）

Kim Ch'anghyŏp 金昌協

Kim Chasu 金子粹

Kim Chip 金集

Kim Ch'o 金貂

Kim Ch'ŏlchun 金哲埈

Kim Chŏngbae 金貞培

Kim Chŏng-guk 金正國

Kim Chongjik 金宗直

Kim Ch'unt'aek 金春澤

Kim Doo-hun, see Kim Tuhŏn

Kim Hyŏng-hyo, see Kim Hyŏnghyo

Kim Hyŏnghyo 金烱孝

Kim Ikhŭi (Ch'angju) 金益熙（滄洲）

Kim Inbŏm 金仁範

Kim Inhu 金麟厚

Kım Koengp'il (Hanhwŏn) 金宏弼
   （寒暄）

Kim Kŭnsu 金根洙

Kim Kuyong 金九容

Kim Maesun 金邁淳

Kim Manjun 金萬拨

Kim Manjung 金萬重

Kim Mujo 金戊祚

Kim Munjŏng 金文鼎

Kim Pusik 金富軾

Kim Sanggi 金痒基

Kim Seryŏm 金世濂

Kim Sisŭp 金時習

Kim Suon 金守溫

Kim To 金濤

Kim Tonguk 金東旭

Kim Tuhŏn 金斗憲

Kim Tujong 金斗鍾

Kim Wije 金謂磾

Kim Yongdŏk 金龍德

Kim Yongsŏp 金容燮

Kim Yongsuk 金用淑

Kimp'o 金浦

Kimyorok poyu 己卯錄補遺

Kinsei ajia kyōiku shi 近世アジア教
    育史

Kinsei kanseki sōkan 近世漢籍叢刊

kisa 己巳

Kisa hwan'guk 己巳換局

Ko 格

Ko 高

Ko Chumong 高朱蒙

Ko Pyŏngik 高柄翊

ko-wu chih-chih 格物致知

Ko-wu pu-chuan 格物補傳

Kobong chŏnjip 高峯全集

Kobong munjip 高峯文集

Kobong sŏnsaeng munjip 高峰先生文集

Kobongjip 高峰集

Kogi 古記

Koguryŏ 高句麗

Koguryŏ sijo Tongmyŏngwang chi wi
高句麗始祖東明王之位

Koh Byong-ik, see Ko Pyŏngik

koin myŏngdŏk sinmin chi sirhak
古人明德新民之實學

kojik 庫直

Kojŏn munhak yŏn'gu 古典文學研究

Kojukkuk 孤竹國

kok 曲

Kōkyō keimō no shomondai 孝經啓
蒙の諸問題

kŏmgyo milchik chehak 檢校密直
提學

Kōnan bunka kaihatsushi 江南文化開
發史

kongbu 工夫

Konggo chikchang tosŏl 公孤職掌圖說

Kongjŏn 工典

Kongjŏn 公田

Kongju 公州

Kongmin (wang) 恭愍(王)

kongsin 功臣

Kŏp'yŏng 居平

Kōrai cho ni okeru jiin keizai 高麗朝
に於ける寺院經齊

Koryŏ 高麗

Koryŏ chunggi ŭi minjok sŏsasi—
Tongmyŏngwang p'yŏn kwa *Chewang
un'gi ŭi yŏn'gu* 高麗中期의民族叙
事詩—東明王篇과帝王韻記의
研究

Koryŏ myŏnghyŏnjip 高麗名賢集

Koryŏjo hanmunhak yŏn'gu 高麗朝漢文
學研究

Koryŏjo ŭi i e taehaeyŏ 高麗朝의「吏」

에대하여

Koryŏsa 高麗史

Koryŏsa chŏryo 高麗史節要

Kosa ch'waryo 攷事撮要

Kosen sappu 古鮮册府

Kosŏ mongnok 古書目錄

Ku K'ai-chih 顧愷之

Ku samguksa 舊三國史

Ku-wen chen-pao 古文眞寶

Ku wŏn i pyŏn ryu 究源而辨流

Ku Yen-wu 顧炎武

Kuan 關

Kuan Chung 管仲

Kuan Tzu 管子

Kuan-yin 觀音

K'uang 匡

Kuang-hung-ming chi 廣弘明集

Kuang-wu 光武

Kuei-chou 貴州

kuei-ssu 癸巳

Kugŏ kungmunhak 국어국문학

kugyŏl 口訣

Kuillok 求仁錄

kujaean 九齋案

Kujaesaksi 九齋朔試

Kukchagam 國子監

Kukchagamsi 國子監試

Kukcho oryeŭi 國朝五禮儀

Kukhak 國學

kukhyul pokche 國恤服制

Kŭmmagun 金馬郡

Kŭmsŏng 錦城

Kŭmsŏng 金城

K'un-chih chi 困知記

K'un-ming 昆明

kung-fu 工夫

K'ung Fu-tzu 孔夫子

K'ung Wen-chung 孔文仲

Kung Yung-ch'ing 龔用卿

Kungmunhak charyo 國文學資料

Kungmunhak sa 國文學史

Kŭnjaejip 謹齋集

Kuo-t'ing lu 過庭錄

Kusaerok 懼塞錄

Kusumoto Masatsugu 楠本正繼

kuŭi 口義

Kuunmong 九雲夢

Kuunmong ŭi kujojŏk yŏn'gu 九雲夢의構造的研究

Kuunmong ŭi kŭnbon sasang ko 九雲夢의根本思想考

Kuyodang 九曜堂

kwagŏ 科擧

Kwagŏ kanggyŏnggo 科擧講經考

Kwagŏ samch'ŭngpŏp 科擧三層法

kwamok 科目

Kwanch'alsa 觀察使

Kwangjong 光宗

Kwangsan 光山

kwanhak 官學

kwanin 官人

kwasil sanggyu 過失相規

Kwibong sŏnsaengjip 龜峰先生集

kwŏn 卷

Kwŏn Che 權踶

Kwŏn Han'gong 權漢功

Kwŏn Kŭn 權近

Kwŏn Kyŏngu 權景祐

Kwŏn Nam 權擥

Kwŏn Po 權溥

Kwŏn Sangha 權尙夏

Kwŏn Si 權諰

Kwŏn Talsu 權達手

kye 契

kyech'ukcha 癸丑子

Kyegokchip 谿谷集

Kyegukpaek 啓國伯

kyejang 契長

kyemija 癸未子

Kyemong 啓蒙

Kyeryong 雞龍

kyesa 癸巳

kyŏl 結

kyŏng 敬

Kyŏngbok (kung) 景福(宮)

Kyŏngguk taejŏn 經國大典

kyŏngjaeso 京在所

Kyŏngje mun'gam 經濟文鑑

Kyŏngje mun'gam pyŏlchip 經濟文鑑別集

Kyŏngje yukchŏn 經濟六典

Kyŏngjong 景宗

Kyŏngjong ch'un'gung ilgi 景宗春宮日記

Kyŏngju 慶州

Kyŏngmong yogyŏl 擊蒙要訣

Kyŏngmongp'yŏn pal 擊蒙編跋

Kyŏngsang (do) 慶尙(道)

Kyŏngsin hwan'guk 庚申換局

kyŏngŭi 經義

Kyŏngyŏn 經筵

Kyŏrhon togam 結婚都監

kyori 校理

kyosŏgwan 校書館

Kyōyaku kyōho to dōgi kyōyaku 鄕約教法と道義鄕約

Kyujanggak tosŏ Han'gukpon ch'ongmongnok 奎藏閣圖書韓國本總目錄

Lan-t'ien 藍田

Lao-Chuang 老莊

Lao Tzu 老子

Lee Chong-young, see Yi Chongyŏng

Lee Choon-hee, see Yi Ch'unhŭi

Lee Sang-eun, see Yi Sangŭn

lei-shu-hsüeh 類書學

li 里

li 禮

li 理

Li-chi 禮記

li-ch'i 理氣

li-ch'i miao-ning 理氣妙凝

li chih ch'üan-t'i ta-yung 理之全體
大用

li chih fa 理之發

Li Ching-te 黎靖德

li-fa 理發

li-fa-chieh 理法界

li-fa erh ch'i-sui chih 理發而氣隨之

Li Fang-tzu (Kung-hui, Kuo-chai) 李方
子(公晦, 果齋)

li-hsien ch'i-hou 理先氣後

li-hsüeh 理學

Li-hsüeh tsung-ch'uan 理學宗傳

li-i fen-shu 理一分殊

Li Ki 禮記

Li K'ou 李覯

li-lei, tsa-li-shu 禮類, 雜禮書

li-she 里社

li-shih wu-ai fa-chieh 理事無礙法界

Li-tai shih-shih tzu-chien 歷代釋氏資鑑

Li T'ang 李棠

li tao 理到

Li T'ui-ch'i chih *T'ien-ming hsin-t'u* yü
li-ch'i-shuo 李退溪之天命新圖與理
氣說

li-tung, ch'i-tung 理動氣動

Li T'ung (Yen-p'ing) 李侗(延平)

Li Yu-wu 李幼武

li-yüeh-hsing-cheng 禮樂刑政

Li-yun 禮運

liang-chih 良知

liang-i 兩儀

liang-neng 良能

Liao 遼

Liao-tung 遼東

Lieh-hsien-chuan 列仙傳

Lieh Tzu 列子

Lin-ch'uan 臨川

Lin Sung-ch'ing 林嵩卿

Lin Tse-chih (Yung-chung) 林擇之
(用中)

Ling-yüan 靈源

Liu Cheng 留正

liu-hsing 流行

Liu Shu-wen 劉叔文

Liu-tien 六典

Liu Tzu-hui (P'ing-shan) 劉子翬(屏山)

Liu-tsu-t'an-ching 六祖壇經

Liu-yü hsiang-yüeh 六諭鄉約

Liu-yü yen-i 六諭衍義

Lo Ch'in-shun (Cheng-an) 羅欽順
(整菴)

Loyang 洛陽

Lu 蘆

Lu 魯

Lu Chiu-ling (Tzu-shou) 陸九齡(子壽)

Lu Chiu-shao (Tzu-mei) 陸九韶(子美)

Lu Chiu-yüan (Tzu-ching) 陸九淵
(子靜)

Lu Hsiang-shan 陸象山

Lu Kuang-tsu 陸光祖

Lü-shih hsiang-yüeh 呂氏鄉約

Lü Ta-chün 呂大鈞

Lü Ta-fang 呂大防

Lü Ta-lin 呂大臨

Lü Tsu-ch'ien (Tung-lai, Po-kung)
呂祖謙(東萊, 伯恭)

Lu-Wang 陸王

Lü Yü-shu 呂與叔

Lun-yü 論語

Lun-yü chi-chu 論語集注
Ma Tuan-lin 馬端臨
Maema Kyosaku 前間恭作
Mahan 馬韓
Makino Shūji 牧野修次
mal 末
malpŏp 末法
Man'gwŏndang 萬卷堂
manp'il 漫筆
Manp'il chasŏ 漫筆自叙
Mansong Kim wansŏp mun'go mongnok
    晚松金完燮文庫目錄
Matsuda Kō 松田甲
Mei-shan 眉山
meibun taigi 名分大義
Meng Tzu 孟子
miao-ho erh ning 妙合而凝
Mien-chai chi 勉齋集
Mien-chai wen-chi 勉齋文集
milbu 密付
Min (Queen) 閔(妃)
Min 閔
Min Chinwŏn 閔鎮遠
Min Chŏngjung 閔鼎重
Min Hyŏn'gu 閔賢九
Min Pyŏngsu 閔丙秀
Min Sŭpchŏng 閔習靜
Min Yujung 閔維重
Min Yuŭi 閔由義
Ming 明
Ming (ti) 明(帝)
Ming Hsüan-tsung shih-lu 明宣宗實錄
Ming hui-yao 明會要
Ming-ju hsüeh-an 明儒學案
Ming-shih 明史
Ming-tao hsien-sheng mu-piao 明道先生
    墓表
Ming-tao wen-chi 明道文集

Minh-tam pao-giam, see *Myŏngsim
    pogam*
Min Shin shisōshi no kenkyū 明清思想
    史の研究
Mirŭksa 彌勒寺
Miura Baien 三浦梅園
Miura Kunio 三浦國雄
Miyajima Hiroshi 宮嶋博史
Miyake Shōsai 三宅尚齋
mo 末
mo-fa 末法
Mo Tzu 墨子
Mogŭn mun'go 牧隱文藁
Mojaejip 慕齋集
Mōri 毛利
*Mori Mikisaburō hakase shōju kinen
    tōyōgaku ronshū* 森三樹三郎博士頌
    壽記念東洋學論集
Morimoto Jun'ichiro 守本順一郎
Mou Tsung-san 牟宗三
mu (yüan) 木(元)
mudŭng 無等
mugen no sekaikan, Kegon 無限の世界
    観, 華嚴
mugŭi 墨義
Mukwa 武科
Munhŏn pigo 文獻備考
munjip 文集
Munjong 文宗
Munjong sillok 文宗實錄
Munkwa 文科
Munkwa ch'ojang kanggyŏngpŏp 文科
    初場講經法
Munmyo 文廟
munŭm 門蔭
Muo sahwa 戊午士禍
muraokite 村掟
Muwŏn 婺源

Myoch'ŏng 妙淸

myŏn 面

myŏng 命

Myŏngch'o Chosŏn ŭi Yodong kongbŏl kyehoek kwa p'yojŏn munje 明初朝鮮의遼東攻伐計劃과表箋問題

Myŏngjae yugo 明齋遺稿

Myŏngjong 明宗

Myongjong sillok 明宗實錄

Myŏngsim pogam 明心寶鑑

Naesi pyŏlgam 內侍別監

Nagong pisŏl 欒翁稗說

Naikaku Bunko 內閣文庫

Naitō Torajirō 內藤虎次郎

Naju 羅州

Nakai Tōju 中江藤樹

Nam Chwa 南在

Nam Kuman 南九萬

Nam Ŏn'gyŏng 南彦經

Nam Ŏn'gyŏng ŭi saengae, sasang mit Yangmyŏnghak munje 南彦經의生涯, 思想및陽明學問題

Nambu haktang 南部學堂

Namgyŏng 南京

Namhae 南海

Namhae toin 南海道人

Namin 南人

Namjŏnggi 南征記

Namjŏng ki-e taehan il koch'al 南征記에對한一考察

Namwŏn 南原

Nan-feng 南豐

Nan-hsüan 南軒

Nan-kan hsiang-yüeh 南贛鄕約

Nan-pei-chi 南北極

nandok 難讀

Nangaku 南學

nei 內

Nei-tse 內則

Nien-p'u 年譜

Nihon Shushigaku to Chōsen 日本朱子学と朝鮮

Nishijima Sadao 西嶋定生

Nishiyama Takeichi 西山武一

No 顧

No Susin 盧守愼

No Yŏngch'an 盧永燦

Noja Todŏkkyŏng sŏ 老子道德經序

Non Konjigi 論困知記

Non sadan ch'ilchŏng sŏ 論四端七情書

Nongga chipsŏng 農家集成

Nongsa chiksŏl 農事直說

Nongsang chipyo husŏ 農桑輯要後序

Noron 老論

nosa 老師

Nulchae Yang Sŏngji ŭi sahoe chŏngch'i sasang 訥齋梁誠之의社會政治思想

Nung-sang chi-yao 農桑集要

Nung-shu 農書

Ŏ Hyoch'ŏm 魚孝瞻

O kwa i i 吾過而已

Ŏ Mujŏk 魚無迹

Ŏ Sukkwŏn 魚叔權

obok chedo 五服制度

odang 吾黨

odo 吾道

Oejip 外集

Ogyŏng ch'ŏn'gyŏnnok 五經淺見錄

Ogyū Sorai 荻生徂徠

ojang 伍長

Okada Takehiko 岡田武彦

Okayama 岡山

Okazaki Fumio 岡崎文夫

ŏllo 言路

ŏnhae 諺解

Ŏnhaengnok 言行錄

ŏnjŏn 堰田

ŏmmun 諺文

Ŏnŏ munhwa 言語文化

ŏnt'o 諺吐

Ŏrok 語錄

oryun 五倫

osŭng 五升

pa-kua 八卦

pa-t'iao-mu 八條目

Pae Kŭknyŏm 裴克廉

Paegak 白嶽

P'aegwan chapki 稗官雜記

P'aegwan munhak e taehayŏ 稗官文學
  에對하여

P'aegwan sorok 稗官小錄

Paek Ijŏng 白頤正

Paek Munbo 白文寶

Paekche 百濟

Paekho chŏnsŏ 白湖全書

Paekho chŏnsŏ haeje 白湖全書解題

Paekho Yun Hyu igi ch'ŏrhak yŏn'gu
  sŏsŏl 白湖尹鑴理氣哲學研究序說

Paekho Yun Hyu ŭi sadan ch'ilchŏng,
  insim tosimsŏl 白湖尹鑴의四端七情
  人心道心說

Paekho Yun Hyu yŏn'gu 白湖尹鑴
  研究

Paeksa sigyo *Chŏnsŭmnok* ch'ojŏn insŏ
  kihu 白沙詩教傳習錄抄傳因書
  其後

Paeksan hakpo 白山學報

P'aerim 稗林

P'aesŏl 稗說

P'ahanjip 破閑集

pai-hsieh 白骸

Pak Ch'o 朴礎

Pak Chonghong 朴鍾鴻

Pak Ch'ŏn'gyu 朴天圭

Pak Ch'ungjwa 朴忠佐

Pak Hŏn 朴憲

Pak Hŭimun 朴希文

Pak Kwangyong 朴光用

Pak Kyegang 朴繼姜

Pak Sang 朴祥

Pak P'aengnyŏn 朴彭年

Pak Sangch'ung 朴尙衷

Pak Sech'ae (Hwasuk) 朴世采(和叔)

Pak Sedang 朴世堂

Pak Semu 朴世茂

Pak Sil 朴實

Pak Sŏngmyŏng 朴錫明

Pak Sŏngŭi 朴晟義

Pak Sŏsaeng 朴瑞生

Pak Ŭijung 朴宜中

Pak Wŏnho 朴元熇

Pak Yŏng 朴英

p'alcho kŭmpŏp 八條禁法

pangŏn 方言

pangyŏk 防役

pao-chia 保甲

Pao Yang (Hsien-tao) 包揚(顯道)

Park Chong-hong, see Pak
  Chonghong

pei-chen 北辰

pen-jan 本然

pen-jan chih hsing 本然之性

Pi-ko t'u-shu 秘閣圖書

Pi-shu lu 避暑錄

p'ien-ch'i 偏氣

p'ien-li 偏理

P'ing (ti) 平(帝)

P'ing-shan 屏山

Pirwŏn chapki 筆苑雜記

pisajok (Ch. fei-shih-tsu) 非士族
po 洑
Po I 伯夷
Po-lu-tung shu-yüan 白鹿洞書院
Pogwang 普光
Pogwŏn'gung 福源宮
Pohanjip 補閑集
poksŏ 卜筮
pŏlch'ŭk 罰則
Pŏmmun 法門
Ponghwa hyŏn 奉化縣
Pŏpchang 法藏
Pou 普雨
poyang 輔養
Poyang chaesang 輔養宰相
Poyangch'ŏng ilgi 輔養廳日記
Poyanggwan 輔養官
pu 府
pu-i pu-erh 不一不二
Pu Indong 夫仁洞
pu-li pu-tsa 不離不雜
Pugongmin 部曲民
pugun 府君
pujehak 副提學
Pujŏn 賦典
Pul sŏ su pŏn ... 佛書雖煩其要不出
　於眞空妙有四字
pulch'ŏn 佛天
Pulssi chappyŏn 佛氏雜辨
p'umgwan 品官
P'ungangnok 楓缶錄
pun'gwan 分館
Pup'yŏng 富平
puyakchang 副約長
Puyŏ 扶餘
P'yoje ŭmju Tongguk saryak 標題音註
　東國史略

p'yojŏnmun 表箋文
pyŏksa wido 闢邪衛道
pyŏlgŏm 別撿
p'yomun 表文
Pyŏn Kyeryang 卞季艮
p'yŏn 篇
Pyŏngan (do) 平安(道)
Pyŏngja horan 丙子胡亂
pyŏngjin 丙辰
Pyŏngjo 兵曹
Pyŏngjon 兵典
P'yŏngyang 平壤
Pyŏnhan 卞韓
Ri Rikkoku to kyōyaku 李栗谷と
　鄕約
Ri Taikei no shishichironben to
　ridōsetsu 李退溪の四七論辯と理
　動說
Richō bukkyō 李朝佛教
Richō jidai ni okeru kei-kiyaku no
　kenkyū 李朝時代に於ける契規約
　の研究
Richō jidai no kyōyaku 李朝時代の
　鄕約
Richō Jinso ōdai no kyōyaku kyōka
　李朝仁祖王代の鄕約教化
Richō jugaku shi ni okeru shuriha
　shukiha no hattatsu 李朝儒学史に
　於ける主理派主気派の発達
Richō no kyōki ni tsuite 李朝の鄕規
　について
Ro Yong Chan, see No Yŏngch'an
sa 士
sa 邪
sabu pin'gack sanggyŏn ŭi 師傅賓客
　相見儀
sach'ang 社倉
Sach'anggi 社倉記

Sach'anggye 社倉契

sach'angpŏp 社倉法

sach'il nonbyŏn e issŏsŏ ŭi T'oegye
  Kobong ŭi ipchang 四七論辯에 있
  어서의退溪高峯의立場

sach'illon 四七論

Sach'ong 史叢

sadae 事大

sadaebu 士大夫

sadan 四端

sadan ch'ilchŏng 四端七情

sado 斯道

Sado 思悼

saekchang 色掌

saengyuksin 生六臣

Saganwŏn 司諫院

Sagye 沙溪

sagyŏn 邪見

sahak 私學

sahak sibido 私學十二徒

Sahŏnbu 司憲府

sahwa 士禍

sahwa 司貨

sai-yü 塞語

sajanghak 詞章學

Sajikche 社稷祭

Sajiktan 社稷壇

sajok 士族

Sakai Tadao 酒井忠夫

samasi 司馬試

samaso 司馬所

Sambong 三峰

Sambongjip 三峰集

Sambongjip e nat'anan Chŏng Tojŏn
  ŭi pyŏngje kaehyŏgan ŭi sŏngkyŏk
  三峰集에나타난鄭道傳의兵制改
  革案의性格

Samgak 三角

Samgaksan 三角山

Samgang haengsil 三綱行實

samgant'aek 三揀擇

Samguk sagi 三國史記

Samguk sagi ŭi yŏksa sŏsul 三國史記의
  歷史叙術

Samguk yusa 三國遺事

Samguksa chŏryo 三國史節要

samgun toch'ongjebu 三軍都摠制府

Samgwan'gi 三官記

Samgyo hwahap non 三敎和合論

Samgyŏng sŏgŭi 三經釋義

samu 事務

samun nanjŏk 斯文亂賊

san-kang 三綱

san-kang-ling 三綱領

San-kuei 三桂

San-kuo-chih 三國志

San-min 三民

San-t'ung-ch'i 參同契

Sang 象

sanghogun 上護軍

sangin 上人

Sangjŏl karye 詳節家禮

sangmin 常民

Sangnye piyo 喪禮備要

sarim 士林

sarimp'a 士林派

Sarimp'a ŭi yuhyangso pongnip
  undong 士林派의留鄕所復立運動

saryŏng 使令

sasil 事實

Sasŏ kyŏlsŏk 四書訣釋

Sasŏ ogyŏngjae 四書五經齋

Sasŏ ŏnhae 四書諺解

sasŏl 邪說

sayuksin 死六臣

se 勢

se 世

sega 世家

Seikyū gakusō 青丘學叢

Seinangakuin daigaku bunrironshū 西南
學院大學文理論集

Seito to itan 正統と異端

Seja 世子

Seja ikwisa 世子翊衛司

Seja kwansok 世子官屬

Seja sigangwǒn 世子侍講院

Sejo 世祖

Sejo—p'aedo e ǒlkin ungji 覇道에얽
힌雄志

Sejo sillok 世祖實錄

Sejong 世宗

Sejong sillok 世宗實錄

Sejongdae ǔi ǒnǒ'gwan ǔi sǒngnip
世宗代의言語觀의成立

Sejongjo e issǒsǒ ǔi taebulgyo sich'aek
世宗朝에있어서의對佛教施策

Seng-ts'an 僧粲

Seng-yu 僧祐

Seoh Munsang, see Sǒ Munsang

Seson 世孫

shan-hsing 善行

Shan-ling i-chuang 山陵議狀

Shang 商

Shang-chih 尚志

Shang-shu ta-chuan 尚書大傳

Shang-ti 上帝

Shang Yang 商鞅

Shao Yung 邵雍

she 社

she-hsüeh 社學

she-tsang fa 社倉法

Shen Pu-hai 申不害

sheng-hsien chih tao 聖賢之道

sheng-hsüeh 聖學

Sheng-hsüeh hsin-fa 聖學心法

sheng mieh hsing 生滅性

Sheng-yü hsiang-yüeh 聖諭鄉約

Shigaku zasshi 史學雜誌

shih 勢

shih 事

shih (solid, substantial, practical, real)
實

Shih-chi 史記

Shih-ching 詩經

shih-fa-chieh 事法界

Shih Hao 史浩

shih-hsien 實踐

shih-hsüeh 史學

shih-hsüeh 實學

Shih-hua 詩話

shih-kung-p'ai 事公派

shih-li wu-ai kuan 事理無礙觀

Shih-lin 石林

Shih-lin kuang-chi 事林廣記

Shih-lüeh 史略

Shih-shih lun 釋氏論

shih-shih wu-ai fa-chieh 事事無礙
法界

shih-shih wu-ai-kuan 事事無礙觀

Shih-shuo hsin-yü 世說新語

shih-ta-fu 士大夫

shijuku 私塾

Shikata Hiroshi 四方博

Shimada Kenji 島田虔次

Shina ni okeru bukkyō to jukyō dōkyō
支那に於ける佛教と儒教道教

Shina shigakushi 支那史學史

Shinajin no koten to sono seikatsu 支那人
の古典とその生活

Shinshaku kambun taikei 新釈漢文大系

Shōgaku 小学

shoin tsukuri 書院造

shu 疏

Shu-ching 書經

shu-niu 樞紐

shu-yüan 書院

shui (chen) 水(貞)

shuki-ha 主氣派

Shun 舜

shuri-ha 主理派

shun 順

Shushi gorui 朱子語類

Shushi gyōjō T'oegye shūchū no igi 朱子行狀退溪輯注の意義

Shushi no shisō keisei 朱子の思想形成

Shushi shōsōhō 朱子社倉法

Shushigaku no denrai to sono eikyō ni tsuite 朱子学の傳来とその影響に就いて

Shushigaku taikei 朱子学大系

Si yō sŏn yu ... 時與先儒有異同, 又 似汎濫釋氏…

sidokkwan 侍讀官

siganggwan 侍講官

sijik 侍直

sil 實

Silla 新羅

Sillok 實錄

sim 心

sim kwan sim 心觀心

sim mu ch'e yong pyŏn 心無體用辨

Sim T'ongwŏn 沈通源

simpŏp 心法

Simgi ip'yŏn 心氣理篇

Simgyŏng huron 心經後論

simhak 心學

Simhak to 心學圖

Simmun ch'ŏndap 心問天答

simsŏng chi hak 心性之學

Simu isipp'alcho 時務二十八條

Simyuk segi ŭi ch'ŏnbang (po) kwan'gae ŭi paltal 十六世紀의 川 防(洑)灌漑의 發達

Sin Chihyŏn 申芝鉉

Sin Husok 申侯溭

Sin Sang 申商

Sin Ton 辛旽

Sin Sukchu 申叔舟

Sin Ton ŭi chipkwŏn kwa kŭ chŏngch'ijŏk sŏnggyŏk 辛旽의 執權 과 그 政治的 性格

Sin Ŭigyŏng 申義慶

Sin'gyŏkchŏn 神格殿

Sinim sahwa 辛壬士禍

Sinji 神誌

Sinjong 神宗

Sinjŭng Tongguk yŏji sŭngnam 新增東 國輿地勝覽

sinmyo 辛卯

sinmyŏng hyangyak 申明鄉約

Sipsao segi nongŏp kisul ŭi paltal kwa sinhŭng sajok 十四五世紀農業技術 의 發達과 新興士族

sirhak 實學

Sisŏ sŏgŭi 詩書釋義

so 疏

sŏ 庶

Sŏ Hwadam kŭp Yi Yŏnbang e taehan sogo 徐花潭及李蓮坊에 對한 小考

so-i-jan 所以然

so-i-jan chih ku 所以然之故

so-i-yŏn 所以然

Sŏ Kŏjŏng 徐居正

Sŏ Kyŏngdŏk (Hwadam) 徐敬德 (花潭)

Sŏ Munsang 徐文祥

So Seyang 蘇世讓

Sŏ Susaeng 徐首生

so-tang-jan 所當然

so-tang-jan chih tse 所當然之則

Sŏ *Yangmyŏngjip* hu 書陽明集後

so-yi-fa-che 所以發者

Sŏ Yugu 徐有榘

Sŏae sŏnsaeng munjip 西厓先生文集

Sobuk 小北

Sŏbu haktang 西部學堂

sodae 召對

Sŏdai keizaishi kenkyū 宋代經濟史研究

sŏdang 書堂

Sogyŏkchŏn 昭格殿

Sŏgyŏng 西京

Sohak chipchu 小學輯註

Sohak ch'oryak 小學抄略

Sohak chusŏl 小學註說

sŏin 庶人

Sŏin 西人

sŏjae 書齋

Sojaedonggi 消災洞記

Sojaejip 蘇齋集

Sŏjŏgwŏn 書籍院

Sojŏnsaek 燒錢色

Sok taejŏn 續大典

Sŏkka uŏn 釋伽寓言

Sŏkkok 石谷

soksu 束脩

soksu ŭi 束脩儀

Sŏktam 石潭

sokwa 小科

Sŏl Ch'ong 薛聰

Sŏl Sŏnggyŏng 薛盛璟

Sŏl Wi 薛緯

Sŏltong 雪洞

Sŏmhakchŏn 贍學錢

Sŏn 禪

sŏnakchŏk 善惡籍

Sŏnbi chŏnggyŏng puin haengjang

先妣貞敬夫人行狀

Sŏnch'o ŭi sabu haktang 鮮初의四部
學堂

Sŏnch'o ŭi Sŏnggyun'gwan yŏn'gu
鮮初의成均館研究

sŏnch'ŏn 先天

Sŏnch'ŏn 宣川

sŏng 誠

sŏng 性

Song Ch'ŏnhŭi 宋千喜

Song Chunho 宋俊浩

Song Chusŏk 宋疇錫

Sŏng Hon (Ugye) 成渾(牛溪)

Sŏng Hon haenjang 成渾行狀

Song Ikp'il 宋翼弼

Song Kŏngsŏp 宋兢燮

Sŏng Nakhun 成樂熏

Sŏng Sammun 成三問

Sŏng Sammun—Taeŭi myŏngbun ŭi
hwasin 成三問—大義名分의化身

Song Sangmin 宋尚敏

Song Siyŏl (Uam) 宋時烈(尤庵)

Songak 松岳

Songgang sŏnsaengjip 松江先生集

Songgye Wŏn Myŏng ihak t'ongnok 宋季
元明理學通錄

Sŏnggyun'gwan 成均館

sŏnghak 聖學

Sŏnghak chibyo 聖學輯要

Sŏnghak sipto 聖學十圖

Sŏngho saesŏl 星湖僿說

Sŏnghwang 城隍

Songja taejŏn 宋子大全

Songja taejon such'a 宋子大全隨箚

Sŏngjong 成宗

Sŏngjong sillok 成宗實錄

sŏngmyŏng chi hak 性命之學

sŏngnihak 性理學

Sŏngniyŏnwŏn ch'waryo 性理淵源撮要

sŏn'gŏ 選擧

Songsŏ soksŭbyu 宋書續拾遺

Songsŏ sŭbyu 宋書拾遺

Sŏnjo 宣祖

Sŏnjo sillok 宣祖實錄

Sŏnjo sujŏng sillok 宣祖修正實錄

Sŏnu 鮮于

Sŏnyo 禪要

Sonzai no mondai 存在の問題

sŏŏl 庶孽

Sŏp'o 西浦

Sŏpo manp'il 西浦漫筆

Sŏp'o sosŏl yŏn'gu 西浦小說研究

Sŏp'ojip 西浦集

sŏri 書吏

Soron 少論

Sŏrong 雲翁

Sŏsae 西塞

sosŏl 小說

Sŏul taehakkyo nonmunjip 서울大學校論文集

sŏwŏn 書院

Sŏwŏn hyangyak 西原鄉約

sŏyŏ 胥餘

Sŏyŏn 書筵

Sŏyŏn chin'gang ŭi 書筵進講儀

Sŏyŏn kangŭi 書廷講義

ssu 私

ssu-fa-chieh 四法界

ssu-hsiang 四象

Ssu-k'u ch'üan-shu tsung-mu t'i-yao 四庫全書總目提要

Ssu-k'u ch'üan-shu chen-pen 四庫全書珍本

Ssu-ma Kuang 司馬光

Ssu-ma shih shu-i 司馬氏書儀

Ssu-pu pei-yao 四部備要

Ssu-shu 四書

Ssu-shu chi-chu 四書集註

Ssu-shu Wu-ching ta-ch'üan 四書五經大全

ssu-tuan 四端

Su Ch'e 蘇轍

Su Shih 蘇軾

such'a 水車

such'aek 水柵

Sudo Yoshiyuki 周藤吉之

sugyu 宿儒

Sukchong 肅宗

Sukchong sillok 肅宗實錄

Sumun soerok 謏聞瑣錄

Sun Ch'i-feng 孫奇逢

Sunch'ŏn 順川

Sunch'ŏnsa 順天寺

Sung 宋

Sung-shih 宋史

Sung Tuan-i 宋瑞儀

Sung Yüan chieh-yao 宋元節要

Sung Yüan hsüeh-an 宋元學案

Sung Yüan hsüeh-an pu-i 宋元學案補遺

Sŭngjŏngwŏn ilgi 承政院日記

Sŭngmunwŏn 承文院

sungyu ch'ŏkpul 崇儒斥佛

Suzuki Mitsuo 鈴木滿男

Suzuki Takeo 鈴木滿男

Szu-shih-erh-chang ching 四十二章經

ta-ch'üan 大全

Ta-hsüeh 大學

Ta-hsüeh chang-chü 大學章句

Ta-hsüeh huo-wen 大學或問

Ta-hsüeh-wen 大學問

Ta-hsüeh yen-i 大學衍義

Ta-hui 大慧

Ta Ming hui-tien 大明會典

Ta Ming i-t'ung chih 大明一統志
Ta Ming lü 大明律
ta-yung 大用
Tabana Tameo 田花爲雄
Tae chŏ chŏn in ... 大抵前人之密付
　單傳在後人便成陳談常法
Tae Han cheguk 大韓帝國
taebang 大防
Taech'ŏnggwan 大淸觀
Taedong 大東
Taegak 臺閣
T'aegu 擇友
t'aegyo 胎敎
Taehak changgu poyu 大學章句補遺
Taehak changgu poyu pal 大學章句補
　遺跋
Taehak chŏnp'yŏn taeji ansŏl 大學全篇
　大旨按說
Taehak samgang p'almok cham 大學三綱
　八目箴
T'aehakchi 太學志
T'aehŏ 太虛
taejehak 大提學
T'aejo 太祖
T'aejo sillok 太祖實錄
Taejŏn hoet'ong 大典會通
Taejŏn t'ongp'yŏn 大典通編
T'aejong 太宗
T'aejong sillok 太宗實錄
taejung chijŏng 大中至正
Taesahŏn 大司憲
Taesŏngjŏn 大成殿
taeyu 大儒
Taga Akigorō 多賀秋五郎
Tagawa Kōzo 田川孝三
Tai Chen (Tung-yüan) 戴震(東原)
T'ai-chi 太極
T'ai-chi-t'u 太極圖

T'ai-chi-t'u chieh 太極圖解
T'ai-chi-t'u shuo 太極圖說
T'ai-chi-t'u shuo-chieh 太極圖說解
t'ai-chiao 胎敎
T'ai-ho 太和
Tai Hsien 戴銑
T'ai-tsu 太祖
T'ai-yi 太一
taigi meibun 大義名分
Taishō daizōkyō 大正大蔵経
Takahashi Tōru 高橋亨
Tamura Yoshirō 田村芳郎
T'an-ching 壇經
T'an Ssu-t'ung 譚嗣同
Tanam mallok 丹巖漫錄
T'ang 唐
T'ang-chien 唐鑑
T'ang Chün-i 唐君毅
T'ang Kao 唐皋
Tang Paegujŏn 唐裴矩傳
T'ang-shu 唐書
T'ang Sung pa-chia-wen 唐宋八家文
Tan'gi kosa 檀奇古史
tangjang 堂長
Tan'gun 壇君
Tan'gun Chosŏn 檀君朝鮮
Tanjae Sin Ch'aeho wa minjok sagwan
　丹齋申采浩와民族史觀
tanjŏn 單傳
Tanjong 端宗
Tanyang 丹陽
tao 道
Tao-ch'ien 道謙
Tao-hsin 道信
tao-hsin 道心
Tao-hsüan 道宣
tao-hsüeh 道學
Tao-i (Ma-tsu) 道一(馬祖)

tao-li 道理

tao-t'ung 道統

tao-t'ung chih ch'uan 道統之傳

Te-an 德安

Ti-fan 帝範

T'i Hsi-lin K'o-shih Ta-kuan hsüan
題西林可師大觀軒

ti-hsüeh 帝學

ti wang chih hsüeh 帝王之學

t'i-yung 體用

t'i-yung i-yüan 體用一源

t'i-yung lun 體用論

T'ien 天

t'ien-jen ho-i 天人合一

T'ien-li 天理

T'ien-ming 天命

T'ien-ming chih hsing 天命之性

Tien-shih 殿試

T'ien-t'ai 天台

T'ien-tao 天道

T'ien-ti wan-wu i-t'i chih jen 天地萬物
一體之仁

ting 定

Ting Fu-chih 丁復之

Ting-hsing shu 定性書

ting-hui 定慧

Ting K'e 丁克

Ting Yao 丁堯

tobuyakchŏng 都副約正

toch'ongjesa 都摠制使

Toch'ŏpche 度牒制

T'oegye chŏnsŏ 退溪全書

T'oegye hakpo 退溪學報

T'oegye kyohak sasang yŏn'gu 退溪教
學思想研究

T'oegye sŏnsaeng ŏnhaeng t'ongnok
退溪先生言行通錄

T'oegye sŏnsaeng ŏnhaengnok 退溪先生

言行錄

T'oegye ŭi saengae wa hangmun 退溪의
生涯와學問

Tōfukuji 東福寺

tŏgŏp sanggwŏn 德業相勤

t'ogwan 土官

togyejang 都契長

tohak 道學

Tŏkchong 德宗

tŏkhaeng

Tokiwa Daijō 常盤大定

Toksŏ 讀書

Toksŏdang ŭi yurae wa pyŏnch'ŏn
讀書堂의由來와變遷

tŏksŏng 德性

Tokugawa 德川

Tomoeda Ryūtarō 友枝龍太郎

Tonga munhwa 東亞文化

Tongbang hakchi 東方學志

Tongbangsa nonch'ong 東方史論叢

Tongbu sŏbu haktang 東部西部學堂

tongbukmyŏn tojihwisa 東北面都指
揮使

Tongguk 東國

Tongguk chŏngun 東國正韻

Tongguk saryak 東國史略

*Tongguk saryak e taehan sahaksajŏk
koch'al* 東國史略에對한史學史的
考察

Tongguk senyŏn'ga 東國世年歌

Tongguk t'onggam 東國通鑑

Tongguk t'onggam chegang 東國通鑑
提綱

Tonggung 東宮

Tongho mundap 東湖問答

Tongi 東夷

Tongmong hunhoe 童蒙訓誨

Tongmong sŏnsŭp 童蒙先習

T'ongmun'gwan 通文館

Tongmunsŏn 東文選

Tongmyŏngwang p'yŏn 東明王篇

Tongsa kangmok 東史綱目

tongsok 東俗

tongyak 洞約

Tongyanghak 東洋學

Tosan sŏwŏn 陶山書院

Tosan'gi 陶山記

tosim 道心

Tosŏn 道詵

Tosŏn'gi 道詵記

tot'ong 道統

toyakchŏng 都約正

Tōyō seiji shisōshi kenkyū 東洋政治思想史研究

Tōyōshi kenkyū 東洋史研究

tsai-ch'in-min 在親民

Ts'ai Yüan-ting (Chi-t'ung) 蔡元定 (季通)

Ts'ao Chien (Li-chih) 曹建(立之)

Ts'ao Tuan 曹端

Tseng Tzu 曾子

Tso-chuan 左傳

tso-yung 作用

Tsuan-t'u tseng-lei shih-lin kuang-chi 纂圖增類事林廣記

Tsuda Sōkichi 津田左右吉

Tsukamoto Zenryū 塚本善隆

tsun te-hsing, tao wen-hsüeh 存德性, 道問學

ts'un-yang 存養

tsung 宗

tsung-lun 總論

Tsung-mi 宗密

Ts'ung-shu chi-ch'eng 叢書集成

Tu-shu lu 讀書錄

Tu Wei-ming 杜維明

Tu Yu 杜佑

tun 遁

tun-kua 遯卦

tung 動

t'ung 通

T'ung chien kang-mu 通鑑綱目

T'ung chih 通志

Tung-fang Shuo 東方朔

Tung Huai 董槐

Tung-i 東夷

t'ung-jen 同人

Tung-p'o 東坡

T'ung-shu 通書

T'ung-tien 通典

tunjon 屯田

tz'u 慈

Tzu-chih t'ung-chien 資治通鑑

tzu-jan 自然

tzu-jan chih tse 自然之則

Tzu-ssu 子思

tzu-te 自得

Tzurezuregusa 徒然草

U(wang) 禑(王)

U an yŏng ch'a ... 又安用此夷禮乎

U T'ak 禹倬

Ubok sŏnsaeng munjip 愚伏先生文集

Ueyama Shunpei 上山春平

Ugye sŏnsaengjip 牛溪先生集

Ŭi chae pu kyo 意在扶敎

ŭibang 醫方

ŭibyŏng 義兵

ŭich'ang 義倉

ŭihŭngsamgunbu 義興三軍府

ŭiri 義理

Ŭirye munhae 疑禮問解

Ŭirye sangjŏngso 儀禮詳定所

Umehara Takeshi 梅原猛

Ŭn t'aesa 殷太師

Ŭnbyŏng chŏngsa hakkyu 隱屏精舍學規
Ŭngje siju 應制詩註
Un'gyŏng 云敬
Ŭnmun 恩門
Uno Seiichi 宇野精一
ŭrhaeja 乙亥字
Wakabayashi Kyōsai 若林强齋
Wan-li 萬曆
Wan-pao ch'üan-shu 萬寶全書
Wan Ssu-t'ung 萬斯同
Wan-yung cheng-tsung 萬用正宗
Wang An-shih 王安石
Wang Mou-hung 王懋竑
Wang Po 王柏
Wang Shih-chen 王世貞
Wang Tan-chih 王担之
Wang T'ing-hsiang 王廷相
Wang Tzu-ts'ai 王梓材
Wang Yang-ming 王陽明
Wang Ying-lin 王應麟
Wang Yüan-mei 王元美
wangdo 王道
Wansan 完山
wei 微
wei 危
wei-chi chih hsüeh 爲己之學
Wei chih 魏志
wei-fa 未發
wei-hsüeh 僞學
Wei-hsüeh-chin 僞學禁
Wei-lüeh 魏略
Wei Po-yang 魏伯陽
wei T'ien 畏天
wen 文
wen-chi 文集
Wen-hsien t'ung-k'ao 文獻通考
Wen-hsüan 文選
Wen-kung chia-i 溫公家儀

Wen-kung chia-li 文公家禮
Wen-kung chü-chia tsa-i 溫公居家雜儀
Wen-lin kuang-chi 文林廣記
Wihwado hoegun 威化島回軍
wijŏng ch'ŏksa 衛正斥邪
Wiman 衛滿
Wo-lun 臥輪
Wŏlchŏng sŏnsaeng pyŏlchip 月汀先生
　別集
Wŏlchŏngjip 月汀集
Wŏlch'ŏnjip 月川集
Wŏnhyo 元曉
Wŏnja 元子
Wŏnja hakkung 元子學宮
Wu 武
wu-ch'ang 五常
Wu Ch'eng 吳澄
wu-chi 無極
wu chi erh t'ai-chi 無極而太極
Wu-ching, ssu-shu ta-ch'üan 五經四書
　大全
Wu-chung i-kuei 五種遺規
wu-hsin chih ch'üan-t'i ta-yung 吾心之
　全體大用
wu-hsing 五性
wu-hsing 五行
Wu-i 武夷
wu-lun 五倫
Wu Ssu-an 吳思菴
wu-tsang 五臟
Wu Wen-ch'eng-kung ch'üan-chi 吳文
　成公全集
wu-wu 戊午
Wu yü wu yen 吾欲無言
yakchang 約長
yakchŏng 約正
yakchung 約衆
yaksok 約束

Yamanoi Yū 山井湧

Yamazaki Ansai 山崎闇齋

Yamazaki Michio 山崎道夫

yang 陽

Yang Chi 楊楫

Yang Chien 楊簡

Yang Chih-jen 楊志仁

Yang Chu 楊朱

Yang Fu 楊復

Yang I 楊億

Yang Shih (Kuei-shan) 楊時 (龜山)

Yang Sŏngji 梁誠之

Yang Taeyŏn 梁大淵

yang-tung 陽動

Yang Tzu-chih (Fang) 楊子直 (方)

yangban 兩班

Yangch'on 陽村

Yangch'onjip 陽村集

Yanggok pugyŏng ilgi 陽谷赴京日記

Yangjam kyŏnghŏm ch'waryo e taehayŏ 養蠶經驗撮要에對하여

yangji 良知

Yangnyŏng 讓寧

Yao 堯

Yao Shu 姚樞

Yao Sui 姚燧

Yasa ch'ongsŏ ŭi ch'ongch'ejŏk yŏn'gu 野史叢書의總體的研究

Yazawa Yasu 矢澤康祐

ye 禮

Yebu 禮部

Yech'ŏn Kaesimsa sŏkt'apki ŭi punsŏk—Koryŏ ch'ogi hyangdo ŭi illye 禮川開心寺石塔記의分析—高麗初期香徒의一例

Yegi ch'ŏn'gyŏnnok 禮記淺見錄

Yeh-lü Ch'u-ts'ai 耶律楚材

Yeh Meng-ting 葉夢鼎

yehak 禮學

Yeji 禮志

Yejo 禮曹

Yejŏn 禮典

Yejong 睿宗

Yemun'gwan 藝文館

Yen 燕

Yen Fu 閣復

Yen Hui 顏回

Yen-p'ing ta-wen 延平答問

Yen Tzu 晏子

Yeron kwa No So puntang 禮論과老少分黨

yesok sanggyo 禮俗相交

Yeŭi mundap 禮疑問答

yi 一

Yi 李

Yi Chae 李縡

Yi Chaeryong 李載龒

Yi Chehyŏn 李齊賢

Yi Chi 李至

Yi Chin 李瑱

Yi Chingsŏk 李澄石

Yi Chŏnggwi 李廷龜

Yi Chongyŏng 李鍾英

Yi Ch'ŏn'gi 李天機

Yi Chŭngyŏng 李增榮

Yi Chun'gyŏng 李浚慶

Yi Ch'unhŭi 李春熙

Yi Hang 李恒

Yi Hangno 李恒老

Yi Hoejae wa kŭ hangmun 李晦齋와 그學問

Yi Hongjik paksa hoegap kinyŏm Han'guksahak nonch'ong 李弘植博士回甲紀念韓國史學論叢

Yi Hŭibo 李希輔

Yi Hwang 李滉

Yi Hyŏnbo 李賢輔

Yi I 李珥

Yi In 李遴

Yi Inbok 李仁復

Yi Inim 李仁任

Yi-Ki 李奇

Yi Kok 李穀

Yi Ku 李球

Yi Kwangnin 李光麟

Yi Kyŏk 李格

Yi Kyubo 李奎報

Yi Min'gu 李敏求

Yi Nŭnghwa 李能和

Yi Ŏnjŏk 李彦迪

Yi Pangsŏk 李芳碩

Yi Pangwŏn 李芳遠

Yi Pyŏl 李鱉

Yi Pyŏngdo 李丙燾

Yi Pyŏnghyu 李秉烋

Yi Saek 李穡

Yi Sangbaek 李相佰

Yi Sangbaek chŏjakchip 李相佰著作集

*Yi Sangbaek paksa hoegap kinyŏm
    nonch'ong* 李相佰博士回甲紀念論叢

Yi Sangjwa 李上佐

Yi Sangŭn 李相殷

Yi Sŏnggu 李聖求

Yi Sŏnggye 李成桂

Yi Sŏngmu 李成茂

Yi Sŏnjo 李宣朝

Yi Sugwang 李睟光

Yi Sukcha 李叔自

Yi Sŭnghyu 李承休

Yi Sungin 李崇仁

Yi Sŭngjik 李繩直

Yi Sunjong 李順宗

Yi Tal 李達

Yi Tam 李詹

Yi T'oegye (Hwang) 李退溪(滉)

Yi Usŏng 李佑成

Yi Yo 李瑤

Yi Yulgok 李栗谷(珥)

Yijo chŏn'gi poksik yŏn'gu 李朝前期
    服飾研究

*Yijo hugi Kŭn'gi hakp'a e issŏsŏ ŭi
    chŏngt'ongnon ŭi chŏn'gae* 李朝後期
    近畿學派에있이서의正統論의展開

Yijo kŏn'guk ŭi yŏn'gu 李朝建國의研究

Yijo kungjung p'ungsok ŭi yŏn'gu
    李朝宮中風俗의研究

Yijo saengwŏn chinsasi ŭi yŏn'gu 李朝生
    員進士試의研究

Yijo sidae ŭi Tan'gun sungbae 李朝時
    代의檀君崇拜

Yijo sŏwŏn mun'go ko 李朝書院文庫考

Yijo surisa yŏn'gu 李朝水利史研究

*Yijo Yangmyŏnghak ŭi chŏllae wa
    suyong ŭi munje* 李朝陽明學의
    傳來와受容의問題

*Yijo yŏryu munhak mit kungjung p'ungsok
    ŭi yŏn'gu* 李朝女流文學및宮中風俗
    의研究

yin 陰

yin-ching 陰靜

Yin Hao 殷浩

Yin Keng 尹畊

yin-ssu 淫祀

yin-yang 陰陽

Yo i wi sŏk … 要以慰釋大夫人憂思

Yŏgong p'aesŏl 櫟翁稗說

yŏgwi 厲鬼

Yŏhŏn sŏnsaeng munjip 旅軒先生文集

Yŏksa hakpo 歷史學報

Yŏksa kyoyuk 歷史教育

yŏlchŏn 列傳

Yŏlsŏngjo kye kang ch'ackcha ch'aje

列聖朝繼講册子次第
Yŏmal Sŏnch'o ŭi kwaŏp kyoyuk
麗末鮮初의科業教育
Yŏmal Sŏnch'o ŭi pulgyo chŏngch'aek
麗末鮮初의佛教政策
Yŏn ha p'il tok ... 然何必獨於釋氏而
深惡痛斥哉
Yŏnbo 年譜
yong 用
Yongch'ŏn tamjŏkki 龍泉談寂記
Yongjae ch'onghwa 慵齋叢話
Yŏngjo 英祖
Yŏngnam 嶺南
Yŏnhaengnok sŏnjip 燕行錄選集
Yŏnp'yŏng tammun 延平答問
Yŏnsan 燕山
Yŏnsan Sŏngsŏnsaeng yuhŏbi 連山成
先生遺墟碑
Yŏnsan'gun ilgi 燕山君日記
Yŏri 於里
Yoshikawa Kōjirō 吉川幸次郎
Youn Sa-soon, see Yun Sasun
yu 儒
Yu Chŏk 俞廸
Yü-hai 玉海
Yü-ho-kuan 玉河館
Yu Hongnyŏl paksa hwagap kinyŏm
nonch'ong 柳洪烈博士華甲記念論叢
Yu Hŭich'un 柳希春
Yu Hŭiryŏng 柳希齡
Yu Kuang-p'ing 游廣平
Yu Kŭn 劉瑾
Yu Kye 俞棨
Yu Kyŏng 柳璥
Yü-lei 語類
Yü-lu 語錄
Yu Paegyu 柳伯濡
Yu sahak sasaengmun 諭四學師生文

Yü-shan 玉山
Yu Sŏngnyong 柳成龍
Yu Sungjo 柳崇祖
Yu Tso 游酢
Yu Yŏn 柳衍
yüan-ch'i 元氣
Yüan-chüeh-ching 圓覺經
yüan heng li chen 元亨利貞
Yüan Huang 袁黃
Yüan Ming-shan 元明善
Yüan-shih 元史
Yubul yanggyo kyodac ŭi kiyŏn e
taehan il yŏn'gu 儒佛兩教交代
의機緣에대한一研究
Yüeh-shih 月氏
yüeh-tan chi-hui tu-yüeh 月旦集會
讀約
Yuhyangso 留鄉所
yugyu (Ch. liu-yü) 六諭
Yulgok chŏnsŏ 栗谷全書
Yulgok yŏnbo 栗谷年譜
Yun Chŭng 尹拯
Yun Haje 尹夏濟
Yun Hyojŏn 尹孝全
Yun Hyu 尹鑴
Yün-ku 雲谷
Yun Kŭnsu 尹根壽
Yun Kwisaeng 尹龜生
Yun Namhan 尹南漢
Yün-nan 雲南
Yun Sang 尹祥
Yun Sasun 尹絲淳
Yun Sojong 尹紹宗
Yun Sŏn'gŏ 尹宣舉
Yun Tusu 尹斗壽
Yun Yonggyun 尹瑢均
yung 用
Yung-chia 永嘉

Yung-k'ang 永康
Yung-lo 永樂
yusaeng 儒生
yusul 儒術

Zettai no shinri, Tendai 絶対の眞理,
　　天台
Zoku Daizōkyō 続大蔵経
Zoku Nissen shiwa 続日鮮史話

Index

NEO-CONFUCIAN STUDIES

MODERN ASIAN LITERATURE SERIES

TRANSLATIONS FROM THE ORIENTAL CLASSICS

STUDIES IN ORIENTAL CULTURE

COMPANIONS TO ASIAN STUDIES

INTRODUCTION TO ORIENTAL CIVILIZATIONS

Wm. Theodore de Bary, Editor